*Pure Love, Pure Poetry,
Pure Prayer*

Pure Love, Pure Poetry, Pure Prayer

The Life and Work of Henri Bremond

Peter J. Gorday

Foreword by
François Trémolières

WIPF & STOCK · Eugene, Oregon

PURE LOVE, PURE POETRY, PURE PRAYER
The Life and Work of Henri Bremond

Copyright © 2018 Peter J. Gorday. All rights reserved. Except for brief quotations in critical publications or reviews, no part of this book may be reproduced in any manner without prior written permission from the publisher. Write: Permissions, Wipf and Stock Publishers, 199 W. 8th Ave., Suite 3, Eugene, OR 97401.

Wipf & Stock
An Imprint of Wipf and Stock Publishers
199 W. 8th Ave., Suite 3
Eugene, OR 97401

www.wipfandstock.com

PAPERBACK ISBN: 978-1-5326-3839-8
HARDCOVER ISBN: 978-1-5326-3840-4
EBOOK ISBN: 978-1-5326-3841-1

Manufactured in the U.S.A.

To Jean Cobb, who first introduced me, gently, to Francis de Sales and the French seventeenth Century, and to Gene TeSelle, who possessed the historian/theologian's greatest gift, the ability to take up beloved texts in such a way that the intellectual inquiry after God is an unending adventure "son vrai maître Fénelon"

Guibert, DS 1: 1937

Contents

List of Illustrations | viii
Foreword | ix
Preface | xi
Acknowledgments | xv
List of Abbreviations | xvii

Chapter 1	Introduction: High Honors | 1
Chapter 2	Aixois Roots and Politics: The First Stirrings of a Devout Humanist | 11
Chapter 3	The English Desert | 24
Chapter 4	Newman and Blondel: Setting the Theological Frame | 43
Chapter 5	Bremond and Blondel: The Circle of Friends | 63
Chapter 6	Returning to Roots | 84
Chapter 7	Pure Love | 104
Chapter 8	Under the Shadow of Sainte-Beuve: From the Literary Soul to the Mystical Soul | 125
Chapter 9	Formulations in Time of War: The "French School" and the Mysticism of Self-Annihilation | 146
Chapter 10	Port Royal I: The Problem of "Devout Charlatanism" | 166
Chapter 11	Port-Royal II: Pascal, Nicole and Anti-mysticism | 188
Chapter 12	Ignatian Mysticism | 208
Chapter 13	1922–1923: First Signs of Integration | 227
Chapter 14	Interlude and Assessment | 247
Chapter 15	Pure Poetry and Pure Prayer | 260
Chapter 16	The "Metaphysic of the Saints" I: Setting the Stage | 281
Chapter 17	The "Metaphysic of the Saints" II: The Main Act | 299
Chapter 18	Bremond's Mysticism: Friends, Foes and Critics | 319
Chapter 19	If We Die with Christ, then We Shall Sing with Him: *Histoire*, IX, and X—then Loisy | 340
Chapter 20	*Histoire*, XI: "The Mystics on Trial," and Bremond Also | 360
Chapter 21	Conclusions | 381

Bibliography | 389
Index of Proper Names | 405

Illustrations

P. 8. Henry Bordeaux arrives at the Institut de France, May 22, 1924, for the reception of the abbé Bremond (photo, Bibliothèque Nationale de France).

P.8. Bremond, looking jubilant and relieved, and in the company of a friend, leaving the Institut at the conclusion of his reception (photo, Bibliothèque Nationale de France).

p. 388. Henri Bremond "au livre." The text of this prayer-card, requesting intercessions for the repose of the soul of Henri Bremond, reads as follows: "Remember before God the abbé Henri Bremond of the Académie Française. Aix-en-Provence, July 31, 1865; Arthez d'Asson, August 17, 1933. 'Let us, this year, learn how to accept as joyously as possible all that the divine tenderness would have us suffer.' From his last letter to his Benedictine nieces. (Photo compliments of François Trémolières)

Foreword

THE ABBÉ HENRI BREMOND (1865–1933) knew a certain notoriety in France during the interwar period. The first volume of his *Histoire littéraire du sentiment religieux en France depuis la fin des guerres de Religion jusqu'à nos jours*, after publication in 1916, would go on to sell more than ten thousand copies. Elected to the Académie française in 1923, he profited from the tribune thus offered to launch the quarrel of "pure prayer." Catholic among writers, writer among Catholics, he labored to maintain a vital communication between these two worlds—literary and spiritual—even at the price of controversies which, in fact, were not always displeasing to him!

Anglophile and anglophone (having been educated partly in the UK, when the Jesuit scholasticate had been exiled from France), he became connected with George Tyrrell, and other actors in the English Modernist crisis, such as baron von Hügel, whose work he translated during the latter's polemics with Blondel. Some of his first essays focused on Anglican writers—even though in time to come he confined his attention to the French Catholic world of the seventeenth century.

Translated during his lifetime, he seems after his death, both in France and abroad, to have sunk into a relative oblivion. The centenary of his birth was the occasion for manifestations of scholarly interest, from which issued fifteen years later Émile Goichot's thesis, conceived as "the biography of an *oeuvre*." Goichot's work has inscribed itself as well in the renewal of the study of Modernism, with Émile Poulat, and in the historiography of seventeenth-century religion, with Michel de Certeau. British and North American critical interest has focused especially on "pure poetry." Since 2000, then, and in turn, most notably in the work of Charles Talar, Bremond's work has also figured more prominently in our understanding of the Modernist context.

A second surge of interest has developed as a result of the new edition of the *Histoire littéraire* . . . in 2006. Peter Gorday participates here in this renewal, and should be congratulated for making better known in the United States this complex and engaging figure, Henri Bremond, who revealed the "spiritual interplay" (*révélatrice des enjeux*) of his era.

(tr. Peter Gorday)   François Trémolières
professeur des universités
L'université de Rennes 2

Preface

HENRI BREMOND (1865–1933), THOUGH now mostly forgotten, deserves better. He should be more robustly remembered as a wise spiritual writer and a gifted, innovative historian. This biography will, I hope, be a stimulus to that end.

Catholic priest, essayist, literary critic and commentator, biographer, "religious psychologist" (his favorite self-designation), as well as historian of religion, académicien from 1924 onward, tireless composer of a vast correspondence with a wide range of figures, aesthetic theorist dubbed the "curé d'art" in sophisticated, high-culture Paris in the years after the First World War—Bremond was all of these things and more. Born and reared in a French era rich beyond imagining, stretching from the Second Empire through the Franco-Prussian War and its aftermath to the early years of the Third Republic, he matured as a person, priest, and literary artist in the *belle époque*, late Victorian-Edwardian milieu of culturally hegemonic France, absorbing many of its currents into his spiritual work. With his major publications in hand, renown came to him during and after the Great War, but it was an unsteady prominence in an unstable, scarred environment filled with ceaseless turmoil in church, state, education, and the arts. Postwar cultural, social, and political changes of every kind signaled a watershed time for human thought, not least of all in the fields of theological and historical scholarship, where changed methods in research, new modes of understanding truth, and altered perceptions of the nature of religion itself, were in dynamic play. The comfortable certainties of the Old Order, already in decline before the war, gave way, despite widespread dismay, to the tormented uncertainties of Modernity.

Living through this revolutionary time, Bremond absorbed it all, struggled with his own demons, and reflected. As a historian, he crafted a mode of analysis in which the texts left by people who pray, who reveal their inner longings for commerce with God, became his central interest. As a student of literary expression, he became enamored of the lyricism, the poetic spirit or *sentiment*, that often surfaces in those texts that bear witness to the most intimate moments of prayer. As a priest, he became convinced that this prayer, which is also poetry, reveals a divine-human encounter in which pure love is the dominant note.

Preface

Popular with a wide readership at the time of his death in 1933, Bremond was lionized by the French *literati*, celebrated by the dignitaries of the church, and fondly recollected by many intimate friends. The funeral mass was celebrated in the cathedral of his native Aix-en-Provence by the archbishop himself and written up in the Paris newspapers. A service of remembrance, conducted by the rector of Paris's Institut Catholique and soon-to-be cardinal, Alfred Baudrillart, took place at Notre Dame. Having received a papal blessing during his last illness, one would hardly have known that one of Bremond's biographies had been put on the *Index*, that he had been disciplined for priestly disobedience, and that a perennial threat of churchly condemnation hung over much of his work.

Supported by many fans who applauded his intellectual daring, he also drew the barbed iron filings of criticism like a magnet. His involvement in ecclesial controversy made him notorious, although his ability to speak to spiritual "disquietude" made him beloved. Faithful friend to many of the Modernist rebels (Jean Baruzi famously called him the "stretcher-bearer" of the Modernist movement), he was also a bitter antagonist to seemingly mean-spirited religious traditionalism, as well as to organized hatred such as he saw in the Action Française movement of the postwar years. His single most famous publication, the massive eleven-volume *Histoire littéraire du sentiment religieux en France depuis la fin des guerres de religion jusqu'à nos jours*, published between 1916 and 1933, registered the nuances of his own development even as it served as a milestone in the historiography of the French seventeenth century.

All the more extraordinary is it, therefore, that after his death he was quickly forgotten by practically everyone except the compilers of church encyclopedias. The attention of French writers turned elsewhere as ideological developments escalated during the stormy 1930s. English translations of his work, proceeding apace in the decade before his death, came to a halt. Catholic scholars, when they chose to discuss his productions, usually categorized him as a "romantic," that label carrying the frequent implication of "overly idealistic and a bit naive." His methods or his constructions or his prejudices or his often ironic, gently mocking style of presentation were easily lambasted as insincere or dishonest. Ecclesial controversialists, often rehashing the issues of modernism vs. traditionalism, found him too elusive, too "chameleonic," in his advocacy of this-or-that position. Interest in him gradually became the preserve of specialists who study early twentieth-century Catholic Modernism or the history of spirituality, especially mysticism.

During, however, the period of the Second Vatican Council, and at the time of the centenary of his birth, the situation in France began to change. Several conferences and colloquia reflected, and stimulated, interest in Bremond. Seminal studies by André Blanchet—especially his biography of Bremond's early years, as well as his magisterial edition of Bremond's correspondence with Maurice Blondel—and by Émile Goichot on the processes that led Bremond to publish the *Histoire*, set the pace for new study. More recently, under the leadership of François Trémolières, scholars

Preface

have advanced progressive analyses of many aspects of Bremond's work, but most significant has been the new critical edition, in 2006, of the *Histoire* with interleaved interpretive essays and supplementary material. The sources are increasingly available (though no *oeuvres complètes* is in sight) for bold, new perspectives on the nature and import of Bremond's contributions not just to scholarship, but also to the spiritual renewal of church and society.

The time has come, thus, for the encouragement of fresh familiarity with, and assessment of, Bremond and his work in English-speaking circles. There has not been a major treatment in the Anglo-Saxon world since Henry Hogarth's biography of 1950. This book is an effort to fill the gap by offering a full-length biography that incorporates perspectives from recent French treatments. The reader will discover in Bremond a writer and thinker of breathtaking scope, genuine perspicacity, and winsome grace. He is entertaining to read, his views always spiced with wit and always discerning. He is a master of the ability to paint with the pen, so that his sketches come alive with flair and nuance. His fondness at times for an idiosyncratic terminology in interpretation should not obscure the fundamental nature of his perceptive brilliance.

In my conclusions I offer a thesis about the structure of spiritual life as Bremond gradually came to understand it—a "nexus" of pure love, pure poetry, and pure prayer. And I particularly highlight his long dialogue with Maurice Blondel as the single most important smelting-furnace of his thought. Many other figures will enter the narrative, as well as major environmental forces and trends—Jesuit debates, Catholic Modernism, the study of mysticism, the war, and so on. It is only fitting that a writer who saw history as a vast cast of speaking and writing characters should himself have lived a crowded life of endless dialogue and unceasing written expression. But within the confused welter, his voice and his composition produced a particular clarity and synthesis from which we can continue to learn a great deal, as Bremond's current French interpreters are robustly demonstrating. Perhaps an American "spin" on the discussion can open even more windows for fresh and invigorating spiritual air!

Acknowledgments

IN THE COURSE OF researching and writing this biography I have incurred three levels of debt.

The first is owed to the tireless librarians and archivists who have retrieved materials for me from various storage sites: the Woodruff and Pitts libraries of Emory University, Atlanta; the University Library of Georgia State University, Atlanta; the University of Georgia Main Library at Athens, GA; the University Library of the State University of New York at Albany; the Perry-Castañeda Library of the University of Texas, Austin. Online resources have been invaluable as well, most of all those of the Bibliothèque nationale de France.

A second level of indebtedness accrues to those two researchers who have laid the foundations on which all work about Henri Bremond must rest: André Blanchet, SJ, and Émile Goichot.

The third level is the most personal. Bernard McGinn first put me on the trail of the contemporary researchers in Bremond studies. Charles Talar and François Trémolières, both busy university professors whose scholarly endeavors on Bremond and his milieu are noted throughout, have then been unstinting with support, commentary, bibliography, and the gift of their own most recent publications. Talar provided —far above and beyond the call of duty—a careful critical reading of an early draft, saving me from some egregious errors, while Trémolières graciously agreed to provide a foreword and a priceless picture of Bremond "au livre." Both men are pacesetting leaders in Bremond studies in this country and in Europe. Thanks are due also to Jon Sweeney, editor of my *Fénelon* for Paraclete Press, for directing me to Wipf & Stock.

Most of all, I am deeply grateful to the late Eugene TeSelle, specialist in the study of Augustine and my onetime PhD advisor at Vanderbilt University, and always diligent reader and critic of my various publications. We started out with patristic biblical exegesis, then moved to Origen, then to Augustine and Augustinian tradition, took a detour with psychoanalysis and David Bakan and Heinz Kohut, continued on with Fénelon, finally landing with Henri Bremond. Gene enthusiastically reviewed, and issued insightful commentary on, the pieces of this haltingly emerging biography at every step.

Acknowledgments

My greatest debt is, as always, to my wife Virginia, unfailingly supportive, ever faithful, steadfast at the copy machine! She has made the conditions under which I could compose this work possible. Bremond (and I) agree with Paul: *Major autem horum est caritas.*

Abbreviations and Short Titles of Frequently Cited Works

BB	*Henri Bremond et Maurice Blondel, Correspondance*, ed. A. Blanchet (3 vols.)
DS	*Dictionnaire de spiritualité ascétique et mystique*
EG	Émile Goichot, *Henri Bremond historien du sentiment religieux*
GT	Alfred Loisy, *George Tyrrell et Henri Bremond*
Histoire	Henri Bremond, *Histoire littéraire du sentiment religieux en France*, Bloud et Gay edition (11 vols., 1916–1933)
HLM	Henri Bremond, *Histoire littéraire du sentiment religieux en France*, Millon edition (5 vols., 2006)
MC	Maurice Martin Du Gard, *Les Mémorables* (3 vols.)
MG	Maurice Martin Du Gard, *De Sainte-Beuve à Fénelon, Henri Bremond*
VB	André Blanchet, *Henri Bremond 1865–1904*

1

Introduction
High Honors

IN THE SPRING OF 1924 the abbé Henri Bremond received the greatest public honor his country could bestow on a historian and writer. Having completed to popular acclaim, but mixed scholarly reviews—even outrage in some quarters—the first six volumes of his *Histoire littéraire*, his projected *Literary History of the Religious Sentiment in France from the Wars of Religion down to the Present Time*,[1] he was elected to membership in that revered bastion of elite French culture, the Académie française. He had made it to the top.

The journey, however, had been a rocky one, and he had been an unlikely candidate. His Provençal roots marked him as a regional and provincial character; his early career as a Catholic priest had been turbulent with departure from the Jesuit order; his involvement with Modernist writers and thinkers had led at one point to ecclesiastical censure; his 1912 biography of Ste. Jeanne de Chantal had landed on the Index of Prohibited Books. He was not a product of the prestigious Parisian Écoles normales, and he had not secured a university position. Further, the principal focus of his best-known historical work—Catholic spirituality in the seventeenth century—might easily have ensured permanent oblivion for all but a handful of readers in a secular society increasingly alienated from traditional churchly discourse.

But, just the opposite happened. Enthusiastically devouring long passages from the often obscure spiritual writers that Bremond cited in abundance, a diverse constituency had been enthralled by the liveliness and sparkle of his presentation, especially by his ability to capture the energy of the inner struggle to secure a place with God as something literary and *artful*, as poetry and autobiographical remembrance and journalistic intimacy and lyrical prayer. In a long tradition hearkening back at least to

---

1. Published in eleven volumes between 1916 and 1933 by Bloud et Gay, it will be referred to throughout this work as *Histoire*, followed by the volume number in Roman capitals, then the page number(s). All translations from French, unless otherwise indicated in the notes, will be my own.

Saint-Simon's famous memoirs from the time of Louis XIV, Bremond had mastered techniques of literary portraiture, of word-painting, in order to make religious affections, specifically the inner life of prayer, aesthetically compelling, not only for people who *do* pray, but also for those who *might*. And the fact that these affections were distinctively *French* only heightened his readership's pride and pleasure in a wartime of desperate patriotic struggle for survival.

The occasion of his induction to the Académie thus marked a moment of extraordinary success for Henri Bremond, a moment whose peculiar significance resided in the kind of historical work that he was attempting to do and in the tenor of his "message," as well as in the validation that membership as an *académicien français* entails.[2]

Though partial imitations exist in other countries, the Académie is an institution unique to France and French society. One of the five learned "companies" that since the Revolution of 1789 and its aftermath make up the Institut de France, chartered originally by Louis XIII in 1637 with precise and strict statutes, it has a peculiar national mandate: to oversee the production of the definitive dictionary of the French language, and, second, to award prizes for distinction in the arts. The Académie functions in effect as an instrument of national unity by means of linguistic unity, with "the office not to create, but to register, words approved by the authority of the best writers and by good society."[3] France being a composite land of quite distinct regional dialects and traditions, with today's multiculturalism adding to the complexity, there is in the work of the Académie the reflecting, and then reinforcing, of an aesthetically-derived social cohesion. Moreover, the work is done not by a group of professors from the universities, but by savants and successful professionals from every walk of life, including generals, diplomats and politicians, as well as artists. As the "arbiters of elegance," the mandarins of excellence, the members of the Académie are not primarily erudite specialists, but figures representative of popular standing and general culture.[4]

For French thinkers of every sort, moreover, election to membership in the Académie can justly be described as the ultimate and official act of recognition of one's "voice," of one's popular impact, in a society where the role of the "public intellectual" remains very strong. That kind of presence of intellectuals in the public mind, whereby they constitute an "intelligentsia," is a very European thing, an acknowledgment that ideas emanating from well-trained thinkers matter in the formation of national purpose and the setting of tone for national life.[5] Dubbed the "Immortels" by long custom

---

2. For what follows, see the three-part essay by Goichot, "Deux historiens à l'Académie," and Sorrel, "Henri Bremond académicien français."

3. Le Bars, *French Academy*, loc. 30.

4. Overview of the history and functioning of the Académie may be found at http://www.academie-francaise.fr, in the *Wikipedia* article "Académie-française," and in Le Bars, *French Academy*, loc. 30.

5. Members of the Académie were often radicalized politically to the royalist/Catholic right or the Republican/secular left, their votes for new members being reflected accordingly. The Académie thus sometimes operated as a bully pulpit whose power for intellectuals could possess an almost sacral status. On the role of public intellectuals in the European context, see TeSelle, "Engaged Intellectuals,"

Introduction

(because presumably their ideas and contributions will live on after them), and limited by statute to a membership of forty, the Académie meets regularly in closed sessions to present and discuss issues of scholarship, public interest, and cultural definition. Members are elected for life by their peers, each member occupying a specific seat in direct intellectual succession to the deceased predecessor.

And so it is no wonder that the early afternoon of May 22, 1924, found Henri Bremond, then fifty-nine years old, both exhilarated and nervous as he prepared to complete his induction into the Académie with a substantive address. Standing on Paris's quai Conti close by the meeting place of the Académie *sous la Coupule*, "under the cupola," of the Palais de l'Institut, he greeted friends and pondered his upcoming "discours de réception." In the traditional green-embroidered coat of an académicien for the first time, he would be officially welcomed to the podium by the Perpetual Secretary, and then begin his initiatory presentation, while new peers and specially invited guests gauged his performance. The purpose of this ritually enacted "discours" is twofold: appreciative commemoration of the work of the esteemed predecessor in the seat in question (the *fauteuil*), and then a sketch of the direction of the inductee's own ongoing work. Continuity and discontinuity are in play, therefore, at the same time, a prolongation of the past and a creative anticipation of the future. Build on your forebear, but improve on him as well!

The relationship of a new member to his/her predecessor can be, thus, a subtle matter. When a sitting member dies, the first step for replacement is a formal nomination, declared by a member in writing to the Secretary of the Académie, of a suitable candidate for the vacated seat. Campaigning then begins with a round of social visits to members by the candidate in order to (gently and by implication) solicit their support,[6] since there will have been other candidates nominated as well for the same seat, and because it is these same, presently sitting members who will cast the decisive yea or nay votes. One of the questions in the minds of the electors will be: is this candidate a suitable/worthy/sufficiently accomplished replacement for our departed and esteemed colleague?

For Bremond, the nominator was the well-known, indeed notorious for many, nationalistic novelist and propagandist Maurice Barrès, and the seat to be filled would be that of the distinguished, though massively controversial, church historian Mgr Louis Duchesne, deceased on April 21, 1922. Complications abounded. Barrès was scorned for his type of hyper-patriotic French chauvinism, including his association with the anti-Semitic, monarchist Action Française, seen by many as fascist.

304–5: "Especially in the modern world—and this, in fact, is one of the defining features of 'modern'—intellectuals have become increasingly independent, filling the role played in more traditional societies by seers and prophets, bishops and theologians."

6. Pierre Arrou describes this socializing as a state of being "*en coquetterie*," and cites a letter of Bremond to his friend and later bibliographer, Charles Grolleau, in which he humorously describes the process as campaigning-without-seeming-to-campaign (Arrou, "Henri Bremond et Charles Grolleau," 53).

3

Duchesne was despised by many Catholics as a liberal proto-Modernist, a historical-critical debunker of saints's legends and an irreverent, Voltaire-like wit in relation to the unspiritual foibles of church history. His landmark history of the church, critically sophisticated but deemed irreverent by traditionalists, went on the Index in 1912. With two such polarizing figures as Barrès and Duchesne to be acknowledged and honored through his candidacy, Bremond in his canvassing, and later in his induction, needed to affirm what he saw as the best in these two, while steering clear of their excesses or blind spots. It would prove to be a delicate balancing act.

What he had the cold comfort of knowing in his nervousness on that afternoon of May 22 was that, as things turned out, he had been elected by a respectable majority of votes on the second ballot, and precisely in circumstances where multiple ballots resulting in a candidate's final defeat were not unusual. In this case, some members would have been indifferent to the election of a churchman to one of the seats traditionally reserved for church representation, while rightist and anti-Duchesne conservatives and politically leftist opponents of Barrès might have joined to oppose Bremond. The Roman Catholic hierarchy, always proud to have one of its own seated at the Académie, while ambivalently supportive of Bremond, threw in its weight.[7] On April 29, with twenty-nine members present (twenty is a quorum) in a session at the Institut, with seventeen positive votes cast (absentees are counted as positives) Bremond had his majority and was in.[8]

The preliminary rituals had quickly passed. As required by statute, the President of the Republic, Alexandre Millerand, had signaled approval of the election, and Bremond then prepared for the "installation," which is a private, closed-door ceremony conducted by a select group of members in the meeting chamber at the Institut. Accompanied by his two "sponsors," the novelist Paul Bourget and Mgr Baudrillart (thus symbolizing the conjunction of secular and sacred), Bremond first read a draft of his "discours," in order to certify its formal adequacy—that is, that it conformed to the requirements for eulogy of predecessor, length, tone, etc. We know, in fact, that Bremond had gone through, and continued at this point to go through, a painful vetting process in the construction of his text. Conflicting input came from a number of associates, with some advising forthright boldness, come what may, but others urging caution and circumspection. As he constantly revised, he wrestled with his need for integrity in the message with reasonable deference to the sensibilities of his audience.

---

7. Sorrel points out that church representation since 1854 had been consistently liberal, thus allowing Duchesne to be elected in a hotly contested rivalry in 1910 (Bremond had written in support of him) (Sorrel, "Henri Bremond," 151–52). A more conservative turn happened with the election of the rector of Paris's Institut Catholique, Alfred Baudrillart, but Baudrillart was supportive of Bremond. See Chauvin, *Petite Vie de Henri Bremond*, ch. 4, for a lively account here.

8. Goichot indicates that the election was "easy," but the session was "stormy," with the rejection of the candidacy of Charles Maurras of Action Française (Goichot, "Deux historiens," 47n2). Bremond was preferred over the archaeologist and historian Claude Jullian, who would, however, be elected soon after.

Introduction

In any case, all went well at the installation and he was led to his seat, vested in the traditional regalia with medallion (with the "Immortels" inscription), and assigned his word for the Dictionary. He also learned who would be the respondent to his "discours," none other than the conservative Catholic, lawyer, and man-of-letters, Henry Bordeaux, a witty, shrewd personification of old-fashioned and nationalistic values. Bordeaux had been charmed by Bremond's portraiture of Francis de Sales,[9] but he was at the same time suspicious of modernizing trends. Bremond thus had good reason to anticipate that his reception would generate sophisticated riposte[10]—as would indeed prove to be the case—to his opening remarks. His big day with its "public seating" was assured, but it would not be easy.

The house was full that afternoon, and it was quite warm. Cardinal Dubois, archbishop of Paris, had his chair up front, with President Millerand seated underneath Bossuet's statue, with Baudrillart and Bourget next to Bremond, M. Bordeaux presiding. The literary critic Paul Souday, in due course an opponent of Bremond's theories, would write the primary newspaper report. Goichot suggests that the size of the turnout reflected the controversy around Bremond after the condemnation of his work on Chantal, as well as the reputation he shared with Duchesne for caustic wit regarding all things ecclesiastical.[11] Surely everyone was expecting great fun. The worst thing for Bremond would have been to be dull, or contrariwise, to engage in empty bravado. His most cautious advisers had warned him against shooting himself in the foot. So he went ahead and ruffled feathers, while being careful, so to speak, to cover his flanks.

His opening emotional tribute was to his nominator Barrès, deceased since the nomination, as an artist who always sought truth in a long tradition of fearless writing.[12] He then continued with praise for Duchesne as one in a long history of historians, including the Protestant controversialist Jean Daillé, who had "the eye, the nose, the ear" for what is genuine and what fraudulent in ancient documents, thus manifesting the "divine part" in the faculties of the historian with the instinct of a poet. Mastery of detail, while possessing the ability to cut to the essence of historical material, as in his (condemned) work on the early church, those were Duchesne's hallmarks, along with a gift for sensing what is mysterious and puzzling in texts, without jumping to premature conclusions.[13]

---

9. Sorrel, "Henri Bremond," 153.

10. Bremond had submitted to Bordeaux ahead of time, at the latter's request, an autobiographical sketch with personal background information, Blanchet has published a text that appears to be that note, "Henri Bremond: Notes autobiographiques." Bordeaux made the most of it.

11. Goichot, "Deux historiens," 34. Bremond's faithful publishers, Francisque Gay and Edmond Bloud, begged him to go easy (ibid., 392–93), and so a *commercial* agenda entered the picture!

12. In his tribute, Bremond, after referring to a liberty that Voltaire (!) had taken in his own opening address at the Académie, said to those assembled, "He who came to me in my solitude to present me for your suffrages, covering me in some degree with his glory, Maurice Barrès, is no longer here to receive me with you" (*Discours de réception*, 7–8).

13. Ibid., 9–11.

One might say that Bremond was here praising Duchesne for his humility in the face of the sources, listening, always listening, and not forcing the material into a preset, thus rationalizing, mold. In that sense, Duchesne's work became a kind of anti-Renan, challenging that great rationalist's constructions, at the same time that he opposed merely pious interpretation of the past.[14] Bremond did not use the term "empathy" here, since he was not schooled in the work of Wilhelm Dilthey, but empathy is what he liked in Duchesne. *Listen to the writer's heartbeat in the text, without imposing.* That is absolutely essential.

Bremond then shifted to the way in which Duchesne straddled the worlds of Catholic scholarship, just coming into its own with the establishment of the Parisian Institut Catholique under the leadership of Mgr d'Hulst and in the spirit of the *ralliement*[15] of Leo XIII, and the scientific spirit of secular research (one can see Bremond glancing at Cardinal Dubois and Mgr Baudrillart here). In a truly Christian soul, claimed Bremond, these two are united without effort. And there is the first of Bremond's battle cries. "In validating for himself and his students the right to accept loyally the rules of historical work, Duchesne served the magnanimous thoughts of the Holy Father."[16] Heavy-handed at times with irony, averred Bremond, as he patiently dismantled pious legends and theologically biased accounts of church councils, Duchesne embodied "an imagination profoundly realist" in the interpretation of history. With an acknowledgment to his own critics, Bremond admitted that there could be, as in family fights, too much "persiflage" on the historian's part, a kind of ill-spirited condescension toward the past in the manner of Edward Gibbon. But all of that is part of scholarship, part of the purification of historical perspective, and no sin against charity.[17] In Duchesne's case, it was a manifestation of the "saint" and the "man" in a single personality.

After some rehearsing of the fact that critical historians have always ruffled feathers, Bremond came to a central point: "Critics are never popular!" They disrupt all of our comfort and our certitudes, sometimes with ephemeral conjectures that will be tested over time and sometimes accepted, sometimes rejected, through a slow process of percolation, as Edmund Burke has taught us.[18] The point is that Duchesne was committed to truth and believed with absolute resoluteness that there is nothing to fear, for it will triumph in the end. And here Bremond got personal. Some of Duchesne's work had involved the toppling of his own idols, some of the saints' legends of his

---

14. Ibid., 13.

15. The decision of Leo XIII to support and encourage a collaborative spirit between the Catholic Church of France and the secular French Republic.

16. Ibid., 20–21.

17. Ibid., 23–26. Bremond made the discerning observation that it was not "among things properly divine" that Duchesne could be a biting critic, but rather "in that uncertain zone, where the profane and the sacred seem to be confounded, where the saint risks hiding the human being, and the human being the saint" (ibid., 25). He might well have been speaking, of course, of his own work.

18. Ibid., 31–33, 36.

beloved Provence! Duchesne possessed the peasant's sense that appearance and reality may be quite different things, even in those customs and traditions that one loves best. Bremond thus forged the argument that the critic who steps on many toes does it out of love for the thing itself, so to speak, and not for its particular manifestations, which may be flawed and disposable.[19]

Thus it was, insisted Bremond, that Duchesne was a true son of the Church, faithful to the end and ultimately submissive to authority. He was a critic and a Christian simultaneously, but he could also be wrong. In fact, says Bremond strikingly, "pure criticism is a myth."[20] Good historical-critical writing is, he says, a kind of poetry, in which the critic's faith-perspective sets the tone, shapes the perception of what is true and powerful, or not, in the past. For Duchesne (and here, we must say, for Bremond as well) the goal was always to get behind the dogmas to the living experience that created them and that is reflected in them, so that the real humanity of past characters, and finally of the Incarnation itself, comes into focus.[21] Submission to the Roman Church is not a matter of bowing to an abstraction, but a matter of immersion in a flesh-and-blood community of belief and practice, always "developing" its faith as new truth unfolds and new questions are being asked. Duchesne thus wrote with a "tranquil audacity about the truth," thereby producing history and not romance, which is the truth of real human beings, not idealizations.[22] Duchesne shows us, says Bremond, that the critic must love what it is he hopes to understand, for, lacking that love he will end up in incomprehension.[23]

It seems that Bremond's intentions were clear at this point. He wanted to send a message that he himself would continue in the same bold historical-critical spirit of Duchesne's scholarship as well as in his loyal churchmanship, but *not necessarily* with the same need to demolish old positions. One can hear in Bremond's tones a gentle dismissal of Duchesne's roughness. Duchesne had been a Breton—blunt, frank, fearless, but deeply faithful—while he, Bremond would be more Provençal—romantic, subtle, colorful and tender. That is the implication. Duchesne had been a bit of a bulldozer, while he, Bremond, would operate with more delicate instruments, more like a spiritual pathologist, distinguishing good tissue from diseased in people's souls, not just their actions.[24]

---

19. In a subtle argument that common sense about one's own beloved regional traditions can link up with the critic's sense that truth and legend need to be distinguished (ibid., 35–41).

20. "Doesn't everyone know that pure criticism is a myth, like the blank slate so vaunted in the *Discours de la méthode*, a chimera?" (ibid., 44). A point that Bremond's mentor, Maurice Blondel, had worked relentlessly to impress upon him.

21. Duchesne made it clear that "speculation and life will always be two different things" (ibid., 48).

22. "His devotion to Rome did not in any way compromise the honesty of his criticism . . . he wanted to write the history, not the romance, of the popes" (ibid., 52).

23. Ibid., 58.

24. In fact, Duchesne was no great enthusiast for Bremond's inward focus, having greeted the first volume of the *Histoire* with courteous, but not enthusiastic, praise. Duchesne thought the history of

Pure Love, Pure Poetry, Pure Prayer

As he rounded off his discourse to a rapt audience, thus, including the evocation of extensive intellectual pedigrees to support his every point (a talent now fully matured at the height of Bremond's development) he paid the customary respects very eloquently, including a compliment, to the current Pope, Pius XI, for his progressive zeal.

Bordeaux's response was urbane, but ham-fisted. Describing Bremond as a "magician," while Duchesne was a "pyro-technician," he defended Duchesne as a true churchman by arguing that his celebrated, sometimes feared, caustic skepticism was more a matter of style, than substance.[25] After a salty reference to Bremond's Jesuit background, Bordeaux displayed his own preferences that ran counter to those of Bremond: Bossuet is superior to Fénelon, John Henry Newman is a dangerously radical and anti-authoritarian character, and so on. In conservative vs. liberal fashion, Bordeaux was mostly interested in opening up some old debates. One can only imagine a sigh of relief on Bremond's part as the occasion came to an end, and his initiation to the Académie was finished. The press reported the event as "wise, moderate."[26]

There is a photograph of Bremond, looking pleased but exhausted, while walking away from the Institut afterward in the company of a (perhaps) Mademoiselle J. Durand,[27] associated with his publisher. Another photo shows him being congratulated by two unnamed gentlemen, while well-wishers, men and women, stand in the background. Grolleau reported that the social occasion afterward was quite well attended.[28] It all looks and sounds very convivial. Did the ecclesiastics in attendance approve? No photo survives to tell us.

---

mysticism, or spirituality, to be elitist and dated, while the history of the skeptical dismantling of old verities is contemporary and relevant (Goichot, "Deux historiens," 42–43). See also Marxer, "L'abbé Bremond," 18–20, for a comparison of Bremond and Duchesne with regard to historical method and goals. Both rejected hagiography, but then their paths diverged.

25. Bordeaux, *Un sourcier*. Chauvin, citing Alfred Baudrillart's musings about, and description of, the occasion, published in the nine volumes of the latter's *Carnets d'Alfred Baudrillard 1918-1942* after WWII, refers to his comment that Bremond seemed "quite nervous" during Bordeaux's remarks, finding the latter's thought "certainly less subtle, but decidedly Christian" (Chauvin, *Petite Vie*, 102).

26. Goichot, "Deux historiens," 35.

27. My speculation! According to a note in EN, 246, the famous photo emanated from "Mademoiselle J. Durand."

28. Arrou, "Henri Bremond," 54. Grolleau indicated that he could not get close to Bremond because of the crowd.

Introduction

Analysis of Bremond's initiation came years later from Alfred Loisy.[29] The core issue, Loisy thought, was the relationship between science and religion. He contended that in truth Bremond had failed to satisfy either side in the debate. The traditionalists hated the skeptical tone and resented the dismissal of saints' legends, while the secularists deplored the idea that a purely objective critical method is a "Cartesian delusion." But, it must be said, Loisy was contemptuous of Bremond's, and Duchesne's, efforts to have it both ways, that is, to stay in the church and be loyal to critical methods, and he sympathized with Bordeaux's jab, that Bremond still had too much of the Jesuit about him, as well as Souday's dismayed response to Duchesne's dismissal of Renan and Gibbon as historians. But Henri Bremond was no hypocrite; by praising Barrès and Duchesne he was articulating his own struggle to define his own hermeneutic, his own empathic way of reading the sources and feeling after their truth, letting their *sentiment religieux* resonate with the present. Bremond's claim was that he saw this method at work in Duchesne, even though Duchesne, always atheoretical, resisted formulating it as such. But he, Bremond would continue it, precisely now as an *inner* history, the history of souls rather than external events.

But in May 1924, Bremond was not quite there yet. He was still in the process of elaborating a point of view that would come out fully only in 1926 and 1927 in the seventh and eighth volumes of the *Histoire*, where he argued that the spirituality of "pure love" is the living heartbeat of all mysticism, which is to say of all prayer, which is to say of the entire life of the church, insofar as it is empowered by God's "sanctifying grace"! The concept of "pure love" had crystallized, come into full view, only in Bremond's 1910 book on Fénelon,[30] but it registered a gathering, cumulative kind of awareness in his thought, developing through many twists and turns.

I want to show in what follows that "pure love" is an interpretative "master key" beyond what Loisy imagined, a key that evolved into the correlated concepts of "pure love," "pure prayer," and "pure poetry." When Bremond suggested that the loving understanding of the competent historian, as exemplified by Duchesne, is a kind of poetry, and that his work *is* prayer, we should take him seriously. Unlike Loisy, for whom the historical-critical methods led to a universal "religion of humanity," Bremond remained resolutely, if at times agonizingly, Catholic, convinced that sensitivity to the divine mystical presence in all traditions leads one deeper into one's own heritage, and not away from it, that "pure love" precisely in order to be pure, must also be grounded in the specifics and particularities of concrete traditions.

Henri Bremond's induction into the Académie may thus be seen as the cresting of a wave. The whole momentum of his intellectual and literary career, not to mention

---

29. GT, ch. 2.

30. For all of the difficulties that we will note with his essay, Guibert was essentially correct (echoing Saint-Simon's famous estimation of Fénelon himself) in stating that for all of his "extravagances," Bremond was, in the boldness of his writing like "son vrai maître Fénelon, de singulièrement prenant, élevant and séduisant" (Guibert, "Bremond," 1937). Guibert thus echoed Bordeaux's "sourcier" as well.

his ecclesial and political trajectory, led to that day and that climactic acclaim, while all that followed was the receding after-play of clarification and the extracting of implications, with an enrapt public looking on. The origins were quiet, correspondingly obscure even, though filled with the elements of an extraordinary intellectual and psychological complexity awaiting sophisticated expression. This would come amid all of the contradictions of modernity in *fin-de-siècle* Paris, a place exquisitely attuned to the *au courant* while always engaged, in Proust's famous phrase, in "the remembrance of things past." An ideal environment for a budding historian determined to write history that "speaks."

2

Aixois Roots and Politics
The First Stirrings of a Devout Humanist

THE YEARS 1903–1910 ARE the pivotal, nodal period in Henri Bremond's life, because they are the period in which three strands of formative influence in his development became tightly interwoven. One strand was the English, culminating in his four different books (1904–1906) on John Henry Newman, then still somewhat unknown to French readers, as well as a study of the English Catholic Erasmian and humanist, Sir Thomas More (1903). Second was the nativist element: book-length treatments of two seventeenth-century Provençal mystics, Antoine Yvan and Madeleine Martin, popular in the local history of Aix-en-Provence, and then of the work of novelist Maurice Barrès, appeared in 1908. And a third marked his increasing intuition that the seventeenth-century debates about quietism, mysticism, and pure love provided the essential key to French spiritual history, culminating in his 1910 book on François Fénelon and setting the stage for the future *Histoire*. Interlarded with the production of these major studies was Bremond's journalistic production: major review essays where, in the course of critically assessing a wide range of biographies, memoirs and new editions of classic authors, he offered interpretations of their work that showed the movement of his own thought as well.

That second strand, the nativist, exposed Bremond's complex relationship to provincial roots that he deeply treasured, but that over the years became increasingly problematic. While spirituality may begin with the earth, it often does not, indeed must not, end there: Bremond loved Provence, but that love gradually grew, became enlarged, reached for the universal in the particular, while never forgetting that the universal always begins with, and returns to, the particular. The essential elements were his Provençal childhood in a distinguished, but politically polarized family, Catholic upbringing and early schooling in an environment saturated with literature, then a vocation to priesthood and entry into the Jesuit order, where in time he would be followed by his two younger brothers, André and Jean.

Quiet, but Seething

The year was 1865 in Aix-en-Provence, when Henri, their second child, was born on July 31 to Pierre and Thomasine Bremond, he a third-generation notary, and she a descendant of the ancient Provençal-Occitan Pons family.[1] The place of birth—to this day still the residence of notaries—was the Bremond family home, decorated with the notary's escutcheon, at no. 34, Place des Prêcheurs, a short distance from the baroque-era Church of the Madeleine, where the family attended regularly and Henri would be baptized as Marie Joseph François Régis Ignace Henri on August 5. He seems to have looked more like his mother,[2] indicating, perhaps, that he would come to share more of her spirit and allegiances than those of his father—which, indeed, proved to be the case. His older brother was Émile, and there would be in due course a sister, Marguerite, eventually to enter the religious life, finally André and Jean.

A group photo, taken when Henri appears to be about eight years old, shows bright, well-dressed children, terribly bored, it seems, by sustaining a pose, with just a sly hint that they are about to say something sarcastic. The family was prosperous and well-regarded in the community, solidly moyen-bourgeois, socializing often with the Catholic clergy, especially the Jesuits. The domestic dwelling is a four-story affair, typical of the time and place, with a street-level entryway area, two levels for the family, and probably the top level for servants and storage. For the most part, the impression is of a peaceful, harmonious and orderly world, a kind of small-town idyll. Or least it seemed so to the Bremond brothers in retrospect.

Today a mid-sized cathedral-university center about thirty kilometers NNE of its overshadowing metropolis and neighbor, the bustling Mediterranean port of Marseilles, Aix was in the time of Bremond's childhood a modest community of about 20,000 inhabitants. Founded, according to tradition, by the consul Sextius Calvinus in 123 BC because of its proximity to an abundant water source, the springs of Aquae Sextiae, the Romans developed it as the chief settlement of southern Gaul. University, church and an independent Parlement grew vigorously during the Middle Ages. After the Revolution of 1789 a certain level of political autonomy was curtailed, but Aix continued to grow in the cultivation of learning and the arts, as well as a focus of Provencal regional culture. It is a place of stately ancient architecture and medieval lineaments, graceful tree-lined avenues, and customs and practices rich with preserved forms. Education is treasured and tasteful beauty is a supreme value. Bremond's memories of

---

1. In addition to the material gathered by Blanchet (VB, 13–28), Henry Hogarth's *Henri Bremond* has interesting detail. Older biographers of Bremond, like Hogarth, were heavily dependent for his early years on the account by Maurice Martin Du Gard, MG, based on interviews by the author with Bremond himself. And Blanchet had the further information that came from the aforementioned memo that Bremond prepared for Henry Bordeaux at the time of his entry to the Académie.

2. Charpin, "Souvenirs d'un Aixois," 28. Dr. Charpin suggests that the possible reason for so many baptismal names is that Henri's mother wanted to maximize his heavenly protection.

the gentle Catholic ambience of old Aix convey an impression of maternal embrace, a "safe place for children," as we now say.

In his 1908 work on the Provençal mystic, Père Antoine Yvan, Henri acknowledged that as he did research in old archives at Aix, he found himself reliving his childhood in "a venerable little world whose scoldings and caresses surrounded my young years," a place where holiness and devotion and virtue flourished. André Blanchet emphasizes how strongly Bremond insisted that Aix possessed in his childhood a striking continuity with the time of Yvan, a place where change came very slowly and the past was lovingly venerated, a place where the religious house founded by Yvan still persevered. Reminiscing in 1925, Bremond recalled "the members of religious orders," dating back to the *ancien régime*, "Carmelites passing by in the old alleys that ran by the Cathedral," as he, with childlike wonder, watched the procession of these holy men and women in their habits.[3] He remembered long walks to local places of interest, often accompanied by mentors and friends, with the pleasant sights and the lively conversations reflective of that precious commodity *amitié*, comradeship. Church and culture were smoothly symbiotic; Christian teaching and discipline coexisted with the humanistic values of polite and lettered society in a comfortable communion.[4]

A charming picture, to be sure, but let us call it "creative nostalgia," since we know that the France of 1865, in the troubled last years of the reign of Emperor Louis Napoleon, despite its cultivated sheen, was increasingly torn by discord. Having successfully smothered down old enmities for a time by means of a relative political stability and widespread prosperity, Louis's empire was near its end. The boy Henri Bremond may not have felt the tensions directly, but the adults certainly did, and with increasing anxiety.

One mark of discontent was the current upsurge in Provençal regionalism, a reaction to the relentless forces of centralization, standardization and homogenization that a painfully modernizing French government attempted to enforce. Post-Revolutionary France had struggled relentlessly with centrifugal forces and national fracturing grounded in old loyalties and more recent class divisions. One result was that local peculiarities and heritage were sometimes downplayed as "provincial" in the familiar and negative sense of that term. We have noted the role of the Académie in fostering a linguistic cohesion for the nation.

But periodically there would be a countervailing dynamic. In the time of Bremond's childhood, a Provençal literary revival, known as the *Félibrige* ("pupil" or "follower"), was in its ascendency, calling for an enhanced artistic status for the Provençal

---

3. Bremond, *La Provence mystique*, 4, and VB, 15–16, including the 1925 citation from a short-lived history of Catholic literature, the *Manual illustré*.

4. Martin Du Gard rhapsodized—presumably because Bremond did so—about Aix as a place that was ideally suited to produce the soul of a poet, where Bremond's "first formation" was marked by "the fountains, gardens, Florentine-style homes, the convents and cicadas," a place where the "flowered cloister" and the "resonant pine woods" (MG, 10–12) were reminiscent of the first church-run school that Bremond would attend.

native dialect of Occitan or the "langue d'Oc." At the center of the movement, and now its most remembered figure, was the popular novelist Frédéric Mistral.[5] It seems that Bremond never took much interest in Mistral and the Occitan movement,[6] but what did interest him intensely by way of this kind of regionalism was the work of Maurice Barrès, who celebrates another region—Lorraine—in his work. Bremond affirmed this kind of literature, despite its vulnerability to jingoism, but ultimately he treated it as a kind of refracting lens, a way of capturing and focusing something larger, which he called in a tribute to Barrès "the religious problem."[7]

What preoccupied Bremond, when he thought of the Provençal legacy, was the idea of character, that distinctive regions are generative of distinctive kinds of personalities. In his study of Antoine Yvan, he argued that this mystic exemplified a type: the peasant saint of Provence. Such a man, claimed Bremond, has a deeply penitential streak which moves in the direction of a mysticism of charity. He is impetuous and brooding, leaning toward the depressive. There is a constant "return of disquietude" in his makeup, with a tendency to frequent changes of direction. His piety tends to be a product of expressions and experiences gathered from his immersion in social life. And yet he is fiercely independent, so that his character "fits poorly with the demands of community life and the yoke of a regular discipline." Yvan was marked by the Provençal love for concrete and sensuous images with a fondness for "exaggeration" in his theological expressions, for radical and extreme statement.[8] There is the implication as well that the capacity for humor, the ability to laugh at foibles and absurdities, is always present. Surely Bremond was describing himself as well as Yvan.

It is no wonder that Bremond's later critics would label him a "gamin," an impulsive imp always loving the joke, the master of "sprightly *brio*."[9] But that is another way of saying "the Provençal type," the daring lover, passionate, colorful, and free-spirited, a "child" (somewhat) tamed by social requirements! There is no question that Bremond

---

5. See Zeldin, *History of French Passions*, II, esp. ch. 1, "The National Identity," and ch. 2, "The Provinces." He notes that by 1859, efforts at linguistic standardization (recall the mission of the Académie) were being vigorously resisted, at the same time that pseudoscientific notions of racial/ethnic superiority were evolving.

6. An exception, however, is in his *Discours de réception*, where he described Mistral and others in the Occitan movement as equal in culture to the best from Paris, at the same time that they defended local traditions, such as saints' legends, not so much for historical veracity as for the spirit they evoked. Thus, said Bremond, "my noble town of Aix, a center of good sense, of atticism, stood ready to accept the critical spirit with a smile" (*Discours de réception*, 38–39).

7. Bremond, "Maurice Barrès," lxiv–lxv.

8. Bremond, *La Provence mystique*, 1–5, 112–14, 155–57. Blanchet builds his whole introduction to Bremond's early life around this material from the study of Yvan, contending that Bremond was "impregnated" with this regional consciousness, particular at his reception into the Académie (VB, 13). Quite true.

9. Blanchet, "L'Abbé Bremond," is rich in psychologically colored insight. He lovingly sketches the "jokester" side of Bremond, highlighting George Tyrrell's hard description of Bremond as a "Mephisto," the image softened to that of the lover of farces, always the master of the *jeu* and alive to the irrational element in things and people.

cultivated this Provençal style,¹⁰ as he viewed it, as part of his persona, and my hunch is that it was learned in his case in the family setting where another kind of tension, the more political kind, ran rampant, and humor, especially heavily ironic humor, is a way of coping with irreconcilable differences and the uncertainties that result.

This second tension—again with roots in the Revolution and its aftermath—was social-political in nature. Jean Bremond referred in later years to the "lively discussions" in the Bremond family circle when they were all children, and that Henri thus learned "to see both sides of a question," having "his natural tendency to propound new and challenging ideas" thus stimulated.[11] Such a benign interpretation may, however, be an understatement or a "cover" for a highly conflicted situation, in which Pierre Bremond, a "legitimist," that is, "an ultramontane Catholic, passionately attached to the older branch of the House of Bourbon," was at odds with his mother, who was a decided Republican and liberal, perhaps even a "Gallican." It was a classic polarity in French society: a Catholic monarchism, aristocratic in origin and hostile to secular and lay authority, versus a more secularly attuned Catholic Republicanism open to lay authority. The one backward looking in many ways, the other forward looking. A Catholicism that looked to the Pope as the source of all authority versus a Catholicism oriented to some degree of autonomy for the French Church. The political "right" versus the political "left," and thus all of the makings of heated disagreements.[12] What exacerbated this inherited division of fronts was the collapse of the Second Empire of Louis Napoleon in the wake of the debacle of the Franco-Prussian War of 1870–71, followed by the founding of the Third Republic.

As a "legitimist" the elder Bremond's narrative, as he orated at the dinner table, would have run somewhat as follows: "The Revolution of 1789, beginning with the horrific days of the Terror, unleashed chaos, misery, murder and mayhem on the country. It catapulted into power a godless (Voltairean!), bloodthirsty, greedy class of parvenus, Jacobins, all rationalizing their grab for control in the name of the 'sovereign people.' And look now at how it has all ended—with a well-deserved collapse! Let us return to the alliance of throne and altar." As a notary in an ancient cathedral and administrative center like Aix, Pierre Bremond would have subscribed to such a point of view, in which business and top-down royal and ecclesiastical rule could work in tandem for the benefit of the whole community. Indeed, Pierre belonged to that stratum of the provincial bourgeoisie that applauded the end of the Second Empire,

---

10. Maurice Blondel, in a letter to Bremond of September 2, 1908 (BB, II, 131), teased Bremond about being a "nephew of Yvan."

11. Cited by Hogarth, *Henri Bremond*, 1.

12. Although Blanchet has Bremond saying that the atmosphere was benign, one of family squabbling with liberal uncles, his mother smiling and patient, she who would gradually wean Henri away from any kind of sympathy with the hopelessness of monarchism (VB, 18, following the Henry Bordeaux memoir).

an empire built, as they saw it, on nouveau, modernizing, and secular commercial interests uncontrolled by traditional values.[13]

The leader of the Third Republic, the respected historian of the Revolution, Adolphe Thiers, had in his youth, while studying law at Aix, actually been influenced by Madame Tassy, Bremond's Republican maternal grandmother.[14] The bitter pill was that as Thiers established republican control, France paid indemnities to Prussia and gave up Alsace and Lorraine. One can almost hear the royalist Pierre Bremond thundering at the family table. Royalist-monarchists like Pierre, often aristocratic in ethos despite being bourgeois, could then ally with local interests, including those of agricultural peasant or worker-proletarian groups, often more inclined than the urban mass to be traditional and religiously observant. The Catholic Church became the voice of restraint and good order in society, therefore of resistance to social change. Royalists would thus be "clerical," that is, supportive of the privileges, power and symbolic presence of the Catholic Church in public life, even while they might not be personally pious and believing. Precisely, moreover, as a "traditionalist" mentality—what we today would call a "family values" or "law and order" perspective—royalism and its accompanying clericalism easily functioned as bulwarks of a localism resistant to control from Paris.

Actually, there is little clear indication that the young Henri in any explicit, consciously held way absorbed such loyalties from his father, who died when his son was nineteen.[15] But there was always a side to Bremond that sympathized with loyalty to ancient traditions, as in his fond remembrance of childhood Aix. And he could be a snob with respect to the social pretensions associated with middle-class life, as when he exuded contempt for social climbers and would-be aristocrats. In his 1910 study of Fénelon he dubbed the ambitious, but insecure, Madame de Maintenon, consort and then wife of Louis XIV, a "parvenu" riddled with spiritual scruples (worse with Bossuet!).[16] But this kind of criticism is ambiguous: it could as well have come from the proud Republican quick to condemn those who "put on airs."

13. I am indebted to many sources for my portraiture here, but especially Magraw, *France 1815–1914*.

14. MG, 12. Mgr Guillebert, Henri's teacher at Sacré-Coeur, later bishop of Fréjus, described the mother's clan as "an honorable family of the ancient capital of Provence, so rich in its illustrious traditions, in intellectual values, the Tassy family." They were liberal supporters of the revolution of 1830. Guillebert's affectionate portrait of the Bremond family ambience was part of a communication to Merry del Val at the Vatican on June 24, 1921, in which he was defending Henri's intentions in *Sainte Chantal*. It is reproduced in Bernard-Maître and Guarnieri, *Don Giuseppe de Luca*, 18–19.

15. Blanchet suggests that Henri "was more respectful and astonished than convinced" by his father's views. Henri described his father as a man of "astonishingly lucid intelligence," and in his professional work as operating with "a dexterity that experts admired a great deal" (VB, 17, and Blanchet, "Henri Bremond," 436).

16. Bremond, *Apologie pour Fénelon*, 72–73. Bremond also referred to Jacques-Bénigne Bossuet, Fénelon's great opponent, as a "meat-eating Burgundian," i.e., a "meathead from Burgundy!" One of the contradictions, or tensions, in Bremond was his respect for "moyen" spirituality, while turning up his nose at anything, as we say, "low-class."

What permanently alienated Bremond, however, from his father's legitimist-royalism—apart from what he saw as its hopeless whimsicality—was that it absorbed regressive elements in late nineteenth-century French society, namely, jingoistic nationalism, colonialism-imperialism, xenophobia, militarism, anti-Semitism. These came to full flowering in the Dreyfus scandal and then the rise of the Action Française of Charles Maurras. Bremond was kindly affectioned toward literary figures aligned with some aspects of these royalist-connected trends, most particularly in the person and work of Maurice Barrès.[17] But, he would come to despise Maurras and Action Française, and his tendency in later years was to harbor strong reservations about any posture in which religion is used for extra-religious purposes, his deepening understanding of the nature of mystical experience being, I shall argue, a major factor. Pure love, pure poetry and pure prayer facilitate a social vision, but not a polity or a strategy for enacting that vision!

On the contrary, the major parental influence seems to have come from his mother's side, from that of her mother Madame Tassy, lover of Rousseau and solidly Republican, though not radical, i.e., socialist. The maternal tradition was what one historian calls "bourgeois Republican,"[18] a blending of the heritage and values of the 1789 Revolution with the economic expansionism that marked French life after the humiliating "lessons" of 1870–71. Such Republicanism embraced the broadly secular and humanitarian side of the Revolutionary heritage, with its commitment to freedom in the social order and a nonsectarian civic allegiance. The "people" would be sovereign, and France's institutions would reflect that fact by means of popularly elected government supported by an enlightened and intelligent citizenry. Society would be meritocratic, not hereditary, in the granting of rewards, with suitable administrative and educational structures in place to ensure the efficient implementation of national goals. Scientific endeavor is the key to progress. While the Church and its clergy have an important role to play in the moral and spiritual health of the nation, an optimal church-state partnership will not give them overweening control. Thus, republicanism need not be anti-Catholic, though it might be "anticlerical," and in the case of Bremond's mother, we may certainly presume that it was not so. The rub would come with the issue of control of the nation's educational system.

Divided political allegiances within families were not unusual in those days. Martin Du Gard's impression, gained from the reminiscences of Henri's younger brothers, that

---

17. Blanchet describes Bremond as "mesmerized for a long time" by the work of Alphonse Daudet (Blanchet, "Henri Bremond," 436n7), whose son, Léon, would become a notorious anti-Dreyfusard.

18. Magraw, *France 1815–1914*, ch. 6, sneeringly, since he writes from a decidedly leftist perspective. A term like "pragmatic centrism" could also be used, since these Republicans, like Madame Bremond, wanted to avoid the anticlericalism of the more radical left. Bremond himself described the family as one of "solidité bourgeoise," "ascendance libéral," and with "le goût de l'aventure" (Blanchet, "Henri Bremond," 434). Acknowledging the dominance for him of the maternal side of the family, Bremond attributed to his mother his gift for irony, which does not become a tragic sense (ibid., 434–35). The distinction is essential for Bremond's self-understanding.

the atmosphere of conversation in the notary's household in Aix was lively and spirited, with "both sides" of an issue being articulately represented, is suggestive. Separating valid insight from dogmatic rigidity must have been challenging for a young thinker. Blanchet notes Bremond's later aversion to ideological constructs and his preference for paradoxical over logical formulations, i.e., his desire to keep both sides of an issue in some kind of dialectical relation.[19] But Bremond could also have been manifesting an aversion for what he later called "asceticism," the idea that we can work our way through to God as long as we have adopted the right position, and then use the right tools in a properly disciplined way. He came to see that such an attitude is the death of all real prayer because it puts a human product in the place of God.

These tensions continued to play out between the adherents of some form of monarchism, on the one hand, and those who believed that there was no turning back what the Revolution of 1789 had begun. In February 1872, the new National Assembly, with a fresh mandate based on greatly expanded male suffrage, met in Bordeaux. Shocked by the disorders of the Paris Commune, and disgusted by the Bonapartists who had instigated the war, the electorate ushered in a royalist majority composed of an alliance between two subgroups, the legitimists and the Orleanists (royalists loyal to the constitutional monarchism of the younger Bourbon line descended from Louis XIII). When, however, the royalists took steps to return the country to full monarchical rule, and the Comte de Chambord, the legitimist Pretender, was invited to take power under certain constitutional conditions, he declined. Deprived thus of a willing monarch, royalism, whether legitimist or Orleanist, was dead, with the elections of 1877, followed by Chambord's death in 1883, being the final straw. No longer a real political force, royalism would have a long romantic afterlife in the dreams of advocates, and would continue as a general conservatism of the political right, tending to morph into fascism, often marked by a hunger for a "strong man" to take control.

A central issue woven into the cultural changes that followed the Franco-Prussian War was the question of whether to resist modernizing forces tooth and nail, or to engage in discerning collaboration. The former position among Catholics often took the form of nostalgic monarchism, the ultramontanism of absolute papal authority, strict adherence to traditional doctrinal statements, and then the massive resurgence of popular cults with relics and saints and the Rosary and Marian devotions and miraculous medals and the supernatural apparitions at La Salette and Lourdes, much of this flourishing in rural and provincial centers such as Aix. In this churchly conservatism piety would be severe and austere, with a focus on the fear of God, and on the final destinies of death, damnation and hell, accompanied by a hunger for the intercession of the saints celebrated in processions and festivals.

19. Blanchet, "L'Abbé Henri Bremond," 25–26, also Blanchet, "Henri Bremond," 436–37. Bremond, in describing these family dinner-table quarrels, contended that when the dust cleared and dinner was over, there was often a "truce," and "friendship" prevailed. Truth, irony, or mellowed reflection? In the *Discours de réception*, he picked up on the image of quarreling ideologues as "an irritated council of cicadas" (*Discours de réception*, 38).

The posture of collaboration, on the other hand, would register the influence of the Enlightenment with a focus on reason, on historical study and interpretation, on the spiritual value to be found in some secular art forms and philosophies, on the importance of independent and creative thought. What is often called "Catholic romanticism," originating earlier in the century with Chateaubriand, functioned as a kind of compromise-formation, where tradition is a way of feeling and passion and beauty and goodness, no longer rigid and doctrinaire, but human and warm, not as something to induce dread but to foster attraction.[20] Romantics can affirm the old authorities as guides but not dictators, as sources of spiritual truth in their essence, though not always in their outward forms. This latter posture was absorbed by Bremond in his early education and became second nature to him.[21]

Humanist Religion

Most pertinent, therefore, for Bremond, who would become a priest-educator and writer, was the impact of these political divisions on the educational system. He loved school and was always a good, in some areas an excellent, student, doing his secondary studies—that is, through age seventeen—at the nearby Catholic collège of Sacré-Coeur, just built on the boulevard Carnot in Aix. The dominant emphasis was literary study with its attendant verbal skills. He remembered the place as firmly clerical, though with moderating influences, being staffed in those days mostly by diocesan clergy.

Two of Bremond's most beloved teachers at Sacré-Coeur, the abbé Guillebert, director of the school, and the abbé Penon—both of whom were to advise him against entering the Jesuit Order—were parish priests who later became bishops (Fréjus, Moulins). Both men were to be supportive in due course of Bremond's work in his banned biography of Ste. Jeanne de Chantal, since both were relatively liberal and modernizing in their thought. Bremond remembered that he developed a great love for Homer and Virgil, learned to appreciate and admire Ernest Renan's style, and was exposed even to the novels of Alfred de Musset and Victor Hugo.[22] He was to become a strong believer

---

20. See especially Gibson, *Social History*, and Harrison, *Romantic Catholics*, both of whom place emphasis on the feminization of French Catholicism during the nineteenth century, as well as the move from a spirituality of fear to one of love.

21. See Cholvy, "La restauration catholique," and Leflon, "Crise et restauration," on the dynamic of historical retrieval as part of Catholic romanticism. These essays concern the project of the editor and publisher Jacques-Paul Migne to restore patristic studies to the nineteenth-century French church, but much of it applies as well to Henri Bremond and his project to recover the mystical piety of the seventeenth-century French Church for a modern project.

22. MG, 12–14. See also Charpin, who lists prizes won in French, Latin, Greek, English, and rhetorical analysis by the young Bremond ("Souvenirs d'un Aixois," 28). Jesuit education very much revolved around competitions and prizes, and Bremond clearly excelled. His teachers loved him. Guillebert described him as "a very intelligent student, lively and quite mischievous" (memo cited in Bernard-Maître and Guarnieri, *Don Giuseppe De Luca*, 18).

in the value of literary studies taught by priests, and was to defend this kind of teaching vigorously once he himself became such a teacher in Jesuit-run schools.

Critical, moreover, for the unfolding of Bremond's career is the fact that several of his teachers at Sacré-Coeur during his mid-teens were Jesuits. Capable and inspiring mentors, they became role models for Bremond, then for André and Jean, as well. Because of later developments in Bremond's frustrating experience with the Order, some second-guessing eventually occurred. Guillebert later, in 1921, was to criticize these Jesuit faculty, particularly a certain Père Pralon, as exercising too much influence over the boys,[23] aggressively recruiting them at an age when they were unformed and vulnerable, thereby seducing Bremond into a lifestyle unsuited for his independent temperament. Maybe some truth here. Blanchet has suggested that Guillebert's opinion was probably influenced by a number of factors, including some *intra muros* anti-Jesuitism among Catholic educators. Bremond himself thought that he owed his taste for historical and literary research, thus for the introduction of critical methods, to Jesuit perspectives. Further, his teachers used a modified form of the Ignatian method of spiritual formation, less rigid and doctrinaire than that to which he was later exposed in his formal training.[24]

I have noted that as in Henry Bordeaux's response to Bremond at his Académie induction, some critics (with varying tones of friendliness or its lack) would accuse him of "Jesuitism" in his style of presentation. The implication was that he had a way of making subtle distinctions by means of which of which radical or unconventional perspectives could be insinuated into an argument. But a more charitable interpretation is that the Jesuits early on began to teach him to discern nuance, allusion and implication in the texts that he studied, i.e., to be a good literary critic. He never forgot the lessons, learned early and well at Sacré-Coeur.

Just at the time that Bremond would have been concluding his secondary education, the French educational system was changing, and thus the status of the "teaching" orders of the Catholic Church. In his childhood the schools operated under the regulatory authority of the Falloux Laws of 1850–51, which attempted to maintain a

---

23. Guillebert described Pralons, one of the Jesuits, as "too absolute and a little narrow," and said he had steered all four of the Bremond boys, now without a mother (who had just died), into the religious life—the three younger boys into the Jesuits, the oldest into the Benedictines. He opined that the Jesuit Order was too rigid for Henri, who was by nature "vibrant and impetuous." When Bremond later left the Jesuits, Guillebert felt confirmed in "my just forebodings" (Bernard-Maître and Guarnieri, *Don Giuseppe De Luca*, 19).

24. VB, 20–23. The source here is a statement that Bremond apparently intended to include in the preface to a critical commentary, announced in 1929 but never published, on the Ignatian *Exercises*. The text is in Guy, "Henri Bremond et son commentaire." Bremond reminisced about the influence of this Jesuit mentor at the Collège, who encouraged him in a more interesting and flexible use of the *Exercises* than was common then. He described this priest as "provoking my petulance [over the use of the *Exercises*], so that I took my revenge on him by announcing that I would enter the Dominican novitiate, and by swearing to him that the writer of the *Provinciales* was the best of all" (Guy, "Henri Bremond," 192). This capable mentor (a "smart, good man") simply outsmarted the sassy, adolescent Bremond, who ever afterward had a high regard for holy cleverness.

balance between ecclesiastical and secular control. Considerable power was granted to the Church by allowing bishops to sit on departmental educational councils, authorizing unrestricted numbers of students to attend Catholic primary and secondary schools, and giving members of religious orders permission to teach without an official certificate.[25] Village primary schools were put directly under the authority of curés, and priests might teach in secondary schools without the university degrees required for lay teachers. Thus, most of Bremond's early schooling was securely in the hands of the clergy, who were largely exempted from state control.

But after 1871, the prevailing view was that the only way to improve the scientific calibre of French students was to laicize education. Thus came the Ferry Laws of 1881–82, by which the whole educational system, public and private, moved in the direction of lay control, uniformity of curriculum, and the requirement for state licensure of all teachers. Technically, the laws were anticlerical without being anti-Catholic. One particular stipulation that would later affect Bremond was the increasing, but controversial, pressure brought on the religious orders for "authorization to practice" in France. This requirement referred back to one of the conditions specified in the old Concordat of 1802 between Napoleon Bonaparte and the papacy, that the clergy of the French Church would take an oath of allegiance to the civil power. The requirement had been indifferently enforced, and the Jesuits had avoided it. But as pressure was brought to bear, their activity became illegal and they were expelled—at least, until the state relented.

Then, on March 29, 1880, the Jesuits were obliged to dissolve. By June 30 they were evicted from their houses, including that on the rue Lacépède in Aix. There was a popular outcry, but it may have been the young Henri Bremond who was most affected. Declaring that this "persecution" was the final straw, he signed a declaration, committing himself to the Jesuit novitiate at just that age (15) when youngsters in the French educational system are completing "collège" and preparing to enter "lycée." The novitiate, or program for priestly formation, for the Jesuit Lyon province, located at Monciel, near Lons-le-Saunier, was about to be moved to a new, English site.[26]

Everything coalesced for Bremond. As he was finishing his secondary education at Sacré-Coeur in 1881 with his *baccalauréat* in rhetoric, then in 1882 with the *baccalauréat* in philosophy, and as the Ferry Laws were coming into play, his vocation for the priesthood ripened. Family influence was strong here, and Bremond later attributed much to his mother. In a 1928 note he claimed that she had been decisive in forming his taste for irony, some of his fondness for imaginative literature (novels!), and finally for inculcating a certain Anglophilia, a deep attraction to the style and

---

25. Magraw, *France 1815–1914*, 137.

26. The institutional disengagement must have proceeded in stages of some kind, especially in light of the fact that there was continuing pressure to undo the Ferry provisions as soon as possible—which in fact happened later. Blanchet covers the turbulence of all of this, which must have made the year 1881, and the first part of 1882, rocky and uncertain for Bremond (VB, 26–28). He would not depart Aix until November 1882.

values of popular English literature, especially the work of Walter Scott.[27] This is to say that while the Jesuits stirred the impulse to literary analysis and subtle thinking, his mother stimulated in young Bremond a certain spiritual and ethical cosmopolitanism, an openness to the values and outlook of urbane culture, a perspective of which he became more conscious especially as he outgrew his provincialism. In Bremond's later terminology, she was both *devout* and *humanistic*, an ideal combination of spiritual values. He could laughingly dismiss the "Jacobitism" and lost-cause mentality of his father,[28] but never his mother's spiritual fortitude and awareness. She died when he was just fifteen.

There was one particular friendship formed at Sacré-Coeur that would have long-term consequences for Bremond. In the list provided by Dr. Charpin of Bremond's fellow students at collège,[29] the one that stands out is Charles Maurras, three years younger than Henri, and fated to outlive him in notorious fashion to 1952.[30] They shared the same Provençal roots, similar bourgeois family backgrounds, some of the same teachers, and many of the same interests. And yet their destinies diverged so radically—Maurras to the founding of Action Française, and Bremond to a bitter antipathy to all that French right-wing politics represented.

The irony is that they both benefitted especially from the pastoral and pedagogical skills of the abbé Jean-Baptiste Penon on the Sacré-Coeur faculty. Bremond enjoyed him as an inspiring teacher of French classical literature and drama, but Maurras, suffering early on from severe deafness, received a special level of attention from this devoted teacher. Frederick Brown has described this teacher-student relationship, how religious ambivalence grew in young Maurras despite Penon's efforts, how he longed for certainty and solid foundations spiritually, aesthetically, finally politically. Penon tried to steer young Maurras to a sense of "Jesus Christ as a real presence and not a remote sovereign," but it was no good—the remote sovereign would turn out to be more useful politically, if not as personally satisfying. In due course, Maurras would link up with another key nationalistic player in Bremond's development, Maurice Barrès, both of whom shared the struggle of "the believer manqué yearning for salvation."[31] Initially grounded in a genuine friendship with shared aesthetic passions, Bremond's relations with Maurras would give way to a gradual cooling, then hostility and alienation as they came to see France's spiritual heritage, including its Catholicism, in deeply opposed ways.

Nonetheless, nostalgia is powerful, especially that of old men after one of them is gone. Maurras recalled observing the four Bremond brothers walking along to collège, the oldest, Émile, in the lead, and the youngest, Jean, struggling to keep up. He

27. Ibid., 23.
28. Blanchet, "Henri Bremond," 26.
29. Charpin, "Souvenirs d'un Aixois," 28.
30. The principal studies are Guiral, "Bremond et Maurras," and Prévotat, "Réactions et sensibilités."
31. Brown, *Embrace of Unreason*, 96, 100.

described them as moving in "an exact rhythm," precisely on schedule, while he himself was rather awed at this display of quasi-military discipline and good order in boys still so young. He remembered class sessions in which the Bremonds demonstrated their argumentative and critical skills.[32] Perhaps there is a bit of wistful envy here on the part of Maurras. Guiral argues that it is clear that while Bremond and Maurras enjoyed a deep friendship early on, it was the politics of Dreyfus and the war that separated them. Thus, the split that eventually led to separation became representative of the kinds of ruptures that would put Frenchmen, all loving their country, at loggerheads with one another. Bremond found his salvation, though in a complex way full of paradox, in spiritual "disquietude," while Maurras settled for the ideological peace of lesser gods.

So it is that Bremond would end up in England for several years and become profoundly and decisively influenced by British literary and ecclesiastical currents. This is the second major "strand" mentioned above as critical to Bremond's development.

Succeeding French governments, sometimes in a mood to compromise with the church by relaxing constraints and sometimes adamantly opposed, would allow the Jesuits back into France, and the debates about church-state relations in education would continue, with the next crisis coming under the Combes government in 1905. We shall have occasion to note some of the divagations as we track Bremond's unfolding Jesuit career.

32. Cited by Guiral, "Bremond et Maurras," 38–39.

3

The English Desert

AT THE END OF 1882, Henri Bremond, precocious and a bit spoiled, but bright, energetic and idealistic, found himself beginning the Jesuit novitiate at Peak House, Sidmouth, Devonshire. It was a whole new departure—life away from home, family, and friends, from the familiar nest of Aix, for the first time. What followed, however, were very good, richly and complexly formative, years for Bremond, even though he moaned and groaned with loneliness or frustration or boredom. Picking up the use of "desert" from an 1891 letter of Bremond's, Blanchet titled his treatment of the period of 1882–1897, the years of Bremond's Jesuit training, the time of "crossing the desert."[1] But "crossing" is quite different from "stuck in." The phrase is intentionally ambiguous, recalling the wilderness wandering of the Hebrews, or the spirituality of the Desert Fathers: one enters a period of darkness, finding mysterious sustenance there, in order to prepare for the light. What doesn't kill you may make you bitter, but by grace it can also make you tougher and wiser, preparing for the best yet. The latter outcome prevailed in Bremond's case.

In later years, after he had left the order in 1904, many perceived Bremond not just as a Jesuit, but a *failed* Jesuit, a dropout. He went through a difficult spell of discouragement, and he always remained ambivalent about his Jesuit formation, but one never senses any self-reproach. Study and reflection led to new perspectives, as he would wrestle in his historical work with the true nature of Ignatius Loyola's religious experience, the original purpose of the *Spiritual Exercises*, and the Jesuit history and practice that, he believed, had misconstrued Ignatius. His eventual claim would be that in his training during the English years he was subjected to a style of formation that robbed Ignatius of his true vitality, a non- or anti-mystical approach that was spiritually devastating. But, rightly understood, the *Spiritual Exercises* could be, he claimed, powerfully enlivening. In time he won a hearing: the whole tendency in modern interpretations of the *Exercises* to ascribe a genuinely "mystical" dimension to

---

1. VB, 29.

Ignatius's intentions, is partly the result of his efforts.² But first, the wilderness, which, indeed, contained manna.

One of the foundations where Bremond studied had a particularly well-stocked collection of classical spiritual writing, including French seventeenth-century authors, such as Surin, whom he would come to treasure. He was also exposed to the literature of the Anglican Oxford Movement, which gave him a chance to see how this Romanizing, Catholicizing thrust within the Church of England was generating in its literary output striking, non-scholastic affirmations of classic forms of devotional life. And that brought him to the work of John Henry Newman, by this time a cardinal of the Holy Roman Church, but being discovered by the French only erratically and haltingly.³ A new world of spirituality thus opened up for Bremond, one very far indeed from Aix, and yet redolent of the best artistically sensitive humanism that he had known in his native setting. He would begin to discover with the English writers struggles akin to his own, namely, an entrancement with the richness of inherited tradition combined with a restless awareness that the old forms no longer "work" spiritually, because the old world—provincial, stable and dogmatic—is giving way to the incertitudes, the disquiets, of modernity. How can we, then, best retrieve, and be refreshed by, ancient wisdom?

Jesuit Formation

Anyone who has ever been through a period of training in a highly regulated environment, where there is a dominant, central theoretical model of formation along with specific techniques for its application, knows that students may either be compliant and adaptable, inclining to find the regimen congenial, or they may be rebellious and restless under constraints. Bremond was in the latter class. The intuition of Guillebert, back at Sacré-Coeur, had been accurate. Bremond was freethinking, free-spirited, sometimes hyper-critical. He may also have been more intelligent, or better prepared, than some of the other novices. In addition, he was moody and subject to black periods of despondency. We recall that he had been a bit of a "pet" back at Sacré-Coeur,⁴ had enjoyed easy security and favored status, and now he was not so "special."

---

2. See, e.g., Egan, *Spiritual Exercises*, ch. 1. For the whole history of Bremond's struggle with the Ignatian tradition, and the controversy that ensued, see Trémolières, "Witness to These Witnesses," which, for the English period and then the tertianship, is an important supplement to Blanchet's foundational account in VB.

3. The most comprehensive overview of Bremond's English years, of his writing on English subjects, and of his unending love for English literary culture, is Neveu, "Henri Bremond et l'Angleterre." Neveu's access to the Jesuit Archives at Vanves, where he could read many of Bremond's intimate expressions of affection for "*le monde brittanique*," makes his essay especially poignant.

4. Bremond described himself as "a little precocious" for an eighteen-year-old, with an "impertinently critical" spirit, but withal, a "true Provencaux" (Guy, "Henri Bremond," 192–93).

Indeed, barracks-discipline can be a refreshing structure as well as a galling penitentiary, even under such an "amiable" director as Père Louis Rosette in the attractive circumstances of the country setting enjoyed by Peake House.[5] Bremond must have been a demanding pastoral challenge. One imagines him as the skeptic sitting in the back of the class, a smirk on his face, ready with the barbed or ironic remark. Any vocation looks more exciting from the outside, and now that he was "inside," things may have seemed a bit more mundane. And so Bremond struggled with a combination of boredom and distaste for mechanical methods of instruction.

Jesuit spiritual formation, grounded in the meditational method and regimen of Ignatius's *Spiritual Exercises*, relies on a discipline of supervised, and progressively more refined, moral self-examination by the individual seeking spiritual maturity. That person is challenged to separate good from evil in his/her life, and then to discern the signs of divine leading, so that the lineaments of personal vocation come into focus. In the strengthening of moral and vocational resolve, an effort is made to strike an optimal balance between obedience to superiors and the life of the community, on the one hand, and obedience to the unique contours of the individual's calling, on the other. Quasi-military in its ability to channel energies, the discipline is rigorous, thorough, and psychologically sophisticated. Ignatius himself wanted the virtue of obedience to be the hallmark of membership in the "Company," with the human tendency to narcissistic assertion reduced to a minimum.[6] This last, so his dominant interpreters claimed and Bremond later disputed, made him suspicious of the privatizing dimension of "mystical" experiences, thus inaugurating the early anti-mysticism that marked Jesuit history. The net result was that Bremond's independent spirit butted into the rock wall of communal discipline. Fortunately, however, he seems to have had patient and accommodating pastoral oversight.

The great culprit here, Bremond contended, was the *La Pratique de la Perfection chrétienne* (a manualized adaptation of the original *Ejercicio de perfección y virtudes cristianas* of 1609) of Alphonsus Rodriguez, SJ, used by his teachers as a guide in the application of the *Exercises*. In his *Histoire* he will take constant potshots at the *Exercises*, thus administered, as "ascetical" or "anthropocentric" or "panhedonistic," the idea being that when methods of meditation are utilized as a mechanics for fortifying the will, they become moralistic and legalistic, finally subservient to the human ego and its demand for control. Bremond would work mightily throughout his career to shift the focus in spirituality from obedience and moral perfection to self-forgetful

---

5. VB, 30, with citations from Bremond's unpublished correspondence.

6. Meissner, *Ignatius of Loyola*, is an outstanding introduction. Appendix B of this work has a convenient gathering of notes from Ignatius on holy obedience. Meissner shares the classic, but rather outdated, Jesuit suspicion of mysticism as self-indulgent, to which is joined Freud's view of the narcissism of oceanic states. Meissner seems to have relented a bit over time; in a discussion of the discernment of spirits in the second week of the *Exercises* he acknowledged that experiences of "desolation and the dark night" were not really considered by Ignatius (Meissner, *To the Greater Glory*, 284–86). Yet these are precisely what began to preoccupy Bremond, as we shall see.

loving adoration of God (i.e., in his later terminology, to the "mystical" or "theocentric" focus). The frightening part is that the locus for the latter is not a bright day marked by easily acquired sensibilities, but rather an interior, silent darkness accessed only by suffering. Bremond's wilderness had begun.

But St. Ignatius and his *Spiritual Exercises* seem also to have made Bremond ineluctably *inward* in his thinking about all things pertaining to God. They formed the matrix for the gradual emergence of the budding "religious psychologist," who would ever afterward find himself engaged in intense focus on the "dispositions" and "states," the movements of the "soul," the obscure inklings and impulses and intuitions, sometimes the stages of development, that mark the individual's journey deeper into God when things work properly—or away from God when things go awry. Bremond cared very much about ethics and politics and institutional dynamics—all of the outward things—but for him they were secondary to things inward. The inner life is more *real*, more immediately present for the individual searching for God and the divine will, where "hearing" God's call to action will always be a venture for the human heart and its "disquietude," its restlessly shifting subjectivity. *That* is the Ignatius Bremond liked. When the goal of Ignatian spirituality is reduced to militarized certainty and unflinching action with regard to one's "mission," Bremond found it to be at its worst, productive of a "great ennui."[7]

Nonetheless, Blanchet has argued that Bremond's buoyant, Provençal spirit kept him going, with some of his later recollections perhaps exaggeratedly morose.[8] In December 1883, the novitiate moved to Ore, Hastings, where Bremond spent two years of "juvenate" (advanced rhetoric) prior to taking his First Vows as a Jesuit. These are vows of chastity, poverty and obedience (thus "simple" or elementary) for a lifetime (thus "perpetual"), along with a vow to continue to final profession and ordination (the advanced vows). Then, in 1885, he was moved to Mold in Flintshire, Wales, a dreadful facility (former prison),[9] for his "scholasticate," or period of instruction in philosophy. All of the descriptions of the curriculum highlight its excessively by-the-book quality: Aristotelian, medieval-scholastic, logical and deductive, etc. In other words, deadly.

Martin Du Gard is the source for the claim that salvation came for Bremond when he had a chance to socialize with a middle-class Protestant family, and then to discover George Eliot and Charles Dickens.[10] André Bremond similarly recalled that in Dickens his brother found "the humor and humanity of almost contemporary

---

7. Guy, "Henri Bremond," 193.

8. VB, 32–34.

9. Described in mind-numbing detail ("the most perfectly cellular system") by Bremond in an unpublished letter cited by Blanchet (ibid., 34). Excerpts from Bremond's letters of this period are contained in a series of volumes, the *Lettres de Mold*, that chronicle the experiences of various members of the Lyons scholasticate at Mold during the 1880s.

10. MG, 15–16. He cites Bremond's later comment that while the English had introduced him to Dickens, this great writer and poet had a "French spirit and a European sense of humor."

English life," and that Bremond's professors at Hastings and Mold encouraged his humanist interests and his "literary gift," since his "literary vocation" was coming to be "recognized and consecrated."[11] Martin Du Gard thought that the Jesuits continued to stimulate Henri's humanistic tastes and inclinations by exposing him to classical belles-lettres of a type that "preceded Chateaubriand."[12] Clearly Bremond, obedient to the standard Jesuit requirement that students become proficient in the language of their surrounding culture, had gained sufficient facility to begin reading works in English as well.

Then in 1888–89 it was back to France for his first teaching assignments (the "professorate"), as a professor of humanities at the École Libre de Notre-Dame, a boarding-school in Mongré, near Villefranche-sur-Saône just north of Lyon, then at Dôle in the Franche-Comté, southwest of Besançon. Indeed, despite their suppression after the passing of the Ferry Laws, Catholic educational institutions were once again thriving in France, and Jesuits were being invited back to teaching positions. Progressive Catholic thought, in the spirit of Leo XIII's *Ralliement*, shared in the great surge of official energy in the French educational establishment directed at the upgrading of standards, including embrace of the sciences and scientific methods, and the widening of access for the general population. Education would be the hope of the future, of a renewed national energy and vigor. The church would partner with the state for the instilling of moral excellence and discipline, to lift horizons and fire aspirations.

The forming of young minds and young sensibilities thus became the church's venue, where it was believed that good literature forms good character, especially if that literature is properly taught. Linguistic and verbal skills grounded in exposure to the best authors along with the development of skills for good verbal expression were primary. Such was the context in which Bremond earned his spurs as a classroom teacher, discovering in the process that he had real gifts for elucidating the work of great writers. He found that he could make the study of literature into a *spiritual* adventure for his young charges. He learned, moreover, that his talent was not for the teaching of religion as such, but rather for religion in its literary expression. His experience in the classroom soon whetted his desire to write, to pursue the kind of literary portraiture, the "religious psychology," that would be his hallmark. His pen, not his voice, would finally be his master instrument, but always geared to the hungers, perceptions, and questions of a popular audience gathered in his mental "classroom."[13]

---

11. André Bremond, "Henri Bremond," 30–31, 37. Blanchet, basing himself on personal acquaintance with André, questioned this reminiscence, preferring the correspondence with Maurras as more determinative of Bremond's gestation during this period (VB, 40). In general, however, I am taking the side of André, that Bremond's absorption of English culture, accompanied by his "childlike" spirit, was at least as potent, if not more so, than his frustrations with Jesuit discipline. See André Bremond: "His master virtue was sympathy, respect for the child and the child's spirit" ("Henri Bremond," 32).

12. MG, 14.

13. I am thus taking the position that Bremond would always remain a bit of a compelling schoolmaster in his writing, rather than a frustrated novelist, as is sometimes suggested (as in Chadwick,

In the Third Republic, education had become a virtual substitute for religion, so high was it held in esteem as the instrument of social transformation. But Zeldin has argued that these were top-down ideals, enforced by the church-state accord, and then imposed by authoritarian, old-fashioned educational methods in an implicit two-tier system: basic education for the peasantry and lower class workers, and advanced levels for the bourgeoisie. A meritocratic system would favor those from more upper-class backgrounds, who would be taught by an increasingly professionalized mandarinate of specialists. The goal was to instill universal values without disturbing the social order. The mark of a truly educated person, an individual of real standing in the community, would be command of the language.[14] I do not think Bremond had any overt quarrel with the ideals and goals of education thus expressed, but one of the remarkable features of his *Histoire* much later would be his attempt to take spirituality out of the hands of theologians and hand it back to the laity, to the "little people" who pray and lyricize, sometimes in a grammar that is not immaculate. There would come to be an anti-elitist strain in his thinking about the religious "sentiment."

Teaching the "Child"

By 1900 the Jesuits in France were running twenty-nine secondary schools that attracted the sons of the aristocracy and the conservative bourgeoisie, and the figure could not have been much different when Bremond first taught at Mongré. They were noted for forming strong, pastoral relationships with students, for a humanistic spirit of interactive learning and for attention to the needs of the individual.[15] In a phrase that would become popular much later, their methods were more "child-centered," more psychologically progressive, than was the case in most of the secular schools. Here Bremond would have his first important say. Over the next twelve years or so he would produce for various publications a series of articles on the education and spiritual formation of children, arguing that traditional methods were quite unsuitable and that approaches more geared to the real needs, interests and abilities of children were necessary. Essential to his project was the evoking of the "child" in the teacher as well as respectful attention to the childlike qualities of the students themselves.

He gathered these essays together in one of his first published collections, *L'Enfant et la vie*, in 1902. Marshalling a long and distinguished line of supporters, he set out his organizing premise by citing the French journalist and littérateur Ximénès Doudan: spiritual health requires that "a certain childhood of the imagination must be preserved for all of one's life." Most adults have forgotten that fact. The sight of some atrocious art at the Paris Universal Exposition of 1900 moved him to argue that adults are merely sentimental about children, especially about the suffering of children, but

---

"Henri Bremond and Newman," 168).

14. Zeldin, *History of French Passions*, II, ch. 4, "Education and Hope."
15. Ibid., 1011, 1031.

that great writers—like George Eliot[16] and Mark Twain—truly understand, and can convey, childhood agonies. He strongly endorsed the use of storytelling in the education of children, referring as example to the work of a contemporary poet, Madame Julie Lavergne, who teaches us that the poet's true gift is to see "the invisible presence of the very good God, who has chosen every creature to be a temple and symbol by its own proper beauty."[17] Most of all he extolled the feminine, the role of mothers (perhaps recalling his own!) in the spiritual formation of children.

The two preeminent essays in the collection concern "the priest and the literary formation of children," and "the education of the religious sense." In the first he constructed an elaborate analogy between the priest in his ministry at the altar, opening the tabernacle for the veneration of the Blessed Sacrament, and the priest teaching the work of Racine to a literature class. The latter is opening a tabernacle as well, so that, as he interprets the text, his face glows, his voice trembles with feeling, and the students are absorbed in the numinous moments. These sacred texts thus become the means of salvation. Since the task of the priest-educator is to excite the imaginations of his students in the face of what is truly beautiful, "no admiration," avers Bremond, "has a better chance of being contagious than his."[18] A sustained intimacy between the teacher and student will then allow the student's soul to open to the text. If the student feels inspired to the kind of sacrifice depicted by Racine, then it is only one step to the sacrifice of Christ! By contrast, a merely secular education is nothing more than "a superstition of taste," in which the texts fall flat and the imagination of the student is dulled.[19]

The second essay is a more modern-sounding exposition of the importance of exposing children to texts at an age-appropriate level, especially religious texts, so that their nascent religious "sensibility" is not prematurely dulled. Stories and historical narratives are the best tools, as Fénelon and John Henry Newman well knew.[20]

---

16. Bremond's first sustained reference to George Eliot's work seems to be in the passages that he cites from *The Mill on the Floss* in "Devant des portraits d'enfants" (EV, 22–26). For Bremond, Eliot had captured the pain of childhood in the anxiety that the child must feel in the face of the incomprehensible unknown.

17. "L'éducation par les contes: vie et oeuvre de Madame Julie Lavergne" (ibid., 46).

18. "Le prêtre et la formation littéraire" (ibid., 125).

19. Their relationship in its early stages, Blondel got Bremond to tone down the clericalism of the argument (which Bremond did), and to take the angle that it is the superficial, nouveau quality of secular teaching that ruins literature ("Blondel to Bremond, December 20, 1898" [BB, I, 138–42]). It is the duty of the priest, then, to restore "soul" to literature, to be "more of a child than the children" and "more man than the men," to inspire that most wonderful of all spiritual states: "admiration." Blanchette, *Maurice Blondel*, 276–78, has an excellent summary of Blondel's views on teaching. One of Blondel's regrets as a teacher "was that he could never know enough about the secret of those young minds whom he had to teach and love, which ones were looking for a word of life or a viaticum for eternity" (ibid., 276).

20. Émile Goichot's work picks up with the comprehensive interpretation of Bremond's life where André Blanchet's leaves off, namely at Bremond's exit from the Jesuit Order in 1904. In EG, 30, he speculates about the theme of the "lost mother" in Bremond's own childhood, referencing Bremond's

Sketches of Arnold of Rugby and Edward Thring depict the strategies and characters of good teachers, although Bremond was quick to scold them when they could forget pedagogical shrewdness and fall into moralizing forms of admonishment with their students. The underlying theme—to be echoed years later in his praise of Duchesne that day at the Académie—is that the spiritual stance of the teacher, or the critic, operates from first to last.[21]

The essays in *L'Enfant et la vie* thus demonstrate as well how strong the English influence had become in Bremond's thinking as he moved into the decade of the 1890s. To be sure, it is difficult to hit just the right balance here. One can argue that Bremond brought as much in a Provençal spirit to the sometimes dour English as he received. While at Mold in 1890 at Christmastime, in ministering to a poor Irish family, he helped them build a crèche in the French style, thus bringing a touch of joyful color into their otherwise drab existence. It may be also that French intellectual sources, such as the work of the moral philosopher Léon Ollé-Laprune, whom both Bremond and Blondel highly respected, were major factors in the eventual *way* Bremond interpreted his English sources.[22] While there is no question that Bremond saw English writers, as it were, through French eyes (how could it be otherwise?), and that Blondel's influence on him was already operative by the time he produced his interpretive essays on English figures, the initial impact of that culture came at a time when he was still quite young and impressionable, more of a "child" himself, more ready to receive than to give.

Maurras Again

Ordained to the priesthood at Mold toward the end of 1892, Bremond then moved on to a year of teaching at Moulins in 1893–94, then back to Mongré for another two years, then a school at St.-Étienne, just outside Lyon, where in 1896–97 he would be teaching students headed for the military academy at Saint-Cyr.

In the forefront of his experience during this period was contact with two personalities destined to be famous in diametrically opposed ways. The first, once again, was Charles Maurras, with whom he corresponded frequently during the last period at Mold, fairly often during his teaching spells, and then more intermittently up to the

---

letter to Blondel, December 5, 1898 (BB, I, 122–24). I would suggest, however, that Bremond's regrets related more to the loss of childhood simplicity than of maternal embrace.

21. See Onimus, "Bremond et l'enseignement des Lettres." The impression that one gets is that Bremond was always more of a classroom magician with young people than a true persevering pedagogue. This may help to explain why he burned out on teaching rather early.

22. This is Blanchet's case (VB, 41–42). Both Blanchet and André Bremond maximize the humanistic-literary aspects of the Jesuit experience for Henri. The story of the crèche comes from André Bremond, "Henri Bremond," 38–39, and is told with great gusto. Of the text composed by Henri, for singing at the crib, André comments: "And the canticle, English words on a Provençal air . . . And the crèche also came from Provence; the Midi, the good Midi, always conquering!" André's ultimate source here was an anonymous essay contained in the Jesuit collection of letters from Mold (VB, 43n1.)

First World War.[23] Their shared love for high literature, grounded in their shared educational experience at Sacré-Coeur, centered on questions of the spiritual import of what they were reading. It soon became clear, when Maurras spoke confidentially, that he had lost his inherited faith, that he had turned instead to literature as the source of a "pagan aestheticism," an "aristocratic paganism" dressed up in a philosophical skepticism.[24]

In fact, from 1886 to 1891, Maurras published in a Catholic periodical a sizable number of essays, in which he revealed that he was coming under the influence of a figure as yet unknown to Bremond—but to whom Maurras would later introduce him—the novelist, Maurice Barrès.[25] Both writers shared the same orientation to an ultra-nationalism. Barrès we will consider later, but the position of Maurras was expressed in his role "as a founding member of the école romane (the Roman school) and an enthusiast of Provençal politics . . . the term 'Roman' ecapsulat[ing] the idea that France's genius belonged to the Mediterranean or Greco-Latin tradition, which had been perverted by Romanticism and its decadent offspring."[26] It seems that Maurras was already well on his way to a religion of the Fatherland under the inspired leadership of a charismatic ruler, and with impure elements such as Jews removed. The seeds of monarchism and fascism were thus being sown, but still germinating in a soil of regional pride with which Bremond resonated. Eventually Bremond will come to espouse precisely the kind of romanticism and anti-rationalism that Maurras despised, although for the time being their literary-critical and aesthetic sympathies were still overlapping.

For Bremond the challenge at this particular stage in corresponding with Maurras was to counter his religious skepticism by clarifying "the religious problem" as such in literature, where some writers in the so-called "Greco-Latin tradition" set themselves in opposition to the gospel. What worried Bremond was that Maurras was becoming arrogant, that his enthusiasm was running away with him, that he was beginning to identify with the pagan energy of a strict social order based on logic and reason, thereby dressing the body politic in the garments of a rigid and authoritarian Catholicism intolerant of the kind of romantic searching that he, Bremond, was coming to favor.

---

23. The correspondence, as yet unpublished, is in the fonds Goichot at the Bibliothèque nationale de France in Paris.

24. VB, 44, 47. Blanchet's analysis (ibid., 43–57) of the unedited correspondence between Bremond and Maurras during this period is subtle. He suggests that it was Maurras more than anyone else that made literature and its interpretation the place, for Bremond, where faith and doubt hang in the balance, the place of "religious inquietude" (ibid., 57). However, Bremond had already encountered similar themes and questions in English literature as well. We might say that Bremond was stimulated by the interaction with Maurras, but not necessarily formed.

25. Brown tracks the early collaboration between Maurras and Barrès, emphasizing their spiritual kinship (*Embrace of Unreason*, 99–110).

26. Ibid., 100.

By 1894 the two men had wound down the correspondence in a state of some impasse, more or less agreeing to stay in touch until they finally became permanently alienated in the opening period of WWI. Bremond would later bitterly regret, despite some early naiveté about it, the rise of Action Française and its cynical alignment with the Catholic Church, but Maurras had touched on Bremond's raw nerve, his "demon," namely, the theological status and import of literature and literary expression. If Maurras had demonstrated that bad theology could be derived from literature, Bremond's task would be to show the opposite, to demonstrate that literature rightly understood, moves one toward, not away from, a gospel of pure love. Granted that he struggled with uncertainty, doubt, and discouragement, at times, Bremond seems always to have moved in the direction of the "full" darkness of God, where love and poetry and prayer operate—as he would learn from mystical writers—never to the empty darkness of cynical despair. Blanchet is right to point to Bremond's use of Newman's "I have never sinned against the Light."[27]

The other contact, much briefer but warmer in remembrance, was with the very young Teilhard de Chardin at Mongré in 1894, where Teilhard was a student. According to Bremond, "one of my classical pupils was a little fellow from Auvergne, very intelligent, first in every subject, but disconcertingly well behaved . . . and it was only long afterwards that I learned the secret of his seeming indifference. Transporting his mind far away from us was another, a jealous and absorbing passion—stones."[28] It would seem that Teilhard was very reticent about what was occupying his thinking, and that Bremond found it harder to be the insightful teacher who really knows his students than he thought it would be! What he remembered about Teilhard and found significant was his passion for a beloved object, which, of course, in Bremond's case is literature. That single-minded focus defines the person, is his "soul." In its own way, that was the Jesuit in Bremond, "discerning the spirit" of an individual, and then affirming that spirit.

The "Desert" Blooms

In August 1897, Henri was ready for the Jesuit "tertianship," the so-called Third Year, in which he would serve a priestly, pastoral ministry of some kind, testing his vocation, engaging in deeper study of the Jesuit Constitutions and the *Exercises*, and preparing for Final ("Great") Vows at the end of the period. He requested a position back in Aix-en-Provence, partly so that he could study with the impressive philosopher Maurice Blondel, professor at the university, whose famous *L'Action*, published in

---

27. VB, 49. For all of the beautiful prose produced by skeptical or historicist writers such as Renan, Bremond was never much moved by their reconstructions. The same will apply to the historicist arguments of Loisy as well, though the two friends never collided on the issue.

28. Cited in King, *Spirit of Fire*, 10–11, and repeated from an article by Bremond in *Le Correspondant* of May 25, 1924.

1893, was making waves among progressive thinkers. In his earliest correspondence with Blondel he indicated that the Jesuit students in England were all reading him raptly, and that he, Henri, wanted a deeper, more sustained immersion. Blondel, only recently become professor at Aix, was glad to accommodate.

The background figure to the impact of Blondel, eventually known as "the philosopher of Aix," on Bremond, is John Henry Newman, but the larger setting is that of the English literary and ecclesiastical milieu that Bremond absorbed, largely through voracious reading, and that he processed in dialogue with Blondel. The results of that exposure were most clearly registered in the essays, written mostly in the period from 1894 to 1900, some of them extended book reviews from his time at the Jesuit journal *Études* in Paris, that he later collected in the two volumes of *L'Inquiétude religieuse* (1901 and 1909) and in *Âmes religieuses* (1902). What we see there is that Bremond "became enamoured with English letters and their romanticism, so that they left a deep imprint on him."[29] To be more precise, however, it was a romantic version of English Protestantism's Puritan heritage that gripped him.

Largely unfamiliar with French Protestantism, it was different in the years that he lived in England.[30] There he came into direct contact with a predominantly Protestant culture that diffused everywhere, even into the lives of English Roman Catholics. In that culture's fascinating Calvinist-Puritan core he discerned above all a high moral seriousness, an earnestness, an ethical purity of heart, a passion for righteousness, that he found immensely attractive, but also disturbing and unsettling. He became an acute observer of the ways in which this seriousness played out in the inner life of gifted individuals, how it worked, how it expressed itself, how it could reinforce a deep relationship with, and perhaps changes in, ecclesiastical allegiance, or alternatively, how it seemed to move some persons away from a faith in God and any sort of churchly loyalty. The representative of these Calvinist-inspired spiritual journeys whom he finally most admired was the novelist, essayist and radical thinker, George Eliot. From early on,[31] her excellence as a writer and a moralist gripped him very tightly, so much so, I think, that the best place to begin considering the English influence on Bremond is with the long, sustained, complex essay on her work that he published in 1906, but that had much earlier roots.[32]

---

29. Debongnie and de Brandt, "Bremond (Henri)," 519. This perspicacious essay, strongly emphasizing the English-Newmannian influence on Bremond, seems to have attracted little attention from scholars.

30. Hogarth, *Henri Bremond*, 8–11, has a good survey of the many essays and reviews that Bremond composed on English church life and literature without, however, much sense of how this interest reflected and shaped aspects of his own spiritual growth.

31. Already in Bremond to von Hügel, March 30, 1899 (Goichot, "En marge de la crise," 220–21) where he suggested that Tom and Maggie Tulliver in *The Mill on the Floss* represent respectively conservative and progressive approaches to moral truth.

32. The essay, "La religion de George Eliot," first appeared in the *Revue des Deux Mondes* for Sept. 15, 1906, and is collected in IR II, 86–162, but apparently Bremond had tried a version of the essay as early as September 1898, as one can infer from a comment to Blondel in a letter of October 1, 1898

Drawing on a number of recent works, as well as a collection of her letters and a biography by Eliot's second husband, John Cross, Bremond assessed the spiritual journey of George Eliot. He absolutely loved *Adam Bede* and *Middlemarch*, especially the former, where he saw her Puritan-derived belief in duty combined with a tender sympathy for human nature. But while he contended that her Puritanism was sincere and genuine, it had, nonetheless, an element of a "facade," of a surface covering something deeper.[33] What one saw behind Eliot's apparent serenity was a subterranean passion that had been learned, he thought, from reading Rousseau, who had created a "tumult of sensibility" that had led to a "maternal sweetness" always trying to break through her nature, in order to express itself, dutifully, as a disinterested love, especially in her mature writings. Passion had transmuted into affection, a fact important to the "tragedy"[34] of her religious evolution. He traced her unfolding from a troubled childhood in a conventional kind of Anglican Calvinism and piety (always described as "quaint" in its village settings, much like the genteel Aix of Bremond's own childhood) to a nonbelieving skepticism and humanism. In the process she had given up a rather cold-hearted religiosity for a life of warm-hearted care for others.[35]

In this analysis of Eliot, Bremond gave sustained attention to her inner dispositions, where she battled with a strong call to saintliness while feeling the pull of the flesh, where her youthful idealism became a recognition of the complexities of egotism and self-love in even the most virtuous. He talked about "an insensible preparation of her soul for a new way of thinking," and "the secret interior work" in her soul, and "the pathetic drama" that played out there. He contended that "the logic of the Calvinist *credo*" makes room only for the lonely personal search, as with Newman, but cannot accommodate "the ardent and unquiet pursuit of a sensible presence of God." She could not hear the heavenly voices however much she yearned to discern them.[36] She desperately sought a way to let her natural capacity for sympathy have unfettered expression—in other words, to let what we could call the "inner humanist" breathe free—but the religion that she knew was always getting in the way with its focus on

---

(BB, I, 80, and note). In letters to P. Valensin of June 12, 1931 and October 19, 1932, Blondel indicated how much he owed to the reading of Eliot: "on the logic of actions, on the proliferation of thoughts when conscience has died, on ideas that incarnate the soul and history of a people" (cited by Blanchet, BB, 84). The most interesting treatment of Bremond's work on Eliot is Goichot, "Trois 'prophètes du dehors,'" where he analyzes Bremond's unpublished thoughts on Charles George Gordon and Benjamin Jowett, as well as Eliot, in terms of their function as genuinely spiritual prophets who spoke from outside the structures of church and dogma.

33. The Puritanism from her English mother, thought Bremond, "La religion," 87–88, and a certain impulsiveness from a French father!

34. But with the use of this term qualified to mean something more like "ironically." See my earlier comment about Bremond not learning tragedy from his mother, but irony.

35. Bremond, "La religion," 88–91. I cite many phrases scattered through the essay, whose richness defies simple summary.

36. Her soul was marked, said Bremond (ibid., 95) by an "instinctive defiance of which she would never be healed." Surely Bremond spoke of himself as well!

"duty," which finally is little more than bourgeois "dutifulness" as opposed to "heroic virtue."

His reading of Eliot is masterful here, but it is clear that Bremond was also providing a window into his own soul.[37] His dissection is far too elaborated in order to be anything less. Deeply moved by Eliot's "poetry of goodness" as exemplified in the characters of Adam Bede and Silas Marner, kindly men who yearn for exalted levels of virtuous excellence, he saw that they always ultimately fall short. They are saints manqués, illustrating the powerful pull of the ideal of disinterested loving along with its practical impossibility in the contingencies of actual existence. Admiring in Eliot the way she used her literary creations as vehicles for pursuing her own spiritual struggles, where Adam and Silas and others functioned as her spiritual representatives—she served the same purpose for him. Her new religion, as inherited faith withered, would be one of reaching out to others in their suffering, a "religion of humanity" marked by the thinness of Comtean positivism, yet capturing something real and powerful in the thrust of a woman's "simple, forgiving heart." Such is the decisive mark of the person who attains to true prayer—something that the religious hypocrite with hours on his knees can never understand.[38]

Having largely given up on ecclesial Christianity, in her art Eliot personified the faith, hope and love that mark Paul's end note in 1 Corinthians 13. The final residue of her Calvinism, thought Bremond, was sympathy with suffering, not the sympathy of the agonized, elect soul that cries out, but rather the sympathy of the "cooler" meliorist, who knows that practical charity is a daily struggle to make at least some degree of improvement. Art would be the moral means. "It is," said Bremond, "perhaps the supreme humiliation and the ransom, so to speak, of the preacher and the artist—that sometimes they pay their share only with the money of a dream. Their power of effort and of sacrifice exhausts itself by celebrating in magnificent terms a virtue that others, thanks to them, pursue with more gusto. Otherwise, it is here that we seek to hide our misery."[39] Therein lay Eliot's "tragedy," that her pursuit of goodness could only be realized in the "dream" of her art. The same would be true for Bremond, as he would come to portray a panoply of characters, for whom, in turn, the same was true as well.

The English Puritan-Calvinist tradition was taken by Bremond as a launching pad, a jumping-off point, but not an optimal landing zone, for ideal development. Much the same was true for the Ignatian method, and for a provincial Catholicism just a shade too self-satisfied, at least as Bremond experienced them: the direction is right, the intentions

---

37. See Jossua, "Le jeune Bremond," esp. 27–28, who has developed the view that Bremond saw in Eliot's spirituality of sympathy, where literary creation served as a vehicle for searching after a God whom she had lost yet desired, a representation of the dynamics of his own deep immersion in literary art and expression.

38. Ibid., 156–57, where Bremond refers to ch. 61 of Eliot's *Middlemarch* and the self-righteous character of Bulstrode.

39. Bremond refers to Eliot's "poetry of goodness," where her lingering prayer to God is for only enough happiness to make her lovingly sympathetic (ibid., 134).

are good, but it fails to deliver by becoming its own worst enemy. And here is the catch: God recedes from view, does not become "sensible," in Bremond's favorite term, a here-and-now tangible reality that "speaks" clearly so as to be "heard" clearly. There is only silence. What Eliot could not see, thought Bremond, was that her very suffering and disillusionment and frustrated groping, her "anxious monotony," are the marks of the hidden working of grace, something necessary for the "fermentation" of a slow development. She lacked the steady patience, the quiet persistence, that are needed, but her heart was pure, and her art became her prayer. As the decade of the 1890s progressed, Bremond was discovering that he needed just that solution also, assuming that he could muster a calm steadfastness—until his art began to emerge.

The English Puritans excelled at educating children, and Bremond dedicated a long review essay to two recent books on Edward Thring, the Anglican priest who took charge as headmaster at the troubled school at Uppingham, "a fine example of that moral fervor—rigid, enthusiastic and mystical—which seems to find itself naturally in the country of Bunyan and Wesley."[40] Thring had that gift of creating a "marvelous contagion" with his students, so that they wanted to imitate his life. He operated with a "puritan enthusiasm" otherwise described as the "cold and impersonal beauty of the *categorical imperative*,"[41] in an environment where "each action, prayer, lecture, class, game, was transformed and received an infinite value."[42] Moral example was his primary educational tool, and he used it with startling effectiveness, instilling demanding discipline, ethical excellence, and nobility of purpose in his students. He brought out in them the best, and more than the best. And he knew all about sin. He was a great believer in collective punishment, contending that "the school is like life, where a small number of bold men will rule by terror over the mob which, law-abiding and timid, does not know its true power."[43] Choosing to place the emphasis in his teaching on "largeness of ideas and first principles," he knew that morality is a function of character in changing circumstances, not of rigid codes. However, averred Bremond in a revealing commentary, there was something chilling and unattractive about the man, for he lacked intellectual playfulness, the zest of new ideas, and the stimulation that comes from disagreement.[44] He was more of a prophet than a mystic, since he is too much of a Protestant to allow for any illuminism, and thus in the final analysis, not the kind of saint that the French can admire, who have more to offer than virtue alone. He had none of the suffering of the true poet, like George Eliot![45]

---

40. "Un Éducateur Anglais," 130. The essay first appeared in the *Revue des Deux Mondes* for September 15, 1902.

41. Ibid., 142.

42. Ibid., 143.

43. Ibid., 160.

44. "One of the humbling aspects of our nature," says Bremond, "is that our sympathies do not necessarily keep pace with our admirations" (ibid., 173).

45. Ibid., 196–97.

Anglicanism

The problem, then, with the spirituality of moral character, admirable and beneficial as it is, is that it runs the risk of stifling the "child" in us, that is, our capacity for admiration, for wonder, for creativity and playfulness, and most important, for a generous and broad humanitarian sympathy for all persons, especially in their suffering. There is the further danger that such morality, though compassionate, becomes bourgeois and conventional, that is, a morality of the comfortable and the privileged. George Eliot thought so, and that became Bremond's complaint about Anglicanism. In an essay about the clergyman Sydney Smith (1771–1845), celebrated for his wit and literary expression, but also honored as a liberal and socially progressive critic, Bremond saw an Anglican of the old school, of a bourgeoisie resistant to change and secure in its social standing.[46] Smith was a good pastor, and his heart was pure, and he was not afraid to advocate for change, but at the same time he saw religion as a means to happiness and the good life. He had no serious "religious inquietude," knew nothing of the true hunger for eternity. But this was the heritage of the English clergy, the heritage of "easy virtues, of comfortable living, and of theological insouciance." Bremond here ventured an early contrast with John Henry Newman: Smith as a young pastor "had found in the Gospel the condemnation of the English bourgeoisie and he strongly reminded his compatriots that the time of the Old testament promises had passed; the material prosperity of England, which Smith would have given as a testimony of the divinity of Anglicanism, made the preacher of St. Mary's at Oxford tremble."[47]

Other Anglican figures attracted Bremond's approval, but then final criticism. In his essays on the teaching of children, as noted, he admired Thomas Arnold (1795–1842), the great humanist headmaster of Rugby and progressive thinker, but then he went on to assess the career of one of Arnold's students, William Charles Lake (b. 1817, dean of Durham in 1869, d. 1897). Lake was a defender of Newman to his Anglican brethren, then a moderate advocate for Catholic liturgical practice, always oriented to the enrichment of the inner life, but never as an archaizing medievalist. His virtue was that he grasped "the idea of the Church," just as Newman had, and this awareness enabled him to be a true pioneer of sacerdotal priesthood within Anglicanism. He represented the death of the old "Anglican dignitary" and the emergence of something approximating the true "Catholic ideal."[48]

46. "Sydney Smith et le chistianisme bourgeois." First in *Études* 65 (1895).

47. Ibid., 21. Smith was a "poor soul, plunged into the egoism of the material," said Bremond (ibid., 22).

48. "L'Assimilation des principes catholiques," 231–32. In an uncollected review ("M. Gladstone théologien") of a work by W. H. Gladstone on the thought of Joseph Butler, Bremond ironically admired, but also critiqued, the Anglican lay thinker, who, having no infallible teaching authority on which to rely, has to put his faith in personal theological speculations. The same reservation occurred in a somewhat later (1900) review, "Que ferait le Christ?" in which Bremond expressed deep admiration for the Protestant desire "to do what Jesus would do" whatever the cost, in a given set of circumstances. One obvious difficulty, however, is that in the absence of an infallible teaching authority, it

Another study focused on the Anglican historian John Richard Green (1837–1883), whom Bremond saw as a further example of the moral intensity of the tradition emanating from Arnold, and in this case typifying the kind of broad-Church Anglicanism, marked by compromise and an addiction to comfortable living, that would evolve toward humanism and rationalism.[49] Green, headed for doubt and unbelief, belonged to "that generation of utopians who believed naively that science expanding into every realm would lead to the golden age."[50] The extraordinary thing about Green, however, was that even as his rationalism increased, so did his respect for the spiritual life, so that in the final analysis he remained "profoundly English." "He was a man who venerated tradition, , a man faithful to ancient habits, fashioned in a mystical way by biblical education and the greatest abundance of religious literature."[51] Green was a man of moral intensity and devotion to duty, the "sweetness" of whose soul "remained Christian among the ruins of its first faith." Having none of the egoism of a Renan, he had something unusual for the English: sympathy for the French after the debacle of 1870–71![52]

However, aside from the special case of Newman in his early years, the Anglican who most caught Bremond's attention—the one for whom he had genuine respect—was John Keble, a veritable "Anglican saint," to whom he devoted a carefully wrought essay.[53] Longtime pastor at his rural parish of Hursley in Hampshire, and a major initiator of the Oxford Catholic Revival, Keble will always be marked by a certain hagiographical glow in Anglican tradition, rather like George Herbert. What most attracted Bremond to Keble was both the nature of Keble's personality and dispositions as it came through in a range of memoirs, but also his gifts as the poet-author of *The Christian Year*. The language of the essay is lyrical, where Keble comes across as an archetype of the Catholic artist, for whom poetry and prayer are intertwined realities. Bremond's terms for describing the person of Keble are "calm, peaceful, trusting," "mild," "moderate," "serene," "tranquil," "peaceful," "musical," "softly feminine," and "poetic."

Keble is the ideal of a pastor. Repeatedly Bremond detected in him a *douceur*, a "sweetness" tinged with sadness, as he nursed an ill wife through many years of suffering, and as he ministered to the suffering in the lives of his parishioners. He was alive to the pain of others, and to his own, but chose always to focus on things of joy and beauty, always maintaining a sunny state of mind. Keble's family background in a clergyman's household is described as tender, loving and affectionate; it has the

---

will prove impossible to get consensus on that question, once the initial burst of enthusiasm is past.

49. "De la foi au doute: J.-R. Green (1837–1883)."

50. Ibid., 253.

51. Ibid., 265.

52. Ibid., 260.

53. "Un saint Anglican," first in *Études*, for April 20 and May 5, 1901. Blanchet indicates that Bremond's articles on Oxford Movement figures, his first publications, began appearing anonymously in 1893–4 in *L'Univers*, a traditionalist Catholic journal. Maurras, when he found out about it, criticized Bremond, finding the Protestants with whom the latter was fascinated "disgusting" (VB, 60–61).

quality of a stained glass window. Bremond's descriptions have a breathless softness, dangerously close to sentimentality. Keble's domestic nest, despite the wife's pain, and despite the fact that they could not conceive, was filled with the children of the parish, an "idyllic" haven at its best. The little ones of the parish that he baptized are tiny regenerate saints deserving of all the best devotion, and he celebrates them in his *Lyra Innocentium* collection of poems. Keble's friendships, especially that with Newman, are marked by humility, honesty and tenderness.

But then came the catch: Keble was "more attached to the sweetness of heaven than to the austere joys of the full truth," since his mysticism of brightness had little room for the darkness of the night, and for the agonized pain of deep penitence.[54] He could not really understand Newman's anguish and the decision to leave for Rome, although in later years he was blissfully happy, surrounded by family and books and music, the rift with Newman notwithstanding. A late visitor to the vicarage of Hursley, found it, Bremond noted, rather disappointing: having planned to confer with a great leader of the Church and looking for an "Athanasius," he found only an "Anglican pastor."[55] Bremond does not use the word here, but in a phrase like "more pious than heroic," he implies it: "bourgeois." So much for Anglicanism at its admirable best and in its ultimate failure, well-intentioned and sometimes with real depth, but always weighted down with too many compromises. Bremond was envious of all of that English domesticity, but, celibate and Gallican, wary as well!

It comes as no surprise, then, that Bremond ventured to explore the spirituality of a number of English Roman Catholics, some converts and some not. Here, too, he saw the English character at work, sometimes in harmony with, and sometimes in some degree of opposition to, his own developing views of spiritual strength and maturity. It became increasingly clear during the decade of the 1890s that he was more and more taken with the idea that "disquietude," a dispositional restlessness, is the hallmark of spiritual depth, and that efforts to baffle down that discontent with either the willful blindness of authoritarian certainty or with the obtuseness of skeptical dismissal are misguided.[56]

Thus, he saw the figure of W. G. Ward, convert, professor, and master logician, as a kind of object lesson.[57] Married, family man, respected Oxford don, converted to the scholastic and ultramontane kind of Catholicism, gifted teacher, deeply sensitive and charitable, Ward exemplified qualities in Catholicism that Bremond would come to loathe. Ward's whole way was to arrive at knowledge by means of mathematical deductions, without the "disquietude of experience." Unlike Newman, he loved

---

54. Ibid., 53.

55. Ibid., 58.

56. The first of the *L'Inquiétude religieuse* collections, that of 1901, included as an epigraph in English Newman's "To be at ease is to be unsafe."

57. "La logique de l'esprit," first in *Études*, May-June 1894. Bremond would later come to oppose the scholastically-minded Ward's criticism of Newman's thought.

the product more than the process, ending up with a religiosity over-developed in theory, and brittle in practice. In such an all-or-nothing approach to religion, thought Bremond, pure ratiocination will finally backfire into a soulless kind of spiritual death.

An example was in his review of the novel, *One Poor Scruple*, by Josephine Hope Ward, writing under the name of Mrs. Wilfrid Ward (Wilfrid a son of W. G.), where Bremond discussed the author's depiction of an "old," recusant English Catholic family, who must deal with a moral dilemma, namely, the fact that one of their circle has broken church discipline by marrying a divorced Protestant.[58] By the end of the novel we are led to see that there are basically two spiritual dangers in moral matters: that of a thoughtlessly loose permissiveness that is without God, and that of a hard, mean-spirited and rigid legalism, both of them manifestations, again, of bourgeois thinking. Both Protestantism and Catholicism in different ways set up these extremes, but when religion is healthy there is the recognition that grace works mysteriously and relentlessly in souls given to God and faced by difficult choices, whatever their imperfections, and however many hard times they must endure. An English quality Bremond seemed most to like in Ward was her "realistic" observation-based portrayal of human foibles.

Bremond sketched Nicholas Wiseman (1802–1865), lifelong English Roman Catholic, first Cardinal Archbishop of Westminster after the Catholic hierarchy was restored in England in 1850, and the central figure in the process of receiving into the Roman Catholic Church the first Oxford Tractarians who were converting.[59] He was chiefly concerned here with the various ways in which Wiseman's English roots made him practical, sensible, and pastoral, as well as patiently sympathetic, with the scrupulosity and moodiness of the Oxford men. Himself a romantic with a romantic's sentimental love for the Church of Rome, he had realized in his own formation the role of Roman joy in dissipating the typically "taciturn torpor" of English culture.[60] Wiseman negotiated, agonizingly and at considerable length, the complex tensions between England's old Catholic families and the new converts, and to his vast credit had the sense to recognize, if few others did, how much these new members added to the community of the Truth! In other words, as for Bremond himself, the English input would be vital.

Finally, Bremond sketched, as many others have done since, Edward Bouverie Pusey, Newman's closest associate in his latter days at Oxford, and the supreme example of a Tractarian who did *not* convert.[61] Bremond took the opportunity here to depict the Oxford atmosphere in the early days of the Tractarian movement, a time in which

---

58. "L'Idéal et la realité." Blondel's comment on this essay (Blondel to Bremond, January 25, 1900 [BB, I, 266]) is interesting. He thought that Bremond was a little confused in the analysis of the "Pharisaism" (*sic*) of some ordinary Catholics, contending that he focused too much on "sentiments and attitudes" in characters, and not on the "distinct principles" by which the characters acted.

59. "Wiseman et les catholiques anglais," first in *Études*, September 20, 1898.

60. Ibid., 139.

61. Bremond, "L'inquiétude de Newman."

young men had become stirred with the ideals of "heroism and sainthood" in a Church grown "too comfortable." The young Pusey, claims Bremond, typified in an English way "the appearance of cold reserve" where "often hide treasures of tenderness," but at the same time he never experienced the "inquietudes of first doubt," an anxiety "dolorous of full light,"—as did his young wife—that is the beginning of true conversion. Bremond opined that "men like Pusey know neither how to show or speak tenderness, but they do not love any the less ardently for that." Eventually, following the death of his wife and in grief that never ended, Pusey was to become "a puritan with his bible tucked under his arm," inhuman, dry, authoritarian, "too obstinate to have been truly pious." Bremond developed at considerable length the contrast with Newman, always discerning in Pusey a "hopeless inertia," "a mysterious and incurable illness of the intellect," a kind of "intellectual immobility." Pusey evinces a deep mental instability masking as firmness. He is "imperturbable serenity" on the surface, and a veritable typhoon in the depths.

Thus, the picture of unhappy Pusey became for Bremond a kind of pendant to that of happy Keble, providing in the process a snapshot of his conflicted relationship to English culture. Attracted to its seriousness and Puritan heritage, he was made uneasy by something that could lack balance, though even more, by something that resisted religious agony while simultaneously succumbing to it. The problem with English character was not a blithe unawareness of the dark depths, but a determined avoidance of them. The dark places of spiritual disquietude can be gracious, but they must be understood to be so and then embraced in a certain spirit before they can yield their treasures. Here was the English deficiency. No wonder that his portrait of Newman himself will manifest real ambivalence.

As Bremond prepared to begin his year of study with Blondel at Aix, he was resonant with the echoes of English influence. Newman's antithesis of the "notional" and the "real" is already present in their correspondence, where, in Bremond's construal, the work of the reasoning intellect ("raison raisonnante") is the "notional," while the "real" is the affectively toned expression of immediate "experience." In the essays on English figures the notional always pertains to the surface of the personality, its outward presentation, while the real is a reflection of the depths, of the inner life often in tension with, if not outright contradiction of, the surface.

He was careful, though, about the way he presented Newman to Blondel, justifying his interest by referring to the work of the Parisian clericalist philosopher and friend of Blondel's, Léon Ollé-Laprune, as well as his desire to read and understand Blondel's *L'Action*.[62] Add to these, he said, "a 'culte' for Cardinal Newman . . . and you will conclude that you could treat me in turn as a student, as your student." The *real* issue was Newman. Would he be acceptable to Blondel? Could Newman be made French?

---

62. Letter to Blondel, March 22, 1897 (BB, I, 31). The tone of the letter is ingratiating, with the reference to Ollé-Laprune one of puffery. He refers to his reading of this philosopher as a "great intellectual blessing." But cf. EG, 31–32.

4

Newman and Blondel
Setting the Theological Frame

From 1897 onward, once he had become Maurice Blondel's student, they continued as friends, interlocutors, collaborators and correspondents for the rest of Bremond's life. The volume of their frequent epistolary communications, both of them abundantly articulate, though not necessarily intimate, is enormous.[1] Blondel, a devout layman and professor, grew to have great respect and fondness for Bremond as a young priest and, as it turned out, aspiring writer and historian. Bremond would always look to Blondel as a senior mentor, philosophical guide and theological censor, someone on whom he could, as we say, "bounce off" ideas and get critical feedback, although only four years separated them in age. Blondel in turn appreciated Bremond's support during his own intellectual and ecclesial trials and seemed to derive benefit from priestly counsel at difficult moments of his life, in personal or family crises, and especially in the evaluation of this or that event of Church politics.

The result of this mutuality was that Blondel made Bremond more thoughtful and judicious, and Bremond made Blondel savvier about ecclesial practicalities and contemporary culture, especially literary culture. There would be difficulties and tensions as well. When differences of opinions arose—especially as the "Modernist" crisis whipped up—they treated one another more circumspectly, positions and counter-positions became more complex, and Bremond became more secretive about his sympathies and range of contacts. Alfred Loisy would become a major bone of contention between them, as would Bremond's behavior at the time of Tyrrell's death.[2]

---

1. In three large, heavily annotated volumes in Blanchet's edition, BB. Blanchet's general assessment of their relationship, in addition to the introduction in the first volume of the edited correspondence, is "Bremond et Blondel."

2. In his introductory remarks to the correspondence, Blanchet was ironically suspicious—a bit too much so—of the level of honesty in their shared communication (BB, I, 7–17). Certainly Bremond was circumspect around what he knew would upset Blondel, but sparks flew often enough and they did not hesitate to cry on one another's shoulders.

Initially, some of their conversations turned around John Henry Newman, and the ideas that Bremond had picked up from Newman. Indeed, much of his mature working theology came from Newman as Bremond understood him, and then as Blondel succeeded in modifying, and possibly restructuring, that understanding.[3] He honored the wisdom that Bremond absorbed from Newman, but critiqued it vigorously as well. The situation was further complicated by Bremond's growing friendships, also from 1897 onward, with the Catholic Modernists Friedrich von Hügel, George Tyrrell, and Alfred Loisy, especially the last, which persisted to the end of Bremond's life—all of whom knew, and approved of, Newman's work in varying degrees. While, however, the influence of these three on Bremond was substantive, it was quite secondary to that of Newman, then of Blondel. Our first task, then, is to assess the impact of John Henry Newman on Bremond.

The Phenomenon of Newman

By the time that Bremond first encountered his writings, John Henry Newman had been a celebrity of Victorian England for several decades. Raised a Calvinist and marked by an evangelical conversion-experience, he had became a student, then Anglican priest, fellow, and tutor at Oxford University when that venerable institution was still a bastion of genteel Anglican privilege and status. As that status eroded, then collapsed, in the aftermath of the Reform Bill of 1832, Newman became a leader in attempts to defend the independence of the Anglican establishment—its doctrine, polity and endowments—by asserting the catholicity of the Church of England over against Protestant sectarianism and Roman papalism. As he became the central character in an ecclesial protest movement, his outspokenness and flamboyancy drew public attention. As the popular preacher at the University Church of St. Mary the Virgin in Oxford, as well as the respected author of important patristic studies, he projected an image of himself as, like his idols, the embodiment of true orthodoxy and churchly freedom from secular control. The true heritage of Anglicanism, enshrined in its prayer books, lay, he averred, in its continuity, rightly understood, with the Undivided Church of the early centuries. He began to polemicize against biblicist Calvinist-evangelicalism and its Reformation heritage on the one hand, and creeping "liberalism" and unbelief in the university on the other. He had a dark vision: as the industrial age advanced, British society was being corrupted and the Church as he knew it had been compromised in its functioning. After a long, agonized, publicly displayed and dramatic exit-process filled with a large and complex polemical literature, he converted to the Church of Rome in 1845.

---

3. In his account, Goichot emphasizes the role of Blondel in forming Bremond theologically (EG, 31–37). No doubt, that is true. But the influence, I believe, came in the form of modifying the more fundamental influence, which was that of Newman. *L'Action* was inherently difficult to assimilate, whereas Newman came much more easily.

Vilified and attacked at length for his "defection" and for "Romanizing," he published in 1864 his classic defense, the *Apologia pro vita sua*, which proved to be a huge sensation. He laid out his whole life as a kind of austere cerebral struggle, with the reader invited to eavesdrop, as he thought his way through to Roman obedience. He presented the matter as a crisis of personal integrity, in which he constantly waited for God's "leading" before taking radical steps. Of course, the account was self-serving (hence an "apology"), since Newman himself was perfectly clear about his motive: it was to demonstrate that "I am a Catholic by virtue of my believing in God; and if I am asked why I believe in a God, I answer that it is because I believe in myself, for I feel it impossible to believe in my own existence ... without believing also in the existence of Him, who lives as a ... Being in my conscience."[4] The seeming candor and self-transparency of the narrative has always enthralled readers.

But not only Newman, they all did it. Many of the principal figures around him, whose careers would be parallel or antithetical to his own, produced personal testimonials and memoirs over the years, and there are great masses of correspondence and diaries and journals to supplement the picture. There is a lively cast of characters from both Newman's Anglican and Catholic periods, some of whom were as colorful as Newman, many of them revealing and even intimate in what they chose to say about themselves, about Newman, and about themselves in relation to Newman.

A tireless wielder of the pen, Newman produced a vast body of writing, the most important of which as far as Bremond is concerned are, in addition to the *Apologia*, his *Fifteen Sermons Preached before the University of Oxford between A.D. 1826 and 1843* (3rd ed., 1872), the *Essay on the Development of Christian Doctrine* (2nd ed., 1846), and *An Essay in Aid of a Grammar of Assent* (1870). To these should be added his letters and sermons. The hallmark of these writings is that they *both* defend traditional Catholic truth, *but also* tend to recast or reframe it within the philosophical currents and historical methods which Newman had come to treasure. While bitterly criticized by his former Anglican and Protestant constituencies for embracing Catholic dogma and claims, he was held in suspicion by Roman theologians for the *way* of his embrace.

But as a vindication of his thought over against his critics, Leo XIII made Newman a cardinal in 1879. His status thus assured, he would always remain controversial. He died August 11, 1890. Thus, in the 1880s and '90s during the time of Bremond's Jesuit education and formation, Newman was a lionized figure, whose work, along with that of his many associates, always invited close inspection. People would try constantly to understand him, for reasons sympathetic or not. The source material was vast, and has become more so.[5] Newman was fiercely introspective and volubly articulate about his introspection, so that a theological assertion often came dressed in the vesture of his

---

4. Newman, *Apologia pro vita sua*, cited in Ian Ker, *John Henry Newman*, 549.

5. Bremond had access to most of it, but Newman's enormous correspondence would not become available until well into the twentieth century.

personal struggles. Hagiographical accounts, hatchet jobs and everything in between have been produced endlessly ever since. His story was large, blatantly public, and rich with detail. A perennial gold mine for the would-be "religious psychologist."

Newman's Mind: Methodological Beginnings

By the time of Bremond's young adulthood the practice of literary portraiture had reached new levels of sophistication as well as new levels of public interest. The classic example, still popular today, is the 1893 biography of Francis of Assisi by the French Protestant Paul Sabatier, but there were many others. Source materials, including often newly discovered or newly edited texts, were assembled and critically sifted; "scientific" perspectives were brought into play with the help of psychological or sociological models; concerted efforts were made to discern the heartbeat, the mind-set, the "spirit," of a character in order to construct a narrative of compelling verisimilitude. Unlike older styles of literary analysis, where moral evaluation often predominated, the newer emphasis aspired to historical objectivity and an understanding of the forces involved in a person's "development." Why did a character behave in such-and-such a way? What factors were at work? Specifically religious experience was explored in the genius-product of the age, William James's *The Varieties of Religious Experience* (1902), since the reading public thrived as well on religious confession and testimonial, the more personal the better—the trend being typified in France by the swell of enthusiasm for the carefully edited and vetted *Autobiography—Story of a Soul* (1898) of the young Carmelite Thérèse of Lisieux. Most notably the "inner life," the subjectivity of the individual, had become more interesting than his/her *beliefs* as such, as the key to understanding behavior and action. Bremond would become a specialist in this trend *par excellence*, which was to become a hallmark of modernizing theology.

So, exactly when and how Newman first caught Bremond's attention is unclear, but he soon functioned as a foil, or contrast-figure, to the other Anglicans of the Oxford Movement, both those who stayed in the Church of England, like Keble and Pusey, and those who converted, like Ward and Manning—as well as old-line Catholics like Wiseman. Newman seemed to Bremond to be a pure "type," namely, the spiritually disquieted soul who truly agonizes in the ways that authentic faith requires, who does not hide from the pain. By comparison with Keble he was willing to face the night of disquietude; by contrast with Pusey he will honestly face anxiety and doubt; by contrast with Ward, he will avoid the rigidity of the syllogism in favor of "the contemplation of truth"; by contrast with Manning, after both had become cardinals, he would be the subtle intellectual rather than the aggressive man-of-action;[6] by contrast with Wiseman the lifelong

---

6. "Manning et Newman." This use of Newman as the magnetic center of the Oxford Movement and its dominant personality would become more or less explicit when Bremond organized his earliest essays on the Anglican clergy, composed between 1894 and 1900, then gathered in the first volume of the *L'Inquiétude religieuse* series, around the headings of "Avant Newman" (the essay on the "bourgeois" Anglican, Sydney Smith), the "Daybreak of Conversion" (including the essay contrasting

Catholic, Newman would always be an uneasy and scrupulous newcomer, suggesting that traces of his former Calvinism remained. By 1901 Bremond was referring to "the life and work of that great man," to "the marvelous influence of Newman," and to "the heart and spirit of Newman," for Newman like no other personified the "disquiet" of the soul that seeks to be "calmed," thereby freeing us in our study of the inner life from "theories" and "abstraction" for "the problems of religious psychology."[7] With Newman, Bremond seemed to say, we may look at the "bare" soul itself!

It is Newman's inner life—the whole gamut of states, perceptions, emergent tendencies and developments, shifts of direction, continuities but also discontinuities with the past (such as conversions), sudden reversals and altered sensibilities, the internalization of various texts and experiences, the functioning of memory, all that made up Newman's progression from Anglican to Catholic, and then from Catholic layman to prestigious prelate—that will be of interest. The eventual word to cover all of this will be *sentiment*, a term that suggested the whole range of human affectivity and perception, the totality of a person's mental state in its characteristic qualities. It is something very close to what we mean today by terms like "temperament" or "personality," that is, general and universal traits combined and expressed in uniquely individual ways that are often molded by cultural context and historical contingencies.[8]

But it is *sentiment* as delineated not by direct observation, but by historiographical imagination—the historian engaged in empathic immersion with his object as a figure of the past—which, in the case of Newman the writer and thinker, would require immersion in the texts that are, as it were, his continuing embodiment. The methodology that Bremond would use is that of belles-lettres literary commentary and portraiture, in the tradition of Saint-Simon and La Bruyère, and as handed down by the nineteenth-century critic Charles Augustin Sainte-Beuve in his *Lundis* and the *Port-Royal*—which we will come to shortly. More than his predecessors, however, Bremond will utilize the perspectives of romantic psychology, that is, the analysis of the passions and moods of his biographical subjects, as these are manifest in their compositions. Thus, he will operate as an exponent of "religious psychology" in the sense of a textually-derived psychology, a mapping of the inner life of the writer as it is enshrined in the spiritual content, as well as the tones, of his/her literary art. What would distinguish Bremond's work, as we shall see, was his marshalling of personal documents—journals, diaries, letters, biographical narratives, contemporary testimonies, and so on—as an underpinning to analysis of a subject's published writings, creating thereby an uniquely "thick" portrayal of that person's inner life.[9]

Newman and Pusey), and the "Days after Conversion" (including the essay contrasting Newman and Manning).

7. The preface to the first volume of *L'Inquiétude religieuse* (IR), vii–viii.

8. The decision of K. L. Montgomery, the English translator of the first three volumes of Bremond's *Histoire*, to render *sentiment* as "thought" was highly unfortunate to say the very least, although "sentiment" would have been even worse.

9. Bremond's sources here were complex, since the term "sentiment" was "in the air." See the

Deeper Reason

Bremond's early use of ideas deriving from Newman came to light in a March 1897, review of some recent work by the French writer, critic, and académicien Ferdinand Brunetière.[10] Known as a rationalist and free thinker, who had shown some signs of moving in the direction of religious faith (he would later convert to Catholicism), Brunetière was a formidable character, and Bremond was brave to challenge him.[11] He had been advancing a theory of faith based on a sharp distinction between scientific and religious modes of knowing, contrary to the more traditional Catholic approach with its efforts to integrate these. Religious believing arose from a moral need, mysterious in origin, and thus "irrational," a "sacred delirium," said Brunetière, not in the sense of contradicting reason, but as a different kind of reason which is not subject to syllogistic demonstration: we believe in God because we need God. The question was whether the use of the descriptor "irrational" for this different kind of morally grounded reason was legitimate. Bremond thought not.[12]

The danger in Brunetière's argument is "fideism," that is, the contention that religious belief is purely a matter of faith, with a consequent, or implied, need for authorities, such as the church, to dictate the content of faith. It would seem that Brunetière had restated and updated Pascal's famous "reasons of the heart," with the philosopher Ollé-Laprune in agreement, that some forms of reason have a "willed" element, so that, while being intellectual, they are not purely "rational," that "doing the truth" may be prior to, even ultimately higher than, "knowing the truth." But then, after citing de Maistre's romantic idea that an "interior sentiment" will show us what is true or false before we consciously reflect, Bremond quickly turned to Newman's

---

discussion by Houdard, "Henri Bremond et la psychologie" (ibid., 125n7) who refers to Marxer, "L'École française," for the idea that the term derived from the philosophic writer Benjamin Constant via romanticism, Protestant liberalism, and pietism, in order to distinguish between outward and contingent forms, including dogmatic language, and the inner essence of an experience. It is an empirically descriptive term that avoids normative judgments of true or false, good or bad. Both Marxer and Houdard argue that Bremond's use of the term provided a way of understanding how the literary expression of an experience precisely as "sentiment" created a textual "internal drama" that could enable its social propagation. Also, as Houdard notes (ibid., 125), F. Strowski's 1898 publication of *l'Introduction à l'histoire littéraire du sentiment religieux en France au septième siècle*, a study of Francis de Sales, was bound to have caught Bremond's notice.

10. "La logique de coeur" first appeared under another title in *Études*, March 5 and 20, 1897. Blondel in his first letter to Bremond, March 11, 1897 (BB, I, 29) very much approved of this essay. Bremond would later dedicate the second of his books on Newman, *La psychologie de la foi*, to Brunetière.

11. Blanchet contextualizes this essay in a very public debate that had been going on between Mgr d'Hulst, founder and rector of the Institut Catholique in Paris, and Brunetière (VB, 84–87).

12. Henri Bremond, "La logique de coeur," 109–11. Brunetière's use of "irrational" lacks "rigor," says Bremond. For background on Ferdinand Brunetière, one cannot do better than Owen Chadwick's account in *Secularization of the European Mind*, 240–43. A disillusioned Comtean positivist, Brunetière had come to believe that science provided no basis for morality, that only religion could perform that function adequately. Therefore, let us put the two of them in quite separate compartments.

conversion-experience, where "adhesion spontaneous, immediate, in the absence of at least apparent reasoning," reveals that a deeper reasoning, an underlying "sentiment," drives the process, so that faith is never "a blind movement of the soul." Newman, more than anyone, he suggested, has described "the mysterious work" by which we realize that faith can never be a purely analytical process, that faith builds its reasoning bit-by-bit (Newman, *University Sermon* 12), and that "sentiment" is a judgment of "sympathy or repugnance" toward the whole of an object.[13]

Instancing the critic Sainte-Beuve's judgment that Racine and Virgil are similar, although there is no clear reason for the claim, Bremond appealed to Newman's dynamic of "natural assent," in which we argue from concrete details and antecedent probabilities to a general conclusion. "In the realm of the conscience this logic [of faith]," argued Bremond, "becomes a natural casuistry much like the procedures of literary sensibility." Reason is involved, but not "raison raisonnante." As in Newman's concept of *implicit reasoning*, where the mind does not rise to the level of an *explicit reasoning* of the kind that analytical science would employ, there is a moral reasoning, that is, a "conscience," that "knows" before it "knows what it knows." The operation of faith is the same, and it is thus Newman who correctly interprets Pascal!

It was Newman's use of the idea of "conscience" in the life of faith that fixated Bremond, as Roger Haight pointed out, and that led to his "existential" reading of Newman. "Conscience" as the morally discerning dimension of personal experience then inspired Newman's "illative sense" as a historiographical method. Bremond, in thus interpreting Newman, was, Haight thought, on target.[14] But Maurice Nédoncelle disagreed, pointing out that for Bremond everything in Newman so quickly became a matter of "conscience in the acquisition and determination of revealed truths,"[15] that Bremond ended up by simply reading himself into Newman. He created a "romantic Newman," where everything is shifted from the head to the heart, and Newman becomes the model Christian, who struggles with darkness, uncertainty, and dryness in his prayer for all of his life.

Owen Chadwick, however, had it best, when he saw that Newman is essentially an English empiricist (as is evident in the *Grammar*, where Newman constantly refers to the Anglican Joseph Butler), with the implication that analysis of a historical figure is not a romantic assimilation of souls guided by the assumption that past and present share the same struggles. Rather, good historical work is a careful vectoring-process in which many details are gathered in order to create an "impression" with a probabilistic level of certitude.[16] Newman employed that method, and Bremond then used it on

---

13. Henri Bremond, "La logique du coeur," 113, and the whole argument, 111–30.

14. See Haight, "Bremond's Newman."

15. Nédoncelle, "Newman selon Bremond," 43.

16. Chadwick, "Henri Bremond and Newman." See also J. M. Cameron, "Newman and the Empiricist Tradition," 87, who argues that the "structure" of Newman's arguments comes from the empiricists, and their "spirit" from Pascal.

Newman. For Newman, as Bremond interpreted him, "imaginative insight," which prefers "the painting of an intellectual picture to the scientific analysis of a logical idea," is the high road of interpretation. He wanted Newman to be completely human, so that all of the strange "antinomies" of his inner life would come to light, "to get inside the mentality" of his beloved object by cutting through the "notions" to get to the "real." "Bremond was the first Catholic mind," claimed Chadwick, "to try to understand the Anglican Newman with a total sympathy; and that also meant that he was the first Catholic mind to treat the whole of Newman, Protestant or Catholic, as a unity."[17]

In communication with Blondel regarding the Brunetière article, Bremond pointed to the last question raised there, namely whether or not the "irrational" understood as implicit thought ultimately implied a pure negation of the importance of conscious understanding, suggesting that this is *the* question in the final analysis. Blondel, already indicating a wariness with regard to Newman, questioned whether Brunetière was quite as much of a fideist as Bremond seemed to think, thus waving a warning flag about Bremond's move to the subjective as such.[18] Nonetheless, Blondel was supportive, quick to affirm what he called a "psychological apostolate" in Bremond, oriented to the "inner experience and spiritual process of the mystics," on whom Bremond was starting to focus and whom he, Blondel, thought poorly understood.[19]

Feeling very much affirmed by his new mentor, Bremond arrived back in Aix in the latter part of 1897. To brother Jean he expressed how excited he was, but also how hard he was working at Blondel's *L'Action*—which he found enormously difficult—while at the same time he enjoyed following Blondel's course.[20] Intense conversation with Blondel assured him that the problem of "religious anguish" must be his focus, and that the contribution of Newman to their discussion was the close connection between the content of preaching and the content of the preacher's life. In the spring of 1898 Bremond thanked his mentor for their continuing friendship, opining that he, Bremond, is no theologian, but Newman's best friends were not thinkers either![21]

---

17. Chadwick, "Henri Bremond and Newman," 197. Hogarth discusses some of the early criticisms of Bremond's work on Newman (*Henri Bremond*, 6–8, and appendix 1, 166–69). Most of it was fatuous, in so far as critics jumped on him for creating a sometimes unflattering picture of Newman. What they failed to appreciate was that Bremond was committed to a "warts and all" perspective. Eventually Bremond would come to recognize how firmly rooted Newman's thought was in the moral philosophy of Joseph Butler ("Bremond to Blondel, May 13, 1917" [BB, II, 320]).

18. Bremond to Blondel, March 22, 1897, and Blondel to Bremond, March 27, 1897 (BB, I, 30–37). Blanchet reproduces (36–37) Brunetière's response to Bremond: it seems that Brunetière aspired to a kind of vitalism in the thinking process itself, i.e., that thought impregnated with lived energy is thus irrational—this view having a rather different thrust from Bremond's direction.

19. Blondel to Bremond, June 19, 1897 (ibid., 48).

20. Cited by Blanchet in the notes appended to Bremond to Blondel, January 7, 1898 (ibid., 54).

21. Bremond to Blondel, April 9, 1898 (ibid., 56).

Études

In August, at the end of the tertian year, he was posted to a chaplaincy at the Collège des Brotteaux at Lyon, where for a year he would teach students headed for Saint-Cyr. In one of his few references to the Dreyfus crisis then convulsing France, Bremond alluded to the "sadnesses" of this crisis, but that its "concrete form" made it especially suitable for the use of literature in clarifying and illuminating moral issues.[22] Early in 1899, Jesuit superiors placed Bremond, much to his pleasure, on staff at their journal, *Études*, in Paris, where he would function in the role of "specialist in religious psychology and literature" until 1903, shortly before his dismissal from the Order. Thanks to the Jesuits, however, it was at *Études* that Bremond would begin to flourish, now having an official and approved outlet for his early reviews and essays.

André Blanchet has argued, after examining records in the Jesuit archives of the Province de Lyon, that Bremond's tertian year was quite difficult for him, even painfully disillusioning, and thus provided the setting for his thinking about the darkness of faith.[23] The notes from his Ignatian "examens," those special instruments of self-examination that are part of the *Spiritual Exercises*, show that Bremond was struggling to attain a decisive clarity about his vocation and a satisfying integrity in his prayer-life. In Newman's kind of language, he was patiently looking for, awaiting, a "leading," a decisive and concrete sign.[24] But as with the "mystical" type of Ignatian spirituality—which Bremond will lovingly lay out in volume 5 of the *Histoire*—in which the Jesuit novice, in his Third Year, is expected to experience a "second conversion," no such sign leading to calm conviction appeared. In fact, just the opposite: Bremond's darkness and disquietude only intensified. It might, then, have been his reading of another Jesuit, Jean-Joseph Surin, that would have convinced him that this darkness and disquietude, rather than being signs of failure, were just the opposite, were, in fact, the true indicators of an approach to the true God. It could also be the case that Bremond was starting to read Fénelon, where suffering-leading-to-love is precisely the work of grace. In any case, what we can see is that in his earliest interpretation of Newman Bremond was moving in a particular direction: the person of spiritual disquietude is the person on true spiritual pilgrimage, the person moving from illusion to reality, the person who really prays, the person living from "soul" and "conscience" Godward.

Bremond was excited about joining *Études* and going to Paris![25] A fortnightly review of "religious science" primarily for clergy, *Études* aspired to be "cutting edge,"

---

22. Bremond to Blondel, October 10, 1898 (ibid., 87–88).

23. VB, 67–82.

24. Newman was complex, however. At one point Bremond cited Newman's sermon "Waiting for Christ" to make the point that in Newman's thought the "sentiment" that should mark a true Christian soul is that of "tender and disquieted devotion" where all is held in suspense and anticipation ("Christus vivit!," 320–21). The concept of the "sign from God" will become dubious for Bremond later.

25. He indicated to Blondel in a letter of August 21, 1899 (BB, I, 227–29) that his plan was to "Blondelize" at *Études* in a "vulgarizing" kind of way, and that it has been Eliot and Newman who have

conversant with cultural currents and trends, but safely orthodox at the same time. As Bremond was coming on board, the magazine, having been relatively progressive in spirit, was starting to move in a more conservative direction, since the ecclesiastical winds were changing. He would live in community with his colleagues at 15 de la rue Monsieur for four years, but never felt at home, describing the place as a "citadel" or "fortress."[26] Surrounded by specialists in the various subject-areas of the publication, in a somewhat stuffy and eccentric ambience,[27] he huffed and puffed constantly about what he saw as hypocrisies or rigidities.[28] While, on the one hand, these years provided him with time to mature in his literary immersion, to become attuned to the spiritual dimension in all literary art, whether believing or unbelieving,[29] he gradually soured. Present at the Jesuit church in Lyons-Fourvières for a ceremony in which a cardinal was present, resplendent in his colorful vestments, the liturgy magnificent and beautiful, but the whole affair reeking of complaisant, spoiled pomposity, he asked in dismay, "Is this what it has all come to?" "Where are the saints?"[30]

Indeed, these years at *Études* marked the key period of transition for French Catholicism as a whole, years in which the anti-Modernist forces of reactionary retrenchment would become dominant and Bremond started to become "radicalized." The general impression that Bremond managed to create in letters to his friends was that he was constantly tormented by the degree to which free thought, creative thought, real spiritual vigor, was shut down by ecclesiastical strictures and the ever-present threat of condemnation for being too outspoken. To von Hügel he expressed his unhappiness more floridly than he was inclined to do with Blondel, comparing his distress with the state of the church to that of Newman in the latter's famous last sermon at Littlemore, as he anticipated separation from his friends: "My Mother, from whom so many good things have come . . . why do you not recognize your children, why do you not utilize their zeal, why do you fail to recognize their love?"[31] Another time, referring to the resistance that Newman had received from the Anglican bishops, he says, "My cross is analogous to that of Newman before his conversion."[32]

---

brought him to this point. Goichot references a letter from Bremond to von Hügel of January 13, 1900, where Bremond notes his "newmano-hügelo-blondélinisme d'aspirations et de besoins" (EG, 31n19).

26. VB, 101–13. Reference to the "fortress" is in Bremond to Blondel, Aug. 13, 1899 (BB, I, 224), cited by Blanchet (VB, 105). The "citadel" reference is in a letter to von Hügel of September 30, 1899 (cited VB, 106).

27. VB, 105. In his letter to Blondel of August 21, 1899 (BB, I, 227–29), Bremond calls the staff of *Études* "a sanhedrin of a dozen members, each in his domain, which he guards jealously."

28. In Bremond to von Hügel, December 3, 1900 he complains about tensions over scientific methods of study and "intellectual emancipation" leading to "emancipation of the heart" (cited VB, 162).

29. This is the theme of Jossua's survey, "Le jeune Bremond," of Bremond's output while at *Études*.

30. VB, 109, where Blanchet cites from Bremond's letter to von Hügel of December 14, 1899. He speculates (108n1) that the occasion was the feast of the Immaculate Conception (108n1). Goichot edited the text, "En marge de la crise, I," 232–34.

31. "En marge de la crise, I," 231.

32. VB, 111, citing from Bremond's letter to Blondel of December 19, 1899 (BB, I, 248–49).

As the time approached for his Final (or "Great") Vows as a Jesuit, he was in a state of turmoil. These vows are renewals of the earlier ones to perpetual poverty, chastity and obedience—but with an explicit and additional vow to obedience to the Society's chain-of-command and whatever service the Society might require. Bremond tossed and turned with all kinds of doubts and hesitations about himself, his vocation, the state of the church. But he went ahead anyway. On February 2, 1900, he took the step, thus climaxing an eighteen-year journey with the Order. His career at *Études* would continue for another four years, and in the interval he would be an aggravation to his Jesuit compatriots, complaining about all matters ecclesial, while producing marvelous essays.

Bremond's Newman

For a while the entrancement with Newman banked down, then flared. The gathering of earlier pieces in the first volume of *L'Inquiétude religieuse* in 1901, with the Newman superscript, "To be at ease is to be unsafe," reiterated his attention to Newman's work.[33] In a letter to Blondel on June 12, 1900, he took up a subtle point with Newman's help.[34] Blondel had been accused of "naturalism," when he had contended that anyone who might receive the Christian message favorably must *already* be the recipient of grace *before* hearing the message. Bremond offered in support Newman's sermon on "the secret power of grace," in which the wise apologist is admonished to pay close attention to the "inner dispositions" of any potential convert, since the preparatory work of grace is always hidden psychologically.[35] Then by the latter part of 1901 Bremond was indicating that he had a book about Newman in the works.[36] In the spring of 1902 he was even more explicit: one French critic had misrepresented Newman and now he, Bremond, was set to make the plunge into Newman in order to set the record straight.[37]

In his December 20, 1902, essay in *Études*, on the Anglican dean of Durham, William Charles Lake, a great sympathizer with Newman, Bremond claimed that Lake had absorbed Newman's "idea of the Church," by means of a more Catholic understanding of priesthood and sacrament, so that religious life could become more intense, more serious, deeper and more inward. Official dedication of the famous Newman statue at the Oratory in Birmingham was a reminder that Newman's heritage is "a defeat

---

33. Actually he had already used this text in a letter to Blondel of October 23, 1898 (BB, I, 103), saying that "he was more and more convinced" by it.

34. BB, I, 294.

35. Although Blondel's argument will always be that such grace is "hidden" *metaphysically*. From his perspective, it is a confusion about the proper analysis of subjectivity that will becloud the whole Modernist movement.

36. Letter to Blondel of November 14, 1901 (BB, I, 386).

37. Letter to Blondel of April 22, 1902 (BB, I, 421).

more glorious than victory," because, by transforming Anglican ideals, he hastened the death of the old Anglican order of the "high dignitary" for something infinitely better.[38] Then, about the time Bremond departed the Jesuits by mutual agreement in 1904 for "something infinitely better," his first major Newman publication would appear, a translation of Newman's fifteenth *University Sermon*, entitled "The Theory of Developments in Religious Doctrine," along with an abridged version of *An Essay on the Development of Christian Doctrine*.[39]

Blondel had enthusiastically anticipated this book, called by Bremond his "little booklet."[40] Temporarily boarding, after official departure from the Jesuit Order, with the hospitable George Tyrrell at the Jesuit residence at Richmond, Yorkshire, he dated the volume's introduction at June 1904. It is his apology for Newman. Acknowledging that Newman, when first received into the Catholic Church, was viewed as "a poorly converted Protestant and a dangerous sophist," he has become, contends Bremond, "the doctor and the glory of contemporary Catholicism," so that "the history of his thought and of his soul" has become, and should be, of pressing interest. Indeed, he is a thinker whose "soul and thought, heart and intellect, cannot be separated." In order to understand his essays on development and assent, therefore, one must know his inner life, where a puzzling "antinomy" in need of resolution appears. Dogma must be immutable, thought Newman, yet it also, clearly, patently, changes and "metamorphizes" historically.[41]

Bremond wanted to show that Newman had resolved the "antinomy." The key, Newman thought, is the infallibility of the Church itself—and thus he can sound like Bossuet denying all variation—where the teaching authority is trustworthy, where the Spirit will always preserve eternal truth in the midst of historical changes. A rationalist, therefore, will recognize that Newman is not his friend, since he preserves dogma, but a faithful Catholic will now see that he need not fear historical analysis, that is, the human reality and contingencies of church history, out of which dogma in its manifoldness has emerged and "developed." In the latter perspective Newman can sound like Bossuet's Protestant opponents—Daillé and Jurieu—applauding variety for its fertility, rather than its sterility, as Bossuet had claimed. The translated material in this volume, Bremond hoped, would thus make the case for Newman's synthesis,

---

38. Bremond, "L'Assimilation des principes catholiques," 235, 237.

39. Bremond, *Le développement du dogme chrétien*. References are to the second French edition of 1906, with an introduction by the Archbishop of Albi, Eudoxe-Irénée Mignot, an important and mediating figure in the Modernist crisis, and celebrated by Bremond later in the pseudonymous defense of Loisy, *Un clerc qui n'a pas trahi*.

40. Blondel to Bremond, March 3, 1904 (BB, I, 485); Bremond to Blondel, May 23, 1904 (BB, I, 495).

41. Bremond, *Le dévéloppment du dogme chrétien*, 1–2, 6–7. He cites Newman's famous dictum: "Great ideas evolve at the risk of corruption. It may not be the case in another world, but here below to live is to change: the more perfect a doctrine is, the more often it has needed to change" (ibid., 6).

showing him to be the man of the hour, especially for French interpreters who were conflicted.[42]

Indeed, Newman's earliest, most substantive influence in France had emanated from the *Essay on Development*, where he had defended aspects of official Catholic teaching against the Protestant claim that these are unscriptural innovations.[43] Catholic apologists, accepting the fact of historical development in dogma, had usually argued that this development is a process of the logical unfolding of the truth contained in the dogma from the beginning, with nothing essentially new added. Newman, however, allowed for genuine historical change in development, this change being understood as the coming to outward fruition, contingent on circumstantial factors, of aspects of a particular dogma's "idea." The development of doctrine, he claimed, is not a *logical* internal unfolding, as in Thomist teaching with an *a priori* definability, but rather a historically manifested series of novel forms dependent on "the sum total of aspects" "commensurate," i.e., recognizable only *a posteriori*, with the original "idea." What ensures the true-to-type character of this development is an infallible teaching authority, the Spirit-guided church, operating by means of its ability to weed out corruptions when they occur.

Thus distinguishing carefully between the "idea" in a dogma and its historical series of authentic cumulative manifestations (thus, *not* an endogenous process as such, but an externally stimulated one, rather like the "expression" of a gene in modern thought), Newman had skated out onto thin ice. The strength of his position was that it allowed him simultaneously to take historical development seriously as adding something genuinely new to a dogma, while not changing its essence, which is the "idea." The surface changes, but the depth does not. Liberal thinkers applauded, but traditionalists were uneasy.

In France, lines of division became clear early on, as rationalist historians eagerly embraced what they thought Newman was saying.[44] The Protestant Auguste Sabatier, as one among many, took the view that Newman was admitting that religious experience is the creative matrix of all dogma, where the outward form is like the body of an organism that is perpetually evolving (thus disposable!). Assimilation to evolutionary theory came very easily, and the dangerous organic metaphor, which in fact Newman had used, always lay ready-to-hand. But a host of other interpreters, more cautious,

---

42. Ibid., 5, 8–12. "Nothing," said Bremond, "is more maladroit than that attitude of mistrust toward one of the most Catholic spirits that has ever lived" (ibid., 10).

43. See Beaumont, "Reception of Newman in France," for an overview of which of Newman's writings were first known in France, and the extent and accuracy of this knowledge. Bremond agonized about what he saw as the inadequate and misleading existing translations of Newman (e.g., Bremond, *Newman. Le développement*, xx–xxii).

44. The best surveys, in addition to Beaumont, "Reception of Newman," are those of Dupuy, "Newman's Influence in France," and Talar, "Newman in France." Dupuy includes Bremond in the group "which, assimilating Newman's thought to the philosophy of Action, appealed to it in support of the doctrines of immanence" ("Newman's Influence in France," 166–67).

insisted that what Newman wanted was something more interactive, more dialectical, that experience shapes dogma while dogma provides the base for the interpretive lens.[45] A further complication lay in the fact that thinkers, who would be considered "Modernist" after the turn of the twentieth century, led by Alfred Loisy, quickly picked up on Newman as seeming to endorse, by implication, the use of critical methods in the study of historical phenomena, including dogma. Thus was the door opened to a historicist reading of Newman, where a dogma is nothing but a historical artifact—a view that Newman would have deplored.

Bremond labored to have it both ways in a manner that would become a characteristic of all his work—respectful of tradition, yet insistent that the actual content of the tradition is not necessarily what meets the eye. His argument was that Newman spoke simultaneously for the importance of the historical approach as essential to valid understanding, *while at the same time insisting that the church in the inner lives of its most holy members is always a sufficient guarantor of the meaning of the dogmas it proclaims.* When the intellect bears witness to what the soul is experiencing, it speaks truly. It is in the lives of her saints that the mind of the church is revealed and validated, for it is there, that we see, Newman insisted, that "the soul and the thought, the heart and the intellect, cannot be separated."[46]

An intermediate step remained, however. Before he could move from Newman's views on the development of doctrine to an examination of the meaning of his inner life, Bremond needed to clarify Newman's understanding of the "psychology" of faith. In his second book on Newman, *La psychologie de la foi*, published in 1905 and dedicated to Ferdinand Brunetière, he offered an anthology of excerpts, taken primarily from the *Grammar of Assent* but spanning Newman's entire oeuvre, structured in such a way as to illustrate in an orderly and synthetic manner the progression by which Bremond believed that Newman had come to his mature positions. The result is a Cartesian-like presentation of Newman's "method," in which Newman explains for the reader how the "adhesion" to religious truth can happen, in effect how *his* adhesion had come about. Bremond's commentary had one central purpose: to show beyond a shadow of a doubt that Newman was deeply loyal to dogmatic truth, to the "deposit of faith," as this deposit is maintained and interpreted by the infallible teaching Church. Newman was *not*, through his questioning of purely logical and deductive methods in theology, advocating a religious skepticism. Quite the contrary, said Bremond, who showed that Newman's long-standing intent was to make the case that no one believes because of a syllogism, that we believe by "assent," and not by "inference," and that assent is commanded initially by the conscience and not the

---

45. Thus, in latter-day revisionist understandings of Newman, such as that of Dupuy, he will come to be seen as the great champion of tradition as the "conscience of the Church" ("Newman's Influence," 169–71).

46. Bremond, *Le développement du dogme chrétien*, 2.

intellect.[47] Let no one doubt Newman's "dogmatism," says Bremond, even if his way of stating it is new and different!

In a telling admission, he acknowledged that for several reasons Newman could be misleading. He did not argue in the careful manner of French thinkers. He used language impressionistically at times and with some degree of imprecision.[48] But, more important, he often modified the straightforwardness and rigor of his thinking out of pastoral considerations, such as the sensibilities of certain readers or of the general public.[49] Furthermore, he was a profound either/or thinker: either one submits unconditionally to Catholic doctrine and authority, or one lapses into total religious skepticism. Truth is of a single piece.[50] Thus, Newman could be viewed by some as a "skeptic in a cardinal's robes." Bremond recognized this ambiguity in Newman, but saved it for later analysis, finding it profoundly interesting, as he did Newman's conviction of the reality of "another world," as well as his deep pessimism about the human condition. The bottom line, though, was that Newman's adhesion was "categorical" and "entire."[51]

Bremond explored also Newman's "theology of conscience" and the role of "natural religion" as a prelude to faith, noting that the role of conscience in motivating faith, Newman's "illative sense" of truth, had been seen improperly by some as tantamount to a "new apologetic." The contention that apologetic arguments, in order to be convincing, require an "anterior adaptation" (i.e., the action of illative judgment) on the part of the potential convert, had, as we have seen, come to be associated with Blondel's case in *L'Action*. As far as Bremond knew, Blondel had not read Newman, and, in any case, both men would be dismayed at the idea that this view had anything "new" in it. Jesus himself had already said, "My own know me."[52] Somewhat later Bremond opined that Newman operated as a true precursor of Blondel's philosophy of action, saying that "if Newman were born sixty years later, he would have written neither the *University Sermons* nor the *Grammar*; he would have written *L'Action*," and that Blondel's philosophy "provides the Newmanian thought with the harmonic notes

---

47. Bremond, *La psychologie de la foi*, 1–5.

48. Ibid., 8.

49. Ibid., 28. This "wise and gentle minimism" on Newman's part represented a "wise and prudent theology" (ibid., 31).

50. Ibid., 24.

51. Ibid., 21.

52. Ibid., 356–57n2.

and explicit justifications that [critics] show us that it needs."[53] We will see later how Blondel responded to this assimilation of his views to those of Newman.[54]

In the meantime Bremond moved on to publish a selection from Newman's sermons, *Newman: La vie chrétienne*, in 1905, which then cleared the way for his blockbuster, *Newman: Essai de la biographie psychologique*, the Newman book for which he is best known, and either loved or reviled.[55] The essential nature of the *Essai* lay in the fact that Bremond put at the center of his exposition Newman's repeated statement that "There are for me but two beings who count, God and myself," suggesting that "all the history of Newman, emotional, intellectual, and literary, is, in fact, nothing esle than the history of his personal relations with God," that such comes close to being "the secet of this great man." "That man," averred Bremond, "could live and die alone."[56] Later he would declare Newman to be, in effect, a mystic manqué, one whose "imagination" was mystical, but not his "heart." "What is mystical is the idea that he has of his place in the universe, of his mission, of the direct and constant influence which God exerts upon him."[57]

After chapters on Newman as a "solitary by choice," as a "suspect" reserved and icy though not insensitive, and then as the sometimes cruel and often sarcastic "controversialist," he depicted Newman, contrariwise, as operating at times with a gentle wisdom that swayed hearts: "Like Fénelon, he is one of those men to whom we can tell everything, because we feel that no revelation will surprise him." But the iciness still protrudes, since "some of this ability is in the distance that he is able to maintain even

---

53. Bremond, "Apologie pour les newmanistes français," as cited by Talar, "Newman and the 'New Apologetics,'" 52n2. In this essay, Talar carefully explores the channels by which Blondel may have become aware of Newman's work, including, but also prior to, his relationship with Bremond. He speculates about Blondel's reasons for expressing wariness about Newman, emphasizing a need to distance himself from the troublesome Loisy, who had shown great enthusiasm for Newman in pseudonymous essays, the "Firmin" articles. I am choosing to emphasize what Blondel saw as his substantive reasons for the distancing, the ones he pressed on Bremond.

54. The ecclesiastical censors passed on *La psychologie de la foi*, after insisting on certain changes, but higher authority thought poorly of the work and during 1907 storm clouds gathered (BB, II, 97n1, for details). In April 1907, Cardinal Richard, archbishop of Paris, received a "severe warning" from the Congregation of the Index (the Holy Office), requiring him to censure *La psychologie de la foi*, and further directing him to have Bremond quietly remove all unsold copies from circulation. No further edition would be allowed. (In fact, there has been none.) The censure thus avoided the Index for Bremond, and, by being secret, protected Newman's reputation (Goichot, "Trois 'prophètes du dehors,'" 42). Goichot had secured a copy of the Congregation's letter. (I am grateful to C. J. T. Talar for direct communication of the last piece of information and the reference, contained in his essay "Assenting to Newman," 270n79.)

55. Bremond, *Newman: Essai de la biographie psychologique*, translated into English by H. C. Corrance as *The Mystery of Newman*, with an introduction by the Rev. George Tyrrell. All references are to the English translation. For an interesting sketch of Henry Clemence Corrance and his beliefs, see Vidler, *Variety*, 160–65.

56. Bremond, *Mystery of Newman*, 16.

57. Ibid., 267, 295.

in the closeness," so that "he thirsts for love, and yet the better part of his life is passed in a desert where he meets only with God."[58]

A modern clinician might say that Newman was depressive and withdrawn (even schizoid, with his talk of "other worlds" that are quite real), fearful of intimacy. We are reminded again that Bremond was constructing a *literary physiognomy of the inner life* ("solitary") and that his categories are those of essayistic portraiture ("controversialist") and empirical description ("icy"). To the dismay of critics, he had no intention of putting a halo around Newman's head, since he wanted his readers to know Newman in all of his gritty humanity, but without passing a moral judgment. For Bremond, Newman was a giant, but a "hard" (a favorite term of Bremond's) giant, his vices being a product of that "hardness," but, by grace, his virtues as well.

Newman's "Autocentrism"

What Bremond was building up to from the beginning of his sketch was his use, outrageous to some readers, of "autocentric" as a key descriptor for Newman.[59] The term was not pejorative (i.e., moralizing or pathologizing), like "egotistical" or "selfish" or "narcissistic." Simply as human beings, we are all "autocentric," each of us in his/her own way.[60] For Newman such a tendency took the form of believing that he was the object of special Providence. He referred everything to himself, especially all of the "signs" that he believed had led him eventually to the Roman Church. Bremond was at great pains to show that Newman built up his whole theological structure out of his personal experience, out of the way that events struck him, out of the way that his struggles made sense, out of the way that his intuitions then fit into a conceptual logic. Newman was a poet, and like all poets, insisted Bremond, he was dependent on the vividness of his imagination, with its intuitive, but certain, grasp of concrete reality. His great essays, then, on the development of doctrine and the forms of assent are ultimately "learned theories" grounded in his "intellectual habits."[61] The poet's use of logic clarifies, but the concreteness of experience is primary.

---

58. Ibid., 56.

59. Ibid., 298.

60. Although it must be admitted that things are slippery and reveal a complex ambivalence on the part of Bremond. He was also able to admit later, in a letter to Loisy, that Newman's claim of "myself and my Creator" as the only two realities had a "frightful" quality—a self-absorption that came out in the *Apologia*—that is disturbing (Bremond to Loisy, June 15, 1913 [Bernard-Maître, "Lettres," 175]). The context was that Bremond was trying to defend Loisy against charges of egotism, and he drew a comparison with Newman. In truth, Bremond could not decide if the self-assertiveness of the lonely artist is gracious or not.

61. *Mystery of Newman*, 76. "By his own [Newman's] admission the 'Grammar' is a series of confidences" (ibid., 75). "The whole of this book [the *Grammar*] is nothing but a long definition of the 'illative sense,' and this 'illative sense' is the name taken by conscience when in quest of religious truth" (ibid., 333).

To understand Newman the theologian, one must understand his "mental habits,"[62] since for Newman nothing presented abstractly made sense; it all had to be run through his personal filter, though, as Bremond argued forcefully, Newman's experience was not of the "convulsive" emotional type, which is narrowly "self-focused" and "self-conscious."[63] Or again as in the treatment of suffering, Bremond compared Newman with Bossuet: the latter had in his preaching a "fusion of the ideal and the concrete," thus manifesting "an impatience... that seeks to bind general ideas beneath a living form," while Newman moved in the opposite direction, "taking the concrete [i.e., his own experience] as his point of departure," only gradually transforming "his slight material by infusing into it the splendid life of ideas."[64] "Autocentrism" as the basis for a working methodology, was Newman's way of brilliantly turning dross into gold. Any good good literary expression of the religious "sentiment," will, Bremond thought, do the same.

But then came a paradox. For all of his determination to think theologically on the basis of concrete experience, Newman never put on a show consciously, but only, and then rarely, revealed himself "unconsciously." That last word, however, meant "in fragmentary expression," "indirectly," primarily in the form of literary allusion and suggestion. "Reserved, timid, English to the backbone, he did not permit the indiscreet to listen at the doors of his inner life,"[65] so that "the exaggerated contemplation of self" does not intrude. Thus, Newman most reveals himself to us by his pregnant silences, which can speak with great eloquence, which is to say by his power to evoke without stating.

In a long chapter, Bremond argued that Newman's reserve was rooted in his experience of the nature of God, before whom fear and trembling (Newman's Puritanism came out here) can be the only appropriate response. Terror at the prospect of hell was always there,[66] but so was the prospect of infinite grace, leading Newman to believe that the active conscience is the very voice of God in the soul. This inward voice, "enthroned within us at the very springs of thought and affection," was, said Bremond, "the history of Newman's conversion."[67] His firm belief in the "other world," the world of angels and demons and supernatural forces—a world often vividly depicted by Newman—a world hidden from us and yet more real than the one we know,

---

62. Ibid., 122–23. "All he wishes to describe is a living faith, his own" (ibid., 123).

63. Ibid., 130–31.

64. Ibid., 162.

65. Ibid., 172–73.

66. With regard to a "God of justice and pity," Newman believed that "near Him, within Him, extremes meet, contradictions are solved, hope and fear unite in a single action, are translated by the same effort; love fearful, terror loving. At the moment when dread seems the strongest, an infallible voice tells the Christian soul that the last word rests with love" (ibid., 212).

67. Ibid., 194.

is an inner world, where "the flood of grace is sedate, majestic, gentle in its operation," where God operates quietly, secretly, slowly, by surprise, by laws unknown and mysterious.[68]

A further paradox lay in the fact that Newman thought of the action of grace quite concretely, as "fire alarms from the first," that are the very opposite of abstract. But since Newman actually suffered from a sense of the lack of some kind of fire within, he came to believe that God's grace was working quietly within that lack—precisely Bremond's personal struggle as well—with the result that a "quiet sweetness" became Newman's signature presentation of self. God is always silently at work melting our hearts, and one day we shall wake up and recognize that working. Faith is solid, but the night is dark. The present is distress and disappointment, but the past is certain, and the future holds joy and peace.[69]

As a finale, "the religious philosophy of Newman," Bremond yielded to the need for a systematic overview, and argued summarily that Newman's thought revolved around three principles: the primacy of conscience, the communion of saints, and dogma as a composite whole. It all served, once again, to defend Newman's orthodoxy against his critics, but with the reminder that "there is nothing more self-centred, more personal, or more independent than the conscience"; that for Newman Christianity was from the beginning "an ethical system, that is, an 'ethos' or living principal of ethical life . . . of vigorous motive power."[70] In two final notes Bremond appealed to Newman, thus, as the basis for a "religious psychology" in the tradition of Sainte-Beuve's writing on Port-Royal, based on "scientific observation," and, with a whiff of William James as well as Blondel, that "Newman's psychology of faith is like an introduction to 'pragmatism' and the philosophy of 'Action.'"[71]

In the introduction that he wrote for the English translation of *The Mystery of Newman*, George Tyrrell linked Bremond with William James, referring to Bremond's sense for Newman's "twice-born quality . . . with the dialectic of opposites," where egotism is both strength and weakness.[72] This likening of Bremond to the Anglo-American empirical tradition was fair enough, to a degree, but what Tyrrell most emphasized was the way in which Bremond tried to create a biography that would challenge both liberal and conservative critics of Newman to reassess their positions, to see that Newman's intentions were valid even if his expression fell short. But Tyrrell's hope was in vain. For his critics Newman continued to exist under the shadow of Modernist patronage, and Bremond's treatment reinforced that perception. In any

---

68. Ibid., 237.

69. The whole chapter here, "The Silence of God," has to be one of the finest things Bremond ever wrote. No wonder he was considered by his critics, e.g. Henry Bordeaux, to be a "seducer" and a "magician."

70. Ibid., 337, 345.

71. Ibid., 345–46n, and 332.

72. Ibid., xii.

case, sparking great interest, the book sold well. One hostile reviewer called it "an impertinent book," and another "a brilliant phantasy."[73] Clearly Bremond, by describing Newman's inner darkness and struggle as well as his holiness and intellectual brilliance, was defining the kind of saint that modern times require.

---

73. Dupuy, "Newman's Influence," 168. The critics were, respectively, Wilfrid Ward, the voice of English neo-Thomism, and Henry Tristram, eventually to be the English twentieth-century editor of Newman's complete correspondence.

5

Bremond and Blondel
The Circle of Friends

BREMOND WAS A TIRELESS writer of letters. He communicated, almost ceaselessly, with a wide range of like-minded correspondents—who often wrote to one another, as well as to Bremond. In the case of Maurice Blondel the relationship was set within a dynamic interplay or dialogue among a number of epistolary interlocutors, all Roman Catholic, all to become embroiled in the "Modernist" crisis.[1] They critiqued one another's ideas in the midst of a constant flow of mutual emotional support, and they were chastised in various degrees, or at least warned, by Church authority, when their ideas and methods became too radical. They published abundantly, their works for the most part now being artifacts of their era, while it is really only Bremond's historical *magnum opus*, the *Histoire*, and Blondel's theology, that have weathered well the passage of time.[2] Blondel was in truth the major thinker within their group, and for all of the intensity and durability of Bremond's relations with the group's members—primarily George Tyrrell, Friedrich von Hügel, and Alfred Loisy—Blondel's influence would be paramount intellectually.

Catholic Modernism

In the period of Bremond's Jesuit formation and profession, from 1882 to 1904, the Catholic Church of France was developing along both internal and external trajectories. The former was marked by the church's painful absorption of historical-critical

---

1. I now use "modernist" as a descriptor for the general cultural trends, and "Modernist" for the specifically Catholic movement that resulted in the anti-Modernist decrees of 1907.

2. Goichot called Bremond's *Histoire* "the one exception, a 'modernist' enterprise that has succeeded," that is, has continued to have a lasting influence as a propagator of the mystical spirituality that it celebrates (EG, 308). See Trémolières, "*L'Histoire littéraire du sentiment religieux*," for contextualizing and analysis of this claim. For a tribute to Blondel's lasting influence within the structure of modern Thomist thought, see Somerville, "Maurice Blondel 1861–1949."

consciousness, where "scientific" methods of study predominate, and the meaning and truth-status of all transmitted knowledge, including church dogma, is subject to perpetual, socially contextualized reevaluation. The question always was, What did such-and-such bit of knowledge mean *then*, and what does it mean *now*? The upshot was that the analysis of "sources" became the central challenge in assessing, clarifying and properly understanding what has been transmitted, these tasks no longer being just the responsibility of tradition-bearing communities as such, but also of the individual who might take such sources to heart. Biblical scholars and church historians, as well as the theologians who relied on their work, had to engage in elaborate processes of purifying ancient texts from corruption, verifying reliability and assessing degrees thereof, teasing apart fact and legend, reconfiguring the continuities and discontinuities of historical developments, so that new meanings could often emerge. But new meanings often, though not always, are at odds with old authorities and inherited views.

The problem is that new meanings often push in the direction of change, so that "historical-critical" easily links up with "liberal" and "progressive," even "free thinking" views in many domains, including the political and social. Radical thinking, dubbed "modernist" or "rationalist," easily inclines as well to naturalistic and even materialistic philosophical views, where such classic categories as "spiritual" and "miraculous" are either eliminated or thoroughly redefined. Traditional confessional theologies across Christendom leaned heavily on age-old views of the supernatural, of miracle, of providential divine working, of a transcendent realm, and historical criticism potentially challenged the whole structure. Only the "positive sciences," it was claimed, can interpret Scripture accurately. The usual verdict of historians, thus, is that the rise of historical-critical modes of understanding is part of the wider process known as *secularization*.[3]

The Roman Catholic Church fought historical-criticism and the tendencies that attach to it as long as possible.[4] The *Syllabus of Errors* of 1864 had already condemned various forms of rationalism and liberalism.[5] But Leo XIII in a series of encyclical letters—*Rerum novarum* (1891), affirming some of the energy and direction of the anti-capitalist labor movements; *Au milieu des sollicitudes* (1892), looking to a better working relationship with the French state; and *Providentissimus deus* (1892), with its affirmation of critical biblical studies—moved to embrace progressive developments. Along, then, came a scholar like Louis Duchesne, blasting away at old legends of the saints and insisting on the human virtues and vices of church history. And many oth-

---

3. All interpreters struggle here with Max Weber's "disenchantment" as the hallmark of modernity. See especially Chadwick, *Secularization of the European Mind*, and then Taylor, *Secular Age*.

4. For context, see especially Carroll, "Philosophical Foundations of Catholic Modernism." Carroll configures Modernism as the need for a "theology of immanence" that can address increasing "agnosticism." Blondel then becomes the central figure.

5. The secular French state was horrified by the Decree. See Spencer, *Politics of Belief*, 192–97.

ers especially in Germany, Italy, France, and England, were doing the same. The older scholastic theology and its associated Thomism was impugned.[6] Important studies of Scripture, of the saints, of episodes and eras in church history, were beginning to appear regularly. There were many new journals that operated as forums for modernist thought. The new Catholic universities in France, the Instituts Catholiques in Paris[7] and Toulouse, cautiously adopted the new perspectives, even as the secular universities accepted them wholeheartedly.[8]

But reaction counter-surged. In political life the old monarchical and nationalistic attitude, jingoistic and xenophobic, then anti-Semitic, became anti-modernist, trying to turn back the clock on social change, while republican politics tended to be modernist in spirit.[9] In the church the mounting reaction came with Leo XIII's death in 1903, then the consequent accession of the conservative Pius X. We have already seen how the interpretation of John Henry Newman polarized into liberal and conservative views. Bremond and his friends were on the cusp of these modernizing developments in the church, becoming anguished, dismayed and despairing as conservative forces gained control. Pius, in the decree *Lamentabili* of July 3, 1907, then the encyclical *Pascendi* of September 8, 1907, condemned it all root and branch. Modern thinking, based in historical-critical method, has become "the synthesis of all heresies," defined as "Modernism" whose central characteristic is "evolutionary" thought (Darwin and historical-critical thinking are lumped together). An anti-Modernist oath to be administered to the clergy was promulgated in 1910.[10]

And then the external trajectory. Pressure for the full separation of church and state in France had grown inexorably in France. The perennial issue was control of the educational system. We recall that Republican anticlericalism had steadily increased

---

6. See McCool, *Catholic Theology in the Nineteenth Century*, 247–67, for the theological background and the clash of the then-reigning Thomism with Modernist currents.

7. Bremond strongly complimented the founder of the Institut Catholique in Paris, Mgr Maurice d'Hulst (1841–1896), the "leader . . . of a vast spiritual crusade" for the rights of scientific work (*La littérature religieuse*, 25). D'Hulst, with a careful eye on Church authority, was yet an outspoken supporter of critical biblical studies, although he was later to dismiss Alfred Loisy for views considered too radical. The successor of d'Hulst would be Alfred Baudrillart.

8. Such as the newly founded (1886) École pratique des hautes études with its section for "sciences religieuses," where Loisy would go after leaving the Institut Catholique.

9. See especially Brown, *For the Soul of France*.

10. The bibliography on Catholic Modernism is vast. Foundational now is Émile Poulat, *Histoire, dogme, et critique dans le crise moderniste*. His description of the horizon that marked the Modernist movement in the minds of many of its supporters is noteworthy: "It is a question neither of a simple social transformation nor of an intellectual renovation, but of the dawn of a new age of humanity, which implies a new and mutual adaptation of humankind and Christianity." Such a perspective is contrasted with "the cult of the past practiced by Catholic intransigents." By the beginning of the twentieth century, says Poulat (ibid., 21–22), the term "modernism" denoted tendencies, influences, and methods that were seen as contrary to church teaching, because they were marked by "Kantianism, naturalism, subjectivism . . . relativism, agnosticism, evolutionism, immanentism, symbolism, individualism, rationalism," and after the turn of the century by Loisyism, when Alfred Loisy had become the personification of all of these "isms" (ibid., 11).

during the last decades of the nineteenth century, that the Ferry Laws had partially wrested control of schools from the dominance of the church, that an uneasy alliance existed between church and state for the "moral formation" of France's children. Then came the political upheavals of the Boulanger affair, increased royalist sentiments in league with the Church, then the explosion of the Dreyfus affair in which the church, for the most part, aligned itself with conservative anti-Semitic sentiment. Under the premiership of Marie René Waldeck-Rousseau, beginning in 1899, a parliamentary majority proceeded to form a solidly Republican, Dreyfusard cabinet eager to effect the Separation once and for all. Suppression of the most aggressive religious orders started in earnest, with anticlerical Socialists determined to eliminate the Orders completely. While teaching Orders like the Jesuits were widely respected, legal restraints were enforced more and more vigorously, and church-sponsored education was viewed as retrograde, overly classical, even tending to be unpatriotic! Diplomatic tensions with the Vatican worsened as a result of all of these pressures, and from December 1902, Émile Combes, the new prime minister, at first hesitantly and then more and more vigorously, enforced limitations on the church. The climax was that in December 1905, the Law of Separation was passed. Anti-clericalism as the glue of the Republican Left had succeeded, the religious orders and all of their schools and other institutions were viewed with great distrust, and the church responded with anger, jealous protection of its remaining privileges, and a middle ground ceased to exist.[11]

As noted, the atmosphere at *Études* gradually became intolerable for Bremond as the atmosphere stiffened, became reactionary, and more controls over freedom of expression became manifest. Vastly complicating the situation, moreover, was the whole network of communication that had gradually evolved, by which he kept in touch with other Modernist figures, as they twisted and turned with the ecclesiastical winds.

Von Hügel

Specialists debate endlessly about the roots of Catholic Modernism, with Leo XIII's *Providentissimus deus* usually seen as the catalyst.[12] René Marlé dated the beginning to a meeting between Maurice Blondel, who was then on vacation in Rome, and Friedrich von Hügel in March 1895, and he contended that their relationship was the real unifying dynamic of Modernism.[13] Von Hügel had read *L'Action* and praised it highly, as

---

11. The whole story is told with verve by Partin in *Waldeck-Rousseau, Combes, and the Church*.

12. The history is complex, but much of the pre-Modernist "modernism" in Catholic circles had operated in terms of resistance to the First Vatican Council and its resultant victorious ultramontanism and authoritarianism. "Temporal power" vs. "spiritual power" dominated the debates. Spencer, *Politics of Belief*, ch. 3, "Ultramontanes and Liberals," is an excellent resource. Catholic romantics could flip-flop in their embrace of the secular state and its ideology, or be massively resistant to it, as is argued by Harrison, *Romantic Catholics*.

13. Marlé, *Au coeur de la crise moderniste*, ch. 1, "Le printemps d'une amitié." Of course, much more of the correspondence has been edited since Marlé's book, but his account is still a good chronological

he would Blondel's *Lettre* of 1896. The two men then began a steady correspondence. It is ironic that they would eventually be at complete and quite bitter loggerheads over another figure in the Movement, Alfred Loisy. Real question exists as to whether persons who were enthusiastic about *L'Action*, a difficult book, really understood it, and we have already seen that Bremond had to struggle with its subtleties. There was thus always the danger that people would talk past one another.

In any case, von Hügel, or the "Baron" as he was known, would prove with his background in diplomatic experience to be a good and useful friend to Blondel, especially as the latter's problems with the Vatican began to crystallize. The Baron was an independently wealthy Austrian of noble lineage living in England, devoutly Catholic, and well connected all across western Europe with intellectual movements of a modernizing type. A student of mystical literature, he had also absorbed progressive German biblical criticism, and had adopted, following Alfred Loisy, advanced views on the literary history of the Hexateuch. Firmly committed to historical-critical methodology, he tended to be an empathic and sensitive, rather than subtle and logical, thinker, always inclined in church politics to mediating views.[14] By the latter part of 1897 he had made the acquaintance of George Tyrrell, Irish Jesuit and intellectual, who had moved in his teaching from liberal views of Thomism to full-blown Modernist ideas. The Baron acquainted Tyrrell with Blondel's thinking, and Tyrrell was impressed.

In June 1898, Blondel first introduced Bremond to the Baron, describing him as "a Jesuit very open and very Anglicizing."[15] But Blondel soon started to become wary of the Baron and the role of philology in theology, and cautioned him against an over-reliance on empirical demonstrations that lead to "the intolerance of a doctrinal

---

ordering of the interactive drama of the controversy. As an interesting aside, apparently the material that appears in this book was first gathered by Henri de Lubac, who testified later that he was not allowed to print it, and so turned it over to Marlé. Some kind of falling out occurred over the way in which the material was presented, and de Lubac angrily, and in slightly gossipy fashion, disowned the book as misrepresentation, especially of von Hügel. See de Lubac, *Service of the Church*, 102–3.

14. His discourse, more mystical than rational, was not that of French university intellectuals, but rather partook of "the noble simplicity of a great international aristocrat following the conventional rules of the old provincial bourgeoisie" (Marlé, *Au coeur*, 32). For many, Von Hügel's thought and writings have not worn well over time and he has come to be treated rather disparagingly, as with Thomas Loome, who sees him as sincere and idealistic, though ultimately naive, given to "an alarmingly false assessment of the religious situation." On the positive side, "what in fact set him apart from his contemporaries was his recognition that only a union of scholarship and sanctity, of a critical spirit with interior devotion, could undertake the task that faced Catholic intellectuals" ("Enigma of Baron Friedrich von Hügel," 215). Lawrence F. Barmann's many strong essays advocate for the Baron, presenting him as a thinker who, in his embrace of historical methods, his sensitivity to church politics, and his study of mysticism, "never lost his balance as a Catholic" ("Mysticism and Modernism," 38). But it was easy to treat him condescendingly. Bremond, referencing Jules Verne's famous novel, once described the Baron to Blondel as "a little above the sun, but full of oxygen," Bremond to Blondel, May 3, 1901 (BB, I, 356). There is a huge literature here, pro and con, with regard to the Baron and his seeming inconsistencies.

15. Marlé, *Au coeur*, 25. The Baron responded: "I am so happy that you have P. Bremond as a comforter; I receive the same treatment from a very fine and excellent Jesuit, P. Tyrrell."

despotism or the temerity of incurably conjectural interpretations."[16] Alluding thus to arguments found in his *Lettre* of 1896, Blondel was putting a warning shot across the Baron's bow. And so they sparred, presaging the future.

At one point, the Baron sounded Blondel out on the idea that we each have a "spiritual I," stable and eternal, at the "fine point of the soul," which is opposed to the empirical, psychological and phenomenal "moi" with its surface phantasmagoria of states. How can one reconcile, asked the Baron, the timelessness of this "I" with the living temporality and succession of the world?[17] In his response Blondel argued that the concept of personality, so beloved by the Baron, is too limiting as a way of expressing divine presence, because it runs the risk of anthropomorphizing projection. In speaking of God, Blondel thought, the language of "substance" is to be preferred, because it better conveys the idea that God penetrates every aspect of concrete existence including personality. Blondel suggested "personalized substance" as a more broadly inclusive concept.[18] Seeing himself early on, and increasingly, as a theological watchdog within Modernist circles, and always on the alert for simplistic or one-sided thinking, Blondel did not for a moment hesitate, albeit with courtesy and affection, to speak his mind!

From their first actual meeting, in early 1899, initiated by von Hügel, the Baron indicated to Bremond his great enthusiasm for Newman's heritage, and his total support for Bremond's budding interest in mystical writers. He encouraged the exploration of specific writers in a way that was an uncanny premonition of Bremond's later work.[19] Goichot has pointed to the somewhat barbarous nature of the Baron's French, his great admiration for progressive Jesuits, and his even greater enthusiasm for the insight with which Bremond wrote about English authors. More than anyone else, the Baron would over the years encourage Bremond's vocation as a writer, specifically as a "religious psychologist." A truly avuncular figure, he would become, in Goichot's phrase, a kind of "prestigious uncle" to Bremond during the ups and downs of the Modernist struggles.[20]

---

16. Ibid., 26–27, citing Blondel to von Hügel, August 18, 1898.

17. This is to say that the Baron had become committed to a "personalism" which would be the signature quality of his thought: God is at work preeminently in the formation of the human person in all of its moral and spiritual dimensions. Von Hügel had a long and important correspondence with Ernst Troeltsch, with whose ideas there was significant overlap.

18. Letter of Blondel to von Hügel of March 22, 1900, cited at length by Marlé, *Au coeur*, 39–40. In general Marlé takes the position that tension between the Baron and Blondel steadily grew as their difference regarding Loisy came more and more into focus, though the Baron tended to deflect this.

19. Selections from the correspondence are reproduced in Goichot, "En marge de la crise." The details in this paragraph and the next are all drawn from this collection with Goichot's commentary. Bremond and the Baron actually met in Lyon on February 10, Bremond reporting to Blondel that he found the Baron to be a man of "an admirable heart, very close to God, very upright and good," Bremond to Blondel, February 10, 1899 (BB, I, 167). In his commentary Blanchet calls the meeting a mutual "seduction" (ibid., n2).

20. Goichot, "En marge de la crise," 213.

Indeed, it was to the Baron that Bremond confided his doubts, his hesitations, his growing discontent, and it was from the Baron that he received the greatest comfort when he left the Jesuits. A few years earlier the Baron had described Bremond, who had begun to be a bit of a link between the two men, to Blondel as "an open, warm, suffering, *very* suffering soul."[21] As they exchanged letters, kept one another informed about reading and research, it became the Baron who aroused in Bremond not only his already emergent interest in the inner life, but even more, the life of grace and holiness in the saints, the life of prayer and personal transformation, especially as this plays out in exemplary lives enshrined in literary deposits. He deplored pathologizing interpretations of florid religious experience, insisting that "abnormal nervous health" may play a constructive part in valid perceptions of the sacred.

Tyrrell

It is right about this time, 1900–1901, that Bremond, showing the influence of von Hügel, first published a programmatic essay on church history, which he now saw precisely as the history of the church's life of prayer.[22] Such a history is the story of the life of Christ in souls, a life which only "religious psychology," a discipline still in its infancy, can grasp. The Church is a "school of sanctity" for "the mystical action of Christ," often expressed in the daily anecdotal detail and particularity of individual lives. He argues that "attachment to Jesus" in the inner life is the essence, where outward forms of piety and devotion are the external signs of what is inward.[23] He cites Newman on the importance of the Incarnation and the sacred humanity, and then underlines an idea taken from the Irish Jesuit, George Tyrrell, that we must feel "the human heart of God," especially as this "heart" is expressed by means of the testimony contained in popular and parochial literature. It is the natural sympathy of human beings for one another, argued Tyrrell, that manifests the supernatural work of grace within. The church needs, thought Bremond, a Christian Sainte-Beuve to tell this story of grace.

Indeed, it was this shared concern for the concretely human, flesh-and-blood realities of ecclesial life, over against its theological abstractions, that formed a special bond between George Tyrrell and Bremond, as together they experienced disillusionment with their Jesuit existence and anti-Modernist conservatism.[24] Their relations

---

21. Letter of von Hügel to Blondel of July 30, 1899 (cited by Marlé, *Au coeur*, 34).

22. "Christus Vivit."

23. It should be noted, however, that this christocentrism in Bremond is temporary, and will wane as the influence of the Baron wanes. Eventually, it will become an issue between Bremond and Blondel as well. Marxer has argued that Bremond here got into a dilemma, even confusion, that he never adequately resolved ("L'École française," 891–99). It is better to say, I think, that as a result of Loisy's work Bremond realized that it is a mistake for Christian thinkers to be (uncritically) christocentric. A good analysis of these pitfalls is TeSelle, *Christ in Context*.

24. Ginter, "Expérience pastorale et réflexion théologique," shows how Tyrrell's pastoral context shaped his formulations. English Catholicism, lacking the university traditions found in France,

would end only with dramatic ecclesiastical consequences for Bremond, when he ministered at the deathbed and funeral of the by then excommunicated Tyrrell in 1909.

A writer since 1896 on the staff of the *Month*, the British equivalent to the French *Études*, Tyrrell had come from evangelical roots, then had became Anglo-Catholic, then converted to Roman Catholicism. Ordained as a priest in the Jesuit Order, he had been a fairly orthodox Thomist, then had embraced increasingly liberal views. Having been introduced to Blondel's work by the Baron, he had drunk even more deeply at Newman's well, finding it profoundly refreshing in some of the same ways that had attracted Bremond. Newman's influence on Tyrrell seems to have been pervasive in a general way, stirring him to think about the essence of Catholicism, then Christianity itself, in modernizing terms.[25] Perhaps it was reference to Newman in Tyrrell's 1897 *Nova et Vetera: Informal Meditations for Times of Spiritual Dryness* that first drew Bremond's attention to the Irish Jesuit, but in any case, after an initial contact by Bremond in the summer of 1898, they were in touch as spiritual brothers sharing many of the same intellectual predilections, as well as similar personal struggles.[26]

While we have only Tyrrell's side of their correspondence, a picture emerges of a rapidly developing comradeship-in-arms in which Tyrrell had the uncanny gift of planting seeds in Bremond's fertile mind—such as the idea that Saint Ignatius had been more of a mystic than later tradition had made him out to be.[27] At the heart of Tyrrell's thinking was the notion that the central meaning of a tradition has to be retrieved by means of historical imagination, backed up by solid research, in order to save that tradition from its rigid and distorting latter-day practitioners. Nothing is more distorting, thought Tyrrell, than abstract theology or logical philosophy, when these are applied to a living religion, since the former are merely *notional*, while the *reality* of a religion is found in the devotion, the prayer, the self-denial in the name of God, *the living thing itself*, on the basis of which abstract thinking, always dangerous, might provide a marginally adequate superstructure. "Devotion and religion existed

---

desperately needed to establish more robust connections with educated English thought—thought, I would suggest, always empirical in spirit.

25. See Leonard, *George Tyrrell*, 15–16, and notes, for discussion, but also, Pierce, "Crossbows, Bludgeons and Long-Range Rifles." The closeness of the Tyrrell-Bremond friendship and collaboration somewhat defies analysis, since Bremond's letters to Tyrrell appear to have been lost (probably destroyed by Tyrrell). Much depends on the picture painted of the two men by Maude Petre in her biography of Tyrrell. Selections from his letters to Bremond were edited and published, first by Maude Petre, then more completely by Anne Louis-David. See Aubert, "Henri Bremond et la crise moderniste," for a good discussion of Tyrrell's influence on Bremond.

26. VB, 98–101. Blanchet describes their relationship from the first as "non, certes, de complicité, mais de solidarité," a subtle distinction that could be applied to all of Bremond's relations with Modernist figures (ibid., 99).

27. Ibid, 100, an "entry by the *porte cochère*," says Blanchet, since, having encouraged Tyrrell to produce a "mystical" commentary on the *Exercises*, Bremond himself would take up the project 30 years later. See also Ginter, "Expérience pastorale," 181–83, and Trémolières, "Witness to these Witnesses," 260–62, for discussion of this encouragement from Tyrrell.

before theology," Tyrrell said, "in the way that art existed before art-criticism; reasoning, before logic; speech before grammar."[28] With regard to truth, there must be "imaginative assent" before there can be "notional acceptance."[29] The life of the Spirit in souls is prior to any kind of outward expression or intellectual grasp, since these even at their best fall short of, and at their worst will freeze or ossify, the living tissue.

Early on, in January 1899, the Baron represented Tyrrell to Bremond as "our mutual friend, a good head, a large heart," very much in the intellectual line of Cardinal Newman.[30] As Bremond got to know Tyrrell, and became familiar with his ideas, he realized, apparently, that he was dealing with another thinker very much in the English traditions that he admired,[31] for he once made the statement that a third of Tyrrell was already found in the work of Matthew Arnold,[32] poet and skeptic son of that Anglican schoolmaster, Thomas Arnold—who, as we recall, had the magic ability to make abstract ideas "real" for his boys. Matthew, having acknowledged the influence of Newman's poetry (that is, *The Dream of Gerontius*), was widely known for his view that religion is symbol and poetry, dressing the ineffable in the clothing of concreteness. It is that same English empirical tradition coming down from Butler through characters like Newman and Arnold to Tyrrell. Like Arnold, "Tyrrell defined faith as necessarily rooted in some kind of experience and not merely in propositions and principles accepted on hearsay.'"[33]

Tyrrell was a bold, but not a subtle, thinker. Not being a historian like Newman or comfortable with dialectical relations, he developed the view that the eternal truths contained in Christian experience are timeless, there being in them no real room for change. Church tradition is a "deposit" from the beginning, which Tyrrell (reflecting his Thomist underpinnings) understood as a "sound form of words," whose outward expression constantly shifts, to be sure, but whose inner reality—something quite different from Newman's "idea" that unfolds—is ever the same throughout the ages.[34] A particular corollary was his increasing conviction, which echoed one aspect of Newman, that the only dependable sign of God's presence in the world is the action of the human conscience. God works in human beings, but not in inanimate and impersonal nature. The kingdom of God, he contended, is the expansion of sympathy

---

28. See Livingston, introduction to *Tradition and the Critical Spirit*, xiii. Livingston considers this essay, "The Relation of Theology to Devotion," first published in the *Month* toward the end of 1899, to be the beginning of Tyrrell's Modernist phase.

29. Pierce, "Crossbows," 59.

30. Letter of von Hügel to Bremond, January 31, 1899 (in Goichot, "En marge de la crise," 217).

31. Neveu has an especially good sketch of the specifically *English* aspect of Tyrrell's influence on Bremond (Neveu, "Henri Bremond," 607–11).

32. Pierce, "Crossbows," 59.

33. Livingston, introduction to *Tradition and the Critical Spirit*, xvii–xviii.

34. From Tyrrell's, "Lex Orandi, Lex Credendi," a November 1899 essay, in Livingston, *Tradition and the Critical Spirit*, 65.

in the human heart, the zone of "divine fecundity," where commitment to the welfare of others immerses one deeper within the Divine Will.[35]

Other than their mutual commiserating about Jesuit training, church authority, etc., it is hard to know how much Bremond took in from Tyrrell. Blondel warmed to him at first. He liked the way in which Tyrrell expressed the view that any science like philosophy is "a symbolism of ever perfectible signs," a "treasure of holy letters" for "the interpretive work of the Spirit."[36] Bremond even described Tyrrell at one point as "Blondelizing" in his thought.[37] When, however, Bremond praised a controversial article by Tyrrell, in which the latter argued that the standard Catholic belief in hell perversely paints a picture of God as vindictive, bloodthirsty and merciless, Blondel registered only qualified approval. He agreed that popular religiosity is sometimes grotesque and distorting, but then he pushed back with an extended reflection, suggesting that the effect of religious imagery varies with the spiritual state of the recipient; pictures of the damned for those who refuse God may represent "the cry of heinous Negation" for some, but be salvific for others who have in them the spirit of justice and charity. Bremond confessed to being a little confused by Blondel's statements, but admitted that Tyrrell may have overstated things,[38] and he admitted that he found Blondel's formulations more edifying, more solid in the expression of ideas that were "immanentist and subjectivist."[39] Before long Blondel would refer to one of Tyrrell's books as "more filigree than architecture," or, as we would say, "all window dressing."[40]

Loisy

And then woven all through the fabric of Bremond's relationships with the Baron and Tyrrell and Blondel was the imposing presence of Alfred Loisy, generally seen as the central figure, and lightning rod, of French Modernism.[41] As priest and intellectual,

---

35. Tyrrell, "Divine Fecundity," in *Tradition and the Critical Spirit*, 185, 198–200, originally a lecture, one of Tyrrell's last, given in 1909. In a letter to Bremond of September 16, 1901 (Petre, *George Tyrrell's Letters*, 52), Tyrrell claims that loving God is so hard when God is hidden, leaving us to conclude that God can be loved only in other persons, the rest being "neo-Platonism." In a hallmark of Modernist thinking, Tyrrell argued that the *words* of authoritative church dogma cannot be the *object* of faith, since that object can be known only *inwardly* and thus as a nonverbal, non-verbalizable reality perceived "through a glass darkly." See Tyrrell "Théologisme" (in response to M. L. Lebreton), 499–505.

36. Blondel to Bremond, August 19, 1898 (BB, I, 71).

37. Bremond to Blondel, January 15, 1899 (BB, I, 153).

38. Tyrrell, "Perverted Devotion," originally published December 16, 1899. Blondel's reservations are in "Blondel to Bremond, January 25, 1900," and Bremond's response, Bremond to Blondel, January 29, 1900 (BB, I, 263–69).

39. Bremond to Blondel, June 7, 1900 (BB, I, 291).

40. Blondel to Bremond, July 14, 1902 (BB, I, 432).

41. Poulat, *Histoire*, 19. "Incontestably it is in France that modernism found its chosen ground [by

specialist in the new critical biblical studies, his rise to eminence had been meteoric, landing him as a professor at Paris's Institut Catholique, from which he was then dismissed in 1893 because of his radical views. Having absorbed much from progressive German biblical scholarship, he called for new modes of interpretation, challenging in a number of anonymous essays, then in widely read published work, the historicity of various biblical texts.

He and the Baron had been in communication since April 1893, and the Baron would be his steady defender at Rome for years to come (though ultimate disillusionment would set in).[42] From early 1897, Loisy and Blondel would be in touch, Blondel initially approving (as with Tyrrell!) of Loisy's attitude and forward-looking views. Indeed, Loisy's early correspondence with Blondel is remarkable for its congeniality and the view that they are very much on the same track, both "innovators" critical of scholastic Aristotle-based theologizing and preaching "in the desert which lies between the fanatics of science and the rationalists of faith."[43] His correspondence with Blondel and the Baron show that Bremond was paying attention to Loisy's publications, and that he was disturbed by the various ecclesiastical strictures and sanctions being gradually placed on Loisy's work.[44] Loisy, aware of some of Bremond's writing, was impressed also; at one point he confided to the Baron that he thought that Bremond should be the next General of the Jesuits![45] Bremond was thrilled with Loisy's teaching when he attended the latter's course on the parables at the secular École pratique des hautes études, Loisy's new venue, in the autumn of 1901.[46] Their correspondence had actually begun earlier, in May of that year, with their shared enthusiasm for Newman much in evidence.[47]

Then came Loisy's bombshell. On November 8, 1902, he published *L'Évangile et l'Église* to initially rapturous reviews. Adolph Harnack's great book *The Essence of Christianity*, a liberal Protestant version of the rise of the primitive Church, having

---

contrast with Germany, Great Britain and Italy]. It had its eponymous personage in Loisy."

42. Under the heading of Bremond's early phrase for Loisy as "the good Noah," Blanchet provides a careful tracking of the growing relationships among Loisy, von Hügel, Blondel, and Bremond from their beginnings until 1904 and the first beginnings of painful ruptures. He emphasizes the tension between intense and intellectually supportive friendship on the one hand, and the growing theological discomfort on the part of Blondel on the other, with Bremond caught in the middle (VB, 157–88). Marlé details the unfolding of Blondel's debates with Loisy and von Hügel in more detail, with Loisy as the man in the middle (*Au coeur*, chs. 3 and 4)!

43. Loisy to Blondel, February 25, 1897, cited by Marlé, *Au coeur*, 35.

44. Blanchet notes from a letter of December 3, 1900, from Bremond to the Baron, that tensions at *Études* were running high over scientific methods of study and "intellectual emancipation" leading to "emancipation of the heart" (VB, 162).

45. Loisy, *Mémoires*, I, 520, as cited by Blanchet (BB, I, 192n1).

46. "Bremond to the Baron, November 14, 1901," but also to Blondel on the same date (ibid., 386–87). Blanchet thinks that the Baron used this passionate endorsement from Bremond in defending Loisy in Rome shortly thereafter (VB, 164).

47. See Bernard-Maître, "Lettres d'Henri Bremond à Alfred Loisy," as the primary resource here.

appeared in 1900, Loisy's book was a Catholic counter-narrative (not a refutation).[48] Seemingly akin to Newman's theory of the development of doctrine, Loisy's view was that the essence of Christianity is inseparable from the history of its traditions; who Jesus was and what he was about is inseparable from the life of the church, that is, the Catholic Church, down through the ages. Christian tradition began, he thought, with the Resurrection, then led to idealizing narratives about Jesus and his work, and gradually to elaborated theories of redemption that account for his significance. The kingdom of God exists in the hearts of those who believe, it is "for all whom God pardons, provided that they pardon themselves,"[49] and is then a collective and objective reality in the community of those who look for a future ripening and perfection.

This eschatology is the "husk" wrapped around the "seed," which is the kingdom foretold by the prophets, which must then germinate by the power of love within the individual soul until the thing itself comes in its fullness.[50] But Loisy was terribly elusive here, arguing that while the "idea of Christ" is essential to Christianity, the truth of such a claim is beyond the purview of the historian. He very much objected to Harnack's view of the sonship of Jesus as something that resided in his unique and perfect knowledge of the Father, preferring to construe Jesus as the center of messianic hopes that others placed on him, so that for faith he is the King for all eternity, a figure of the timeless future.[51] What Loisy constantly underlined was the idea that Jesus is an eschatological figure, that his identity was all wrapped up with what he would be in the final kingdom, not what he was at present. How he actually, historically thought of himself is indiscernible from our texts.

There is, then, said Loisy, no essence to the gospel, since Jesus as a redemptive figure is generated by the collective life of the church, ever changing through the centuries—although he did not state the matter quite that baldly. What he said is that the natural thrust of Jesus and his gospel message was toward the formation of a society that would grow and develop, the "society of Jesus' friends," and "in order to be at all times what Jesus desired the society of his friends to be, it had to become what it has become."[52] It is this collective entity that continues to carry the "impulse of the Spirit," that looks for the kingdom. Every step in the history of the church is "a deduction from the preceding," so that "the historian cannot say that the total extent of the movement is outside the gospel. The fact is, it proceeds from it and continues it."[53] A living faith must be acted out as a collective and continuous life. The community's

48. References are to the 1903 Christopher Home translation of Loisy, *Gospel and the Church*.

49. Ibid., 61.

50. "What is traditional is the husk; what is personal the kernel" (ibid., 63). "Love, therefore, is not an end in itself; charity leads to the kingdom, sacrificing the temporal to gain the eternal" (ibid., 70).

51. "It is somewhat rash to-day to maintain that the essential significance of the title of Son of God was different for Christ Himself, and that its real justification was the consciousness of God as Father" (ibid., 92–93).

52. Ibid., 150.

53. Ibid., 165.

teachings, its dogmas are immutable, but interpretation changes, always striving for a balance between loyalty to the past and new needs in the present. Divine in origin, they are "human in structure and composition."[54] "It is not indispensable to the authority of belief that it should be rigorously unchangeable in its intellectual form and its verbal expression. Such immutability is not compatible with the nature of human intelligence."[55] The conclusion, *contra* Harnack: "This little volume is full enough if it has shown how Christianity has lived in the Church and by the Church, and how futile is the desire to save it by a search after its essence."[56]

Traditionalists, seeing Loisy's presentation as a brilliant defense of the Catholic Church and its dogmatic apparatus, applauded, while Modernists, who viewed it as a defense of change and evolution and progress in the statement of dogma, applauded as well. Loisy looked like Newman all over again. Two passing statements by Loisy might have caught Bremond's attention, because they are representative of his future work. The essence of Christianity, Loisy argued, cannot be "a metaphysical entity . . . a logical quintessence . . . [and] the gospel will always need a body to be human."[57] *Pure love*, as Loisy well knew, would eventually serve as Bremond's restatement of the contention that the Gospel must be at the same time eternal and temporal, infinite and finite, redolent of both heaven and earth.[58]

Before long, however, more careful readers began to notice that for Loisy everything in Christian belief is, we would say today, a "construction," something fabricated by the church in every age, since nothing *definable* is "given" or "deposited" in the beginning. Christianity begins, not with Jesus, but with the Resurrection as an ineffable church-creating event, the church in turn producing out of its communal existence new images of Jesus. Harnack had pictured Jesus as the founder of Christianity, but for Loisy it is the church responding to a now historically invisible Jesus, that engenders Christianity. Inclined at first like many to see his work as a profound apology for Catholic Christianity, Bremond later acknowledged that he had failed to discern at the time the full seriousness of the challenge being issued by Loisy.[59] But other critics caught on much sooner, and official condemnation would come before long.

Blondel himself quickly expressed serious reservations, after Bremond asked him for an opinion.[60] The matter escalated into a three-way conversation between Blondel,

54. Ibid., 211.
55. Ibid., 217.
56. Ibid., 277.
57. Ibid., 14, 121.
58. Loisy, *George Tyrrell et Henri Bremond*, ch. 4, "A Religious Philosophy." Loisy's eschatology was to become more mystical and even more inward over time until he arrived at the "Religion of Humanity" stage.
59. In the pseudonymous Sylvain Leblanc, *Un clerc qui n'a pas trahi*, 19–20, where he claimed that he was "too indifferent to the religious problem," to be fully aware of what was at stake in *L'Évangile et l'Église*.
60. Bremond to Blondel, November 23, 1902 (BB, I, 445).

Bremond and the Baron, the latter two defending Loisy, with Blondel at the beginning of a sustained attack. From this point on, from the beginning of Blondel's critique of Loisy, his theological influence on Bremond begins in earnest.

Blondel

Bremond, Tyrrell, von Hügel, and Loisy all claimed to be familiar with Blondel's thought from their reading of his 1893 classic, *L'Action. Essai d'une critique de la vie et d'une science de la pratique*, and then the 1896 *Lettre sur les exigences de la pensées contemporaine en matière d'apologétique et sur la méthode de la philosophie dans l'étude du problème religieux*. And they all claimed to be positively influenced by these works, having picked up on Blondel's critique of traditional philosophical methods. And they all thought of him as a successor to Newman. While there is some truth in their collective perception, the reality is more complex.

L'Action, originally Blondel's doctoral dissertation of 1893 at the École normale in Paris, was controversial in every way from the beginning, because it had so many facets in the eyes of critics. Some philosophers found it to be too theological and some theologians found it too philosophical. Some found it too scholastic and traditional in its style and method, while others thought it too modernist and radical in its spirit and conclusions. Probably the genius of the work is that it was all of those things in measured proportions, all counter-balancing one another for the sake of a central, highly ambitious vision.

In what came to be called "the method of immanence," Blondel set out to show that it is in the subjectivity of taking action that we reveal a hidden depth, where we "undergo" being itself and become "attached" to it.[61] That depth appears in the gap, "an inexplicable and disconcerting disproportion,"[62] that Blondel claimed to discern between what we know and will, and what happens when we convert intention into action. He coined the distinction of the "will willing" and the "will willed" as the starting point for a dialectic in which moral choices are revelatory of the nature of the consciousness with which those choices are made. "The truth essential to every consciousness and the movement common to all wills" become operative in action, whereby the desire to love and to exercise freedom are manifest in acts that fail to attain their inherent horizon.[63] Science (the laws of practical necessity), morality (goodness or its lack) and metaphysics (the realm of being itself) will all intersect at this center of

---

61. *L'Action*, 3. All references are to the 1984 English translation, by Oliva Blanchette, of Maurice Blondel, *Action (1893): Essay on a Critique of Life and a Science of Practice*.

62. Ibid., 4.

63. Ibid., 13. "At each stage [the 'tiered forms of morality'] he shows what the will must integrate as part of what it wills necessarily, but at each stage he also shows what is willed at each intermediary stage is still not equal to the power of willing" (Blanchette, *Maurice Blondel*, 69).

life, precisely at the point where action occurs. Thus, we can see, averred Blondel, "the hidden truth that souls live by and that perhaps they may die of for eternity."[64]

The whole work is then a systematic application of these theses to different arenas of human endeavor. Arguing that there is a "natural orientation of the will" that human beings cannot avoid, that takes a mysterious "something" for its object, something not contained in itself, and thus "transcendent,"[65] Blondel engaged in his own restatement of the scholastic *desiderium naturale*, by which we by nature, and thus necessarily, seek God, without knowing that we are doing so. The very structure of "action" is impossible otherwise. This is Blondel's radical claim. Willy-nilly, we seek God in every choice that we make.

Blondel's analysis of scientific method as a particular form of action was important for his later criticism of Loisy, because he contended that the positive sciences are fundamentally incoherent; they presuppose for their operation a "subjective element" that they themselves cannot produce. This element is an "ideal" or a priori factor, in which experience and deduction are united. In other words, science is adapted to the nature of things without being able to account for their nature. Applied to each of the sciences in turn, this contention shows why empirics are always an approximation at best, and that "every scientific discipline requires the postulate of action to subsist, and that action must become, if the will remains consistent with the initial movement of knowing, the object of a proper science. It does not resolve the antinomy of the positive sciences except by raising problems of another order."[66] The scientist always operates from an unexamined metaphysical stance, which, when examined, exposes the "gap" pointing to transcendence.

In a concluding passage that would, perhaps, have the most effect on Bremond, Blondel suggested that religious dogmas are "expressive signs" that speak to the "dispositions of wills" in their various receivers, welcome or scandalous as the case may be, offering "the infinite only under the guise of the finite."[67] Some are illumined and some are hardened by these "signs of contradiction," that "recapture being under sensible species," where what is worthy to be received is so "only in virtue of what makes it contemptible and hateful to others."[68] In other words, dogmas as "signs" expose our need, and how far we are in our own devices from meeting those needs. Thus nature cries out for the supernatural, while not in any way "proving" the reality of what it seeks!

Blondel's final contention was that religious practice is the putting into action of what we cannot know because it is beyond us while being demanded by our being; we

---

64. *L'Action*, 13. We catch a glimpse here of the reason for Blondel's discomfort with Tyrrell's summary rejection of popular images and thinking relative to the idea of hell.

65. "The necessity of the supernatural will appear precisely out of the consciousness of this inevitable failure" (Blanchette, *Maurice Blondel*, 69).

66. Ibid., 88.

67. Ibid., 364.

68. Ibid., 366.

can only grope after it, all the while letting our interiority of knowing and willing be constantly refashioned in what Blondel calls "the beautiful expansion of the inner life." "Like the philosopher or the artist whose subservience to signs and forms prevents him from remaining complacent with confused intuitions, the religious soul finds a help against itself in the demanding rigor of the letter . . . [and] under this constraint, it renews itself . . . by projecting them [these religious sentiments] into the body of an act."[69] Let the will, he said repeatedly, constantly return to its principle in order to be renewed, thereby revealing what its principle is. With such reasoning Blondel could affirm Bremond in his program of "religious psychology," as long as he stayed clear about what such psychology is—not a mere empirics, but rather an exploration of this putting into act through the working of consciousness of that which manifests its essential being.

For Blondel the transitory character of particular dogmatic signs and expressions arises not so much from temporality itself, as from an inevitable inadequacy to their object. This is reminiscent of Newman, to be sure. But the difference lies in the fact that Blondel is thinking metaphysically, while Newman was a historian. The problem that would dog von Hügel, Tyrrell and Loisy is that they could not decide which register to land in with regard to dogma, and thus there would be a confusion which Blondel was quick to spot and then probe mercilessly by questioning their ability to make theological pronouncements on the basis of historical reconstructions. And Bremond was caught on the horns of the dilemma, inclining painfully to either side, but ultimately, I believe, to that of Blondel.

L'Action was for some time known only to a small circle, but what first brought Blondel out into the open in combat mode was the *Lettre* of 1896, actually a series of journal articles, in which he clarified his method in *L'Action*.[70] His target was the traditional apologetic use of "facts" as "evidences" for Christian truth-claims. His core assertion was that there cannot be a demonstration of the existence, or even the bare possibility, of the supernatural in facts, but only its *necessity*—as a true philosophical method would require. One can then yield in faith to that necessity, or not. Thus is shown the ambiguity of all manifestations of the divine, which arouse desire, making the soul feel an absence, but not mandating submission. Consequently, the sciences of human nature remain intact in their sphere, describing the natural causal nexus, whereas faith involves a leap, but a *rational* one justified by a true philosophical analysis. Science and religion are put in their proper places, but at the same time are indissolubly joined. "In short, just as it has been necessary to condemn the false separatism which isolated the religious problem from philosophical problems, so must we

---

69. Ibid., 376.

70. All references are to the 1956 English edition of Maurice Blondel, *Letter on Apologetics* and *History and Dogma*.

condemn the false separatism which isolates the work of speculative thought from ascetical efforts and from the painful teaching which is given to us by life itself."[71]

According to Talar, as mentioned, while there may have been some mediated influence of Newman on Blondel, he was at some pains to distance himself from the Cardinal, primarily because Loisy and others had co-opted him, and because of the charge of "subjectivity" being brought against his own thought as well as that of Newman.[72] Indeed, as conservative criticism of his work mounted, in which a misguided "psychological" interpretation of his stress on subjectivity tormented Blondel, he became defensive.[73] The appearance of Loisy's blockbuster was the last straw. Intense epistolary exchanges followed, in which communications between Blondel and the Baron, a defender of Loisy, as well as between Blondel and Loisy himself, were central. The principals gradually became exasperated with one another, the climax being Blondel's published rejection of Loisy's thought in his 1904 *Histoire et dogme: Les lacunes philosophiques de l'exégèse moderne*, which was then followed by the Baron's rejoinder.[74] Through it all Bremond had some tense exchanges with Blondel, was utterly preoccupied with his process of leaving the Jesuits, and then got into the middle of things by producing a French translation of the Baron's spirited rebuttal to *Histoire et dogme*. The upshot for personal relations was that things would never be warm again between Blondel and the Baron, while Bremond would maintain compartmentalized relationships with Blondel and Loisy for the remainder of his life (things rapidly tapered off with the Baron after 1909).

While Blondel, as mentioned, tended to keep Bremond closer to the orthodox side of the debate, Loisy would represent his rebellious side, especially after Tyrrell's death. On the one hand, he would always, in a way uncongenial and problematic for Blondel, maintain a fondness for the risks and surprises of historical-critical methodology in approaching the interpretation of texts. On the other hand, he developed, with Blondel's applause, a deep veneration for the classic expressions of Christian piety in different "golden" ages, especially the seventeenth century, this orientation being quite foreign to Loisy, outside of the pale of Tyrrell's interests, and even a bit alien to the Baron, who was really a medievalist with a mono-focus on Catherine of Genoa. If Blondel kept Bremond on the "inside," it was Tyrrell initially, then Loisy, who kept him on the "outside edge of the inside,"[75] the Baron playing the role of spiritual therapist in the earlier years.

---

71. Ibid., 197.
72. Talar, "Newman and the 'New Apologetics,'" 55–56.
73. Somerville speaks of a "veritable purgatory" for Blondel ("Maurice Blondel," 381).
74. Both Poulat and Marlé, in the works cited, structure the rise of Catholic Modernism as a process that began with the publication of Harnack's "Essence" and Loisy's reply, followed then by the range of responses and debates, and concluding with Blondel's pronouncements on the nature of dogma.
75. Borrowed from a self-description by Richard Rohr, OFM.

Responding to a query from Bremond, Blondel voiced the essence of his critique of Loisy just after New Year's 1903.[76] Many of the ideas in Loisy's book, he insisted, are commonplaces—such as the concepts of organic growth in the history of dogma, of transformations that modify the letter without changing the spirit, of the maintenance during the transmittal process of profound analogies along with the suppression of apparent resemblances, the conviction of vital exigencies by which the church is instinctively inspired to be at each moment of its history what it must be so as to subsist—but there are two problems. The first is the pretension that one can systematically separate all that is historical in the same matter from all that is metaphysical or theological, as if "facts" had a sufficiency that automatically yields real explanations. What happens instead, he argued, is that the supernatural is suppressed, so that what should be transcendent in the facts is subordinated to, if not eliminated by, what is "historical." The second objection lay outside of Bremond's purview and related more to debate with the Baron: Loisy's claim that Jesus himself seemed unclear about his identity and role, leaving it to others, i.e., the incipient church, to think what they would, to make redemptive capital, about him.

Blondel had thus homed in on what would come to be called the problem of "the messianic consciousness of the historical Jesus," one of those issues in New Testament interpretation that has never been completely resolved, given the literary complexity of the gospels. Loisy belonged to the evolving tradition of exegetes who have considered the issue ultimately irrelevant for sound interpretation of the gospel of the kingdom, while Blondel represented the classical view that the two-nature Chalcedonian Christology of Christian orthodoxy cannot be sustained without the ability of exegetes to reaffirm the view that the human Jesus was aware of his own divine nature.

Blondel's first objection was, on the contrary, vitally important to Bremond, and we have seen it surfacing clearly in his Académie address of 1924, in which he defended Duchesne with the view that all historical-critical interpretation operates with presuppositions that shape what the interpreter discerns and how he fits those discernments into larger patterns of meaning. The fundamental question will be the appropriateness of the interpreter's particular presuppositions to the nature of the material which he is interpreting.

Jesuit Crisis

In the meantime, however, the crisis with the Jesuits, and of the Jesuits, worsened. On July 24, 1902, the government of Émile Combes, once again cracking down on the church, closed nearly 2,700 schools, and drumbeats for the dispersal of the unauthorized teaching Orders intensified. As the situation at *Études* eroded, Bremond was complaining to Blondel that "there is a vague feeling that I am not a Jesuit man in the

---

76. Blondel to Bremond, January 4, 1903 (BB, I, 451–53.)

way that Rome understands, and it is true, my life is lamentable."[77] As he fretted over the approaching condemnation of Loisy, however, he managed to focus his attention on other writings, including the publication of his first *L'Inquiétude religieuse* collection, the *L'Enfant et la vie* collection, and then in 1903 his extended portrait of the great Reformation-era English Catholic and humanist Sir Thomas More.[78] Tellingly, Bremond picked up on the famous "man for all seasons" description of More as "a friend for all hours," thus presaging the role that he himself would play through the Modernist crisis.[79]

Bremond presented More as a burdened child, early dedicated to legal work, so that "like many others, he devoted the best of his time to work he did not care for,"[80] his real passion being for the Erasmian humanism then manifesting itself in cultured English circles. In More's embrace of Italian Renaissance spirituality via the influence of the Dutch Erasmus, Bremond saw the kind of "Christian asceticism that could go courageously even to the 'folly of the Cross' [combined with] a kind of exaltation of humanity that threatened a return to paganism."[81] "By contemplating Thomas More as he lived," said Bremond, "we shall the better understand how a Christian can renounce nothing of what is nobly 'human,' and still remain faithful to the 'hard words' of the Gospel."[82]

In the course of laying out the events and developments of More's illustrious career, Bremond articulated some gems: "[It] is his [More's] glory to have... wedded to the thoughts of faith and the experience of the Christian life, this English prose, which is one of the noblest, strongest, and sweetest tongues ever found by the gospel for the interpretation of its message";[83] More, this "friend of Erasmus was a forerunner, both in tone and doctrine, of St. Francis de Sales";[84] "an analogous example of generosity in prudence [is found in] the conversion of Newman";[85] at his final imprisonment and martyrdom More "remains thoroughly English to the end, neither trying any flights beyond his nature, nor searching for great words... there was nothing in it new, forced or affected."[86] In *Thomas More* Bremond was beginning to trace out a line of descent, a tradition, as it were, within Catholic tradition—an early sign of the momentum in

---

77. Bremond to Blondel, March 11, 1902 (BB, I, 408).

78. Bremond, *Le Bienheureux Thomas More*, 4, with reference to the 1920 English translation, *Sir Thomas More (The Blessed Thomas More)*. Blondel would later claim to see something of Bremond himself in the depiction of Thomas More ("Blondel to Bremond, March 3, 1904" [BB, I, 484–85]).

79. Bremond, *Sir Thomas More*, viii.

80. Ibid., 13.

81. Ibid., 19.

82. Ibid., 21. Exactly what Bremond, somewhat later and after more sustained reflection, would say of Francis de Sales.

83. Ibid., 143.

84. Ibid., 147.

85. Ibid., 151.

86. Ibid., 201.

the direction of the *Histoire*. Then came Bremond's departure from the Jesuits in 1904, and, following the book on More and the essay on Eliot, some waning of his English fixation.[87] No more "flight beyond his nature" for Bremond; he was headed home.

In the meantime Blondel published *Histoire et dogme*. It is his polemic against "extrinsicism" and "historicism" in biblical exegesis, the former being the view that historical facts are merely signs that allow for "gross perceptions" of the eternal dogmas being signified, the latter the assumption that historical analysis has the power to make metaphysical claims. "What . . . eludes the historian is the spiritual reality within the phenomena, that which eludes the deterministic nexus," he averred. In fact, "real history is composed of human lives; and human life is metaphysics in act."[88] The challenge in exegesis is one of keeping faith and history in proper relation, and it is precisely the work of Tradition to do just that by formulating and correctly evaluating the received Deposit in experience and act. Subjectivism in interpretation is thereby avoided, Tradition being the safeguard, so that "the universal gift of the Redemption, which is the divine reality," is preserved.[89] In the words of James Somerville, Blondel was here intent on outlining "a positive solution to the problem of scriptural exegesis that would take account of the newer critical methods without sacrificing any of the traditional values."[90] It was the whole problem of Modernism in a nutshell, where the only alternative to Blondel's effort seemed to be "a blind fideism cut off from objective certitude, where religious feeling wells up within man [*sic!*] to become crystallized in dogmas."[91]

Loving both Blondel and Loisy, Bremond, vacationing by this time at the Italian lakes, tried to intercede.[92] He let Blondel know that he and the Baron were both convinced that Blondel misunderstood Loisy, that in fact the historian *qua* historian occupies a privileged terrain that is his proper field, as in claiming that the resurrection-event is a fact. He then took up Blondel's refrain that "the supernatural cannot be naturalized," and offered the analogy that in every prayer the supernatural order is already present and at work. The implication is that the resurrection is, so to speak, a "charged" event unlike the death of Louis XIV, which is not.[93] But he was unclear

---

87. Cf., however, Neveu, "Henri Bremond." Granted that Bremond's love for all things English persisted, his increased orientation to French spirituality became dominant.

88. Blondel, *Histoire et dogme*, 236, with reference to Blondel, *Lettres sur les exigences*, in the English version, *Letter on Apologetics and History and Dogma*, 236. We have already seen the grounding for these statements in *L'Action*.

89. Ibid., 281.

90. Somerville, "Maurice Blondel 1861–1949," 388.

91. Ibid., 389.

92. Bremond to Blondel, March 10, 1904 (BB, I, 486). Recall Bremond's description of himself to Henry Bordeaux at the time of his reception at the Académie: "[I have] this tendency to reconcile everything, so that nothing good is lost. That is the true liberalism, which is not at all a doctrinal minimalism" (Blanchet "Henri Bremond," 437).

93. Bremond to Blondel, March 1904 (BB, I, 489–92), an unusually long letter for Bremond.

about the modality, or character, of the supernatural "presence" within the natural, appealing to Blondel's focus on subjectivity, the consciousness of the human actors, as the key factor, but unsure about how to move beyond the bare affirmation.

During the last part of 1903 and the first part of the next year, while the whole uproar with Loisy was at its height, Bremond was in the midst of his final crisis with the Order.[94] Superiors who knew how unhappy he was, allowed him to do some traveling. He spent time in Italy, where he met Modernist figures such as Antonio Fogazzaro, and visited with Tyrrell, then living at the Jesuit house in Richmond, Yorkshire. And, of course, he corresponded with everyone. In that correspondence we get a general picture of nervous collapse paradoxically combined with considerable productivity (as with the *Thomas More*). Clearly he needed to find a new inner balance. Blanchet is emphatic that the departure from the Jesuits was by mutual agreement, was amicable, was executed in a calm, respectful way. A complicating presence was that of Maude Petre (1863–1942), an Englishwoman, intellectually trained, Superior of the Daughters of the Heart of Mary, a religious order liberal in its discipline and grounded in Ignatian spirituality, who had become a Modernist confidante of Tyrrell's (later his biographer) and then penitent to, and counselor of, Bremond during and after his departure from the Jesuits.[95]

While Tyrrell was utterly sympathetic with Bremond's increasing need to exit the Order, as was Loisy, and the Baron was supportive though anguished, Blondel found it all rather immature and was impatient. But departure became official on February 6, 1904: Bremond was dismissed from the Order, and he claimed to Blondel that it was because of his support of Loisy.[96] Indeed, there seems to have been no other reason than intellectual and spiritual unhappiness, combined with the need to get on with his proper work as a writer, historian and "religious psychologist." And then, of course, to work out where he stood in the impending Modernist controversy, how he would metabolize the heritage of Blondel and the others, and how that heritage would be enshrined in his mature work. And all of this, just as his first book on Newman was coming out, and he was gaining a public readership that would make him both beloved and notorious.

---

94. Traced out in great detail by Blanchet (VB, ch. 4, "La crise"). Blanchet suggests at one point that in the midst of the uproar reflected in his sustained correspondence with Maude Petre, Bremond had picked up the idea from Eliot of leading "an undogmatic clerical life" (ibid., 226).

95. Blanchet has a substantial treatment of her role as an intermediary between Bremond and Tyrrell, an "amitié à trois," as he suggests, citing one of her letters (VB, 199–213). Basically Bremond agonized with her as he prepared to leave the Order, while she sympathized with his "sufferings" and shared Modernist intellectual misgivings. There was never any question, however, about her primary loyalty: Tyrrell.

96. Bremond to Blondel, February 9, 1904 (BB, I, 479–80).

6

Returning to Roots

BY EARLY 1904 BREMOND was clear that his vocation was to write, and, specifically, to write as a historian of "religious psychology" across the range of its literary expression. High theological literature might have a place, but it would be secondary to the analysis of an author's "inner life"—the individual's "sentiment," "soul," "subjectivity," "conscience"—as found in experience-near compositions, especially those dealing with prayer. As a matter of temperament, he had discovered that he needed to work at his own pace in his own kind of surroundings, and for the most part alone. He simply could not thrive in a regimented and authoritarian environment, however moderated. He needed the freedom of the independent scholar, and now, having left the Jesuit community, he had it.

After some negotiating of his status as a new "secular" priest, he was "incardinated" as a "free priest" into the archdiocese of Aix by François-Joseph Bonnefoy, the understanding and supportive archbishop.[1] As far as material resources go, he had some modest income from family inheritance, but finances would always be shaky and worrisome. His main challenges were to get himself settled down and resituated, and then, critically, to refine and focus his field of work.

He quickly discovered how cherished he was by a circle of friends, old and new. A generous outpouring of offers of hospitality flowed in, but his first impulse was to cultivate some time on his own. Initially the whole situation was complicated by the ongoing struggle between Blondel and Loisy, with himself maneuvering somewhere in the middle. We saw that in February and March of 1904 he was settled in the Italian Lakes district, where he communicated his concerns about *Histoire et dogme* to Blondel, who had already let him know of a sad correspondence on the matter between himself and the Baron. He had in the meantime labored to make the best case that he, now a "vagabond," could for Loisy, representing him as a man of deep faith

---

1. Blanchet's last pages describe a certain amount of thrashing around on Bremond's part, as he put out a variety of "feelers" to friends and church contacts for possible employment. One gets the sense, however, that he simply needed to be "independent" (VB, 260–69).

"who had helped me keep my faith in the divinity of our Lord," and as a man with a true interior life, though obscured by a certain boorishness of expression.[2] Blondel, even as he was shaking his head over Bremond's departure from the Jesuits,[3] and agonizing over the whole situation with Loisy, tried to pacify Bremond on the matter, as mentioned, with some elucidation of the issues. But then, learning that Bremond was going to exercise his gifts for "clarity and penetration" by producing a French version of the Baron's defense of Loisy—a work that he saw as sometimes imprecise and rambling[4]—Blondel was hurt. A little later Bremond described Loisy to Blondel as "a true Noah," insisting that "the Church will be glad to have this ark when the flood has passed [the flood being the assault of modernizing rationalism on the whole structure of Christian belief]." And he wrote similar things to others.[5]

The focus shifted, then, as Bremond's publications on Newman began to appear. By assimilating Loisy and Blondel to Newman he was intellectually comfortable, but only tenuously, as cracks started to appear. Back in Aix in late 1904, in an unedited letter to Wilfrid Ward, he wondered if Newman had been consistent with himself when he insisted on the reality of the *depositum fidei* as the dynamic core of the process of development, and he acknowledged that Newman would have condemned Loisy. To Loisy himself he revealed that his publisher Bloud would have been horrified if he had linked the name of Loisy, now *persona non grata* in orthodox circles, with that of Newman.

He worked at pacification. To Loisy he said of Blondel, "I think that he suspects that you are less heretical than he thinks," and he offered the assurance that Blondel was well-intentioned toward him.[6] To Blondel he sent soothing and playful letters from Italian and German locales, indicating that his second Newman book (*Psychologie de la foi*) would be "a true anti-intellectualist manual," and that he had found among the Germans a sympathetic voice in that of the Munich philosopher Deutinger, who in 1840 had been teaching "pure Blondelism!"[7] To Loisy he indicated that he thought Newman "illogical" in wanting to remain so dogmatic, and that Blondel had the same problem.[8] One is reminded of the young Bremond back at the parental home in Aix, listening while the adults argued opposing political positions, then laughing (wearisomely?) at the rigidity of their polarized antitheses.

---

2. Bremond to Blondel, February 27, 1904 (BB, I, 482). The last expression is "the half-sufficiency of a country parvenu."

3. Blondel to Valensin, February 29, 1904 (cited BB, I, 483n1), where Blondel speculated that the influence of Maurras and Barrès on Bremond was at work.

4. Blondel to Laberthonnière, May 16, 1904 (cited BB, I, 493n1).

5. Bremond to Blondel, May 23, 1904 (BB, I, 494 and 495n4).

6. Bremond to Loisy, December 27, 1904, in Bernard-Maître, *Lettres*, 16–17, citing (BB, I, 17n2) Bremond to Ward, November 29, 1904.

7. Bremond to Blondel, February 24, 1905, and May 18, 2005 (BB, II, 11–13).

8. Bremond to Loisy, June 5, 1905, in Bernard-Maître, *Lettres*, 18–19.

Dogma or Life?

In a curious essay, substantial in length, Bremond showed signs of starting to turn the corner. It is a review of two novels by the young Austrian Catholic writer Enrica von Handel-Mazzetti (1871–1955). Both books—*l'Année mémorable de Meinrad Helmperger*, 1905, and *Jesse und Maria*, 1906—are stories in which children are either converted to, or deepened in, Catholic piety by the examples of holy lives, rather than by dogmatic browbeating. It is the modeling of Christian goodness that is the best advertisement for truth, says the novelist, and Bremond was in complete agreement, noting the similarity here to Eliot. The idea is that children know intuitively what is true and false, while lacking the conceptual tools for philosophical expression, and it is often female writers and thinkers who are most attuned to that fact. In this way, said Bremond, "the religious problem" is "incarnated" from the world of abstractions into "the world of real souls."[9] Bremond sent a copy of the Handel-Mazzetti piece, a peace offering, to Blondel as soon as it first appeared in print, and would soon call her "a German George Eliot."[10] Blondel was very approving, and in addition sang Bremond's praises for the work on Newman now appearing, though he resisted Bremond's idea that there was "a functional identity" between his own thought and that of the Cardinal.[11] An amicable tone returned to their relationship as references to Loisy were dropped, and they could discuss Newman's thought in a softer atmosphere.

Much of the discussion here inevitably returned to the (ultimately unsolvable) problem of how Christian dogma originally began, that is, the question of the "deposit of faith" and its initial form. After much going back-and-forth with Bremond, who persisted in likening his thought to that of Newman and Loisy, Blondel, in a long letter just before Christmas 1905, registered a muscular response. He agreed with Bremond and Loisy that it is a bad thing to create a material, intellectual, fixist view of the original *depositum*. However, he contended, the separation of revelation and dogma is another kind of error, this time idealist, into which Newman sometimes carelessly fell, an error in which a thinker deems that objects as such are not intrinsically intelligible.[12] But, he contended, one must see that human reasoning powers operate on concrete manifestations that, precisely in the indisputable clarity of their concreteness, are pointers to "divine secrets." The problem is that Newman has been taken too

---

9. Bremond, "Les Romans de la baronne de Handel-Mazzetti," first appeared September 1, 1905.
10. Bremond to Blondel, May 29, 1905, and June 20, 1905 (BB, II, 15–19).
11. Ibid., 18–19.

12. The reference here is to Blondel's 1898 article "L'iilusion idéaliste," where he reiterated the claim from *L'Action* that in his analysis of the act, where knowledge and will are joined, the classical conflict between realist (the object is "real") and idealist (the subject is "real") philosophical positions is overcome. Both are "real" simultaneously and in conjunction. The implication was that Newman, by making the "idea" of a dogma its true reality, was taking the idealist position, thus allowing himself to escape, or avoid, the objective reality of dogmas as they actually and concretely exist. Blondel, anxious to avoid the charge of subjectivism in his own thought, saw subterfuge here, a sign of individualist resistance to submission.

literally, in a way that misconstrues his contrast of the "notional" and the "real" by turning him into a dogmatic anti-rationalist. But he was no such thing. In fact, said Blondel, for Newman the synthetic judgment of faith entails an intuitive grasp "of the whole" (as with Leibniz) in which the parts may be unintelligible at first, but which require the submission of the thinker to their assumed, if yet undefined, wholeness. The whole is prior to the parts, and it is out of that that we live and act. The "real" and the "notional" are thus bound together, not in a timeless unity, but rather in a historically evolving, ever-changing unity of definition. What we must do, therefore, is to work with a "conciliating life," where analytic and scientific elucidation is possible, and where "painful docility is justified with regard to love and faith," thereby being loyal to the light that was that of Newman.[13]

At the most fundamental level, what Blondel was assaulting in this riposte to Bremond (and Loisy) was the assumption that antitheses at the level of thought are merely covers, nothing but the reflection of contradictions deeper within a personality.[14] Bremond would struggle with this issue thus posed for the rest of his career in the way that he constructed his portraits, particularly in how he construed the interactions between experience and personality on the one hand, and an individual's reflective processes on the other. Is experience always prior to thought, or does thought sometimes shape and precipitate experience? When the time came to analyze the nature of mystical experience, or poetic inspiration, or spiritual experience in general, does conscious ratiocination matter? It is another form of the polarity of "rational" and "irrational" in human nature, where Blondel refused to let the former simply collapse into the latter at worst, or be graded much inferior at best, as in Henri Bergson's thought and a number of other movements with which Bremond would contend in late career. Blondel would unrelentingly, and to Bremond's great benefit, hit on him incessantly about this well into the future, because in fact a great deal was at stake.

An immediate implication, however, was evident in an essay that Bremond called "an introduction to Blondelian sainthood." The context was his recent personal visit to an Italian convent, where the life of Ste. Catherine de Ricci was celebrated.[15] By focusing on the inner life and the "religious psychology" of chosen individuals, Bremond had become increasingly interested in sanctity, and specifically "real" sanctity as over against the official or "notional" representations of that sanctity in more-or-less can-

---

13. Blondel to Bremond, December 15, 1905 (BB, II, 43–46).

14. Thus, Blondel insisted that Newman represented a "synthetic practice," but not a "synthetic view," i.e., despite contradictions in his thought, he was unified at the level of practical obedience. In a characteristic note, however, when the final Newman came out, Blondel praised it highly, admitting that when it came to psychological analysis he was out of his depth (Blondel to Bremond, January 19, 1906 [BB, II, 51–52]).

15. Bremond to Blondel, March 11, 1906 (BB, II, 63). The context here is a long letter detailing the storm of ecclesial criticism falling unjustly on Tyrrell. Bremond also bewailed, while admiring Teresa of Lisieux's History of a Soul, the "insipid abundance of pseudo-pious glosses" and "poetic baggage" currently being imposed on it. "La légende d'argent" first appeared November 1, 1904.

onized lives of the saints. The real forms are always hidden and obscure, Bremond contended, by contrast with posthumous cults that aggrandize and inflate in lugubrious ways. He had been discovering the *Lives* of the Desert Fathers, as well as the *History of a Soul* of Teresa of Lisieux, and he loved their simplicity captured in captivating texts. Becoming holy is a gritty daily business with all of its little, usually unseen, tasks and humiliations. When the "silver legend" (i.e., not the "Golden Legend" of hagiography) of a saint is told, it is the story of the most timid soul told by the least cultivated of pens.

All during 1906 the tension of ecclesiastical condemnation continued to mount. In due course both Loisy and Tyrrell would be excommunicated, while the Baron managed to steer clear. Blondel walked a tightrope. Though eliciting from the outset various levels of criticism from official theologians and periodically coming under review in Rome, he always had defenders in high places. But he would be engaged in a kind of churchly guerilla warfare for the rest of his long career. Bremond was just beginning to be treated with suspicion by ecclesiastical watchdogs, given his troubles with the Jesuits, his associations with and defense of Modernist figures, his liberal and Modernist interpretations of Newman, though there was not as yet, despite a muffled censure of *Psychologie de la foi*, any movement toward public condemnation of his work.[16] That would first come only in 1913 with *Sainte Chantal*.

The French Turn

His publication, then, in 1907, of *La Provence mystique au XVIIe siècle: Antoine Yvan et Madeleine Martin* marked not only his growing interest in the psychology of sanctity when it is captured in literature, but also—and just as important—a return to his roots. Though the process is obscure,[17] several steps were involved, the first being his steadily growing interest in the concreteness, often involving ethical dilemmas, of personal holiness.

In the 1900 review, already referred to, of Josephine Hope Ward's *One Poor Scruple*, there is the issue not only of a judgmental moralism, but also the question of sanctified character. As the central character, Madge Riversdale, member of a stiff, stodgy, provincial "old" recusant British Catholic family of Victorian times, must deal with the fact that they are a model of bourgeois piety, where there is "no natural sympathy for holiness, mysticism, or heroism" despite their fussy obedience to the Commandments. Her scrupulosity about marrying a divorced Protestant whose ex-wife is still living constrains her to wrestle with the question: Would it be an unpardonable sin to enter into such a union? Bremond, impressed by the realism of Ward's portrayals, noted that in the case of Madge, a "worldly frivolity" covers a base of "solid faith,"

---

16. But see ch. 4, n54, above.

17. Goichot's treatment here, under the rubric "De l'expérience chrétienne à la sainteté française" somewhat glosses the transition (EG, 48–50).

where religion protects her soul and requires her to struggle with difficult choices. This, said Bremond, is the "drama of holiness" intended by the Church in order to guide her soul to heaven. Messy as her life is, the ideal of the great saints draws Madge on, and she goes ahead with the marriage. She must live with the fact that "the moral life is not prideful and that, in a humbled love, the fear of hell is, more easily than one thinks, the neighbor of the love of God." The final lesson for Bremond here was the idea that souls given to God must endure darkness, fully conscious of personal imperfection and the painful ambiguities of faithful living, but that grace will work mysteriously in the process.[18]

In fact, Bremond was starting to move away from a fascination with English moralism as such—Puritan or Catholic—with a recognition of its limitations. George Eliot would always be for him a supreme example of great moral and ethical stature, clear proof that spiritual maturation moves in the direction of pure love, but she was, withal, a skeptic by the end. Now he was beginning to scan the horizon for lives marked by a sustained drive heavenward, so to speak, this drive being hidden in the confusions of real human struggles. Flawed humanity radiating transcendence was what Bremond wanted here, and what he believed he saw in Ward's novel.[19]

Blondel was moved by Bremond's review and gave it substantial attention with a critique that derived from *L'Action*.[20] In Madge Riversdale, he suggested, what we see is the way that ordinary moral struggles (what Bremond called the "prose" of her life, with all of its bourgeois scrupulosity) remain ordinary while simultaneously revealing their adherence to an ideal reality (the saintly "poetry"), thus raising the individual on occasion to heroic levels. But he also cautioned Bremond against separating Madge too completely from her mundane family. In assessing the spiritual status of individuals one must distinguish between what is simply narrow-minded and limited in people, usually because of group-thinking, and what is genuinely deformed and perverse. He contended that some Christians can simply be painfully obtuse in their thinking, be "narrow," without needing to be demonized by criticism. In other words, Blondel seemed to be saying, the pastoral challenge with such souls is one of drawing out that element in their moral conscience and moral decision-making that has the potential to take them beyond their limited horizons, to keep them moving, so to speak, forward and higher. This "Blondelian" way of thinking about sanctification as a process of letting the supernatural arise into the space which the natural makes for it

---

18. The two titles of the essay are revealing. First published as "Prose et poésie chez les catholiques d'après un roman anglais," then retitled as "L'idéal et la réalité dans la vie catholique" for inclusion in the first *L'Inquiétude religieuse* volume. Citations are ibid., 257, 278–79, 290–91.

19. Tyrrell also reviewed the novel in "Two Estimates of Catholic Life," originally in the *Month*, May 1899, noting the way Ward brought "largeness" into ordinary lives, where "the sublimity of mystic beauty" from the other world is allowed to shine through.

20. Blondel to Bremond, January 25, 1900 (BB, I, 266). This critique may have been the basis for the change of title that Bremond gave to the review when he collected it.

and for which the natural hungers, sank in with Bremond, ready to break out robustly in the years ahead.

A second piece fell into place about this same time, when Paul Thureau-Dangin (1837–1913), liberal Catholic and Republican, historian and member of the Académie, published the first volume of his *Histoire de la Renaissance catholique en Angleterre au XIXe siècle* in 1899. Bremond would have formulated the narrative differently, more in terms of "soul"-history, but the appearance of this work took the wind out of his sails. Following a hint given by Goichot, who had referenced a letter from Bremond to Wilfrid Ward just after Thureau-Dangin's volume appeared, Owen Chadwick speculates that Bremond now gave up any idea of analyzing the Oxford Movement as a kind of Anglican *Port-Royal*, i.e., as an archaizing movement of ecclesial reform.[21] He kept up producing sketches, primarily the series of works on Newman, but his inclination to a comprehensive treatment now waned, despite some continuing encouragement in this direction from the Baron.[22] What stands out in this process, moreover, is the idea that Bremond was even considering, with special encouragement from Maurice Barrès, a work in the spirit and tradition of the great Sainte-Beuve—whom we consider below—historian, literary critic and arch-example of the belles-lettres portraitist, known to him, and admired by him, ever since school days in Aix.[23]

And then a third piece. His interest in the history of French Catholic spirituality was steadily growing.[24] While he had been publishing review essays on aspects of French Catholic spirituality since 1899, the manifestations of this developing trend are in the second *L'Inquiétude religieuse* collection, published in 1909, where Bremond included essays on Pascal and Lamennais, the whole set being introduced by a reference to a famous passage in Joseph de Maistre's *Soirées*, where the writer asks himself, in the midst of a religious ceremony: Who is it here that *really* prays?

Perhaps there was a stimulus in the fact that he was doing his publishing through the firm of Edmond Bloud (liberal Catholic, Republican, died as a member of the

---

21. Chadwick, *Henri Bremond and Newman*, 172, following Goichot (EG, 46), citing Bremond's letter to Ward of July 23, 1899. The significance of this remark will become clear below in the extended treatment of Bremond's interpretation of Port-Royal.

22. In correspondence with the Baron, Bremond had talked at one point about "a great history of the religious sentiment in nineteenth-century England," Bremond to von Hügel, December 29, 1900, cited by Goichot (EG, 45).

23. Bremond to Blondel, January 15, 1900, "One would like to see a history of prayer, of the relations between God and souls, and of all of the manifestations of religious feelings [*sentiments*]. . . . One would now like to see a true savant undertaking this experimental study of the life of Christ in souls" (BB, I, 257–58).

24. Bremond tended, I think, to predate this development a bit, when in a letter to Loisy of April 7, 1916 (Bernard-Maître, *Lettres*, 178–79), just after the first volume of the *Histoire* had been published, he related that during his Jesuit training in England, he had first been exposed to "Nicole, Surin and the others [from the seventeenth century]," who spoke "a pleasant French," rather than in scholastic jargon. That may be true, but the impulse to serious study of these writers came only later with encouragement from Barrès (as pointed out by Bernard-Maître, ibid., 179–80n5, following Maurice Martin Du Gard).

Résistance in 1942). His Newman volumes sold well as part of a new series marketed by Bloud, "La Pensée chrétienne," an ambitious (already 20 titles!) effort to produce translations and re-editions of "classic" works in scripture studies, church history, liturgics, homiletics, and spiritual writings of all sorts. Bremond wrote a fifty-page conspectus and rationale for the series that was a comprehensive survey of religious writing in modern French history.[25] He took the view that there is a close correlation between ecclesiastical vitality and vibrant theological and spiritual writing in a wide range of modes—nonfiction and scholarly, fiction old and new, creative poetry, and a host of others. The renewal of Catholicism in post-Napoleonic France was ably assisted, he argued, by monumental publishing ventures, including the vast *Patrologiae* of J.-P. Migne, the many sketches by C. A. Sainte-Beuve, and the grandiose educational ventures of Lamennais, his disciple bishop Philippe-Olympe Gerbet (1798–1864), and the historian Charles Forbes René de Montalambert (1810–1870), summed up in their 1835 plan for a "Université catholique." Bremond's interest in Gerbet thus sparked, he would go on to author two works on this erudite priest-savant, thereby, and by implication, setting out his own vision of a humanistic-ecclesial French literary culture of the future.

Finally, in the shift of Bremond's interest to the history and character of French spirituality, there was for him a return to the soil, at the center of which was his relationship with Maurice Barrès, and, in a degree, to Charles Maurras once again.

Barrès/Maurras

Up until, and during, the First World War, the now unknown novels of Maurice Barrès (1862–1923) were immensely popular. He played an active part in parliamentary politics for most of his life, and was elected to the Académie française in 1906. His literary productions are often characterized with the label "romantic nationalism." Bremond read them all as they came out and was enchanted, after, as mentioned, Charles Maurras had first made him aware of Barrès's work.

He and Barrès actually met under highly fortuitous, but significant, circumstances. Martin Du Gard told the story.[26] In January 1900, Bremond was asked to fill in for a colleague who had been scheduled to give a series of Lenten addresses at the Catholic cathedral in Athens. After delivering his talks in the form of reflections on the influence of Hellenic thought on the development of Christian dogma, he ended up spending several months in Greece. At the time, as he confessed to Blondel, he was in the midst of his intellectual wrestling with the problem of "aristocratic art," an issue that bedeviled his episodic correspondence with Maurras. Evoking an inner struggle, he drew a contrast, he told Blondel, between "aristocratic" art and another kind, which

---

25. *La littérature religieuse d'avant-hier et d'Aujourd'hui: À propos de la nouvelle collection "La Pensée chrétienne."*

26. MG, ch. 2.

he associated with several writers whom he liked, marked by "a common tendency [which is] more social, less egoist, less refined." He spoke of a kind of "humanist tendency [the aristocratic kind] which has often triumphed, but to which I have never yielded without remorse," even while he was ascending to the heights with George Eliot.[27] Admitting to Blondel that he might be "shocking the Greek part of his soul," he opined that aristocratic art owed more to Virgil than to Jesus Christ. He confessed that he was leaving for Athens with "barbarian ideas" tossing and turning inside his conflicted head.

As it turned out, Maurice Barrès was traveling in Greece at the same time, and so they met, talked, shared the sights, and became friends. Actually, according to Martin Du Gard, both men, "these urchins in front of Phidias," when they viewed the Parthenon, were less than enamored—a fact that disturbed Maurras in his later reflections,[28] and that Martin Du Gard read as an anticipation of Bremond's later root-and-branch rejection of the "idolatry of order and reason" and the "pagan Catholicism" that for Maurras would end up in fascism.[29] Nothing more dangerous than the love of an abstraction, thought Martin Du Gard when he wrote the remembrance in 1927, supernatural charity always being the love of the concrete and the particular. But that was retrospect, the matter being not yet so clear in 1900.

Bremond's memorial to their meeting was *Le charme d'Athènes*, dedicated to Barrès, written as a meditation on the experience of encountering the Acropolis, that supreme representative of the classical world.[30] Contrary to his expectations, Bremond says, he found the aesthetics of the Greek ruin strangely confusing and off-putting (the fact that it was covered with scaffolding did not help), debased by time and destruction, and he could not resist an unfavorable comparison with the grandeur of Notre Dame in Paris.[31] In fact, feeling that the people and countryside of Greece were more "charming" than the ancient ruins, he devoted most of his narrative to an elaborate contrast of the classical temple with the Christian church of Daphné, the "delightful" old Cathedral constructed by French Carthusians in the thirteenth century, on the road between Athens and Eleusis.

What thus entranced Bremond was the simultaneous awareness of the Christian and French adaptation of the classical forms, on the one hand, and their strange

27. Bremond to Blondel, February 13, 1900 (BB, I, 271).

28. Noted by Blanchet (VB, 118).

29. MG, 24–25.

30. First published in 1905 as a booklet, then reissued in 1925 by Jean and André Bremond, with additional essays. Citations are from this latter edition. One should also include here, moreover, the memorial tribute that Bremond wrote for Barrès, "Maurice Barrès," in late 1923. Recalling the circumstances of their meeting, and celebrating the excellence of Barrès's art, Bremond hailed him as "the best kind of romantic, a man of 'prudent realism' in politics, and as a philosopher an heir of Pascal" ("Maurice Barrès," 990). In religion, says Bremond, Barrès, while not adhering to Catholic dogma, attempted to unify church and country spiritually.

31. Bremond, *Le charme d'Athènes*, 17. He includes a comparison with Hagia Sophia, as well, where Byzantine Christianity has transformed the classical aesthetics.

allure, on the other. Recalling Charles Maurras, that "most fervent of the lovers of pagan Greece," he acknowledged in the "scornful silence" and classical harmonies (the "proportions") of the Parthenon a seductive "force grave and all-powerful," a maternal embrace. But this is a mother, lovable as she is (Bremond cites Augustine's "late have I loved you"), who can never comprehend Pascal and the *Mystère de Jésus*.[32] Now, however, that Jerusalem has converted Athens, it is "the true house of every Frenchman who comes this way!"[33] The message is clear: Maurras with all of his Greco-Roman classicism, i.e., rationalism, and Renan and others as well, are put in their inferior place, and French humanistic Catholicism, here assimilated to the "romantic nationalism" of Barrès, is affirmed.

In a memoir that Barrès composed the month before his death, he testified to the deep meaning that this Athens encounter with Bremond still held for him. Consistent with his regionalist nativism, he had contended all along that ancient Greek culture remained a closed book to him, just as all cultures must be for persons not born into their blood and soil. "Barrès had vomited out the Greece of professors, and he was not tempted to forge a Barrésian Greece," said Blanchet.[34] The upshot was clear in Barrès's novels, like *Les déracinés*, that portray the spiritual struggles of young men and women who are seduced away from their roots by philosophical systems with universal pretensions, that stimulate their adherents to become alienated from their roots, thus making them "false" and "untrue" to themselves. Much better, much more satisfying it is, argued Barrès, to return to the springs where we were born, to accept our natural culture with all of its limits, but also with all of its idiosyncratic greatness.

Bremond would argue that Barrès was not being narrow here, or merely provincial, that there is in fact a dialectic in the work of the latter, in which the attraction of the particular and the pull of the universal constitute a creative tension that is spiritually rich. Thus it is that even in *Le charme d'Athènes* Bremond was careful to avoid total dismissal of the Hellenic heritage, alien though it be, because in fact it has its own "charm," and he concluded that essay with a lyrical hymn of praise to the profound beauty of Athens and the Acropolis, at the same time that its resistance to Christ evoked a profound melancholy, an anguish with a "lesson of infinite price."[35] What Maurras wants, and finally Barrès as well, has deep appeal, but an appeal fraught with peril. The concern with race purity, the xenophobia, the anti-Semitism, of nativist tendencies, lay close by.

Indeed, studies of the regressive forces at work in French culture after 1870, particularly those that focus on the precursors, dynamics and after-effects of the Dreyfus

---

32. Ibid., 41–43. He judges that there is in the Parthenon "something very feminine and proud in this queenly attitude that seems to wait coldly for human homage" (ibid., 34).

33. Ibid., 46.

34. VB, 125, with reference. The Barrès-Bremond correspondence still remains, unpublished, in private files.

35. Bremond, *Le charme d'Athènes*, 48.

Affair, tend to lump Barrès and Maurras together as demonic twins.[36] But Bremond saw things differently, recognizing early on that Maurras hated the close friendship that had developed between himself and Barrès, and that Maurras was enraged by Bremond's essay on Athens.[37] A major difference between Maurras and Barrès was that the latter sincerely affirmed a kind of Catholicism that moved him closer to Bremond, a Catholicism of old churches and regional pieties and observances and colorful local characters, i.e., folk-religion ("home and hearth" culture) in all of its indigenous and unself-conscious vigor, while Maurras, by contrast, eventually affirmed, without actually believing, a politically useful Catholicism of papal authority and militant discipline and order. The first version of religion is romantic, while the second is doctrinaire, ideological and legalistic. Aside from friendship itself—something always precious to Bremond—we can see why he was eager to affirm an attractive side in Barrès, where love of the *patrie* ennobles and exalts, but not necessarily in exclusivistic terms.

French national pride had become intense, militant, prickly, almost obsessive, during the decades of the 1880s and 1890s, as traumatic disasters and humiliating scandals followed in a seemingly unending succession. There was the collapse of the Union Générale banking and investment scheme in 1882 (managed by Catholics, but blamed falsely on Jews, thus giving rise to a virulently anti-Semitic literature); the chaotic implosion in utter bathos of the Boulangist political movement in 1889; the financial incompetence associated with DeLesseps and Eiffel in 1893; the disgrace of the church and the army in the Dreyfus Affair that began in 1894, leading to disputes that separated France and, seemingly, every French family into Dreyfusards and anti-Dreyfusards; the Fashoda incident of 1898, in which the French government, in a way that seemed weak to an enraged public, compromised with Britain over territorial claims in east Africa, and so on.[38]

The list continues through the run-up to WWI, especially as military forces began mobilizing, there were more confrontations, alliances began to form, an arms race accelerated, and nationalistic fervor took over with "war fever" in the air and

---

36. At least that is the tendency of the latest treatment by Frederick Brown (biographer of Émile Zola), *Embrace of Unreason*, as well as in the concluding section of *For the Soul of France*.

37. Blanchet, VB, 127–57, working from unedited correspondence, carefully traces out the Bremond-Barrès interaction, noting similarities in, but also contrasts with, the parallel correspondence with Maurras. Barrès, while sharing the energy for national revival, was completely resistant to Maurras's monarchism, but, as Blanchet mentions, he also failed to recognize how "wide and extensive" Bremond's sympathy actually was. When it comes to religion, "their friendship creaks (*grincait*) along" (ibid., 143).

38. I take most of my list from Brown, *For the Soul of France*. Bremond had no illusions about the situation. In an 1899 review ("Les étonnements d'un Anglais en France") of a two-volume work by an Englishman who had surveyed contemporary French life, Bremond admitted that the country in its public and political life was a shambles, that the ideals of "liberty, equality, and fraternity" had become in significant ways a travesty. The redeeming feature, à la Barrès, was the solidity and decency of the French peasant family, always faithful, devout, and patriotic in the best sense!

everyone's national pride feeling insulted. Although Bremond had been insulated from much of this during his years of Jesuit training, from the time that he was at *Études* the angry turmoil was obvious, especially its ecclesiastical ramifications. The 1905 Law of Separation was, among other things, punishment of the church by the Republic for siding with the monarchist and anti-Dreyfusard right during the Affair. Bremond thus found himself caught in a bind, where modernizing trends easily produce a fierce sense of identity—ethnic, racial and religious—along with a surge in populist "pride." Would French nationalism be ultimately good or bad spiritually? Are particularisms inherently divisive?

Martin Du Gard has described the extent to which Bremond and Barrès not only became, but remained, good friends for the rest of Barrès's life.[39] They shared an interest in the educational formation of children, and of family life, especially the role of the mother in cultivating a sensitivity for what is beautiful. Both were concerned with the "natural child" and his tastes and receptivities. Bremond was also eager to support Barrès's work, often reading, critiquing and editing his proofs, so that he referred to himself as "the servant who trims Racine's lamp." After WWI, when Bremond was living in Pau, Barrès would visit from time to time, where they enjoyed long walks and literary conversation. Martin Du Gard visited them there, conducting interviews. "For myself," said Martin Du Gard, "I do not know anything more moving than the spectacle they present of a perfect happiness of head and heart."[40]

The question of their degree of spiritual concord remains open, if only because intense friendship for Bremond could obscure, as with Loisy as well, underlying philosophical tensions. Blanchet argued that in setting themselves over against Maurras's kind of "abstract" monarchist nationalism, Republicans and nationalists had nothing to offer but their romantic patriotism.[41] In religion, it is clear that Bremond was the giver, for he introduced Barrès to the world of Catholic literature and spiritual thought, especially Pascal, over whom Barrès especially enthused. When he had thoroughly enjoyed the first collection of *L'Inquiétude religieuse*, especially Bremond's use in the headings of the famous citation from St. Ambrose, "God was not pleased to use dialectic in saving his people," Barrès offered a gift in return. In an epochal moment for Bremond's career, he spoke the magic words: "Go ahead and be a Christian Sainte-Beuve." Blanchet carefully drew the conclusion: "Let us not say that it is an accomplished fact, that Bremond owes to Barrès the idea of an *Histoire du sentiment religieux*. But Barrès was without doubt the first who, once the project was announced, encouraged

---

39. MG, ch. 6: "The Education of a Son—Barrès and Bremond. Under the Sky at Pau."

40. MC, I, 308–11, for a description of his visit with the two men at Pau in March 1923. Barrès testified that Bremond had "opened heaven to him" with "the sentiment, the nostalgia for the divine," precisely by introducing him in depth to various holy individuals. He indicated that Bremond was his "literary director." He seems also (at least in Martin Du Gard's representations) to have baited Bremond, who carefully avoided this, with his right-wing political activities.

41. VB, 136.

Bremond to persist in it. And it was an immense 'Christian library' that Bremond ended up putting at the disposition of the 'unquiet' in the Barrèsian manner."[42]

Indeed, it was precisely in the use of this term "inquietude," disquiet, that a special kind of bond between Bremond and Barrès subsisted, as they both affirmed this element of spiritual restlessness, a feeling after something elusive, but immensely attractive, in their shared passions. Barrès found himself intensely interested in French individuals, specifically those from Lorraine, who were saints, and Bremond found himself more and more drawn to saintly individuals who were French. Thus, the two disquieted seekers found common ground.[43]

In the religious realm they shared an interest in Pascal and Lammenais, both of whom would receive multiple essays on interpretation, early and late, from Bremond. In the case of Félicité de Lamennais (1782–1854), brilliant ecclesiastical reformer, educator, thinker, and ultimately disillusioned papalist, Bremond saw the truly creative figure in nineteenth century French Catholicism. In a 1909 essay he asked about a possibly "mystical" dimension in Lammenais's development. Could he be seen as one born with a mystical bent, one for whom the duty and effort of prayer is one of the "dry forms of sacrifice"? Suffering acute spiritual distress early on in his career, Lamennais wrote eloquently about his difficulties, so that, while not being a true mystic, he could at least make an approach to such experience by means of his artistic consciousness. Commenting on Lammenais's agony on the eve of his ordination, Bremond said of him that "even if he cannot participate in this [mystical] life directly in every way, he will live it at least by celebrating it in his writings, and the same pen that has cursed the day when it is consummated for him in the supreme sacrifice, will also depict the emotions of the new priest and the joyous liberty of a blessed servanthood." The mystic and the writer are intertwined in one personality.[44] Thus Lamennais experienced the distress of not arriving, while knowing with certainty that the place of arrival indeed exists, and can, to some degree, be embraced vicariously through artful representation. The description of Lamennais sounds again like George Eliot, but applied, Bremond seemed to say, to Barrès as well.

In 1908 Bremond published a large assessment of Barrès's work, along with a selection of illustrative excerpts from the novels. He made a strenuous effort to show that there is more to Barrès than just the passing glitter of a regional writer, that his fixation on his native Lorraine (as in *Un homme libre*, 1889) functions as the kind of symbol in which a romantic writer seeks the heavens. This symbol is a gateway to the

---

42. VB, 141.

43. Blondel disapproved of all of this, having little sympathy for French nationalism, but Bremond, after just publishing a short article supportive of Barrès, tried to reassure him as, for example, in Bremond to Blondel, August 30, 1900 (BB, I, 319): "Barrès . . . is captivating . . . he has not the first suspicion of the moral life [but] the man is better than his books." And so on. Blondel slammed him pretty hard a bit later by contending that there is more "aesthete" than "ascete" in Barrès ("Blondel to Bremond, July 5, 1902" [BB, I, 429]).

44. Bremond, "La détresse de Lamennais," 59, 61.

universal, rather than the mere sign of the classic writer for whom his native nook is world enough. He claimed that Barrès, in writing about his beloved country and its customs, is a true romantic "in spite of himself," transcending the particularities of place and time. Barrès's chosen instrument for displaying that transcendence is the tortured individual, whose solitary existence is actually a solidarity with all persons. Barrès's "cult of the self" (from the title of his first trilogy), though seemingly egotistical, is, therefore, deceptive. In fact, as Barrès's notion of "barbarians" (from *Sous l'oeil des barbares*, 1888) showed, the philistines are those who would seduce the natural self, the true self, of the rooted individual away from his native ground by means of their sophistic "systems." The central issue in Barrès's early novels is that of understanding how it is that the true self emerges when one docilely accepts one's proper limits—a point, Bremond claimed, where Barrès thought that "the master axiom, religion or a human prince . . . will show the footpath whereby his destiny will be achieved."[45]

In the tradition of the historian Hippolyte Taine, who thought that the contingencies of race, climate, place (the "milieu") of historical events explain their true nature, Barrès went on to show in a variety of characters how "the inherited sentimental garden of the parents" constantly beckons the drifting individual back to home, but only after, and in the midst of, the hurly-burly of artistic and intellectual life, where "exasperated individualism" finally accepts the fact that it cannot think its way through to salvation. The problem for Barrès in all of this, Bremond thought, is that he could not break free from analyzing analysis, that is, could not free himself from the philosophical habit of analyzing his own frustration, thus becoming more frustrated. Where he seemed to end up was in the "cult of the hero," where frenzied egotism gives way to the "magnificent discipline," where "the necessary hierarchies" and "the principle of order" come to be respected. "Napoleon symbolizes," noted Bremond, "in the thought of Barrès, that class of hero toward whom an irresistible force entrains us and that our instinct imposes on us."[46] But—an essential qualification by Bremond—this "hero" is only a temporary embodiment of the ideal, in which "national learning" can gush forth as a religious impulse, which, by implication, can lead to Christian dogma.

Bremond was, in effect, testing Blondel's theory of "immanence" by homing in on a particular kind of desiring and action that do not understand their own inherent metaphysical horizons, thus are doomed to fail, without the addition of supernatural grace. Barrès became a test case, in order to see where the dialectic leads over time. In a telling passage, Bremond described Barrès's vision of the ecstasy-followed-by-depression dilemma of the modern individual in this way: "Forgetful of self, he revolts consciously against his limits, he is carried violently towards the external world, in a burst of enthusiasm and of conquest; then, soon, turned to an ironic smile and deceived by an inner watchman who never sleeps, he becomes discouraged with himself

---

45. Bremond, *Maurice Barrès*, xx.

46. Ibid., xlii. We can, therefore, see Barrès finally moving in the direction, though not all the way, to Maurras. He wanted a Republican, not a monarchist, redeemer.

and takes bitter pleasure in contemplating his powerlessness; finally, pulling himself together, he accepts the mediocrity of all that is human and resigns himself to bearing an unhealable misery."[47]

The "religious problem" in Barrès is then resolved when the artist gazes at the Christ in Leonardo's *Last Supper* and sees the message: all can be accepted, because all is forgiven. Humility is learned, action is enjoined, and we have the basis for a Catholic apologetic, thought Bremond. He argued that Barrès had embraced, at least by implication, "the poetic aesthetic" of Catholicism, with its ethereal beauty and solemn rites, had begun to love the old saints, though he had not yet come to believe as they believed. The "disquietude of the soul" leads the individual step-by-step to God. Barrès has shown that classical discipline and freedom in Christ (i.e., romantic independence of spirit) can be integrated under the guidance of the Church, so that dogma functions as a stimulant, not a barrier or straitjacket. Differently stated, it is Barrès's self-transcending romanticism, that which makes Lorraine a symbol, a way-station and not a stopping-place, that redeems his nativism—or so, at least Bremond thought![48]

Indeed, this exhaustive essay and tribute to his friend served for Bremond several purposes: to distinguish himself and Barrès from Maurras's kind of nationalism (they are "romantic," while he is "classical"), to further refine his own field of endeavor (French spirituality), and to experiment with the kind of apologetic he was learning from Blondel (as he read literature through a theological lens). Increasingly, the challenge was to see how the traditional literature of French Catholic spirituality with all of its inwardness could be made appealing and meaningful for a secular, but aesthetically sophisticated, society (as represented by Barrès). With encouragement from the very Barrès whom he hoped to nurture with his efforts, he saw that the time was ripe for a Christian Sainte-Beuve.

Gerbet

Bremond, flowingly productive in these years just after leaving the Order, moving in the direction of more and more concentration on French spirituality, generated study after study. Just after the essay on the two Aixois saints, Antoine Yvan and Madeleine Martin, came a major composition on the nineteenth-century scholarly bishop—already alluded to in the promotion that he wrote for his publisher Bloud—Philippe-Olympe Gerbet, close follower of Lammenais and consolidator of his heritage. And

---

47. Ibid., lvii.

48. As mentioned, Blondel came down hard on all of this, as in Blondel to Bremond, February 26, 1908 (BB, II, 123). He saw in Barrès only an exaltation of the "free man" in aesthetic terms, the very kind of undisciplined and anarchistic, uncommitted character, who settles for lesser gods, he had so strongly criticized in *L'Action*.

not by accident did it appear in the same year, 1907, as the anti-Modernist papal decrees. Bremond knew how to provoke, even if he did it quite indirectly.

Before his death, Gerbet, bishop of Perpignan, had produced the pastoral direction, *Sur diverses erreurs du temps présent*, which would serve as a major source for Pius IX's 1864 anti-liberal *Syllabus*. Many remembered him thus as a traditionalist. But in a way that marked him as a true follower of Lammenais he was convinced that the best way to fight error is with progressive, humanistically conceived educational methods. His principal work, *L'Université catholique*, came off, in fact, as a kind of French equivalent to Newman's *Idea of a University*, a vastly conceived program for renewed Catholic spirituality by means of a renewed non-scholastic pedagogy at the university level. The liberal nature of Gerbet's vision made him interesting and attractive to Bremond, just as the church of his own time seemed to be turning back the clock. The underlying message in *Gerbet* is that it is a good thing to love Catholic tradition, but only if such love is intelligent; respecting the past does not entail disrespect, or fear, directed at modernity.[49] By reminding his readers of the nature of the nineteenth-century French Catholic theological revival, as it existed before the First Vatican Council and the rise of anti-modernism, Bremond showed them another and better way.[50]

After a review of Gerbet's career and his status as the true follower of Lamennais, Bremond underlined the manner in which he made himself the prime expounder of the movement's intellectual heritage, creating an alliance between faith and science, charity and industry, power and liberty, in which Catholic philosophy could take history seriously.[51] Indeed, Gerbet had argued in a quite remarkable *Essai d'un système de philosophie catholique* (1832) that Christianity gathers together all of the wisdom of the world religions for the purpose of educating all people, since it is "the immanent source of the perfecting of humanity."[52] Church history should be taught as the gradual accumulation of wisdom from many spiritual and cultural sources, so that in this latest period it is the humanistic sciences, with their historical and social frameworks of meaning, that constitute "common sense."[53] The great Oratorian Cartesian,

49. The main study is *Gerbet. Introduction*, but as illustrations of the spiritual and aesthetic qualities of Gerbet's composition, Bremond published, with introduction, a separate edition in 1908 of two chapters of the *Université catholique* in *Gerbet: Dernières conférences d'Albéric d'Assise*. In the introduction of the latter, he referred both to Sainte-Beuve's rapturous descriptions of Gerbet's work and to Lamartine's description of him as the "Christian Plato" (Bremond, *Gerbet: Dernières conférences*, 4).

50. The tradition here ran from De Maistre and Louis de Bonald through Lamennais and Gerbet to Louis Bautain, sometimes called the "French Newman," and then, methodologically, on to Blondel, according to McCool, *Catholic Theology in the Nineteenth Century*, ch. 2, "French Traditionalism." Platonic rather than Aristotelian in inspiration, as well as Gallican in Church-state relations, it would end, for the most part, with the First Vatican Council and the subsequent dominance of Thomist thought.

51. *Gerbet. Introduction*, 38–40.

52. Ibid., 54–55.

53. Traditional French Cartesianism, as theologians had embraced it, was at work here in the

Nicolas Malebranche, with his concept of the "vision in God," was held up as a special example of progressive thinking. Theology, said Gerbet at his special school at Juilly, is the basis of all social progress, and that is why Christian nations have surpassed all others in science. Theological development and intellectual development of all kinds go hand-in-hand.[54]

In the first part of *L'Université catholique*, the "Discours préliminaire," Gerbet laid out a whole course in the liberal arts, organizing its structure around a concept of "natural rhythm," in which "the universe, in its ensemble, presents itself as a dwelling-place, as the palace of man and the temple of God," a palace whose beauty and architecture of nature are cathedral-like.[55] The mathematical science of infinities came into play here as well, leading to Christian metaphysics as the pinnacle of the curriculum. All study is a preparation for holiness, for the love of God, since the contemplation of earthly realities should lead by degrees to the contemplation of heavenly ones. Higher learning must be deeply respectful of the secular sciences, while claiming to synthesize them at a higher, theological level. It is Blondel before Blondel. In Richard Niebuhr's typology, it is not "Christ against Culture," but "Christ the transformer of Culture." F. D. Maurice was doing something similar in England just a little later.

Against Sainte-Beuve, Bremond contended that for Gerbet this vision is not rationalist, since "his religious philosophy is a prayer," and Gerbet came across as an artist of prayer with his delightful use of images in the manner of painters and poets. He wanted to use images in such a way as to systematize, to unify thought into a totality, so that reason tries to grasp "an essence of Christianity" within all of the fragmentation and partiality.[56]

Problems began both for Lamennais and Gerbet in the implication that this "common sense" could be a sufficient basis for discerning what is theologically true and what not. The result easily became a kind of history-of-religions approach to faith-traditions in which Christianity would be the logical climax of all spiritual striving. Resistance to that conclusion could, then, be viewed as culpable by forgetting the fact, said Bremond, that in the final analysis the emergence of faith must be supernaturally inspired. Any distinction between the "order of faith" in believing, and the "order of concepts" in dogma, where the latter are "symbols" of the former, would be judged unacceptable (since the resultant concepts *are* the reality). Such thinking anticipated the complexities of the Modernist controversy fifty years later, because it allowed Gerbet to be simultaneously progressive and traditionalist, especially when

---

concept of the "common sense" (a derivative of Descartes's "clear and distinct ideas") that prevails across human cultures, superior to individual intuition and ultimately leading to truth. Alec Vidler sums up this stance: "Since the nature of God and the nature of man are constant, and do not vary from place to place or from time to time, and religion is the expression of the relations between them, there can be only one true religion in the nature of things" (Vidler, *Prophecy and Papacy*, 88).

54. Gerbet. *Introduction*, 72–75.
55. Ibid., 86.
56. Ibid., 173–81.

official pressure was applied. Nonetheless, thought Bremond, he was ahead of his time and an inspiration! Bremond was well aware of the Cartesianism in Gerbet's Gallican theology, where concepts are all-important, and the path to skepticism is laid open (Newman's temptation!).[57]

It is important, however, for Bremond's increasing focus on the poetic nature of spiritual striving, that he showed how Gerbet tried to get around the problem of a "natural" theology. The relationship between religious beliefs and scientific can be explicated, Gerbet thought, by means of an analysis of the nature and function of language in forming concepts. Language by virtue of its social nature bonds human intelligence to universal ideas, thereby serving as the common factor of both religion and science by expressing the zone of overlap between the two. As the bearer of heritage, tradition, and authority, the concepts generated by language are then the individualized breeding ground for disbelief, as well as the means for coming to faith when these individual perceptions and doubts are overridden by the social principle. Catholicism is grounded in the forms of community life and traditions, which are then communicated to the individual in the form of "speech-symbols," "metaphors," and "emblems." The "metaphorical structures" of dogma, socially comprehended and transmitted, historically conditioned in outward forms, enlighten individual lives. The "order of faith," thus socially constituted, has priority, the "order of concepts" being only the individual appropriation in the form of intellectual grasp. Religion and society are not separate spheres. It is the skeptical side of Alfred Loisy ahead of his time, the conviction that religion is an ideal construct, a social product captured in ever-changing conceptual expressions. Gerbet died on August 7, 1864.

The Crisis with Tyrrell

And now Bremond had one more agonized struggle before the English "desert" was definitively passed, but with permanent aftereffects. The context was Tyrrell's death and Bremond's ministrations to his friend at the end.[58]

By early 1909, it was clear that Tyrrell, after a stormy time, was not doing well. Subsequent to a running battle with church authorities, on February 1, 1906, he had been expelled from the Jesuits and declared *suspens a divinis*, that is, forbidden to administer sacraments, though he could be admitted to Holy Communion. Since no bishop was willing to take him under wing, the suspension did not simply "secularize" Tyrrell (as in Bremond's departure from the Jesuits), it stripped him of priestly

---

57. I summarize here ibid., 185–200, 270–88. The material is as dense and compacted as anything Bremond wrote, until he came to *Histoire*, VII and VIII.

58. Bibliography is large and complex. The principal foundational accounts are those of Alfred Loisy, esp. GT, 13–29, Martin Du Gard, MG, 62–70, and Maude Petre in her 1912 *Autobiography and Life of George Tyrrell*. Blanchet provides a list of sources and comprehensive treatments in BB, II, 143n1. E. Goichot expands that list in "En marge de la crise," 125–26n3, and then provides important unedited source material in "Sur 'L'affaire Tyrrell.'"

prerogatives. Then on October 22, 1907, as a punishment for his published criticisms of the Anti-Modernist decrees, he was "excommunicated," the exact implications and ramifications of this act being ambiguous.

Cut free from all Church financial support after leaving the Jesuits, Tyrrell had bounced around,[59] then stayed for periods of time with a small Premonstratensian community—a French monastic congregation in exile—at Storrington, Sussex, where the prior, P. Xavier de Fourvière, was also the village curé. He then lived in a cottage built for him on the grounds of Maude Petre's nearby home, Mulberry House. Petre had herself left her Order, under ecclesiastical censure, in 1907. There, on July 6–7, 1909, Tyrrell experienced a disabling left-side paralysis, diagnosed the next day to be a result of the acute nephritic condition known as Bright's disease. He quickly lapsed into alternating states of semi-consciousness and unconsciousness. On July 9, Petre sent a telegram to the Baron, who arrived the next day. They sent for a diocesan priest, Fr. Dessoulavy, who, struggling to understood Tyrrell's communications and confession, nonetheless gave *conditional* absolution.[60] It seems that "technically," in his excommunicate state, Tyrrell could receive full absolution only from the Pope himself. By conferring the "conditional" absolution, the confessor thought to avoid any kind of official censure. Likewise, when Tyrrell's friends were to request a Catholic funeral for him, they would be refused on the grounds of his excommunicate status.

Then, after some ups and downs in Tyrrell's condition, Petre asked the prior of Storrington to administer Extreme Unction, which he did, although Tyrrell seemed unconscious, thereby making the giving of the viaticum impossible. Loisy in his account was very defensive about all of this, insisting that at this point the prior did not treat Tyrrell as excommunicate, and that a priest of the diocese of Southwark, within which Storrington was located, had sacramentally cared for him prior to any ministrations from Bremond. In response to another telegram from Petre, Bremond arrived on July 12. The three friends—Petre, the Baron, and Bremond—were all convinced of Tyrrell's ultimate loyalty to the church and the faith, and thus of his eternal destiny. During a lucid spell for Tyrrell, Bremond read prayers and gave absolution *in extremis*. Tyrrell died on July 15. Petre and the Baron, in order to forestall some gathering criticism, quickly published a letter attesting to Tyrrell's wish for the sacraments, his full penitence for sins, but also his refusal to publish a retraction of what he had written in all sincerity because he regarded it as the truth.

---

59. After leaving the Order, he had convalesced with Bremond for a spell at Freibourg-am-Breisgau, from which Bremond vigorously defended him in print. Thus it is that Loisy, quoting a famous saying from his successor at the École normale, Jean Baruzi (originally in *Problèmes d'histoire des religions* [Paris, 1933]), would refer to Bremond as having not really been a true Modernist, but instead "the Red Cross worker, the burier of the dead and the stretcher-bearer for the wounded of the movement." It is noteworthy that Blondel himself, as early as his letter to Bremond of April 18, 1906 (BB, II, 72), had described Bremond's vocation as that of "caring maternally for the wounded."

60. Charles L. Dessoulavy (1875–1944) would be stripped of his teaching position at the Southwark seminary by Mgr Amigo, bishop of Southwark, as a result. See Vidler, *Variety*, 175.

Questions immediately arose thus about the integrity of Tyrrell's repentance, and there were various documents that verified Tyrrell's position of defiance regarding retractions. The bishop of Southwark, Peter Emmanuel Amigo, therefore, refused to give permission for a Catholic funeral, although he indicated that, with a written testimonial as to Tyrrell's repentance from one of the ministering priests, including Bremond, he would relent. Complicated negotiations then ensued, related in detail by Loisy, about all of this, but the upshot was that Bremond decided, supported by Petre, that there was ample precedent for a priest to say certain prayers over the deceased, when that individual's ecclesiastical status was unclear. And that is what happened. The prior of Storrington concurring, Bremond read prayers and spoke, unvested, at Tyrrell's burial in the Anglican cemetery, in a gravesite purchased by Petre and a relative of Tyrrell's. Loisy called Bremond's action "un geste magnifique," "the action of a good man, a Christian, a Catholic, a priest"—which indeed it was.

Bremond thus paid tribute to a friend whom he pictured as sharing the life of John Keble on the one side, and the Catholic Church on the other. He thanked everyone present for their faithfulness to Tyrrell, and recalled Newman's similar journey. Tyrrell had, he said, believed in the Church as the "social organization of the Christian idea" (perhaps the phrase resonated with Bremond from his recent study of Gerbet), and in the dogma of the communion of saints. "We know," said Bremond, "that, for him, the Roman Catholic Church, as a fact, stood for the oldest and the widest body of corporate Christian experience, for the closest approximation, so far attained, to the still far distant ideal of a Catholic Church." He said farewell to Tyrrell, noting that "as for our personal loss, it is beyond words. He was the one to whom we turned in all of our anxieties."[61]

Three days later, Mgr Amigo telegraphed the prior of Storrington: "Do not allow Bremond to say mass." The decision was immediately confirmed in Rome by cardinal Merry del Val. Only the Pope had veto power. Bremond was in up to his neck. Having crossed the English Channel once more in a good cause, the anti-Modernist flood had swamped his boat.

The pain of this experience would dog Bremond for the rest of his days, as he would always live under a perpetual ecclesiastical shadow, the most heartbreaking episode of which would be the condemnation of his *Sainte Chantal*. Immediate consequences, as we shall see, were brief, but the long-term ones were more serious. His greatest comfort was the man who signaled a major step forward in his inner life, that exponent of the French-humanist spirituality of "pure love," François Fénelon.

---

61. Text of the address reprinted by Guinan, "Portrait of a Devout Humanist," from vol. 2 of Petre, *Autobiography*. See also Martin Du Gard, who described Bremond's "admirable allocution" as "words of irreproachable discretion, exquisite words of invincible sweetness, all inspired by the sympathy that only religious friendship can give" (MG, 64).

7

Pure Love

MAYBE THERE WAS SOMETHING about the way that George Tyrrell and Maude Petre cared for one another as spiritual support that struck Bremond. There is absolutely no clear indication of such a thing, but we might recall that Maude had at one juncture come to Bremond as a penitent, and she had been one of his supporters in the days right after his departure from the Jesuits. It is noteworthy as well that over the next several years, as he built to the beginning of his magnum opus, his two most important books would involve male-female spiritual companionships, namely those between François Fénelon and Jeanne Guyon, and Francis de Sales and Jeanne de Chantal.

Aftermath

In any case, following the Tyrrell incident, the first imperative was damage control. Bremond had to run an ecclesiastical gauntlet, although nothing was so intimidating as having to deal with Blondel, who, unsympathetic with what he saw as simplistic overstatement on both sides of the controversy, felt that the Church's anti-Modernist decrees simply did not apply to him.

Indeed, Blondel was convinced that he was innocent of the core accusation contained in the decrees—that the heterodox Modernists try to draw the supernatural out of the natural.[1] But the situation was galling. On the one hand, he shared with Bremond real indignation at the establishment of the "committees of vigilance" now mandated as watchdogs in every diocese over Catholic teaching and writing, "enforcers" of the anti-Modernist mood. On the other hand, he took the position that while Tyrrell was intellectually in the right, morally he was in the wrong to challenge directly the authority of the bishops, thus precipitating his excommunication.[2] The atmosphere was filled with suspicions and accusations. A running critique of New-

---

1. Blondel to Bremond, September 21, 1907 (BB, II, 103).
2. Blondel to Bremond, October 4, 1907 (BB, II, 112).

man, and of Bremond's interpretation of Newman, picked up steam among Catholic interpreters,[3] with the very real fear that Bremond, perhaps even Newman himself, would be condemned as a Modernist.[4] The problem, for Blondel and Bremond, was how to carve out free working space, where they could pursue their scholarship with integrity, while simultaneously submitting to the authority of the Church. Could they be "modern," be truly critical scholars, without being Modernists?

Bremond's criticism of the Baron became more pronounced at this point, since von Hügel seemed to have a way of gliding past the authority issue (as a layman not dependent on a Catholic institution, as was Blondel, he indeed had a larger zone of freedom). Just after visiting Tyrrell and the Baron at Storrington, Bremond had written to Blondel that the Baron "is always the same, as if nothing had happened, constructing, and living in, his impossible Church."[5] At the same time, Bremond was involved in the process of producing a French translation of Tyrrell's *Medievalism: A Reply to Cardinal Mercier*, a head-on and angry critique of all that Tyrrell found antiquated and retrograde in the Catholic Church.[6] Dismayed at the Baron's "I'm above it all" attitude, yet determined to be both honest and loyal in adherence to the Church, Bremond looked for a posture that was neither rebellious nor craven. It is as if he were telling himself that there is no way to avoid conflict, but there is a way of sanctification in the midst of it. Here, when he needed an example, he found one ready to hand.[7]

It is no wonder that Bremond's attention turned to a serious study of François Fénelon, seventeenth-century archbishop of Cambrai, major character in the Duc de

---

3. Neveu, "Henri Bremond," 612–16, provides a good overview of the initial French critical response to "Bremond's Newman." He highlights the complex French resistance to Bremond's trumpeting of an English thinker.

4. Dupuy, "Newman's Influence," 168–69. French interpreters could not decide if Newman was an idealist (Blondel), a nominalist (Lebreton), or "too original, too personal a thinker to be followed with safety" (Grandmaison, "Newman considéré comme un maître," *Études* 109 [1906], n.p., cited by Dupuy, "Newman's Influence," 169), and so on. But always the biggest criticism of Bremond's interpretation was that it was too "psychological." However, popular culture thought otherwise: in 1906, Bremond's *Newman, Essai* received a prize from the Académie (BB, II, 78n3). There was also a carping debate about whether Bremond had translated some of Newman's language accurately. See the bibliographical note by Blanchet in BB, II, 91–92n2.

5. Bremond to Blondel, August 26, 1908 (BB, II, 128). But he also wrote to the Baron later that afterwards Blondel had been absolutely obnoxious, pontificating to him about the "invalidité of my prayers on the grave" (Bremond to von Hügel, August 13, 1909 [Goichot, "En marge de la crise," 140]). The irony is that von Hügel ended up eventually voicing the same criticism, as Bremond would reveal to Loisy in 1913 (Bremond to Loisy, June 1913 [Bernard-Maître, *Lettres*, 176, cited by Vidler, "Variety of Catholic Modernists," 124–25]).

6. Bremond to Blondel, November 8, 1908 (BB, II, 134). Blanchet suggests that Blondel would have been greatly saddened to hear this, believing that his *L'Action* had been very much misused by the Baron and by Tyrrell (BB, II, 135n3).

7. For comprehensive treatment of the many factors that played into Bremond's decision to construct a major interpretation of Fénelon and his spiritual heritage, see especially Talar, "Prayer at Twilight." He argues eloquently for the centrality of the *Apologie* to Bremond's entire intellectual unfolding and for its status as a monument of Modernist thought.

Saint-Simon's portraits of Louis XIV's Versailles and its imbroglios, and defender, in opposition to Jacques-Bénigne Bossuet, of Madame Jeanne Guyon and her "quietist" teaching about "pure love." Fénelon, in the drama of his personal history, was a kind of quintessential "man-in-the-middle," since he had submitted to a papal censure for his controversial ideas while retaining his freedom of conscience as a faithful priest. He might serve as a model for the present, Bremond seemed to think, if the dynamics of his spiritual journey could be properly set in context and properly elucidated.[8]

In choosing to focus on Fénelon, Bremond was homing in on a classic character both in French church and literary history. As a churchman and theologian, he was usually and officially seen as rightly condemned for heterodoxy, since the quietism associated with his name is spiritual poison; Bossuet was right in leading the spiritual charge against him. But as a literary figure, he was most celebrated for his universally admired and politically idealistic imitation of Homer's Odyssey, the *Adventures of Telemachus*—which Louis XIV had seen as a criticism of himself—as well as for the elegant and widely celebrated prose, largely free of quietist excesses, of his spiritual letters, as well as his treatise *On the Education of Daughters*. A long tradition thus developed in sophisticated French society, whereby one group saw Fénelon as the "swan of Cambrai," the prime example of literary excellence, papal loyalism and spiritual depth (at his best), while an opposing group saw Bossuet as the "eagle of Meaux," muscular, militantly Gallican and baroque in expression, as well as impeccably orthodox. "Fenelonians" and "Bossuetists" thus routinely sparred, the former always insisting that their champion had been mistreated, the latter that their champion stood strong against spiritual error. Bremond was, therefore, entering the lists of some old, old debates.

What always complicated matters for the defenders of Fénelon was his association with Guyon. The usual strategy was to argue against the standard view, going back to Bossuet, that she, an evil woman, had seduced Fénelon into some bad spirituality. Catholic writers usually excoriated her, although a strong Protestant tradition venerated her, but definitive evidence was always lacking. The evidence could be read either way. The publication in early 1907 of Pierre-Maurice Masson's volume *Fénelon & Mme. Guyon, documents nouveaux et inédits*, helped to change the picture by establishing the high reliability of a trove of correspondence from the early period of the Fénelon-Guyon relationship. More nuanced, mediating interpretations of Guyon and her spirituality emerged, in which it was seen, that her influence on Fénelon was substantial without being definitive. While absorbing her insights, Fénelon clearly remained independent in his thinking. The net result was a spirituality of real depth and power, a spirituality more in accord, ironically, with Bossuet's best writing than had

---

8. Thus Talar rightly ("Prayer at Twilight," 44–45), following Alistair Guinan, "Portrait of a Devout Humanist." That Bremond *explicitly* identified his own position with that of Fénelon is clear from a letter of August 1909, to the English churchman, A. L. Lilley, in which he described himself as giving to the authorities "a very calm, half-Fenelonian, half-Voltairean answer," humbly accepting the church's chastisement with a sort of "*perfide ingenuité.*" He accepts the sentence "as a soldier," but with the implication that "*je reste sur mes positions*" (Bremond to Lilley, August 8, 1909 [cited Vidler, *Variety*, 43]).

been thought. The inevitable question arose: had the Church misunderstood, acted wrongly even, in punishing Fénelon?[9] Has the concept, and implications, of "pure love" been misunderstood? Church condemnations of bold and innovative thinking seem to result in disastrous backfire, then and now.

Coincidentally, and reflective of his growing fascination with the age of Louis XIV, Bremond published that same year a short book of selections, with an introduction, from the writings of Pierre Nicole (1625–1695), a Port-Royalist and Jansenist moral theologian. Bremond admired Nicole for his psychological insight, wise and discerning, into the nature and subtleties of self-love. He was, averred Bremond, a Christian La Rochefoucauld, unsparing in his acute awareness of human foibles, but also able to depict those perversities with a light, sometimes amusing, touch. Articulating some of the character of his own emerging project, Bremond noted that Nicole "always elucidates his psychological analyses in the supernatural light of Christian dogma . . . [and that is] his originality, proper grace, and charm."[10]

Blondel considered himself well edified by *Nicole*, using it as a healthy distraction from the ego-driven Modernist turmoil.[11] A little later, while being skeptical of Barrès, he nonetheless, in carefully guarded praise, thanked Bremond for his "harangue" about Barrès, calling him the "defender of taste, of traditions, of 'home.'"[12] In June 1909, Bremond indicated to Blondel that he was working away on his own *Fénelon*, clearly showing where his affections lay: "It seems to me that Bossuet reasoned always in a skewed way, and that his own mysticism contradicted formally the theoretic mysticism of the controversy and left right on the side of Fénelon."[13]

Then the storm broke with Tyrrell's death, and Bremond (the very day of Tyrrell's death) sent a long explanation to Blondel, who, having read the newspaper accounts, immediately expressed strong disapproval. You should, he said bluntly to Bremond,

---

9. A jumping-off point for Bremond was a 1909 review, "Fénelon et la critique psychologique" (cited by Talar, "Prayer at Twilight," 43), of Albert Delplanques's 1907 study, *Fénelon et la doctrine de l'amour pur*, a book that so irritated him by its unjust treatment of Fénelon that he felt he had "a duty to dispute them [the Bossuetists]." The works, however, that received the fiercest pounding from Bremond were L. Crouslé's *Fénelon et Bossuet. Études morales et littéraires*, of 1894 and E. Levesque's essay that appeared in the *Revue Bossuet* for July 25, 1909. Crouslé, a Sorbonne professor, and Levesque, a Sulpician priest, both ardent Bossuetists, accused Fénelon of bad faith and dishonest dealing in his relations with Bossuet during and after the Conferences of Issy. Much of Bremond's argument is then an elaborate rebuttal of the conclusions of both scholars, in the course of which he engages in a massively sustained critique of Bossuet's methods and motives as a polemicist not only with Fénelon, but also with the biblical scholar Richard Simon. Clearly both Tyrrell and Loisy were in the back of Bremond's mind. On Levesque, see above p. 162, n. 53..

10. Bremond, *Nicole*, 11.

11. Blondel to Bremond, September 2, 1908 (BB, II, 130).

12. Blondel to Bremond, March 3, 1909 (BB, II, 139).

13. Bremond to Blondel, June 28, 1909 (BB, II, 141). Blondel's complex reactions to Bremond's position are detailed by Blanchet, BB, II, 160n. Blondel thought Bremond's arguments in defense of Fénelon a bit forced and "elliptical."

have simply engaged in silent prayer, without public observances, at Tyrrell's grave.[14] Bremond had tried initially, and to no avail, to forestall this perception.[15] Blondel softened later, after Bremond acceded to Rome's requirements for reinstatement, and after he had convinced himself that Bremond was a bit clumsy where fine distinctions of thought or practice were concerned. To the Jesuit, Auguste Valensin, he wrote that Bremond "is wise in religious psychology, [but] is no theologian or canonist, and not a Modernist, because ideas have very little existence for him."[16] We may be grateful that that statement seems never to have come back to Bremond. Loisy and others in the Modernist camp were immensely supportive, of course. Mgr Bonnefoy, back in Aix, was pastoral and understanding, but not exculpatory![17]

As Blondel had foreseen, Rome's concern with a breach of discipline on Bremond's part was not over the absolution given in private (parodied in the conservative press as a "sacrilegious comedy"), but the public prayers at the graveside. On August 3, 1909, Bonnefoy was notified from the Vatican that Bremond had been suspended from priestly duties not only by the bishop of Southwark, but now by order of the Holy See. Lifting of the suspension would require a formal submission. After Bremond produced the necessary official document, co-signed by himself and Bonnefoy, he was further required to write to Mgr Amigo in Southwark, expressing regret and repentance, along with a statement of formal adherence to the anti-Modernist decrees. On November 5 Bremond signed the Oath, and his restoration was complete. Inevitably some applauded, and some lamented.[18]

A secondary drama cranked up, when letters, written in mid-October by the prior of Storrington, claimed that Bremond, in ministering absolution to Tyrrell, and in his behavior and words at the graveside, had clearly disobeyed the instructions that he, P. Xavier de Fourvière, had given him. Bremond let it go, and the long and the short of it was that his friends, apparently rightly, were convinced that he "covered" for

---

14. Blondel to Bremond, July 28, 1909 (BB, II, 143–44).

15. Bremond to Blondel, July 22, 1909 (BB, II, 143).

16. Included by Blanchet in a long note (BB, II, 150–54), detailing Blondel's exasperation with the situation, and Bremond's self-defense.

17. The latest updating of scholarship on this "Tyrrell affair" for Bremond is that of Augustin Laffay, OP, "L'abbé Bremond suspendu *a divinis* en 1909." Bonnefoy seems to have been particularly effective in "cooling Bremond down," and pouring balm on the situation, as is clear from the materials gathered in Goichot, "Sur 'L'Affaire Tyrrell."

18. Bremond shared with the Baron his dismay at Blondel's criticism (Goichot, "En marge, de la crise" 140). Very supportive of Bremond's actions at Tyrrell's graveside, von Hügel was in turn deeply disappointed when Bremond signed the letter of submission and expostulated at length in a letter of December 31, 1909 (BB, II, 142–43). As Goichot points out, the relationship was never as close again (ibid., 144–46). Loisy was furious with the Baron (GT, 39–40).

the prior and took the fall in the final analysis.[19] Case closed and damage control more or less completed, although the shadow and the scars always remained for Bremond.[20]

Apologie

Bremond pushed forward. His sense of humor and of the irony of things always helped him, when even the conservative Church press applauded the appearance of the second collection of *L'Inquiétude religieuse*.[21] His new book, the *Apologie pour Fénelon*, received the imprimatur in May 1910.[22] Blondel was rapturous with praise in a way that suggested that the two men were once again, perhaps more than ever, in synchrony.[23]

The central issue in Bremond's interpretation was the question of whether Fénelon's submission to Church authority had been sincere. Bossuetists, often referring to Saint-Simon's descriptions of Fénelon as crafty and sly, always charged him with hypocrisy and duplicity, with "trimming," when he defended himself. Newman had had to face such charges from representatives of the Protestant British public, and from conservative churchmen in the Roman communion. Cynical calculation or craven kowtowing, or both? Blondel knew all of this in his own way, and Bremond was coming to know it. Therefore, Bremond's book would be an "apologia," a *Pro Fenelone*,[24] a kind of exoneration before one's accusers, parallel, it seems, with Newman's *Apologia*.[25]

Like a playwright defending his intentions to the audience and disclaiming any malice, Bremond started out with the claim that he was completely impartial. Admitting that he was clearer about Fénelon than Bossuet, he would give equal consideration

---

19. The whole sad drama is laid out schematically by Blanchet in notes (BB, II, 150–54). He cites Martin Du Gard's report that Bonnefoy urged Bremond in the final analysis to let Xavier "have his say," and then to move on (BB, II, 155).

20. Among some progressive thinkers and writers outside of France, Bremond was greatly admired for the courage of his ministrations to Tyrrell. See especially Ernst Troeltsch, "Father Tyrrell [was] . . . one of the purest, most religious characters of our time. He was excommunicated, but in the hour of his death he found a courageous priest who gave him the last rites" (*Christian Faith*, 45).

21. Critics at the traditionalist *La Croix* on October 21, 1909, praised Bremond as "a very unsure theologian and an ill-advised canonist [but] incontestably a first class litterateur and a subtle psychologist." Cited by Blanchet, BB, II, 147n.

22. But it was a brutal process. Blanchet reproduces part of a letter of April 28, 1910, from the abbé Wehrlé, the official censor assigned the first review and approval of the manuscript, to Blondel, detailing the difficulties. In light of Bremond's reputation, Wehrlé was put under enormous pressure from the archbishop. His final judgment was fascinating: while one could carp at details the overall tone of the book was so powerful, that details faded into insignificance; "No part is modifiable," he said (BB, II, 168–69).

23. Blondel to Bremond, 'end of January 1910,' (BB, II, 159). Was Blondel being honest? See n16 above.

24. *Pro Fenelone* was, in fact, the title that Bremond himself had given to the original series of articles on Fénelon, but he later renounced it, as he explains in the "Notes complémentaires" to *Apologie pour Fénelon*, since it smacks too much of a Ciceronian legal brief (*Apologie pour Fenelon*, 477).

25. Laffay, "L'abbé Bremond," is especially good at showing the extent to which Bremond, in formulating his intentions for *Fénelon*, was working out his own "psychology of submission."

to both men, and he would not in any way attempt to revive the ideas contained in the *Maxims of the Saints*. He then explained the structure of the drama about to be presented as a five-act production and delineated the principal characters: Madame de Maintenon, Fénelon, Bossuet and Madame Guyon, supported by secondary pro- and contra-Fénelon representatives, followed by a gallery of interested groups, such as Protestants, the great religious orders, and Jansenists. He provided some essential background on two points. First was his contention that the official description of quietist spirituality as a passive "sleeping devotion" that lends itself to immorality, derived from the condemnation of Molinos, had little to do with reality, at least among French practitioners. In fact, quietism was the effort to overcome scrupulosity and distraction in the devotional life. Second was his claim that a quick examination of Fénelon's early relationship with Bossuet showed clearly that he loved and respected, but did not envy, this great pastor, and that the later criticisms, rather than being mean-spirited, were friendly, and even badinage. Their opposition was not grounded in personal animosity.[26]

With Guyon, he wanted to show that Fénelon was not her "champion," but rather her defender against unjust attacks. He was not in some way besotted with her, as critics claimed, but considered her to be wise, good, devout, and filled with spirit, though, said Bremond, she wrote too much![27] In fact, she was a visionary and a spiritual director, from whom Fénelon learned in a way that seemed to contradict the natural male-female hierarchy, but the Gospel mandate to become "like little children" overrode such scruples—and, says Bremond, "lyric expression does not burden itself with analysis."[28] Fénelon was deeply moved by her teaching of "pure love," came to believe in her "suppleness in the hands of God," and was clear about her limitations as well as strength (as the recent publication of their correspondence clearly showed).

Fénelon's skill was that he homed in on what was essential in Guyon's teaching, namely, a doctrine of "pure love" grounded in "pure faith," where the "dry piety" of "an amorous activity completely secret and hidden" is key.[29] This is a love that can love without the accompanying feeling, where the reality of love and the feeling of love are quite distinct. Fénelon is Dante to her Beatrice, in the sense that one who is in the darkness of faith looks to another who is pure light. He experienced in her the reality of the divine, and submitted as a child, simple and vulnerable, in order to learn. "Fénelon is pure and orthodox . . . but she is right and good," said Bremond.[30]

26. Bremond, *Apologie pour Fénelon*, ch. 2: "Fénelon and Bossuet Before the Conflict." Quite true. See Gorday, *François Fénelon*, 171: "I pray to God for him with all my heart," said Fénelon at the time of Bossuet's death. Bossuet had also been a close and helpful mentor in Fénelon's early career, and they shared an assault on Malebranche. They had much in common.

27. Bremond, *Apologie pour Fénelon*, 38. He refers to "irritating extravagances" on the part of Guyon.

28. Ibid., 41.

29. Ibid., 42, citing from one of Guyon's letters to Fénelon in Masson, *Fénelon & Mme. Guyon*, 17.

30. Bremond, *Apologie pour Fénelon*, 46.

Pure Love

As the scenario unfolds, it is the redoubtable Madame de Maintenon, powerful consort of Louis XIV and center of Versailles intrigues, who would play the darker part. Various groups at Versailles vie for Maintenon's support with layer on layer of internecine fighting, but it is a feminine animosity that is decisive. Particularly as her cherished school of Saint-Cyr begins to rumble with discontent about spiritual teaching emanating from Guyon and Fénelon, Maintenon turns against them, enlisting Bossuet as her hammer. The net result is an extended ecclesiastical process of examination, led by Bossuet, in which Guyon and her work are condemned, and Fénelon's defense, but careful restatement, of her views in the *Maxims* is finally condemned as well. But it is all engineered by Madame de Maintenon, with Bossuet as a willing servant. A major irony, said Bremond, in a sop thrown to the traditional Fenelonian-Bossuetist antagonism, is that the two of them agreed on "pure love" all along, but Fénelon submitted, and Bossuet triumphed—and Bremond promised in his last chapter to show that in fact there was no substantive difference between them.[31]

In the censure that he received, Fénelon acknowledged the superior wisdom of the Pope, "who understands his book better than he understands it himself," but he was clear that the Pope cannot understand his private thinking, and this he does not renounce. Thus, said Bremond, Fénelon was not "simple," but that fact did not make him "duplicitous." In fact, the *Maxims* itself being condemned, a subsequent cascade of clarifications by Fénelon met with approval, and it is these that have stood the test of time as the mystical doctrine of Fénelon, the doctrine of pure love.[32]

In the second part of the *Apologie*, Bremond discussed the whole history of attempts to drive a wedge between Fénelon and Bossuet, thus creating a false antithesis. But it is in the final "*Revanche* of pure love" that Bremond rose to full stature. In fact, he said, the doctrine of pure love was alive and well for later generations, and continues so to the present. Fénelon, he contended, was not a mystic, but as a "synthetic, systematic thinker,"[33] looking for the point where everything coheres, the essence, the thing itself (anticipating Kant), he *mysticizes* "pure love."[34] He saw that this pure love is something lived, however difficult it may be to expound in a philosophically lucid fashion. Extracted from Scripture and Tradition, it is the childlike simplicity of the evangelical life, and as such the point at which the soul encounters the presence of the living God. Developed as the life of prayer, it is the calm, unifying, simplifying enlarging work of the Spirit, that naturally leads to action, but does not force it by means of ecstasy. This pure love is prayer that no longer requires pleasure as a driver, that courts love without delectation, that rejoices in the divine precisely in the darkest night. The

---

31. Ibid., 180.
32. Ibid., 184. For a recent treatment of this whole history, see Gorday, *François Fénelon*, chs. 5–7.
33. Bremond, *Apologie pour Fénelon*, 453.
34. Ibid, 455. Bremond describes this "mysticizing" as having the effect of "rendering more efficacious and more noble the counsels of simple human wisdom."

fundamental agreement of Fénelon and Bossuet would be registered in the work of Jean-Pierre de Caussade and Nicholas Grou in the next century.

A sustained presentation and argument beyond anything Bremond had yet composed, this long *Apologia* for Fénelon blended converging streams: analysis of the life of the soul in terms of motivation and desire and the working of grace; concern with the development of dogma, not abstractly, but in the modality of living application; the passion for literary expression and the construction of dramatic as well as novelistic narrative; the theme of the restless and disquieted individual (autonomy) over against the authority of the all-powerful, all-knowing representatives of the community. There was as well the dialectic of historical opposition, that of Fénelon and Bossuet, out of which came a synthesis—the doctrine of pure love—that would outlive the temporary particularity of the disputants to achieve lasting and universal status. And there was an exploration of the dynamics of male and female partnership as well as male and female collision in the work of the Spirit.[35] Thus multi-determined, the *Apologie pour Fénelon* was the product of crystallized and conglomerated forces in Bremond's inner development up to 1910, the trauma of the events surrounding Tyrrell's death functioning as the catalyst for creative energies.

And there was the visceral dimension as well. In the conclusions to the book, Bremond underlined something that he felt Bossuet never could grasp: "Pious egotism [that is, where pleasurable 'consolations' from God are expected] will never taste the 'bare faith' of Fénelon, the 'void,' the seeming dryness of the doctrine of pure love." Bremond saw Bossuet as an exponent of that perverted Augustinianism, like that of the Jansenists, that generates injustice, the destruction of souls, the fear of true eloquence, and fear-driven submission. Thus the conflict of quietism proves to be "an eternal conflict."[36]

Henry Hogarth contends that "it [the *Apologie*] was the best romance of the year 1910."[37] And there is no doubt that many read it that way. Martin Du Gard represented it as a kind of defense by Fénelon of the honor of a woman over against Bossuet's cloddish dismissal of the feminine.[38] Allowing for some truth in the idea that Bremond was a frustrated novelist, his main purpose was to work out the pain of Tyrrell's death, the politics of the Modernist crisis, and then to focus, to clarify, to generate thrust for

---

35. Of course, Bremond was criticized for this. He later noted this criticism to Blondel (Bremond to Blondel, November 12, 1915 [BB, II, 282]), when he was working on Jean-Jacques Olier, founder of the Sulpicians, who had been spiritually enlightened by Marie Rousseau.

36. Ibid., 468–69, and n2, referenced by Goichot, EG, 52. His treatment (Goichot, EG, 52–53) of the *Apologie* is too brief.

37. Hogarth, *Henri Bremond*, 17. The *Apologie* was published by Perrin, more of a mass-market publisher than the more limited and churchly Bloud.

38. MG, 73: "Bossuet had for women and the feminine in general only defiance . . . [but then came] la noblesse si naturelle de Fénelon [a phrase best left in French!]." The extent to which Fénelon's defense of Guyon can be construed as Gallican gallantry is illustrated by Michael de la Bedoyère's 1956 recounting, *The Archbishop and the Lady: The Story of Fénelon and Madame Guyon*.

the work ahead. Now this hero will serve both as a spiritual point of convergence in the past and a launching pad for the future. As a point in the past, he will come in the structure of the *Histoire* to represent the "twilight" of seventeenth-century mysticism, the end of the line that begins with Francis de Sales, before its somnolence in the eighteenth century, and then gradual rediscovery in the nineteenth. As the voice of the future, his idea of "pure love" would become dominant, the nucleus of all spiritual renewal in the Church.[39] Had he lived to finish the great eleventh (and perhaps the twelfth) volume of the *Histoire*, the Fénelon-Bossuet quarrel over quietism would have been the capstone. It was where he was headed, even though he did not quite make it that far.

Politics

And so, we have Bremond about the middle of the year 1910 starting to ride a modest crest, officially rehabilitated with the Church, though held in suspicion by some, and starting to be popular with a progressive audience, ecclesiastical and secular.[40] His living situation had evolved through time spent in Aix, especially at family property at Vinon, brief spells of travel, then an apartment in the Paris suburb of Neuilly. Things had calmed down a bit.

Two transient episodes involved potential ecclesial employment. Back in February 1906, there had been the possibility of his serving on the staff of the new bishop in Fréjus—a small diocese close to Aix—who happened to be his old teacher, Guillebert. There were signs that he was interested in a pastoral charge, but he also wanted time to write—so it all came to nothing.[41] And then, in 1907, there was a strange affair involving the Italian Bourbon-Parma family, Catholic progressives who thought highly of Bremond and who, at the time of the Modernist decrees, wanted to recommend him for a Vatican prelature! He was tempted, but soon deflated when a (false) rumor came that his books on Newman were (again) being considered for the Index. He then awkwardly backed away from all of this as quickly as he could.[42]

---

39. As Loisy recognized, rightly, taking the theme of "pure love" as the introduction to Bremond's "religious philosophy" (GT, ch. 3). Talar is right to make the claim that "for the rest of Bremond's life, Fénelon always stood in the background of his published work," or, in Joseph de Guibert's words, Fénelon would always be Bremond's *"vrai maître"* (Guibert, "Bremond," 1937; for the idea, see Talar, "Prayer at Twilight," 45).

40. But it is also true, as pointed out by Blanchet, that these years were "painful," particularly as Modernist friends were disciplined and *Sainte Chantal* went on the Index ("Redécouverte de Bremond," 16).

41. Bremond to Blondel, February 27, 1906 (BB, II, 53–54, and 54n1) and Blanchet, "Redécouverte de Bremond," 15.

42. Bremond to Blondel, June 4, 1907 (BB, II, 96–97, with discussion by Blanchet, 97n1). Blanchet commented on this peculiar incident also in "Redécouverte de Bremond," 15–16. It seems that this family had been in contact with Bremond at least since 1903, and that, in trying to function as an intermediary between them and the Vatican, he had had some kind of spat with Charles Maurras. He

Political involvements always simmered at the edge of his consciousness, primarily as a tension between the Catholic right and the Catholic left.[43] Action Française, growing steadily in vigor with a daily newspaper from 1908 onward, continued to expand the influence of its nationalist and reactionary themes. As momentum accelerated during 1906 and 1907 toward the anti-Modernist decrees, Maurras had thrown his weight on the side of conservative and traditionalist thought. Let Catholic dogma and practice be an unchanging monolith supplying moral backbone to the French state, he said, while decrying Modernism, with its call for the separation of Church and state, as indicative of weakness, moral compromise and dogmatic uncertainty.

Blondel, whom Maurras had come to see as the most dangerous representative of Modernist theology, was fiercely, volubly, publicly opposed, arguing that the Maurrassian exploitation of traditionalist, scholastic, and authoritarian theological thinking was a destructive union of positivism and Catholicism. Maurras had succeeded, thought Blondel, in eviscerating Catholic faith by turning it into a pseudo-scientific ideology of state control.[44] The core theological problem, as Blondel saw it, was "monophorism," that is, "an over-simplification, or an all-too-human simplification of the relation between the natural and the supernatural, or between the divine and the human." The result was "a sort of theocratic tendency" marked by "theological enormity and political insanity," in which God's grace is simply imposed on the natural order by fiat, because in itself the natural order is devoid of all such grace. Bad theology, thus, produces tyrannical politics.[45]

Bremond was in complete agreement, though his resistance to Action Française was reasoned through in a manner more literary and historical. There was the "pagan aestheticism" and the "Gallo-Romanism" in Maurras's approach to literature, and the complexity created for Bremond by his entanglement with nativism in the person of Maurice Barrès. In a 1908 roundtable discussion on the "religious question," conducted by Frédéric Charpin for the popular magazine *Mercure de France*, in which both Bremond and Barrès participated, the latter (at that time a parliamentary deputy from Paris) expressed the view that, while not being a faithful believer, he would "uphold

---

had a close friendship with two princes of the family, Sixte and Xavier, brothers to the empress Zita of the Austro-Hungarian empire. Then, in 1917, Bremond became involved, through the machinations of this family, in a fruitless effort to activate the Vatican in peace negotiations ("Bremond to Blondel, January 21, 1917," and August 19, 1917 [BB, II, 311 and 324, with notes]). Sixte would be an attendant at Bremond's funeral.

43. For general historical and political context, see Magraw, *France 1815–1914*, ch. 7, "An Intransigent Right." Magraw's bias is to emphasize the power of the political right in its alignment with conservative Catholicism, and mostly to downplay Catholic alliances with the left as over-idealistic, naive, and futile. But see Bernardi, *Maurice Blondel, Social Catholicism and Action Française*, for a quiet different view.

44. Blondel's thinking here is summarized by Alexander Dru in the introduction to Maurice Blondel, *Letter on Apologetics*, 27–33.

45. There is an excellent discussion of the connections of "monophorism" with Action Française in Blanchette, *Maurice Blondel*, 242–60.

and defend menaced Catholicism, because I am a patriot, in the name of the national interest." He contended that human beings are ineluctably religious animals, and that only Catholicism "assimilated and attenuated" can draw forth the human potencies of the nation. But Bremond responded with a caveat. While acknowledging that religion was enjoying a revival as something intrinsic to normal health and vigor, and foreseeing a great surge in "religious psychology," he warned that a problem arises when Catholicism comes sweeping back in an utterly exterior, "Roman," way, resulting in a Charles Maurras.[46]

Alexander Dru has convincingly suggested, at least by implication, that Bremond saw in the person of Bossuet, and in his resistance to the inward, quietist spirituality of Fénelon, a throne-and-altar ideology allied with external forms of authoritarianism, thus a kind of forerunner of Maurras's political use of Catholicism.[47] In any case, critics now began to tie Bremond more closely to Blondel and the latter's charge against Maurras of "monophorism," in order to suggest that he was advocating a soft Modernist approach to the teaching of Catholic truth. One example that particularly galled was the blast aimed at his review, noted above, of the Handel-Mazzetti novels, printed in the second *L'Inquiétude religieuse* collection, where Catholic representatives are pastoral and attuned to the hearts of their listeners, rather than authoritarian.[48] Bremond's resistance to the ideology of Action Française was, so to speak, more humanistic and visceral, Blondel's more a bit more cerebral and academically theological, though they ended in the same place.[49]

But political involvement on the other side of the spectrum had come to seem problematic as well. The Catholic left was represented by the Sillonist movement of Marc Sangnier (1873–1950), a devout Catholic committed to democracy and the rights of organized labor.[50] His movement, Le Sillon ("the Path"), starting out among student study groups, branched quickly from 1893 onward into a large and popular effort to enroll Catholic laity in labor reform, and then to move the whole church in the direction of a full embrace of the politics of the Republic. Church authority, from Leo XIII and then Pius X on down, was largely supportive, until the reaction that followed the 1905 Law of Separation. The Sillon then became the counterpart to

---

46. Charpin, *La Question religieuse*: for Barrès, 165–67; for Bremond, 230–33.

47. Dru, introduction to Blondel, *Letter on Apologetics*, 22–24. Dru was stretching the argument a little. In fact, in *Bossuet, textes choisis*, II, ch. 7, Bremond saw Bossuet, and his support for the Gallican Articles of 1682, as the prime example of a seamless throne-and-altar alliance in which no "antinomy" could occur, comparing it with Pius IX's hope of allying with the Comte de Chambord for a revival of the French monarchy. It was more his father's pious dream than a fascist nightmare.

48. References are in BB, II, 179n4, attached to the letter of "Bremond to Blondel of December 26, 1910." The larger context was the all-out assault by conservatives on Blondel's "method of immanence."

49. Prévotat, "Réactions et sensibilités maurrassiennes," explores the reactions of Maurras's followers to Bremond's growing criticism of the movement. By the 1920s, they were dismissing him as a hopelessly apolitical and irrational romantic/mystic.

50. For an excellent overview of Sangnier and the *Sillon*, see Vidler, *Variety*, ch. 8.

Action Française, so that between the two them the entire political field was covered.[51] Both movements, dominated by the personality of a strong leader, quasi-military in organization, and heavily dependent on popular newspapers, eventually suffered papal condemnation, Le Sillon in 1910 for being too liberal, Action Française in 1926, despite bitter resistance, because of the agnosticism of Maurras.[52]

Leaders of the Sillon, progressively social in their thinking, early on saw themselves in alliance with Blondel's ideas. In late 1896, and 1897, they applauded Blondel for what conservative critics saw as his "Kantian tendencies," that is, his apparent emphasis on practical reason and the categorical imperative rather than the aridities of scholastic deductive theology or rationalist science.[53] Blondel was leery, however, again not wanting at this early stage of his thought to be seen as too aligned ideologically. If traditional Catholicism was identified with the political right, then Modernism gravitated to the left, and Blondel operated with an essentially pragmatic mentality.[54]

To all intents and purposes Bremond seems to have been of the same mind. In fact, he was on occasion sarcastic about the politics of the right and of the left.[55] Nonetheless, after Sangnier and his movement were struck down in a letter from Pius X to the French episcopate on August 25, 1910, he claimed in retrospect to have been greatly saddened at the same time that he admired Sangnier's unflinching submission.[56] In communication with Charles Péguy in 1910 he expressed approval of the latter's separation of a genuine religious mysticism from politics, but then went on to criticize the disciplining of the Sillon by Rome, contending that it seemed to "accept, channel and make eternal the differences of classes."[57] Then in a 1915 article he lamented and celebrated a number of French writers already killed in the war,

---

51. Petit, *L'Église, Le Sillon, et L'Action Française*, is a valuable comparative study of the two movements.

52. An important study is Prévotat, *Les catholiques et l'Action française*.

53. Blondel to Bremond, April 14, 1897 (BB, I, 41–42, with important references by Blanchet, 42n1).

54. Blanchette discusses the "Testis" articles produced by Blondel in 1909–1910, where he supported a "social Catholicism," but insisted on a "paradoxical method" in which concrete social programs would be constantly critiqued in the light of new experience (*Maurice Blondel*, 236, and the whole section, 233–42). The idea, in accordance with *L'Action*, was that they would not thus lose their transcendent horizon.

55. The reference here is to an obscure popular article, published as a book review in late 1911, in which Bremond, with heavy-handed irony, poked fun at an author who was a supporter of Sangnier. Blondel and others were quite annoyed, and there was a minor flap in which Bremond admitted that he had overplayed his hand with an excessive and somewhat clumsy use of irony. See BB, II, 192–93, where Blanchet discusses this curious incident.

56. The source is Bremond's comment to Martin Du Gard (MG, 102–3, cited by Blanchet, BB, II, 175n1). According to Magraw, the Sillon was "condemned for using a 'disfigured and degraded Christ' to pursue its 'social dreams,' for allegedly subordinating religion to politics by supporting popular sovereignty" (*France 1815–1914*, 279). Sangnier had responded with dignity to Pius on August 31, 1910, submitting completely.

57. Cited in Blanchet, "Péguy et Bremond," 10.

including individuals sympathetic with Action Française as well as with Le Sillon.[58] Patriotism and unity in a shared heritage, yes (he was about to publish the first volume of the *Histoire*); but nationalistic jingoism, no. Even though Maurras and Bremond had shared a last warm moment a few years earlier, when both had participated in a congratulatory subscription for their Sacré-Coeur teacher P. Penon, now appointed bishop of Moulins, Maurras was outraged at Bremond's affirmation of Le Sillon, and from that point on any mutual good will was finished.[59]

The Golden Age

Exactly how it is that Bremond was to become so immersed in the spirituality of the French seventeenth century is, as suggested, a bit of a mystery, perhaps best resolved by imagining a vectoring convergence of factors. We have seen the decline and collapse of any intention to construct a grand history of English religious literature, even though his love for English writers would remain unabated. We have seen the Baron's enthusiastic support of his interest in mysticism. We have noted Barrès's encouragement of a "Christian Sainte-Beuve," as well as his own rising to that lure. His nativist turn with the 1907 work on the Aixois saints, as well as the encouragement of his publisher to focus on French ecclesial literature, played their part also. A growing interest in Fénelon probably had catalytic force.

To this last, moreover, we should add the fact that in 1907 Bremond published a substantive review of the new Visitandine critical edition by Dom Benedict Mackey of the writings of Francis de Sales, in which a fresh volume containing Francis's letters had just appeared.[60] Bremond was deeply moved by the rich spirituality of Francis himself, but also of the Salesian community and tradition that embodied this spirituality, especially as a literary heritage. That appreciation led him to Jean-Pierre de Camus, early exponent of Francis's thought, but also to Jeanne de Chantal, Francis's first disciple and collaborator, as well to Jeanne's first biographer after the founding of the Visitation, Mère Françoise-Madeleine de Chaugy (1611–1680). All of these characters

---

58. Bremond, "De quelques jeunes écrivains."

59. Details and sources, BB, II, 282n2. In correspondence with a friend, the abbé Monbrun, on November 26, 1915, Bremond said of Maurras, "I consider him a fool."

60. "Les lettres de François de Sales," first in the journal, *Archives de philosophie chrétienne*, then gathered posthumously in abbreviated form in AH. He was aware, also, of the aforementioned Fortunat Strowski's 1897 study of Francis, as well as Strowski's major study, just appearing, of Pascal, both works focusing on the "sentiment religieux" of their central characters. In the appendix to *Histoire*, I, "The Visitation of Anneçy and Jean-Pierre Camus," Bremond used this fourteenth volume of Francis's collected works as a lever against the historical authenticity of Camus's popular account of Francis's life, thus much preferring Mère de Chaugy's account with regard to the founding of the Visitation. His preferences here would become an issue of debate with the Sisters of the Visitation, when they objected to his portrayal in *Sainte Chantal* (Trémolières, "L'abbé Bremond à l'Index," 155–56). Bremond later, in 1922, paid eloquent tribute to the quality of Mackey's critical work and the fineness of his discernments in explicating Francis de Sales's thought ("Pour qu'on lise S. François de Sales").

would loom large in Bremond's later work, and he would in time, in the *Histoire*, make Francis the foundational figure of French seventeenth-century spiritual history, the opening arch-exponent of "pure love," with Fénelon providing closure at the end of the century. The pieces were starting to fall into place from 1907 onward. But there were intermediary steps in important essays and collections.

The first was a compendium of excerpts, with a critical introduction, from the writings of Esprit Fléchier (1632–1710), priest, poet, skilled pastor, great pulpit orator, member of the Académie, finally bishop of Nîmes. Mostly forgotten today, his funeral discourses were great favorites during his era, and he was well respected by Louis XIV. Bremond celebrated him as "one of the most considerable bishops of *ancien régime* France," a man who exemplified "the interior music" of serious faith combined with "justness of thought." Fléchier showed how a great spiritual teacher's life penetrates his artistic range, especially his preaching and composition. He was saintly, said Bremond, but in a quiet and unspectacular way that does not draw attention to itself. Urbane, yet simple; simple, but pleasing in expression; direct and not "precious"; and with the marvelous ability to capture great thoughts in well-turned phrases. He had that ability of "interior observation" by which we can recognize the great portraitist, able to convert a person's "inner structure" into artful prose.[61]

Soon thereafter Bremond published an essay on the preeminent theorist and authority for French poetry, Nicholas Boileau (1636–1711), whose *Art poétique* (1674) had long functioned as the gold standard governing form and matter in versification.[62] Taking Boileau as the ultimate representative of doctrinaire conservatism in aesthetics, Bremond attempted a dethronement. Boileau, while having good moments, was merely "precious," lacking spirit and verve, a mere "bourgeois" in his art, averred Bremond. His ultimate sin was that he lacked real inwardness. Arguing against the exaltation of Boileau by Sainte-Beuve and Brunetière (both Bossuetists as well!), Bremond contended that Boileau with all of his rational rigidity about poetry embodied the ultimate bankruptcy of the classical ideal.

Indeed, by the time of this essay on Boileau, it had become clear that Bremond was taking a stand against the usual reading of the seventeenth century, where Boileau is the aesthetic master, Corneille the great dramatist, Pascal the preeminent spiritual writer, and Bossuet the ecclesial champion, favoring instead a "romantic" (the term yet to be defined) reading, in which a line of descent from Francis de Sales to Fénelon is the true spiritual heartbeat of the era, with (as we shall see) Racine the supreme dramatist.

It comes, then, as a bit of a surprise to find that Bremond had also been working for some time on a large selection of texts, with critical introductions, from the work of Bossuet. Following, as with the study of Fénelon, some piecemeal publication, the

---

61. See Bremond, *Fléchier*, introduction (3–21). Repeatedly, Bremond emphasized the "music" of Fléchier's expression, and his gift for "interior observation." He was also Provençal!

62. "La légende de Boileau," first published March 10, 1911.

complete text came out in three volumes in 1913. The excerpts are grouped under the three periods into which Bremond divided Bossuet's life: the years of his youth and early preaching and writing, the time of his episcopate and role as preceptor to the Dauphin, and the period in which he functioned as bishop of Meaux. The extensive introduction and commentary amounts to a small biography. Bremond admired Bossuet's talent, his genuine piety, his strong character, and his good intentions, but in the end found him unlovable. He was a man of contrasts. Genuinely pastoral and at times beautifully "lyrical" in expression, as a stately figure of the *grand siècle* he was pompous. Marked by a grandiose vanity and a contrived self-importance early in his career, he was moderate and accommodating with the Jews and the Protestants. Profound as a teacher, he tended, nevertheless, to operate with a "sublimity too dense" in his role as a preceptor as well as with too much severity. Bremond described Bossuet's praise of absolute royal power ironically, arguing that it was unrealistic—a kind of laughable inflation that exposes the weaknesses of the authoritarian personality. In the conflict that eventually erupted with Fénelon, Bossuet depended, thought Bremond, on "lyrical elevations," the power of lofty words, over against "the dryness, the silent reality, dark and active, of pure love, which is to say the love that does not speak."[63]

On the subject of Gallicanism and the freedom of the French church over against the papacy, Bremond thought that Bossuet wavered and equivocated. He compared Bossuet's uncertainty about Louis XIV as a spiritual leader with the awkward alliance in the nineteenth century between Pius IX and the French royal Pretender, the Comte de Chambord. One has to be raised in a legitimist family, said Bremond, to feel the power of this conjunction, where Church and throne are such bonded realities that an "antinomy" is inconceivable![64]

The ultimate fault, thought Bremond, was that Bossuet's understanding of an unchanging Catholicism allied with a political order is rigid and simplistic. It was Newman who understood, by contrast, that it is *Catholicism* that changes while Protestantism is essentially immobile! Sadly humiliated in the end, Bossuet had beautiful expression and a forceful personality, but truth lay elsewhere. And to that "elsewhere" Bremond now turned.

Jeanne de Chantal

The Baron, we recall, had early on supported Bremond's interest in the spirituality of the inner life, especially the life of prayer, and especially the life of *mystical* prayer. He enthused as well about Bremond's budding interest in the Quietist controversy.[65] That was one factor. And then there had been Bremond's study, through portraiture, of the progress of the nineteenth-century English cultural heritage in literary, educational

---

63. Bremond, *Bossuet: texts choisis*, II, 157.
64. Ibid., 219.
65. A subject well discussed by Portier and Talar, "Mystical Element of the Modernist Crisis," 4–6.

and ecclesiastical circles—a heritage marked by artistically rendered moral reflection grounded in empirical modes of observation and analysis. But we noted, also, his view of that heritage's deficiencies. His Jesuit Third Year in France was the bridge period, where he began to take the view that Catholicism rightly understood overcomes the deficiencies in the English legacy, while salvaging the advantages. The paradox, however, is that he would use methods honed in the English "desert" to better understand that literary French Catholicism that is his own native turf. And this use of what he had learned would affect, first, his method for constructing a historical recital—essentially a series of portraits—and, second, his understanding of the process of historical development as one portrait follows another chronologically.

The latter element came from Newman, as tempered and refined by Bremond's exposure to Blondel's critique. We will see in *Histoire*, VII and VIII, a version of Newman's theory of development applied to the history of the religious sentiment in France in the seventeenth century. What Newman proposed as the "idea" in a dogma, the thing that comes more and more to expression through historical unfolding, will become in Bremond's treatment of France's seventeenth-century golden age of spirituality the relentless trajectory not of a dogma, but of an "essence," which is the idea of "pure love," experienced in the life of prayer, and manifested in texts rich with poetic power. If he had lived to complete his *Histoire* as he intended, he would have shown that the direction established in the seventeenth century has continued down to the present as the true heartbeat of Catholicism.

But the first element—the method of using portraiture as primary building-blocks for a narrative—was ready for refinement and demonstration. He needed, as it were, a foundational portrait, a character of true saintliness, of a holiness flamboyantly reflective of a rich and well-developed inner life, an inner life grounded in prayer and sufficiently illustrative of pure love at work in the contingencies of human existence. This character would serve to make the "notion," the abstraction, concretely "real." He could take what he had learned from his series of English sketches, those paragons admirable for their Anglo-Saxon moral seriousness, but ultimately lacking in appeal to French tastes, and add to it his desire to be a "Christian Sainte-Beuve," to improve upon the techniques of that great French romantic historian Charles Augustin Sainte-Beuve—whom we discuss in the next chapter. Having already encountered Francis de Sales, he spotted the person he needed, an individual who met all of the requirements, and who, in addition, stood at the very beginning of that fascinating seventeenth-century spiritual unfolding: she was Jeanne de Chantal, or better, Jeanne de Chantal as captured in her relationship with Francis de Sales, where in their shared work they set the train of "pure love" in motion.

Bremond knew that these two canonized saints had enjoyed a long, warm, and mutually fecund friendship, that together they both experienced degrees of mystical prayer and experience, that Francis was acting as her spiritual director and guide at the time when she founded the Order of the Visitation for women. The story of their relationship had great potential for a great telling, since the sources are exceedingly abundant, detailed and colorful. As mentioned, new critical editions of primary texts were just appearing, and the time was ripe for an exposition that would be soundly critical, not just hagiographical. Bremond rose to the challenge and his *Sainte Chantal* was published, with official approval from the ecclesiastical censors, in the spring of 1912. It would land on the Index in 1913.[66]

By showing, withal, the effectiveness of his critically sophisticated method of presentation, by portraying saintliness in a non-supernaturalized way, Bremond was working his way theologically. He illustrated what the conventional thesis of grace-completing-without-canceling-nature looks like in human terms, where saints keep all of their idiosyncrasies and failings even in the expression of the *charisma* given to them. But there is more. As in Blondel's criticism of "monophorism," grace is not just imposed on nature as a kind of supplement, but—as Bremond's study of the contrasting, but collaborative and effective, personalities of Francis and Jeanne showed—the divine gift seems to *arise from or within* human nature, i.e., "immanently," *rather than arriving from the outside*. By implication, moreover, he wanted to begin to show that the heritage of Francis and Jeanne was antithetical to another line of development in the seventeenth century, namely, that of Port-Royal and Jansenism, his first essays on the subject appearing in 1910. Finally—and this is the one that really got him into trouble—he wanted to illustrate specifically in the case of Francis how a very human love undergirded that saint's widely acknowledged and transcendent masterpiece, the *Treatise on the Love of God*.

Out of all of the sources for Chantal's life, and in accordance with his method, Bremond made the most of Mère de Chaugy's *Mémoires*, because they are practical, down-to-earth, packed with gritty detail, realistic. Indeed, his descriptions of Chantal's childhood and marriage have a colorful, novelistic quality that we now take for granted in biographies. He saw her as a lively, charming, and poetically inclined young woman, but also genuinely vain and worldly—"spoiled," we might say, with "daddy" as her hovering protector. Her personality sparkled, and she was not, averred Bremond, prematurely pious, but enjoyed to the full her marriage with a good and strong man, and truly grieved his early, tragic death. But then came her "mystical flowering," a depth of experience that should not close her off from us, insisted Bremond, but rather should help us to see that "the mystics remain our brothers" (*sic*!) if we approach them with humility.[67] And, of course, he related the famous story of her listening to Francis preaching during Lent, and her deciding on the spot that this was the man to be her director, the result being that she will eventually show to him, with insight from some subsequent Carmelite experience that he will adapt for his *Traité*, the true nature of Teresa of Avila's spirituality.[68]

66. All references are to the 2011 re-edition of the original text.
67. Bremond, *Sainte Chantal*, 63.
68. Ibid., 69.

Francis turned out to be skillfully patient with an overly intense directee.[69] At one point she inscribed the word "Jesus" on her chest, and then told Francis about it with "a touch of coquetry" that showed her to be (unwittingly?) seductive and tender.[70] The tone is sensual, but not carnal (a critical distinction for Bremond, though we can easily understand how the Sisters of the Visitation could first applaud *Sainte Chantal*, then have serious second thoughts).[71] But then Chantal went on to speak of the light of God appearing at the "fine point" of her soul (Francis will make much of this later), precisely in the midst of her deepest darkness. Bremond's comment is eloquent: "When God encounters and presses us, night precedes his action, envelops him, hides his retreat and covers his traces. But when it is a question of mystical graces, the night of man, I daresay, adds itself to the night of God, graces twice as dark, since they come from the abyss and return to the abyss, hollowing out, it seems some new depths in the soul that receives them."[72]

The idea for Bremond is that the life of mystical prayer grows in a hidden place in the soul, especially if outwardly the mystic remains human in the most ordinary ways. "Shouldn't we remind the pessimists that the wound of the Old Adam is healable, and must not we show everyone that the hundredfold promise to those who give up their life is not a vain word?"[73] Poetry, always a characteristic of the mystics, becomes more evident in some of Chantal's writing. Her continued grieving for her husband transmutes into friendship with Francis. Her vanities constantly reappeared, and Bremond confessed to some puzzlement on "the mystery of the feminine soul."[74]

The story of Chantal's coming to Francis's episcopal see at Annecy in order to win his support for a special vocation especially fascinated Bremond, for it somehow evoked the "bitter roots" in Francis's spirituality (Francis resisted her efforts for some time), for all of its reputed "sweetness." Bremond argued that Francis, once convinced of Chantal's "charism," was the guiding spirit in forming the Rule for the Visitation,

---

69. Ibid., 55: Francis, says Bremond, worked with a "smiling wisdom." Just before the appearance of *Sainte Chantal*, Bremond had published an overview of the ongoing, official critical edition of Francis's *oeuvre* ("Saint François de Sales et sainte Chantal"). The essay was his way of clearing the ground for his selection and weighting of sources.

70. Bremond, *Sainte Chantal*, 81–82.

71. There was, thought an early Visitandine critic, a little too much here of Francis's "friendship" with Jeanne arising in a "natural" way (Trémolières, "Bremond et la Visitation," 202). Vatican denunciations of literary Modernism during the 1920s will lambaste the supposed "eroticization of the sacred" by many Catholic authors. See Amadieu, "Mysticisme, modernisme et littérature," esp. 110–13, for description and analysis.

72. Bremond, *Sainte Chantal*, 93–94.

73. Ibid., 99.

74. Only after a lengthy treatment of intense fluctuations of mood and perception on the part of Chantal, where both she and Francis struggled to discern their meaning, does Bremond make the statement that "while these two personnages groaned together over their shared deception and over the mystery of the feminine soul, the Baronne [Chantal] continued cheerfully certain mysterious visits [seemingly supernatural occurrences] that have greatly disquieted several of her biographers" (ibid., 107).

that he intended it as a "Carmel for the weak," that is, women too frail to endure Carmelite austerities, but aspiring to a comparable spirituality. He argued now that in their personal relationship Francis came to experience a "great interior suaveness," an "infinitely consoling particularity," that somewhat mystified him, but that, at least partially, reflected a "beauty" and "heart" in Chantal that elicited the like from him. They complemented one another, in that "she thinks, she loves, she lives in the light," and that "a shadow very sweet and very stimulating is projected from her over his life." Bremond compared this relationship with that between Guyon and Fénelon, but observed that the latter was less animated, much "drier." In discussing Francis's official request to Chantal to start the Visitation, Bremond noted that "of the sacrifice that Francis reckoned one day to ask of that soul, and that by the same token she asked of herself, they would both suffer, but she much more than he." Bremond referred to their "heroic dialogue" and said, "I know of nothing more beautiful."[75]

Bremond went on to describe Chantal's many practical abilities in organizing the Visitation, especially her genius for reading people, for discernment of souls—a grace that Bremond always greatly admired. Chantal could be tough and hard on people, but with a French gift for the ironic phrase that could put a bit of humor on a difficult situation. As her death approached, said Bremond, she experienced great spiritual darkness, something typical of the mystics. He closed his description of their relationship with passages from the *Treatise on the Love of God*, 10.3 and 11.20, passages that he interpreted as Francis's theological commentary on his love for Chantal: "Even while our heart is employed in sacred love we may still love God in various ways and also many other things along with God," and "divine love uses all the passions and affections of the soul and brings them under its obedience."

Sainte Chantal, lavishly and richly illustrated by Bremond with a wealth of colorful description, sold quite well. At first members of the Visitation loved it. It is a touching, tender book, abundantly documented and packed with detail, obviously written with great affection for its central characters. But, the initial enthusiasm quickly evaporated as closer reading by the disciples of Ste Jeanne de Chantal produced a different reaction, then complaint to Rome, then official censure.[76] He was forbidden to reissue the book, when his publisher urged him to do so, unless he made changes. He refused, and thus the book went out of circulation for good, the ban never to be lifted.

---

75. Ibid., 181. Citations drawn from ch. 5, where Bremond drew heavily on the volume of Francis's letters that he had carefully reviewed in 1907.

76. The Vatican process behind this condemnation was first studied by Blanchet, *Histoire d'une mise à l'index*, but now must be updated and supplemented by reference to the materials and analysis supplied by Trémolières, "L'abbé Bremond à l'index," and "Bremond, et la Visitation." Included as an appendix to the first essay is the report by the Roman censor regarding *Saint Chantal*: it is clear that the core complaint is directed at the supposed Modernist tendency to confuse grace and nature, to imagine that the former bubbles up out of the latter. Blondel had spotted the essential problem quite clearly.

The problem, it seems, is in the pious need for edification when reading the life of a saint. The Holy Office in Rome, deciding that the original censors had been naive, and after consultation with critics, decided that there was a problem of "tone," that Bremond had written his work too much in the skeptical, slightly mocking spirit of Renan and of Modernist heresy. Blanchet's researches into the Vatican file showed that there were never specific objections to this or that passage in the book, but only a generalized discomfort. Bremond had strong defenders—particularly Guillebert, now at Fréjus—but pressure from the Visitation, combined with, it seems, a certain desire in some quarters to hit back at Bremond over his Modernist associations and support of Tyrrell, decided the matter. Bremond was devastated.

Tired of the turmoil in Paris, and tired of bouncing around between Aix and the capital and the homes of various friends, Bremond finally made a nest for himself that he would use for the rest of his life, and where he could pursue his grand project.[77] The commune of Arthez-d'Asson is in the Basses-Pyrénées region, now the Dept. of the Pyrénées-Atlantiques, in the old Béarnais, Occitan-speaking, region of Aquitaine in southwestern France. The regional capital is Pau, where Bremond would often ensconce himself with research at a well-stocked library. He loved his garden cottage in Arthez and would receive a stream of visitors there for many years. He named it "Littlemore" in memory of another thinker, trying to venerate ancient tradition in a modern way, and finding the upward climb rather steep. A great deal of work lay ahead.

---

77. He referred to his "niche" in Arthez, a healthy and comfortable place for work on his "big book" (Bremond to Blondel, July 25, 1913 [BB, II, 218–19]).

8

Under the Shadow of Sainte-Beuve
From the Literary Soul to the Mystical Soul

With the furor over *Saint Chantal* abating by the end of 1913, Bremond was poised to begin work on his great project. We have seen that it would be specifically a French history, a history of the inner life in French souls, a history of the hidden work of grace in souls at prayer, a history of the literary expressions of the experience of this grace, a history in which central themes and direction would emerge as the work progressed. Though he did not use this terminology (which comes, as explained further on, from Certeau), he increasingly saw the seventeenth century as the setting in which the transition to "modernity" anticipates the "Modernist" problematic for the life of prayer. He decided at the outset that it was the first half of the century, not the age of Louis XIV, that was critical, because the literature of saintliness then flourished prior to a time, in the latter part of the century, of increasing rationalism.[1]

In the introduction to the first volume of the *Histoire*, Bremond described his methods and goals. The intention is to produce a *literary* history of the soul in its inner life, utilizing primarily the printed deposits of individual, personal, intimate religious experience. "High" literature—the dogmatic or speculative treatises of theologians, official Church pronouncements, biblical commentaries, liturgical texts—would be strictly secondary, if used at all. While taking note of such texts when necessary, he will privilege the "low"—journals, diaries, memoirs, correspondence, but especially "didactic writings," and early biographies often written by contemporaries—much of which he would exhume from forgotten monastic libraries and private collections.[2] The purpose is to include the testimony of "little people" as well as the mighty. The question would always be one of deciding how wide to cast the net in choosing texts,

---

1. *Histoire*, I, xvi–xvii. The way that Bremond had made this point back in the *Apologie pour Fénelon* was to argue that it was Guyon (of the older generation) who was the mystic, while Fénelon (of the younger generation) only wrote theology *about* mysticism.

2. *Histoire*, I, xvi. References to passages in *Histoire*, I–III, will be to Montgomery's English translation.

and, of course, there would be all manner of source-critical issues with regard to dating, degree of corruption, the relative historical reliability of one witness over another when they conflicted, and so on.

Bremond never stated in unambiguous fashion his personal spiritual agenda for the *Histoire*, probably because it remained somewhat inchoate in the early stages of organizing the material. But it was there as a kind of blending of what he had learned from writing the books on Fénelon and Chantal. As a *historian* he was working with Newman's thought: he would display a genuine process of development, of the implicit becoming explicit in the literary expression of the religious sentiment across the course of the seventeenth century. This development would start with an "idea" that unfolds over time, namely, that of "pure love" from Francis de Sales to Fénelon, gathering richness from various witnesses but not changing in essence, through interplay with a changing historical context. As a *theologian*, he would work, broadly, with Blondel's metaphysics, or method of immanence, in which it is understood that spiritual experience and insight emerge, as with Francis and Chantal, not from an authoritative tradition of revelation, but out of the willful process of human consciousness aspiring to action that seeks truth and goodness. So far as the history of the religious sentiment goes, that aspiration crystallizes in the lyricism of "pure poetry," which is "pure prayer" seeking after saintliness in communion with other human beings and with God.

Blondel's task, in endless communication with Bremond as his project evolved, would be that of reminding him that his theories and those of Newman do not sit together easily. The issue of the natural and the supernatural will be ever-present as one of determining in what sense, and in what ways, natural human processes give rise to, or tend toward, supernatural resources. If God's grace is somehow operative in human nature from the beginning, what does it mean to say that that "grace" still needs "grace" of a different and higher order? How does what is "immanent" become something "transcendent?" More specifically, there will be the convoluted issues of knowledge and willing as Blondel's two modes of human consciousness. How does the tension of natural and supernatural play out in what human beings can *know* and can *will* in the course of spiritual development? For Bremond, these questions took the form of asking *what* his historical subjects came to know and willed as they loved, made poetry and prayed, and then *how* they knew it.

In the course of his explorations Bremond will coin his own idiosyncratic vocabulary to describe what he believed that he was discovering in his sources. But we should not allow this terminology to obscure the underlying structure that slowly crystallizes. That structure of love, poetry and prayer, with its particular kind of solution to the perennial queries—what is it that one comes "really" and not just "notionally" to know when one prays, and what, then, is it that the one who rises from prayer must do?—will be his response to the challenges, difficulties and promise of the Modernist project.[3]

3. If, for a moment, one uses categories derived from the thought of Thomas Aquinas, a major

We should see as well that Blondel's affectionate, though at times testy, harassment of Bremond for greater clarity on these questions, is structured into the very essence of the Modernist problematic. Modernism wants to say that religion is not dogma or ecclesial structures or outward forms of any kind, but is something behind and within, and ultimately apart from, all of those things. Religion is the agony of the "disquieted" and restless individual soul searching inwardly for God, resting in a hidden, even "absent," God in the private place of inwardness, then being changed by this God.[4] Outward things mislead and divert and even deceive the searching soul, tempting it to find peace at the surface, instead of in the depth. It is the individuals whom Bremond in the *Histoire* will celebrate as "mystics" that know all of this, who function as Modernists *avant la lettre*, while the rest of us have to discover it through struggle and by having our own mystical potential, as Bremond understood this, unleashed.

Blondel's *gift* to Modernism, as we have seen, was the "method of immanence," with its turning away from "extrinsicism" and "monophorism"; but his *challenge* was strikingly bold: the method can come to its full potential only when the human "space" ready for supernatural filling gives up its own will by "submitting" to God's will.[5] For Bremond, attuned to Blondel at heart, that will can be discerned not so much by harkening to the current hierarchy of Church authority (he is a rebel there, while sensing that all it produced in an "issue with authority" is a pathos of bloody noses and bruised egos), but only by returning to the texts (this is the *real* battle, he might have said), beautiful, sincere and withal disturbing, left by holy persons, in order to listen to their "devotion" afresh.[6] Thus, the *Histoire*.

When Bremond came to the formal question of organizational structure, of how to give his own kind of literary shape to the history of souls that he wanted to write, an imperative model lay ready to hand, that of Charles Augustin Sainte-Beuve in his great *Port-Royal*. Then, the conceptual pair of "devout humanism" and "mysticism" would provide the desired thematic coherence, and, finally, the concept of the "French School" would bestow historical particularity on his overall treatment. The first constituted the flexible skeleton, so to speak, and the second the vital internal organs

---

challenge that Bremond faced in thinking through the meaning of the lives that he portrayed was that of understanding how a "real apprehension" can lead to Blondel's "real adhesion" and not merely "conceptual adhesion." It is one form of the classical and ever-recurrent issue of the relation between knowing and willing that goes back at least to Plato and Aristotle.

4. Marxer, "L'abbé Bremond ou la subjectivité," 14–15, refers to the progression from "inquietude" to "admiration" as the quintessential modernist spiritual pilgrimage, where, for Bremond, the admiring "poetic act" is a form of the Thomistic apprehension of the "real" through the darkness of mystical "knowing." But the question of *what* is "known" remains problematic.

5. For example, in a letter to Bremond of July 22, 1913 (BB, II, 216), he counsels "mystical submission in the passive manner and method of the saints" for the whole group, including Bremond, who are restlessly agitating for the resuscitation of a suppressed Modernist journal.

6. In a laudatory review in *Les Nouvelles Littéraires*, December 29, 1928, after *Histoire* VII and VIII had appeared, Henri Gouhier said that in the *Histoire*, Bremond "looks at the soul that prays, which is to say, at the ideas that *hum* [my emphasis] in the prayer." Such is the *religious sentiment*.

of this new body, the third the intellectual self-consciousness.[7] Understanding why Bremond made these particular choices can give us essential insight into his evolving grand design. First the literary style and narrative structure.

Sainte-Beuve

In the whole process of his education at home and in the schools of Aix, Bremond would have come early to know the name of Sainte-Beuve. If Newman is the principal influence on Bremond as historian, Blondel as theologian, it is Sainte-Beuve as literary stylist and portraitist.

At various points in Bremond's career, influential figures—the Baron, Blondel, Barrès—encouraged his vocation in the field of religious psychology in the mode of a "Christian Sainte-Beuve." He himself indicated in an early essay, the "Christus vivit" piece in the first *L'Inquiétude* collection, that increasingly he felt ready to accept the Sainte-Beuve challenge. In the preface to the first volume of the *Histoire* he indicated that he would walk in the footsteps of "Newman in England and Sainte-Beuve in France ... [whose] main object is to penetrate into a soul's Holy of Holies ... and the particular *nuances of its secret* ... [by means of] the truth of their inner lives, their methods of prayer, their personal individual experience of the realities of which they speak."[8] Indeed, operating in the classic tradition of the Duc de Saint-Simon and La Bruyère, Sainte-Beuve was generally acclaimed as the master French literary historian and biographical essayist of the nineteenth century, a verbal painter who could capture a soul in the multitude of external details—deftly chosen, artfully represented, and modulated with a certain lightness of touch—a skill in which the historian's insight and the novelist's craft merge, and where the outer is a gateway to the inner. Sainte-Beuve had set the standard, and Bremond was determined not only to learn from him, but also to improve upon him.[9]

Charles Augustin Sainte-Beuve (1804–1869) had been a journalist, literary critic and writer of poetry and fiction in Paris during the reign of Louis-Philippe and the Second Empire of Louis Bonaparte, closely associated with the Cénacle, the circle of writers around Victor Hugo. His greatest influence came through an early collection of *Portraits littéraires* (1831), a now-forgotten novel, *La volupté* (1835), a long series of literary portraits in the newspapers (the *Lundis* and *Nouveaux Lundis*, or "chats," from 1851–1870) and then his masterpiece, the *Port-Royal*, published in five books from 1840 to 1859 (2nd ed., 1869; 3rd ed., 1867). A colorful figure from a provincial background, he was a disappointed lover and romantic poet, a would-be religionist

---

7. We might—to follow out the metaphor—think of the pure love/pure poetry/pure prayer nexus, as I have described it, as the circulating blood of the organism!

8. *Histoire*, I, v.

9. It is thus tempting to describe, then dismiss, Bremond as merely a "romantic" historian. But the discerning reader should resist this temptation, the descriptor "romantic" being ambiguous.

and longtime friend of Lamennais in the latter's liberal phase (who gave him access to a large theological library), and an outspoken supporter of Republican views and policies. Eventually he became a professor at the Collège de France, a member of the Académie, and a senator in Parliament.

Composition of the *Port-Royal* was undertaken by Sainte-Beuve as a massive effort to define the canons of French taste by means of a historical survey directed at a movement of cultural assertion.[10] Very much aware of the importance of the Port-Royal-associated characters of Pascal and Racine in national history, and needing a field of study for purposes of a publication that would gain him academic credence, Sainte-Beuve in the 1830s had became enamored with the story of the seventeenth-century women's monastic foundations known as Port-Royal, one in Paris and another, with a boarding-school under the care of male "Solitaries," at Port-Royal-des-Champs, a marshy valley just outside Paris. Reformed Benedictine communities led by charismatic superiors, and hungry for discipline, they had embraced, from 1640 onward, theological emphases and practices emanating from the Flemish bishop and interpreter of St. Augustine, Cornelius Jansen (1585–1638). These had been mediated to Port-Royal primarily through the influence of a pastor and spiritual writer, Jean Duvergier de Hauranne (1581–1643), known as the abbé de Saint-Cyran, and a highly influential Sorbonne professor, Antoine ("the great") Arnauld (1612–1694), by whom, and through the agency of the Port-Royal schools, either directly or indirectly, large numbers of French thinkers, artists and public figures were profoundly influenced. The history was turbulent, filled with charges of heterodox teaching, and efforts at papal control. Port-Royal rose and it fell in a colorful drama.

Sainte-Beuve, with access to important primary sources, told the whole story, with extended portraits of many of the leading lights, as well as a host of important, auxiliary figures. In fact, so numerous were the many connected to Port-Royal as friends or teachers, or artists, or penitents, or debate-opponents, or scholars, or thinkers of every stripe, that Sainte-Beuve was able to create in the course of his breath-taking narrative a kind of gallery of Parisian high culture in the time of the Fronde and of Louis XIV. Substantial depictions of major characters not implicated in Port-Royal, such as Francis de Sales and Nicolas Malebranche, find their way into the account as well. And, of course, Pascal and Racine get major treatment. *Port-Royal* comes off in encyclopedic fashion, and with a great mass of material, as a Parisian *Who's Who?* of the era.[11]

Religiously, Sainte-Beuve was complex. Lapsed from Catholicism, yet hungering for spiritual satisfactions, he loved the story of fiercely held belief, stern discipline,

---

10. Fumaroli calls Sainte-Beuve's *Port-Royal* "at the same time the most singular and the purest expression of national character and especially French 'taste'" (Neveu, *Érudition et Religion*, intro, 1).

11. The *Port-Royal* has never been translated into English, but for a time it captured the attention of informed English readers, curious about religious experience and its portraiture. William James cites it, primarily to illustrate the "heroic" firmness of the grace-filled life, and then the extraordinary lengths to which religious obedience could go (*Varieties*, 255, 309). For James, the *Port-Royal* exemplified *extremes*.

penitential rigor, and proud independence that made up the ethos of Port-Royal. Even while disdaining some of them, Sainte-Beuve saw various denizens of Port-Royal as moral heroes, and he sketched them lovingly and tenderly. Ironically, while having no sympathy with the scholastic theology favored at Port-Royal, with its Augustinian machinery of grace and free will and predestination and divine wrath with sinners, he worked "to defend the doctrine objectively against those who saw no more in it than an hallucination."[12] Through their writings Sainte-Beuve analyzed the dispositions and perceptions of the Port-Royalists, marveled at their strengths and virtues, and deplored their weaknesses and vices. He hated their obsession with physical miracles, but loved their Gallican resistance to attempts at papal control. Their doctrine of sin had great appeal—primarily because of its supposed secular derivative in the world-weariness that marks the work of the Port-Royal hanger-on, La Rochefoucauld. Augustinian sinfulness became a romantic lament for the sadness of life.

Convinced that Port-Royal as the original expression of "Jansenism" maintained its true vitality only up until the time of the papal condemnations beginning in 1705 (after which Jansenism became just theological quibbling), Sainte-Beuve evolved a highly differentiated picture of its many florid individuals, about which, however, he became increasingly discouraged as the story unfolded. Unable to accept their Catholic faith himself, he foresaw their inevitable destruction and ultimate tragedy in their obsessive and pedantic theologizing. On the other hand, he discerned a set of ideals that had transformative power then and now. If only, he thought, we today could recapture their spiritual fraternity, emulate their devotion, be inspired by the moral energy that made them great! He wanted France to be a kind of secularized counterpart to Port-Royal, that is, a nation with the spiritual substance, but not the religious window dressing, of a church. What we can hear in his analysis is something we have already heard: let the church be the moral backbone of the nation, as long as we do not have to submit to all of the dogmatic baggage.[13]

In short, Sainte-Beuve had constructed an idealized picture of a past community, sympathetically reconstructed with the literary historian's eye for rich detail and anecdotal color, that could animate contemporaries by evocation.[14] The saga of Port-Royal is a nation's saga. Bremond, when he later addressed the subject directly in a 1919 essay,[15] clearly recognizing a somewhat outmoded romanticism in Sainte-Beuve,

---

12 Nicolson, *Sainte-Beuve*, 152.

13 Nicolson emphasizes that "Sainte-Beuve's surpassing gift of narrative, of portraiture, and of variation" was his real forte, "that he was no theologian and his bouts of contrition were not permanent" (ibid., 154–55).

14. In an early biography of Sainte-Beuve, that of Othenin d'Haussonville, the author notes that Sainte-Beuve originally formulated *Port-Royal* as a series of lectures to a predominantly Protestant, liberal-academic-Calvinist and Arminian, audience in Lausanne, Switzerland. He piously referred to Port-Royal as "the school of Jesus Christ," thus playing up Port-Royal's moral fervor and playing down its theology (*Sainte-Beuve, sa vie et ses sources*, 164).

15. "Sainte-Beuve ou le romantique impénitent,"

argued nonetheless that he wrote with "soul," with "heart," with the spirit of a poet who has turned to history and recognizes that good historical narrative communes with its subjects. Sainte-Beuve had a way of intuiting a "presence" in the object, and in the images held up by the object, that is religious in nature. That "presence" is God's grace, reaching out to us *through nature*, thus preparing for supernatural grace. This "profane mysticism" in Sainte-Beuve, as he worked at his depiction of Port-Royal, manifested his "antennae" homing in on spiritual realities. Sainte-Beuve "felt before he wrote," thus putting himself in a separate class from Gibbon the rationalist, who could not understand what he does not love.

But Bremond was far from uncritical in his idolizing of Sainte-Beuve.[16] Admiring Sainte-Beuve's kind of historiography and its spirit was a far cry from agreeing with his interpretations, especially if—and this is critical—the historian himself is not a person who prays, perhaps even is a skeptic, and so is tone-deaf to the life of prayer in the objects of his study. Romantic empathy, in order to be effective, calls for the *whole soul* of the interpreter, and this is precisely where blind spots can manifest themselves. Sainte-Beuve seemed to be leaving something essential out.

What mattered was Sainte-Beuve's central technique: let a writer's works interpret the writer's life, and then let the life interpret the works in a closed loop.[17] A writer's biography, Bremond thought, should enlighten that writer's treatises and vice versa, the premise being that "the saint and the writer . . . are complementary to the other, luring on, restraining, rounding into completeness," and "the greater number of spiritual masters 'lived' their books and have told their own life-stories in writing them."[18] The classic challenge to that view would come from Marcel Proust early on, in his contention that the creative energy in writing does not come from the artist's "social self," but from a "private self" that cannot be accessed biographically. The interplay of actuality (the "real") and inventive imagination is thus more elusive, more *textual*, than Sainte-Beuve thought.[19] But Bremond shared some of that Proustian reserve: let the life of the artist interpret the work, but let it be the "real" life of the artist, that is, his life of prayer, access to which is gained only when one makes living contact with the poetry present in his text.[20]

---

16. A quite definitive assessment here is that of Laurent Thirouin, "Deux visions de Port-Royal," HeL, 79–80, who presents Sainte-Beuve as "model and tutelary father" for Bremond, and yet the former's religion is only "a Christianity of desire." I will return to this essay, which posits, following Certeau, a kind of oedipal rivalry of complicity and disengagement between Bremond and Sainte-Beuve, when we come to *Histoire*, IV, "The School of Port-Royal."

17. *Histoire*, I, xiv–xvi.

18. Ibid., xv. He disparages Strowski's study of the "religious sentiment" in Francis de Sales as too confined to doctrinal writings, thus too "speculative" (xiv).

19. Proust, *Contre Sainte-Beuve*, esp. 121–47: "On the Method of Sainte-Beuve." Bernard de Fallois argues that the character of Swann in *Swann's Way* was created by Proust as a "hidden" Sainte-Beuve precisely in order to illustrate the futility of Sainte-Beuve's aesthetic (ibid., "préface," 21).

20. It is thus that Marxer, joining with those critics who complain about Bremond's sometimes lack of historical exactitude with regard to "textual diffusion" as well as the nuances of critical purification

And there was also the problem that Sainte-Beuve wandered or meandered through the history of Port-Royal, so that he ended up including anything and everything in a kind of leisurely guided tour with side trips through an endlessly fascinating museum. Focus is lost. The way that Bremond said this is that Sainte-Beuve "avails himself of his 'lion rights'" as he works through the history, but that he, Bremond, will operate otherwise, because he has a particular vision for ordering his material.[21] He is more like Newman here, with definite ideas, an a priori, of what it is that develops through the course of the narrative. He referred, somewhat mysteriously,[22] to the "mystic keep," that is, the "Mystical Life," that would constrain his range of interest. And he laid out a format along that line for three volumes: *The Coming of Mysticism*, followed by *The Triumph of Mysticism*, and completed by *The Retreat of the Mystics*. He had decided at this point that "mystical" was a more useful term than "sanctity," since (citing another) "for all those who, in endeavoring to develop their personal religion, gropingly seek their Creator through the desert of the daily task, the mystics stand, each in his appointed class and place, as witnesses."[23]

Devout Humanism

So, accept Sainte-Beuve as inspiration, we might say, and then push beyond him, recognizing that what *we* need is a literary history of the religious sentiment that empowers us in the present in a way that failed with Sainte-Beuve when he communed with his beloved, but failed, Port-Royal.[24] Convinced that the practice of mystical prayer provided the best window into the peculiar inwardness of seventeenth-century piety, Bremond then settled on the concept of "devout humanism" as the comprehensive ideological construct that best unified both the theological thinking and the inward orientation of spiritual writers high and low. The first volume, therefore, of the *Histoire* would be titled not "The Coming of Mysticism," but "Devout Humanism." The beauty of the latter choice would be that it served two purposes simultaneously: historical description and contemporary critique. Suitably retrieved, the concept suggested

---

in his favored sources, argues that Bremond approached texts "in a metaphysical manner, where the mystical experience is potentially opened up, and the printed page is the distillate or mediator of that experience" ("L'abbé Bremond," 23). Trémolières makes a related point when he argues, following Certeau and against Joseph de Guibert, that Bremond could be right on target with what he "reported" about a text, while being wrong in what he "argued" ("The Witness to These Witnesses," 272).

21. *Histoire*, I, xiii.

22. "Somewhat mysteriously," because it would turn out that he had wrestled with whether or not he should do a whole exposition of the nature of "mysticism" in the general introduction to *Histoire*, I, and then, on the advice of others, decided against it, reserving the subject for an appendix to vol. II.

23. Ibid., xxii.

24. Nicolson cites Bremond, who was commenting on the skeptical tone in Sainte-Beuve toward the end of *Port-Royal*: "The story of *Port-Royal* is in this sense the story of a conversion that failed" (*Sainte-Beuve*, 144).

a mandate for the present, a counterforce to the authoritarian dogmatism of anti-Modernism, a Catholicism more humane, yet truly faithful.

Goichot has traced out Bremond's use of the concept as a coalescence of a number of thematic trajectories and political agendas.[25] In the midst of prolonged correspondence with friends, and with potential publishers, he struggled with different formulations for the structure and naming of what was shaping up as a large multi-volume work, as well as with matters of theoretical coherence, keeping an eye simultaneously on factors of church authority, public interest, terminological clarity and precision, and, of course, the demands of the material itself. Most notable were the various arguments pro and con about the choice of the term "sentiment" for the title, but "devout humanism" and "mysticism" were debated as well. Every choice had advantages and disadvantages. In the midst of all of this fine-tuning, Bremond produced a second essay on Félicité Lamennais that can serve as a clue into the final choice of "devout humanism" in close pairing with "mysticism."[26]

In that essay he commented on two recent books that had condemned Lamennais for being a continuator of the radical ideas of Rousseau, ideas that turned him into a traitor to Catholicism. We recall that in his earlier study of Lamennais Bremond had described him as a failed "mystic," for whom the life of prayer early on had been powerful. And then it withered, grace seemingly disappeared, and Lamennais despaired. We saw also in the study of Gerbet, Lamennais's most influential follower, that a theology which honored the developing spiritual truth found in all of human experience, the "common sense," led inexorably to a deep immersion by believers in all of the arts and sciences of the human heritage and the modern state. Gerbet was an admirable humanist, a believer who looks with humility and wonder on all that human diligence at its best has produced that is good, beautiful and true. But Bremond also saw with both Lamennais and Gerbet that unless that humanism is undergirded by, and solidly grounded in, the experience of the "presence," i.e., the "mystical" experience, it cannot thrive.

Now, in this successor article on Lamennais, Bremond argued that in the course of his development Lamennais began, as his conflicts and intellectual instability worsened, and as he was subjected to increasing violence, to experience "the silence of God." The grace of God seemed to have been withdrawn in some way that we cannot discern, said Bremond, though the result is quite visible. Consequently, Lamennais could no longer preach the love of God, for his springs had dried up. In the case of Francis de Sales, Bremond would make much of Francis's statement that "nothing human is foreign to me," but Lamennais would serve as the cautionary tale: take away prayer and the quest for holiness, and a robust, spiritually motivated humanism collapses. But it must be *mystical* prayer (yet to be defined) in the face of silent darkness. A sustainable, truly "devout" humanism cannot survive without that foundation.

25. Goichot, "'L'humanisme dévot' de l'abbé Bremond."
26. "Lamennais et les origines du romantisme catholique," first composed in 1913.

With the spirituality of devout humanism, thus, as his starting point, and Francis de Sales as his pacesetter, Bremond was then off and running. At the beginning of *Histoire*, I, he distinguished between two types of humanism, both originating in that medieval tradition that, delighting in the Greco-Roman classics, passed on this taste to the Italian Renaissance, where it flourished in the Cult of Man.[27] This "natural" humanism starts out as a literary culture, luxuriating in new discoveries, flamboyant in expression, marked by "that curiosity and sympathy which incline us towards all manifestations of activity and all aspects of human history."[28] "Masters of a new earth and new skies, men felt themselves more man."[29] Humanity thus is never contemptible, but always to be excused, defended and exalted. Such humanism is optimistic about human goodness, and sees beauty in all aspects of human nature.

Christian humanism then enters the picture by means of a highlighting of the drama of Redemption, where the focus is not on sin—as in gloomy Calvinism—but on consolation, encouragement, and an orientation to the potential in human nature for infinite goodness. Natural man has been injured by the fall, but not profoundly corrupted, retaining real free will and, when empowered by actual grace, capable of holiness. Such humanism, contended Bremond, was at first aristocratic, but then made canonical by Trent, and is represented by Catholic writers, teachers, artists, and all who create a Christian humanistic culture of beauty. "Without neglecting any of the central truths of Christianity, it [Christian humanism] brings forward by preference those which appear the most consoling, encouraging, in a word *human*, which to it seem the most divine and the most conformed to Infinite Goodness."[30] What such humanists do is to "blend natural delights with the Christian life, thus sanctifying and increasing their charm."

Then one more ingredient is added to this Christian humanism in order to make it a truly "devout humanism," and this is the quest for personal holiness. Such a quest, the hallmark of Francis de Sales's absorption of Christian humanism into the goals of the Counter-Reformation, thus ministers to "the needs of the inner life," integrating the best elements of humanist tradition with the age-old Christian quest for a practical

---

27. Thus Bremond never entered into those debates about "premodern" versus "modern," in which a fundamental originality in the Italian *quattrocento* is highlighted. He was very mindful of elements of continuity in the Renaissance with medieval forebears, including the Provençal troubadour tradition, as in his 1908 study of Antoine Yvan.

28. *Histoire*, I, 9.

29. Ibid., 8. The great Paul Claudel thus vigorously applauded Bremond's early volumes of the *Histoire*, then became disillusioned as Bremond championed the spirituality of "self-annihilation" in the later volumes. Claudel could not understand that the latter was grounded in the former. See Blanchet, "Claudel lecteur de Bremond," for sources and discussion.

30. Ibid., 11. Thus, the moral philosopher Charles Taylor also affirms Bremond's project, where he takes "devout humanism" as an example of the ideal of cultivating the love of God precisely as the desire for "a transformation which goes beyond ordinary human flourishing," i.e., a human flourishing that is more than human, thus directed at God and requiring God's grace. This is *human-defined-as-more-than-human* (*Secular Age*, 510).

saintliness that fulfills the deepest yearnings of human nature.[31] We see Blondel's theology everywhere in Bremond's foundations.

Thus stated, there is absolutely nothing remarkable about "devout humanism." In fact, it can easily be argued, as some have done, that Bremond over-stretched the term "humanism," so that it becomes a catch-all umbrella for everything that he did not like about some expressions of Catholic tradition, which he will come to associate with Jansenism and Port-Royal, as well as with the conservative and authoritarian movements of the post-1870 Church.[32] Such retrograde Christianity, Catholic or Protestant, overplays the doctrine of sin, turning Christian faith into an intellectual exercise in obscurantism by resisting the accomplishments of secular culture, and it turns Christian practice into a legalism by mandating (what he interpreted to be) a self-glorifying self-improvement through asceticism. The story of Christianity, in effect, will become a battle of humanists and anti-humanists, past and present. What would complicate the picture, and keep it from being a simple cartoon, is that Bremond could, and did, recognize genuinely humanistic elements in those that he would describe as anti-mystical and anti-humanist. Anti-humanists are more humane and more devout when they pray, said Bremond, and humanists are devout precisely when they do not cease to pray.

The first figure that Bremond set up for praise in the *Histoire* was the French Jesuit Louis Richeome (1544–1625), a Provençal dubbed the "French Cicero." Comparing him to such later word-artists as La Fontaine, or Théophile Gautier, or John Ruskin, Bremond described him as pedagogue, poet, and painter, with "an inexhaustible supply of sketches."[33] He exemplified Fénelon's "childlike spirit," loving the world of nature, and convinced that by virtue of baptism every Christian has the power to overcome sin, if only we will trust God and make the effort. "Instead," said Bremond, "of depressing us by a realistic painting of our corruption, he addresses himself to the noblest instincts of our nature." Instead of whipping us for our sin, as Port-Royal would do, "he incites us to heroism by treating us as heroes."[34] The war of the soul with sin is turned into a game, a tournament, in which the soul struggles valiantly, then is aided by grace at the critical moment, and sails on to victory. There is a juvenile playfulness in all of this, said Bremond, that combines "the freshness and riot of

---

31. *Histoire*, I, 15.

32. Bremond was sometimes criticized for a too generalized use of the term "humanistic" in defense of his understanding of Catholic tradition. It is also true that Bremond operated too much under the shadow of Jacob Burckhardt's interpretation of the Italian Renaissance, as did all interpreters at that time. For a trenchant, but balanced, critique of Bremond's use of the concept of humanism, see Le Brun, "L'humanisme dévot." The principal objection raised by Le Brun, who follows Henri Gouhier, is philosophical: because "humanism" usually refers to the *sufficiency* of human nature for all things, the idea of a *Christian* humanism is ambiguous and confusing. Bremond would struggle mightily with these distinctions later when he came to the subject of "pure poetry" (1032–33).

33. *Histoire*, I, 28.

34. Ibid., 48.

youth and the subtle humorous wisdom of kindly age."[35] But the wisdom is scattered, fragmented, anticipatory of more adequate statement. It would take Francis de Sales, a generation later, to give this spirituality a systematic, coherent expression, and then with Pierre de Bérulle, to turn it into the "French School."

The first of several treatments of Francis de Sales, has him as a master synthesizer of past wisdom and the supreme disseminator of Christian humanism in popular form with the *Introduction à la vie dévote*, and then in systematic form with the *Traité de l'Amour de Dieu*. In all of Francis, averred Bremond, "nature and grace meet . . . adjusting themselves to each other, mingling with perfect ease." "The Salesian spirit is the most exact and perfect expression of Devout Humanism," rejoicing in the beauty of human nature, while advocating the disinterested "Pure Love of the mystics," in an unquenchable optimism. Central to Francis's understanding was the classical view that we have a "lower self" and a "higher self," but he insists that the higher self is the "real self," a dimension of the soul accessible through the act of faith and the exercise of charity. It is the fulfillment of human potential, something that Sainte-Beuve, viewing Francis only as a poet, could not understand. Francis's writing will become "the charter of the Higher Mysticism in France of the seventeenth century."[36]

In several richly written chapters involving a parade of writers, Bremond displayed a virtual cornucopia of the literary output of devout humanism—hymns and canticles, poetry, drama, scholarly study, biographical sketches of holy lives, religious "romances"—all of it marked by mirth and play, by a persistently "childlike" and thus "mystical" spirit, by the practice of prayerful recollection, by an exuberant and unquenchable optimism, by the movement toward "pure love" as the spiritual ideal. Multitudes of illustration and citations make the point that devout humanism was from the first interwoven with aesthetic efflorescence, in which writers captured lyrically the dynamics of the inner life as a great human adventure. The common intuition, running through it all, is that human beauty of expression, sometimes consummately elegant and sometimes excessive and hyperbolic, can be, whatever its level of excellence, exquisitely expressive of divine goodness. Thus, in this first volume of the *Histoire*, Bremond put his readers on notice that the journey ahead would be a dazzling, fireworks-filled procession of artful religious penmanship. It is no wonder that the *Histoire* was a hit with the general public.

It was clear also that he would grind away relentlessly at this Salesian thesis. Treatments of bishop Jean-Pierre Camus (1584–1652) and the Jesuit Étienne Binet (1569–1639) displayed the growing influence of Francis de Sales, but it is the relatively unknown Capuchin, Yves of Paris (c. 1590–1679), that Bremond promoted to the status of "the archetype of Devout Humanism."[37] He had discovered and perused

---

35. Ibid., 51.

36. Ibid., 64, 82, 94, 99, 100, for citations.

37. Ibid., 331. Yves is an ideal figure for Bremond, because he spans the distance between Italian ecclesiastico-humanist roots and its importation into French circles of influence.

Yves's work while on a visit in Rome, finding him to be a Christian Platonist and contemplative of refined sensibility. Yves focused in a remarkable way on the wonders of nature, meeting God everywhere in all created things, and then in the manner of the Florentine neo-Platonists developing a theory of participation in the hierarchical structure of being. This is to say that "contemplation with Père Yves here reaches at least the frontiers of mysticism, thus once more verifying the great law of the normal evolution of Devout Humanism."[38] Devout humanism develops naturally into mysticism. They are inseparable.

Bremond will often point to the Platonic philosophical inspiration of writers in the devout humanist tradition, arguing that with Yves they "invariably tend, sometimes with a certain exaggeration, to platonize Christianity [while endeavoring] yet more to Christianize and supernaturalize Plato."[39] Such devout humanism, claimed Bremond, with its optimistic conception of the universe, "so far from softening the holy rigour of the Gospel, insists upon its straitness.... Devout Humanism, to be logical, cannot stop short of Sanctity, nay, if God will, of the Mystic Union."[40]

At the very end of this first volume of the *Histoire*, Bremond offered a first definition of mysticism: it is "that natural disposition which leads certain souls by a sort of sudden compulsion to seize with direct and daring love on the spiritual beneath the veil of sense, the one in the many, the order amid the confusion, the eternal in the transitory, the divine in the created."[41] Citing the Jesuit theorist Léonce de Grandmaison at length, Bremond portrayed natural mysticism as a moment, or series of moments, in which the mind allows intellection to cease, so that a calm "receiving" and "savoring," an "interior silence," can allow "an understanding . . . of the unknown" to crystalize. Mysticism is the awareness of *depth*. And then comes the final statement: Since mystical moments allow for a suspension of the human ego and its "base obsession," "with all its *logical* [my emphasis] tendency, with all its élan, Devout Humanism insists on Pure Love." The word *logical*, used a number of times by Bremond for the trajectory he traced, is Newman's "development" applied not to dogma as such, but to a dynamic unfolding of the "idea" contained in the outward form, where in the inner life of the soul obeys a "compulsion" and "seizes" the "real." It is the Modernist project: the Thing Itself, rather than mere outward forms.

The second volume of the *Histoire*, published almost immediately after the first, simply continued the story-line already established, through a host of characters, folding in the apophatic Dionysian tradition of Benedict Canfield, then the founding figures of the French Carmel, ending with, once again, Francis de Sales and Jeanne de Chantal, this time focusing on them as mystics. Bremond suggested that the establishment of the Visitation was, in effect, the creation of "an Academy of Pure Love," in

38. Ibid., 347.
39. Ibid., 355.
40. Ibid., 395.
41. Ibid., 400.

which the Sisters could practice "the simple presence of God, through an entire abandonment of themselves to the holy Providence."[42] But there was an essential qualification: this practice was framed at such a level of ordinary daily routines and duties that natural, frail and imperfect humanity was always in evidence, without prideful attempts to be perfect or to imagine that they were angels.

At the end of the second volume came the long awaited, and long delayed, theoretical treatment of the nature of mysticism, where Bremond, having decided not to address the subject in the general introduction of the *Histoire*, was finally ready to engage a range of thinkers on a widely disputed subject. It is a remarkable overview and synthesis, one that went through considerable revision before reaching its published form. Some background and context are imperative for proper understanding.

Mysticism

Like "devout humanism," "mysticism" was, for Bremond, a richly determined concept, rapidly picking up steam in his own time, prior to its virtual explosion in our own. Its history is complex.[43]

The distant background was in the "mystical theology" that had become, alongside dogmatic and moral theology, one of the three separate disciplines of Catholic theological reflection and exposition by the end of the fourteenth century. In this structure some theology would be speculative, some practical, with mystical theology tending to bridge the divide by being a theology of experience, on the one hand, while often utilizing a speculative anthropology for various purposes, on the other.

In terms of *experience*, the typical focus was on those "extraordinary" or "ecstatic" spiritual states, in which some individuals claimed to enjoy especially intimate union with, or participation in, the divine Being itself. The purpose of mystical theology was to spell out the nature of this mystical experience, often conceived as an ascent, or "ladder," with prolegomena, physical and spiritual accompaniments, distinct stages and graded facilitating ascetical disciplines. Debates existed about the external marks of mystical states, the degree to which normal human functioning ceased in such states, the extent to which such states should be encouraged or discouraged by pastors, and if desired, how to assist their development. All schools of thought agreed that the final unitive consummation with the Godhead, an "ineffable" state, could be described only privatively in the apophatic tradition, or with metaphors, the most

---

42. *Histoire*, II, 421, 423.

43. Bibliography is, of course, massive. The best theoretical introduction, with a sketchy historical overview, is Solignac et al., "Mystique." The best historical overview and analysis of late nineteenth-century and twentieth-century developments in the study of mysticism, especially by major Roman Catholic thinkers in the Thomist tradition, is McGinn, "Theoretical Foundations," which should be supplemented by Schmidt, "Making of Modern Mysticism." The best philosophical exploration of the meaning of mysticism in contemporary thought is Certeau, "Mystique," but it should be supplemented by Katz, *Mysticism and Philosophical Analysis*.

famous of which is the mystical marriage, in the kataphatic tradition. Most writers agree that human knowing and willing are gradually combined in the mystical ascent, so that the experience of union and deification, or, alternatively, the fully consummated experience of divine "presence," is best described in the language of loving relationship.[44] Bremond gravitates, as we shall see, to the apophatic language, to the *unspeakability* of the divine, as well as its unknowability, and thus to an *affective* as well as a cognitive-intellectual apophaticism.[45]

In terms of *speculative anthropology*, a body-spirit, or body-mind-spirit configuration was sometimes used by writers as a key to sacred hermeneutics. It is the spiritual dimension of our natures that allows us to interpret the *mystical* sense, or the *mysterium*, contained in nature or in biblical texts. The spiritual or *mystical* individual, as part of the mystical ascent, can discern the deeper, divine meanings hidden behind the surface, or literal level, that is, the *body*, of the physical, material world.[46] Bremond, in his use of mysticism for his own theological constructions, will make great capital of the idea that mysticism, as in poetry, is a way of discerning deeper levels of meaning.

Mystical theology accelerated, then, during the sixteenth century, easily linking up with the Reformation/Counter-Reformation emphasis on greater spiritual aspiration, especially in the search for "perfection" in the Christian life and the increasing elaboration of theologies of "grace." The Spanish Carmelites, most notably Teresa of Avila and John of the Cross, were prime movers.[47] Mystical theology contributed greatly to the development of "interiority," with a theology of the inner life that combined the acquisition of virtue with a journey into closer inward relationship with God. As various elites "specialized" in ascetical disciplines of all sorts, mystical experience became a desideratum in the form of "contemplation," or a broad spiritual awareness, as a normal dimension of all true prayer, for all serious devotées. The seventeenth century then saw a shift toward the "practical" in all areas of theology, Catholic or Protestant, with the consequent rise of pietistic movements in which richness of emotional fervor combined with the cultivation of disciplined devotional habits eventually gave way, as part of modernity, to endless hybridization with technologies for improving the quality of life, including its moral depth. The distillate for Bremond of this phase of the development of mystical understanding will be the "theocentric-ascetic" tension in true mysticism, and the unending debate about the "moral" component in mysticism.

The reaction came, however, in the eighteenth century, with an increasing suspicion of irrational excess. Mystical experience was more and more associated with the religious fringe, with "enthusiasm," "illuminism," and fanaticism, thus acquiring

---

44. See Louis Dupré, "Christian Experience of Mystical Union," for an especially helpful discussion.

45. Certeau, "Henri Bremond," 43.

46 Henri de Lubac, SJ, would become, in many publications, the great expositor of the "tripartite anthropology" in relation to the mystical interpretation of Scripture.

47. At this point in the history, Michel de Certeau, "Mystique," becomes the best guide.

the derogative connotation that still lingers. Michel de Certeau has noted that mysticism became the pathology for some, but also the essence for others, of vital religion, and Leigh Eric Schmidt contends that by the eighteenth century in Protestant circles "the term [mysticism] was socially situated within debates about the fundamental comportment of religious people."[48] The question was asked: is religious "ecstasy" or "rapture" essential to vital religious experience? Reasonable people denied it, and contended that correct doctrine is more important. Catholics associated "mysticism" with the aberrations of Fénelon and Guyon, while Protestants linked it with hyper-emotional fanaticism. Bremond will labor energetically to show that the core of mystical experience does not require any of the florid external manifestations, many of which may indeed be pathological.

But then in the nineteenth century, as a result of the romantic-transcendentalist turn in culture, religious people began to issue a qualified "Yes," or they at least came to affirm the importance of deep passion and immediacy in relation to God as a desideratum, as something ultimately more important than bare doctrine—now known as "rationalism" in religion. It is in this romantic context that mysticism came to be associated with the "vital" element in religion, its heartbeat, as opposed to the verbal formulations that are the outer surface. And in Victorian language mysticism comes to be the "poetry" of religion, with doctrine as its "prose."

It is, then, only one step to saying that we can do without the prose. This is the point at which the forces of modernity, of the human and the personal and the inward, became the fuel of Modernism in the churches toward the end of the nineteenth-century. The linkage is easily made with the historical-critical reading of texts for their "true" meaning, where correct interpretation is a matter of going "deeper" into the text, not staying at the surface. This is the context in which Catholic modernists embraced mystical spirituality fervently, and it is the point at which Bremond entered the lists.[49]

Bemond was, in fact, playing a part in an enormous surge of interest in mysticism in specifically Catholic circles.[50] Of particular importance to his theoretical thinking were two Jesuits, the Belgian Joseph Maréchal (1878–1944), from whom he took the idea that mystical experience consists essentially not of outward phenomena which may be pathological, but of the consciousness of the immediate presence of a transcendent being, and Léonce de Grandmaison (1868–1927), from whom he took the view that there is across cultures a non-intellectual intuition of God, with or without

---

48. Certeau, "Henri Bremond," 875, speaks of the "paradoxical forms" of mystical experience, "abnormal and strange," on the one hand, and an "announcement of the 'essential,'" on the other. Schmidt examines, in particular, the American contribution to the connotations of the term, whereby its steadily expanding use has helped to precipitate the current fascination with "spirituality" (Schmidt, "Making of Modern Mysticism," 277, 284–95).

49. While there are many studies of mysticism in the writings of each of the Catholic Modernists, the best comprehensive collections are essays are those edited, or coedited by C. J. T. Talar, MM and MMM..

50. See especially Portier and Talar, "Mystical Element," and Losito, introduction to MMM, as well as De Pril, "La théologie catholique," for context.

theistic language, that prepares the way for truly supernatural experience. For both thinkers mystical awareness is part of human nature as such.[51]

L'Échelle Mystique

The best way of approaching the "Appendix" to *Histoire*, II, is by way of the "Échelle mystique" or "Mystical Ladder," which is the most complete of several versions that preceded the published form of the "Appendix." It has been known since 2004 from documents bequeathed to the Bibliothèque nationale de France by Goichot, and reveals more of Bremond's original intentions than are evident in the Appendix in its finished state.[52] When we recall, also, that the "Appendix" was Bremond's substitute for the discussion of mysticism he had originally intended as part of the general introduction to the *Histoire*, we can better see that he delayed full revelation of his views, knowing that a hornet's nest would be stirred.

His central theme in the "Échelle," and the analogy that drives the whole essay—an argument completely missing in the published version—is the idea that "natural mysticism" is best understood in terms of the inspiration that a poet experiences, when a transformative moment of sudden awareness occurs, where the writer feels "acted upon." In that action a "simplification" of the poet's jumbled and confused perceptions occurs, so that his material crystallizes into a meaningful unity that can be expressed artistically. A "higher knowledge" is bestowed, and energy begins to move. There occurs a mysterious calm, a stillpoint, in which "the heart has no other sentiment than a sweet and peaceful taste of God, who nourishes it effortlessly as milk nourishes infants."[53] No special knowledge is given cognitively, but the poet "feels," "touches," "possesses," with a sense of being "possessed" by the strange presence. Initial sluggishness is followed by an eruption of energy. A depth is revealed or "given" beneath the surface of things, showing that ultimately a merely mechanical, deterministic universe makes no sense. Bremond called this experience a natural anticipation of the beatific

---

51. The critical work is Maréchal's 1927 collection, *Studies in the Psychology of the Mystics*, which contains the enormous essays on "The Feeling of Presence in Mystics and Non-Mystics" (1908–1909), and "Empirical Science and Religious Psychology" (1915). Grandmaison's famous essay was the 1910 "L' élément mystique dans la religion." He was strongly supportive of Bremond, and strongly endorsed the whole project of the *Histoire*. As the director of *Études* in Paris after Bremond's departure, he represented more flexible and liberal views.

52. Printed, for the first time, in HLM, I, as "L'Échelle mystique," with a critical introduction, in which Trémolières explains the convoluted relationship between this preliminary text (one of three versions) and the published end product. He reproduces the list compiled by Goichot, who demonstrated the close connection between portions of "L'Échelle" and Bremond's use of this material in the 1926 *Prière et poésie*, thus displaying the "Ariadne's thread" of his whole undertaking (HLM, I, 827–28).

53. A well-worn image to be sure, but one essential for Bremond, who referred to sources in Grou and Alvarez (HLM, I, 831n1). The better source, however, is Francis de Sales and such passages as the *Treatise on the Love of God*, 5.2, where "the milk our souls draw forth from the breasts of our Lord's charity is of incomparably greater value than the wine we press out by human reasoning."

vision, a true "preparation for the state of grace." It is the sacred being revealed in the profane. It is Newman's movement from the "notional" to the "real."

But there is, averred Bremond, nothing easy about these mystical moments of inspiration; they come only with hard work and suffering. He speaks of "the dry and mortifying virtues... courageously practiced before the appearance of the heroic [i.e., poetic] signal."[54] He is at pains to distinguish the moment of inspiration, the mystical encounter, from any product that is produced. Adding nothing to the dogmatic corpus of Christianity—with no "content," we might say—this moment is a trigger, an initiator, ultimately ineffable, so that mystical *theology* can only be a post hoc reflection, in which the "ecstasy of the encounter," the actual contact with the *Real*, can never itself be literary material. Bremond speaks of "mysteries" in the experience, where there is the transformative sense of penetrating beneath the surface of things to an invisible world, a world solid and real, with an awareness that the experience as something "given" and unable to be generated intellectually or morally must be experienced "passively." Thus it is that such "natural mysticism" is precisely *mystical* because it constitutes the "necessary condition" for supernatural mysticism.[55]

The published form of this essay on the nature of mysticism, the "Appendix," likewise left out the next section of the "Échelle," which is a long discourse on the understanding of "devotion" in the work of Francis de Sales, and the relationship between "devotion" and "mysticism." Devotion is the ordering of the human will in the direction of charity, and for the purpose of serving God. It is a profoundly inward orientation, initiated by grace at that "fine point of the soul" which is deeper than sensory experience, deeper than the surface of the soul, and the locus of properly mystical experience. It normally requires a measure of ascetical effort, but must not be confused with that effort or the rigors of structured meditation. In a slight reference, much diminished from the "Échelle," Bremond highlights Sainte-Beuve's emphasis on the "ray" that must animate every true writer, the "ray" that is his proper mysticism.[56]

The next lengthy section of the "Échelle," on the theme of "ecstasy" as the proper name for mysticism, is constituted, then, by the same reduced material that forms the first major part of the published Appendix. This is where Bremond leaned the hardest on Maréchal and Grandmaison, against the views of Augustin Poulain, SJ, (1836–1919), to argue that mystical experience does not consist essentially of the bizarre outward phenomena, of strange visions and private revelations, since, in fact, it is deeply inward, non-sensual and void of intellectual content as such. It is experience continuous with a broad variety of mental states, thus universal, thus accessible in principle to all. The point, though, is that such experience at the "fine point" *leads* to

---

54. HLM, I, 832.

55. Ibid., 836n1, where Bremond claims to speak "in all rigor," that is, so that the natural/supernatural distinction is not confused.

56. Ibid., 842. This is material that Bremond will hold for the opening sections of *Histoire*, VII, where he will expound Francis de Sales's "philosophy" of prayer.

insights, gives birth to art, stimulates discovery, etc. It is not light, says Bremond, but is a generator of light.[57]

The remaining sections of "Échelle," constitute the latter part of the Appendix as well. On the question of what is "learned" from the mystical encounter, Bremond sides with the tradition of "amorous knowledge," but, he warns that such "knowledge" is not that which comes from "consolations" or pleasurable experiences of love, but rather it arises from a single-minded focus on the object of love, on God. Such love is thus "pure" or disinterested—it is love itself—it is the love extolled by Fénelon, and then by de Caussade, in which one loves God solely as "our sovereign good" and "our sovereign beatitude." It is here that the suffering of the mystical ascent appears, since the process of beginning to experience such love must include the painful stripping of the human ego "in the frightful night" where "a light dwells," the night of self-abandonment.[58] This is where the "scandal of quietism" arises, in the fact that love can be learned only by a mysterious purification that defies rational analysis, that transcends all ascetic efforts, since it must be endured passively in order to become a source of strength. The immediate intuition of God, so emphasized by Maréchal, is thus a well-known process of "progressive despoilment," with parallels in neo-Platonism and in Islamic spirituality, a "mortifying simplicity" that is the key to a rightly understood quietism, despite the bitter criticisms directed toward it.[59]

The general conclusion is that "devotion is the flower; the Mystic Union is the fruit; but, while the flower does not survive the fruit which is its completion, devotion derives from the Union a new vitality, in fact carries it on, exploits it, if the term were not too vulgar."[60]

Given the revisions that Bremond made to the "Échelle," before its appearance as the "Appendix," we thus see that when the time came for Bremond to define mysticism, to explain its relation to devout humanism, to position himself for the long trek through the seventeenth century, the true starting point was a combination of the analogy with poetic inspiration combined with an explication of "devotion" in the work of Francis de Sales, the result being a spirituality of self-abandon in the spirit of pure love. But he decided that any straightforward statement was premature, preferring at the outset to operate strictly under the umbrella provided by Maréchal and Grandmaison, and in dialogue with the positions of Poulain. Nonetheless, the overall result was clear: mystical devotion is the living heartbeat of the church's life in all ages, for it is the heartbeat of life itself.

Critical response to Bremond's thinking about mysticism would be, as we shall see, fast and furious, with every element in his characterization a bone of contention. But his cards were (beginning to be) on the table.

57. Ibid., 857.
58. Ibid., 865.
59. Ibid., 867–70.
60. Ibid., 871, and *Histoire*, II, 445.

Lights Extinguished

From the literary soul to the mystical soul, with devout humanism as the mediating element, the seventeenth century being the field of activity, Bremond thus refined his project, as his trajectory picked up speed in the years 1913 to 1915. *Histoire*, I, would come out from Bloud et Gay at the end of 1915 and the turn to the new year, with II to follow shortly. He moved back and forth between Arthez-d'Asson and an apartment in Paris, 16 Rue de Chanoinesse, where, with a friend and fellow Newman-scholar, Canon Ernest Dimnet close by, they could both gaze at the buttresses of Notre-Dame. His life had become books, books, and more books, with excursions to provincial collections.

But then, one major interruption, as "the lights started going out all over Europe." War came in August 1914, right in the midst of Bremond's final gathering and ordering of materials for the first two volumes.

In their immediate prewar correspondence, Blondel and Bremond, very much aware of the mounting atmosphere of militaristic nationalism, constantly lamented the accelerating furor around Maurras and Action Française. And they were attuned to early indications that eventually the Vatican would move to condemn this cynical co-optation of Catholicism in the cause of right-wing politics. The time was not yet, however, and they buzzed constantly about efforts to start or restart Modernist journals and other outlets for ideas. Bremond was clear that an archaizing return to the past in the form of purist revivals does no good. At one point, recognizing the dangers entailed in corporatism, he vented strong resistance (which he would develop much later in *Histoire*, X) to Dom Prosper Guéranger's efforts to reinstate medieval liturgical forms and practices on the premise that a corrupt "individualism" had crept into Catholic worship.[61] Likewise, he also never showed any real interest in, or respect for, the backward-looking and nationalistic cult of Joan of Arc, then sweeping France as a religious endorsement of Gallican triumphalism.[62] Love of the past must not, cannot mean a naive return to the past!

As war broke out, followed by escalating turmoil and dislocations, Bremond and Blondel had trouble staying in touch, but finally Bremond was able to inform his mentor that with his Jesuit brother Jean already operating as a chaplain/stretcher-bearer with a unit at the front, he, like everyone else in France, was now anxiously scanning the casualty-lists. In fact, he told Blondel, he had tried to enlist. Having secured permission from the archbishop, he submitted his application, but brother Jean moved to block it on the basis of age—Bremond was forty-eight years old. He then offered

---

61. Bremond to Blondel, May 23, 1914 (BB, II, 246). Bremond was here anticipating his later distinction between bad romanticism (looking backward) and good (looking forward).

62. The one exception known to me appears in a little booklet Bremond wrote, *Sainte Catherine d'Alexandrie*, for a series on "Art and the Saints," where he analyzed the evolution of the legends, and associated artwork, around the fourth-century Catherine of Alexandria, a vision of whom was supposed to have been had by Joan of Arc before going into battle. Both women show that faith and a holy life are stronger than rationalist philosophy!

himself to the bishop of Bayonne for replacement parish work or seminary teaching, but was ignored, the implication being that Modernist associations had tainted him.[63] So, unlike a former student of his, enlisted and in the trenches, one who adored rocks and was developing his own form of pure-love mysticism, Bremond would have to sit out the war, researching, writing, and fretting.

Theological wrestling continued non-stop, however. In the autumn of 1914 he put a question to Blondel about the "introduction" (i.e., the "Échelle," which would become the "Appendix" in *Histoire*, II) that he was writing on mysticism. Referring to a disagreement between two experts, Augustin-François Poulain, SJ, already mentioned, and Auguste Saudreau (1859–1946),[64] he noted the former's view that mystical encounter, an experience intended by God for only select individuals, produces "experiential intellectual knowledge" with inevitable "concepts" of some kind, while the latter took the position that mystical experience as contemplation, the goal intended by God for everyone in the normal course of spiritual development, is "the experiential feeling of presence." Bremond favored Saudreau, a Thomist like Maréchal, by drawing attention to poetic inspiration, where there is the "feeling" of a presence. It is a "feeling that is not felt," said Bremond, this being the very same experience that is central to all prayer.[65] He indicated to Blondel that critics were accusing him of metaphysical pantheism with all of his talk about "'the fine point of the soul,' where the true self remains attached to God in the midst of the darkest night." The critics then complain that this is "Augustinian" and "ontologism," i.e., suggestive of some kind of transformative divine initiative *demanded by* nature itself. He is, Bremond reveals, thus in a state of "tumultuous dryness."[66]

Blondel's response was slow in coming. The war disrupted everything and complicated all communication, but he was stirred and piqued, needing some time to think. He would finally answer in bits and pieces, but only definitively in a 1924 essay on mysticism. The build-up to that essay, following the world-changing event of the war and its aftermath, will be instructive.

---

63. Bremond to Blondel, September 20, 1914 (BB, II, 250–51, with Blanchet's note on details, 251).

64. Both discussed by McGinn, "Theoretical Foundations," 278–79, and much more fully by De Pril, "La théologie catholique." The latter formulates the contrast between Poulain and Saudreau in terms of Ignatianism (each individual's vocation is unique) over against Thomism (we are all on the same continuum toward contemplation).

65. Bremond to Blondel, October 16, 1914 (BB, II, 253–55).

66. Bremond to Blondel, December 26, 1914 (ibid., 258–60). The charge of "ontologism" is obscure to the modern reader, but it reflected debates about the influence of the Catholic philosopher Antonio Rosmini-Sabati (1797–1855) in Italian Modernist circles, especially in the work of Antonio Fogazzaro—with whom Bremond was in correspondence. For a comprehensive treatment, see De Giorgi, "Saints, visionnaires, hérétiques et poètes."

9

Formulations in Time of War
The "French School" and the Mysticism of Self-Annihilation

WAR CHANGES EVERYTHING, BUT the questions raised are perennial: Can this carnage lead to new life? Can love triumph, in the final analysis, over hate?

On September 3, 1914, as European hostilities rapidly escalated, a new pope, Benedict XV, was consecrated. A career church diplomat, he rapidly became known for his efforts, futile as it turned out, at brokering peace negotiations among the belligerents. He was instrumental in promoting Italian neutrality at the outbreak of the war, and ended up concentrating on a variety of humanitarian projects for refugee relief and the welfare of noncombatants. After war's end, he facilitated renewed relationships—strained by the Dreyfus Affair and broken off after the 1905 Act of Separation—between the Vatican and France. Less punitive toward the Modernists than had been his predecessor, Pius X, he was positively regarded by many progressive thinkers, so that dogmatic quarreling abated for a time.[1] The *Union sacrée* of church and state in France, whose high point was the canonization of Ste Joan of Arc in 1920, marked, as well, a war-driven alliance of all of the French for the sake of national survival and final victory in "the war to end all wars." These were the glory days of Maurice Barrès and Charles Maurras.[2]

Bremond entered into much of the fervor as a faithful priest and loyal citizen. But he was also very much aware that there were mixed feelings among the Modernist coterie, especially in light of the fact that friendships, the sharing of ideas and common purpose, as well as persecution before the war, had created tight bonds among French, German, Italian, and British participants. Being internationalist in practice and spirit,

---

1. Blanchet points out that one of Benedict's first moves, after consecration, was to suppress an organized group of Vatican "integrists" who agitated for the condemnation of Modernist writings (BB, II, 204n3).

2. The story well-told by Brown, *Embrace of Unreason*, part 1.

concord within the group tended, on the one hand, to gravitate against the antagonistic nationalism produced by wartime conditions, while on the other hand, the reality was that friends now found themselves to be foes. The new status quo contradicted, painfully, the old affections. In the spring of 1915 Bremond indicated to Blondel that the Baron had addressed this situation in a series of well-done articles in a collection, *The German Soul and the Great War*.[3]

The Baron had there confronted views held by two German writers, Friedrich Naumann and Ernst Troeltsch, in which they had argued that the kingdom teachings of Jesus apply to each person in his private individuality, while the state must operate by a different standard, namely, that of the *realpolitik* use of military power. These two spheres must not be confused.[4] The Baron saw in such views an overly logical compartmentalization typical of the German soul's tendency to "system," thus opening the door to great kindness in some situations and limitless cruelty in others. The solution lies, he said, in the eradication of "Pan-Germanic swagger" by the war, so that the state can be reformulated as a moral sphere penetrable by supernatural perspective. To the Baron, Bremond wrote on May 2, 1915: "I cannot repress how deeply I feel ashamed of such of my countrymen—and then amongst them the most Germanised—who take their parable in such a violent, unjust and low tone, against whatever has been, is, and will be German. Of course this awful war has made terribly known the failure both of Catholicism and Christianism—but also of *humanitas* and urbanity and moral dignity."[5]

Bremond was also aware of Loisy's thinking about the war. In a letter during the third year of conflict he told Loisy how much he liked the latter's latest book, *La religion*, along with the earlier *Guerre et religion*. In the latter work, according to Bremond, Loisy had shown that the war is a product of the Germans' identification of God with their tutelary genius, "an embodiment of its brutality." The larger issue, however, was that of Christianity itself, in which the ideal of the kingdom, a thing of pure hope (in Loisy's construal), had become debauched by the Catholic Church into a corrupt German patriotism. And France had done the same thing with its *Union sacrée*. His hope for the outcome of the war was that it would facilitate the evolving conversion of traditional religion into a "religion of humanity," built on conscience, reasonable standards, and obligation to the whole human community mediated through one's own country and heritage.[6] Bremond suggested that in this line of argument Loisy

---

3. Bremond to Blondel, May 4, 1915 (BB, II, 266).

4. Excellent summaries of these essays and discussion in Barmann, "Baron Friedrich von Hügel." In a 1904 essay, Troeltsch actually contended that Jesus' teaching of the kingdom can influence the policies of the democratic state, but only to a limited degree and only at the level of foundational values. "The very meaning and nature of Christianity prevent its having a direct political ethic" ("Political Ethics and Christianity," in *Religion in History*, 190). Naumann's positions were quite similar.

5. Cited by Arnold, "Joseph Sauer," 123n38.

6. See Talar, "Alfred Loisy and the Great War," 18–31, for summary and analysis of this work.

had remained faithful in spirit to a true mysticism—though he regretted some lack of clarity about what would happen to priests in Loisy's kingdom![7]

While it may seem that Bremond did not reflect on the war to any great extent or at any great depth, only indicating some degree of sympathy with others on the matter, appearances are deceiving. In fact, letters to Blondel show that he was very mindful of the horrors of what was going on, and remained in a constant state of some anxiety about developments.[8] When we keep in mind that from the outset he wanted the contents of his history to be both a worthy portrait of the unfolding of devout humanism and mysticism in a past era, but also a message to his own time and a gateway for others into the mystical life, we would expect the nightmare of the war, lacerating the soul of the nation, to register deeply. It is no accident that Bremond focused increasingly on the sacrificial, self-giving aspects of devout humanism, and that he saw the assertion of such a humanism, when it is rightly conceived, as an inevitable process of combat with spiritualities that distort the gospel.[9] As Teilhard de Chardin noted during this same period: the struggles of war sometimes require, and facilitate, the best that humankind has to offer, thus making space for the reassertion of ideals.[10]

Several interacting trajectories of thought began to converge. First, in his ongoing conversation with Blondel and others Bremond continued to clarify the character of mysticism, particularly the question of the nature-grace dynamic. Second, in his implementation of a structure for *Histoire*, III, he made a critical decision: he would adopt and develop the concept of the "French School" as a historical container for the unfolding of devout humanism. And he would expound this concept in at least three

---

7. Bremond to Loisy, August 14, 1917, in Bernard-Maître, "Lettres d'Henri Bremond à Alfred Loisy," 180. Bremond appears to have been poking fun, but for commentary on the way in which this drollery reflected a growing split between himself and Loisy on the contemporary function of a mystical spirituality, see Trémolières, "Mystique et église," 331. In a note appended to the letter from Bremond to Blondel, September 11, 1917, Blanchet cites a letter of that same day (August 14, 1917) from Bremond to another friend, Monbrun, in which he summarizes Loisy's view that it is religion that gives people pure power to kill, that the existing religions have failed to deal with the war, and that a better religion will emerge from the ashes of the war. He suggests that Loisy is in the process of returning to the views of Comte and Eliot on a "religion of humanity" (BB, II, 326–27, and 329n6).

8. One might note also his 1916 review of work by the English Jesuit Herbert Thurston on prayers for the dead. Sensitively written, with an awareness of the pastoral comfort afforded by such prayer, the review includes Bremond's supplementing of Thurston's English materials with French sources, ending with a citation from Mère Angélique Arnauld on the "baptism of blood" and the final redemption that thus awaits God's elect (Bremond, "La priere pour les morts").

9. In a 1915 essay, "Fénelon et la guerre," Bremond let his views be known in his indirect kind of way. As archbishop of Cambrai, Fénelon was pastor, exhorter, critic, advocate for a miserable peasantry and soldiery in the hands of incompetent aristocrats, and ultimately peacemaker from 1700 to 1712 in the disastrous War of the Spanish Succession that raged through Flanders between Louis the XIV and his English-Dutch opponents. Through a rich selection of materials, Bremond held Fénelon up as the model of a just-war theorist who works unrelentingly for peace, who is a patriot, yes, but a Christian first! Just what we need right now, implied Bremond.

10. For instance, the February 1919 essay of Teilhard, "The Promised Land," 280: "The Impulse set in motion by the war was a deep-rooted instinct to preserve the race and add to its greatness."

modalities. There would be the history of personalities and institutions making up the French School. There would be descriptions and assessments of the spirituality of the French School, which, as Bremond saw it, highlighted themes of the nothingness of humankind and of all things, the centrality of the Incarnation and the self-emptying of the God-man, union with the states of Christ through adoration and self-offering, and the two faces of life and death in devout self-annihilation before God.[11] And, third, he would begin to give serious consideration to what he saw as the counterpoints to the French School: the asceticism of Ignatian spirituality on the one hand (addressed mostly in large footnotes), and the moralistic and anti-humanistic spirituality of Port-Royal.[12] In due course, the handling of these last would prove unmanageable in a single volume, and thus Bremond found himself simultaneously spinning out material for what would eventually become vols. III, IV and V of the *Histoire*. Consequently, these three volumes would all be published about the same time—IV on Port-Royal and V on Jesuit mysticism in 1920, and III on the French School, after a delay, in 1921.

Mysticism: Challenges!

In order to complete preparations in late 1915 for the publication of *Histoire*, I, Bremond had to gain the requisite approvals from church censors. The first obstacle was the granter of the *nihil obstat*, Ubald d'Alençon, a Capuchin, who, concerned about particular passages where Bremond seemed, especially in the treatment of Yves of Paris, to confuse the natural and supernatural levels in mystical experience, called for changes. Bremond complied, quickly receiving the desired approbation on August 10, 1915. But he complained about it to Blondel, who generously sympathized by finding the censor's complaints off the mark. Having, however, given with the right hand, Blondel took it back with the left, and went on at some length to review the projected essay (the original draft on "the mystical ladder," which Bremond would abbreviate to the "Appendix," *Histoire*, II) on the nature of mystical experience.[13]

While making the shrewd observation that Bremond's concrete way of writing confused dogmatic thinkers, Blondel still was not pleased with the way in which Bremond had assimilated "the natural mysticism, aesthetic, etc., to the properly supernatural mysticism." "There is not only," he averred, "a difference of degree, object, mode, but a heterogeneity between certain affective or intellectual states which 'realize' our life, or the concrete life of things in us, and the transcendent, growing, transforming

---

11. This is the summary of anticipated themes for vol. III that he offered to Blondel in Bremond to Blondel, May 2, 1916 (BB, II, 292–95).

12. Ibid., where he also included a proposed outline for *Histoire*, III. He departed from this outline considerably as he came to see that the Port-Royal material would require a separate volume.

13. Bremond to Blondel, August 8, 1015, and September 13, 1915 (BB, II, 270–73). Blondel to Bremond, September 18, 1915, with an appended memo (BB, II, 274–78).

action of God in the deiform soul."[14] In other words, Blondel, was being exceedingly cautious about the Modernist "subjectivism," or conflating of the natural and the supernatural in the inner life, with which conservatives were always charging him. And he was suggesting that while Bremond seemed to have put the natural/supernatural distinction, as we might say today, on a dimensional continuum—where "supernatural" is a heightened level of the "natural"—they should rather be considered "categorically," as being in quite different classes altogether.

And he then raised a fundamental and awkward issue, suggesting to Bremond that, despite his intentions, he tended to make mystical experience too "ex-centric" to everyday life, a matter of high inspiration and illumination, when in fact it is more ordinary, obscure, anonymous, hidden away in humble piety. What then happened, Blondel opined, was that Bremond ended up more, willy-nilly, with Poulain than Saudreau (i.e., mystical experience is only for a few, rather than a general *desideratum*). He challenged Bremond to take his stand rather with John of the Cross, where even the most supernatural experience is marked by "the evacuation of sensible graces and divine visions," precisely because John could thereby make all of the necessary connections between the highest nuptial union and the most childlike prayer. The problem, Blondel told him, is that you still have not worked out, in the matter of nature and grace, the correct dialectic of rapprochement and separation. This is why the censor, Ubald, jumped on you.

In essence, Blondel was accusing Bremond of creating an "elitist" view of mysticism, by likening it to poetic inspiration—normally thought of as "high" art—although Bremond's intention had been just the opposite. One way to approach the problem was to say, as Blondel did, that Bremond had still not thought through the question of knowledge, and then of the "notional," in mysticism. If it can be said that something "known" contributes to the production of high literature, then it would seem that this "known" has content of some kind, over and above what the recipient already possessed. An ambiguity may have resided here in Bremond's reliance on Maréchal, who, being a Thomist thinker, was committed to the position that the mystical apprehension of a "presence" is essentially intellectual, and not affective, i.e., that intuition perceives an Object that is real. Bremond, as we saw in the "Échelle," wanted to argue that mystical apprehension is "amorous knowledge," thus primarily affective, adding nothing cognitive to human awareness. Blondel had him in a bind: wanting to avail himself of a Thomist thinker, he tried to avoid Thomist implications.

Furthermore, the claim that mystical experience contains no notionally definable content raised the question again of what is meant by the "darkness" of mystical states, indeed of faith itself. It seems that what Bremond wanted to say at this point was that faith possesses only a "moral" certainty—in Newman's sense, that is, a "certitude"—but not an intellectualist "certainty." Thus, there is no "grasping" of the object,

---

14. BB, II, 274–75.

only a resolute "feeling after it"; faith proceeds by means of a "dark Presence" but well-illuminated "ends."

Blondel made it clear to Bremond that he took Saudreau's position: there is only a difference of degree, not nature, between the most visionary state and the simplest prayer. What the mystic must realize is that the "illuminations" that are experienced are not "revelations," but, are limited to lighting up already-known dogmatic truths, making them more accessible by, as it were, a more gracious pedagogy of "plastic and verbal inventions." The great spiritual trap of the mystics is to imagine that they grasp something that the ordinary believer does not grasp; in truth, they may only grasp it a bit more tightly. Blondel was here trying to remind Bremond, in a different context, of a criticism that he had voiced regarding the latter's understanding of Newman, i.e., of indulging in an inverted rationalism. By saying that Newman was all "real" and no "notional" in his vision of truth, Bremond had fallen into a "rationalism of the real" when he was attempting to avoid a notional rationalism. The result was an intellectual pride trying to avoid intellectual pride. Now Bremond was risking the same trap when he likened mystical experience too much to the authority of poetic inspiration, which now becomes rationalist in the form of an aesthetic elitism.

Bremond, as always a bit subdued by Blondel's critique, thanked him for his "precious remarks," and then squirmed. Since we are already baptized, he wondered, can we not assume that our natural means are already operative in a "supernatural order," that is, as already graced? Isn't all "grace" as such supernatural? Blondel's response: "The continuity of the fact of the supernatural and of nature, in the actual order of history and of psychology, does not prevent an actual heterogeneity, nor the onerous, mortifying character of its practice."[15] Differently stated, Blondel's "immanent" working of grace within nature is not a simple identification of the two! The pain of loving, that is, the purifying process, marks the boundary line.

Shortly before the publication of *Histoire*, I, Bremond revealed to Blondel that part of what he was struggling with, as he worked away at delicate material that would go into vol. III, was the fact that the founder of the Sulpicians, Jean-Jacques Olier, had been deeply influenced by a woman, Marie Rousseau, with whom his director-directee relations appeared to have been compromising. Things got quite concrete here. It was again the question of "nature" and "supernature" in understanding the dynamics of actual love-relations, as with Fénelon and Guyon.[16]

The solution that Bremond will in time come to is this: what makes love "natural" is the pleasure it brings, and what makes it "supernatural" is its prolongation, precisely when pleasure is gone and, thus, the possibility of sanctification emerges. Granted that the problem is not thereby ultimately solved since "pleasure" remains ambiguous, this framing of the issue in terms of love will be ultimately privileged for Bremond.

---

15. Bremond to Blondel, September 24, 1915, and Blondel to Bremond, September 29, 1915 (BB, II, 278–81).

16. Bremond to Blondel, November 12, 1915 (BB, II, 281–82).

Again the relationship between "devout humanism" and "mysticism" is critical here, since love as the quintessentially "human," and mystical prayer with its "darkness" as the quintessentially "devout," are brought into intimate, mutually reinforcing, conjunction.

But, Blondel was not the only interlocutor from whom Bremond accepted criticism and reflection vis-à-vis the essay on the nature of mysticism. Relations with the Baron had generally improved, and not only did he stay abreast of the Baron's reflections on the war, he also sent the old sage a prepublication draft of *Histoire*, I, with the proposed introduction. The Baron responded with a twenty-page memorandum, summarized by Goichot.[17] The background to his remarks is found in the dialogue he had maintained with Ernst Troeltsch for some years, especially after latter's publication of *The Social Teaching of the Christian Churches* in 1911, with its typology of religious fellowships, where "mysticism and spiritual idealism" characterize one "type" over against those of the "sect" and the "church." He had learned, averred the Baron, two things from Troeltsch about mysticism, namely, that the mystic has a totally gratuitous experience of the "Absolute of faith" as the constant amid the relativities of historical expression, and second, that this experience is secondary to, and derivative from, the objective existence of the concrete aspects of ecclesial traditions. Thus he argued the case with Bremond for the immediate presence of an objective Reality in the experience of the mystic, as well as the transcendent character of this Reality over against the subjectivity of the mystic.[18]

Von Hügel then hit on what he saw as another kind of contradiction that arose in Bremond's thinking, when he utilized Joseph Maréchal's thought. The latter, eager to erect a solid wall between true and false mysticism with the argument that the false type is full of natural manifestations inflated to a high degree (visions, auditions, etc., that is, all of the "pathological" phenomena), argued that the true type is natural as well, but in a different way (quiet, inward, poetic) which is then expanded to a supernatural level. But, the Baron pointed out, since both types are equally "natural," the decision to affirm one and deny the other is arbitrary. The conclusion is that we must not disparage the exalted, illuminative, rapturous state of the grossly flamboyant mystic, but should affirm this "mystical hymn to joy" as a proper component in mysticism as much as the other.

The Baron had a good point, because he had picked up on Bremond's prior preference for one kind of mystical experience—the quietist type manifesting poetically—as "the real thing." The Baron, wanting to be inclusive, was ill-disposed to Bremond's tendency to oppositional types. As it turned out, however, Bremond would not hear

---

17. EG, 84–87. The memo, in the St. Andrew's, Scotland, archives, is thus far unedited.

18. It should be recognized as well that in the background of the Baron's reservations about Bremond's formulations, though this did not become explicit, was his unhappiness about the absence of a clear christological element. Blondel would complain about this as well, and Marxer, "L'École française," sees it as the root cause of Bremond's (supposed) misunderstanding of Bérulle's doctrine.

it. Goichot's comment is on target: "Hügel attributed to the abbé his own spiritual optimism, the luminous climate of his inner life, and for him the system transposes and confesses personal witness; but Bremond had lived only *the silence of God*."[19] True enough, but one can also say that for a complex of reasons Bremond had chosen to favor pure-love mysticism, and its potential for highlighting the "dark" side of mystical experience, as the essential expression of his favored era and writers. In other words: Francis de Sales and Fénelon were champions for Bremond in a way that they were not for the Baron.

Further complications entered the picture in the debates about the role of ascetical disciplines in preparing for, and regulating, mystical experiences. It is the issue, going back to the sixteenth-century Carmelites, of "acquired" versus "infused" grace, the former being that grace that accrues to ascetical efforts, the latter being that which comes as utter gratuity when human effort reaches its limits. It is really another facet of the nature-supernature problematic, this time in the modality of behavioral disciplines that either assist, or retard, the inward life of prayer and receptivity for progressively advanced states. Bremond will address the issue directly in *Histoire*, IV, on Port-Royal, and in V, on Ignatian mysticism, but from the beginning of *Histoire*, III, and his treatment of the "theocentric" French School, side-glances at Port-Royal "anthropocentrism" and Jesuit "asceticism" will become omnipresent.

The French "School": Bérulle

At the turn of the year, 1915–16, then, *Histoire*, I and II, appeared in quick succession and to mostly rapturous applause.[20] Apart from Bremond's gifts for style and presentation, which made his material engaging and entertaining for a wide readership, his decision to celebrate a golden age of French spirituality struck a positive note in a Church and country that sorely needed a boost in self-esteem. The Modernist-traditionalist doctrinal turmoil in the church, combined with the prewar political struggles of church and state, as well as the scandals, setbacks and internecine factional infighting of the political left and the right, combined with the unbelievably horrible ravages of the war, necessitated the need for balm that soothes, encourages and unifies. Just as the *Union sacrée* was being affirmed, Bremond's volumes reflected, and helped to satisfy, a national need, for they directed loyalties into a shared heritage that all groups, liberal or conservative and churchly or secular, could affirm. Bremond's stock rose;

---

19. EG, 87.

20. Among others, Bremond would receive enthusiastic praise from P. de Grandmaison at *Études*, where all had been forgiven (Bremond to Blondel, January 29, 1917 [BB, II, 313n3]). In a letter of august 16, 1917, Blondel mentions that Bremond had won the Broquette-Bronin prize of 10,000 fr. from the Académie for *Histoire*, I and II. In the attached note, Blanchet cites Bremond's letter to Monbrun of August 26, 1917, in which he indicates that Lavisse (the anthropologist of religion), seconded by Barrès, and supported by Duchesne, had engineered the vote (BB, II, 323n1). I discuss the critical response to the first volumes of the *Histoire* below, ch. 14.

even the condemnation of *Sainte Chantal* looked like an insult to French sensibilities from a Germanophile pope!

The principal sour note came from Maurras—by this time he and Bremond were alienated—who referred to "the holy and diabolical author of that *Humanisme dévot*" who has taken "the curious spirits of a picturesque history" and made "playthings" of them.[21] Buoyantly, Bremond forged ahead on *Histoire*, III, which, potentially, could be an even bigger hit.

Having described in his first volume the first French flowering of devout humanism in the work and life of Francis de Sales and the Salesian "school," then its expansion into a range of literary and poetic forms of expression, then its "archetypal" form in the figure of Yves de Paris, in the second volume Bremond had turned primarily to the founding of the French Carmel in such figures as Mme Acarie and Jean de Saint-Samson, then some of the great Benedictine abbesses of the earlier part of the century, serious about monastic reform and the deepening of piety, finally to Francis and Jeanne once again as mystics. But all of these developments, important as they were, did not constitute the full implementation of devout humanism and its associated mysticism at the center of French life. For that he needed solid Parisian institutional foundations—for, after all, Paris is the heart of the nation—and he found them. First, in Pierre de Bérulle (1575–1629, cardinal 1627), founder of the French Oratory, and his successors Charles de Condren (1588–1641) and François Bourgoing (1585–1662), and then, second, in Jean-Jacques Olier (1608–1657) and his establishment of the priestly Society based at the Parisian parish and seminary of Saint-Sulpice. They are the chief actors in the drama of the "The Triumph of Mysticism," and the leading lights of "The French School" of spirituality.

Exactly *how* Bremond came to the concept of the "French School" and became utterly transfixed by it is unclear. The massive edifice of the parish church of Saint-Sulpice is located very close by the offices of Bremond's Paris publisher, Bloud et Gay (Francisque Gay, an influential and progressive lay Catholic, had joined the firm in 1909). The curé of the parish during the war years was Georges Letourneau (1850–1926), well-known author of an important book on spiritual formation that utilized classically Sulpician methods and materials. He was, despite being anti-Modernist in spirit, an outspoken fan of Bremond's volumes as they were starting to appear, and he had also been a defender of *Sainte Chantal*. Goichot describes him as a formidable figure with strong and traditional views, but energetic and creative. On the subject of mysticism, he supported Saudreau and was highly critical of Jansenism.[22]

When, therefore, Bremond decided to take the "French School" concept and bring it front and center in his history, Letourneau must have been pleased. Indeed, though he was probably not the creator of the idea of the French School, he had in

---

21. Cited by Blanchet (BB, II, 292n3).
22. EG, 125–26.

his own work promoted the notion, making Olier the central figure.[23] Things would, however, eventually turn sour with Letourneau in a manner analogous to the disillusionment of the Visitation nuns with Bremond's picture of their beloved founder. But not at first. The change came only when Letourneau had in hand the first draft, sent to him by Bremond for review, of the proposed sketch of Olier—for whom there just happened to be an active canonization process currently underway in Rome. Initially, however, all was wine and roses, because Bremond needed the concept of the French School as the vital link between Francis de Sales and Fénelon at the two ends of the century, first because of its mystique of self-giving, "self-annihilating" love in prayer and action, and second, because of the inherent appeal of a distinctly Gallican spirituality just as (1916!) France struggled for survival. One could say that it was Bremond's counterpart to what Barrès and Maurras were doing politically,[24] but with the difference that it turned in the direction of love rather than hate.

So first Bérulle. Bremond says that the story of the French School is essentially that of the "Oratorian School," with Bérulle as its founder, but his successor, Charles de Condren, its greatest writer, and finally Bossuet(!) its "indisputable disciple," "all French to the backbone."[25] Bérulle had been instrumental, most notably, in bringing the Carmel with its Teresian spirituality of simple, passive prayer from Spain to France, but he had then proved to be too much of an individualist for the discipline entailed. He tried a vocation with the Jesuits, but discovered that neither "active combat with the world" (Carmelite) nor "choosing a state of life" (Jesuit) was to be his spiritual focus. Immersed in study and prayer, he came to see intimate communion with the Incarnate Lord in terms of a "perfect forgetfulness of self and of all conditions," that would become the hallmark of his life and thought.[26] Further, "to be religious without being religious," that is, to live out a life of high devotional discipline, but as a secular priest, would be his goal.[27] Thus, in 1611 he brought to France the Oratory, the order founded by the Renaissance humanist and saint, Philip Neri, consisting of groups of priests living in unvowed scholarly communities. In this way, argued Bremond, Bérulle affirmed his "natural spirit," thereby remaining faithful to the ideals of devout humanism, even though as a cardinal "he was not the man for so delicate a mission,"

---

23. Ibid., 126n5, and 128n11. Goichot refers here to the article by Rayez on the French School in *DS*, 5:782, where the author somewhat cynically suggests that Bremond took up the term from Letourneau's use in 1913 in order to give his material "audience-appeal" and "glitter." François Marxer traces the usage back to Charles Baudry, professor at Saint-Sulpice from 1846 to 1861, whence it came to Mgr d'Hulst at the Institut Catholique and then to Letourneau ("L'École française," 885–86).

24. So also Marxer, "L'École française," 888. Marxer sees the whole "French School" concept as a narrowly "nationalistic" construct that overly systematizes Bérulle and is too focused on mysticism. To distinguish what Bremond was doing from Maurras's nationalism, the term "ethnocentric" might be better.

25. *Histoire*, III, 1.

26. Ibid., 12, citing Bérulle.

27 Ibid., 14.

when he became embroiled in the failed negotiations for the marriage of Henrietta of France to the Prince of Wales, the future Charles I.[28]

Admitting that Bérulle was a tedious writer—his two principal works being the *Élévation à Jésus et à Marie* and the *Discours de l'état et des grandeurs de Jésus*—Bremond saw the essence of French School teaching as comprised in the special descriptor that he crafted for Bérullism: "theocentric."[29] By this term Bremond meant that Bérulle made the adoration of God rather than the seeking of personal salvation (termed by Bremond the "anthropocentric" view) the principal focus of the spiritual life. Thus initiating a "Copernican revolution" in spirituality, said Bremond, Bérulle's own image was that the soul must revolve around its God as the earth the sun. The "anthropocentric"[30] enemy of a proper theocentrism in the spiritual life is self-love; therefore, self-annihilation is its antidote, leaving the soul unencumbered for the adoration of God. It is the classic paradox of the giving up of one's life in order to gain life, but with an extraordinary ratcheting up of intensity that caught Bremond's attention early on.

The language is counterintuitive. One would think that "humanism" would be "anthropocentric," with God as the goal of a distinctively human aspiration and goodness, yet the terms were radically opposed for Bremond, at least as he interpreted Bérulle. Herein lies the nerve center of the French School, and it is a major window into the development of Bremond's wartime spirituality and his future work. It is also the place where Bremond gave Blondel his due, i.e., yielded to the demand for an ultimate disjunction of the natural and supernatural, however "immanent" might be their connection.[31]

Bremond argued that the theocentrism of true Christian spirituality had been implied in Christian teaching from the beginning, as in the thought of Augustine and Bernard. But Bérulle's genius was to make of theocentrism a "religion," i.e., to give it dogmatic "teeth," even as Francis de Sales had made it a proper "devotion," i.e., a warm-hearted piety.[32] Speaking of Bérulle's special calling that theocentrism be "freed

---

28. Ibid., 15–16.

29. "A barbarous, but unavoidable [term]," said Bremond (ibid., 17). Clearly Bremond's intentions were not anti-christological, but it is also true that he never embraced the outright christocentrism of Scotist tradition, where the Incarnation is the organizing pivotal event of cosmic history. For him, as in his interpretation of Bérulle, the Incarnation is an invitation into the symbolic structure of Christian experience.

30. First used by Bremond, where he immediately associated it with the kind of Ignatian teaching he experienced in his younger years as a Jesuit (ibid., 18).

31. Suggestively, this is where Alfred Loisy showed the least interest in Bremond's work. This is why Trémolières, "Mystique et église," can formulate the difference between the two in their appreciation of the contemporary role of mystical spirituality as a difference in their views of the role of the priest "outside of the church." The French School exalted the self-annihilated priesthood as the mystical representation of the Incarnation.

32. *Histoire*, III, 26. It is also true, as Marxer notes, that Bremond saw in the first Oratorians a kind of refined and courtly spirituality, an austere "respect for God," as opposed to the "provincial

and expanded, simplified and brought into the light of common day, offered to and dominating the prayers of all,"[33] Bremond identified with that mission. The problem is that in so many other spiritualities, and without realizing it and certainly without intending it, people end up making God "the ministrant (*serviteur*) of their inner life," thereby betraying, in the words of Amelote, Bérulle's first biographer, "sacred courtesy in Christian manners."[34]

Instead, said Bremond, Bérulle wants us to approach God in such a way that "respect is admiration, and prayer a song," so that "overwhelmed by the Splendour and Majesty of God, [we] yet rejoice in magnifying this overwhelming and celebrating it in hymns of praise."[35] In short, Bérulle wanted our whole relationship with God to have the quality of a lyric poetry that fires the soul, that stirs the imagination, that inspires and ennobles—Bremond uses these words constantly—so that the moral and spiritual beauty of divine purpose, and divine power, and especially, the divine God-in-manhood of Jesus Christ fill the mind and heart of the devotee. It is the aesthetic quality of the Bérullian spirituality that captivated Bremond, and brought him very close to the equation, later made explicit, of pure prayer with pure poetry. A spirituality of pure doing (Ignatianism), and a gloomy and sin-centered spirituality (Port-Royal and Jansenism), would be anathema.

Bérullian spirituality in all of its theocentric aesthetic was robustly christocentric as well, especially as a psychologically framed application of dogmatics.[36] Bérulle worked with the standard two-natures Christology, Jesus God and Man, the two natures perfectly joined, but not in any way mixed, in one Person. The practical implication that he drew is that human nature in all of its psychological and historical contingency is the means of access to the divinity: one contemplated the divine presence in, and by means of, the sacred humanity of Jesus. Part of Bérulle's genius was that he innovated a devotional mode: the preferred way of prayer is identification through "elevations" with the inner "states" of the Incarnate Word. Through the use of pious/mystical imagination one enters adoringly into Jesus' spiritual "state," not his actions, at each moment of his life and ministry. After encountering the divine presence in him, one's own inner states are "imprinted" with the qualities of his state. Bérulle's preferred metaphor for the divine presence in Jesus was that of a shining Light illuminating the soul of the worshipper as he/she prayed in a state of "eleva-

---

familiarity" more typical of Francis de Sales's style of devotion ("L'École française," 880). Certainly there are implications of class issues here.

33. *Histoire*, III, 22. Bremond speaks here of "the evolution of Christian thought and consciousness." Surely Newman is in the background.

34. Ibid., 28–29. However, Bremond was troubled here with Bérulle's tendency to use a hedonic language in referring to the "divine caresses," accusing him of some "confusion" in his "rhetoric" (ibid., 28n1)! True courtesy should not expect "caresses."

35. Ibid., 30.

36. Ibid., 332, "For all of the leaders of the French School metaphysics and ethics, contemplation and action, theory and practice, cannot be separated or even distinguished."

tion." In the language of Catholic piety the "heart" of the worshipper communes with the "Heart of Jesus," or "the heart of Mary" (the latter profoundly important also for Bérulle), and this sharing of inner "states" between the worshipper and Jesus constitutes an entry into the presence of God, a true mystical rapture. Bérulle is clear: start with the "heart" and its need for change first, and only then, can Godly action follow.[37]

But the kicker comes when one asks about the nature of what is encountered inwardly when one identifies with the "states, mysteries, perfections and qualities" of the Incarnate Lord. Often, said Bremond, what comes is the silence of God and the darkness of faith, in which "His grace does not quench our own quasi-nothingness, but on the contrary, by rendering it God-like, it 'consummates' it." There is an annihilation of the old Adam, the "supreme annihilation" of which the mystics speak. There is the implication as well that this "annihilation" of a distracting self-love enables the soul to lose itself in a contemplative "state" of utter focus on the "Other." For Bremond, Bérulle became a Founding Father of the modern spiritualities of "attention" leading to compassionate action.[38] Bérulle's core perception is that the human will cannot be forced by fear and commandments, but must be induced, not into obedience, but *adherence*. Bremond tells us: "Adoration and adherence have precisely the same object; in the former, we recognize the infinite grandeur of this object, abasing ourselves in lyrical absorption before Him; in the latter, we endeavour to unite ourselves with this Object, and to take Him for our own."[39] Differetly stated, Bremond is not eliminating the need for mediation, but he relativizes the instruments of mediation, so that they do not become the final goal. The process of "elevations" must stamp out the "culte de moi" and replace it with the "culte de non-moi."[40]

Bérulle applied this adherence specifically to the "states" of the Word Incarnate, so that (theoretically) the will of the devotee is replaced by the will of God, and the appropriate *askesis* is the result. Bremond called the resulting type of ascetical discipline not a "science of morality," but paradoxically, a "mystery," in which ethics is not an "imitating

---

37. Ibid., 35–107. Bremond cites François Bourgoing: "By 'Elevation' they (the French School) understood that 'kind of prayer . . . which moves along the path of marvel, adoration, reverence, humble gaze, homage, honour and other such exercises as tend wholly and simply to glorify God, without any return on ourselves, without asking or desiring aught for ourselves'" (ibid., 99). Bremond entitled the section of text that deals with this subject "Elevation or Lyric Adoration."

38. Marxer argues that Bremond failed at this point to take with complete seriousness Bérulle's christocentrism, in which the believer identifies with Jesus' state of self-emptying through a willed imitation, so that self-annihilation is not ontic in the Rheno-Flemish sense, but ethical and ascetic, keyed to successive moments in Jesus' own historical progress ("L'École française," 891–92). Consequently, Bremond may have been too quick to take the view that self-annihilation in Bérulle is equivalent to the purely quietistic, timeless neantism of a pure destruction. But, what if the "annihilation of self" is the *sine qua non* for "pure love"?

39. *Histoire*, III, 108.

40. Ibid., 41. "If the young Barrès could base his *culte de moi* on the Exercises of S. Ignatius, the *culte de non-moi* inculcated by the French School, a veritable initiation in poetic enthusiasm, will prove no less interesting."

of Christ," but a "putting on Christ."[41] Concretely, Bérulle taught that those who embrace his teaching will go through the four stages of desire to do God's will, ratification of that will by our own will, exposition, i.e., the imprinting of God's will on our own (like an "electrotyping," says Bremond), and submission. "The originality of the French School consists in realizing the existence of the Divine Electricity, so to speak, which Providence puts at our disposal, and in desiring and learning how to use it."[42]

Condren

With all of the major figures emerging from Bérulle's "school"—Charles de Condren, Jean-Jacques Olier, Vincent de Paul, the Jesuit Jean-Baptiste Saint-Jure, Jean Eudes, and many others—it is a matter, then, and as with the followers of Francis de Sales, of working variations on the teaching of the master, although in the case of Olier we will see a particular heightening of the theme of self-annihilation.

Bremond's sketching of Charles de Condren, Bérulle's successor as superior of the Oratory, is especially striking. It is one of his most charming mini-biographies, since he genuinely admired Condren for his intelligence, his deft maneuvering with the royal court, his military virtues, and the maturity of his spirituality. "To destroy and annihilate self, to cease to be—all Condren's doctrine is summed up in this," averred Bremond.[43] The sheer psychological practicality is evident. In his approach to exorcisms, for instance, Condren operated in a manner quite unlike the approach of his contemporaries, who would try, in staged public sessions, to "interpret" the voices of demons coming from possessed persons. Instead, Condren officiated at exorcisms only in private, treated the demons as grandiose forms of self-glorification by the possessed person ("narcissistically invested projections," we might say today), spoke to them in contemptuous terms, then dismissed them as ridiculous.[44] It is clear that Bremond liked this Condren's common sense, a no-nonsense approach to the inner life that homed in on human need with laser-like precision.

In the way of many immediate followers, Condren tended to be a systematizer of Bérulle's thought. Phrases like "the abyss of our nothingness" and "to be reduced to nothingness for His Honour" occur constantly in Condren's writing. He emphasized that creation, rightly understood, implies our nothingness before God, and this fact forms the "links of religion," whereby offering grateful sacrifice back to God is the ultimate reality-based act of human freedom. Our fall in the Garden, says Bremond,

41. Ibid., 113.

42. Ibid., 118, 120.

43. Ibid., 258. Condren's original biographer, Amelote, in a citation that Bremond describes as possessing "erudite subtlety not without charm," compared Condren to "a certain type of man who you will say belongs to a particular species. One might say that it was fortunate for the followers of Origen that such a one had not been born in their century; they would have taken him for a convincing proof that the souls of men had formerly belonged to the angels" (ibid., 248).

44. Ibid., 270–73.

leads to the coming of the Redeemer, then a renewed capacity for adoration and praise on the part of the creature. This is "the theocentric *felix culpa* of the French School."[45] Condren argued that this renewed capacity for the sacrifice of self, and of sinful self-love, is in fact a self-fulfillment through adhesion to God in Christ. Bremond admired Condren's delicate balance here, a balance that made him a true humanist, and that Olier tended to lose later.

In one of many footnotes that make the *Histoire* such rich reading, Bremond highlighted Condren's ironically expressed good sense by relating a vivid story in which he counseled a penitent who felt that she was completely unworthy to receive absolution, no matter how miserable she was.[46] But Condren knew how to break through the self-love that refuses forgiveness by means of a (scarcely) veiled egotism; he had the gift of using the language of self-annihilation in an empowering, not disempowering, way. Another example is in the French School's use of the "victim" language—notoriously subject to misuse when co-opted by self-love—with Christ as the divine Victim. Rightly exercised, "victim" denotes a choice that is knowing and free because grounded in loving identification with the Incarnate Lord, and in the offering of one's own self in service, with all of the costs thereby entailed.[47] The result in Condren's best teaching is that this ideal "imposes on those who desire to follow it faithfully, without faltering and all through their life, an almost supernatural heroism."[48] Condren wanted to avoid all morbid self-examination and introspection, by turning attention to the ideal and its attraction and away from the self as such, because he believed that empowerment came from a focus on the goal and not the weakness of the aspirant.

Thus, claimed Bremond finally, Condren condemned all mysticism based on sensuous experience, insisting that "the meeting between God and ourselves [is] in the innermost parts of the soul," at Francis de Sales's "fine point of the soul." The paradox here is that a spirituality that so emphasizes human nothingness can be at the same time so lyrical, so sensuous, so to speak, in admiring a (theoretically) non-sensuous ideal. In Bremond's own time, it becomes the dialectic of surface and depth: the surface (physical, sensuous, phenomenal) deceives (should be treated as "nothing") while the depth (invisible and immaterial) reveals (should be treated as the "real").

---

45. Ibid., 313. "Fortunate then was the fall of our first parents, not only because it has won us such a Redeemer, but also and above all because in some way it has won for God Himself an adoration and a sacrifice worthy of Him."

46. Ibid., 331n2. After citing Amelote's description of this incident, Bremond continued: "After this, none could call de Condren unpractical. The case of Mlle. de la Roche [the lady in question] is by no means uncommon in the confessional [one might add: in the therapist's office also]. How is it to be dealt with, if not by such subtle reasoning as that to which he had recourse?"

47. Ibid., 334n1. Bremond has the interesting observation: "We need a work resembling Newman's *Grammar of Assent*, a textbook of voluntary adherence, distinguishing between the *unreal* and the *real* assent of the will, if so be that the will itself does not play a decisive part in the *real assent*, in the realization of such assent." The issue is one of adherence to the good within oneself, understood as the beginning of an adherence to God's will.

48. Ibid., 338.

Bremond thus saw in the French School that suspicion of the surface, the outward, the formulated, which is Modernism *avant la lettre*.

And then Olier

Where things start to complexify is with Jean-Jacques Olier, because Olier was a troubled man, albeit a central figure in the development of the French School. On the one hand, Bremond argued that Olier had an unbalanced side to him, that he manifested aberrant behavior as well as exaggeration and one-sidedness in his thinking. On the other hand, he wanted to show that God's grace can take this kind of man and do very good work through him, transforming his personality to a remarkable degree in the process. Here was a challenge to Bremond as a "religious psychologist," and he rose to it with ill-concealed gusto.

The final version, however, of Bremond's treatment of Olier, which now appears in *Histoire*, III, is a substantial modification of the first version, which he had submitted to Letourneau for review, and which the latter vehemently rejected as a caricature. Stunned, Bremond compromised with the curé of Saint-Sulpice, retaining some features in the characterization that displeased Letourneau, but discarding others. In the final text Olier's neuroticism is somewhat played down, as is the large role that Marie Rousseau played in stimulating, as well as executing, Olier's vision. The result in the finished text is something of a whitewash. The original version, preserved in Bremond's private notes, has been recently printed with commentary in the Millon re-edition of the *Histoire*. In what follows regarding Olier and his significance, I will be citing from both versions.

Olier as a young man was a student of Condren's, who then became involved in religious "missions" with Vincent de Paul, and ended up working in the parish of Saint-Sulpice. After a period of parish renewal, he organized a seminary whose program of formation was based on his adaptation of Condren's teaching, as well as a society of priests living under a shared devotional discipline. Before long, the special ministry of the Society became the revitalization of seminary supervision and teaching. Further, the ethos was one of aristocratic independence, with member-priests allowed to keep their own property. Eventually, the "gentlemen of Saint-Sulpice" will provide the seminary ambience for François Fénelon.

Bremond originally titled his chapter on the life of Olier "The Singularities of M. Olier" ("Initiation of Jean-Jacques Olier" in the published version) in order to make the point that Olier was a truly original character, unlike the standard picture which saw him merely as a continuator of Bérulle and Condren. The word "singularity" suggests, however, "oddness" and "peculiarity" as well as "individual uniqueness." And there came the rub. In his journals and diaries, said Bremond, Olier was harshly severe, agitated, overexcited, prone to exaggeration, and it is clear that he suffered from "nerves," was tasteless and tactless at times, with an "unhealthy exaltation" of expression, like Madame Guyon.[49] In the published version, however, Bremond reduced this description (unfortunately!) to "feminine weaknesses" in Olier, which came out in his preparation for priesthood, where in time he had a crisis of vocation.[50] He seems to have gone through a period of real mental illness, a personal "martyrdom," marked by morbidity, extreme penances and neurasthenia.

But under Condren's direction, he began to stabilize, despite continuing ups and downs, becoming an advocate of the "death to self" which is the antidote for "self-exaltation." He went through demonic temptations, became depressed and ridiculous to his peers, paranoid, megalomaniacal. Bremond then described a remarkable return to health for Olier, in which "the poet" overcame the chronic neurotic.[51] Humility and self-effacement followed, he resumed constructive work, and "the persevering energy of the saint conquered the weaknesses of the neurasthenic." An interior divine working guided him as would a parent a child. Condren taught him not to listen to his own crazy insides, to avoid any devotion that requires "consolations" from God, but to focus outwardly on Christ and Christian work. "Self-annihilation," thus makes perfectly good sense here, because the "self" being discarded is pathological.

In the original version Bremond engaged in some polemic with the Sulpician defenders of Olier, who adamantly avoided the seriousness of their hero's illness. But the result, insisted Bremond, is that they then cannot appreciate what grace is able to do in a person and how it sometimes works.[52] And the same went with the large role that the complex Marie Rousseau played. Marie was a serious Catholic who had cycled through a number of spiritual directors, all of them obtuse to her particular experience, because they could not understand a mystic, says Bremond. A cabaret-keeper's wife in the neighborhood of Saint-Sulpice, she became convinced that it was her role to work for spiritual renewal in the parish. She had visions, she became theatrical, she prophesied, she kept a diary in which she described her unusual episodes, and Olier became enraptured with her writing. Bremond considered her work inferior to that of Guyon, as Olier's writing would be to that of Fénelon.[53] One problem is that Olier was

---

49. HLM, I, 1354–55.

50. *Histoire*, III, 367.

51. Ibid., 393. Olier was, said Bremond, as compared with Condren "more ardent, more tender, more arresting, in a word, more of a man and a poet." Such was "the glorious and beneficent reverse side, of [his] weaknesses."

52. HLM, I, 1359–60. Bremond highlighted Olier's capacity for attaching himself to persons who were admirable, and from whom he could learn. Ultimately this tendency grew into his fondness for the saints, said Bremond, who then became ideal sources for him. The Sulpicians must have disliked this section, however, because it provided the setting for Olier's attachment to Rousseau.

53. Ibid., I, 1362–63, 1375. The treatment of Rousseau is extensive, and Bremond debates with Sulpician scholars throughout. It is no wonder Letourneau was appalled by all of this, seeing it as Bremond's hitting back at the Sulpician Levesque (an ardent Bossuetist and anti-Fenelonian defender of Olier, who had criticized the *Apologie pour Fénelon* (as discussed in the editor's introduction, ibid., 1351–52). On Bremond's debate with Levesque, see EG, 134–37, where it is clear that the polemic in which a saintly male can be accused of too much involvement with a female figure can cut in many

overly credulous with her, and he expressed himself emotionally and sentimentally with regard to their relationship. It is all puerile, said Bremond, but nonetheless gracious. One suspects that here Bremond was taking the Baron quite seriously, having hearkened to his complaint that it is unfair to privilege one kind of "natural" dimension in mysticism to the exclusion of other "natural" components.

In the published text, under "The Excellence of M. Olier," Bremond went on to characterize Olier's teaching as a heightening, intensification, and a lyricizing of the core ideas of the French School, raising its tenets, said Bremond, to the level of poetry. In this way he is actually a match for the Anglicans Herbert, Vaughn and Traherne. The idea of self-annihilation in adherence to the saints especially appealed to Bremond, because Olier was able to develop it with a particularly colorful and attractive fervor. In a personal note, Bremond claimed to see in Olier the kind of "spiritual father, equal if not superior in prestige to his [own] teaching colleagues, nay, as I know from my own experience, [to] be met with, but very rarely."[54] Especially compelling was Olier's picture of self-forgetful modesty on the part of the priest, who exudes goodness but is unconscious of it. Olier popularized and operationalized the characteristic emphases of the French School—filtered through his personal experience—with the result that devotional life became a form of personal rehabilitation, a therapy even, freeing the individual from a self lost in its own pathology precisely in order to gain a renewed self based on identification with the Ideal.

There may have been a certain measure of naiveté on Bremond's part, where he may have been led astray by Letourneau's earlier approval of his picture of the Francis de Sales / Jeanne de Chantal relationship with all of its human foibles, where the depiction of the flaws of *someone else's* saints can even be amusing. And granted that the politics of the canonization process for Olier (he has never been approved) complicated things. Yet more was at stake.

Bremond was, in effect, throwing up a red flag about the use of the concept of "self-annihilation" in French School spirituality. Powerful as it is, it lends itself to misuse, even abuse. There is the psychological problem of masochistic submission to sadistic authority.[55] And it is vulnerable to the ideology of "following orders," as when, in a standard criticism of the trench warfare of WWI, troops were repeatedly told to sacrifice for the motherland in useless, suicidal assaults. As Bremond interpreted Olier, he was likely at times, especially in his illness, to abuse the idea of self-annihilation, until, with Condren's common sense, he began to straighten out. It is the problem of distinguishing between a sound versus and an unsound understanding

directions.

54. *Histoire*, III, 397n1.

55. It is no accident, of course, that Freud was developing his theories of sadomasochism and the death-instinct at precisely this same time. For a helpful and relevant discussion of Freud's view that the "death-instinct" is an essential dialectical partner with the "life-instinct" in maintaining the directionality and vitality of life, see Porter, "Love of Life."

of the "nothingness" that human beings are understood to be, and then the practical consequences of that "nothingness." Bremond will not work all of this out definitively until he gets to the "Metaphysic of the Saints" in *Histoire*, VII and VIII, but with the treatment of the French School, the problematic was becoming more precise, more focused for him. Eventually the question will crystallize as an exploration of the nature of self-giving love, and the issue of what kind of loss of self is required by authentic loving, where the Bérullian ideology of self-annihilation is subsumed by the Salesian and Fenelonian language of "pure love." But not yet.

It should be noted as well that Bremond's use of Bérulle as the means for identifying a "French School" of spirituality raises a number of questions, outlined most recently by François Marxer.[56] First, critics have questioned his interpretation of Bérulle, arguing that Bérulle's thought was more multifaceted, more of a constant work-in-progress, and more dependent on some uncritical reading of patristic sources, than Bremond acknowledged. Second, there is the claim that it would have been more accurate for Bremond to think in terms of an "Oratorian School" or "Bérullian School," since so many other groups such as the Carmelites and the Jesuits were left out. Third, the whole concept of a "school" feels artificial, when a term like "current" or "tradition" might have been more accurate, given the number of threads that Bremond tries to weave into the constraints of a "school." Finally, and most substantive, Marxer complains that Bérulle was ultimately christological in his thinking, rather than Dionysian, as Bremond construes him. For Bérulle the ideal of "self-annihilation" is the kenotic self-emptying of the Cross that results in self-giving service, not the cancellation of self in mystical silence. Thus, Marxer sees here a christological "failure" in Bremond's notion of theocentrism. Blondel will rap on Bremond precisely at this point, and we will see his sharp response.

The central issue, once again, is that of understanding the "nothingness, the death of the *moi*," that is the result of self-annihilation. What is left? Is it the "real" me in place of the "false" me? No, for that would be an anticipation of existentialism and some modern psychology. Rather, it is the movement from surface to depth, toward the "fine point" of the soul, which will turn out to be the place where God holds in potency the "self" that grace will make me to be. Marxer has stated it well when he suggests that the "I" that I am at this moment is the one that will die in favor of the "I" that I am becoming, that belongs to the future and thus to eternity—not an existential I, but a mystical and hidden I. It is this latter "I" that defines reality, and that will turn out to be, as Bremond contended, the one that each of us was created to be and that baptism enables, in the mystical life of prayer, for every believer.[57]

56. For this paragraph and the next, François Marxer, "L'École française," 885–91. Marxer updates the argument most recently in "Entre religion et métaphysique," especially the conclusions, 311–15. Nonetheless, the concept of the "French School" lives on, as in Thompson, ed., *Bérulle and the French School: Selected Writings*.

57. Marxer, "L'École française," 903–5, although he criticizes Bremond for taking Condren too literally, as well as too metaphysically, making him too passive, and ignoring the "as if" aspect of

In the course of thus formulating his picture of the French School, it had become clear to Bremond that the two alternative currents of tradition in the seventeenth century, namely, the Jesuits and the Jansenists (Ignatianism and Port-Royal), would require separate treatment, first as foils or counter-movements to what he saw as the mainstream, but then as sources of sharpening and refinement. Because they contained valid as well as invalid sub-currents—that is, French School emphases along with distortions—these alternatives would make their own distinctive contributions to the river of "pure love" gathering strength as the century progressed.

Turning first to Port-Royal, Bremond girded up his loins.

Condren's doctrine of sacrifice. Condren writes "as if" we were rocks or animals, not freely willing subjects, though he knows better. Sacrifice is a "choice," as we say, not a mere acquiescence to being. The issue comes up later with Chardon and Piny in *Histoire*, VII and VIII.

10

Port-Royal I
the Problem of "Devout Charlatanism"

BREMOND WAS FACED WITH questions. Early on he had wondered about the reality of prayer: where does one see the genuine article? And what is it in the first place that makes it genuine? How does one separate what is "true" and "real" in religious devotion from that which is not just merely "notional," but ultimately specious and unreal, a mere charade despite the (sometimes) best intentions of the practitioner? The question is made all the more difficult when one recognizes that the true and the false are often present in subtle combinations inextricably interwoven.

In the course of *Histoire*, III, Bremond had answered the above questions with the term "theocentric." Genuine, true, real, from-the-depth, steadily pure, prayer puts all of the focus on God, *and not on the self of the one who prays*. The paradox or seeming contradiction is the claim that such prayer is not only "devout" but the manifestation of devout "humanism," as well as being truly "mystical." Thus, theocentric, devoutly humanist and mystical, along with the core idea of the "annihilation of the self," all become more or less synonymous terms for Bremond, their antitheses being self-centered or egotistical, that is, "anthropocentric."

At this point, from 1917 and up until reception into the Académie in 1924, Bremond was operating with his own version of what we have come to call the "hermeneutic of suspicion," that is, the interpretive process in which surface appearances are critiqued in order to "uncover" deeper levels of meaning and of reality. This is the Modernist challenge: first to analyze received truth in order to show what is misleading, wrong-headed, hopelessly archaic, downright hypocritical, or malignly oppressive of one group by another, in traditional forms. But then, second, to retrieve the old forms by means of deeper understandings that transfuse fresh blood into old bodies. "Mysticism," for instance, had often been a term of derision for pathological and exhibitionistic religious experience, but now, in conversations with theorists like Poulain and Saudreau and Maréchal, it could be renewed. The upshot, however, was that in the

Histoire Bremond, having identified the genuine article in the French School, would now be on the lookout for false manifestations, which, to be sure, would often be mixed with some good elements some of the time in some persons. In *Histoire*, IV, "The School of Port-Royal," he would deal with the first major false manifestation.

We recall that Bremond's first intention had been to minimize Port-Royal in the narrative, including it only as part of the countervailing forces, culminating in Bossuet, that would pull down mysticism by the end of the century.[1] It would function as a negativity, a mere sideshow at best.[2] Further study, however, began to put things in a different light. Not only were there too many connections between prominent figures at Port-Royal and the leaders of the French-School, there was also, when Bremond took a closer look, too much actual mysticism and admirable spirituality at Port-Royal despite the shortcomings.

He was coming to see that, in any sketching of the spiritual landscape of the era, he could not ignore Pascal, that giant associated with Port-Royal and a massively (the word is not too strong) venerated figure in the history of French culture, by Protestants as much as Catholics. Dealing with Pascal would mean taking on the whole Port-Royal/Jansenist phenomenon, with which Pascal was inseparably identified.

Bremond was also becoming a bit more dialectical in his thinking about historical change. In order to highlight the goodness of French School spirituality as the fruit of a true developmental process, he needed to show how aspects of counter-spiritualities, such as Port-Royal, were taken up into future manifestations. The matter is subtle, but we might recall that in his study of Fénelon Bremond had argued that the depth of the Swan of Cambrai and the muscular force of the Eagle of Meaux ultimately operated from the same premises, as would become evident in de Caussade and Grou a generation later. Port-Royal and Jansenism, antithetical to the French School, concealed some genuine concord that will leave its mark on the shape of future developments.

And, as mentioned, and in a way freighted with oedipal overtones, Bremond could not resist taking on "father" Sainte-Beuve, showing where the master was wrong and doing him one better.[3]

Consequently, the *Histoire* in its coverage of the seventeenth century was about to become a much longer work than Bremond had originally imagined. Now, instead of single volumes on the rise of the mystics (II), on the triumph of the mystics (III), and the defeat of the mystics (?), there would in due course be three volumes on the conquest of the mystics (IV, V, VI, all being prepared at the same time), and only in the

---

1. As in, for instance, the communication, dated by Goichot sometime between the spring of 1911 and the summer of 1912, from Bremond to his friend, the art historian André Pératé, where he referred to "sa [mysticism's] défaite par la revanche active du jansénisme, qui est à l'opposé" (EG, 67).

2. This is the approach that he took in *Histoire*, I, in the chapter "Devout Humanism versus Jansenism," where he argued that Jansenism simply represented the negative resistance to devout humanism, that there are "two philosophies of Christianity: that which we have called Devout Humanism and that which may be styled Eternal Jansenism" (ibid., 308).

3. The view, once again, of Thirouin, "Deux visions de Port-Royal."

last unfinished volume XI would Bremond approach circumstances toward the end of the century, with Bossuet at the center, surrounding the condemnation of mysticism. "The School of Port-Royal" could, therefore, be fitted into the overarching structure as refinement and focusing, but the work would be more extended, and, as we shall see, more controversial than ever. The struggle over Olier in the third volume had been painful, but time-limited, whereas turmoil over volume IV would continue for the rest of Bremond's life and well beyond. Indeed, it has continued down to the present day, sparking the most sustained objections and criticisms, beginning with Blondel. The "School of Port-Royal" caused Bremond more sleeplessness and agony in composition than any of the other volumes or individual portraits,[4] and it is the one he would most have liked to revise if he had lived long enough to do it.[5] Our question at the outset must be, Why was it so hard?

Port-Royal: Symbol and Problem

Two interconnected and overlapping, yet separate, phenomena, both of them constituting major trajectories in the "literary history of the religious sentiment" that was Bremond's agenda, should be teased apart. These are Port-Royal and Jansenism. The second may be seen as the hardening-of-the-arteries, so to speak, a sclerosis of the first.

As discussed in my earlier treatment of Sainte-Beuve's *Port-Royal*, that great literary critic's decision, in mid-nineteenth century, to devote a major historical analysis to the leading personalities of a pair of obscure seventeenth-century monastic communities immortalized them. Already known generally as part of the milieu that bred Blaise Pascal, "Port-Royal" now became a symbol of all that Sainte-Beuve conceived to be freedom-loving, artistically creative, and morally admirable in traditional French culture.[6] It became a symbol, and precursor, of the French spirit that the Revolution would then crown with victory, and that would always serve as a reminder of what can be retrieved and reactivated in a new day for new challenges. It is the Gallican spirit, moral and spiritual, though yet to be unencumbered from the baggage of religious, dogmatic language.

But, for churchmen it was also a symbol of French Catholicism at its independent best. First of all it was a reform movement in the spirit of the Counter-Reformation, and we recall that the Counter-Reformation, or better the "Catholic Reformation," was the Roman Church's concerted effort to respond to the Protestant challenge, to clean house, and to renew ecclesial life. The reforming Council of Trent had in one of its last

---

4. Bremond to Blondel, September 11, 1916 (BB, II, 304): the material on the abbé de Saint-Cyran is driving him crazy in a "prodigious imbroglio." Bremond to Blondel, May 13, 1917 (ibid., 320): he describes the Port-Royal material as "a dreadful strife." Bremond to Blondel, December 11, 1917 (ibid., 332–33): proofs of IV are being sent out for critical comments, of whom Blondel is the "*pars maxima.*"

5. Probably he would have upgraded his treatment of Saint-Cyran, as is suggested by the more favorable evaluation contained in "The Assaults on Pure Love" in *Histoire*, XI.

6. And precisely at a time when Bonapartism threatened those freedoms!

sessions, in November 1563, formulated the *Decretum de regularibus et monialibus* specifically to address abuses in monastic foundations.[7] When Jaqueline Marie Angélique Arnauld, daughter of a prominent family in Parisian legal circles, had become abbess of the little country women's community of Port-Royal-des-Champs in 1602, she was ten years old. The nuns owned private property, had servants, and the Rule was not observed with care. Trent meant to change all of that, but it would take time. After 1635 Saint-Cyran's influence on Angélique and others, following their earlier efforts, would be decisive in their reforming project.

Second, Port-Royal would come to represent theological innovation and renewal, especially in response to Protestant theologizing about grace, and the means of grace, in personal salvation. The reappropriation of the theology of Saint Augustine was central here,[8] and there was in place a pattern well-established by Catholic humanists for instituting programs of reform based on new readings of the patristic heritage. With Protestant reformers sharing in this "back to the sources" mentality, the Protestant-Catholic split can sometimes be seen as a matter of reading the Augustinian heritage differently. Fresh interpretations of the Bishop of Hippo, especially of his anti-Pelagian compositions, became a staple of "school"-debates in the Catholic theological faculties, giving rise, as at Louvain and the Sorbonne, to radical theses followed by internecine disputes between the teaching Orders, about original sin, free will, the operation of grace, and predestination. Things became so heated, as well as so generative of heterodox thinking, that papal authority tried to shut down the furor with the decrees *De Auxiliis* in the early seventeenth century. A Louvain-trained thinker, however, Cornelius Jansen, poured gasoline on the flames with his *Augustinus*, published in 1640, in which he offered views of Augustine that flew in the face of positions held by the Jesuits.[9] As mentioned, it was then the abbé de Saint-Cyran, who would feed the spirit of Jansen's Augustinianism into the Port-Royal process of reform, thereby stirring up a hornet's nest with the powerful French Jesuit establishment.

Third, Port-Royal will come to represent Gallican resistance to papal authority when Rome, responding to Jesuit alarm about developments at Port-Royal and a supposed "conspiracy" against the theological authorities, tried to squelch Port-Royal resistance to the theological censorship that followed the suppression of the *Augustinus*. The eruption came in 1653 with the Five Propositions controversy, when the Roman authorities, backed up by the Sorbonne,[10] summarized the (supposed) objectionable

---

7. See O'Malley, *Trent: What Happened at the Council*, 238–40, for discussion.

8. See Neveu, "Augustinism janséniste et magistère romain," and "Le statut théologique de saint Augustin au XVIIe siècle," who lays out the whole history by which Roman authority eventually felt compelled to "regularize" and "relativize" Augustine's role in theology, fearing an "Augustinian fundamentalism." Censure of Dom Mabillon's Maurist edition of Augustine in 1690 would be the final straw.

9. Thus it is that the claim is often made that "Jansenism" is a "phantom-heresy" created by the Jesuits in order to stigmatize their Port-Royal opposition. In fact, the *Augustinus* itself received a quick censure from the Vatican in 1641.

10. Sorbonne theologians were in charge of regulating doctrinal expression "under the authority

Jansenist theses being taught at Port-Royal and then required a formal disavowal from the nuns.[11] Never-ending debates followed about whether Rome, despite its authority (the "droit") to articulate correct doctrine, had correctly understood the book at issue (the "fait"), that is, the actual nature of what Jansen had been saying.[12] This debate continued on into the 18th century, well beyond the papal decrees culminating in 1713 in *Unigenitus*,[13] which is considered the formal condemnation of Jansenist thought root-and-branch. Resistance would continue for a long time, finally transmuting into a rigidly disciplinary, rigorously dogmatic Catholicism that went beyond Roman standards. "Jansenism" would eventually become a synonym for a kind of "ultra" Catholicism, and thus the very thing against which Bremond and the Modernists were rebelling.[14] Over time its Gallican element became a hyper-nationalism, as we will see much further on in a novelist like Georges Bernanos.

Finally, there was the cultural power of Port-Royal. In 1625 Angélique Arnauld, distressed by the unhealthy conditions, moved the women's community from Port-Royal-des-Champs to Port-Royal-de Paris in the faubourg Saint-Jacques in Paris (where Pascal would first attend services conducted by the charismatic Antoine Singlin [1607–1664], Saint-Cyran's successor, at the chapel). A men's community continued at the country location with a school, the famed Petites écoles de Port-Royal, begun in 1643 and led by the able scholar/physician Jean Hamon (1618-1687). As mentioned, these would become a fashionable training-ground for two generations of elite thinkers and artists, many of them characterized by some form of the Port-Royal

---

of the Most Christian King," with the Chancellor of France often presiding in cases that called for the intervention of the monarch. See Gres-Gayer, "Magisterium," whose pro-Gallican thesis is that in 17th-century Paris magisterial authority still lay in the hands of those who had knowledge, rather than power.

11. The condemned Five Propositions, not actually assigned to Jansen's book, but assumed to be a summary were: (1) "Some commandments of God are impossible to the righteous though they desire and strive to fulfill them, according to the power they possess at the moment; and they lack the grace which would render these commandments possible; (2) In the state of fallen nature, resistance to interior grace is impossible; (3) In order to deserve merit or demerit, in the state of fallen nature, man is not required to enjoy the freedom which excludes necessity; it is enough for him to enjoy freedom from constraint; (4) The semi-Pelagians admitted the need for interior and prevenient grace for every action, even in the act of initial faith; but they were heretics because they claimed this grace to be such that the human will was able to resist or obey it; (5) It is a renewal of the semi-Pelagian heresy to say that Christ died for all men without exception" (Krailsheimer, intro., *Pascal: The Provincial Letters*, 29).

12. Actually, the droit/fait distinction was introduced only by Nicole after the Formulary of Alexander VI in 1661 required an oath from clergy and religious that they did not subscribe to Jansenist teaching.

13. A long tradition thus began of interpreting *Unigenitus* as an assertion of Roman power over the ancient rights and privileges, i.e., the "Gallicanism," of the French Church, see Gres-Gayer, "The *Unigenitus* of Clement XI: A Fresh Look at the Issues." *Unigenitus* condemned Jansenist theses that derived from the work of Pasquier Quesnel (1634–1719), and it was fiercely resisted primarily by *Parlement*-circles supportive of Port-Royal.

14. Bremond calls Jansenism "a religion of terror" in which God commands the impossible and predestines some persons to eternal hellfire (*Histoire*, IV, 179).

pessimistic outlook on human nature, ranging all the way from dark tragedy (Racine) to a worldly street-wise cynicism (La Rochefoucauld). Salon-culture, under the leadership of sophisticated, aristocratic women, provided an ideal setting for the diffusion of Port-Royal influence, often softened into secularized forms.

So, Bremond was dealing with all of this large heritage when he embarked on *Histoire*, IV. Sainte-Beuve had been uninterested in the Jansenist phenomenon after the destruction of Port-Royal, considering post-*Unigenitus* developments degenerate culturally as well as theologically-fixated. But that fact exposed, Bremond thought, a spiritual tin ear, since Sainte-Beuve could not see how the spirituality of the early Port-Royal was already latent with the corrupting forces that would emerge along two vectors with more and more clarity.

First was an exaggerated sin-consciousness grounded in a terror of the holy God, leading to scrupulosity, rigorism, and a harsh judgmentalism toward the Jesuits, and then toward any spirituality judged to be morally permissive. The sacraments must not be profaned by inadequate penitential preparation, they said; there must be true "contrition," or sorrow, for sin, not just the weak "attrition," or fear of judgment, of the Jesuits. Second was the whole notion of "election"—a bugaboo that became Bremond's primary complaint about Pascal—which he believed led to a prideful sense of specialness, and an inordinate emphasis on privileged "signs" that certified one's status as a member of God's elect. And then, third, came the classically Jansenist concept of "victorious delectation" in which one's assurance of salvation is marked by sensuous, felt, palpable delight. Bremond's later word for this last would be "pan-hedonism," always a trap, he thought, in the spiritual life, where, despite our constant thirst for reassurance, God comes only in the "dryness" of an eternal silence evoking pure love. All of the Port-Royal emphases lead to the "anthropocentrism" that distorts the inner life, the life of prayer. But the clincher was the rejection of mystical spirituality as Bremond understood it, that is, the "theocentric" focus. Careful analysis of the "religious psychology" of the principal Port-Royal figures would, Bremond thought, illustrate the inner working of these debased teachings.

From the perspective of the factions within church-historical scholarship, Bremond was caught between opposing forces. He could not be neutral about Port-Royal. One *either* found the whole Port-Royal/Jansenist movement, as with Sainte-Beuve, to be an admirable example of spiritual power (religious, intellectual, political), *or* one decided, as in standard church historiography, that the movement was fundamentally heretical, sectarian, disobedient to proper ecclesial authority, and corrupt spiritually. Unlike Sainte-Beuve, Bremond, while focusing most of his attention on the same pre-*Unigenitus* period, would in time incorporate in his perception of Jansenism some Jansenists whom he to some degree admired, such as Pasquier Quesnel (1634–1719) and Jacques-Joseph Duguet (1649–1733).[15] Indeed, on the basic question of whether

---

15. The question is subtle, however. Though he profoundly disliked Jansenism, Bremond had to admit on a number of occasions that individuals influenced by Jansenism made significant contributions

to be for or against Port-Royal, Bremond took a notably middle position, deciding to affirm many good qualities in the leading representatives of the movement, while offering trenchant, sometimes devastating, criticism of their shortcomings as he perceived them.[16] Port-Royal would be a cautionary tale rather than a scene of corruption pure and simple.

Knowing that much of the controversy about the nature and meaning of Port-Royal depended on the discerning assessment of complex primary sources, Bremond offered a careful, critical survey of the range of available records and accounts, remaining delicately attuned to the inevitable elements of party-bias and the factor of character-assassination often contained in polemical work.[17] Unlike the Quietist controversy, which revolved around a small number of distinct individuals fighting out their differences in a high-profile public drama marked, so to speak, by hand-to-hand theological combat, the story of Port-Royal and Jansenism was much more diffuse and prolonged, with a wide panoply of characters and divergent tendencies. We recall that Sainte-Beuve took six volumes to tell his version of the story, and Bremond would take into account an even larger range of material that included judicial and archival records, as well as strictly literary accounts. The essence of his narrative will, however, be contained in sketches of four thinkers: Saint-Cyran, Antoine Arnauld, Blaise Pascal, and Pierre Nicole; of a saintly woman, Agnès Arnauld, and of a male "half-saint," the "solitary" Tillemont.

Saint-Cyran

Bremond launched his treatment of the "School of Port-Royal" with some of the criticisms of Sainte-Beuve's interpretation that we have already seen. While Sainte-Beuve opened the way to a properly psychological analysis of the leading individuals of Port-Royal, he did not, as mentioned, focus on their life of prayer or share their faith, thereby missing what most matters, "the commerce of the soul with God," the

---

to the mainstream. We will see this in *Histoire*, IX, X, and XI.

16. For a sample of more recent scholarship: Doyle, *Jansenism*; McManners, *Church and Society*, vol. 2; Cognet, *Le jansénisme*; Orcibal, *Les origines du Jansénisme*, and *Jansénius d'Ypres*; Abercrombie, *Origins of Jansenism*. The older bibliography, which is massive, is gathered in Dupuy, "Jansénisme." As will be discussed further on, one of Bremond's most trenchant recent critics, Cognet, "Bremond et Port-Royal," takes him to task for ignoring the important 1922 work of Augustin Gazier, *Histoire générale*, 2 vols., as well as Gazier's strongly pro-Jansenist views about Pascal.

17. Given the complexity of primary sources pertaining to Port-Royal, *Histoire*, IV, ch. 4, "Saint-Cyran Conspirateur," section 1, is a remarkable source-critical assessment by Bremond of the materials relating to the trial of Saint-Cyran on charges of a conspiracy against the theological power-structure of France. Supposedly, he and Jansen were the masterminds of a plot to establish the writings of Saint Augustine as the supreme authority in doctrinal disputes. The subject is complex and obscure, to say the least, but Bremond carefully sorted out the documentary sources, showing that the charges were ultimately hysterical and ridiculous. Was he polemicizing against the Anti-Modernist papal decrees of 1907?

"personal religion" that is the real essence of a religious movement. And, even more, he did not see that Port-Royal from its inception was Jansenist in essence, that there is no point in separating the pre-*Unigenitus* from the later, since they are of a piece.

Furthermore, he then suggested, what we actually find in the prayer-life of Port-Royal is not something separate and distinct, but rather a variant in different forms of the teachings and practice of the French School.[18] When the Port-Royalists move away from that solid ground, they become idiosyncratic and unbalanced, lapsing from the properly theocentric emphasis into anthropocentrism. It is the task of the religious psychologist to point to these indicators and to reflect on their meaning.

Contrary to Sainte-Beuve's view, said Bremond in the second chapter, we do not see anything like a "Jansenist-style" of discourse, where a particular kind of apologetic for Christianity is mounted in language evocative of their distinctive spirituality.[19] Sainte-Beuve thought that this style possessed a biblical simplicity and austerity, as well as a lawyerly logic, in marked contrast with the usual stilted, flowery and orotund rhetoric of the period.[20] But Bremond contended that Sainte-Beuve merely showed his ignorance here of wider Christian literature. Something of the same could be said for the so-called Jansenist "rigorism" in penitential practice—a factor often pointed to in characterizations of Port-Royal because of Arnauld's 1643 work *De la fréquente communion*—but in fact the Port-Royal teachers only repeated French School perspectives.[21] The key to their central failing was the absence of what we might call "uplift," the ability, as with Olier, to facilitate a shift in the penitent's mood from self-reproach ("anthropocentric") to aspiration for the vision of God ("theocentric"). Thus the individual ended up trapped in scrupulosity.

In his sketching and analysis of Jean Duvergier de Hauranne, the abbé de Saint-Cyran (1581–1643), the towering eminence and theological mentor of early Port-Royal, Bremond moved into the substance of his presentation. The general impression is of a good and sincere man, but also a weak one eventually led astray. After living in Paris for a time, where he absorbed a range of influences from important spiritual sources, be became a friend and collaborator early on with Cornelius Jansen, sharing the latter's visions for church reform. He then fed these quasi-Augustinian visions into the reforming efforts at Port-Royal, thereby creating the resistance to papal authority

---

18. Of three of the characters reviewed in this chapter, Bremond said of them that "Saint-Cyran is only in essence a Bérullian, though feverish and a bit muddle-headed; Mère Agnès would have made an excellent Visitandine; and Tillemont a Benedictine" (ibid., ii).

19. See Cantillon, "Les Marques du style," for a discussion of this claim by Bremond, esp. 181–84. Involved here was Bremond's intuition that a spirituality generates a "style" of expression as a "social product."

20. Sainte-Beuve had argued that the legal background of the Arnauld family created a particular "genre d'éloquence" for Port-Royal. Sainte-Beuve, as cited by Bremond, had described their discourse as aimed at "moral utility" in an unvarnished, somewhat repetitious style (ibid., 9).

21. Bremond would reaffirm this view much later in *Histoire* IX, in an appendix, where he discussed *De la fréquente communion* by Arnauld as a typical and laudable effort of the period to encourage greater seriousness in reception of the Eucharist.

that would eventually surface. He left a rich corpus of writing, mostly spiritual letters, along with a rendering of Jansen's own work on spiritual discipline, as well as anti-Jesuit and pro-Gallican tracts. This later material, including the *procès* of his trial for conspiracy, survived in abundance, becoming a goldmine for anti-Port-Royal polemicists.

People loved Saint-Cyran or hated him, canonized or despised him with little middle ground. In mediating Jansen's Augustinianism to the Port-Royalists, he gave their community its distinctive spiritual stamp, and in the process elevated himself in the eyes of Port-Royal to something like the status of a saint and, eventually, a martyr. Sainte-Beuve loved him uncritically ("a sovereign genius," "an incomparable character"),[22] seeing him as the personification of all that was best in Port-Royal. Let us, said Bremond in effect, display the chinks in this man's spiritual armor, in order to separate him from idealizing Jansenist propaganda and legend (to which Sainte-Beuve had seemingly succumbed), but also from prejudiced and demonizing Jesuit historiography. A balanced picture was in order, Bremond thought, especially in light of the fact that "no truly critical and comprehensive evaluation" on Saint-Cyran had yet been done.[23]

In "the Misery of Saint-Cyran," Bremond described him in a series of biting phrases as "an unhappy man," as "fatally vowed to impotence," as "eaten away by incurable weaknesses," as "a great man *manqué*." Affecting an austerity that women found to be very seductive (though he was actually light-hearted), he was banal in much of his spiritual counsel (though he sometimes said very profound things), commonplace in his virtues (though genuinely virtuous), as "prodigiously preoccupied with himself" (precisely when he tried to focus on others), and, most damningly, as the purveyor of a "devout charlatanism" in which he constantly painted himself as a saint (without being aware of his grandiosity).[24]

Bremond perceived Saint-Cyran to be self-defeating in his behavior and statements, so that at the very moment when he would say something profound or engage in an admirable action, he would (as even Sainte-Beuve had noticed) seem to say or do something that undid the goodness of the original expression. Bremond hypothesized here a "hereditary psychopathology" in Saint-Cyran's family line, which manifested in his correspondence as "a sweet megalomania," "a grandiose melancholy leading to despair," and finally an "intellectual and moral ataxia."[25] Although Bremond does not

---

22. Ibid., 37. Bremond described Sainte-Beuve's judgment here as "grave préjugé." Sainte-Beuve dedicated all of volume 2 of the six books of his *Port-Royal* to "Le Port-Royal de M. de Saint-Cyran."

23. Ibid., 37n1. Of course, Jean Orcibal's work (n15 above, of which vols. IV and V contain an edition and evaluation of Saint-Cyran's work) in more recent years has changed that. Since middle positions are perennially unpopular, Bremond was seen by his critics as either too affirming of some aspects of Port-Royal, and by others as not affirming enough.

24. Ibid., 36–49.

25. Ibid., 50–67, all of this accompanied by an early woodcut portrait of Saint-Cyran that shows him as smiling and cunning, though with a sadness in the eyes (ibid., 54).

use the language, in Freudian terminology the diagnosis would be obsessional neurosis with strong narcissistic tendencies. And yet all of this is accompanied by great suffering, by rivers of devotional expression, and by sincerely given, and sincerely received, veneration from the inhabitants of Port-Royal, especially during the time of Saint-Cyran's imprisonment and trial.

But Saint-Cyran was also a man with "a soul naturally and passionately religious," "on the threshold of a high mysticism," a "deep soul . . . full of God."[26] Though Sainte-Beuve erred in comparing Saint-Cyran to the saintly Sieyès, moderate voice in the throes of the 1789 Revolution, it is nonetheless true that Saint-Cyran was no sectarian. Bremond discussed at length the assessment of Saint-Cyran given by Vincent de Paul, who knew him well, and concluded, approvingly, with Vincent's early observation (which later hardened) that Saint-Cyran was "a holy man, incapable of wishing evil, or of creating heresy or schism, very united with God and very edifying, but also addled, confused and incoherent."[27]

When he came to discuss the supposed conspiracy, the Augustinizing "cabale" associated with Saint-Cyran, Bremond essentially dismissed it as a comedy of errors, misunderstandings and imprudences so far as Saint-Cyran was concerned. It was true that he and Jansen had huddled together for years on matters of church cleansing and renewal ("vague projects," said Bremond).[28] But by becoming involved in court intrigues and political maneuvering, especially against the Jesuits,[29] and by scheming and dreaming grandiosely, he was in over his head. However, he wanted *reform*, not *schism*, and, foolish and vain as he was, he then played into the hands of others.[30]

Bremond contested the idea that with Jansen Saint-Cyran was the father of a true dogmatic Augustinian "Jansenism." When in 1642 Rome issued its first

---

26. Ibid., 67. "Le meilleur et le vrai Saint-Cyran, l'homme de prière, l'histoire le soupçonne à peine," says Bremond with gusto.

27. Ibid., 78. After discussing Vincent de Paul's later, sterner view, when he testified at the trial of Saint-Cyran, a view based, said Bremond, on "reasoning," he contended that the earlier and more compassionate view was based on "a series of intuitions, controlled and confirmed by mutual counterbalance, during a long intimacy with Saint-Cyran" (ibid., 80–81). In other words, the morally-generated or illative judgment was the more accurate!

28. E.g., ibid., 120. He thus agreed with Pascal's famous satire on this supposed conspiracy in the sixteenth of the *Provinciales*.

29. "One blushes," said Bremond, "to record the tawdriness of all of this," where he acknowledges that Saint-Cyran had definitely soiled his hands with anti-Jesuit plotting, but he was a bungler (ibid., 117, and n3).

30. The best-known popular account of Port-Royal in English, Ronald A. Knox's *Enthusiasm*, chs. 9 and 10, is a virtual running commentary on both Sainte-Beuve and Bremond. Knox found everything about Port-Royal distasteful, and a prime example of the evils that occur when Christians, in the spirit of "enthusiasm," try to be too unworldly. With regard to Saint-Cyran, he contended that this man was a true threat to state and church, that Richelieu was wise to rein him in, and that he is the true father of Jansenism. In general, Knox was antipathetic to all of the French School language of "self-annihilation," including its later use by Fénelon, and, therefore, tended to disagree with many of Bremond's assessments, especially where the latter tried to hit a nuanced and sympathetic balance.

condemnation of the *Augustinus*, Saint-Cyran reacted bitterly and encouraged resistance at Port-Royal, leaving the banner, after his death the next year, to be picked up by Antoine Arnauld. The irony, said Bremond, after a detailed examination of early correspondence between Jansen and Saint-Cyran, was that for the former the *Augustinus* was a pure product of the library, not the oratory, i.e., an erudite intellectual exercise reflective of "school theology," while for Saint-Cyran, it functioned mostly as a jumping-off point, superficially understood, for a practical program of spiritual renewal. Jansen cared about ideas, while Saint-Cyran cared about the interior life.[31] The tragedy was that Saint-Cyran became embroiled in a battle of competing dogmatic orthodoxies, when dogma was not really his métier, and he had not in fact taught the soon-to-be condemned (1644) Five Propositions (though the recalcitrant nuns of Port-Royal would make him their posthumous champion). One recalls here, ironically, Blondel's comment about Bremond after Tyrrell's death, that he cared little about theology!

Then, in his chapter on "the Religion of Saint-Cyran" Bremond first painted a highly positive picture. Saint-Cyran, he said, having been initially trained by the Jesuits, was a man of a "sweet" and good natured piety, with a confiding and affectionate relationship with God, full of joy and humility with regard to the Eucharist, serious about the life of prayer and holiness, intent on a "simple interior adoration," a solitary and meditative man at heart. He had a poetic side to his expressiveness, and he generally kept a good balance between prayer and action, though he was vulnerable to the intellectual agitation of trying too hard. He was a sincere man (a "good priest," says Bremond) who took himself rather too seriously ("imprudent," says Bremond).[32]

Trouble arose at several points. He tended to become scrupulous in preparation for Holy Communion, and seemed not to know how to use sacramental confession in a competent and assured way. As a result he began to lean to excessive self-examination, i.e., rigorism, in his teaching at Port-Royal. Second, he began, unwisely, to distinguish overmuch between serious and not-so-serious Christians, expecting higher standards of unworldly holiness for the former. Third, he started to become excessively inward, focused on a direct, unmediated relationship with God, and thus leaned in the direction of an illuminism. The psychological result of these three aberrations is a megalomania that masks inner weakness (we might say, an "insecure narcissism"), spiritual self-satisfaction, and then a self-isolating tendency that does not brook criticism and review.

Effective insofar as he expressed good French-School devotion, Saint-Cyran became increasingly destructive as his weaknesses took over. The second generation of those at Port-Royal would take up for the most part his unhealthy side, thus paving the way for a full-blown Jansenism. The sad thing, said Bremond, was that

---

31. Ibid., 123, 127. It is the "notional" versus the "real."
32. The whole section, ibid., 129–48, but esp. 147–48.

Saint-Cyran's goodness died with him, while his "puerile vanity,"[33] exploited by others, finally did him in. He showed good sense in prayer, but only there. It is a criticism that Bremond will bring against others associated with Port-Royal, especially Pascal, that there is a kind of haunting beauty in the intensity and aesthetic excellence (at times) of their interior life, but than a shattering and obvious self-importance in the pattern of outward action.

I think that Bremond had hit here on the dilemma of the reformer and of reform movements generally. Intentions and vision and goals are all worthy, but something about the sense of "specialness" that easily infects the mentality of the reformer gets in the way, may even vitiate the whole effort. If the reform movement itself then comes to embody the leader's shortcomings and vulnerabilities, because these align themselves with the psychic needs of the followers, then history is littered with the results.[34]

More broadly, one could say that in his exposure of the "devout charlatan" in Saint-Cyran, Bremond pointed to that tendency in all of us, including the saints. Real spiritual growth, he seemed to be saying, consists of weeding out the charlatan.

The Arnauld Sisters

Next came the Arnauld family, who, long distinguished as jurists, became involved at the small, convent-community of Port-Royal in 1602 when Angélique (1591–1661) became, as said, the abbess at an exceedingly young age. As she grew into a woman of resolve, and her horizons were raised, Angélique gradually instituted Counter-Reformation disciplinary reforms, initially under influences from Bérulle and Francis de Sales, but eventually from Saint-Cyran. Bremond did not like Angélique,[35] much preferring her younger sister Agnès (1593–1671), who would be elected abbess in 1636, and whom he considered a better representative of the early interior life of Port-Royal. This preference reflected, of course, his dominant view, meeting Sainte-Beuve halfway, that there was a healthy core of spirituality in Saint-Cyran and the early Port-Royal.

Bremond argued that Agnès had received her spiritual formation much more robustly than had Angélique under devout humanist influence. He noted a calm,

---

33. Ibid., 175.

34. This is to say that Bremond would have agreed with most of Knox's criticisms, that Port-Royal, and thus Jansenism in general, was sectarian, that it saw itself as "the true Church," that it limited salvation to "the few," that it was rigorist, that it propounded an "ultra-supernaturalist morality," etc., but, once again, Bremond would have bitterly disagreed, and rightly, with Knox's disparagement of the "sweet" side of Port-Royalist devotion as self-deluding, since for them grace, if it was real, had to be *foncièrement délectable* (a view stated by Nicole, see below) (Knox, *Enthusiasm*, ch. 10, esp. 224–25). Knox, a level-headed and practical Englishman, was hostile also to mysticism, as his following chapters on quietism showed.

35. In Bremond's estimation, she was rigid, not personable, and imperious. "She governed more than she directed" (*Histoire*, IV, 177, 182).

peaceful, un-agitated tone in her manner—a giveaway for Bremond, in the tradition from Fénelon, that self-seeking or self-securing is absent from the individual. Citing with approval a long passage from Sainte-Beuve, in which one can see a psychological kinship between the two great male portraitists in the sentimental way that they could depict women, he described Agnès's piety as "tender, affectionate, engaging, of an extreme and highly nuanced delicateness."[36] His sustained analysis of a reproduction of a famous painting of two Port-Royal nuns engaged in prayer is striking: one of the women is Agnès in a radiant heavenward-looking posture of petition, the other is an ill younger sister looking quietly resigned to her state. While the painting has often been interpreted as a representation of distorted Jansenist devotion, Bremond took the contrary position that "this tableau conveys excellently, but uniquely, the poetry of Christian prayer, considered, so to speak, in two typical modes ('deux états moyens'), [namely] the prayer of children, and the prayer of those who are not so any longer, but who will become so by the help of grace: both of them mild and confident, but in different degrees."[37] Thus, he said, we see in the painting a healthy integration of nature and grace, precisely because there is no sense of the "terror of God," as if one had to give up one's fragile and needy humanity in order to be close to the divine.[38]

The influence from Francis de Sales on Agnès was, Bremond thought, palpable. He pointed to the way in which she chose repeatedly to warn against brooding over faults, noting that when we do so, we are engaged in a form of self-love. Such an individual refuses the humbling that comes, when one acknowledges one's imperfections, and seeks grace to remedy them. It is a refusal of repose and peace by feasting on disquietude. Sainte-Beuve found it all "too subtle" and impractical in value, but he could not have been more wrong, averred Bremond with considerable conviction.[39] Another example was in her ability to adopt a playful or light-hearted tone with correspondents whom she found a bit pompous or fussy, to use a bit of humor in a "rustic" way to make a good point; and she hated affectation.[40] The word that Bremond kept using for her was "jolie," all of it reminiscent of devout humanism and totally unlike what Jansenism would come to be. Because she was truly French School in spirit, resisting scrupulosity in preparation for the Eucharist,

---

36. Ibid., 180–81. Bremond's citation continues: "If she had lived in the world, people would have spoken of her as joyfully light-hearted ('comme des précieuses du bon temps') and of the best quality." Perhaps a little snobbery on Sainte-Beuve's part!

37. Ibid., 179.

38. The way that Bremond will make this point later in *Histoire*, VII, is that both petition and resignation are two modes of trust, in which one casts oneself adoringly on the divine mercy. The trust *is* the prayer.

39. "Il se trompe grandement," said Bremond, adding, "the temptations of the devout life have a subtlety to which one can respond only with a greater subtlety" (*Histoire*, IV, 189).

40. Ibid., 193.

eighteenth-century Jansenist editors declined to include her correspondence in official collections.

A Male "Solitary"

Then, before turning to the next Arnauld, Bremond detoured to consider another kind of Port-Royal character that he genuinely admired, one of the group of penitent "Solitaries" or male hermit monk-scholars at Port-Royal-des-Champs. Le Nain de Tillemont (1637–1698), best known for his massive (16 volumes!) history of the patristic Church, fascinated him. A prodigy who had received all of his early education and formation at the Port-Royal school, Tillemont's classical training was superb, based on access to original texts in a large library. Viewing Greco-Roman antiquity as both profane and Christian, his religious formation assured "a rigorous doctrinal orthodoxy." "Positive theology rather than speculative" was his preference, and his methods were highly disciplined in terms of chronology and strict textual source-criticism. He began working early on with the Maurist editions of patristic work, collaborating with Dom Mabillon and the scholars of Saint-Germain-des-Prés. Absolutely dedicated, detached, austere in ascetic discipline, constant in devotion, and much celebrated, he died a revered figure.[41]

However, problems began when a certain perspective on oneself was lost. Bremond thought that these Solitaries became self-righteous in their habits and orderliness, and then ended up with a "functional humility" (rather than attitudinal or dispositional) derived, they thought, from an imitation of the "Desert Fathers" that made them "Pelagians in a new genre." Their "desert" was not Catholic, where one seeks after holiness in a conversation with tried saints, but operated rather as a kind of self-constructed Robinson Crusoe island. In a reference to Tillemont's fondness for idealizing and romanticizing figures from the early Church, Bremond described the Port-Royal tendency to create "an island of august phantoms," which gives rise to a "counter-sense" when it is separated from living tradition. This is why, Bremond argued, it is important to read Augustine through the eyes of, for instance, Francis de Sales, and not to take him "straight up," as it were. It is that danger of primitivism that hovers over all reform movements, so that a reconstruction of the early church simply becomes a mirror-image of the interpreter's isolation and frustrations with the present. Bremond suggested—again in a biting phrase—that a purely bookish education makes one stiff and brittle and archaic and narrow, like dry cisterns! The problem with sectarians is that they do not know how to laugh at themselves.[42]

What is most touching in Bremond's portrait of Tillemont, however archaeologically-minded, narrowly dogmatic, and psychologically tight that worthy might have

---

41. Preceding paragraph based on Neveu, "Sébastien Le Nain de Tillemont." The essay is in part a reflection of Neveu's full-length biography of Tillemont.

42. "It is the lack of humor that makes sectarians" (ibid., 252).

been, is the way in which he saw this scholar "pen in hand," producing highly lyrical and rhythmic devotions with an absolutely sincere effusiveness that starts out in an over-scrupulous fashion and ends up with the spirit of "a child." Tillemont examined himself only in dialogue with God, and did so with real elegance. He kept a keen eye out for self-love in his motivations, operated with a tormented conscience, and often manifested the inner life of a fretful child filled with self distrust. He was constantly afraid of loving something too much, including his books and work! Naive and subject to paranoia, Tillemont was a certain kind of educated saint, living in a resuscitated past rather than the present.

Perhaps the most striking aspect of Bremond's characterization here, once again, is the struggle for fairness in the calculation of virtues and vices. One has no trouble is recognizing in the sketch a form of the modern critique of the book-bound scholar or pedant, but in order to avoid caricature there is a strong counter-balancing effort to be sympathetic. There is also the insistence that spiritual inclinations at their roots (emotional, dispositional, affective, etc.) and manifest in "lyrical" expression, are always essentially pure (come from the "child"), tending to become degenerate only at the level of verbal and systematic formulation, i.e., dogmas. There is also, of course, the assumption that the "real" always precedes the "notional" in time, always requiring rebirth of the "notional" in an endless process. Again, Blondel will issue cautions. Does emotion precede cognition, or is it the other way around?

In any case, Bremond wanted to deal with one whom he considered the dogmatist par excellence and true father, though inadvertently, of a thought-out Jansenism, Antoine Arnauld.

The "Great" Arnauld

What Bremond had against "the Great" (to distinguish him from his lawyer father of the same name) Antoine Arnauld (1612–1694), brother of Angélique and Agnès and highly respected Sorbonne theologian, was that he *rationalized* Port-Royal, took what was still filled with the poetry of French School piety and turned it into a cold and soulless logical system, converted the "real" into mere "notions."

Arnauld is best known to posterity for the book *L'Art de Penser* (*Port-Royal Logic*), created late in his career with Pierre Nicole, and thus he is associated with a rigidly deductive mentality, i.e., a scholasticism such as Bremond detested. The sadness of this, thought Bremond, is that Port-Royal had real devotional spirit, in which desolation and suffering, based on actual deprivation and persecution, played a large part. It had the moral beauty of a tormented conscience, with the "cruel imagination" of an implacable Christ subjecting his elect to the pains of hell, although counterbalanced by the "noble flower" of tenderness as with Mère Agnès. But with Arnauld, lacking in a genuine interior life, obliviousness and insensitive to suffering, everything hardened.

In 1643, the year of Saint-Cyran's death, Arnauld took his teachings and stiffened them into the *De la fréquente communion où les sentiments des Pères, des Papes, et des Conciles touchant l'usage des sacrements de pénitence et d'Eucharistie sont fidèlement exposés.* Later he defended the Five Propositions censured by Rome, turning himself into the prominent public advocate for early Jansenism and arch-enemy to the Jesuits whom he bitterly castigates for moral laxism. He was also a well-known Cartesian in his philosophy, thus entering into debates with the brilliant Oratorian Malebranche about the nature of concept-formation as the mind's "vision in God," and later he became an outspoken defender of Gallican privileges and fierce opponent of Calvinism. Exiled at least twice, supported at one point by Louis XIV, he became the theoretical thinker to whom Pascal turned for grounding. The late work on logic, including a turn in the direction of Thomist theology, immortalized him. Truly, he was everything that Bremond hated, embodying in his personal testimony, Bremond thought, "the monstrous and candid simplicity of a doctor who is only a doctor."[43]

This kind of individual cannot be a mystic, since he lacks the inclination to inner silence and fundamental humility that are the prerequisites; he is self-satisfied because his intellect, sharp and clear, has made him so. There is an exteriorizing, dehumanizing quality to Arnauld. Bremond's critique here is important for his own future development. It is the charge that for Arnauld words have become a substitute for soul, but not an expression of soul. The individual has, Bremond thought, no poetry in him, he never sings, he just pontificates. At this point he aimed a shot at the "sectarian intellectualism" to which he claimed the French temperament is peculiarly vulnerable. The clever precision of my words sets me apart from, and above, the common run of humankind. Intellectual mastery becomes a substitute for the love of God. Sainte-Beuve saw the same thing by claiming that the second generation of Port-Royal had turned "scientific," i.e., hyper-rational, dissecting everything relentlessly, and creating the illusion of truly living within the soul of religion.[44] In his later work Bremond will turn this hunger for the lyrical side of spirituality into the quest for "pure poetry."

And so, Bremond argued, it was the way that Arnauld created a systematic negativity toward the Jesuits that became the starting point for true Jansenism. Earlier devotional needs and insights got woven into a new unity. A piety derived from the *Augustinus* is now lived out at ridiculous lengths, although it is only after *Unigenitus* that it will crystallize into a devotional mood and style, with men like Quesnel and Duguet, and then go on to a long future history. Moreover, Bremond was willing to

---

43. Ibid., 287. Bremond makes this comment in the context of describing the way in which Arnauld seems to have used the opportunity of defending the ladies of Port-Royal, when they refused to take the oath of disavowal of the Five Propositions, as a platform for his own vanity. To Bremond, Arnauld, admired for his intellect, is little more than a cold-hearted exhibitionist. Sainte-Beuve, on the other hand, was dazzled (the word is not too strong) by Arnauld's dialectical talents.

44. Ibid., 305.

spread the blame: the Jesuit historian Rapin, a major source for the details of the Jansenist quarrels, was as vitriolic and one-sided as his adversaries, insensitive to what was genuinely religious in them. He was a good example, Bremond claimed, of how the adversarial spirit infects, then poisons, a debate. A good point, one might say, but then Blondel thought that Bremond was making himself part of the problem.

In February 1918, Bremond sent the first proofs of *Histoire*, IV, along with material that would later comprise volume V, to Blondel for review and comment. The sections of IV included the introductory material and the blocks dealing with Saint-Cyran, Mère Agnès, Tillemont and Antoine Arnauld, but not Pascal and Nicole, since they would require more extended treatment.[45] Clearly he was anxious to see how Blondel would react to his general picture of Port-Royal and Jansenism, since he knew that the response to his upcoming interpretation of Pascal would involve a separate set of thorny issues.

Blondel Responds

Blondel's "timid protestation" (Blondel's phrase) to Bremond's assessment is arresting and illuminating.[46] Bremond responded to Blondel in a note included in the published subsection of *Histoire*, IV, on Arnauld and as a kind of appendage to the negative comment he had made on the uncharitable and mean-spirited flavor of the Jesuit Rapin's history of Port-Royal.[47] Blondel was troubled by Bremond's dismissal of Arnauld as a cold-hearted rationalist devoid of genuine religious sentiment, and thus with the idea that "notions" represent the loss of a prior purity in "experience." It was time, Blondel thought, to fight Bremond on some of this.

Blondel suggested that Jansenism arose not, as Bremond seemed to think, as "a sort of spontaneous generation, by an almost unconscious conjuncture of multiple deviations and without provocation," resulting, as in Rapin's construal, in an "abuse of the eristic spirit and a Pharisaic [sic] confidence." On the contrary, he argued, "devout humanism" itself had created the problem by degenerating in the direction of a "worldliness and laxism" that had failed to recognize "the serious incomprehensibility of the Christian life." The problem, then, was that the Jansenists in their well-intended efforts reacted wrongly when, instead of relying on "the method of the saints," they fell into "a pretense of austerity," and an "embittered zeal," so that in the end they resorted to "means completely natural, under the color of a pure supernaturalism." It would be "more edifying," Blondel thought, for those who

---

45. This is Blanchet's correct inference (BB, II, 346n1) after analyzing Blondel to Bremond, March 2, 1918 (ibid., 343–46), in order to ascertain exactly which portions of *Histoire*, IV, would have been available to Blondel in draft form.

46. Ibid., 345. One senses that Blondel read Bremond's proofs very soon after arrival and with considerable interest. Reproduced by Bremond, along with his response, in the final text of *Histoire*, IV, 316n2.

47. *Histoire*, IV, 316–17n2.

encouraged the rise of Port-Royal to take responsibility for it. Apologizing for the "scrawl" that he had written, since he was sick in bed, he indicated, combatively, that he would have more to say on Pascal later.

Bremond did not take it lying down. In his response "to one of the theologians who have been pleased to review the proofs," he willingly owned the phrase "a sort of spontaneous generation," laughingly referring to Pascal's use of the image of Cleopatra's nose, i.e., the idea that a contingency of nature changes the whole course of history, since Jansenism, he thought, was a true monstrosity, an unpredictable freak of nature determining much that followed. He denied that devout humanism was evolving in the direction of moral laxity. As an escape hatch, he did allow that casuistical moral theology was becoming too rationalistic and insufficiently religious in its thinking. And he allowed that with Saint-Cyran one did see a sincere effort to redress the balance. But, he absolutely denied that he was simply bashing the Jansenists, when others, mean-spirited Jesuits, bore responsibility as well. After all, he had insisted that there was some of Arnauld (i.e., a cold-hearted quarrelsomeness) in "both camps."

Blondel did not take it lying down either, but he held off until he had seen the material on Pascal, and then responded at length and in detail (a memorandum of ten full pages in BB, II) on November 30, 1919. I will consider that response in the next chapter after reviewing Bremond's treatment of Pascal and Nicole. Clearly they agreed that there was something profoundly wrong with the spirituality of Port-Royal as it evolved, and that that "something" manifested as rigorism and an arrogant sectarianism, but as diagnosticians they operated in the differing modalities that make their exchanges interesting. Bremond saw character flaws and spoiled interiority, while Blondel saw bad thinking, i.e., a confusion of the natural and supernatural leading to corrupt practice. Blondel's constant warning to Bremond was that you can't do away with the "notional," because if you try to do so, it will (so to speak) come back to bite you. An overreliance on thinking or bad thinking, which is it? Bremond took the former view, and Blondel the latter.

Huysmans

In order to set up a contrast, moreover, that can illuminate Bremond's concerns, let us consider a Catholic novelist, whose work he loved, and who operated as a kind of subconscious, occasionally conscious, current in Bremond's sensibilities. This person is not a "devout charlatan," but instead is a mystic and a true convert to Christian faith, the Flemish-French art critic and novelist Joris-Karl Huysmans (1848–1907). Bremond had first glowingly reviewed his work during the years at *Études*, but he would have been reminded of Huysmans through an indirect connection while he was assembling his Port-Royal materials.

In the summer of 1917 he indicated to Blondel that he was planning soon to line up an apartment in nearby Pau in order to continue some of his research. He had discovered two libraries there, one of which had belonged to a certain Leclaire, who had been at one time a co-oblate with J.-K. Huysmans at the Benedictine monastic community of Ligugé.[48] The newfound collection was especially rich in mystical writings, writings which would have put him in mind of Huysmans as just the kind of paradoxical Catholic and artist that he had come to admire. It is just possible as well that the collection included work by Jean-Joseph Surin (1600–1665), the Jesuit mystic who especially fascinated Bremond and who would receive major treatment in *Histoire*, V. The common thread with Huysmans is the idea that material expression in religion displays an inner reality that is manifest only at the extreme edges, only where expression is florid and intense, thereby exposing the ironic, the absurd, the impossible, by its rawness.

Huysmans is well-known as the arch-example of the "decadent" period of French naturalist writers, that is, those who pushed Zola's methods of realist, detailed description of the material conditions of life, especially among working-class and bourgeois French, to their aesthetic limit. Huysmans's most famous novel, *À Rebours* ("Against Nature") of 1884, building on his experience as an art critic, displayed his masterful gift for converting the sensory qualities of painting into the verbal format of literature. Elaborate descriptions (verbal cascades, actually) of food, horticulture, architecture, scientific apparatus, dress and grooming, interior decor, etc., etc., carry the recreation of physical ambience almost to the point of absurdity, especially where tawdry or distasteful detail, i.e., decadence, is involved. His characters revel in cultures of decay, where dirt and grime peeps through the layers of makeup, thereby giving us a glimpse of the "reality" behind appearances, or, as he would later have said, the spiritual truth that exists nowhere else other than in its physical embodiment. And once that spiritual truth is discerned, thought Huysmans, surfeit, disgust and disillusionment are in store for us. He thus had none of Zola's idealism, and there are no upbeat representatives of a bright future, with the help of science or anything else, in his books. A realistic view of the decadence behind all of life can only bring us to a final pessimism.[49]

And thus it is that when Huysmans began to take an interest in religion, it was the aesthetically dark, chthonic, earthy side that fascinated him, and his novel *Là-bas* of 1891 enshrined that fixation. He then by degrees began a journey of conversion,

48. Bremond to Blondel, August 19, 1917 (BB, II, 325). Robert Baldick tells us that Léon Leclaire and his wife were longtime associates of Huysmans, and after he and they had spent time at Lourdes, they settled in Pau in 1904 (*Life of J.-K. Huysmans*, 460).

49. Thus it is that Huysmans could be fascinated with, and even duped by, the kind of religious excess represented by the controversial mystic, Cécile Bruyère, as discussed by Talar ("Les Trois Céciles," esp. 255–58, along with an earlier discussion of Bruyère in Talar, "The Modernist and the Mystic," esp. 86–100). Identifying the essence of mysticism with its bizarre, even pathological, manifestations, Huysmans never could have appreciated Fénelon in anything like the way that Bremond did. Where there is a zone of overlap, however, is in the fact that both Bremond and Huysmans would have considered Guyon the *true* mystic, with Fénelon only an abstract theorist on the subject.

captured in a series of novels that charted his progress. For Huysmans there was absolutely no interest in abstract or theoretical discourse of any kind; from beginning to end religion is tantamount to the "stuff" of religion—buildings, books, art representations of all kinds, liturgy and music and rituals, the clergy with their vestments and trappings, communal foundations and settings. Sights and smells and sounds *are* reality, but—and this is critical—it is a translucent reality, not the flattened and one-dimensional realism of Zola leading to positivism. And so the question here for Bremond was one of wondering: what is it about Huysmans's conversion, given his artistic sensibility, that might qualify it as "genuine"?

His first assessment of Huysmans was a 1903 review of *L'Oblat* just after it was published. Tracing the experience of a protagonist who is becoming a Benedictine oblate, Huysmans lavishly illustrated the emotionally and physically demanding nature of the process, constantly evoking the suggestive power of an artistically filled environment which is a "house of prayer." Symbols abound on every level. The idea is that ambience *elicits, shapes and formalizes* invisible dimensions, dimensions that are existent in no other way, and that have massive formative power for the individual experiencing them. One has no trouble here seeing a kind of Catholic romanticism—which includes, be it noted, a sense for dark depths as well as bright heights—that goes back to Chateaubriand, and that led Bremond to think that a new *Génie de christianisme* was in the making.

When he came to write his review of *L'Oblat*, Bremond highlighted an "allure" in Huysmans, "as original and savourous as the classics, our masters, have ever suspected." He was charmed by "the taste of holy things" in Huysmans, by his sense for "daily reality," so that sacred art operates "in the face of the comedy that plays out for our miserable humanity."[50] In one particular scene elaborated in piquant detail, where Huysmans described a woman visitor to the monastery, who arrives with an absurd equipage and in a flutter, yet having a holy and pure quality about her, Bremond saw the artist's gift for showing how transcendence peeps out, through the finely delicate use of irony, through the grit of a mundane, even comical, situation. Seemingly extraneous detail contributes in almost magical ways to the total texture of a scene.[51]

There is in Huysmans, Bremond thought, a "naive attachment to the usages of the past," that gives "some kind of archaic sweetness to a monk's obeisance," so that consecrated lives and art enter into an alliance, the result being that prayer and art have a symbiotic interaction.[52] Bremond does not use the word, but he is reacting to the Symbolism in Huysmans, that compositional technique by which the artist discovers/extracts from the physical object a "materialization of everything," where there is "an attempt to translate all human activity and the most spiritual, by more or less corresponding sensations." In the case of Huysmans the writer Bremond called this

---

50. *L'Oblat*, 329.
51. Ibid., 329–30.
52. Ibid., 335.

materialization "a literary system," in which the author is "pasteurizing our literary faculties of all their microbes of clichés that obsess us," so that materialization occurs precisely "by images of vulgarity and ugliness."[53]

The point of Bremond's review was that Huysmans is a genuinely Christian artist, who comes at ceremonies and symbols with a childlike wonder that has its own purity, so that his devotion is truly "savorous" (Bremond's favorite word for Huysmans), thus offering us a "real meal," not something tasteless and unappetizing. A bitter pessimism has become a magnificently lyrical "apotheosis of sadness."[54]

Art, then, is the key, but only because art and life are inseparable, as Bremond argued in his second essay on Huysmans, collected in the second of the *L'Inquiétude religieuse* volumes in 1909.[55] Imagination and devotion are inseparable, especially if "art" is understood to be that by which I express myself, that which I "construct" in order to communicate to myself and others what I am experiencing. One can even argue that "experience" itself is utterly inchoate, unfocused and deeply elusive, until it is given artistic expression. What Bremond came to see in Huysmans was the way in which immersion in the material fabric of the ecclesial milieu conveys the grace contained in the lives of the saints, especially when the magisterium of the community, the Tradition, has endorsed the elements of that fabric. But it is a *human, very human* fabric radiant with the light of eternity. When this evoking and shaping and forming works effectively, one sees the kind of art that Huysmans produced.

Furthermore, Huysmans's art reflected a profound continuity with its pre-conversion state, so that post-conversion grace captures nature for a new project, brings out its "vibrant original" character, said Bremond. Thus, Huysmans preserved after his conversion his "literary habits and artistic independence," so that "rough and refined all together, supple and brutal, naive and sophisticated, this willful pen that described formerly with cruelty the most miserable distresses, would express nonetheless . . . as much of good as of evil, the anguishes of repentance, the joys of grace rediscovered, the splendours of the liturgy, the nuances of the cloister, the tenderness of pious life, the ardors of the stigmatized, all the shades of Christian mysticism."[56]

There is more in this strongly aesthetic approach to religious experience than a mere aestheticism,[57] or fixation on trappings, although Bremond himself, as we shall see, will be later accused of that. Neither Huysmans nor Bremond was particularly focused on detail as a means to an end, that is, a perfectionism of some kind (the organizing of detail is the way to get it *right*); rather, detail for them is *revelatory*. And it is so in the way of exposing the real nature of a person or situation or tradition; thus,

---

53. Ibid., 336.

54. Ibid., 328.

55. First in *Le Correspondant* for June 10, 1907.

56. "Huysmans," 284.

57. The opinion of Blondel, see Blanchette, *Maurice Blondel*, 179. A good indication that Blondel had a bit of a "tin ear" for romanticism and art generally.

it has to be *telling* detail. The genius of Huysmans from which Bremond learned is the fact that what the details reveal may become clear only in some larger context, to which they may have an ironical or paradoxical, relation. The lives and works of saints, when they have human reality, are a stream of these details. And literary expression is the mode-of-choice (at least for writers) for capturing the way in which concrete detail, embedded in sometimes obscuring assemblages, functions.

In writing a "literary history of the religious sentiment," the literature that interested Bremond is that in which mystics chose to crystallize their experience through records filled with telling details. I think that Huysmans probably helped Bremond along in this respect, then functioned as a kind of unacknowledged guardian angel (so to speak). In any case, the example of Huysmans shows why he found so much of Port-Royal to be "devout charlatanism," that is, the substituting of logically worked out and obsessively maintained forms as the means of grace, or, differently stated, the substituting of rationalism for vital and concrete artistic expression.

One particular telling detail is in the fact that the actual Huysmans toward the end of his life found himself at Lourdes. He was a very sick man, in terminal pain and desperate, and it helped him to be in that throng of sad people, all eager for healing, and all believing. Even his final agonized illness was graphically concrete in an all-too-human reality that submerged him in the mass of humankind. He was not looking for magic, just the assurance of powerful symbols, so that he could, as we say, "own" the sacral potential of his suffering and go in peace. It was reported after he read Bremond's review of his 1903 novel that he was stunned and gratified to realize that this Jesuit reviewer truly understood his suffering, its nature and its sources.[58] There is at least the suggestion that he would have disliked Port-Royal and Jansenism as much as Bremond did, and for essentially the same reasons. The experience of God made him more humble, not less.[59]

But still, Bremond had Blondel to deal with. Much depended on the treatment of Nicole and Pascal, especially the latter.

---

58. Reported by Baldick, *Life of J.-K. Huysmans*, 437. "But perhaps the letter which pleased Huysmans most of all was one from the Jesuit critic Henri Bremond, who wrote to him, 'Do you know that your page on Christ's Betrothal to Suffering is of sovereign beauty?' Quoting this appreciation to Leclaire, Huysmans remarked, 'At last, someone who has understood!'" Bremond maintained regular contact with the Société de J.-K. Huysmans in Paris, and in 1927 contributed to an appreciation of Huysmans's work, "le Souvenir de J.-K. Huysmans," in which he praised Huysmans for his ability to produce "non-egoistical art" out of his suffering ("Autour de *L'Oblat*," 209).

59. Such, however, is the subtlety of spiritual temptations, as Bremond well understood, that "election to damnation" is still election, i.e., specialness, and thus, at least potentially, sectarian (as Bremond thought). Though Huysmans was "of" the crowd at Lourdes, he was still a bit "above" it, I think.

11

Port-Royal II
Pascal, Nicole and Anti-mysticism

IN HIS PREFACE FOR the second collection of the *L'Inquiétude religieuse* essays, in 1909, Bremond raised the question of genuineness in prayer. Who is it, especially in the midst of elaborate ceremonial, that really prays?[1] It was an evolved question, one that had emerged gradually out of prior questions, some of them stimulated by his studies in English religiosity. One of these involved conversion and discerning what it is that makes a conversion "real." In the preface to the first *L'Inquiétude* collection, in 1901, he wrote, "Nothing is more mysterious—few things are more riveting—than the inner history of a soul that is coming to, or returning to, religion. This soul commonly does not know the road it has followed and is mistaken, quite sincerely mistaken, when it tries to formulate for others the rational motivations that have determined the choice. . . . Insiders and outsiders, both are curious to know what these converts are thinking. Have they found complete peace, and have all of their disquietudes been calmed? Looking from a distance, have they believed that the Church that has attracted them is too perfect, too wonderful (*belle*), and does the austere joy of their sacrifices come to be mixed with the shadow of deception?"[2]

Usually the answers to such questions are a subtle mixture of "yes" and "no," depending on how one defines terms. Bremond, in his study of religious biography and autobiography, was keenly aware of the gap that exists between immediacy and its expression. The convert often cannot explain herself accurately and must use narrative and forms of expression that easily mislead, if the nature of religious testimony is not understood clearly. Stories of conversion, therefore, held special interest as a way of assessing the content of experience clothed in literary garb. Does the clothing reveal or hide? And *what* does it reveal or hide? What does the convert unwillingly,

---

1. "Avant-propos," ii.
2. "Avant-propos," vii.

accidentally, indirectly, show us about the nature and experience of conversion *in concreto*, so that we might assess its "reality"?[3]

It will be no surprise to discover that in Bremond's estimation a true conversion moves the soul in a theocentric direction, that is, away from a focus on self to a focus on God, eschewing the devices of anthropocentrism, such as a demand for pleasure in the experience, or a catering to a (sometimes unconscious) egotism as in scrupulosity. Genuine conversion encompasses "self-annihilation." And, as with the inner life of prayer, there may be a mixture of both theocentric and anthropocentric elements in uneasy combination, so that the task of the religious psychologist is to show the components in operation and to tease them apart.

There could be no better way, therefore, of examining the spirituality of Port-Royal than that of analyzing both the prayer and the conversion-experience of its most famous exponent, namely, Blaise Pascal, and then of analyzing the anti-mystical thinking of its most famous theoretician, namely, Pierre Nicole. Here is the conclusion in advance: we will discover in these two men, in different ways, a serious disjunction or split between their thinking, or verbal expression, and their praying. What they do when they pray, or when they allow us to catch glimpses of their devotional fervor, seems radically separate from what they say or think. They think Jansenism, but in the reality of their communion with the divine there is something different. Their textual expressions both reveal and hide something real, but flawed, in their conversions.

Let us see how Bremond came to his conclusions, what Blondel had to say in response, and what critics have been saying more recently. A great deal was at stake here for Bremond, in fact the integrity of his whole project in the *Histoire*.[4]

Pascal

Pascal, scientific and religious genius, is a veritable institution for French culture, sacred and secular. Born at Clermont-Ferrand in 1623, bereft of his mother early on, he was raised, along with an older sister, Gilberte, and a younger, Jacqueline, both of strong personality, by an indulgent and attentive magistrate father, Étienne. Eventually a tax-collector in Rouen, Étienne saw to it that Pascal received the best education and had every opportunity to excel. His consequent rise to success in cultured Parisian circles was meteoric, leading to wide recognition. He was a prodigy in mathematics

---

3. As in postmodern literary analysis, unconscious process may be revealed in the "ruptures" and "aporias" and "displacements" that occur in discourse. Such "signs" of repression are a reminder of Bremond's contention that language at the metaphorical-symbolic level may reveal much more unintentionally than does intentional, discursive exposition. I owe this insight to Eugene TeSelle, private conversation.

4. Therouin has suggested (rightly, I think) that in the "dialogue" with Sainte-Beuve that Bremond has fashioned in *Histoire*, IV, he has given us "a meditation and a source for the whole Bremondian enterprise. The *Histoire* could be defined globally as an anti-*Port-Royal*; the enterprise is like a contest with the *chef-d'oeuvre* of the nineteenth century" ("Deux visions," 63).

and physics, and, as often happens with prodigies, had a complex and troubled personality. Family relationships were emotionally intense and, especially in the case of Jacqueline, determinative of much in his life. She will accompany Pascal on his journey into the spirituality of Port-Royal, and Gilberte, married as Gilberte Périer, will become the chronicler of this journey.

With the success of Antoine Arnauld's *De la fréquente communion* (1643), and the death of Saint-Cyran that same year, Jansenist influence in the Rouen area had grown. In January 1646, a parish priest and disciple of Saint-Cyran, arranged for two Jansenist physicians to attend Étienne Pascal after an injury. These gentlemen exposed the family to the work of Jansen, Saint-Cyran and Arnauld, and it in this context that Pascal experienced his "first conversion" (as it is known) from a posture of nominal Catholicism to that of a strong dogmatic fervor.

Then, as his scientific work progressed, Pascal became increasingly committed to empirically based methodology grounded in rigorous techniques of observation, measurement and mathematical exposition. As a result, he became convinced both of what scientific reason can do, but equally, of what it cannot do. He came to see a chasm of some sort between the "mind" and the "heart" in human nature. At the same time, he was exposed (late 1647), with Jacqueline, to the preaching of Singlin at the Parisian house of Port-Royal, and was deeply moved. Jacqueline herself quickly decided to become a nun, but Pascal was ambivalent, and their father was opposed, thus initiating a family drama that ended only after the patriarch's death. By 1651, when Pascal was developing his famous theory of the void, Étienne had died, and Jacqueline finally entered the convent at Port-Royal. Somewhere in 1654, while pursuing work on probability theory, and amid intense interactions with libertine friends, on the one hand, and a deeply spiritual Jacqueline, on the other, Pascal experienced his "second conversion," the "night of fire," and went to live in Paris near Port-Royal.

He decided to help Port-Royal during the furor over the Five Propositions, and did so by defending their community against the Jesuits in the eighteen *Provinciales*.[5] In 1656 he got caught up in the incident of the Miracle of the Holy Thorn, in which a young Périer niece at Port-Royal claimed to have been cured of an organic disorder by a displayed relic. Strongly touched by the whole matter, Pascal planned an *apologie* for the Christian faith seemingly based on such "signs," and in 1657–58 he wrote most of the *Pensées* as a would-be preamble, it seems (this is much debated). For several years Pascal would bounce back and forth between his scientific work and controversies over his religious writings. Persecution mounted for Port-Royal, with intense debate over the signing of the Formulary of Alexander VI in 1661. Pascal was disappointed

---

5. This is the point at which many of Pascal's latter-day defenders argue that his loyalty to Jansenism was really adventitious, more a product of personal friendships, than of deeply held convictions. And there is the fact that Pascal never lived at Port-Royal, but was always just a lay visitor.

at the submission of Arnauld and Nicole, who utilized the "droit/fait" distinction to justify their decision to sign. He died in 1662.[6]

Knowledge of Pascal's work was immediate. The *Provinciales*, well familiar to a wide audience that enjoyed the controversy immensely, were rendered into English as early as 1657. The *Pensées*, pieced together by Pascal's first Jansenist editors, appeared in 1670, but have been supplemented and rearranged ceaselessly and controversially in many editions down to the present time. Voltaire, in his famous "Letter XXV" in the *Letters Concerning the English Nation*, wrote an "anti-Pascal," debating a host of Pascalian theses that he considered misanthropic, and thus marking debates about Pascal's true meaning. The age of the Enlightenment, the eighteenth century, saw him primarily in terms of the tension between reason and revelation, and thus tended to castigate him, as did Voltaire, for doubting the epistemological powers of disciplined human rationality.[7] The nineteenth century cast him as a romantic, rightly exalting the truth-claims of the "heart" over those of the "mind."[8] The moody, brooding quality of his cosmic awareness—where, for instance, in the classic example, his vision of Kant's "starry sky above" is not accompanied, as for Kant, by rational certainty and respectful awe, but instead by raw terror—has always had great appeal, with the result that his sensibility can be compared with the emotional tones of Goethe's *weltschmerz* or to Kierkegaard's existential sense of the spiritual opaqueness of life without faith.

Indeed, what Pascal really thought about the human condition, about the powers and limitations of scientific, instrumental, objective rationality, about the nature of God and of faith and of grace, about how to defend the truth of Christianity in terms of prophecy and miracles, about prayer and redemption, about the Jewish people and final divine judgment, are subjects for perpetual debate. A particular interest has been the effort to correlate his scientific interests and insights with his reflections on the terror-inducing vastness of the cosmos, i.e., his philosophy, with his vision of the utter and dreadful Holiness of God, i.e., his theology. How are mathematical and divine infinity alike and unlike, and how does one lead to the other? There are many directions in which one can go with Pascal. Both skeptics and believers find comfort in him; both Protestants and Catholics love him.

For Christian interpreters of Pascal, the issue of his Jansenism—the extent to which he really was a Jansenist, to what extent a faithful Catholic, and how to tease

---

6. I have been heavily reliant here, with modifications, on the excellent outline in Jean Mesnard, *Pascal*, 11–20.

7. Bremond noted in "Pascal, l'abbé de Villars" that Voltaire's kind of criticism of Pascal, namely, that his "wager" (it is better to bet on the reality of God, just in case Christian claims are true), was actually an act of despair in the face of the supposed helplessness of human reason in relation to God, emerged early. It quickly appeared after the first publication of the *Pensées* in the humorously written work of the abbé de Villars, cousin of Bernard Montfaucon.

8. For example, Sainte-Beuve, in one of his *Lundi* sketches, said of Pascal that the integrity of his suffering and moral struggle vanquished all of the eighteenth century. See Sainte-Beuve, *Portraits of the Seventeenth Century*, vol. 2, ch. 6, "Pascal."

these apart—has been endlessly fascinating. The church condemned him as a wrong-headed sectarian, but somehow the heart has always known better. The matter is complicated by the difficulties entailed in producing critical editions of his works. And this is where Bremond first began to engage the challenge of how best to assess Pascal spiritually.

His first essay on Pascal's conversion[9] started out as a long review of the recent scholarly edition of Pascal's collected work by Léon Brunschvicg, the multivolume biography of Pascal by Fortunat Strowski, and then, more saliently, E. Jovy's edition of a hitherto unknown diary by the parish priest, Beurrier, who ministered to Pascal at the time of his death.[10] He argued that the real issue in interpretation is that of producing a truly unified picture of Pascal (as with Newman) in which the seeming contraries could be resolved. There is Pascal the controversialist, but also the man of prayer; there is Pascal the Jansenist, but also the Catholic; there is Pascal the intellectual, and there is the mystic. How to integrate all of this? The clue is in the distance that Pascal moved from his first to his second conversion, and the relevant evidence is in the famous fragmentary texts of the *Mémorial*, describing the "night of fire" in his second conversion, and the *Mystère de Jésus*, an extended meditation on the truth of Jesus as transcending the corruptions of Church and society.

A central problem, Bremond suggested, is that interpreters have fallen into overstatement when they see Pascal's first conversion as an embracing, pure and simple, of Jansenist doctrine. There were, in fact, elements of deep devotion at work in this first conversion, averred Bremond, and it is also true that Pascal was left with a hunger that rigorist disciplinary demands could not satisfy. At the same time, it is quite clear that Pascal became disputatious, scholastic even, in his Jansenist way of arguing for Christian truth. He began to develop an actual metaphysic that would later undergird the *Pensées*. In other words, there were aspects of the "real," as Bremond understood it, in this first conversion, although the "notional" predominated, with the result that the heartfelt "movement of charity," while tasted with the help of Saint-Cyran's doctrine, had not yet fully materialized. His sister Jacqueline remonstrated with him about this, but to no effect. Backsliding and some skepticism followed.

Then in the *Mémorial*, with the "night of fire," in the second conversion, Pascal became a "child" of the kingdom, which is simply to say that Pascal began to "feel" God. It was not that Pascal had doubted, really, but rather it was a matter of the desolation that came from a yearning that seemed impossible to fulfill. What he wanted

---

9. "La conversion de Pascal."

10. In "Le sécret de Port-Royal," Bremond contended that in Beurrier's *Mémoires*, as printed by Jovy, we can definitely see that Pascal died as a good Catholic, not a sectarian and a heretic. In truth, the passages cited are a bit ambiguous, and pro-Jansenist interpreters have challenged Bremond's reading. Then in a follow-up review of further work by Jovy, "La pauvresse de Pascal," Bremond further polemicized against the purely Jansenist sources for Pascal's life, arguing that they obscured and omitted too much, and discussed the tradition that Pascal had made a good confession to a priest of Saint-Sulpice just before his death.

was to "possess" God, to love God alone. The first conversion generated desire for God, and the second the attainment of that state where the divine presence is felt to be working within. Both are necessary and indispensable. The philosophical proof of God is a start, and loving God is the theological finish. Bremond contended further that the dogma of the Incarnation filled the experience of the "night of fire," and that it is the "reason of the heart" that knows this dogma to be true. It was not that Pascal discarded dogma, it was that he finally got to what dogma is really all about. Thus— though Bremond did not yet use the phrase—Pascal became a "devout humanist" (even a bit of a "modernist") in the "night of fire"!

The implication of Bremond's formulation seemed to be that genuine conversion is the awakening and stimulation of an appetite, but without a factitious "satisfaction." Pascal's "night of fire" was thus his heartfelt recognition of the nature of the God he had encountered, but not understood, in the first conversion. The heart hungers, but it will prove to be the mode of hungering that is itself the satisfaction, given the infinity of God and, we will see, the demands of "pure love" in a relationship with God. The *Mystère de Jésus*, focused on the suffering Christ in Gethsemane, provided the confirmation.

Bremond concluded the 1909 essay with the thought that Pascal actually should be canonized, that he became a genuine saint, as we can clearly see in the devotion of the *Mystère*, but that his Jansenist starting point will always pull him down, like so many other compromised "demi-saints."

Then came Bremond's comprehensive assessment of Pascal in *Histoire*, IV, where he was broadly consistent with his earlier efforts: Pascal was both Jansenist and Catholic, as was Port-Royal itself, the Catholic dimension operating more at the level of prayer than of doctrine. And Pascal's prayer arose from his life, not from a formed and fixed system.[11] But Bremond nuanced the matter by suggesting that the contrast is not exclusively between prayer and doctrine in Pascal, but between Catholic and Jansenist elements found *both* in the one and the other.[12] Indeed, there are Jansenist elements in Pascal's prayer, as, for example, in the way he would note repeatedly, even as he prayed, that the very ability to pray is itself the "sign" of an efficacious grace, since the one who prays can do so only if God's electing grace is already operative—much in the way that the ability to fulfill the commandments is also a sign of efficacious grace. Non-elect sinners and skeptics will not even try, not even ask for grace, thought Pascal. Thus, even in the most intimate moments of prayer, Pascal is aware of, filled with assurance of, his special chosen status.

---

11. *Histoire*, IV, 321. In a striking phrase Bremond speaks of a "'watertight bulkhead' (*cloison étanche*) between speculation and life" in Pascal.

12. Ibid., 322n1. Here Bremond claimed to be correcting his earlier 1909 essay, where he felt that he had over-compartmentalized Pascal's Jansenist and Catholic aspects into prayer and doctrine exclusively—though, he averred demurely, he had been following the opinion of a well-known pro-Jansenist scholar!

Bremond believed that he saw real sweetness and joy in Pascal's "night of fire," but he also contended that these are characteristic of piety in both Catholic and Jansenist modes. In the Catholic kind of devotion the joy resides "in the simple hope of the Christian," which is the certainty of God's eternal love and charity, while in the Jansenist it is the aspect of inner assurance that comes more into play, that is, the sense that *I* have been chosen and that *my eternal salvation is certain*. One result is the perpetual seeking after affect as the definitive sign of election, i.e., a hankering after constant *re*-assurance as in an unhealthily dependent relationship. There is presupposed a seeming pessimism that arises when believers contemplate the follies of the reprobate, and then a boundless hope that comes when they turn the spotlight on themselves: God is terrible to *them*, but infinitely merciful to *us*. The wonderful words of Jesus, "let not your hearts be troubled," apply only to those for whom Christ has died, and in fact he has not died for all. Pascal said, "Although he has not died for all, he has died for me."[13]

Even the fear of God, thought Bremond in his interpretation of Pascal, insofar as the believer continues to experience it, is a sign of election and thus can itself produce a pious and joy-filled humility in the mode of a *lusus pedagogicus*,[14] that is, a game in which a good teacher (God) teaches us that, contrary to appearances, one thing exists only for the purpose of leading us to another thing. In this case, the disposition of fear leads to the inducing of another disposition: if I feel fear in relation to God, that helps me to realize how much in fact God loves me. Everything comes back to the essential ineluctable foundation: God has chosen me! It is as if fear itself operates as a teasing mask![15]

Thus it is that Bremond thought that he saw in Pascal alongside the passionate and lyrical and the, at times, deeply moving devotion, a corrosive element of the "for me" in everything, with reliance on the "signs" of salvation/election as the toxic catalyst. For Bremond, it is as if Pascal were constantly abandoning his own maxim, learned in his two conversions—that to seek God is in fact to have found God—in favor of the predestinarian doctrinal structure of Jansenist thought. In the dynamics of his spiritual journey an emphasis on "signs" enabled Pascal finally to hear, directly from God, that he, Blaise, was truly loved and could love in return. The assurance from

---

13. In a complex note Bremond discussed the question as to whether Pascal completely repudiated, or conditionally accepted, the "for all" in Christ's saving work. He took the view that Calvin had been "supralapsarian," i.e., double predestination had applied from all eternity and thus before the fall, whereas Jansen and Pascal were "infralapsarian," i.e., double predestination comes into play only after the fall on the basis of what God had foreseen from all eternity. Practically speaking, the result would be the same for the believer: inner assurance (ibid., 323n1).

14. Ibid., 335n3.

15. The reference here is to the passage in the *Mystère*, where Pascal has a dialogue with Jesus as follows. Jesus: "If you knew your sins, you would lose heart." Pascal: "In that case I shall lose heart, Lord, for I believe in their wickedness on the strength of your assurance." Jesus: "No, for I who tell you this can heal you, and the fact that I tell you is a sign that I want to heal you. As you expiate them you will come to know them, and you will be told: 'Behold thy sins are forgiven thee'" (*Pensées*, 315).

the Church that all are loved, there from the beginning, was not, it seems, enough, but he needed something akin to the Protestant emphasis on the "inward testimony of the Holy Spirit," in which "sensible devotion" brings "assurance."

In order to better grasp what happened to Pascal in the "night of fire," as well as to ward off numerous misunderstandings,[16] Bremond then offered a diptych, a parallel pairing of two kinds of conversion experience, one Protestant and one Catholic. Pascal's conversion, he suggested, lay in a midpoint between these two. In the first, that of the thirteenth-century mystic and Benedictine St. Gertrude of Hackeborn, there was a more or less standard Catholic pattern: an initial gentle and obliging sweetness (a "glimmer" rather than a "sign"), followed by dryness and moral struggle.[17] Pascal is different, since for him the time of dryness indicates the silent withdrawal of God, so that the fire, when it comes, is sudden and unexpected. For Gertrude the vision of God is quieter, being, as Bremond says, "only a lively realization of what she [already] believes," and it serves as the trigger for the process of "sanctification," with the implication that this ongoing sanctification is tantamount to salvation itself. For Pascal, by contrast, there is a kind of "Methodist" moment of the regenerative impact, filled with the all-sufficient content of salvation. Bremond saw here in Pascal a kind of "nervous exaltation," whereas, by contrast, Gertrude's visionary imagination, as it is formed by her conversion, is little more than "a picturesque transposition of an act of faith."[18]

The other comparison focuses on the experience of the Protestant evangelist, Henry Alline, whom William James had discussed in *The Varieties of Religious Experience*, and whose conversion James had likened to that of John Bunyan in *The Pilgrim's Progress*.[19] Bremond saw this type of conversion as typically American-Puritan, where the unregenerate sinner broods over, not just his sins (a Catholic would consider them quite venial) but his obdurate *sinfulness* and active resistance to grace. There is no more-or-less here, says Bremond, and what Alline yearns for is not sanctification, but for a sense of particular election, that is, for an experience in which God "speaks" to him, and certitude follows. The sudden blow from heaven will resolve all. The steady assurance that he now belongs to the elect is quite different, insisted Bremond, from the view that "for us Catholics hope must suffice." For Pascal the Jansenist there can be no hope prior to certitude, no hope without the "sign," no hope without the "for me."

---

16. Bremond gently took Barrès to task for a speculative understanding of what was revealed to Pascal on the "night of fire." Barrès had advanced the idea that what came to Pascal was a revelation of "the truth that disciplines the world of the soul," and a "rule of life" that science by itself cannot give us. Pascal already had all of that well before the "night of fire," thought Bremond (ibid., 355n1).

17. Ibid., 359–63.

18. Bremond indicated his disagreement with William James's characterization, in *The Varieties of Religious Experience*, of Gertrude's experience as a typical "crisis" moment leading to "mind-cure." His difficulty with James, he avowed, was that this psychologist lumped too many disparate experiences—Catholic, Puritan, mystical—together under a common heading, and he did so because he was unwilling to recognize that the social/ecclesial setting is essential to the shaping of experience (*Histoire*, IV, 363n1).

19. Ibid., 364–66.

Bremond insisted that Pascal's experience came *between* those of Gertrude and Alline, that there was, in truth, a deeply mystical, thus Catholic, dimension to the "night of fire," that transcended Jansenist implications, that can be seen in the kind of joy he experienced, but then quickly clouded with perverse doctrine.[20] His very use of the dictum, "you would not be searching for me if you had not already found me," marked a trajectory going back to St. Bernard and St. Augustine.[21] What is different for Pascal, Bremond thought, is the fact the joy thus generated is again a reminder of the indefectibility of the grace now given: all is assured! Perhaps, then, Bremond suggested, there is a better word for Pascal's joy than "joy," and he offered a survey of "Pascal's religion" in order to crystallize that word.

He concluded by describing what we would call Pascal's "belief system." Having no confidence in a "natural" or "rational" experience of God, Pascal is convinced that God can be known only in the encounter with Jesus Christ, where there is a simultaneous awareness of both our utter sinfulness and the gift of redemption. Since the knowledge of God and the knowledge of our sin are coefficients, religious duty is a matter of fear-driven obedience, not of loving adoration. Any vision of the goodness of God is so dependent on Christ that Pascal ends up with the kind of Christology that is an exaggerated christocentrism without the Creator. There is no real basis for an ongoing sanctification, only a kind of holding back of the tidal wave of sin, with ultimate escape for the elect. Misery will always be the human state. God can only be held in fearful reverence. By contrast, thought Bremond, in the correct understanding of redemption the whole cosmos is made worthy to sing the praises of God. Bremond does not end up offering a substitute for "joy," but his implication is of something closer to relief: as the ship sinks, I find myself in a lifeboat and am thankful.

Blondel's Critique

Blondel's reaction to this assessment of Pascal, when Bremond first sent it to him, was complex and needs to be set in context.

The mood during the early months of 1919 was grim. In late winter Bremond indicated to Blondel that, as far as he was concerned, things were going from bad to worse. We are passing through dolorous days, he wrote, in which it is clear that "our poor victory" is producing nothing but torment. Specifically, he was deeply distressed about the trial currently in process of the assassin of Jean Jaurès; he referred to the condemnation of the *Sillon* and the despair that had followed; and he expressed distress about a new series of books on "Catholic Moralists," that he thought rationalist and anti-mystical in spirit. He also shared with Blondel an animosity toward the work of Jacques Maritain, associated at this time with Action Française.[22] And on occasion

---

20. Ibid., 367.
21. Ibid., 377–78.
22. Bremond to Blondel, March 10, 1919 (BB, II, 373).

he and Blondel commiserated about the "American Wilson" and the machinations of the Versailles Treaty. Vengeful cynicism seemed to be in the air, with religious affiliation and its divisiveness feeding the mood. Perhaps some of the ferocity in his attitude toward Jansenism, and toward Pascal, arose from a degree of association in his mind between this legalistic, sectarian Catholicism and the right-wing religious-political alliance he saw emerging around him.

In a series of letters through the spring and summer he gave Blondel glimpses of the direction in which he was heading with Pascal, summarizing aspects of the coming presentation. Possibly as a softener, he claimed at one point to be "Blondelizing" Pascal by arguing against the simplistic thesis that Pascal was a Jansenist at the notional level and a Catholic at the real/prayer level, in favor, as described above, of the view that Pascal had a "double life" at both levels.[23]

After letting Bremond know that he was awaiting the treatment of Nicole "without flinching," and the treatment of Pascal "with trembling,"[24] Blondel girded up his loins and settled in with the text as soon as he received it. Upon finishing the "good pages" (Blondel's phrase) of Bremond's finished analysis, he prepared a long memo, referred to in the accompanying note as "dolorous remarks," and dispatched it to Bremond at the end of November.[25]

The spirit of Blondel's critique can be summed up in the words "you have subjected [Pascal] to a unilateral interpretation and a repugnant doctrine." But the actual elaboration of this critique was more nuanced, showing that there was substantive agreement on a deep level. In truth Blondel and Bremond shared a similar evaluation of Jansenism itself, but where they differed was in their assessment of the extent to which Pascal himself was infected with that spirituality. It became clear that Blondel fundamentally liked Pascal more, and thought him sounder in his theology, than Bremond ever did. It would always prove impossible for Bremond the (ex-)Jesuit to warm to Pascal.

Once he had finished scolding Bremond for "banal prejudices" and "historical inexactitude," Blondel launched into the substance of his critique, a substance which is best understood with some fleshing out from his definitive essay on the subject, written for a special issue of a leading philosophical journal at the time of the Pascal tricentennial in 1923.[26] Many of the basic ideas that are expanded in that essay are already present in the earlier memo, but we can use the essay in order to clarify Bondel's logic. As stated, he wanted to defend Pascal by distancing him from Jansenist theology, while making it clear that Jansenist theology itself was quite corrupt.

---

23. Bremond to Blondel, June 4, 1919 (BB, II, 383).
24. Blondel to Bremond, September 15, 1919 (BB, II, 392).
25. Blondel to Bremond, November 30, 1919 (BB, II, 396–98 for the letter, 398–408 for the memo).
26. "Le jansénisme et le anti-jansénisme de Pascal," discussed by Blanchette, *Maurice Blondel*, 302–5.

It was immediately clear in the memo that Blondel distrusted Bremond's theocentric/anthropocentric distinction, while preferring the more traditional natural/supernatural dichotomy. It is not hard to see why, when one considers that Blondel's whole approach to theology, beginning with *L'Action*, was *by way of* a philosophically constructed analysis of purposeful human striving. In *that sense*, starting "from below" in order to work through to the possibility of God, theology must be, in the usual signification of the word, "anthropocentric." For Blondel, theological statement goes astray when reflection on the divine-human interaction ends in some kind of confusion between the "order" of the supernatural and the "order" of the natural, when one encroaches on the other. The problem with the human ego, he contended, is not its "natural" self-assertion as such—as Bremond sometimes seemed to think—but in its *undue* assertion, i.e., its assumption of supernatural capacity.[27]

The Jansenist error, Blondel suggested, lies in a covert supernaturalizing of the natural, and naturalizing of the supernatural. God is humanized, and the human ego is divinized. The latter occurs when there is a demand for an inner assurance of election, for the confidence that one is saved, and that grace will never fail, these constituting the ego's presumptuous desire for a certainty that only God can possess. Thus Blondel agreed with Bremond that the ego *is* the problem, but in wanting a more precise, less misleading, formulation that allows for the human "precursors" of grace, Blondel was (as Blanchet has pointed out)[28] creating difficulties for the idea of a truly disinterested, utterly adoring prayer as central to mystical experience. Bremond, his spiritual radar attuned, sensed a threat to the whole French-School terminology of "self-annihilation" and a "pure love."

In the memo of November 1919, Blondel suggested that the joy felt by the Jansenist is not based "solely on the egotistical confidence of the individual who is conscious of his election," but arises earlier from "the logic of its [Jansenism's] initial and fundamental conception . . . which is a doctrine of goodness." The reference here was to what he would call in 1923 the "ideological geometry" or "the invisible armature" of Jansenist thinking manifested in the sect's peculiar "obstinacy" and "tenacity."[29] "Goodness" in this construal is applied specifically to God, who—contrary to the usual picture of the Jansenist God as "rigorous and sombre"—is seen as immensely liberal. Liberal because, having originally created Adam and Eve as creatures who "naturally" possessed "supernatural graces" (i.e., immortality, beatitude, etc.), he has then, following their fall and the resultant punishment *en bloc* to all of their descendants, had the "goodness" to rescue a band of the chosen Elect for salvation. In effect,

---

27. It should be noted, again, that here Blondel is responding not just to Bremond, but to the central charge brought by Vatican critics against Modernism, that it confuses the natural and the supernatural orders by reducing the latter to the former!

28. Introductory editorial note included with Blondel's memo in the letter to Bremond of November 30, 1919 (BB, II, 398).

29. Blondel, "La jansénisme," 132.

said Blondel, "nature" and "supernature" are indiscriminately mixed before the fall, and then human beings are "de-naturized" after the fall: in other words, human beings before the fall naturally possess a supernatural capacity, but after the fall that which was "natural" for them no longer accrues to them. God's magnificent goodness in Election after the fall then becomes a continuation of his magnificent goodness in Creation before the fall.

It is *this structure*, argued Blondel, that produces the Jansenist "monstrosity," with the sad result that the original incorporation of the divine destiny into human nature at the beginning leads to the present pathetic condition of humankind. One can see that all of the "hardnesses" of Jansenist thinking and practice thus make perfectly good sense. Humankind is totally spoiled, salvation must be entirely gratuitous from the outside, Election must operate by a "victorious delectation" which irresistibly overcomes the captive state of humankind. This is not about "egotism" and the psychological hankering after assurance, Blondel thought, but rather the product of an ideological mind-set, obsessed with a certain kind of predestinarian thinking, from beginning to end.[30]

Two particular consequences follow, thought Blondel. The first is that the Jansenists insisted on reading Augustine in a rigid and schematic way untrue to his thought. Augustine's writings became an arsenal of citations and authorities for the formulation of "propositions," all constructed in an either/or structure for disputation. "Mummified texts" and a petrified tradition are the result. Meanings are given propositional form in a way that destroys the "reality" of what Augustine intended to convey. What Blondel particularly objected to was the way in which "contrarieties" in Augustine's thought were then methodically ironed out in order to produce a system that excludes, we would say, paradox or dialectical tension.[31]

The other result, which in fact brought Blondel around to Bremond again, was that the Jansenists engaged in "a notional fashion of envisaging spiritual realities, a ratiocination of the facts of the soul or the givens of history, a ratiocination that takes itself for the meritorious reality of living, for the full reality of the tradition, at the very moment when it transposes in declarations, gestures, in ink, that which is of the order of actions, of direct experiences, of positive revelations." Bremond could hardly have asked for a stronger qualifying of the value of the notional in itself. With the Jansenists, Blondel thought, there has been a "functional alteration" of religious meaning, in which grace has become purely extrinsic and all true inwardness has been lost.[32]

30. Preceding paragraph based on "Jansénism," 132–36, but also Blondel's note on *Histoire*, IV, 386 (where Bremond asserts that the Jansenist God is "infinitely lovable"), in the 1919 memo (BB, II, 402).

31. "Jansénisne et anti-jansénisme," 136–38. See also Abercrombie, *Saint Augustine*, ch. 4, "Pascal and Saint Augustine," who exemplifies the more common view that Port-Royal "scholasticized" Augustine, thus distorting him. Blondel is more subtle: Port-Royal *badly* scholasticized Augustine.

32. Ibid., 138–40. When grace is thought of extrinsically, as an imposition from outside, the recipient becomes dependent on ecstatic experience of some kind as the sure sign that grace is operating, whereas when the work of grace is thought of intrinsically, then grace can work slowly and silently,

Pascal, Blondel contended, after an initial flirtation, worked himself free of all that bad thinking. Having dismissed Jansenism as "extrinsicism" (grace operating externally to created human nature) and a perversion generated by scholasticism in theology, Blondel had substituted his own theological *bête noire* for Bremond's "anthropocentrism." Now he was in position to take a direct shot at Bremond.

In the 1919 memo he slammed Bremond hard for exalting a "devout humanism" that leads to "a naturalism pure and simple" because it lacks a proper place for the indispensable mediatorial work of Jesus Christ.[33] The passage from nature to supernature requires, Blondel averred, a "dilatation infinitely onerous,"[34] and it is this that we see in Pascal. After accusing Bremond of a "phobia of Pascal," of being "struck with an anaesthesia from your extremist thesis" (about the source of Pascal's joy), and generally of "unilateralism," in 1919, in 1923 he laid out the case for Pascal as a progressive apologist, ahead of his time, for Christian faith. The core idea was that, unlike the Jansenists for whom an apologetics was inherently impossible in light of the chasm separating the saved from the damned, Pascal the philosopher, always respectful of concrete human reality and the structures of willing, knowing, and acting in human life, developed in the *Pensées* a powerful picture of how it is that human beings by nature seek God without knowing that they seek God. In fact, thought Blondel, Pascal repeatedly took an element of Jansenist thought and then turned it in a non-Jansenist direction in order to show that we can find God deep within by exploring truths that answer to the world as we know it, but that simultaneously point beyond the world as we know it. Thus it is that Blondel saw his project already in Pascal. Some of the pages in the 1923 essay must be among the strongest that Blondel ever wrote about another thinker.[35]

Bremond's initial response came out in a note to a sympathetic supporter, the abbé Monbrun: "Sir, I tremble. Yesterday's postal vehicle, running from Toulouse to Pau, must have been smashed to pieces by some infernal locomotive released by Saint-Cyran." He then briefly touched on a number of points, referring to Blondel's general antagonism to the "devout humanism" concept. Most saliently, and rightly (in my opinion), he contended in the face of Blondel's charge of a-christism that in fact it is a commonplace of mysticism that the high point of experience is that of God, and not the Christ. What he shunted aside, however—at least for the moment, since it will come up again in regard to "pure poetry"—was the idea that the attainment of the vision of God may require a *donum superadditum*, given the chasm between nature

---

more ambiguously (?), deep within.

33. BB, II, 404. Blondel was aiming at Bremond's contention that in French School spirituality adoration is directed solely toward God without concern for human benefit. Blondel wanted to argue that Pascal saw rightly that such adoration is impossible unless one has received a prior salvific assist.

34. Ibid., 404, 406.

35. Blondel, "Jansénisme," 160: "His [Pascal's] Jansenism is superficial, borrowed, occasional, equivocal . . . His anti-Jansenism, unconscious at first and for a long time, is deep, personal. . . . [His] sense of concrete and psychological realities, not the genius of abstraction and the superstition of ideology" would win out.

and supernature. The problem was to convince Blondel that devout humanism is not just humanism pure and simple, and he had not succeeded in doing that. In a reply, Monbrun advised him to stick to his guns.[36]

Blondel, however, now moving into the *panchristic* phase of his thought, kept up more gently on the a-christic issue.[37] Debate centered around John of the Cross and whether this sixteenth-century Spanish Carmelite mystic did, or did not, teach that explicit christology played a part in the higher reaches of mystical ascent. Blondel clearly took the affirmative side.[38] But in one of his most self-confident rebuttals ever to Blondel, Bremond expressed himself with unusual care, contending that he agreed with the general view that "the Christ is constitutive of every creature and of all beatitude . . . but that the mystical experience in itself (which is not a revelation) arrives at that point *formally*, they [approved mystical writers] all deny with one voice, St. John of the Cross leading the pack. . . . Doubtless, when that experience (so rich when one compares it with rational comprehension; so poor in itself) changes into the beatific vision, we will then see that the God attained by the aforesaid experience is the trinitarian God, and that it was Christ himself who produced this attainment." "How is that explanation?" asked Bremond, a defiant tone in his voice.[39] Blondel, seemingly satisfied for the moment, left him alone after that, and their conversation moved on again to the subject of mysticism.[40]

Moreover, it was in that same letter in late winter of 1920 that Bremond indicated that the Nicole chapters would soon be on their way for review. While their differences over Pascal would never be resolved, Bremond would inch closer to increasingly

---

36. Bremond to Monbrun, December 3, 1919 (BB, II, 410–11). Blanchet reproduces excerpts from an ensuing back-and-forth correspondence with Monbrun and Cavallera. In a letter of January 6, 1920, Bremond indicated to Monbrun that he had been afraid of causing Blondel distress in the treatment of Pascal, because he thought that Blondel might see there "the death of his own philosophy." In a November 1920 note to Loisy he opined that he probably ought to back off some, given Pascal's status as a Father of the Church, since he wanted to remain somewhat in the good graces of his friends of the "Blondel group" (BB, II, 412–13).

37. Bremond did a song-and-dance with Blondel, insisting that he would make substantive changes to the Pascal material, when, in fact, he did not (Bremond to Blondel, January 12, 1920 [BB, II, 426]).

38. Blondel to Bremond, January 31, 1920, where Blondel supplied a detailed commentary on John of the Cross, *Cantique spirituel*, str. XXXVII. Blondel was convinced that the christological element in John's mystical theology was the safeguard against demonic illusions in the mystical ascent. Blondel was also reading a draft of Bremond's upcoming treatment in *Historie*, V, of Jean-Joseph Surin and the devils of Loudon (BB, II, 432–33).

39. Bremond to Blondel, February 21, 1920 (BB, II, 436–37). The sheer force of the statement should confirm the view that in the end Bremond could not, and would not, follow Loisy into a new Comteanism.

40. It is clear also from Bremond's letters to Loisy from 1919–1921 that his interpretive lens in the *Histoire* was slowly moving away from "devout humanism" as such to "mysticism" in particular—and thus to a dimension in religious experience not unique to Christianity. See Bremond to Loisy, November 28, 1919 (Bernard-Maître, "Lettres," 277). This development moved in lock-step with Loisy's own progression.

nuanced views of Pascal.[41] But Blondel was eminently pleased with what Bremond had written about Nicole.[42] They were much more in harmony with one another about the thinker and writer whom they saw as the embodiment of some of the worst rationalist and anti-mystical aspects of Jansenism.

Nicole

Pierre Nicole (1625–1695) is most remembered as a scintillating essayist on moral topics (*Essais de morale*, 1671–1678), a kind of overtly Christian La Rochefoucauld. Bremond, it will be remembered, had some years earlier written the introduction to a short collection of excerpts from Nicole's work, extolling his keen insights. Nicole displays a rare gift in his anatomy of human behavior for smoking out the subterfuges of self-love, and thus showing us that we are not virtuous precisely when we are most inclined to think that we *are* virtuous. He calls us to a high ethical standard and will not settle for moral mediocrity or subterfuges. The revelation that we are sinners through and through can then lead to genuine humility and a new foundation for the true pursuit of virtue rather than the specious efforts that usually suffice. Nicole does all of this in the best traditions of essayistic moral exhortation from classical times through Montaigne and down to the present. Reflected as well, of course, is the Jansenist perception of the original sin-based wretchedness of the human situation and the bondage of the will.

But Nicole was also a confrère-student-mentor with Pascal (the dynamics of the relationship are debated) and a follower of Antoine Arnauld at Port-Royal. The result of their collaboration was a series of works polemically directed against Calvinism, defensive of Port-Royal, illustrative of the principles of formal logic, hostile toward quietism (specifically Molinos and Madame Guyon), and finally dogmatically constructive (as in his final Thomist volumes on the theology of grace). What most interested Bremond was Nicole's *Traité de l'oraison* of 1679, and then the *Réfutation des principes erreurs des quiétistes* of 1695. The posthumous volumes, *Traité de la grace générale*, 1715, would serve as the prime example of how Nicole gave a kind of Thomist legitimacy to Jansenist spirituality, thus perpetuating its influence long into the future after *Unigenitus*.

In the first of his two chapters, "Pierre Nicole, or the Jansenist in Spite of Himself," Bremond offered the thesis that it was Nicole who had originally advanced the idea that Jansenist teaching is a logical system that had never actually been condemned

---

41. Bremond's last substantive piece on Pascal, "En prière avec Pascal," was first delivered as a sermon-lecture at Mass in Clermont Cathedral, July 8, 1923, then partially printed in the special collection on Pascal in *La Revue Hebdomadaire* 28 (July 14, 1923). Bremond slowly warmed to the devout side of Pascal.

42. Blondel to Bremond, February 28, 1920 (BB, II, 438). Blondel described the Nicole material as "vraiment de *bonnes* feuilles"!

by Rome. Using the "right" vs. "fact" distinction, he argued that Rome had exercised its proper authority in condemning the Five Propositions, but had mistakenly construed the content of what it claimed to be condemning, i.e., failed to understand Jansenism accurately. Nicole then advanced his own understanding, with the help of Thomist ideas, of the Jansenist stance on fallen human nature, human free will and the working of God's grace in salvation. The effect, thought Bremond, was that Nicole preserved the Jansenist moral ethos, the rigorism, while shedding the Augustinian dogmatic infrastructure. The end result was a confirmation of Blondel's ideological vision of Jansenism, with Nicole's view that salvation is more a matter of the head than the heart: one must believe rightly, and Christian living must be examined conscientiously at every moment, because it is by believing rightly, *then* practicing rightly, that we are saved. The floodgates are opened to doctrinal hyper-intensity and scrupulosity. Bremond called this end-product the "spirit of Jansenism," rather than the actual doctrine,[43] and it is this spirit, essentially a moralism decked out with Thomist trappings, that will inform the future, thanks to the elegant literary expression of Nicole, the "Jansenist in spite of himself."

After some particularly dense exposition of Nicole's thought, in which he attempted to show that this "obsessive" (Bremond's word repeatedly) moralist was not entirely obtuse to the virtues of mystical prayer,[44] Bremond came to his point.[45] Nicole's assault on mysticism was premised on the view that mystical experience, except for a very few, is "visionary," i.e., is an idiosyncratic and prideful "illuminism," grounded in the mystic's desire for the "extraordinary" and for "novelty." He advocated the view that all true prayer begins with a "holy desire," but a desire limited to the form of articulated petition.[46] Moments of this holy desire are the product of direct supernatural infusion like a jolt of electricity from above, but these moments are not "mystical," since that term is reserved for counterfeit experiences in which the jolts reflect contamination by worldly desires, which must be carefully distinguished. At this point, thought Bremond, rationalizing scrupulosity got in Nicole's way, since he was avoiding a more sensible view, namely, that in an "inner quiet" mystical contemplation enables the formation of "conscience," which is the ineffable action of the supernatural in the natural and by means of the natural. Indeed, mystics claim to be "invaded" by an impulse, but the result is a trusting inner stillness, not an agitated puzzling and second-guessing of

---

43. *Histoire*, IV, 467: "In his discrete and judicious way, he transposes the Jansenist spirit, more common at that time, than Jansenism itself; he mounts from the heart to the head, and by doing so he moves all of the venom upward."

44. Ibid., 499: "à la longue, une sorte of exaspération chez ceux qui le lisent," says Bremond, of those who try to read Nicole.

45. Ibid., 501–42, is the critical section. In the portion, 525–42, where Nicole emphasized the importance of human effort, assisted by "natural" grace, in prayer, his Thomism comes to the surface.

46. Bremond contended that Augustine himself saw desire in much broader terms. Surely Bremond was right. See Eugene TeSelle, "Augustine," esp. 28–30. Augustine's mysticism is an affective yearning for the ultimate capacity to enjoy God in the final state of Rest.

the Holy Spirit. This is the place where pure love will, indeed, separate the true from the false in all of our desiring.

Thus, Nicole was quite right to emphasize grace as the basis of prayer, but his anxious tendency to endless reexamination results in the sense that all prayer may be a form of self-delusion. His intention is praiseworthy: he wants to instill fear, but not desperation, in those who pray, for, after all, this is the Holy God to whom you pray. At the practical level, however, this intention becomes a counter-productive sophism, in which a form of self-doubt ends up as doubting God. For most people such compulsive self-scrutiny is a disaster that leads to total darkness and self-obsession. The "courageous optimism" of the French School is much to be preferred, where human peace operates confidently within the larger field of divine peace and the two are not mutually exclusive.

The problem for Nicole is that method is preferred to illumination, and thus he was attracted to a certain use of Ignatian meditation, where the mind is structurally positioned for the reception of grace by means of "good thoughts" and "right teaching." What happens, however, in Bremond's view is that the human who prays is the object of attention rather than God. But Nicole ran into a contradiction here: if human efforts are contaminated by sin, so that all we can do is to "rest" in God, as the quietists claim, what can we do? Nicole answered by arguing that efforts at moral purity do in fact "facilitate" the approach to God. Bremond countered with the view that human efforts should be seen as "inferior" to grace, so that we see ourselves not as "sin," but as "nothing," that is, as always vulnerable to sin because of our metaphysical nature. It is not activity as such that is bad, but its constant tendency to get waylaid by self-love. Take efforts seriously, but not *too seriously*, we might say, and laugh a lot. Impossible for Nicole.

Mystical writers, said Bremond, do allow for methods of meditation, if people find them helpful, while insisting that "methods" can be our own worst enemy. The latter leads to four traps. First, we see ourselves as needing to be repaired—this is Nicole's fixation on original sin, a fixation that backfires by producing anxious scrupulosity, when, by contrast, the "internal abasement," i.e., a posture of self-forgetfulness, makes more sense. Second is the moral preoccupation with diligence in our duties (am I doing the correct things correctly?), thus destroying the spirit of beauty and joyful adoration in religion. Third is the rationalist obsession with clear ideas as the gateway to God, whereas the mystics know that wordless silence is better. Fourth is "victorious delectation," in which the Jansenists have the view that grace operates only by co-opting the human insistence, given the deep corruption of sin, on good feelings as indispensable reinforcement for correct desires. The problem, then, is that a positive attraction or good feeling becomes a "gusher of emotion" as the sign of operant grace while dryness is the sign of its absence. Rationalism gives way to emotionalism. The mystics insist that maturity in prayer will lead beyond such dependencies.

The ultimate sin of the mystics, Nicole thought, is their quietist inclination to passivity and inertia, in which contemplative prayer is simply a silent waiting for God. Mystics are lazy and act as if prayer were a form of falling asleep, and their glimmerings of moral truth remain fragmented and inchoate. All is confused and muddy with the them. But God is not known in confusion, said Nicole

Assessment

Bremond's "The School of Port-Royal" appeared in mid-1920 to a flurry of critical interest, part of which was a veritable hornet's nest.

First of all, there was the issue of historical accuracy in the expanding availability of sources, the critical assessment of those sources, and then soundness in the exercise of judgment in relating sources to one another and to the larger context. Bremond's predominantly literary methods have always been vulnerable to critique, especially in regard to Port-Royal, and he has absorbed some solid blows. The large work of Augustin Gazier, renowned expert on Jansenism, would appear in 1922, the fruit of his privileged access to valuable sources, and Gazier was highly critical for years of Bremond's opinions concerning Pascal and Nicole. Louis Cognet picked up and affirmed this critique in his acidulous 1966 assessment,[47] where, he made the claim that, despite his obvious efforts to differentiate among the Port-Royal characters and to evaluate them separately, Bremond created an artificial and over-generalized construct in the whole notion of a "school of Port-Royal."[48] Other authorities have complained that Bremond over-simplified and caricatured at times.[49] And there was, of course, the larger issue of a "literary history" as a methodology in the first place, and whether such an approach is really "historical." All of these issues swarmed, and continue to do so. Scholarship on Port-Royal, its people and doctrine, and its aftermath, is a perennial project.

Alain Cantillon, in the most recent treatment of Bremond and Port-Royal,[50] has examined the range of ways in which French historians have viewed Pascal, and by extension Port-Royal and Jansenism. By the beginning of the twentieth century, with improved access to sources and less partisan reconstruction, totalized views were

---

47. Louis Cognet, "Bremond et Port-Royal."

48. An expert on seventeenth-century French spirituality, Cognet was strongly disapproving of Bremond's view that the religious milieu at the beginning of that century was not as decadent as often thought. He opened his *Les origines de la spiritualité française au XVIIe siècle*, ch. 1: "The Milieu of the Spirituals" with a criticism of Bremond, followed by a highly sympathetic sketch of Saint-Cyran as a reformer and a ringing endorsement of Jean Orcibal's more recent scholarship on Port-Royal. One gets the sense that in the post-WWII environment Cognet, Thomist and opposed to the Salesian voluntarism on which Bremond rested, was clearly on the side of a more militant, triumphant Catholic trend, and that Bremond looked weak.

49. Most of the standard criticisms were summarized in Jean Mesnard, "Bremond and Port-Royal." Mesnard was a Pascal specialist, with a number of books and critical editions of Pascal to his credit. He felt that Bremond never truly grasped the nature of Pascal's "conversion of the heart."

50. "Détruire et sauver Port-Royal."

passing out of fashion. One did not have to be completely pro or con. Thus, we see Bremond trying to develop portraits of the principals that are nuanced and more delicately faceted, or Blondel trying to rescue Pascal, though Jansenizing, from Jansenism as such. "Port-Royal" itself was coming to be seen as less of a unitary phenomenon.

Cantillon has also pointed to the fact that Pascal in particular was a crux-point in church-state debates by the beginning of the twentieth century. Clearly Pascal can be taught from a secular, scientific, philosophical perspective or from a theological and ecclesiastical one. University-based critical editions of Pascal, quite secular in tone, were being produced from 1900 to 1914, precisely while church and state were being legally separated, and in the midst of great controversy, and precisely while the Modernist crisis was at its peak. Who shall own Pascal? In 1923, during the tricentennial, a great mass of interpretation was generated, including the impressive collections in which essays by Bremond and Blondel appear, and that I have cited. It is quite clear that Pascal could be presented as refreshingly modern and free-spirited and humanistic, or darkly sectarian, or faithfully Catholic, or as a loyal Frenchman with all of the native characteristics of blood and soil! In his two last, short pieces on Pascal, Bremond mellowed, made him out actually to be a bit of a mystic, one who knew that conversion begins with the heart, the process in which the center of our souls is drawn to what is lovable, after which there is an entraining of the mind in the form of an explanatory logic.[51]

In the final analysis for Bremond, argued Cantillon in closing, the object in evaluating Port-Royal and the Port-Royalists, was not to "rehabilitate," but to "re-appropriate." Granted that he had a sustained sparring-match going with Sainte-Beuve, and wanted to one-up him in a kind of "free variation," his goal was entirely different. He wanted to use Port-Royal and Jansenism as gateways into the deeper life of mystical prayer, but to do so in such a way as to open the gates to all and sundry, to argue that such prayer is an accessible and desirable reality for everyone, but only if it is rightly understood as what it actually is: learning to sit quietly, listening, in the presence of the living God, knowing that Love will define a direction and provide the means, so long as the devious human heart continues to trust and does not lose itself in the search for pleasures conscious and unconscious. In the quest for such prayer, even colossal failures are profoundly instructive, and there are always bright lights even in the darkness of failure.

The question also arose of whether in his critical stance toward Port-Royal and the Jansenists Bremond was simply pro-Jesuit. Alfred Loisy, in his 1936 defense of Tyrrell and Bremond, pointed to Henry Bordeaux's response to Bremond's "Discours à l'Académie," where there is the suggestion that Bremond's advocacy of Fénelon over

---

51. "Pascal et les mystiques." Bremond had another word on Pascal in 1928, "Pascal et Valéry," when he responded critically to an evaluation of Pascal by Valéry in the special 1923 *Revue Hebdomadaire* collection. He argued that Valéry overplayed a basic irrationalism in Pascal, derived from his fear of the vastness of the universe. Bremond was more inclined to attribute Pascal's fears to nervous disorder, as testimony from Pascal's doctors seemed to suggest.

Bossuet was a replay of the Jesuit-Jansenist debate. The Jesuits were defending a view of Christ as tender, inviting, pardoning, loving infinitely with open arms, over against a Christ who invites and pardons and loves only some persons, and who refuses to soften. But, averred Loisy rightly, Bordeaux was scraping up the old anti-Modernist charge that "pure love" is morally lax and flabby, a kind of "Catholicism lite" (we might say). André Bellesort, the successor to Bremond's seat in the Académie, would later twit Bremond in similar fashion on the same issue. It was the Action Française mentality again, since it was clear that Bremond had no intention of endorsing the standard Jesuit methods of drilling a priestly army.[52]

And so another case in point would be that of the seventeenth-century Jesuits and their "asceticism." True mystics arose there as well, Bremond would argue, and in their light we might better understand what Ignatius intended, although his followers (most of them) deviated. We can also take a closer look at the difficult fracture line between mysticism and the demonic (Jean-Joseph Surin), where emotional break-down may be a break-through as well. Nature and supernature can work simultaneously in some very strange ways!

---

52. Alfred Loisy, GT, 89–92.

12

Ignatian Mysticism

BREMOND WAS SLOW, DESPITE his frustrating experience, to launch any kind of sustained critique of the Ignatian tradition. There had been an early opening in such a direction in the conversations with Tyrrell as the two of them began to rethink the content of the *Spiritual Exercises*, wondering if their Jesuit teachers had misled them as to the real nature of Ignatian principles. Tyrrell had intimated that Ignatius may have been more of a mystic than was usually assumed in standard, perhaps overly regimented or mechanical, presentations. But then the matter was dropped, until, in Goichot's happy phrase, there is a "return of the repressed" for Bremond in the immediate post-war years, and it takes the form of an obsession with Ignatianism.[1]

It is helpful to recall that Bremond worked on *Histoire*, III, IV, V, concurrently, the latter two volumes being published in 1920, and the first in 1921 after the delay over the Olier dustup. This meant that he was exploring Bérullism and the French School, Port-Royal, and "The School of Père Lallemant and the Mystical Tradition in the Society of Jesus" (the subject of vol. V) all at the same time, and thus there is a kind of interflow among the treatments. Connections between III and V are especially important here, because it soon became clear to Bremond, as he explored the seventeenth century more deeply, that he wanted, on the one hand, to critique the Ignatian tradition as he knew it from his own experience, while, on the other hand, he wanted to hold up for approval a genuinely mystical, but sidelined, stream within that heritage.

Jesuit tradition had historically been resistant to an emphasis on mysticism or contemplation in spiritual formation, precisely because Ignatius, fond of the regimented rigor of military training, had wanted to make his new Order and discipline an apostolate for practical ministry in society, not an enclosed community of prayer

---

1. EG, 186. Goichot's analysis (ibid., 183–208) of Bremond's treatment of Ignatianism, and that of Goujon and Salin, "Henri Bremond et la spiritualité ignatienne," as well as Trémolières, "The Witness to These Witnesses," and De Pril, "La théologie catholique," are of prime importance here. The older discussion is Bernard-Maître, "Les exercices spirituels."

and mortification. The problem with "mystical experience" from Ignatius's perspective, aside from its elitist implications, was that it opened the door to "illuminism," where individuals would claim "private revelations" from God or extraordinary privileges or status, or an excuse for moral laxity. There was also the danger, as well, of psychopathology or mental aberration in unbalanced individuals. The core issue, in other words, was that mystical experience was equated with an uncontrolled, indeed uncontrollable, subjectivism easily leading to pure fantasy on the part of the individual.[2]

But it is also the case that the use of the *Exercises*, Ignatius's prime training manual, was aimed at helping the individual Jesuit discover and affirm his unique vocation for service, and thus allowance is made for the nuances of private religious experience as well as the differing capacities of differing persons. And this fact began by Bremond's time to open the doors a bit for a more customized approach. Nonetheless, a hard division between the normally expected ascetical approach to spiritual growth, sometimes understood under the rubric of "acquired grace," and a more mystical approach, where an individualized "infused grace" is the norm for highly exceptional individuals, remained in place. The former is marked by aggressive and required disciplines of self-denial and sensual restraint for everyone, while for the latter (a smaller group) there is the state of passivity where the knowledge of God is intuitive and given, where adepts (very few) would come to know a true loss of self in the infinity of God (mystical union, mystical "night," mystical presence, etc.). It is this traditional three-stage structure that Tyrrell and Bremond wanted to challenge with the idea that aspects of the second and third stages belong to the fullness of the interior life *from the very beginning for all persons, and that it is critical not to over-play the ascetical aspect.* As he studied Ignatian tradition, Bremond started to see warrant for his desired point of view, but it would be an uphill struggle.[3]

Much like Letourneau at Saint-Sulpice, Jesuit reviewers had given robust praise to *Histoire*, I and II, and they very much appreciated Bremond's stance in volume IV on Port-Royal, but then they started to have reservations when they saw the treatment of Ignatius and the Jesuit tradition in drafts of III and V. The principal interlocutor here was a Jesuit scholar at Toulouse, Ferdinand Cavallera (a specialist on Jerome).[4] Enthusiastic at first about Bremond's attempt to stimulate interest in prayer and inner life, Cavallera became increasingly hostile as he saw that Bremond wanted to create

---

2. I am dependent on the psychoanalytically oriented treatment of the subject by Meissner, *Ignatius of Loyola*, esp. ch. 5: "Mysticism and Spiritual Life." The new and comprehensive collection, *A Companion to Jesuit Mysticism*, with the essay by Donahue, "The Mysticism of Saint Ignatius of Loyola," is now a complete update.

3. De Pril, in the latest treatment of the subject, makes it clear from a look at Joseph de Guibert, SJ's, 1930 work, *Études de théologie mystique*, that the Ignatian suspicion of mystical experience was still alive and well at the end of Bremond's lifetime ("La théologie catholique de la mystique," 99–101).

4. Described as a "moderate progressivist" in the Modernist struggles by Goichot (EG, 189n20). The official reviewer for the *nihil obstat* of *Histoire*, IV, he had praised Bremond for his treatment of Pascal.

a clear separation between Ignatianism and his beloved French School. He and Bremond entered into a debate that became voluminous and increasingly acrimonious, extending through most of the 1920s in rival periodicals, about the true nature of the *Spiritual Exercises*, about Ignatius's original intentions, and about the place of mysticism in the development of the Jesuit Order. As we shall see in this and later chapters, some of the debate had a very "in-house" squabbling character about it, but there were truly substantive issues at stake.

Goichot has suggested[5] that the driver, the thing that really kicked up the dust for Bremond and his critics, was that by volume III he had established himself with a reading public, he was becoming bolder in statement, and he was increasingly clear about his central trajectory: the French School and its devout-humanist/mystical/theocentric piety as the mainstream, with everything else as subsidiary or antithetical. In this construction, the stream rises during the seventeenth century, goes subterranean with Fénelon at the end of the century, reemerges with de Caussade briefly in the eighteenth century, has a vibrant resurgence for a short time with Lamennais and Gerbet in the nineteenth until suppressed at Vatican I, finally surfaces again with Modernist thinking in the twentieth! Everything good seemed to move like a train in the direction of Loisy, but with Blondel waving the necessary warning flags and cautions everywhere. As this big picture started to come into view, critics like Cavallera, now alarmed, began to nip relentlessly at Bremond's flanks. But they should have seen it coming sooner.

From the beginning of the *Histoire*, the notion of "devout humanism" had been formulated by Bremond as the Renaissance-derived antithesis to medieval scholastic theology. In his formulation, Trent and the Counter-Reformation carried this humanist model forward as the Catholic Church's response to the spiritual vacuum that had given rise to the Protestant Reformation. Catholic renewal thus had at its core an upsurge of that devout humanism and tendency toward mysticism synthesized by Francis de Sales, by Ignatius and, most of all, by Bérulle's French School. The substantive question that arose was, then, that of defining what it is about devout humanism that makes it right or truly fruitful, while its scholastic antithesis—as well as derivatives of scholasticism—are wrong and ultimately sterile.[6] Bremond's first formulation, as we have seen, was the contrast of "theocentrism" and "anthropocentrism," the former being an exclusive focus on the glory and goodness of God as the purpose of religion,

---

5. EG, 183–85. He notes also that by the time Bremond came to the "French School," he was already clear that he wanted to evolve a "philosophy of prayer" for our own time, anticipating *Histoire*, VII and VIII, and "the Metaphysic of the Saints." Goichot is also clear that increasingly, with the publication of *Histoire* III and V, Bremond was tracking not only a "natural process of maturation" in ideas, not just an "evolution," but "a development in Newman's sense of the term, a progressive making explicit of the implicit, more perfect to the extent that it grips the conscience more clearly and in a more assured way" (EG, 184). The *content* of this philosophy of prayer is then the issue.

6. Houdard's masterful overview and integration, "Humanisme dévot," highlights the "hybrid zone" that Bremond created, a "zone of ambiguity," an "undecided zone," in which literature (thus poetry), freed of authorities and "opening out" to transcendence, would become the preferred place for speaking about religious experience.

the latter a concern with human benefits and the service of the human ego as that purpose, with the paradox that the former is more "humanistic."

In order to make his case convincing, Bremond resorted to the use of foils. We recall that he had described the admirable nature of John Henry Newman by comparing him with other Anglicans. Likewise, he could better define what devout humanism and mysticism are by describing what they are not. His historical judgment was that the spirituality of Port-Royal, and then of the Jesuit Ignatian practice as he had experienced it, are descendants of scholasticism, each in its own way opposed to the French School. The irony is that when he described the spirituality of Port-Royal as overly logical, overly rational, overly mechanical and exterior in its understanding of grace, cold and methodical in application, his Jesuit readers should have taken sharp notice. Applauding Bremond's castigation of Port-Royal, primarily in the persons of Arnauld and Nicole, as a perversion of the role of human understanding, or *ratiocination*, in salvation, they were then astounded when he argued that Ignatianism in its dominant self-understanding involves a perversion of the *will* in salvation, a distortion that he terms "asceticism" or "ascetism." He meant here a rule-bound, methodically instilled approach to prayer, but also a view of the purpose of prayer, not as silent adoration, but as a reinforcement of the human will for action. False views of the role of intellect and will, the mind and the heart, cognition and affectivity (in contemporary formulation), covers the waterfront, so to speak, in any analysis of human functioning, and Bremond now had his two foils to the French School.

Bremond seems here to have intentionally avoided the traditional Augustinian language of Pelagianism, or the Pauline language of works righteousness, though in essence, of course, he was accusing Port-Royal and Ignatianism of just those things. By using, instead, his neologisms of "theocentric," "anthropocentric," "ascetist," he could operate in a more psychological rather than doctrinal dimension, labeling tendencies, or emphases, rather than consciously thought-out or hard-and-fast positions, thereby acknowledging how elements mixed at the "real," rather than "notional," levels. With Port-Royal it was their life of prayer as opposed to their pronouncements, but for Ignatius it will be something larger, a fully developed, but as yet unacknowledged, current of mystical interpretation of the *Exercises*, alive and well alongside the dominant "ascetic" tradition. A retrieval of the mystical strain would be Bremond's rescue of his own Jesuit roots, where he had "a bone to pick" with a loved and loving, but (in his opinion) incompetent parent—something quite different from the contempt he felt for Port-Royal.

The Battle Begins

We recall that in his first presentation of the spirituality of the French School, where he had pointed to Francis de Sales as the School's proximate source, he had argued that "theocentric" devotion descended from Augustine himself by way of Bernard's treatises on holy love. When Augustine wrote the *fecisti ad nos* (i.e., "you have made us for yourself," at the beginning of the *Confessions*), he had strongly implied, thought Bremond, that the "we are for God" takes priority over the "God is for us," as Bernard of Clairvaux then formalized in his teaching that "that man should love God, not only for His Goodness toward him, nor for the fear of chastisement, but solely for God Himself." "Theocentrism" was, to be sure, only latent in this tradition, Bremond admitted, but waiting for the Counter-Reformation to make it patent, the implicit "idea" coming to explicit expression. He drew a provocative parallel in Newman-like fashion with the way in which advocates had hesitated for a long time to state the gradually crystallizing dogma of papal infallibility, although the "dogma" was "in their bones," so to speak, "only the word was alarming to them."[7]

And then in the first of two long footnotes Bremond turned to the work of Henri Watrigant, SJ, respected historian of the Counter-Reformation and authority on varieties of meditational methods. Watrigant had attempted in a Thomistically-flavored 1907 study to show that Ignatius's focus in the *Spiritual Exercises* on the "final end" of humankind actually had a long lineage stretching back to the patristic Church.[8] But it was unfortunate, said Bremond, that Watrigant tried to marshall passages that would provide *explicit* proof for his thesis, showing that this or that Church father anticipated Ignatius, when, in fact, he could find very few. Actually, said Bremond, Ignatius's focus had become explicit only in quite recent sources, whereas *implicitly* it had in truth been in operation in unstated ways much, much longer. Indeed, theocentric ideas were bound up with anthropocentric ideas so tightly that disentanglement becomes a subtle task for the historian as well as the psychologist. Not only, I think, was Bremond showing the signs here of Newman's theory of development, in which an essence passes through countless transmutations in response to historical contingencies, but he was also showing that a kind of "illative" method, a progressive moral discernment, would be his instrument of investigation. We see that "theocentrism" is present throughout the tradition, just as we see the presence of Ignatius's concern for the "final end," because a host of converging and accumulating indirect indications produce a high level of certitude for that thesis, even if irrefutable evidential certainty is impossible.

In the next note in *Histoire*, III, Bremond praised Watrigant for showing that Ignatius was in effect a direct predecessor of Bérulle.[9] Ignatius's real intention, argued Watrigant in a discussion of the so-called "fundamentum" or cardinal principle of the *Exercises*, comes out when he reminds the individual on retreat "that God created human beings so that they might praise, reverence and serve our Lord God, and by this means to save their souls."[10] Ignatius's definitive emphasis, said Watrigant, is on the

---

7. *Histoire*, III, 6–8.

8. Ibid., 21n2.

9. Ibid., 22–24n1.

10. Puhl, *Spiritual Exercises of St. Ignatius*, 12, sec. 23 "First Principle and Foundation," "Man is created to praise, reverence, and serve God our Lord, and by this means to save his soul." The Latin

offering of praise, not the gift of salvation. "Pure charity for the glorification of God" is always primary. Exactly right, thought Bremond, but then he castigated Watrigant for proffering this view in a somewhat apologetic way, since the Jesuit scholar expressed some diffidence about offering an unconventional interpretation. You see, said Bremond, that even Watrigant, right as he is, qualifies and weakens his insight, thereby watering down its essential theocentrism.

The problem then, Bremond contended, is that subsequent Jesuit commentators on the *Exercises* have routinely contravened Ignatius's original intention with anthropocentric distortions. In fact, Ignatius designed his *Exercises* for "elect retreatants" who are "capable of approaching by the 'motive of pure love the glorification of God,'"[11] so that "directed from the beginning towards pure love, [they] will not break ground towards interested love; in other words, this admirable little book [the *Exercises*], the wisdom and practicality of which is sometimes contrasted with the 'reveries of the mystics,' is no more than an enticing manual leading to mysticism, although it may be, and in truth is usually, given another meaning." It is the true Ignatius that Bérulle may well have glimpsed, even as he turned away from an early flirtation with the Jesuits.[12]

In subsequent references to Ignatius, as volume III unfolded, Bremond would take the occasional swipe at anthropocentric-leaning interpretations of the *Exercises*, usually by setting up a contrast with Bérulle. The young Barrès, we are told, found the *Exercises* to be the basis of a "Culte de moi," but he, Bremond, would make the French School "Culte de non-moi" no less poetic and interesting![13] While the methods of Bérulle reflect pure contemplative joy in adoring the Incarnate presence of God in the baby in the manger, Ignatius's methods are envisaged by a "rival, not hostile school" (!) as "more practical and more popular." Jesuits, Bremond tells us, do not regularly practice the "composition of place" in imagining Gospel-scenes, as "fervently and felicitously as the founder of the Oratory," for whom a rapturous "gather[ing up of] every act and word" of the Word Incarnate is essential.[14] With regard to worship of the Incarnate Christ, Ignatius as "a militant and practical genius," envisions himself in service to "the King of the supernatural world and the finished model of our moral life," and the result is that "the retreatant who follows the Exercises never loses sight of himself"; for Bérulle, the worship of Christ as King and Model operates by means of

---

is: *Homo creatus est ut Dominum Deum suum laudet, ac revereatur, eique serviens tandem salvus fiat.*

11. Bremond citing Watrigant (ibid., 24n).

12. Thus it is, says Bremond, that these reflections on Ignatius in the context of treating Bérulle are justified (ibid., 25). In his discussion of the unfair assessment of Bremond meted out by Joseph de Guibert, SJ, in his *DS* article on Bremond, Trémolières cites the passage in which de Guibert complains about Bremond's tendency to hang "historical paradoxes . . . upon two lines of a single text" ("The Witness to These Witnesses," 270). Bremond's treatment of the "fundamentum" may be an example. But, as Trémolières points out, where Bremond's approach was "intuitive," or as I am suggesting, more "illative" in Newman's sense, Guibert's objection is otiose. A single surface detail may, in fact, indicate great, hidden depths of significance.

13. *Histoire*, III, 41.

14. Ibid., 47–49.

a participatory dynamic in which the worshipper is filled with divine Spirit glorifying itself, i.e., the humanity of the worshipper is "carried up into" (as it were) the divine Presence.[15]

Bremond even speculated that the terminology of Bérullism with its "elevations" and "states" and "adherence," etc., has found a home in French language-use that has been denied to the more Ignatian stress on "actions."[16] Finally, Bremond made a definitive statement: Ignatius taught an "almost Stoic" and "reasonable" procedure of "practice makes perfect," while the Bérullian *askesis* was one in which change occurs only by means of a prior identification with Jesus' inner states, the "Christ living in us."[17] Perhaps one could state it this way: for Bremond Ignatian spirituality, *as it had been taught to him*, lacked proper inwardness, a kind of "soul lyricism," and the result was a heartless pragmatism—which becomes moralism—as applied to the Christian life.

However, having criticized Ignatian spirituality as "practical," Bremond backtracked slightly when he offered the thesis that it is "methodic" instead, the term "practical" being better preserved for the results in living, as it were, of any approach to the inner life. Bérulle is "practical" in his concern for the fruits of contemplation, but it is Ignatius who is "methodic," having created, claimed Bremond, a "spiritual gymnastic" that embodies "a calculated system for arriving at an end." Ignatius had a gift for "taking to pieces . . . the *human* mechanism of prayer, with a view to stimulating and oiling the natural play of the faculties it sets in motion; the result being the scientific method in question." One result is that for the Jesuit "the master virtue is energy; [while] for the Bérullian, religion." It is Martha, rather than Mary.[18] The Jesuit speaks of "resolves" following meditation, the Bérullian of "co-operation." Ignatius is "grammar," while Bérulle is "poetry." Ignatius is the athletic process of attaining virtue, and Bérulle is submission and self-annihilation. It is precisely here, though just in passing, that Bremond suggests, after a great deal of debating with Jesuit sources, that there is a linkage with the Port-Royalist Nicole, who held out for method against the opinion of many of his cohorts.[19] The obsession with method allows rationalists of quiet different stripes to hold hands, we might say, and anticipates the modern criticism of "technique" as dehumanizing.

Perhaps his most colorful psychological polemic against the use of the *Spiritual Exercises* to which he had been exposed was Bremond's characterization of what is called the "particular examen" in Ignatian method, and then the contrast that he constructed with Condren's "general examen." The particular "examen," as the name

---

15. Ibid., 51–53.
16. Ibid., 54–55.
17. Ibid., 60–61, 68.
18. Ibid., 93–97.

19. Ibid., 97–98n1. Eventually, said Bremond, Saint-Sulpice in its application of Olier's teaching, evolved a "programme," but not a "method." Clearly Bremond was struggling with terminology here, and was still thinking through his critique.

suggests, is a detailed procedure by which the individual searches his conscience and memory for specific failures in the daily struggle to master certain vices and to develop certain virtues. Bremond emphasized the "day and night" quality of such self-examination, and with touching detail he admitted that it does indeed produce moral discipline. But he also thought it produced a "do it yourself" kind of strenuous mentality (though without reference to Theodore Roosevelt or William James!).[20] Condren, on the other hand, developed an "examen" in which everything is framed not as "How well am I doing?" but as "How do I look from God's perspective?" The result, contended Bremond, is a faithful following without faltering that leads to (in a phrase already cited) "an almost supernatural heroism." He suggested that the Ignatian moralism, an anthropocentric *ascetism*, is "liable to paralyze or vitiate action rather than stimulate it," while Condren's program will truly enable it.[21]

It is striking, however, that Bremond was willing to acknowledge real power in both approaches, when he refers to Ignatius and Condren as Leibniz and Newton or Caesar and Pompey. Both are giants. But there is a dilemma. Does strong moral character result from the effective intervention of a commanding, but wise, general (Ignatius) or from the empathic attention of a skilled mentor who stimulates the natural capacity and desire for working ideals (Bérulle-Condren)? In truth, probably both at different times and for different individuals, and we have all had teachers of both types. But, Bremond's conviction, of course, was that the first had been overplayed (recall the war-context in 1916), and the time had come for the second. Thus, he was careful to respect both approaches, while favoring one over the other—at least so far as his personal experience had gone!

Finally, Bremond, having pursued this guerilla war with Ignatius all through his exposition of the French School, raised the question. Does all of this mean that Ignatius is hopeless? Specifically, does it mean that "the Ignatian discipline is incompatible with a prayer of quietude, that it simply deadens the mystic action of God? Assuredly no," Bremond contended, and he would show it in his volume V.[22] And then this: "Nothing is easier than to adapt the *Exercises* to the mystic initiation, and on my part I am disposed to believe that if they are not directed towards that end, they depart from the intention of S. Ignatius." There we have it: Ignatius, *rightly understood*, is, after all, quite mystical, quite theocentric. The challenge is to show just how, so that by a certain

---

20. Truly, Bremond could go on endlessly here. At one point, he argued that in the "preparatory prayer" that precedes each meditation in the *Spiritual Exercises*, where the retreatant asks God that "by his grace, all my intentions, acts and operations may go straight to the praise and service of his divine majesty," there is "an expansion of the Ego, voluntary and conquering," a hasty pushing for action as soon as possible (ibid., 394–95). One can only conclude that the young Bremond must have felt very, very pressured by his Jesuit directors, and then very deflated when the program did not work for him as expected.

21. Ibid., 336–41.

22. Ibid., 425.

alchemy an anthropocentric/asceticist opponent of the French School—as Ignatius's interpreters typically have made him out to be—proves in fact to be an ally.

The "School" of Louis Lallemant, SJ

After the very large interlude of "the School of Port-Royal," Bremond turned in *Histoire*, V, "The School of Louis Lallemant and the Mystical Tradition in the Society of Jesus," to a succession of seventeenth-century Jesuits, whom he considered as representatives of a genuine Ignatian mysticism, though they had been largely ignored, because, after all, as he reminds us, "the Society preferred ascetics to mystics."

The foundational figure is Louis Lallemant, SJ, (1578–1635), teacher and professor, then Master of Novices, at several Jesuit locations in France, director of the critical Third Year program of the second novitiate (the make-or-break final year in Jesuit formation, we recall), finally rector for some years of the Jesuit collège at Bourges. He created a "school" of spiritual formation "far more original, twenty times more sublime, twenty times more austere," Bremond averred,[23] than anything that ever came out of Port-Royal.

Lallemant is sometimes compared to Balthasar Alvarez (1533–1580), a Spanish Jesuit who made efforts to develop a contemplative dimension in Ignatian practice. Lallemant not having been a writer, however, his theories were handed down by his faithful disciple, Jean Rigoleuc (1595–1648), then given literary form and polish by Jean-Joseph Surin (1600–1655). Much of the preservation of the tradition of Jesuit mysticism, including portions of Surin's *oeuvre*, was the work of a courageous priest, Pierre Champion de La Mahère (1632–1701), who produced a *Vie* of Rigoleuc in 1686, and a *Vie* of Lallemant as well as a compendium of his ideas in 1694. But by that time, and because of the Quietist controversy, anti-mystical thinking was in the ascendant. Given, then, the suppression of Surin's books after the Loudon experience and his own breakdown, Lallemant's work also went into eclipse as a submerged and subversive voice, resurfacing to some degree in the eighteenth century, with Jean-Pierre de Caussade and Jean Nicolas Grou.

In his sketching of Lallemant's views, Bremond highlighted the way in which this gifted teacher could strike a compromise between a genuine mysticism, on the one hand, and a classic Ignatian practicality, on the other. Emphasizing the regular habits and military discipline typical of Jesuit training with its focus on service, he also taught the importance of a "second conversion" reminiscent of Pascal, where the heart is inflamed with the desire for perfection. This latter transformative experience is, Lallemant thought, the beginning of a true interiority, where the contemplative life can begin, where the individual can give not only the fruits of his labor, but his very own self, to God. Such teaching, noted Bremond, is always subject in Jesuit circles to

---

23. *Histoire*, V, 4.

charges of "illuminism" and seeking after "extraordinary" experience, but Lallemant persisted by taking the position that exterior action must be interiorly grounded, or else it will be contaminated by self-love. The good Jesuit, therefore, must go beyond the practical "examen" precisely by cultivating an inward sense of being always in the presence of God. Such experience of this presence will be "crucifying" because it will be accompanied and shaped by self-abandonment to God, so that belief and obedience are thereby deepened, and that which was heretofore merely "notional" assent will become "real." This is all theocentric, contended Bremond, but in an anthropocentric and ascetically Ignatian kind of way. The main thing, however, is that Lallemant thereby established a fragile beachhead for mysticism within the Order.[24]

There follow two chapters in which Bremond assessed Rigoleuc's ideas as well as those of some minor figures associated with the Jesuit missions in Brittany. Bremond was struck by Rigoleuc's "critique of action," that is, his idea that action is merely exterior and narrow, but that interiority, especially if it is marked by an absolute resignation to suffering, is wide and deep. This suffering may well be that of an inscrutable interior void, where the individual has no sense of "feeling" for God, so that love for God must be hidden in the form of a disquietude-without-assurance. This state, says Bremond, is a genuine example of the dryness of the mystical night, and, of course, he drew the contrast with Pascal's need for the "sign."[25] At some point Rigoleuc believed himself to be damned, as did Surin, but in the "second conversion" infused prayer and confidence finally came to him.

In fact, the Breton missions, colorfully described by Bremond, were marked by supernatural, mystical and quietist phenomena of all kinds. A special feature of this evangelistic activity was the enthusiastic and widespread use of Jesuit retreats, and the development of individualized protocols for the application of the *Exercises* as instruments of conversion. Indeed, the use of such protocols, clearly encouraged by Ignatius himself in the text of the *Exercises*, is a hallmark of their modern use. And thereby came a paradox, Bremond thought. "The retreats are one of the glories of the Company of Jesus. By a singular contrast, the Order which has worked the hardest for the centralization of Catholic forces actively developed at the same time that individualism which is one of the characteristic traits of modern Catholicism, as it is of all interior progress. I know that this word of individualism rings poorly in certain ears and that several people have made it the synonym for Protestantism and *Rousseauism*.

24. Ibid., 66–67. The preceding paragraph is a summary of ibid., ch. 1: "The Spiritual Doctrine of Lallemant." One problem is that in recounting Lallemant's teaching, Bremond had to be dependent on Champion, where the account is mingled with Rigoleuc's transmission of that teaching. There are, thus, subtle distinctions to be made between Lallemant and Rigoleuc in terminology, as, for instance, in treating the slippery concept of "purity" (ibid., 36n3).

25. Ibid., 76–77. The thought here is striking. Bremond contends that in the *Mystère de Jésus* Pascal yearns for God in a disquieted, felt, sensible way which itself becomes the possession he seeks, i.e., the yearning precisely because it is "felt" is the sign itself. But in the mystical formulation, faith that we have truly found God and God has found us in the middle of desolating dryness is the mark that "we can perfectly love God without knowing that we love Him."

Alas! Is not the author of the *Spiritual Exercises* also the founder of the Company of Jesus, that is to say, the Order the most hostile to the idolatry of private judgment or of one's own understanding, and the most disciplined there ever was?"[26] Clearly Bremond saw in the mystical side of the Ignatian tradition that which was present in the seventeenth century, but had been denied to him in the nineteenth.

Surin

And then came Surin, a figure whose depth and complexity almost matched that of Pascal, yet a figure vastly more compelling. Part of the reason is that Surin is in some ways more modern than Pascal: for the latter the "night" of faith is one of doubt and searching—a kind of epistemological groping, painful in its terror to be sure, but with a cerebral quality that somewhat mutes the terror—while for the latter the "night" shares space with encroaching "demons," raw and dark forces that are more than frightening, since they will eat you alive. We have to think just a bit in order to connect with Pascal, but in the immediacy of all-consuming emotional torment we recognize Surin instantly, as did Bremond.

Surin is, of course, best known for the affair of the "devils of Loudun" and Aldous Huxley's famous novel and the movie made from it, and more recently, from Michel de Certeau's treatment (see below). And fascination with the exorcist-theme is perennial. But Bremond was primarily concerned with Surin's spiritual writing, particularly the *Catéchisme spirituel* (1654), which went on the Index in 1695,[27] and then various letters and dialogues. Thus, he began his treatment with a discussion of the history of Surin's work and of the early biography by Boudon.

Despite Bossuet's great liking for Surin's writings, there is a long history filled with suppression and the derailment of attempts at publication in a manner not unlike Fénelon's *Maxims of the Saints*. And yet, noted Bremond, his work has continued to be in demand and has been much appreciated, though there is always the overhanging shadow of Loudun and Surin's consequent mental illness. In fact, Bremond's final judgment on this man, after reviewing his teachings in a highly favorable way, is quite extraordinary, drawn as it was from a modern psychiatric evaluation. This last came from the medical scientist, Henri Delacroix, who said of Surin, as well as of some other mystics, that their lives show "great intuitions of affective and intellectual character," so that "there is a great continuing impulsion, internally coherent and tenacious, which disposes their lives (and the work of the spirit) like an inflexible and clear willing."[28] In psychiatric language, this is to say that Surin suffered from the "idée fixe,"

---

26. Ibid., 139.

27. In an amusing aside (ibid., 155n1), Bremond was so bold as to dismiss the whole idea of the Index, given its history, as essentially idiotic (ibid., 155n1). He was definitely becoming more outspoken and combative.

28. Ibid, 309. Bremond saw here a strong affirmation, since Delacroix is not, he says, "one of ours,"

but that he did so in a way, and to a degree, that baffles rational analysis of any kind by teasing the boundary line between mental states and conditions of the soul.

After a careful tracing out of Surin's background, Bremond made the summary point that central to this man's merit was the fact that in his work he was "prudent, down-to-earth, timid, positive, and, as they say, practical." These very qualities enabled him to be both mystic and pragmatist in such creative ways that, along with Lallemant, he actually continues to be read and used by some Jesuit directors, despite contrary impressions held by some.[29] In the intensely religious milieu in which Surin was raised, ecstatic religious phenomena including female demonic possession, mostly among Carmelites, were taken quite seriously. Bremond saw here a point of infusion from Teresa of Avila. In fact, the whole discussion of Surin's formative period was marked by interaction with female correspondents and interlocutors; he was thus providentially prepared for what would come in Loudun in 1634.

From 1632 to 1638 a group of Ursuline nuns of Loudun, led by their Superior, Jeanne des Anges, claimed to have been in a state of demonic possession induced by a local priest, Urbain Grandier, who was subsequently tried and condemned and executed after a highly dramatic process involving both medical and priestly examinations under the authority of a royally appointed judge. Documentation of the whole process is extensive (thus a gold mine for reconstructions), including detailed witnessing from "possessed" nuns from whom "demonic voices" spoke during highly suggestive interrogations. The whole proceeding, staged in public exhibition, lent itself to colorful theatrical representation. Bremond took an agnostic position on the "reality" of such possession, allowing for its possibility even if, as is likely, elements of a more psychological hysteria are present as well.

Surin was brought into the situation in order to function as an exorcist for the nuns, since a "mass delirium" had settled into the whole group and was contagiously spreading to the wider community. In a sustained discussion of the practice of exorcism in Church history, Bremond argued that a ritual with humble and ordinary beginnings (one renounces the devil and all his works at baptism or prays for release from evil spirits, etc.) had turned into a circus, a maniacal spectator-event that had become a travesty. But the key idea that he wanted to convey was that Surin, already sick and troubled by the time he got to Loudun, was dragged into a mess in which he endured the pains of hell and was profoundly humbled.

The other major factor for Bremond was the person of Jeanne des Anges herself, whom he interprets as an example of the false mystic (again the foil!). After careful discussion of her biography, he turns to the psychiatrists Charcot and Janet (in a way

---

i.e., was a skeptic, but yet was deeply moved, precisely as a scientist, by what he saw in Surin and others (ibid., 310n1). On Bremond's respect and fondness for the work of Delacroix in interpreting mystical experience, see Portier and Talar, "Mystical Element," 11–13, and Talar, "The Modernist and the Mystic," 99–100, but also Houdard, "Henri Bremond et la psychologie," 126–27, 133–35.

29. Ibid., 158 and n2.

highly unusual for him, given his reluctance to pathologize) for a diagnosis of hysteria, while insisting, with a reference to von Hügel, that her religious dynamics were separate.[30] She was marked, thought Bremond, by a quality that seems to be true of all false piety, namely, grandiose vanity, the kind that has great aspirations and imagines that it has fulfilled them. In reality, she was undisciplined, bored and disliked, the Ursuline community at Loudun being a miserable little hothouse. It was not that she was insincere; in fact, she tried hard, but lacked perspective on herself. In a detailed treatment, Bremond showed that Surin tried to rescue Jeanne by taking the view that her possession could be treated as a prelude to sanctity, that God would use her illness as a stepping-stone to health and holiness. But he failed, and experienced a deep breakdown in the process, having to be separated from her in the end. Accusations that he mishandled the process have dogged him ever since and have played a part in bringing him under a shadow.

What then truly interested Bremond was the depth of Surin's suffering, during and after the exorcisms, and its implications for his spiritual writing. At the heart of that suffering was not only the post-Loudun physical illness and rejection that Surin endured (Bremond thinks that this was a bit exaggerated by Surin), but also his deep conviction, following a statement by one of the demon-possessed women, that God had damned him to eternal perdition. Believing what the woman said, despite all of the efforts to talk him out of it, Surin was convinced that *now* he had two options: to love God with all of his heart, or to despair. This is Francis de Sales's "impossible supposition" which again functions as the "limit-case" for truly loving God: even though God damns me and thus I have nothing to gain, I will love God in any case. Unlike de Sales, however, Surin did not push through the obsession in order to reveal its absurdity, but rather he clung to it.[31]

Withdrawing from external things, Surin immersed himself in prayer and threw himself totally onto the mysterious and ineffable divine Presence. He practiced Jesuit discipline, holding himself to the most rigorous moral standard, and yet sought no consolation from God, because there was none to be had. Bremond called this combination Surin's "mystical moralism," "an astonishing synthesis," seeing in it a combination of Ignatian hardness with a profound inwardness in which only the Holy Spirit

---

30. Ibid., 205n1. Doubtless, one of the factors that influenced Bremond's studied even-handedness about exorcism was the fact that Auguste Saudreau, one of his favored authorities on the nature of mystical experience, had come out strongly with the view that demonic possession is a reality. Saudreau was thus critical of Bremond's handling of Jeanne des Anges because of the latter's (moderate) skepticism: this criticism hurt Bremond (Bremond to Blondel, March 8, 1918 [BB, II, 350]). See Goichot, EG, 102–6, for a discussion of the correspondence between Bremond and Saudreau on all of this. In fact, Bremond very much anticipated the modern view (in the year 2018!) that spiritual genius and psychopathology occupy overlapping, probably inseparable, domains.

31. The perennial quality of the "impossible supposition" and its derivatives in Catholic art is worth noting, as in Graham Greene's *Heart of the Matter*, where, however, it is not so that much that "God has damned me," as it is that "I have damned myself," but nonetheless, "I shall love God to the end."

can give guidance and direction. There was no *action* that could help Surin, only a passive love waiting on God. Surin called such prayer a festive "repast," though it is not an illuminism that brings pleasure and a sense of spiritual superiority.[32]

And so it is that for Surin, the only inward motion that matters is "consent," saying "yes" to what God has decided, miserable though that may be.[33] Intellectual objections are, thought Surin, just so much evasion. The mystics know better, he said. Thus, Surin resisted an arid scholasticism, said Bremond, insisting that it is only the purely loving heart that can know the reality of God, and that there is no payback for such a heart. Bremond contended that, at least in the case of Surin, this is what "devout humanism" comes to in the end. What is promised in such a perspective, and with such practice, is "an operation by which the soul looks upon universal truth" precisely by means of loving detachment from all things. This "truth" is a divine wisdom of not-knowing, a "wise ignorance," in which God is approached easily by means of the perfect docility of a child. But the "taste" of God will always remain "confused," because God is silent and privations are painful.

Jesuit Response Pro and Con

With his side comments on Ignatius in *Histoire*, III, and then the full treatment in volume V, there was no question that at the time Bremond was poking a stick into a hornet's nest. There was the perennially sensitive issue of the status of the Jesuit Order in France, and there was also the fact that the Retreat Movement was enjoying great popularity in the 1920s. The use of different forms of the *Spiritual Exercises* as a tool for conducting retreats was invaluable, and the Jesuits were quick to defend it.

Cavallera responded soon after seeing a draft of *Histoire*, III, and Bremond reproduced part of his letter, with his own commentary as a rejoinder, in an appendix to *Histoire*, III, in its published form.[34] With heavy sarcasm, he described his correspondent as "one of the most liberal-minded men I know," grateful that this individual does not "treat me as the beadle or sacristan of a little chapel," since both of us simply want

---

32. Ibid., 259. The whole section, ibid., 267–310, is quite remarkable. At one point, Bremond says of Surin that he tried "to explain the inexplicable, to describe the indescribable" (ibid., 292).

33. Ibid., 287–88. "Abnegation is for him [Surin] a virtue, an exercise, a voluntary and laborious entrainment. Aided by grace, it produces in us its effects natural and supernatural, reducing little by little our instinctive cowardice while multiplying our capacities for heroism. But the mystic penetrates deeper. Behind the human effort just described, he perceives the divine activity, God himself hastening to cover this 'nudity,' to fill this 'void,' to populate this desert and to 'deify' this 'nothingness'" (ibid., 289). Bremond describes this discourse as a combination of Dionysian mysticism and Ignatian spirit, and thus a true Ignatian mysticism.

34. Some of the argumentation was carried out in the newly founded journal, the *Revue d'ascétique et de mystique*, whose editor, Joseph de Guibert, SJ, tried to mediate as a pacifier. He would eventually have all of his own criticism, in the *DS* article on Bremond, of the latter as a great writer and poor historian. See Olphe-Galliard, "Cinq lettres," and then the comments of Trémolières, "The Witness to These Witnesses," 264–74.

"neither . . . to exalt or belittle Ignatian spirituality, but simply to define it." Turning to Cavallera's first charge that he, Bremond, had rather overplayed his enthusiasm for Bérullism, while needlessly derogating Ignatius, who, after all, was quite theocentric, as the Jesuit motto "To the greater glory of God" testifies, Bremond riposted with a kind of smirking irony that he was simply being a "historian" in his description of the import of the French School in the seventeenth century. He claimed that he had engaged in strictly nonpartisan description of a number of "schools" in that era, that his "critical faculty" constrained him to present the subject "in its best light."[35] He pointed out (rightly) that he had been careful to argue that Ignatius was one of the predecessors of Bérulle in his theocentrism. The problem has been that "the rank and file of Jesuits," who are not of the mystic élite (such as Surin), have *detheocentrized* Ignatius. He curtly dismissed Cavallera's annoyance that he, Bremond, has agreed with an Oratorian writer who had made the rhapsodic statement that the Oratory bears "greater love to Jesus Christ": nonsense, says Bremond, since statements like that are meaningless anyway.[36]

Cavallera went on to plead the case that the *Exercises* are strongly focused on "the disinterested worship of Jesus," contending that Bremond had overplayed the idea of a self-interested "rational basis" for engaging in Jesuit formation. He contended that there had, in fact, been a close spirit of agreement between Ignatius and Bérulle, an agreement which Bremond strongly denied by restating his view that most Jesuits had been opposed to Bérulle's mysticism.[37] Dripping with sarcasm, Bremond insisted that the shift from Ignatius to Bérulle is like going from Calais to Dover, or from Bourdaloue to Fénelon, or from Macaulay to Coleridge, where each member of the pair can be taken quite separately, or by degrees be converted into the other. Bérullism has been easily "Ignatianized," as one can see in the Jesuit mystical élite, but it is also true that Ignatius as Rodriguez interpreted him is what most Jesuits have experienced, this latter being quite different from Bérulle.[38]

But the really substantive element that emerged in the early phases of the debate involved a doctrinal issue, as Goujon and Salin have pointed out.[39] Cavallera raised the spectre of quietism in mystical prayer, and quietism was something that had been officially condemned back in 1695. He suggested that Bérulle leaned in the quietist direction through his theory of "adherence" to the "states" of Jesus, where the working of grace is understood as an infusion into the soul of the adoring, utterly "passive"

---

35. Goujon and Salin note this statement by Bremond as an example of his "methodological chameleonism," the idea being that Bremond could "put on" the habiliments of the tradition or individual he was describing without revealing his real sympathies("Henri Bremond," 422). But that does not seem quite right—one has no doubt where his sympathies lie as he lays out his material, but it is the use of irony in the process of assessment that makes him seem furtive and elusive .

36. *Histoire*, III, 578–79, and notes.

37. Ibid., 579–80, and notes.

38. Ibid., 581–82, and notes.

39. Goujon and Salin, "Henri Bremond," 423.

worshipper. But in classic mystical theology, such an experience would characterize the prayer of only a very few elite practitioners, the true mystics.[40] Thus was raised again the Saudreau/Poulain debate about whether mysticism is part of the norm, an aspect of all humble and true prayer, or something extraordinary and only for adepts. Cavallera was also coming out into open combat by giving voice to the traditional Jesuit suspicion of the hankering after "advanced" states of prayer.

Bremond went on the defensive, knowing that he was vulnerable. The charge of quietism, or "semi-quietism," hit a raw nerve, since he was already under suspicion with the Vatican's doctrinal watchdogs after his work on Fénelon, and, of course, *Sainte Chantal*. And he also knew—since he was already beginning to prepare materials for *Histoire*, VII and VIII, "The Metaphysic of the Saints"—that he was about to issue a grand synthesis in which he would reveal that the thematic bundle of devout-humanism/mysticism/theocentrism has as its core the spirituality of "pure love." But that concept was tainted by inevitable quietist associations. At this point, as Goujon and Salin put it, Bremond decided to "play dead," and the debate about the *Exercises* went into abeyance until the summer of 1926, at which point, now an académicien, Bremond would have *Histoire*, VII and VIII, ready with all guns blazing.[41]

Certeau

If we ask the question of what was truly at stake in Bremond's unrelenting, dogged advocacy for a true Jesuit mysticism, the answer lies in his assessment of Surin, who represents the point of convergence, the place where all of the threads of the fabric, so to speak, weave themselves into a unity. Certainly there are other figures in the course of the *Histoire* whom Bremond loved and admired more than Surin, but no figure fascinated and awed Bremond more in terms of subtlety and integrity, by the mysterious depth and intensity of his writing. This troubled Jesuit created, and embodied, a synthesis of metaphysics and the mystical practice of prayer in a way that foretold the ideal blend to which Bremond himself would aspire as he composed the succeeding volumes of the *Histoire*. In his suffering and in his interpretation of that suffering Surin hit the target squarely, thereby elevating what can seem like a tiresome bit of intra-Jesuit scholasticism about Ignatius into something much more profound.

That profundity was gathered up by the postmodern Jesuit and thinker Michel de Certeau, some of whose inspiration came from Bremond. Certeau produced critical

---

40. The implied reference here is to the traditional idea of the "ligature," or "binding," of normal human capacities, that the mystic is supposed to experience in the ecstasy of union with the divine. It is as if the human subject goes into a kind of limp paralysis in the divine embrace. Bossuet used this argument against Fénelon in the debates at the Conference of Issy in 1694 in order to make the point that "passivity" in prayer, as the Quietists taught it, is not normal and ordinary, but only for an elite few who may experience the ligature.

41. Goujon and Salin, "Henri Bremond," 423–24; Goichot, *Henri Bremond*, 193–94. Loisy, of course, loved every moment of this debate, and celebrated it in GT, ch. 4: "The Quietism of Fénelon."

editions of Surin's *Guide spirituel pour le perfection* (1963) and the *Correspondance* (1966) and then a major interpretation in his *La possession de Loudun* (1970), where, among other things, he reflected on the significance of Surin's exorcistic experience. In the midst of all of this work, he produced for the 1965 Cerisy-la-Salle colloquium his masterful assessment of Bremond's accomplishment in *Histoire*, VII and VIII, "Henri Bremond et 'La Métaphysique des Saints," as a harbinger of major postmodern paradigm-shifts in the understanding of spirituality. For Certeau, Bremond's whole project in the *Histoire*, including his treatment of Surin, and, more fundamentally, his analysis of mystical consciousness, has opened a vital window into the spiritual struggles of the modern age.

In *The Possession at Loudun*, Certeau developed a broad picture of the "gradual disintegration of shared meanings" that marked the seventeenth century, one sign of which was the phenomenon of witchcraft trials and demonic possession.[42] In this time of crisis the language of orthodox fidelity along with stable conceptions of nature and truth collapsed, and there arose simultaneously a language of "interior strangeness," a language that registers the existence of "fissures" and "interruptions" in social dynamics, where there is an obsessive concern for "reality" versus "appearances."[43] Certeau's postmodern terminology was his way of understanding the cultural impact of the waning of traditional structures of ecclesiastical authority and the waxing of individualized and anti-authoritarian mystical experience, especially among women, in the seventeenth century. Most germane here, however, was Certeau's understanding of Surin's dialogues with the "demons" in the Ursuline nuns of Loudun.

Analyzing Surin's functioning during the public exorcisms, Certeau emphasized that the priest was operating in "the camp of the possession," where he was "inside" a "progressively circumscribed 'place,'" operating by its own laws.[44] We might say that Surin went to work in a historically and culturally defined milieu or "field," in which the determined significance of his actions transcended the man himself. Believing that the nuns were possessed, he saw it as his duty to take their "voices," mixed with elements of truth, seriously. His challenge, following St. Thomas Aquinas, was to recognize that these voices would be a blend of "truth and vanity," to realize that "truth and vanity crisscross, as do paganism and Christianity," but that "one must not believe the demon even if he says true things." The implication for the exorcist, said Certeau, is that having to find the truth in lies "is a religious situation that is symbolized by the

---

42. References are to the English translation, Certeau, *Possession at Loudun*. In the more comprehensive *Mystic Fable*, Certeau referred to the rise and fall of seventeenth-century French mysticism, as depicted by Bremond, as a mark of the "deterioration of frames of reference" (ibid., 153).

43. In the words of one analyst: Certeau's "intellectual strategy" was "an endeavour to discern and to make ethical and aesthetic space for particular forms of interruption" (Ahearne, *Michel de Certeau*, 3).

44 *The Possession at Loudun*, 203.

labor of discerning truths mixed in with the statements of the possessed," since "the truth seems to lose its way in lies."[45]

It was Surin's accomplishment, thought Certeau, that he recognized the necessity of condemning the public spectacles and moving the exorcistic conversations to private places, where "decisive choices" could be made.[46] He thereby created a new "experimental science," i.e., a setting, not unlike the psychoanalytic session, where objective safety and honesty could allow the exorcist "in a disinterested and prudent spirit" to separate truth from illusion. At the same time, it was Surin's downfall that he failed to observe the Thomist wisdom. Deeply serious and deeply convinced of the import of his mission, Surin thought that he could outsmart the demons, since he had carried on a similar struggle within himself for years, "seeking God in the depths of anguish, beating at the doors of his own limits," and now "he *perceives* the adversary."[47] Though he was describing Surin, Certeau probably could not have better described Bremond himself.

Certeau went on to describe Surin's place in the creation of a "financial and psychological enclave" for practitioners, space set aside for the profitable pursuit of exorcistic displays. He portrayed the blossoming of Surin's ascetical disciplines and his deterioration, his growing sense of "two souls" at work in himself, followed by his elaboration of historical accounts of the events at Loudun, finally a "literature of triumph," in which Jeanne des Anges became a veritable and miraculously healed saint, while he himself descended into madness. Around Surin there then emerged a group of "mystics," endowed with a "suspect spirituality," where each person is "like a child in the bosom of Our Lord, having as little care as at the age of eight."[48] Certeau spoke more ironically regarding the outcome of Surin's struggles than had Bremond, but he recognized the kinship in their interpretations, as well as their shared sense that something culturally earthshaking was going on.

That "something" is this: the "demons" are the spiritual internalizations and writhing embodiments of social/cultural upheaval, Surin was their crucified sacrifice, and Jeanne des Anges their narcissistic sales-representative! And God is the voice of "pure love" at "the fine point of the soul," if one can only listen closely enough, and in silence, through it all.[49] Surin's message and Bremond's message seem to coincide.

---

45. Ibid., 148–49, with a reference to the *Summa theologica*, IIa–IIae, quaest. 9, art. 2. What has happened here, in Certeau's view, is that the "I" of God speaking *through* the mystic has become inseparable in practice from the "I" of the mystic herself, since, in the dynamic of modernity, subjectivity has become the privileged locus of divine presence. Disentangling the two becomes an essential, but inherently impossible, act of discernment, if the subject is demonically possessed. See the astute commentary on Certeau of McIntosh, *Mystical Theology*, esp. 68–69.

46. Ibid., 148–50.

47. Ibid., 204.

48. Ibid., 204–12. The final chapter is "The Triumph of Jeanne des Anges."

49. An interesting follow-up study to the interpretive work of de Certeau is Sluhovsky, *Believe Not Every Spirit*, who has argued that in the context of the advent of modernity frenzied possession

So, it seems that Bremond was on to something. His concern for greater affirmation of, greater access to, and greater practice of, mystical approaches to the inner life, and the relationship with God, was one registration of an "interruption," a "fissure," a sense that came over many people in the post WWI years that a new age had begun, an age in which inner disquiet and pervasive spiritual misery, masked by frenzied hedonism and outbursts of "demonic" rage and aggression, were the surface symptoms of profound social disturbance.

By contrast with the Superior of the Loudun Ursulines, in *Histoire*, VI, Bremond took a break with another seventeenth-century female figure, this time one that he deeply admired, Marie of the Incarnation, followed by a crowd of "little people," the *turba magna*, who, forever unsung, aspire to holiness and who struggle with the hunger for God. This volume, more than any other, won for him the affection and esteem of contemporaries, thus launching him into the process that led to the Académie and, finally, the recognition and validation that he deserved.

---

became a voluntarily induced experience, in which the possession, reflective of one's "nudity before God," could be seen as either divine or demonic. There are psychoanalytic overtones to Sluhovsky's thesis, similar to "regression in the service of the ego," as in Bakan, *Sigmund Freud and the Jewish Mystical Tradition*. See, most recently, Sluhovsky, "Mysticism as an Existential Crisis."

13

1922–23: First Signs of Integration

WITH *HISTOIRE*, IV AND V, then III, behind him, Bremond entered a period of emerging, but not yet realized, synthesis, and of public recognition and honors, but private struggle and crisis.

The first indications of a synthesis came in *Histoire*, VI, published in 1922, where he dealt with Marie of the Incarnation, who truly represented for him, as he said, "the highest summit of mysticism."[1] His treatment of her would be Bremond at his best, without the polemics or special pleading or fireworks connected with controversial subjects such as Jansenism and Ignatianism, but also without the elaborate historical construction as with the French School. His exploration of Marie's inner life, of her personal trials and experience of prayer, is affectionate and celebratory, lyrical even, as well as loaded with all of the paradoxes of true saintliness, as if he were loudly saying to us: "Here is the real thing!"

The public recognition was his election to the Académie, but the run-up was painful in some ways, and his aggressive embrace of the theme of "pure poetry" in what followed unleashed another round of vituperative controversy. The cultural ambience of dislocation was volatile, since these are the years in post-war France of exploding unrest artistically and politically, years of enormous creativity and mounting turmoil, years of searching for new and viable expression on the part of spiritual thinkers. Everything was in ferment.[2]

One very fortunate thing for Bremond's physical circumstances happened in the autumn of 1921. During the previous December he had undergone some surgery at Pau for a digestive disorder accompanied by very high fever. During recovery he had befriended a Miss Johnston, an English nurse living in the area.[3] The following

---

1. *Histoire*, V, i.

2. Cobban's descriptor, "muddied waters" (*History of Modern France*, 126), serves well. Weber (*Hollow Years: France in the 1930s*), while mostly dealing with the slightly later period, pertains to the '20s as well in its opening section, "The Wilderness Called Peace."

3. Blanchet cites a letter from Miss Johnston to Blondel of January 4, 1921, with this information

October, he informed Blondel that Miss Johnston had purchased a home in the Pau area, that included a "cottage enclosed in the home's park," which she had offered to Bremond for his work. He accepted her generosity, and "baptized" the dwelling "Littlemore"[4]—a playful reminiscence of (and identification with?) Newman's place of sojourn and retreat as he transitioned from Anglicanism to the Roman Church. This retreat would serve Bremond well for the rest of his life, and would be the place where many visitors sought him out. But Miss Johnston herself disappears from the historical record.

And there had been less felicitous developments as well. One of them involved his abortive efforts to land an academic position at the university level. He was somewhat diffident about this, since his real vocation lay in writing, not in classroom teaching, but he took the possibility under serious consideration on three quite different occasions. In December 1918, he had asked for Blondel's advice and counsel about applying to the Institut Catholique in Paris, since the incumbent in the chair of Church History had just died. He gave three reasons: he could try out his ideas for the upcoming *Histoire* volumes on his students, he could challenge his students to focus on religious sentiment as the "real" rather than on "theses of pure curiosity with little real nourishment in them," and, being condemned to a "sordid economy," he could generate some "gagne-pain" (put bread on the table). A little defensively, he suggested that *Histoire*, I and II, had earned him sufficient academic credibility as a historian, though he was quite aware that in advancing himself for a professorship, he, like Blondel, was running real risks.[5] It came to nothing. Blondel picked up on the cry for financial help, and quickly offered some sustenance.[6] But within a short time Bremond gave up on any placement at the Institut.[7]

(BB, III, 12n1). Apparently Bremond had her write to Blondel in order to reassure him.

4. Bremond to Blondel, October 13, 1921 (BB, III, 16). Blanchet tells us that Miss Johnston's house was named "Les Charmettes." The parallel with Tyrrell's sojourn on the grounds of Maude Petre's home at Storrington is uncanny. The arrangement would probably be frowned upon today as "inappropriate," but apparently was not so in the period under consideration.

5. Bremond to Blondel, December 13, 1918 (attachment to letter of November 29) (BB, II, 360).

6. Blondel to Bremond, December 16, 1918: "And also, if, in order to balance your books, you need a bit of cash ('un bout de papier'?), you know that you have *promised* always to have recourse to me" (BB, II, 363). Nothing the least bit petty here, even though they were fighting about Pascal et al.! Blanchet notes that later on Bremond accepted the offer (BB, II, 364n1).

7. Bremond to Blondel, December 31, 1918 (BB, II, 366). Although a communication from his friend Monbrun, who taught at Montpelier, warned him that teaching is no bed of roses, the reason that he gave was that he would be putting Alfred Baudrillart, the Rector, in a tough position. Out of friendship and respect, Baudrillart might offer him the position, but then the wrath of the Vatican would fall on Baudrillart: "I would be putting the Rector uselessly to the torture" (BB, II, 367n2). Baudrillart would later make it up to him in the election to the Académie. In fact, because of the condemnation of *Sainte Chantal*, some cloud would always hang over Bremond. Blanchet discusses the politics of this decision regarding a place at the Institut for Bremond (*Histoire d'une mise à l'Index*, 197–201).

The second venture was more complex, involving a position on the Catholic faculty at the University of Strasbourg. It was a unique kind of situation, reflective of the more Germanic heritage with which Strasbourg is associated. Strasbourg is a state university, but the only one in France with a specifically Catholic faculty within the university structure, a faculty both academically accredited and also canonically licensed by the Catholic Church for the preparation of students for priesthood. Thus its appointments are subject *both* to the secular and ecclesiastical authorities. It was a tempting situation, since the available appointment was in "religious psychology" and would have given Bremond an ideal platform.[8] Blondel was thoroughly supportive, noting that he himself had been at one time turned down at Strasbourg, but that Bremond could bring the necessary light![9] To say that the politics proved complicated would be an understatement.[10] All sorts of questions about Bremond's orthodoxy and obedience to the church hung in the air and (to change the metaphor!) torpedoed his vessel. He brought a noteworthy amount of anxiety to the situation, partly in regard to his own financial security but also (revealingly) about the need to give support to a cousin and five orphaned children as well as dowries for two Benedictine nieces. He also worried about keeping the pace on his twelve or fifteen(!) upcoming volumes.[11] In the end, he was passed over.

A third effort was initiated by Loisy toward the end of 1920, when he nominated Bremond for a post at the Collège de France. Writing to thank Loisy, he justified the nomination by noting that his work to date was not narrowly "confessional," but historical and objective, not containing "his own philosophy." He suggested that in the *Histoire* he was not engaged in Catholic apologetics as such, but rather was invested in an effort to appreciate the seventeenth-century mystical stream. He would at some point juxtapose other streams, such as those of Anglicans and "dissenters," the whole analysis marked by "the same curiosity and comprehensive sympathy." Recognizing that an "avalanche of soutanes" constantly created difficulties as a kind of "phantom sacristy," no one , he thought, really appreciated what he felt he was trying to do. Even Barrès—grateful as he was to this man—used him, it seemed, in a shortsighted fashion (quite true). He thus thanked Loisy for his efforts, while acknowledging that he

---

8. Bremond to Blondel, May 26, 1919 (BB, II, 379).

9. Blondel to Bremond, May 30, 1919 (BB, II, 380). It is remarkable that Bremond could follow this kindly letter, having just accepted some financial help from Blondel (Bremond to Blondel, May 26, 1919), with one of his most concerted blasts against Pascal (part of the immediate build-up to *Histoire*, IV), Bremond to Blondel, June 4, 1919 (BB, II, 381–84).

10. Discussed by Blanchet with relevant texts in *Histoire d'une mise à l'Index*, 201–34.

11. Bremond to Blondel, December 21, 1919 (BB, II, 415). This is a long, fretful letter. One senses that the close infighting of academic/ecclesiastical jockeying for position was not Bremond's forte, for all of his interest in such. Let it be said, however, that it was not to Blondel's taste either. He commiserated certainly, but both men were always highly dependent on "friends in high places." Blanchet's comment (BB, II, 417n1) about his own efforts to explain what was going on at Strasbourg is amusing: "we have tried to shed light on this whole business."

was exhausted with defending his work. His plan was to continue to scrape together enough income by journalistic and popular writing.[12]

It is no wonder that by year's end of 1920 he was in the hospital with "stomach pains," and one realizes in a fresh way what a relief it must have been when his nurse-angel, Miss Johnston, offered him "Littlemore" in Pau as a free and charming place for his writing. We can see as well what a triumph election to the Académie would be, a genuine secular and ecclesiastical coup for a man with many friends, but at least as many critics, and frustrated by roadblocks!

And so, Bremond ground away at his projects in his Pyrenees bases at Arthez-d'Asson and Pau, now and then back and forth to Paris, with the occasional visit to Aix. Living conditions were spartan, he cultivated a small garden at Littlemore, and his head swirled constantly with his own ferment, with offshoots and implications and addenda to his ongoing projects.

Marie of the Incarnation

Marie of the Incarnation, Marie Guyart Martin (1599–1672), the central character of the first part of *Histoire*, VI, offered in the concrete detail and color of her life an opportunity for Bremond to synthesize much of the thought of the earlier volumes, even as he anticipated the abstract and thematic exposition of *Histoire*, VII and VIII. Furthermore, Marie was a relatively unknown and unproblematic character for analysis, free from any massive body of prior interpretation, free as well from portrayal by Sainte-Beuve. There is thus a relaxed and lyrical quality, an easygoing flow, to Bremond's presentation. He was not fighting battles here, or competing, just relaxing into his art.

The means for constructing a literary portrait of Marie are complicated by the fact that the two primary sources, an early biography as well as the collected edition of her writings, emanate from the labors of her son, the Maurist Benedictine Dom Claude Martin (1619–1696), a character as colorful as his mother.[13] They had an exceedingly convoluted and ambivalent relationship, grounded in the fact that in order to pursue her vocation as an Ursuline nun after the death of her husband, the young Marie Martin had, painfully but firmly, entrusted her young and unwilling son Claude permanently to the care of relatives.[14] The history of Marie and the history of Claude

---

12. Cited by Blanchet, ibid., 453–54n1. See also Bernard-Maître, *Lettres*, 285–86. There was some special pleading here on Bremond's part, and an example of his "chameleonism" in conforming to Loisy's prejudices.

13. There is an excellent modern introduction, with selections from Marie's writings, in *Marie of the Incarnation*, ed. Mahoney.

14. Bremond thought that Dom Claude misrepresented his mother's mysticism both by downplaying it and rationalizing it. In a long note, he indulged in some careful source-critical analysis to make the point. Claude had a relationship with Pierre Nicole at Port-Royal, from whom Bremond thought he saw a pernicious influence. There was also, he contended, an effort on the part of the Saint-Maur

thus intertwine. In order to probe this complexity Bremond inserted into his treatment of Marie, several chapters on Dom Claude, whose biographer was yet another Benedictine, Dom Edmond Martène, a gifted and insightful writer with a complex relationship with Claude! When we look at Marie, therefore, we are often looking through her son's eyes, but partly as those eyes have been interpreted for us by a third party. Bremond delighted in all of the reverberations, which become convoluted and imbroglio-like for the modern reader, but which for him added human depth and texture to entanglements of life in the "communion of saints."

In his first chapter on Madame Martin, the "French Teresa" (as he calls her, following Bossuet),[15] and after establishing a lineage of influence that he traces to Louis Lallemant and French School roots, Bremond laid out her family background, with connections to the Versailles *dévot* circles around Fénelon (at one point he claims that *mystically* she embodied everything that Fénelon knew, without the polemical context).[16] Her childhood of unruffled piety and simplicity stirred in Bremond echoes of his own work with, and about, children, such that he recalled aspects of the Swan of Cambrai's *Treatise on the Education of Daughters*, and then the work of the contemporary American J. B. Pratt on the "religious consciousness" of children.[17]

In one of the two *Relations* that Marie wrote for her Jesuit spiritual directors, she described her childhood experience of watching others at prayer, beginning to imitate them, and then hearing internal "voices" or "interior words," that would lead her, Bremond contended, to short spoken prayers and then "the prayer of quietude" which is a hallmark of mysticism.[18] The point is critical for Bremond: the first gateway to mystical prayer is the child's directness and simplicity, uncluttered by rational considerations and equivocations.

And yet the child knows the purity of suffering, as we saw earlier. This aspect comes out in Bremond's retelling of Madame Martin's "abandonment" of Claude as she committed herself to conventual life. There is a poignancy here, as "she did not

---

Benedictines to avoid imputations of quietism to their order (*Histoire*, VI, 3-9).

15 Though, as Bremond points out, Bossuet picked up the phrase from Claude, having just read the *Vie* of his mother (*Histoire*, VI, 9, and n1). A touch of irony on Claude's part (?).

16 At the very end of his assessment of Marie, though it should be said that he is praising her as a "moralist," that is, an analyst of interior states and their relation to personal holiness (*Histoire*, VI, 173). We are reminded again that what matters for Bremond with mysticism is its role in making people *human and humane*, because all will follow from that.

17. *Histoire*, VI, 13, notes. For discussion of Fénelon's *Treatise*, widely influential in 19th c. America, see Gorday, *François Fénelon*, 46-49. The work of James Bissett Pratt (1875-1944), especially *The Religious Consciousness: A Psychological Study*, 1920, was widely influential ("an excellent work," says Bremond). A student of William James, Pratt emphasized the dynamics of early childhood in religious formation, later was much interested in Buddhism. My hunch is that Loisy put Bremond on to him.

18. The "prayer of quiet" or the "prayer of simple regard" will get careful attention from Bremond only in *Histoire*, IX and XI, especially the latter. Bremond could not quite decide if mystical experience is primarily "busy," i.e., artistically expressive and externalized, or "quiet," i.e., non-expressive and internal. Clearly it is both, but he is still looking for the right way to combine these. A certain kind of "dry" and subtly allusive poetry will be the answer.

leave him because of inconsideration or hardness of heart, nor for the purpose of getting rid of him," nor did she do so in obedience to an illuministic "leading," but rather as a result of "interior appeals" that finally could not be denied. Claude threw fits, tried to get her back, ran away, but in the end, after he also became a monk, she was able to say to him, "See, it was all to your good; your 'abandonment' turned out to be advantageous." Marie suffered mightily as well; her decision not to give him a parting caress was agonized, so that she wondered for a long time: "Was she not mistaken, victim of an egoistical illusion and an unregulated fervor?"[19] The second gateway to mystical prayer is the acknowledgment, always with a remnant of painful ambiguity, of painful choices leading to loss as well as gain. Bremond admitted that, had he been her spiritual advisor, he would have counseled her not to abandon her son, but then he realized that a heavenly calling must take precedence over earthly cares, and that there is ultimately an insoluble quality to these cases of conscience. Mystical prayer requires pathos.[20]

And then Bremond emphasized the ways in which Madame Martin grew from childhood into a well-balanced, sensible, unscrupulous sort of person, one who could be honest about her shortcomings without engaging in self-punishment. She could mix devotion with play, always retaining a certain gaiety and lightheartedness in her approach to the spiritual life. This is where he describes her femininity as a great asset, so that, as he says, "her style has not taken the veil."[21] We are reminded of Mère Agnès at Port-Royal here, but with a larger element of sparkle, a twinkle in the eye, so that with charm or vivacity Marie argued or pleaded or cajoled with an "involuntary coquetry" that disarmed those who disagreed with her.[22] Bremond was fascinated by her ability to mix melancholy with "great jubilations for God," to describe her surroundings with delicious detail, to combine holiness with good sense. "She takes men and saints as they are: she renders full justice to their virtues, and sweetly resigns herself to their miseries." Common sense, practicality, no self-pity or brooding over insults, etc. Let us say, then, that the third gateway to mystical prayer is an inner life largely unencumbered by scrupulous self-absorption.[23]

19. *Histoire*, VI, 58–59. One senses that in the vividness of his descriptions here Bremond was picking up on what he loved so well in Charles Dickens, the depiction of childhood anguish and the long-term devastations that result.

20. There is a strange detail. Bremond references one contemporary of Marie's, who mentioned that she "laughed" as she turned young Claude away from the convent, whose doors he had been assaulting. An "infinitely dolorous" laugh, said Bremond (ibid., 71n). Indeed.

21. "Except for some inevitable contaminations, Marie of the Incarnation remained what she was as Madame Martin. She did not try to change her voice, or diminish her freshness, or reverse her tone or mannerisms with the somewhat faded unction of a certain kind of devout literature" (ibid., 105).

22. Bremond uses phrases like "smiling malice" and the "venial sin of impertinence" to describe what we today would call her "operating style" (e.g., ibid., 107).

23. That being said, Bremond was at pains to show that she was *self-aware*, but not *self-satisfied*. She could recognize the pridefulness of some of her activity, be repentant, but not be immobilized thereby (ibid., 110n2).

Then came "mystical transports," "ecstasies," "ravishings," in which she experienced "a great door opening," followed by a stable internal disposition consisting of "states of tendency, of attention, which become in turn . . . possession and privation." This is, says Bremond, "an inquietude, which stimulates without weakening, these presentiments, this attentiveness." There we have the "surest index for distinguishing true contemplatives from false or mediocre ones, when they are quickly persuaded that they have attained the seventh heaven."[24] So, actual mystical prayer occupies an "intermediate region" where it is hard to distinguish a mystical state, that is, an interiorly stable state of intuitive awareness of the divine Presence, from ordinarily graced activity.[25] At this point, says Bremond in a critical statement, mystics begin to be like poets, and there is a likeness to the playfulness of childhood. The fourth gateway thus is the gift of a poetic consciousness, by which the individual can abide in a simultaneous awareness of the co-presence of heaven and earth, can glimpse signs of the invisible behind the visible.

Indeed, in the introduction to *Histoire*, VI, Bremond made it clear that the language of the mystics has nothing in common with our ordinarily "abstract, conceptual, desperately mediate" use of language, but rather is "experience-immediate," and is based on "impression, contact, a sentiment of presence, intuition." The "natural sense" of language is "adapted" and "transposed," so that contemplatives must he studied as poets are studied. What separates poetry from prose is its different sense of what is "real."[26] As an example, he referred to the "lights" that Marie claimed to discern in her mystical experiences; one must not think, he averred, that these "lights" had notional content of any kind (i.e., they are not "revelations"), contrary to the ordinary connotations of the word, but rather they emphasize the living, real *contact* that Marie had with God.[27]

Bremond went on at some length thus in a number of passages to highlight this claim that mystical language is a kind of poetry, where individual words somehow *convey* experience without pretending as such to *describe* it, or, certainly, to conceptualize it. Referring to the non-rational character of mystical experience, he contended that "we should admit the prodigious contradiction that we profane people work on the mystics. Willy-nilly, we reduce them to our measure, we place them in the intellectual, sentimental, literary order, which not only is not theirs, but which, in some degree, is the negation of their own order. This is to confuse the genius with the orthography."[28] So we might say that the fifth gateway to mystical prayer is the capacity

---

24. Ibid., 24–25, 26–28. Bremond scolds Dom Martin for being too preoccupied with the *theology* of his mother's experiences here, rather than the *experience*.

25. Marie spoke of an "impression" that occurs, beyond all affectivity or intellection, in the contact with God, which Bremond (combining with Francis de Sales) locates in "the sacred zone" at the "center or apex of the soul" (cited ibid., 37).

26. Ibid., i–ii.

27. Ibid., 32n2.

28. Ibid., 46.

for an experience-near poetic consciousness that can express itself with a sufficiently compelling and proper language. At one point, Bremond says that Marie's speech is a form of inspired *singing*.

At this point Bremond had made two advances on his treatment of the nature of mysticism in the "Appendix" to *Histoire*, II. First, there is the focus on mystical *language*, not just mystical inspiration, as something analogous to poetry. And, secondly, we see him ratcheting up the claim that conscious intellectual activity on the part of the subject is anathema to mystical intuition, yet simultaneously qualifying that claim, perhaps in response to concerns voiced by Blondel, who was about to produce his own definitive essay on mysticism. In fact, mystics do learn something about God from their experience, although that "something" is elusive and paradoxical.

In the first two years of her time with the Ursulines Marie went through an exceedingly difficult time, all detailed in the two *Relations*. Out of that struggle came her theoretical reflection on the mystical life. The first part, she said, is the "agony and death of the powers," by which she meant the putting down of the intellect, which is the enemy of interior silence and repose.[29] The result is that mystics appear to be asleep, when in fact they are in a state more like what we would call "suspended animation," though marked by an amorously (because God is love) "playful" mental posture, waiting with ardor for God to appear.[30] She also described this state as a "strange agony," where all of the mystic's flaws are thrown into relief. Analogies to the beginning of a love-relationship, with flirtation, uncertainties, exposures, the awakening of desire, etc., are obvious, though again with a childlike directness and simplicity. The intellect, she said, is "dragged along" in all of this, reluctant but obedient. One is also struck by the element of risk, of daring experiment, in the process as well.

Then came what she called "the subterranean life of the powers during contemplation," which designates the way in which the intellect will be fueled intuitively for a descriptive language that surpasses intellect.[31] She says that she is "instructed," although nothing is learned, that she experiences "light" when, in fact, all is darkness, etc. Bremond, with an image from Théophile Gautier, compared her to a blind person

---

29. Ibid., 139–42.

30. Ibid., 142–43. After citing Marie's description of her "ligature," or state of being, as it were (*comme*), "suspended and rendered entirely incapable of proper and ordinary operations," Bremond goes on to describe this state as the "curious *psychologie*" of "the knowledge of one's nothingness." We are thus reminded that phrases such as "self-annihilation," etc., usually refer to the suspension of all other attention or orientation to the point of induced paralysis, the passivity, the pure receptivity, of the mystical state.

31. Ibid., 146. Bremond cited Claude's question to his mother: how does the constant object of your contemplations represent itself to you? She referred then to "impressions in the imagination" (*impressions imaginaires*) which are subsequently "unstably changed intellectually" (*incontinent changées en intellectuelles*). Marie saw here the process by which imagination clothes with a "body" that which surpasses sense, so that it can occupy a "space" accessible to sensory modes of perception. Claude perspicuously saw here exactly what St. Thomas said of mystical language, that it proceeds from the imagination, so that the intellect can then work on it (ibid., 152–53).

who is given a sense of what "red" and "green" mean, though having no natural eyes with which to see them. Thus, one "sees" the Incarnate Word and the Trinity, but all is ineffable and must be expressed symbolically. Furthermore, having made contact with the source of all holiness, the mystic, empowered for sanctification, now begins to be energized for the moral life, as the subterranean resurfaces. The intellect, that which is "natural," having been bypassed in the suspension of powers, is brought back into play for a new, supernaturally transformed, life of freedom, not unlike Bremond's claim that Jesuit asceticism, when modified by a more mystical approach, freed the natural powers of the individual for their "proper creativity." The final result, moreover, in terms of the theory of mysticism, is that the inner person remains united with God (invisible, stable, steady-state internally) while the outward person, the empirical "self," interacts in constant fluctuation with the external environment, subject to all of its vicissitudes.

And a Word from Blondel

For Bremond, therefore, what marks the true mystic is the willingness of the individual to enter into the process of giving up the "powers" in order to regain them on a different basis, having intuitively encountered the God who is Love-dwelling-in-darkness (beyond the reach of language and thus emotionally crucifying) in the process. The result is that the mystic "sees" and "hears" in ways much like those of poets. The polemical edge here: those who insist on a "rational" approach to reality never grasp what is "real," but always exist in idolatries of their own making.

Precisely, said Blondel. Potential idolatry is always the issue. What he would insist on, and never stop jabbing at Bremond about, however, is that the "irrationalism" of poetic inspiration can be just as vulnerable to fascism as a hyper-rationality, and thus everything will depend on the conscious "distillate" and consequent moral action, including the intellectual and philosophical integrity, that flow from the mystical experience. True must be critically separated from false, as Blondel elaborately argued in 1924, in "Le problème de la mystique."[32] A true mysticism, said Blondel, is never "the exaltation of blind forces," the detection of which is the philosopher's task, so that intellect and will are properly united in "action" by the gift of a supernatural knowledge.[33] This is why it was so important, in his last word on Marie, for Bremond to say that her spirituality of direct experience produced "conviction," out of which she spent the balance of her life in the famous Canada missions, at Quebec, contributing to

---

32. "True mysticism may be illogical, but never a-logical," cited by Kerlin, "Maurice Blondel," 64–65. Blondel was preoccupied as well with distinguishing his own kind of prayerful philosophizing, where faith and reason collaborate, from Maritain's dogmatic separation of the two.

33. See now the comprehensive essay of Marxer, "Entre religion and métaphysique," who explores Blondel's thinking about mysticism in relation to his dialogue with other Modernist figures, making the formulation of christology the decisive point of differentiation.

the rise of a new civilization. The process of first-passive-then-active-and-expressive comprises, once suitably critiqued, all of the "gateway" elements described above. Or, at least, so said the "French Teresa."

One noteworthy aspect of his characterization of Marie, moreover, is that Bremond never described her as an obsessively tortured individual—unlike her son Claude, who would later undergo intense mortifications and penances—despite the fact that at one point she considered the "impossible supposition" that God had damned her, though she would love God forever. She thus illustrated the possibility of being in great spiritual pain with an aching sense of abandonment, yet without turning that consciousness into self-punishment.[34]

Even Claude came out in a good place, said Bremond, going on to become an exemplary Benedictine abbot, always marked by the human foibles and frailties that his biographer Martène was not afraid to record, but eventually, with Mabillon and others, becoming a great exponent of the Maurist tradition of devout scholarship. His earlier mental illness seems to have been a prelude to a gracious wisdom in spiritual direction, while Martène as his disciple and biographer modeled the same commonsense ability to distinguish what was of "nature" and what is of "grace" in his hero's actions. What one of Edmonde Martène's later critics described as "puerilities" in some of his narrative about Claude seemed to Bremond to be just the human stuff that makes grace real and concrete in the fabric of a life. Otherwise, said Bremond, we get nothing but "fairy-tales" about the saints. He concluded his account of these two Benedictines with the words used in that Order's festal calendar of prayer: "Sancti Claudi et Edmunde, orate pro nobis"![35]

The "Large Crowd"

Now Bremond's task, as he saw it, was to show that this mystical spirituality was not a thing of elites, but the experience of a wide range of seventeenth-century folk, including rich and poor, lay and clerical, peasant and aristocrat, Norman, and Breton, and Provençal, and Auvergnat, and Burgundian, men and women, especially women. This he does in the second part of *Histoire*, VI, with a gallery, a panoply, the "great crowd" of Revelation 19:6 (Hebrews 12:1, as well), a "bizarre construct" of "wandering

---

34. The passages in her *Relation of 1654* where she describes her process with the "impossible supposition" could do with some psychological analysis (*Marie of the Incarnation*, 141–47). My reading is that as she considers her status as "the lowest, most debased creature in the world," utterly deserving of Hell, and yet determined to love God nonetheless, she is simultaneously heartened not just by the thought of God's mercy, but also (with a twinkle?) by the thought of losing the "friendship" with God that she presently enjoys. She is like Job on his dunghill, yes, but the memory of so many lovely moments with God, the divine Lover, is always foremost! Very feminine, Bremond would have said.

35. Ibid., 226. My summary of this chapter hardly does justice to the amount of energy Bremond poured into appreciating the erudite and devout Benedictines of Saint-Maur. Some of this was an anticipation of his later treatment of the Rancé-Mabillon dialogue about the spiritual value of humanistic learning in *L'abbé Tempête*.

musicians,"³⁶ a whole range of characters, all of whom exemplify aspects of mystical spirituality, while not enlarging or augmenting it. Their stories are filled with amusing anecdote, colorful episodes, some outrageous incidents, strange quirks and all manner of eccentricity. A whole range of dusty biographies and spiritual writings in obscure libraries came to Bremond's assistance here, so that he had a real sense that he was resurrecting a rich, but undeservedly forgotten, past. He was beginning to do what we have come to call "social history" or the history of manners.

Bremond was also beginning to show signs of becoming more familiar with attractive aspects of William James's *The Varieties of Religious Experience.* Just as James painted broad-brush dimensions of religious experience by means of leapfrogging from one anecdotal account to another, often citing the most "purple" passages from personal testimonials of all kinds, Bremond does much the same with his French characters. The idea is that all of these instances illustrate this-or-that distinctive property of a hypothesized, or inductively derived, mode of religiosity. Both James and Bremond are concerned primarily with the lived reality, the practice, the experience, of distinctive religious types, not the "notional" theology from which they operate and by means of which they explain themselves. Both authors claim to see intimations of a Presence locked into impossible language: Bremond cites James's letter to J. B. Pratt, in which the pragmatic philosopher ascribes to religious experience "something familiar, a distant air that sings in the caves of my memory, but that I can't identify," and to J. H. Leuba he says that "there is a feeling in me that awakens when I hear others speak of this experience [which he has not had himself]." This is the "mystical germ," says Bremond, something "very common" and "found in all simple believers."³⁷ And now he sets out to show that.

He starts out by sketching the life and writing of Jean Bernières (1602–1659), a Norman layman, government official and man of deep piety. His writing was mediocre, but became widely popular, his spirituality was utterly Bérullian, he was anti-Jansenist (like all of the others), and he had a following of disciples.

There is the Norman priest Jean-Chrysostome (1594–1646), well known from Henri-Marie Boudon's (1624–1702) biography. Jean-Chrysostome spoke the language of "pure love" in a way that leads straight to Madame Guyon a little later. And then Boudon's own history is celebrated in a richly detailed narrative full of ecclesiastical politics and calamities. Many, many personalities pass through the narrative, which reads like a novel. Boudon's mystical spirituality carried him through his toils and troubles.

There is a section on the "flamboyant mystics" and the "mystics of silence," mostly women in religious orders. Jeanne de Matel (1569–1670) is a very flamboyant

---

36. *Histoire*, VI, iii–iv.

37. Ibid., ii–iii. "In reality, we are all mystics, at least potentially, just as we are all poets, and for the same reason." A fundamental difference between James and Bremond, of course, is that James was constructing a "typology," while Bremond was interested in a "development."

character, devout, earthy, passionate, deeply mystical. Marguerite Romanet (d. 1663) and Catherine Ranquet (1602–1651) and Antoinette de Jésus (d. 1678) receive sympathetic treatment. Bremond was often using a single source here, and his characters appear in vignettes based on the available material. There is a cinematic quality about the way that he passes from one character to the next, usually with generous citations of primary passages illustrative of their devotion. The point that he always comes back to is their musical, lyrical, poetic quality of expression along with its associated "childlike" quality.

His section on "mystical France" is then a kaleidoscopic overview of the whole country, region-by-region, with brief illustrative examples of mystics in each area. Included are Flanders, Picardy, Champagne, Lorraine, the Paris area, Franche-Comté, Burgundy, the Lyonnais, Auvergne, Savoy, Dauphiné, Comtat, Provence, Languedoc, Guyenne, and Périgord! There is little more than a list of names with passing comments, but all with indications of bibliographical sources. Bremond makes it clear that he is resurrecting forgotten sources.

After more than 200 pages of such survey, Bremond presciently concluded volume VI with a more in-depth treatment of a single character, Jean Desmarets (1595–1676). The presentation served two purposes, one thematic and the other political. The first is that Desmarets illustrated, in a particularly vivid way through his literary productions, the marriage of devout humanism with artistic expression that is the hallmark of mystical spirituality. But, second, Desmarets was a founder of the Académie française in the time of Louis XIII, the first holder of Seat 4, and first chancellor. It must be no accident that Bremond concluded volume VI in 1922 with just such a figure, precisely as his own candidature for the Académie was showing the first signs of crystallizing.

The Sieur de Saint-Sorlin, Desmarets—both man of letters and man of action—was an accomplished dramatist, poet, effective minister under Richelieu, spiritual writer and polemicist against Port-Royal. Having led a libertine life in his youth, he experienced conversion to a religious perspective largely in the contemplative tradition of Bérulle. Bremond was fascinated most by his composition, the *Délices de l'Esprit*, a long work in the popular dialogue-form, of a "savorous originality," where a contemplative and devout practitioner, Eusèbe, works overtime to convert a skeptical freethinker, Philédon. Calling it "mystical propaganda," Bremond argued that *Délices* is a model exemplification of "the poetry of Christianity," in which the heritage of pagan poetic literature, especially in Seneca, is overshadowed by biblical symbolism as a guide for the inner life. "The excellence of Christian poetry," says Bremond, serves as an entrée to the "tasting of heavenly delights,"[38] where "the disposition to believe"

38. As noted elsewhere, Bremond had a particular fondness for the metaphor of "taste," and for the images of eating and drinking as applied to aesthetic pleasure and for the kind of consciousness that aesthetic pleasure creates. The truth contained in a work of art is somehow metabolized by the recipient. Following Desmarets at one point, he describes the process of reading something in the spirit of love as not a *praelectio*, but a *praelibatio* or *degustatio* (ibid., 465–66).

can be stimulated by the "ladder of [aesthetic] pleasures," and the non-believer can begin to experience "without hardness of heart, without presumption of spirit, and without any sensual interest" the experience of God speaking in "the superior part of the soul." The key idea for Desmarets, is that "it is impossible that an intellect, master of itself, can refuse a truth that the will has already made its own." All of this, Bremond averred, is what "Chateaubriand does later, but is already further down the pike . . . in the place where, with John of the Cross and Surin and Marie of the Incarnation, 'ineffable certitudes' arise in a place beyond reasoning and words."[39]

What is most remarkable, moreover, in Desmarets is the conjunction of the "man of letters and authentic convert," where "the interior life and literature are joined." He created in the *Délices* an elaborate analogy derived from architecture and interior design, wherein the stages of the mystical life are likened to a configuration of rooms, apartments, and furnishings, all of this coordinated with the symbolism of the heavenly city in the Apocalypse. One proceeds through these rooms methodically and in ascending order so as to reach Holy Prayer, where God dwells in the silence of eternity. While admitting a certain element of conceit and exaggeration here,[40] Bremond was stunned by the artistic cleverness and appeal of the analogy.

One wonders: this concurrence of artistic/spiritual expressiveness and its mystical depth with political involvement and leadership: could something of the same blend function in the France of the 1920s? Could membership in the Académie be an instrument? Could it be a counterbalance to the destructive ascendency of the Action Française?

"Positioning" for the Académie

Sure enough, in a letter to Blondel in the spring of 1922 Bremond indicated that Barrès and others were urging him to stand for the seat at the Académie recently vacated by the death of Duchesne. He was consumed with hesitation because of the "purgatory" involved in campaigning, and there is the possibility of looking like a fool.[41] Within a week, moreover, he had convinced himself that the whole process would be insufferable, that he would be "a pitiful figure in the mêlée," given that others were already hot on the trail.[42] But by mid-summer he had changed his mind. Barrès, that "unquiet nature," had assured him that his chances were excellent, Henri Bergson had indicated

---

39. Ibid., 445–50, 465 . He refers to Desmarets as the "Plato of Richelieu," but also as seduced by the false pleasures of the world (ibid., 453). At one point, Bremond cleverly describes the dialogue between Eusèbe and Philédon as one in which they agree that the important thing is "not to believe, but to 'feel' and to love" (ibid., 463). But the question of the object of that love remains open.

40. Ibid., 518. "Some fragile soldering" in constructing the analogy, Bremond thought, yet "a simple poetic artifice, destined to render more attractive the exposition of the common doctrine."

41. Bremond to Blondel, May 2, 1922 (BB, III, 32). As noted by Blanchet (BB, III, 33n1), he discusses the whole history in *Histoire d'une mise à l'Index*, 248–54.

42. Bremond to Blondel, May 10, 1922 (BB, III, 36).

that he considered Bremond a "born philosopher,"[43] and Alfred Baudrillart was signaling strong support.[44] And, coincidentally, Charles Maurras had also announced that he was running for a seat, Maurras who "exasperates and wearies people," for whom "several will vote out of fear [since] the A.F. has become a bureau of defamation, an agency of terrorism."[45] No question, he will run. By October, he was in Paris, staying at 7 de la rue Méchain, an apartment right above the home of a friend, the abbé Arthur Mugnier,[46] a hospitable ally, himself a fixture and a bit of an *arbiter elegantiae* in the Parisian literary salons. Mugnier would open doors and grease wheels.

In the meantime, Blondel had indicated to Bremond that he was doing some serious thinking once again about the nature of mystical experience. After expressing great enthusiasm for *Histoire*, VI, Blondel homed in on the issue of the role of thinking, of intellection, in mystical prayer. He began to sound Bremond out on the question of "the normal conditions of our mental activity, insofar as they are preparatory to, and concomitant of, the mystical life and infused contemplation." He framed the question as one of exploring the nature of the Spirit-bestowed gifts of wisdom and understanding, wondering about these in relation to mystical experience, and then by implication linking them to Newman's famous epitaph, "ex umbris et imaginibus," that is "from shadows and images [into the truth]."[47] The implied question to Bremond was: how do you tie these together?

In his response Bremond did an end run by means of a speculative concept with a long history, but popularized by Francis de Sales, namely, the "fine point of the soul" as the place of divine-human encounter. Mystical experience as it occurs at this location takes the form of an *amor complacentiae, a* desire to be well-pleasing to God—that, and nothing but that, pure and simple, says Bremond. Everything comes back to the cultivating of the fine point, where the "true me" is both actively oriented toward the unique good, but at the same time is equally passive, since the unique good is the soliciting source. Bérulle and Condren emphasize that the "fine point" operates

---

43. Initially Bremond was enthusiastic about Bergson's support and welcomed Bergson's likening of his ideas about the intuitive nature of mystical experience to his own theories. See Bremond to Loisy, November 4, 1921 (Bernard-Maître, *Lettres*, 50). This will change later, as he and Loisy became more critical of Bergson.

44. Chauvin relays the information from Baudrillart's notebooks that he had become a supporter, though a somewhat reluctant one, of Bremond. He makes the saints human as well as divine, thought Baudrillart drily (*Petite Vie*, 87).

45. Bremond to Blondel, July 6, 1922 (BB, III, 39–40).

46. Bremond to Blondel, October 30, 1922 (BB, III, 41). Mugnier (1853–1944) was the personification of the colorful, witty, high society priest litterateur of the era. Having himself been disciplined for Modernist ideas, hostile to Action Française, he lived privately as a kind of confidant and confessor to the rich and famous, always supportive of artistic endeavors. Chauvin indicates that Mugnier knew well Jean Cocteau, Paul Valéry, Paul Claudel, and even Marcel Proust (*Petite Vie*, 85). Excerpts from his famous journals have been published as Arthur Mugnier, *Journal de l'abbé Mugnier (1879–1939)*. There are many amusing references to table-talk, epigrams and *bons mots* with Bremond and others.

47. Blondel to Bremond, January 8, 1923 (BB, III, 49).

1922–23: First Signs of Integration

religiously, because everything is from God, while nothing is from the human recipient—and *in this sense the human recipient is nothing*. As with Fénelon, self-love is the only obstacle.[48] The question of knowledge thus hung in abeyance. Blondel indicated that he had been discussing the matter, i.e., of mystical knowledge, with the Dominican Thomist Garrigou-Lagrange, pleading that "supernatural contemplation is not false hair added on like a wig, but the luxuriance and actuation of the highest powers of the soul." And then he added puckishly, "I was going to say, of the *understanding*: but you restrict yourself to interpreting this term in the discursive sense. I remain a little grieved about that."[49]

It appears that both men were preparing their essays for the 1923 Pascal celebration, and Bremond had the added pressure of knowing that his performance might be critical to his candidature for the Académie, since académiciens, some of them avid Pascalians, would certainly be reading and assessing his work. Blondel, we may recall, would passionately argue the case for a renewed, purified exercise of the intellect for Pascal after his conversion, while for Bremond Pascal's intellect was purely secondary, and ultimately inconsequential, to the purity, or lack thereof, in his conversion experiences. The two continued to spar before, during and after Bremond's Clermont presentation in July, Blondel especially working to maintain a light, playful spirit in their interaction.

And then came an exchange that was, I believe a wake-up call for Bremond, a clear indication that if he did not take more seriously Blondel's call for a "real" knowledge accruing from mystical experience—that is, a knowledge which is truly a "knowledge"—he would find himself in genuine trouble. The communication came from Jacques Maritain, well-known Thomist philosopher and writer, who had developed of late a strong interest in mystical spirituality and a strong interest also in the creative arts. Blondel and Bremond had, of course, known of Maritain's work for a long time, were largely disdainful, and especially so because of Maritain's well-known association, at this stage of his career, with Action Française.

Maritain wrote because he had been stirred by Bremond's view of Pascal. Addressing him as "monsieur l'abbé et cher ennemi," Maritain approved of Bremond's dismissal of Pascal's spirituality (at least as Maritain read Bremond), but then went on at length to accuse both him and Blondel of confusing the natural and supernatural orders, a confusion in which Blondel, he says, clumsily equates mystical knowledge with a "philosophical counterfeit."[50] Mystical knowledge, insisted Maritain, is not *at all* available to human beings in the natural order, period. The supernatural knowledge vouchsafed to the true mystics is a "despoliation and a nudity," thus utterly transcendent, beyond the highest metaphysic. St. John of the Cross, insisted Maritain, is best

---

48. I am summarizing from Bremond to Blondel, January 1923. The exact date lacking, but certainly after Blondel's preceding letter (BB, III, 51–52).

49. Blondel to Bremond, January 12, 1923 (BB, III, 55).

50. Blanchet prints the note along with Bremond to Blondel, September 1923 (BB, III, 73–76).

understood through the eyes of St. Thomas, where mystical experience is reserved only for the few who have already passed through all of the normal graces given to the baptized. There is no greater danger to true mysticism than that of *naturalizing* it by means of a philosophical exposition as Blondel does. Save yourself, urged Maritain finally, and after lengthy exhortation, from that mistake. Bremond quickly passed the note to Blondel for comment.

Blondel responded with a communication composed for Bremond, but meant to be shared with Maritain.[51] What is Maritain afraid of? he asked. He, Blondel, shares the desire to avoid confusing the natural and the supernatural. He then proceeds to his own argument, which, of course, quickly becomes a highly nuanced wrestling match. The essence, however, is clear and is already presupposed in the image cited just above, where Blondel says that it is a mistake to picture the supernatural operating *extrinsically* on the natural, i.e., like putting a wig on a bald head, or, as he says here, seen as a "pedagogical and orthopedic garment" alien to the human mode of knowing and acting. Supernature must not be conceived as a "contra-nature," which in fact is what Maritain does. On the contrary, argues Blondel, "the contemporary masters of the ascetical and mystical life return more and more to the traditional idea that the highest states of union are the blossoming and prolonging of the initial graces of piety," for, otherwise, "the psychology of the saint is totally excentric to that of a normal human being." He attacks remorselessly the idea that normal and natural human thinking has to be suspended for supernatural inspiration to operate.

In fact, says Blondel, in "real" knowledge we cooperate with God, since the goal of God's redemptive work is not to superimpose something alien on human nature, but rather to free human nature from its bondage in order for true creativity to begin. Supernatural knowledge, says Blondel, is the knowledge that God is love, and this knowledge cannot be "naturalized" in any way, nor can its operation in the mystic be naturalized when it manifests as the "real" knowledge grounded in a living relationship. In fact, it is this knowledge that fortifies the believer against all presumptuous claims on the part of the natural, science included. The working intellect is enlarged and empowered by such knowledge, a knowledge that cannot be acquired otherwise than from intimacy with God. To think otherwise is to make Christianity inhuman.

Actually, essays by Blondel in 1924 for a collection on mysticism done in *La nouvelle Journée*, and in 1925 in response to Jean Baruzi's thesis about mystical knowledge in John of the Cross, add little more to the argument.[52] His main concern was to walk a narrow line between a "naturalist" interpretation of mysticism that reduces it to psychology, and a "supernaturalist" that runs the risk of making it inhuman as well

---

51. Included with Blondel to Bremond, September 20, 1923 (BB, III, 79–89).

52. See Marxer, "Entre religion et métaphysique," 267–72, also Trémolières, "Foi mystique et raison critique," 60–62. Baruzi had argued that the mystic—in this case, John of the Cross—breaks free from all concrete embodiments and images in order to arrive at a state of "pure knowing" which is completely metaphysical. No, said, Blondel, for that is utterly inhuman, contrary to the nature of love itself, which requires an ontology of concreteness.

as inaccessible to ordinary modes of understanding. In the final analysis, asserted Bremond, all natural knowledge is a bare openness to the transcendent, a prepared readiness, so that in the passivity of waiting, an *afference*, a penetration, can occur, the expression of which will be metaphor and symbol with *some degree* of "real," not merely figurative, content.[53]

For Bremond, now down with the first signs of arteriosclerosis, and consumed with campaign-visiting for the Académie, it all came down to two things: first poetry, and then, second, getting ready for his induction address, should he be elected, on Duchesne. He says to Blondel: my effort to understand mystical experience is the effort now to understand the poetic experience as analogous to the mystical, to grasp their differences as well as their shared grasp of the "real." Of Blondel's "real" knowledge and of poetic knowledge, he says that "the interior mechanism that puts into motion these two knowledges would be identical with the natural mechanism that comes into play in mystical experience. There is a difference of intention, and still more of object, and more of a practical orientation, this last elevating us and steering us in the direction of holiness." What is "real" in this is "a contact between the soul—my own—and God." This is "the most fugitive of all knowledge, vaguely felt."[54]

Romanticism and Poetry

In September 1923, Bremond indicated that he had begun a technical study of the dynamics of classical versification in the history of French poetry, specifically of the use of the eleven-syllable "Alexandrine" line—three anapests followed by an iamb—and its derivative forms. In examining Victor Hugo's practice, for instance, he was entering into the current literary debates about the virtues of "classical" versus "romantic" prosody, as well as differences of opinion about prose versus poetry as vehicles of "melodious" expression.[55] This study would come to fruition in the coming year with the publication of *Les Deux Musiques de la Prose*, but for the moment he was simply letting Blondel see how his focus was evolving.

More proximately, Bloud et Gay came out with his collection of essays on romanticism, *Pour le romantisme*, which is a gathering of pieces old and new on Sainte-Beuve, Walter Scott, Lamennais, Barrès and, most significantly, the académicien Nicolas Boileau (1636–1711), whose *L'Art poétique*, championed by modern exponents like Ferdinand Brunetière, was considered to be the ultimate authority for classical principles of versification in French culture. As noted earlier, Bremond argued vociferously that there had been enough silly idolatry of Boileau in the form of rigid adherence to mechanical rules of composition. But, in an "all-cards-on-the-table"

---

53. Summaries of these essays and discussion in Blanchette, *Maurice Blondel*, 305–21.

54. Bremond to Blondel, end of September 1923 (BB, III, 91–92) and Bremond to Blondel, October 1923 (BB, III, 94–95).

55. BB, III, 92.

manner in the volume's introduction, he called for a renewed Catholic romanticism in current poetry, where a robust freedom of expression, of disquietude even to the point of "anarchy," could reflect the fact that poetic/romantic experience and mysticism, while not being identical, reveal that the inspiration of the poet is the first step on the ladder that opens to grace.[56]

The question now as he began to prepare for his potential Académie address was how hard to push in the face of certain opposition, much of it anti-Modernist and anti-romantic in spirit.[57] Like any scholar faced with the need to shrink his goals and methods into the space of a popular address, he had to find a way to articulate an essence and some basic principles. He had the further challenge, moreover, of piggy-backing his own project onto that of an esteemed predecessor. As he confided to Blondel, he had decided to start with the fact that Louis Duchesne was formed in a generation of church historians not yet troubled by philosophical questionings such as those of Loisy. This generation had no need, yet, for the kind of synthesis that Blondel has championed. Thus, his, Bremond's, initial impulse was to come out strongly in favor of the work of the Modernists. He wonders how Blondel might see that?[58]

Blondel waffled just a bit in response, revealing the delicacy of the situation. He made it clear that he did not want his work to be associated with that of Loisy, though he admitted, yes, Duchesne worked in a less complex era of criticism.[59] As the discussion continued, Bremond contended that Duchesne rightly understood the humanity of church history with all of its foibles, but that he lacked a way of uniting historical perspective as a science with a sense of the living Christ at work in the totality. He noted Blondel's claim that history cannot be a "separated science," which would become an extrinsicism once again, but must grapple with the inner life of that which it studies. Duchesne had a sense of this, but couldn't develop it.[60] Blondel agreed that the problem in most church histories is that the "empirical and notional" is taken for the "real," and "historicism" is the result. He urged Bremond to adopt a position in which the extrinsic and triumphalist history of Bossuet and the historicism of Loisy are both rejected in favor of the "interior, eternal, mystical face" as the true driving

---

56. *Pour le romantisme*, ix–x. Here he levels a shot against the current "neo-classicists and neo-rationalists," and thus "anti-mystics," who call for a resurgence of the authority of Boileau. His target is Charles Maurras, Jacques Maritain and their allies.

57. Indeed, criticism of *Pour le romantisme* came pouring in from traditionalist critics, such as Paul Souday, who would become a major opponent in the debate over "pure poetry." See Bremond's notes to Blondel of late January to mid-February 1924 (BB, III, 129–34). This was all happening in the midst of a renewed flap about whether Bremond's *Histoire* would be put on the Index. It turned out to be much ado about nothing (list of correspondence and comment by Blanchet, BB, III, 132–34). Involved as well were efforts on the part of Bremond's partisans to get the judgment on *Sainte Chantal* reversed.

58. Bremond to Blondel, October 1923 (BB, III, 94–95).

59. Blondel to Bremond, October 26, 1923 (BB, III, 96). Duchesne was a *simpliste* in his use of critical method, said Blondel.

60. Bremond to Blondel, November 13, 1923 (BB, III, 99–102).

force in the history of the church.[61] As Bremond submitted revisions of his drafts to Blondel, the latter replied with detailed line-by-line critique that was enthusiastic, but cautious about Duchesne's churchly loyalty and scholarship, the mistreatment that he had received, and the work yet to be done. Stay the course, insisted Blondel, but go light on the irony![62]

Actually, Blondel was a bit sarcastic about the whole process of walking on eggshells, with all of the maneuvering to avoid ecclesiastical discipline on the one hand, and secular ridicule on the other.[63] Take Duchesne out of the whole brouhaha about Modernism! said Blondel. I think that he was somewhat insensitive to Bremond's position as a priest, versus his own as a layman, but he was also naively unattuned to the fact that in championing the mystical/poetic Bremond had created not just an aesthetic (as Blondel tended to see it) but a political entity as well. The forces that would oppose Bremond in the Académie were politicized through and through, associated with the right-wing and reactionary tendencies in French society that had aligned with Catholic conservatism. Right down to his election and induction at the Académie Bremond was commenting anxiously on Maurassian-influenced publications and individuals, whom he imagined to be ganged-up on him.

Probably Blondel's more-or-less ultimate word to Bremond as the election approached was fair, however: exercise "critical sincerity . . . with the submission of a child."[64] We say to people, "just be yourself," to mean much the same thing, though (probably) without the mystical edge implied by Blondel. He also could not resist the urge to say wisely to Bremond one more time: do not take the element of "understanding," the *donum intelligentiae* informed by grace, in mystical experience pejoratively, for then you set yourself up for attack as a pure irrationalist by the defenders of "reason."[65]

In the meantime, Maurice Barrès suddenly died, thus injecting an element of real poignancy into the flow of events. Bremond had held Barrès in high esteem right to the end (a judgment which history has failed to support). The warmth and eagerness with which Bremond sang Barrès's praises in the obituaries probably reflected the tactical situation in which Bremond found himself at the moment, since Barrès had been his patron with the literary world. Still in all, one cannot forgive Bremond for having written that this man "was the genius of 20th century Catholicism."[66] My sense of it

61. Blondel to Bremond, November 18, 1923 (BB, III, 103).

62. Blondel to Bremond, January 25, 1924; February 9, 1924 (BB, III, 127–28, 134–35).

63. See the whole exhortatory and impatient letter, Blondel to Bremond, February 12, 1924 (BB, III, 139–43). It is an extraordinary attempt on Blondel's part to get Bremond to lift Duchesne (and thus himself!) out of the bloodbath of anti-modernist polemics. Fond hope.

64. Blondel to Bremond, February 17, 1924 (BB, III, 591). He also saluted Bremond's decision to include pointed praise of the spirit and initiatives of the new pope, Pius XI.

65. Blondel to Bremond, March 8, 1924 (BB, III, 149).

66. Chauvin observes drily: "One could not have stated the matter more strongly" (*Petite Vie*, 93). Hogarth's comment that for Bremond "his affection and the charm of the style [in Barrès's novel, *Un*

was that once more Bremond was in a Tyrrell-like position, where friendship trumped all. More considered reflection later always tended to more balanced views.

And so, election and induction at the Académie came and went, congratulations flowed, but so did new challenges. Having won the votes of supporters, secular and sacred, Bremond now had to show that they had not been mistaken. The way to do this was to hasten his master synthesis in *Histoire*, VII and VIII, and to unleash his crusade for "pure poetry and pure prayer." There is no doubt that as an académicien he now had leverage, "clout," that he could count on and that would make people listen.

---

jardin sur l'Oronte] had made him oblivious of Barrès's lapse from Catholic sentiment," is fair enough, though a little starchy (*Henri Bremond*, 128n1). It suggests that where friendship was involved, intelligence went out the window for Bremond. Not true.

14

Interlude and Assessment

THERE IS A SEA change, though certainly not a rupture, in the momentum and spirit of Bremond's work after his accession to the Académie. On the one hand, ecclesiastical standing, while always tenuous, became less of an issue (the church would be most reluctant to censure an académicien), and, on the other, his focus now turned decisively to the secular audience from whom he wished to receive a hearing. His ties with the literary world increased while old theological embroilments either diminished, as with the Modernists, or petrified, as with the Jesuits. His friendship with Blondel, his theological mentor, remained as strong as ever, while the friendship with Loisy intensified. A new scholarly friendship began with an Italian Benedictine, Don Giuseppe De Luca. The field of his interests continued to grow, while his forays into theory or comprehensive reflection became more ambitious. All of these changes registered in the later volumes of the *Histoire*, different in approach from the preceding.

His personal existence was that of a scholarly bachelor, living independently under priestly discipline, in modest circumstances—in other words, that of the "abbé," a secular clergyman without cure, dependent on his own resources to make a living. Bremond wore the traditional soutane with collar and tabs when engaged in ecclesiastical or public functions (as at the Académie induction), otherwise the standard Roman collar and street garb in his daily pursuits. He participated in clerical meetings from time to time, and occasionally functioned liturgically by celebrating Mass or hearing confessions on canonically permitted occasions. But, otherwise he was free to pursue his own projects, mostly his reading and writing, for generating income, his circumstances all, of course, being subject to review with his bishop. Since he was a priest, his publications required the approval of ecclesiastical censors. His main task was to avoid becoming a "scandal" to the church, and the degree to which his work might be in service of the church was a matter of his own particular vocation and productivity.

His cultural and social context as an abbé was something unknown outside of the French ambience. The institution of the abbé began in the seventeenth century as that of an individual in holy orders, living on a benefice, but non-resident. It was ideal for aristocratic sons needing an income, while possessing (normally) some degree of religious commitment, but averse to hard work. Naturally, levels of ecclesiastical discipline with abbés varied considerably. In the eighteenth century the more talented ones became prominent writers, freethinkers, artists, scientists and learned figures of all kinds, especially if they had been trained, possibly as Jesuits or Dominicans, to rigorous standards.[1] In the nineteenth century it was less likely that such clergy would have aristocratic roots, but they usually had private means of some kind supplemented by other sources of income. And, provided that they possessed real professional or social ability, they could be well-respected members in a local cultural scene that often had high regard for intellectual excellence, and that would see them as representative of Catholic religion in the midst of their secular activity. Bremond fit into that group.

He loved his Pyrenees bases at Pau and Arthez-d'Asson, but in Paris he had operated transiently from various more-or-less satisfactory apartments. Then in the first part of 1925, after a train wreck that left him physically unhurt but badly shaken, he looked for a more stable, long-term Parisian home.[2] This would be 16 rue de la Chanoinesse, in a side street by Notre Dame, an exceedingly modest apartment that he described as a dream come true, primarily because of its excellent view of the Cathedral from a roof-terrace. A visitor, a friend from the Société J.-K. Huysmans, described the apartment as being "in an old building, a tiny lodging of a poor student, furnished with a bed, two or three chairs, a stand with wash-basin and water-pot, and a table covered with books and papers."[3] Another friend, Canon Ernest Dimnet, a fellow Newman-scholar, lived close by.[4] The perfect pied-à-terre, we might say, for a scholar who would spend much of his time at the Bibliothèque nationale!

Of course, there was also goodly time for socializing, and this seems to be where, especially among some younger men, a certain amount of "cult" around Bremond began to form. Probably Arthur Mugnier was a catalyst here, since he and Bremond had been meeting at least since the early years of the war, and Mugnier was gifted at creating luncheons where the literati could gossip. These were settings in which Bremond's wittiness shone.

---

1. McManners has a lively, slightly sardonic chapter on this subject (*Church and Society*, I, 647–82).

2. Reported to Blondel, Bremond to Blondel, sometime in March 1925 (BB, III, 194–95). Blanchet includes here an excerpt from Bremond's letter to Monbrun of March 30, 1925, with further details and his ecstatic description of his new apartment. There is also a wonderful photograph of Bremond standing out on the "spacious terrace," looking very pleased in his soutane, while gazing at a buttress of the Cathedral.

3. Descaves, "Henri Bremond." Descaves had been a close associate of Huysmans.

4. Hogarth, basing himself on Dimnet's memoirs, describes Bremond's bookish neighborliness (*Henri Bremond*, 150–51). He would, said Dimnet, wander into the friend's apartment in order to inspect his library. "This worshipper of literary beauty went through books as a hotel-porter goes through a time-table and yet missed nothing."

Mugnier's diary for many of these events confirms a supposition that comes naturally, namely that Bremond had become an important mediating voice in elite artistic society, where lay thinkers and critics, eager to build rapport between Catholicism and modern culture, gathered. Two names in particular stand out. Charles Du Bos (1882–1939), literary critic and essayist, had been a regular attender at least since 1921, and was instrumental in introducing Bremond and Paul Valéry in June 1922. Du Bos would write an important essay on Bremond shortly after the latter's death, in which he would celebrate Bremond's ability to hold up, in the face of widespread modern skepticism and unbelief, the mystics as messengers, in Bremond's words, from "the country of truth," which is the inner life.[5]

Another was Maurice Martin Du Gard (1896–1970), cousin of the better-known novelist and Nobel laureate, Roger Martin Du Gard. Maurice was the founder of the fashionable *Nouvelles Littéraires* in 1922 and its senior editor for many years. He is famous for his *Les Mémorables*, a long series of interview-conversations and ironically-tinged sketches with literary figures, including a number with Bremond.[6] I have made generous use of his book on Bremond, derived from interviews, *De Sainte-Beuve à Fénelon: Henri Bremond*, published in 1927, including a full bibliography of Bremond's work to date. As mentioned, Bremond claimed to be a bit embarrassed (and flattered?) by the adulatory quality of this book, the title of which speaks for itself.

Thanks again to the good offices of Mugnier, a budding poet, Marie Noël, was introduced to Bremond in November 1924: he went on to become strongly and persistently supportive of her devout versifications, a kindness for which she was deeply grateful and for which she memorialized him in 1959. She reports that in her first interview with him, he said, "You have made your communion, I trust! Laughter is an excellent preparation for Communion."[7]—and so on with many such remarks. One may safely say that Bremond had become a secure part of the "scene" by 1924! But his major impact in the world of belles-lettres would come only with the discourse on "pure poetry," delivered to the Académie on October 24, 1925, and then the works in 1926 on pure poetry and pure prayer.

In the meantime, however, the major impact of the volumes of the *Histoire* seems to have been where we would expect it, namely, in ecclesiastical circles, and especially in places where the writing of the lives of the saints was a major preoccupation. One of the libraries that Bremond mined in his researches was the Brussels collection of the mostly Jesuit Bollandist Society, esteemed official hagiographers of the Church, committed to critical methods in their researches for the famous *Acta Sanctorum*,

---

5. Du Bos, "Henri Bremond," 1332–33. For the meeting with Valéry, *Journal, 1921–1923*, 106–8 (entry for June 10, 1922). For an overview of Bremond's influence on Du Bos, see Marxer, "Cette curiosité," 1059–63, who tracks a line of influence from Bremond through Du Bos to Henri de Lubac.

6. These were reissued by Gallimard in 1999, with an introduction by François Nourissier. Martin Du Gard had a colorful career, politically leftist, yet somewhat clouded later by association with Vichy.

7. Noël, "Souvenirs sur l'abbé Bremond," 340. Her recreations of whole conversations with Bremond are priceless.

and thus with a controversial history of unmasking "legends." The current director, Hippolyte Delehaye, had written to Bremond in November 1921 to congratulate him on the historical-critical quality of *Histoire*, I and II, taken as a whole.[8] In fact, the *Analecta Bollandiana*, the official publication of the society, would be steadily positive in its reviews.

But Bernard Joassart, in assessing the range of churchly reviews of the *Histoire*, has argued that critics rarely assessed the work from such a total perspective, since they usually homed in on specific issues, such as genre, style or details of historical fairness. In general, Joassart asserts, Jesuit reviewers, as at *Études*, were positive, most people were charmed, and fundamental issues of the whole nature of the project were not raised. The matter of "style" stirred the old charge of "chameleonism," where Bremond was accused of being, in essence, a constantly moving target as to his own views. Thus, the use of an ironic tone could confuse and then anger some readers. Implicit in this criticism was the genre question, since Bremond seemed to move from "history" to "novel" to "learned exposition" in his mode of presentation. And, of course, the matter of historical accuracy and balance had been posed acutely in the cases of Port-Royal and Ignatius. But the core issue, as Joassart emphasizes, following the opinion of one critic, Paul Peeters, SJ, was the nature of hagiography itself: how does one write the history of a saint who is, after all, a real human being? Joassart picks up a phrase from Goichot, that Bremond was operating on "the frontiers of hagiography."[9]

The issue never goes away, though it is clear that Bremond made progress on it, as Hippolyte Delehaye rightly thought and as many people opined as well. There is the inherent challenge in any kind of biographical writing, where, in most cases, the author attempts to be historically accurate about the central character and his/her virtues and vices, while walking a narrow line between uncritical debunking or idealizing. There is the danger of anachronistic constructions, or the imposition of an ideologically-driven hermeneutic of interpretation (e.g., psychohistory) as well. There is also the danger of disturbing vested interests, as with Olier and the Sulpicians or Ignatius and the Jesuits. Landmines are everywhere, and in the case of the "saints," the problem approaches unmanageability, because the central theme of interest is "holiness" or "a sanctified inner life." As Bremond well realized, if a writer makes a saint too human, he/she runs the risk of a kind of de-sanctification; but to Bremond's everlasting credit, he knew that it was a risk that had to be run spiritually and theologically. Otherwise, as he said, we have fairy-tales and horrible theology. Bremond did not use a "process" terminology, but he implied it. We must see "saints" as people who

---

8. Portions of their correspondence have been published and annotated by Joassart, "Henri Bremond," and then contextualized by the same author in "Réception de l'*Histoire littéraire*."

9. Ibid., 60. The reference is to Goichot's essay, "Henri Bremond: Aux frontières de l'hagiographie," where he underlined Bremond's determination to re-think the notion of "sanctity" in human terms. See also Amadieu, "Mysticisme, modernisme," 107–10, who, following Trémolières's analyses, develops the theme of "naturalized hagiography" as part of the wider problematic of the "naturalizing of the supernatural" in Modernist literary expression, including Bremond's work.

are both deeply flawed but authentically growing in the relationship with God; they are on the way, without being there yet—and here is the catch—though *inwardly* they have been there for a long time, i.e., in *real* contact with God. That is why true saints are also mystics.

Furthermore, there is the question of whether the techniques of literary portraiture, as Bremond used them, are the best instrument for good biography. Henry Hogarth cites a caution voiced by Wilfrid Ward, after reading Bremond's final work on Newman, that "ingenious writing cannot unravel a complex personality, though it may heighten the colours of its apparent contradictions."[10] Ward was pointing to an aesthetic problem, such as wondering if the best of portrait paintings ever really "captures" its subject, when, in fact, it can only "display" its character with an intelligibility sufficient to engage our own world of meaning at a substantive level. Bremond's technique of assembling telling details, coordinating that assemblage with what is otherwise known of the character under consideration, then massaging the whole into a picture, is about as good as it can get. We must be dependent on his intuitive ability to gather the "telling" details. No doubt, Ward would have painted a different picture of Newman!

It seems that the further question of the status of the first six volumes of the *Histoire* precisely as *history* was thus just beginning to arise. Bernard Hours, in the best study of this subject,[11] has noted the reluctance of "scientific" historians to take Bremond's work seriously, but he has argued as well that Bremond was path-breaking here in his experimentation with the *genre* of historiographical writing. Hours cites Michel de Certeau's view that Bremond, in writing a *literary* history had created a work that combined psychology, history, philosophy and theology in a *sui generis* hybrid that was ultimately metaphysical (as *Histoire*, VII and VIII, would show). By utilizing the work of historians such as Picot (history of pious practices as seen in the biographies of saints) and Strowski (history of didactic teaching, as in Francis de Sales), and then creating a synthesis at the level of literary analysis, he was pioneering what would become the "history of the appropriation and reception of a discourse."[12] It was only later, and mostly posthumously for Bremond, that focused evaluation would come, that something like the "inner life" of individuals, or groups, or an epoch, would engage serious historians. Thus, at the point in Bremond's career where we find ourselves, he is a titillating novelty for the general public who have never seen church history written in such an iconoclastic and entertaining way, an attractive exponent of "soul" for the artistic world, and a disturbing challenge for church scholarship.

---

10. Hogarth, *Henri Bremond*, 112. Actually, Hogarth more or less agrees with my comments above. Bremond was accused of being an "impressionist," and Hogarth makes the shrewd observation that Bremond "did not intend to exhaust the subject, but only to record what he saw at the moment." In fact, Bremond was deeper than that, but Hogarth has the right idea.

11. "Les historiens et l'*Histoire littéraire*."

12. Ibid., 192–93.

Perhaps no one has elaborated the context here more comprehensively than has François Trémolières,[13] who has underlined the ways in which Bremond upset the status quo for church historians. As we saw in his discourse of reception at the Académie, Bremond was determined to overcome a kind of "schizophrenia" in Catholic, especially Sulpician, historical scholarship, where critical study was rigidly separated from the teaching of doctrine, in order to absorb, in effect, the new understandings coming from the "science of religion" which had flourished in France since about 1880. But, it should be noted, he operated with a careful technique of merger, keeping a simultaneous eye on church and society. On the one hand, as Trémolières points out, he insisted on appealing to the classical interpretive categories of "ascetical and mystical theology," finessing, for instance, the views of Poulain and Saudreau on the nature of mysticism, but on the other, as a historian his way of approaching church history had the effect of "opening" it to the categories of secular critique, thus to raw experience, on the premise that "nature" and "supernature" must manifest an inner continuity. His way of writing history had the effect of constructing, we might say, a conversation between church and society on the meaning of spiritual experience, in which there is no "outside of the church."[14]

Trémolières has pointed as well to the way in which the Jesuit Order bifurcated after the Dreyfus crisis into conservative and progressive camps, so that, once finally deprived of their position in the public educational system, the progressive side became "a nursery of vocations," thus spawning a character like Bremond, who is committed to historical method but has less of a place within the traditional structures. Jesuit research into spirituality, including mysticism, became his favorite area—particularly because of his English experience—but this was a field increasingly freed from doctrinal control. Then came a kind of "moratorium" for the Jesuits during the war (Teilhard de Chardin is an example), where they were freed for creative work under lay auspices. The net result was that Bremond's interest in prayer could be shaped by a new lay environment in which mysticism, not subject to ecclesiastical control, is for everyone, not just the elite.[15]

Increasingly Bremond's readership would be less and less overtly theological, and it would be more and more non-confessional. The idea of a "literary history of sentiment" is thus a laicized idea for the general public. It is proletarian history, so to speak,

13. The content of this paragraph and the following is mostly from Trémolières, "Situation de Bremond."

14. Trémolières, "Situation de Bremond," 803–4; but see also Trémolières, "Une entreprise 'moderniste,'" where he refers (118) to Bremond's "de-partitioning" of church and society at the price of an "incessant mobility" in his interpretive work, as well as Trémolières, "Bremond et la 'poésie pure,'" 246, followed by Trémolières, "Mystique et église." In all of this, Trémolières carefully distinguishes Bremond's views from those of Loisy, as well as from Duchesne.

15 "Situation de Bremond," 814–20. Trémolières describes the spate of new journals given over to spirituality that appeared in the years just after the war. An example is *La Vie catholique*, started by Francisque Gay, and where Bremond would publish for the rest of his life. Blondel noted this founding in a letter to Bremond of October 2, 1924 (BB, III, 105, and n2).

freed from Catholic dogmatic intellection, on the one hand, but also from the forces of rationalism aligned with conservative and right-wing ideologies on the other. Bremond champions the rebel Fénelon over against Bossuet, the darling of the academic establishment, while he batters Sainte-Beuve's Port-Royal, which is the pride-and-joy of official French historiography, and he exalts the scorned "little people." The poetry and prayer of mystics, embedded in pure love, transcends the sacred/secular distinctions and divisions, but also those of class and aesthetic sophistication.

The early description of Bremond by Joseph de Guibert, in which that authority dubbed Bremond a "romantic," has stood the test of time, although Bremond was careful about using it because of its association with Rousseau, whom he deplored. Trémolières has argued, following Certeau, that Bremond was actually pushing beyond romanticism as such, looking for a way of lifting discourse about the inner life out of its parochial "localization" in the church. Differently stated, he was looking for a way to affirm a core religious experience manifest in countless forms, while being able to step back and critique those forms in terms of their *purity* (his chosen working term) with criteria derived from the forms that he knew and that had formed him. The general public, but especially artistic individuals, sensed this search and resonated with it. With "pure poetry" as his "non-localized" domain of choice, especially after his election to the Académie, he would, while constantly being accused of "chameleonism," become celebrated as (in Cocteau's or Fumet's phrase) the "curé d'art."[16]

Furthermore, as the *Histoire* progressed, Bremond moved closer to psychological analysis of his characters. We have observed his greater use of the work of William James and other Americans on childhood development, as well as occasional reference to Pierre Janet on hysterical phenomena, but also, and most importantly, to the ideas of the psychologist Henri Delacroix (1873–1937), who had published two large works in 1899 and 1908 on the psychological nature of mystical experience. Delacroix saw mystical experience as a product of the repressive effect of Christian morality and doctrine on the psyche, where subconscious agitation is restrained and converted into creative energy. The mystic's interpretation of this eruption of energy, particularly as described in literature, is that she has been invaded by the divine presence and is now morally bound. In other words, "the subconscious serves as the vehicle for an exterior action, for the grace of a transcendent God."

Sophie Houdard has suggested that for Bremond, Delacroix's psychology perfectly undergirded his view that mystical prayer issues in religious genius for individuals

---

16. Trémolières, "Situation de Bremond," 824, 819. The subject here is huge. Verbal portraiture, as well as poetry, can be seen as form of "word-painting," and Bremond clearly resonated with representational art of all kinds. Most recently, Talar "Marriage, Mystical Style" (unpublished), has explored Bremond's art-critical approach in his 1917 pamphlet, *Ste Catherine d'Alexandrie*. Trémolières has often commented on Bremond's "chameleonism," where, for instance, it has the function of the "necessarily approximative character" that he assumed as a historian located between Modernism and traditionalsim, between the sacred and the secular ("Situation de Bremond," 804).

and societies, thus instantiating the operation of grace on nature.[17] The reader may remember Marie of the Incarnation's "morose laughter," and "infinitely sad smile," at abandoning her son, Claude: thus was revealed in the mother, and later in the son, the internal churning of a psychologically describable, *but also* a mystically charged ferment, resulting in a very high level of moral resolve for both, though in different ways.

The net result at this point seems to be that Bremond had created, in a phrase evoked by Trémolières, a kind of "literary modernism," in which literary art becomes the vehicle for the expression of spiritual experience and the primary modern register of religious consciousness, particularly where that literature portrays the mystical experience of saints.[18] Jean-Pierre Jossua has pointed to the subversive aspect of Bremond's use of *sentiment*, a term inevitably provoking of censure, given the traditional fear of "enthusiasm," as an effort to replace doctrinal truth with aesthetic feelings.[19] More precisely, however, what Bremond had done was to create the presumption that the literary expression of a religious experience is a constituent of the experience itself, that it captures and crystallizes, so to speak, the subjective "inner" quality of the experience, thereby making it more palpable, thus more "real." Without the literary expression, the experience would be more inchoate and unfocused; it would be mere "whisperings," so to speak, and not a clear "voice," though "clear" will always be ambiguous, given once again the infinity of God. Blondel would raise questions.

Les Deux Musiques

In fact, Blondel was very pleased when he had a chance to look at Bremond's new essay, *Les deux musiques de la prose*, after it appeared just subsequent to his induction into the Académie.[20] It is Bremond's first shot across the literary bows and is a good example of his ability to mix serious analysis with a playful twist.

He wrote the work, he said, in order to respond to critics who had disapproved of his views in *Pour le romantisme*, especially the depreciation of Boileau. Ecclesiastics accuse him of modernism, while right-wing secularists, like Paul Souday (1869–1929), literary essayist for the *Revue de Paris*, claim that he is simply clerical. The latter complain that Bremond constantly appeals to some mysterious, undefinable quality in poetry. But in the process, retorted Bremond, they deny all poetry, and thus all Christianity, where everything hinges on the ability to "hear" a "rhythm" in what is

---

17. Houdard, "Henri Bremond," 133–34. And see also Gumpper, "La crise moderniste," where Delacroix is treated as apart of the new "psychology of religions" being absorbed by ecclesiastical thinkers in the opening years of the twentieth century.

18. Trémolières picks up on a phrase from Caspar Decurtins, in order to expand the concept of "Modernism" beyond the theses condemned by the anti-Modernist decrees ("Note sur Henri Bremond," 113).

19. Ibid., 107.

20. Blondel to Bremond, June 15, 1924 (BB, III, 162).

being said, the most beautiful, the "sweetest" rhythm being that which is "unheard." This last is where the soul opens outward, and we touch the Infinite.[21]

The body of the essay is taken up with an aesthetic question: the prevalence in French prose of poetry-like rhythmic structures, particularly the eight-syllable phrase or clause that typifies a wide array of classic texts. His purpose is to reject Boileau's rigid separation of prose and poetry. He uses a number of historical examples to illustrate the preeminence of poetic rhythm in prose, but also the wide diversity of opinion on the precise nature of this rhythm, particularly the debates about the so-called "Alexandrine" configuration of emphases in French line-composition. There is a general consensus that this rhythm reflects natural rhythms throughout nature, especially that of human breathing. The Jesuit Castel (1688–1737) related this synchrony of speech rhythms with the sounds of nature, when he argued that all living things make their own sounds, which are a cry from the heart, the "song" that comes from the soul.

Having settled on the eight-syllable structure as the mainstream of the tradition, Bremond claimed that it is reflected in French everyday speech in a multitude of ways. It is through this structure that speech remains embedded in memory, and becomes evocative of reality itself. Children should be taught this early on, so that they do not become rationalizers of texts, asking "What does it mean?" but rather learn to "listen" to the text, so that it resonates with interior life. This is why for children as children belief in God is intuitive, and the progression from logic to rhetoric to verse, drawing ever closer to the real, with humanities as the crown of the curriculum, makes perfectly good sense.

The argument and appeal of *Deux musiques* is thus fairly clear in its provision of an objective ground in poetry and prose for the kind of resonance and evocatory power that Bremond sought to define. That being said, the "unheard" melody of some compositions remained a bit elusive. Bremond was at pains to show that the octosyllabic structure can be quite subtle, indeed, in some texts, but that its presence is essential to the power of the text and what is being expressed there. In due course, Paul Valéry's verse will be the prime illustration, though not quite yet, and though ironically Valéry did not fully agree.

Bremond displayed as well the kinship in his thinking with the Pythagorean-Platonic-Augustinian tradition of deriving metaphysics from the experience of aesthetically/intellectually perceived harmonies. The always open question with Blondel will be that of determining what kind of verbalizable intellection is then possible.[22] He was also anticipating what he would later do in *Histoire*, IX and X, where he will

21. *Les deux musiques*, 107–13.

22. In a communication, Bremond to Blondel, July 29, 1924, Bremond refers to the "hysterical neo-Thomist" view of *intelligence* being advocated by Maritain and others, and contrasts it with "the voracious and Blondelian view" (BB, II, 170). But Blondel threw the ball back to him, Blondel to Bremond, August 2, 1924, by agreeing that mystical knowledge has its "aesthetic, ethical and metaphysical 'homology,' especially with children and geniuses," but that he was still looking for enlightenment from Bremond here (BB, II, 171).

analyze the role of written texts of prayer and hymnodic compositions partly in terms of their rhythmic properties.

Romanticism Again: Guttinguer

What was happening, of course, is that increasingly Bremond the "modernist" and Bremond the "romantic" were coming to be seen, by his critics, as more or less synonymous, with traditional scholastic orthodoxy as "rational" and "classical." Having indicated his sympathy with nineteenth-century Catholic romanticism, from Chateaubriand to Lammenais to the novelists whom he admired, Bremond was now compelled to defend this "romanticism" even as he qualified his use of the concept. Furthermore, as against its detractors, he needed to show that this romanticism can lead to real faith, that in the past and in the present those who love poetry stand on the edge of the mystical abyss, into which they sometimes fall.

Bremond could not resist the temptation to show that even Sainte-Beuve, beloved of the classical traditionalists, was himself a romantic at heart, and that even though he did not become Catholic because of his romanticism, he had a deep relationship with a man who did travel that route, the minor novelist Ulrich Guttinguer (1785?–1866). It seems that Sainte-Beuve at one critical point in his career had entered into a complex six-year collaboration with Guttinguer to produce that author's 1836 story of a religious conversion, *Arthur, religion et solitude*. Bremond believed that the story of their coauthorship had not been properly told as a contribution to a "history of Catholic romanticism, a history so deplorably neglected," and when *Arthur* was reissued in 1925, he wrote an introduction, and then a separate long essay, to set the record straight. The heart of the story, gradually emerging as the narrative unfolded, was the way in which Guttinguer's struggle to master the emotions arising from a tortured relationship with his lover slowly gave rise to an enchantment and taste for life that became a gateway to a "universal charity." All of nature became sacramental, in a way that bespoke "the genius of Catholicism," and that led Guttinguer to penance, desert austerities, and finally peace with God.[23] Supernature emerged from the beauty of nature and the suffering nature imposes.

Although Blanchet has suggested,[24] probably rightly, that *Le Roman et l'histoire d'une conversion: Ulrich Guttinguer et Sainte-Beuve* seems to be "the least spoken of and least read" of Bremond's works, it is an important register of how his thought was developing. Having described Sainte-Beuve as a true romantic at heart—with his love of nature, his love of poetry, and his view that because of self-love life is hard and inevitably marked by failure, but that beauty triumphs over all—he could not, Bremond claimed, abide the dogmatism of the rationalists like Gibbon, who, lacking the

---

23. *Le roman et l'histoire d'une conversion*, 78.
24. BB, III, 203n4.

"insights of love," write bad history as a result.[25] Himself an "impenitent Romantic," he shared deeply in Guttinguer's suffering and spiritual search, so that by a kind of emotional contagion, both men will move on to write their own novels of passionate loving, deep despair and remorse, rage and forgiveness. They create literary representations of themselves, in which the central characters discover the spiritual nature of their struggles and draw closer to God. Life and literature intersect, but only Guttinguer goes all the way, with Sainte-Beuve remaining a "Christian so far as *sentiment* goes," a "mystic manqué."[26] Love leads to art/poetry, which *sometimes* leads to God.

Apparently Bremond drew some fire from traditionalists because in the book on Guttinguer he seemed to be praising a man who engaged in adultery.[27] The criticism is nugatory, of course, but even Blondel teased him about Ulrich's being a bit much for pious Catholics.[28] So, the book was something of a bust, though, I would suggest, especially revelatory of how Bremond's thinking was progressing as a refinement of the "romantic" label.

The "Manual"

Another now virtually unknown work by Bremond, yet one also imbued with the spirit of his long-term designs, was published early in 1925, the *Manuel d'Histoire de la Littérature catholique*. It appears to have been the brain-child of Georges Goyau (1869–1929), supporter of Bremond as well as deeply devout, liberal historian of Catholic thought and académicien, and the Catholic publisher, Éditions Spes. Containing survey essays by different (lay, not clerical!) writers on Catholic literary production from 1870 to the present, it covered a range of fields from theatre and journalism to philosophy, fiction, and historical writing, but the most notable element was the immensely long "introduction" by Bremond. In this mammoth essay (116 pages),[29] Bremond took it upon himself to sketch out with masses of bibliographical detail his hopes for many more volumes of the *Histoire*, bringing the whole project down to the twentieth century. In a breath-taking accumulation of books, essays, collections, compendia and writing of all kinds, emanating from Catholic authors humanistic in their style and progressive in their thinking, he painted a picture of late nineteenth-century French Catholicism as culturally engaged by means of the extraordinary artistry of its rich literature. Yet much of this production was unknown to, or forgotten by, his

25. "Sainte-Beuve ou le Romantique impénitent," 201.

26. Ibid., 216–17.

27. See the excerpt from a letter of Bremond to the abbé Ludovic Beaudou, a friend, of December 9, 1925, cited by Blanchet (BB, III, 234n2). Retired teacher and priest at Montauban, Beaudou became an admirer of Bremond's work from 1920 onward, and helped to broker his relationship with the Dominicans. Duclos, "L'abbé Louis Beaudou," gives excerpts from the correspondence.

28. Blondel to Bremond, January 24, 1926 (ibid., 238).

29. Blanchet indicates that the editors (unsurprisingly, perhaps) shortened this piece to 76 pages in the 1939 reprint (BB, III, 180n2).

contemporaries who were inclined to think of Catholic faith as dogmatic and (to its critics) as obscurantist.

In other words, he painted a picture of the French Church of his own time as moving in the direction of all that the Modernists stood for, even though retrograde reaction had hidden that fact. With great masses of citations from a broad range of authors, he rehearsed much of the history of his own formation at the hands of humanistic educators, but at the same time he made the case that it has been *art*, not scholastic theorizing, that has been the life-blood of the Church. Most notable in this art has been the writing of biographies, now lying in dust on library shelves, biographies by the hundreds of many devout figures, in which the living tissue of their faith is enshrined in pungent and piquant narrative. Bremond's longing for a renewal of the hagiographical genius of the Church is abundantly evident, and he saw here in the late nineteenth century the seeds of a renewal. He invited the readers of this introduction to send him notices of biographies that he had missed or of which he was unaware. At one point he celebrated the poetry of Marie Noël as a strikingly beautiful example of contemporary Catholic composition. The scope of Bremond's project is breathtaking, his wheels spinning very fast as he rose, empowered and energized, by his election to the Académie!

To Blondel he described this introduction as written "at a gallop" (indeed it runs hard), but also as "filled with dynamite," because of the liberal progressive names that he chose to highlight.[30] He also admitted that the essay had become "encyclopedic," though he could not resist the temptation to "upend the enemy" and hoped that Blondel would not be scandalized by what he chose to emphasize.[31] By pointing to certain figures as "saints," and minimizing others, he was letting his version of recent church history, conceived from a literary point of view, be known to all and sundry. In a payback to d'Hulst and Alfred Baudrillart, he claimed that the true continuators of authentic Catholic spirituality of the French School, where the imperative to love God and neighbor is central, are those who have embraced, as in the founding of the Institut Catholique, critical methods of historical study. Blondel expressed a few reservations or differences of opinion but generally liked what Bremond had done, seeing it as a prelude to his own constructive work.[32]

In effect, the introduction to the *Manuel* was a kind of "Here I Stand" on the part of Bremond. He was now letting his critics and supporters know his position on the drift, the evolution, the development of the Church's inner life down to the present. Absolutely convinced, in his construal of the church's literary history, that the anti-Modernist church of Pius X was a spiritual dead end, he now saw that the Church's constructive engagement with all of the "natural mysticism" of culture, especially

---

30. Bremond to Blondel, December 27, 1924 (BB, III, 179).

31. Bremond to Blondel, January 23, 1925 (BB, III, 183–84).

32. Blondel to Bremond, January 24, 1925 (BB, III, 186–88). Blondel (somewhat presciently) though that Baudrillart was a Bonapartist or fascist.

where the culture struggled as in poetry to articulate spiritual perception, was critical. And it was now clear that the mystical heritage of the French School in its many branches was the primary tool for forging that engagement.

And so, the opportunity had come. Recognizing that Bremond had been hitting at the issue of the relationship between poetry and religious experience, the leaders of the Académie now invited him to address one of the regular weekly sessions on the subject. Bremond eagerly accepted, framing his address as an exploration of the nature of "pure poetry." The subject was in the air, with recent publications by Maritain and others on the "correct" Catholic approach to the artistic explosion currently going on in 1920s France. Now it would be Bremond's turn. He looked forward to October 24, 1925, with delighted anticipation, for, unlike his "discours de réception," this reading would be entirely on the turf of his own project.

15

Pure Poetry and Pure Prayer

FROM MAURICE MARTIN DU Gard, present at the event as a member of the invited public, we have a tantalizing description of the situation "sous le Coupole," that is, at the Institut de France, on that October 24, when Bremond addressed his fellow "Immortels" of the Académie. It was the annual general meeting, and the situation is instantly recognizable to anyone who has ever sat through the presentation of a series of learned papers, perhaps at a scholarly conference in a warm place (before air conditioning). And Bremond's paper would be the last of the presentations that day!

After, in his report, dishing out some ironic abuse to the presenters who preceded Bremond at the rostrum, either because of their banality of style or the highly esoteric and/or trivial nature of their subject, Martin Du Gard took a deep breath (as it were) and commiserated with the convener, as that worthy stood up and indicated to the audience that there was just one more paper to be heard. Then, in this somnolent atmosphere, a priest "of fine bearing and great simplicity [we recall that Martin Du Gard rather idolized Bremond], with an un-premeditated air and an impatient, ironically effervescent" manner, in secular dress (Bremond had decided to emphasize the "unpriestly" nature of his subject), rose to address an unusual topic for an ecclesiastic: the controversial issue of the nature of poetry. His decision to link poetry with prayer would be most unexpected.

According to Martin Du Gard, the whole room suddenly woke up. He reminds us that Bremond was dealing with enemies, people who had opposed his entry into the Académie because he favored Baudelaire and Verlaine as poets, and because he preferred Fénelon over Bossuet and Francis de Sales over Arnauld. "Stunningly erudite"—Martin Du Gard continues—he is "well-born" (snobby here!), a "devout humanist with a devout air," "liberal by tradition and nature," a "royalist without a trace of the court-priest" (snobby again—Martin Du Gard liked old-fashioned aristocratic understatement), totally at ease with children and with an invincible sense of humor that leads to compassion without ridicule (nice compliment!), he then addressed the group with "Jesuit clarity and gravity," with "the culture of precision and interior discipline" formed in him by the Jesuits (true enough).

Martin Du Gard also noted that the presiding officer at the session introduced Bremond not as "monsieur l'abbé," but instead as "monsieur Henri Bremond," thereby startling those who saw him primarily in churchly terms as Duchesne's successor.[1] They were surprised as well that he chose to address a "profane and dangerous topic." Bremond spoke, said Martin Du Gard, calmly, strongly, solidly, and, as he did so, aspired to act in the spirit of Boileau himself, that Boileau who saw that musician-artists are ultimately contemplatives for whom prayer is the staff of life. Indeed, on this basis Bremond would soon champion the poet Paul Valéry for membership in the Académie. The brunt of his presentation, said Martin Du Gard in an over-simplification, was to show that true poetry, while not excluding reason, operates above and beyond it. On that basis the poet is "sacralized" and "heaven is opened to him."[2]

In the introduction to his narration of what took place at Bremond's reading, Martin Du Gard compared its importance to Fénelon's famous *Lettre à l'Académie* of 1713. No doubt, the comparison is over-stated, but it is also indicative of a long-standing and complex set of issues that perennially troubled French literary theory, often summed up as the "Quarrel of the Ancients and the Moderns." Some background is imperative, and can help us—tempted to think that theorizing about the nature of poetry is hardly an explosive matter—to begin to grasp what was at stake in Bremond's choice of such a subject, and why the response was so intense. We can also move more deeply into the whole nature of his project in the latter volumes of the *Histoire*, where an understanding of the religious "sentiment" is framed less in terms of the earlier thematic of "theocentric devout humanism" and more as a matter of the "mysticism-poetry" correlation.

"Ancients" and "Moderns"

Recall that the founding of the Académie française by Cardinal Richelieu in the time of Louis XIII was, among other things, an act of centralization, an effort to standardize and normalize the French language at a time when it was still a scattering of many local, fluid dialects. The principal mission of the Académie was to produce a dictionary that would become the authority for official documents, for literary expression in all of its modes, and for an educational curriculum. It would help to unite the French people under the rule of the monarch, and it would become the arbiter in disputes about usage, spelling, orthography, etc. The life of a nation and its beautiful language would be permanently intertwined.

---

1. See Trémolières, "Bremond et la 'poésie pure,'" esp. 238–46, and the idea, following Goichot, that Bremond was here engaged, in a "'stratégie' d'ensemble de son oeuvre" (ibid., 246).
2. Maurice Martin Du Gard, "La croisade de la poésie pure" (MC, II, 485–88).

One question was about geography. In passing, we noted back in the first chapter that one of the many controverted issues in the establishment of this central authority was the ongoing status of local linguistic phenomena, whether such localisms should continue to find valid expression, or should continue to exist at all. Bremond's native Provence had been one hotbed of such debates, with its Occitan traditions, but other parts of Celtic France, such as Brittany, had their own concerns, as did German-speaking areas such as Alsace and Lorraine.

But a second, even more fundamental issue was historical. Inherent in the challenge to build a centralizing and "authoritative" dictionary was the question of the extent to which past usage or precedent would function as an ironclad norm, with little or no allowance for novelty. From the time of the Italian Renaissance, this issue had taken one particular form in humanist circles: the status of the classical languages, as well as the classical literary genres, of Greek and Latin, specifically Ciceronian Latin, over against the newer vernacular tongues and new forms of expression, as acceptable artistic vehicles. Should literature be an endless exercise in imitation of timeless models of excellence, or should we break free from the past, while giving it all due respect, in order to create new and possibly better forms of art? This aesthetic dilemma evolved in seventeenth-century France into Charles Perrault's well-known "Quarrel of the Ancients and the Moderns." Should authors writing in French continue to obey norms and forms established by earlier writers, who themselves imitated the classical models—or not? The newly established Académie took up the issue with gusto, and it became perennial, sometimes vitriolic.[3]

Of course, the referents of "ancient" and "modern" constantly changed with the passage of time. By the nineteenth century, literary critics saw the seventeenth century as the Golden Age, the age of Corneille or Racine or Moliére was taken as the norm for dramatic production. Bossuet had become the "classic" for oratory, and so on. What had become "modern" was the literature of romanticism beginning with Chateaubriand, culminating in poets like Baudelaire and Verlaine, and realist novelists like Zola and Huysmans. Political valences shift as well. What counts as "ancient" *may* be more "liberal" than what counts as "modern," especially if more recent art happens to be marked by a conservative or reactionary turn—or vice versa.

And then there is genuine paradox. On the one hand, we might say that Bremond was an "ancient," that is, one who favors the authority of the past over the present. After all, much of his career to 1925 was spent in assembling and analyzing vast quantities of material from the seventeenth century, on the premise that we have much to learn from this literature about how to live in the present. He is constantly looking to the past in order to discern spiritual truth still valid for our own age. Thus it is that he has a traditionalist or conservative feel about him: he listens to ancient texts over and over again in order to discern the divine presence. He *loves* the old texts.

---

3. See most recently Norman, "Quarrel of the Ancients and the Moderns."

On the other hand, and as he insisted repeatedly in various ways, he is no repristinator, no uncritical admirer of the past who wants to purge the present of its decadence in order to return to a Golden Age. Being the historical critic that he was, central to his efforts was the idea that the past has to be *interpreted* as something relative to its context and thus to be appropriated for the present only in critically purified modalities. And if we ask the question, What does "critically purified" mean? the answer might be "in ways consistent with modern forms of understanding and experience, including the modern understanding of how ancient texts originated and operated." But then Bremond becomes a "Modern," who favors the present over the past, while in his own way deeply respecting the past.

The "Ancients vs. Moderns" debate had resolved in Bremond's time into the tension between the people he saw as "rationalists," that is defenders of the authority of the Greco-Roman classics as enshrined in the aesthetics of Boileau (based on Aristotle and Horace)—and in theology the Aristotelian scholastics—and the "romantics," whether ecclesial from Chateaubriand onward, or secular as with Baudelaire et al.[4] In the former truth is expressed "notionally" (Bremond would have said) and according to strict rules, while for the latter it is rendered in terms of the language of experience, of feeling, of "sentiment," of the "real." Politically, the "rationalists" or "classicists" tended to be conservative upholders of order, inclined toward monarchism and militarism, tended to be hyper-nationalistic and vulnerable to fascisms, while the "moderns" or "irrationalists" or "romantics" tended to be social-democratic, called for social change, and welcomed cultural experimentation and subjectivity in the arts. Thus (to get to the core of the matter) Bremond was seen by his traditionalist critics as having written, in essence, a romantic history of the seventeenth century, in which he had chosen to frame everything as "sentiments" and to restrict his focus to "literature," a medium peculiarly suitable for free individual expression as well as a freethinking openness to disorderly experience.

What confused his critics, however, was that as someone passionately interested in the religious life of a past age and its meaning for the present, he looked and acted like an "Ancient." In that respect he really was more like von Hügel, less like Loisy, while his way of approaching the past makes him look more like a "Modern." And then he adopted that ironic tone which led to charges of "chameleonism," thus infuriating some critics. When, therefore, he prepared to deliver his address on "pure poetry" to the assembled Académiciens, no one quite knew what to expect: would he be more "Ancient" or more "Modern"? The answer is both—at least after a fashion.[5]

---

4. A good analysis is DeJean, *Ancients against Moderns*. So far as the political connections go, Leo Strauss, the ideologue of contemporary conservatives in the United States, was a great defender of the value of the Greco-Roman classics for modern society. The question always, however, is: in what mode? We saw how Bremond and Blondel both condemned Port-Royal for the way in which they used the past ideologically.

5. As suggested, this was Fénelon's answer as well. At one point in his *Lettre à l'Académie*, he followed both Aristotle and Horace by declaring that poetry is "without doubt an imitation and a

To gain a sense for the passions that inflamed these debates, we might recall that the young Marcel Proust, that personification of modernism in literature, thrived on going as an adolescent to see the plays of Racine, feeling strongly whether or not this or that performer rendered a part correctly, i.e., according to established norms.[6] One has only to dip into the diaries of André Gide to discover much the same: he adored Racine (a "sharpness of outline") and Shakespeare (a "sublime fitness"), and reflected endlessly on the structure and internal dynamics of their compositions, seeing that in the latter "all poetry laughs, weeps, and vibrates," while "Racine is at the summit of his art."[7]

Clearly Bremond wanted to bridge the divide. He very much yearned to make the case that the mystics, the living heart of the "ancient" tradition, its vital core, are perennially "modern" when understood *correctly*. But it was an uncertain case, until, that is, he could think through how it is that mystical experience *expresses itself with a timeless content*, and then could clarify and articulate the connection between the expression and the experience. In a more contemporary formulation, he was looking for the *language* of mysticism, its characteristic *discourse*, in order to understand how that discourse functions so as to point to an "Other" by means, so to speak, of a revelatory mask that discloses and conceals simultaneously. His challenge was one of deciding how to formulate the nature of the verbal expression in such a way as to avoid the trap of rationalism, where words begin to substitute for experience.

While Blondel's insights would prove indispensable for thinking through the theological implications of his arguments, it would be the literary/aesthetic challenges, as represented preeminently by his idol, Paul Valéry, that would serve as the critical zone of contest. In his address to the Académie that October, in dialogue with a range of critics, and then in the the books on poetry of 1926, he kept his process of exploration moving forward.

Pure Poetry

The address, "La poésie pure," looks like it might have taken twenty minutes to a half-hour at most to deliver. Surely not a great strain on a tired, slightly too warm audience![8] His presentation was quite bald and direct, intended to prolong a conversa-

---

painting" (thus speaks the venerator of the Ancients), but later he is quite clear that he wishes for the Moderns to surpass the Ancients in all those areas where they are deficient, while never forgetting that "the emulation of the Moderns would be dangerous if it had the effect of causing us to despise the Ancients and to neglect their study" (V, 78–79; X, 122–23).

6. For the influence of Racine on Proust, and the whole artistic-literary milieu in which he lived and moved, see Tadié, *Marcel Proust: A Life*, 65–66.

7. *The Journals of André Gide*, II, 178–79 (entry for October 27, 1933).

8. References are to the text published along with the "clarifications," in which Bremond responded to various critics of the address, by de Souza, *La poésie pure*. Bremond's ideas on "pure poetry" have been a special field of interest for North American scholars. The best survey and analysis of the

tion inherited primarily from a range of nineteenth-century writers about the essence, or "pure nature," of poetical composition.

He opened with a gambit intended to sidestep, or transcend, the ancients-moderns controversy by contending that the recent theoreticians on the nature of poetry, such as Poe, Mallarmé, Baudelaire, and Valéry, are actually quite traditional in their thinking. The issue of the nature of "pure poetry" has, in fact, a very long pedigree. Many writers have expressed the idea that there is something "ineffable," something mysterious that bespeaks "secret graces" and "ineffable charms" in poetry. Though it is immensely difficult to pin down this "something," we owe to it that "transforming and uniting action" that we call "pure poetry."[9]

That this "something" really does exist, every child and every peasant knows, they who can penetrate the surface play of contradictions and antitheses in order to detect "with infallible intuition" the "pure" over the "impure." This pure element is often present in its fullness from the first words of the composition, as it weaves its spell over our affections. It is as if an "electric current" flows through poetry deeper than the straightforward sense, as instanced, for example, in the work of Gérard de Nerval.[10]

He then argues that what is "impure" in a poem is the rational, logical, intellectual, discursive level of meaning, where all of the rules of prosody come into play, where a posturing eloquence trying to say something significant becomes didactic. But then the poet no longer speaks *as a poet, for whom the ineffable is the essence.*[11]

He contends that as a poet the author makes words "sing" by means of a "delicious orchestration," in which the "musical resources of language" come into full play. Thus, poetry is verbal music. The harmonious mechanics of the verse, found in varying degrees in prose as well, exert an "attracting force" on the soul like a magnet hidden in a rock. A soothing takes place, in which the soul is distracted from its "anti-mystical imperialism" (!) "in order to transport us into those blessed darknesses, where the claws of the three concupiscences can no longer find the opportunity to seize us."[12] This is the kind of spell, averred Bremond, in which the mystics call us to quietude, where we yield to a power greater than ourselves. Citing various examples to make his

---

immediate debate that Bremond triggered among his French contemporaries is Decker, *Pure Poetry, 1925–1930*, and the best contextualizing of "pure poetry" within the overall flow of Bremond's thought is Moisan, *Henri Bremond*. While Decker's study is limited to aesthetic theory, and both writers honor the close association between "pure poetry" and mysticism for Bremond, neither attempts to locate the concept theologically, that is, in terms of the dynamics of "pure love."

9. Ibid., 15–16.
10. Ibid., 18–19.
11. Ibid., 23. "La qualité proprement poétique, l'ineffable est dans l'expression."
12. Ibid., 27. A reference to 1 John 2:16–17: "All that is in the world, the lust of the flesh and the lust of the eyes and the pride of life, is not of the Father but is of the world. And the world passes away, and the lust of it; but he who does the will of God abides forever" (RSV). Bremond was either being intentionally cryptic with his hearers, or he assumed spontaneous familiarity with Scripture! Probably the former.

point, Bremond then concludes with the idea that "the elements of the poem—words, sounds, colors, lines—create for us a reunion with prayer."[13] Fini. Audience stunned.

Shortly before his presentation, Bremond had sent Blondel a copy and asked for his opinion. Specifically, he wondered ironically if "I have attenuated the blasphemy against declared reason sufficiently: impure" (i.e., if "impure" was a sufficiently modest word for describing the damage done to poetry when "reason" is misused), and he chafed about being limited in the length, thus the depth, of his remarks. He anticipated that the "brilliant dialectician Maurras" would be on the attack.[14]

Blondel responded playfully at first, assuring Bremond that he would look over the text; "Evidently, pure poetry is mysticism perfected and *vice versa*," he jibed, though he promised to go easy on the use of irony in his comments.[15] Trying to make room for the proper use of reason, while recognizing its dangers, he first suggested that Bremond might think in terms of the scholastic concept of "concordance," where there is "a solidarity between the discursive and the poetic and mystical." "There is no disincarnated or absolutely de-rationalized poetry," he averred, "and there is no question of an absence of reason, or a counter-reason, or of an un-reason, but rather of a more comprehensive intelligence, concrete. . . . Pure, or purifying, poetry is like a viaticum, a presentiment, a foretasting, *in via*, not *in termino*." Thus, agreed Blondel, poetry should not be didactic, but just itself, thereby escaping discursivity as such.[16] But a little later he pressed Bremond to urge his listeners "not to mingle together the ways in which concrete thought operates before and then after notional thought—a distinction which you have discerned," nor to confuse "that which is implicit to immediate experience ['l'implicite spontané'] and that which is implicit to the knowing faculty ['l'implicite savant'], lower intuition and acquired contemplation, the aesthetic and the mystical," for otherwise they have confused Rousseau with John of the Cross.

On that basis, then, Blondel was moved to the following claim: "at the deepest level, the most invincible level of living reason, *there is no atheist* [Blondel's emphasis], [but] when reflective reason ['raison raisonnante'] comes into play, there is the risk that atheism will arise, and by various failures of insight, will take form." "For volitional and religious reason, *making God real* [Blondel's emphasis: 'réaliser Dieu'] is quite difficult, and some degree of atheism is hard to avoid," he argued.[17] But, he went on to

13. Ibid., 15–27. Bremond actually creates an interesting connection between Boileau, insisting that this authority highlighted the importance of eloquence "not in order to say nothing, but in order to say *something*," and Baudelaire, who emphasized the incantatory, "suggestive magic" of a poem. The implication is that latter-day rationalists—like Maurras—miss out on what the founders of rationalism, like Boileau, really were intending.

14. Bremond to Blondel, September 1925 (BB, III, 216–17). He was being careful, I think, in his choice of words with Blondel. He does not disparage "reason" as such, only "declared reason," or, as we would say, "declarative expression."

15. Blondel to Bremond, September 17, 1925 (BB, III, 217).

16. Blondel to Bremond, September 21 (?—date slightly uncertain), 1925 (BB, III, 218–19).

17. We recall from *L'Action* that the human will in deciding to act exposes the metaphysical "gap" that requires God without proving God.

assert, natural reason can make progress without prejudice to infused gifts, which, in any case, must be assimilated verbally in order to be as fully elaborated as possible.[18] On the day of the address, he urged Bremond to a full-scale assault on Maurassianism and Thomism in the name of "devout humanist mysticism"![19]

Perhaps Blondel's strictures did make a difference to Bremond's presentation. At that point in his address, where he described mystical-poetic inspiration as that which can deliver us from anti-mysticism into "the blessed darknesses, where the claws of the three concupiscences can no longer seize us," he touches on the moral power generated by pure poetry that is pure prayer. The language is from John of the Cross (and the NT, see ref. above), but the resonance is to the fact that Bremond was preparing *Histoire*, VII and VIII, where he would begin to analyze in earnest the concept of "pure love" as the spiritual punch of the mysticism-poetry nexus. He was returning to Fénelon's idea that in mystical experience there is an encounter with God whose nature is to empower the human soul for Pure Love. Therefore, the experience of poetry is a *morally cleansing, morally transformative* experience, in which the normal dynamics of human desiring are somehow transcended. Bremond does not actually say as much, of course, in the Académie address—that would be going too far in the august and secular assembly—but he implied it. And it is Blondel who is pushing him to that level of reflection.[20] The formulatable content of mystical experience will be this Pure Love, but the formulation cannot be rational (at least not *entirely* rational) because the content is not rational! There is the bind.[21]

The response to Bremond's remarks on that autumn afternoon was lively. He astounded some and angered others. By the end of November, he indicated to Blondel that he had started to publish some replies, but he also mentioned something else: the delight that he was experiencing now that Paul Valéry had been elected to a vacant seat at the Académie. Bremond saw in this election (November 12, 1925) a "vindication" of what he himself had said in his opening remarks about pure poetry, that Valéry and other romantics, usually considered pejoratively as "moderns," were more consistent in their work with classical theory—when that theory is rightly understood—than people realized. Naturally, representatives of Action Française were outraged.[22] Bremond loved it.

---

18. Blondel to Bremond, September 28, 1925 (BB, III, 220).

19. Blondel to Bremond, October 24, 1925 (BB, III, 222–23).

20. They had recently had a conversation about Jean Baruzi's book on John of the Cross, and Baruzi's strong case for the emergence of a real "doctrinal synthesis" as the product of John's mystical dark night. Blondel insisted that Baruzi's thesis led to a resurgence of rationalism once again (and then to a thinker like Schopenhauer), Blondel to Bremond, August 20, 1925 (BB, III, 212–13).

21. This is why Jacques Le Brun, *Le Pur Amour de Plato à Lacan*, traces the idea of Pure Love in the western philosophical and literary tradition by arguing that pure love is a "figure," a haunting image that suggests, an allegorical representation that "murmurs" (Certeau), not a rational construct.

22. Bremond to Blondel, end of November 1925 (BB, III, 224).

Pure Love, Pure Poetry, Pure Prayer

Valéry

Bremond's fascination with the poetry and thought of Paul Valéry is understandable, because Valéry was a remarkable figure. A giant in the world of French art between the wars, essayist and poet, philosopher of art, popular lecturer and speaker, a kind of spokesman for culture to a multitude of different kinds of groups, educational organizer and visionary, finally first holder of the Chair of Poetics at the Collège de France, degraded during WWII by virtue of his resistance to Vichy, he died in 1945.

Originally a product of the circle around the symbolist poet Stéphane Mallarmé, he is best understood as a reflection of the ironically colored, slightly world-weary *belle époque* aestheticism of prewar France, with its impressionistic modes of representation, as this was then modified by the massively shattering experience of WWI and its aftermath. He is thus a forerunner to Camus and Sartre on his dark side, but marked at the same time by a preoccupation with childlike "purity" in art, a trembling immediacy, that made him religiously attuned, without being in any way conventionally religious. In his personal life he was a dull bureaucrat who longed to spread his wings, and in the course of time did just that, being welcomed into the Académie on the basis of his famous early poems and essays on aesthetics.

Charles Du Bos arranged, on June 10, 1922, at his home on the Ile Saint-Louis, the first meeting of Bremond with Valéry. He reports in his journal entry that Bremond had requested this meeting in order to sound Valéry out on the idea that there is a "solder" between pure poetry and mystical states.[23] Through the English literary critic Middleton Murry, Bremond had heard of a supposed reference by Valéry to a "mysticism without God." Du Bos noted that Valéry had written that "in the heroic epoch of Mallarmé's symbolism, that genius had functioned almost like the founder of a religion," though there had been no pomp or charlatanism or anything of the sacerdotal about him. When Valéry had then continued, at this 1922 meeting, to encapsulate what he so venerated in Mallarmé, he articulated a combination of qualities that he imitated in his own verse: Mallarmé had "constructed a universe that was his own, to which he possessed the key, and which, at the same time, gave him a means of opening up and making resonant all of the phenomena that presented themselves to him."

Valéry was thus stating his core conviction, endlessly repeated, regarding the nature of good poetry, that the poet, by the skillful and well-wrought use of language, manages to make his private experience public in a way that speaks universally. When, according to Du Bos, Valéry asked Bremond for an opinion about his work, Bremond responded, "The last chapter of my fifteenth volume will be on you; I want to show that at the point to which we have come, religious mysticism has devolved into the state of pure poetry that you have described, and that more and more it has constituted [poetry] as its unique receptacle."

23. Du Bos, *Journal: 1921–1923*, 106–8.

Pure Poetry and Pure Prayer

At that same meeting, Bremond and Du Bos pressed Valéry for some clarity on the matter of "pure poetry." The latter contended that for him that phrase denoted "a state in which the spirit works on materials already prepared and immobilized by the activity of attention: this state will vary in length . . . but will be relatively short." The act of artistry, the craftsmanship, the fashioning by conscious intention of the spontaneous moments of inspiration into finished verse, is absolutely critical, opined Valéry, underlining the central importance of hard and conscious work on the part of the poet. Apparently the conversation broke off soon after, but Du Bos indicated, probably rightly, that a certain tension remained in the air. He suggested that Valéry had remained silent about how the "first verse" comes to the poet, while being clear about the "second verse," that is, the poet's conscious fabrication, using the rules of prosody and form, as he works over the initial inspiration. But the question of that "first verse" would remain open.

Valéry, in fact, would go on many times over the years to express himself on the matter of poetic composition, which he took as an especially problematic form of all artistic or aesthetic construction. Seeing himself as a tormented son of Descartes, for whom consciousness is both absolute in its demands (we must have precision) and always somehow inadequate in its expression (but precision will always fail)—thus endlessly in process, seeking an ever-elusive perfection of expression[24]—he struggled to capture the paradoxical nature of the "poetic act." To that end he had his own way of stating the poetry/prose distinction. The latter, he contended, is a self-extinguishing form of expression whose intention is to convey information of some sort, and then to pass away once that transmission is accomplished. It is comparable to the desire for food, which, once satiated, ceases to exist for a time, or like walking, which ends when its goal is accomplished.

By contrast, poetry is marked by the "desire to desire," i.e., the desire for an experience which is infinitely prolonged and thus has no satiation or destination other than its own continuation. The example is dancing, which, always artful, feeds only on itself in an endless, infinite self-regeneration![25] Thus, as a text, poetry simply evokes, stimulates, suggests, etc., in an ever-repeating process of self-reference that is simultaneously concrete in its use of language and universal in its open-ended range of connotations. Prose is all cerebral activity (Cartesian consciousness), but poetry engages the whole psycho-physical human organism (the body returns), only to make its peace, so to speak, with Descartes by returning to the need for rule-driven form and verbal artistry. What makes the act of poetic composition thus paradoxical is

---

24. This is the drift of the famous *Monsieur Teste* novel, begun in 1896 and augmented for the rest of Valéry's career. There is a curious kind of parallel between Teste and Proust's Swann with their endlessly self-reflexive analysis of consciousness over against the physical and sensuous environment.

25. Alexandre Kojève would not begin his famous Parisian lectures on Hegel until 1933, but Valéry's analogy between the working of poetry and a desire which, in order to be itself, does not drive toward satiation or extinction sounds Hegelian. But, of course, the deeper roots are in Plato and Augustine!

that it uses finite instruments, words with all of the rules and rhythms and criteria of exact composition, to express the infinite that transcends all rules. What makes poetry especially difficult, if not ultimately impossible, contended Valéry, is that, by comparison with music or the plastic arts, the material at hand, namely language, is much more fluid and uncontrollable than the physically constrained elements of harmonics or the laws of chromatics.[26]

Valéry was, however, willing to meet Bremond halfway. On the one hand, he belittled the idea that the poet was a mere passive receptacle of inspiration from some transcendental source, a mere transmitter of oracles, as it were, but on the other, he acknowledged something mysterious and "given" in artistic inspiration. He could on occasion use the word "mystical" with respect,[27] and, in his "discourse of reception" at the Académie, after describing at length the status of classical French art as a paragon of "conscious intelligence," he admitted that strict rules had long reached a level of absurdity, but that in the work of some few chosen artists there had been produced "miracles of purity, of precise force and of life . . . incorruptible works which make us bow, in spite of ourselves, before their divine perfection: Goddesses, they attain a degree of naturalness that is supernatural."[28]

Notice Valéry's measured use of this quasi-theological language: he was careful to emphasize "precise force" as the point of "supernatural" (or "mystical") intrusion in the poet's creative process, thus carefully avoiding any suggestion of a "passive" or *au hasard* dimension in inspiration. Where he clearly allowed for the truly uncontrollable, and finally gratuitous, nature of poetic effectiveness—and here he anticipated a vast surge of later development—was in the infinitely pliable nature of language and linguistic efflorescence. On this level, the poet found him/herself adrift on, so to speak, God's infinity of ultimately unforeseeable possibility. He also knew that much depended on what a reader brought to a poem, how he *heard* it, thereby introducing an uncontrollably interactive component to poetic meaning.

---

26. Valéry was massively articulate and expressive with regard to his aesthetic theories, but he always returned to a fundamental contrast between poetic expression and non-poetic expression. And he was also constantly insistent on the disciplined, crafted nature of poetic expression. Essays over the length of his career are gathered in Valéry, *Art, Esthétique, Poésie (9 Conférences, Discours et Propos 1923–1939)*. The most helpful piece is "Propos sur la poésie," Conférence faite à l'Université des Annales, le 2 décembre 1927.

27. For instance, In his paper on Pascal for the same 1923 colloquium in which Bremond also participated, Valéry spoke of the "secret movement of naive mysticism" by which Pascal, then Kant, derived the moral law from gazing at the vast solitude of the universe. But, he said, such disquietude is the product of cerebralization, whereas it makes more sense to tolerate the human tension of being nothing and everything simultaneously, of realizing that I am both a bit of dust and a living presence at the same moment. *That* tension is what causes us to see a living Being at the heart of the universe and then to write poetry about that experience ("Variation sur une 'Pensée,'" 164–65).

28. Valéry, "Fragment from 'An Inaugural Address before the French Academy,'" 146.

In an introduction that he wrote to a series of interviews by the journalist Frédéric Lefèvre with Valéry,[29] Bremond argued that Valéry needs to be saved from himself, that all of his emphasis on precise crafting is the damning heritage of Descartes as seen in Monsieur Teste, his *alter ego*, with the result that greater precision finally issues in "impurity," an obsession with verbiage. While both men agreed that didactic poetry is an abomination, they disagreed on the ultimate power, thus the role, of language. Bremond contended that good poetry, like mystical experience, issues in silence, because words are finally—not just contingently, but essentially—bankrupt, the "intellect scoffing at the fine point of the soul." Good poetry gently "suggests," it intimates and conjures, rather like the effect of any evocative discourse, where a chain of association, escaping the actual words themselves, is set loose in the mind of the listener.[30]

Consequently, what is involved in poetry is a different kind of understanding (Valéry agreed) which gives way to the enchantments of love and tenderness (too sentimental for Valéry), thus finally dispensing with language entirely (Valéry disagreed completely). Good poetry *is* music, thus breaking down the distinction between poetry and prose. In fact, averred Bremond, Valéry is filled with mystical inspiration, and he offered an interpretation to make his case, suggesting with the help of Paul Claudel's distinction of "anima" and "animus" for "soul" and "intellect" in art, that Valéry knew very well that exactitude is possessed only in "the moment itself" and that language will finally fail.

Bremond will return to his understanding of Valéry later in his 1930 work, *Racine et Valéry*, but for the moment he needed to turn to his own focus on pure poetry and pure prayer in order to make his case. The admiring dialogue with Valéry would operate as a constant backdrop for the remainder of his career.

Theology then reentered the picture as Bremond, having to deal with Blondel's first responses to his lecture on prayer and poetry, further refined and enlarged his thinking.

Prayer, Poetry and Blondel

Having indicated to Blondel that he was being accused by critics of "pure subjectivism" in his approach to poetry,[31] Bremond received in reply a fictionalized scenario, in

---

29. Preface to Lefèvre, *Entretiens avec Paul Valéry*, xxiv.

30. Bremond saw one of Valéry's recent additions to the *Monsieur Teste* series, "A Letter from Madame Émilie Teste," as a response to his criticisms of the latter's views. In the preface to Lefèvre's interviews, he included long citations in which Teste reflects on "scholars, lovers, old men, priests, and the disillusioned; all *dreamers*, of every possible kind" (ibid., xxxi–xxxii). At one point, Madame Émilie says to her parish priest, "my husband often reminded me of a mystic without God" (Valéry, *Monsieur Teste*, 31).

31. That is essentially the case. In the summary of criticisms-with-responses (the "clarifications") appended by Robert de Souza to the published version of the lecture. Paul Souday led the charge by

which Blondel imagines himself to be responding to the same charge of "subjectivism" from an imaginary character.[32]

A certain abbé Paul Vallée had, according to the fiction, offered to Blondel a critique in the spirit of "fraternal correction." Blondel acknowledges that the labels of "subjectivist" and "modernist" belong together, but denies that they apply to him, because they also imply relativism, phenomenalism and individualism in doctrine, where the subject makes himself the center of a unique perspective. The whole problem here, the basis for the false accusation being aimed at him, he says, is that classicist rationalism has developed a radically impoverished understanding of reason, truth and art.

"Reason," says Blondel, must not be taken as equivalent to "clear and certain ideas," that is, to "discursive and overly logical simplifications," where a "factitious order" is imposed on the real, to which we must then subject ourselves. He then went on to note that in scholastic thought "the intellect is completed in the act," so that "knowing and acting are identical." The function of *ratio* is to analyze, without pretending to grasp the whole of the object, since it is *intellectus* that will seize by contemplation the functional unity of the object in all of its beautiful reality and simplicity. From that perspective, then, mysticism and pure poetry are not subjective caprice at all, and one must remember that the most egregious error is to imagine that the essence of a dogma is the verbal formulation itself.

Blondel then goes on in this same letter to point out that the most common mistake in our own times is to be unaware that there is a *science* of the subject, in which the subject belongs to the real, where the subjective is seen as an object and can itself be understood. The result of this widespread error, that wishes to reject the "subjective," is that a hidden subjectivism then colors all of our assumptions about the "real," this subjectivism itself remaining unexamined. The resulting understanding of the "rational" then leads to grievous misapprehensions. The "subjectivism" of which he, Blondel, is being accused is in fact that which takes proper account of the functional aspirations, highest emotions, and most comprehensive views held by the subject in discerning the "real."

But, as he made clear to Blondel, Bremond was uncomfortable with scholastic distinctions.[33] What he needed, it seems, was a way of making the point with a

---

accusing Bremond of abdicating from all reason and logic in his approach to the meaning of poetry. In reply, Bremond cited Edgar Allen Poe: "The great modern heresy is to make the Truth the supreme object of Poetry . . . between Poetry and Truth there is no sympathy" (*La poésie pure*, 37).

32. Blondel to Bremond, December 1925 (BB, III, 226–27).

33. Bremond to Blondel, end of December 1925 (BB, III, 228–29). While recognizing his need for greater theoretical precision, he added: "I should say, moreover, that I have always resisted St. Thomas's 'poet': a technician of memory" (BB, III, 228). In other words, scholasticism seems to be only another form of rationalism.

different, more psychologically inward terminology. It was this that he would lay out in 1926 in his major treatment, *Prayer & Poetry: A Contribution to Poetical Theory*.[34]

As a digest of abstract thinking, *Prayer & Poetry* is probably the most ambitious, systematically conceived, and lucidly clear book that Bremond ever wrote. He started with a definition of the task: to trace the relationship between prayer and poetry by means of an analysis of the "poetic state," where the inspirational dynamic of poetry operates. Mystical experience will, he believed, bring essential clarification.

The first seven chapters are an overview of the theory of poetry from Plato down to the nineteenth-century romantic authors. Plato established the idea that poetry is distinct from rational discourse, with its own object of knowledge in the particular rather than the universal, so that poets, those "charming and magnificent lunatics," are wise without being able to explain their wisdom. In the case of Aristotle who contended that poets are rational, since they manifest "practical reason," there is, thought Bremond, a "de-poetizing" of the poet, with no room for the ineffable. Thus is born from Aristotle for the Renaissance humanists the problem of "aesthetics," in which meditation on the mystery of poetry is structured around the study of forms and rules and other technical matters. With Boileau everything became technique, logic and clarity, although he possessed a "naturally poetic soul," delighting in details and implicitly rejecting rationalism without being able to state the matter openly. In the period after Boileau, Fontenelle and his follower LaMotte, the adherence to rules becomes absolutely definitive for poetry, the conviction being that even the "magic" of the poem will eventually be subjected to rational principles.

This rationalist aesthetics will become the focus for combat in the Académie, where fear of the irrational becomes normative. A major protest comes from the Jesuits, who, in their *ratio studiorum*, maintain some of the mystique of poetry. Bremond pays special tribute to a little-known Jesuit, Jean-Antoine Ducerceau (1670–1730), who took a Fénelon-like approach to poetry by reflecting on the "something else" that truly makes a poem poetical, although ultimately he lapsed into a rationalist analysis of that "something." Then in romanticism poetry was restored, when its own proper wisdom was recognized. Bremond cites as an example the view of Charles Magnin, that "poetic sentiment" is marked by "that super-excitation of the intelligence, that momentary vertigo of the heart and thought" which is "the poetic state." "Imagination" becomes the chosen term, where poetry has as its object not truth, but the *real*. Baudelaire exalts the mode of symbolism as the primary vehicle for the imagination, and then Matthew Arnold recognizes that poetry is an interpretive act that puts us in intimate relation with objects so that their "secret" is revealed. A. C. Bradley, professor of poetry at Oxford from 1901, recognized that in the poetic act there is a moral intuition of that which is *perfect*, but irreducible to ideas. The end result of this history,

---

34. References are to the 1927 English translation, *Prayer and Poetry: A Contribution to Poetical Theory*.

says Bremond, is that ineffable experience must be imparted by the poet in such a way that the "shock" of the experience, its "contagious shining," grips the reader decisively.

Bremond then paid his debt to Blondel by stating that "if poetry is a reality, one of the forces of nature, it cannot escape the critical examination of reason."[35] The reference is to Blondel's 1924 essay on the nature of mysticism, and the argument that reflection on the nature of that which is trans-rational, if it is to be philosophical at all, must still be rational; therefore, the mystical-poetic state can he understood, if the mode of understanding is *proper*.[36] The challenge, then, is to honor the romanticist insight that the poetic gift has access to a knowledge all its own. Mystical experience will provide the key. Since the mystic and the poet share a common psychological chemistry, with "analogies of form and communities of mechanism" between mystical and psychological processes, we see that grace fulfills nature.[37] The grace that leads to prayer is the same as that which leads to poetry, since both "are signs that we have a higher faculty . . . capable of receiving God, though incapable of apprehending him."[38] Prayer will lead on to an opening to higher grace, to a supernatural gift, thus leaving poetry behind, but they travel in tandem for part of the distance, having started from the same impulse. Following Maréchal (who is following Aquinas), Bremond claims that the human intelligence "aspires to God before it knows him," thereby leading to the claim that the poets help us to understand the mystics better.

In fact, argues Bremond, a whole range of moral and aesthetic experiences have a mystical dimension, when they "grab consciousness" in such a way that it relaxes into a beauty or attraction which is indefinable. Poetic experience is one of these, in which there is a moment of "enriching simplification" that breaks through the normally scattered and fragmented nature of consciousness so that "something" is glimpsed. That moment has a quality of "peaceful repose" which is the "resting in God." Further, there occurs a comprehension of the "real," following which the poet-mystic will seek an "idea" in order to express that "real." Again following Maréchal (who followed Hume), Bremond here suggests that an "impression" is formed, in which the "living being" of what has been glimpsed calls for "realization" in outward expression. An "image" or "sketch" is the result, all of it marked by "pacifying simplification."[39]

---

35. Ibid, 80n1.

36. Ibid., 80n. Bremond cites Blondel's use of a saying from Aristotle, "If we ought to philosophize, well then, let us do so. If not, we must still philosophize in order to know the grounds of denial."

37. Ibid., 87, from Joseph Maréchal, n1. Clearly at this point Bremond is presenting material, as noted earlier, that he eliminated from the published "Notes on Mysticism" at the end of *Histoire*, II.

38. The authorities cited by Bremond throughout here are primarily Maréchal and Grandmaison on "natural mysticism." It is in the very instant, says Bremond, of poetry suddenly becoming prayer, that a supernatural intervention has occurred.

39. Ibid., 92–93. Bremond has here a delightful reference, from Nicolas Grou, to "that simple prayer in which the mind has no other object before it than a confused and general view of God, the heart has no other feeling than a sweet and peaceful tasting of God, which nourishes it without effort, as milk feeds children." One problem here, of course, is the psychologically regressive nature of this language, leading to the Freudian charge of "infantile." In due course, Bremond does an end run

Nothing is taught, insisted Bremond, in this simplification, but there is first an inertia, then a surge of energy for action, which, for the mystic, comes from "the fine point of the soul." The invisible object experienced in the moment of inspiration or vision takes on a palpable quality that is experienced as "given" externally, and not reducible to a physiological stimulation as such.

For the remainder of the argument, then, Bremond appeals to Claudel's use of the "animus" and "anima" distinction, which he sets in parallel with "the fundamental dogma of mystical philosophy," the distinction between the surface self and the deep self (or what he also calls the "I" and the "me"). The surface self, corresponding to the "animus," is orderly, bourgeois and analytic, while the deep self, the "anima," is mystical and poetic.[40] Francis de Sales is Bremond's chief source here—as we shall see in *Histoire*, VII, which Bremond was composing at this same time. Here he cites Middleton Murry to the effect that religion and literature have "the same everlasting root," in which both move in the direction of the "grandeur of the human soul and perhaps its more than mortal destiny," with Christian faith then removing the "perhaps."[41]

As one might expect, Bremond describes at length and with gusto the nature of the "anima," emphasizing the sense of passive receptivity that marks its nature, so that the mystics claim to be "acted upon" and to become "adherent" to the gift that is experienced. The profane poet sees the supernatural but cannot name it, thereby needing to fall back on an undue reliance on linguistic tricks. Remarkably, Bremond now highlights "the necessary collaboration of the 'animus' and the 'anima,'" since the latter will be "sterile" without the former. Therefore, what we see in religious history are prodigious efforts at the expression of ineffable experiences. The sheer volume of expression testifies to its import, this expression serving to communicate the sense of certitude that characterizes the mystic when the ecstasy has passed.

An ineffable experience *must* be communicated, suggested Bremond, so that it is not lost but, in a sense, multiplied, consolidated, prolonged at the level of practical living. Perhaps Bremond was listening to Valéry's view of the nature of poetry as the

---

around the charge through an ultimate repudiation of the sensual quality of the language.

40. Bremond's use of Claudel seems adventitious, more a matter of convenience than of deep conviction. Paul Claudel (1868–1955)—world-famous poet, playwright, eventually diplomat—had been part of the pre-WWI contingent of Catholic converts (like Péguy) whose intensity and theological conservatism had aggravated Bremond (see the reference by Blanchet, BB, II, 247n4). But they ended up sharing similar views on poetry and aesthetics, and were united in opposition to Maurrassian rationalism and politics, although Claudel's sympathies here were complex and controversial (BB, III, 214n1). In the use of the Anima/Animus terminology, Claudel had developed a kind of Female/Male cosmological dualism totally foreign to Bremond's mentality. See, e.g., Barjon, *Paul Claudel*, 49–55.

41. Bremond, *Prayer & Poetry*, 129, citing Murry's 1925 work, *To The Unknown God*. Murry (1889–1957) was a modernist literary critic and radical political writer, strongly oriented to the religious and ethical dimension of literature. Indeed, one of the hottest criticisms that would be aimed at Bremond's notions of pure poetry would come from the journalist-critic Paul Souday, who argued that Bremond had succumbed to the assumptions of Anglo-Saxon literary analysis. As Decker points out, Souday took Bremond to task for "cette détestable anglomanie" which was the product of Bremond's years in England (*Pure Poetry, 1925–1930*, 115).

induction by means of a crafted text to an ever-recursive reflection, but his actual appeal was to a modified, non-Aristotelian, understanding of the effect of "catharsis." In this view an artistic formulation by the "animus," the rational mind, is done in such a way that it induces in the individual a bearable encounter with deep, dangerous perceptions and emotions, and thus makes contact with the "anima," the result being a "purging" of the very same passions that the art arouses. By taking his reader down into a very dark place, but in measured amounts, the poet or mystic allows light to begin to shine through the darkness in what is ultimately a medicinal process. One is enabled to have "contemplative" distance on that which has been aroused precisely by experiencing a manageable dose of it. For the mystic-poet, moreover, this catharsis by means of a descent into the furnace is tantamount to the union with God, an encounter with the Absolute, where, as Baudelaire insisted, the soul is "ravished."

Now, claimed Bremond, this poetic/mystical catharsis/union operates by laws which can be, to some extent, understood in terms of aesthetic rhythms, forms, etc. Again following Maréchal, Bremond insists that there is actually a process of multiple purgations and deliverances, but the essence is as follows: "First of all, the deeper soul, relieved of the importunate activity of *Animus*, becomes dilated, aspires to the real, with which union is at last possible; then *Animus* himself receives as the necessary recompense for the abnegation to which he has consented, a refreshing and redoubling of activity."[42] The surface is renewed from the depth.

The conclusion is that the poet is an "evanescent mystic," still chained to words, and therefore not yet supernaturalized, but on the same ladder with the true mystic. The "happy choice of harmonious words" is the necessary substitute for the silent adoration, or act of love, which is the joy of the mystic; speaking substitutes for being. The poet is a half-saint, as Blondel recognizes, and "the strange and paradoxical nature of poetry" is that it is "a prayer which does not itself pray, but which makes others pray."[43]

Only the philosopher Blondel, says Bremond, has struggled with these tensions, in which it is clear that in any truly mystical experience "*Animus* and *Anima* collaborate in an act of love, of love in the perfect sense of the word."[44] Strangely enough, Bremond concluded with a citation from Maritain: whatever is beautiful "tends of itself to unite us to God." But the last word is the best: for all of the power of poetry (from the Jansenist Hamon!), "it is easier to love if one remains silent than if one talks!"[45] But a question remained.

---

42. Bremond, *Prayer & Poetry*, 185. The parallel that Bremond alludes to is Maréchal's description of contemplation as a progressively purificatory process, in which the devotée repeatedly returns to certain words mechanically reiterated until a "breakthrough" occurs, which then, for Bremond, is like the reader of a poem constantly returning to the text for deeper encounter with its multiple meanings.

43. Ibid., 189–91.

44. Ibid., 194.

45. Ibid., 194–95.

Pure Poetry and Pure Prayer

What Is Prayer?

Blondel raved; he loved it—though, of course, with qualifications.[46] He thought that Bremond's reference to Maritain was deplorable, and, though he called Bremond's use of Claudel "marvelous," we know from elsewhere that he had a very poor opinion of Claudel.[47] What he urged on Bremond was somewhat closer attention to the psychological developments that directly precede poetic or mystical consciousness as well as greater refinement in the understanding of the preconscious and conscious elements in the experience itself. On a philosophical level, he posed the issue of the relationship between the particular and the universal, that is, the degree to which, and the modes in which, general human experience is contained in each individual's unique experience. He offered as well a provocative suggestion regarding poetry in the form of drama, noting that dramatic art, as exemplified by the Oberammergau passion play (an experience both men had shared many years earlier),[48] has the ability to "de-center" us as we watch, "purifying us from temporal and spatial illusions, thus the egoism of the 'I,' so as to exalt and confer on the 'me' a sort of universality and perenniality." On the whole, he very much liked Bremond's accomplishment and the direction in which he was moving, while looking for greater precision and coherence.

Bremond noted the critique with good humor, indicating to Blondel that he was already beginning to deal with some of his concerns via the *éclaircissements* ("clarifications") appended to the published text of his Académie address.[49] In aligning poetic inspiration with mystical experience, he was homing in on the role of "pleasure," or "passion," noting that for the poet there seems to be a sense of operating "below or above" any sensate awareness, while for the mystic there is the loss of "felt devotion." In a claim that aggravated his critics, but that will play a major part in *Histoire*, VII, both the poet and the mystic, he averred, make contact with a dimension in which ordinary human hedonic functioning is either bypassed or transcended.

Indeed, in that volume, soon to appear, he will argue the case that the poetic/mystical state ultimately results not just in the elevation or exaltation of the human subject, but in its *effacement*, in a cancellation of any self-consciousness on the part of the person lost in the divine infinity. The question of the particular and the universal has been thereby answered after a fashion. It is the loss of the self in order to find the self: precisely as I lose myself in God, or in the All, I cease to be an individual ego, but have become a drop in the ocean of cosmic consciousness, etc. The use of language and

---

46. Blondel to Bremond, September 10, 1926 (BB, III, 247–52).

47. Blanchet in a substantial note gives the references, including Blondel's view that the Anima/Animus distinction is a "specious myth" (BB, III, 251–52).

48. See Bremond, "Les acteurs d'Oberammergau," an early (1900) essay, written as a review of a work by Blondel's brother, in which Bremond highlighted the understated realism of the production, where the boundary between the ordinary lives of the actors and their roles as sacred personages disappears.

49. Bremond to Blondel, September 21, 1926 (BB, III, 252–55).

all forms of expressiveness ceases, and silent adoration begins. If the mystic says, "I have become the All," the romantic poet, following in the steps of Baudelaire, can say "I am Another," with the implication that the individual "I" has become Everyman. It is by the clothing of this experience in language that the poet/mystic re-individualizes him/herself and returns to hedonic functioning.

Blondel's response to Bremond's announcement of the direction in which he was thus moving is pregnant, because he saw another danger. "I believe that you are right to say of poetry that it is a prayer which does not really pray, which mimes prayer, which, using some of the resources of the deep soul, provides at reduced price an 'ersatz' of the religious solution: good as a vehicle or apparatus for de-rationalizing *animus*, it awakens and stimulates *anima*, but remains good only as nostalgia for a fuller satisfaction of which it remains radically incapable; it becomes perilous in the measure that it considers itself as perfect, independent, as attaining an object at the same time ideal and real in a way that only the religious solution can present or anticipate."[50] Differently stated, Blondel thought that without a progression into true prayer, poetry would lapse into the anarchy of surrealism and fascist futurism, i.e., pseudo-religion. The problem for the "religious solution," Bremond thought, was in the implications of the loaded phrase "nostalgia for a fuller satisfaction." How can the loss of self be a "fuller satisfaction"?

In the first two chapters of *Histoire*, VII, where Bremond returned at this time—late 1926 to early 1927—to the "primacy of prayer" and the "philosophy of prayer," with Francis de Sales as his guide, he made a concerted effort to define the nature of prayer and to clear away some misunderstandings. He had realized that he could further defend his conjunction of poetry and prayer, partly by more careful exploration of the psychology of the one who truly prays, but even more by means of a more careful assessment of prayer itself, of what it is and what it is not.

The opening of this seventh volume, "The Metaphysic of the Saints,"[51] is headed by several texts that serve as a lapidary preview of Bremond's intentions. There are three passages from the sermons of Bossuet, in which that eminence emphasized, first, that prayer is an "attentive listening 'at the center of the heart' to the word of Jesus Christ," and then, second, that consent and adhesion both happen at that same place, the result being that there is "an accommodation of the will to the very depth of our essence." Newman is cited to make the point that this "new birth . . . sets the soul in motion in a heavenly way," and then there is a text from the Jansenist, Hamon, to the effect that God is most pleased with prayers that have no end.

Thus, we have an implied picture of prayer as an activity in which there is a progressive, continual remolding, at first passive and receiving, then becoming active and responding, where the will, the moral capacity, is the special place of encounter, the

---

50. Blondel to Bremond, October 5, 1926, the cited words all being emphasized by Blondel (BB, III, 256–57).

51. *Histoire*, VII, vii–viii.

place where the human spirit moves from an earthly (false) place to a heavenly (true) place. By means of this collocation of citations, Bremond implied a position consistent with the claims that he was making in his work on poetry and prayer. The description thus constructed is allusive, one that would make sense to his secular audience as a picture of the movement of the soul when it either prays or makes poetry. Although the secular audience might be reluctant to embrace the description as *religious*, they would feel the "tug" in the direction of transcendence. It is a form of Blondel's metaphysical "gap" in the act of willing, where the heart seeks God without knowing what it seeks, now formulated psychologically.

In his opening section of *Histoire*, VII, Bremond suggested that the two formal components of prayer are commerce with God, a "state" of interaction, and then the request that the individual makes of God.[52] This becomes "an elevation of our soul towards God so as to render our homage, expose our needs, and ask his graces." With regard to the element of "request," he looks to writers who take the position that "interested" requests are not essential or constitutive of prayer, as are the "disinterested" ones.

"Elevation" or "ascent" to God is thus the essence, with petition as entirely secondary. The natural human desire for God is quite legitimate, along with all of our needs, but with maturity the desire to give takes priority over all else, argues Bremond. With adoration foremost, requests become primarily a form of trusting love, not a "demand." Granted, he says, that primitive religion is a congeries of fear-based supplications, it is the element of an immediate all-powerful divine presence that is primary, with a sense of human lowliness as the response. Among other authorities, he cites the English authority on mysticism, Evelyn Underhill, to the effect that "instinctive awe and adoring prayer" constitute the "germ of religion," the first response of human beings to God. The petition for daily bread is thus freed from all egotism when it is subordinated to the prayer for the coming of God's kingdom![53]

But it is in the second chapter that Bremond made the explicit connection with the poetry-prayer nexus, when he considered Francis de Sales's "philosophy" of prayer. There is a parallel, he once again affirmed, between Claudel's "animus" and "anima" and the thought of de Sales, when Francis describes our two selves, the one more conscious while the other is more unconscious, the latter often determinative of the thrust of the former. This deeper *anima*-self is Francis's "fine point of the soul," this notion representing Francis's use of a long Christianized tradition of the neo-Platonic "mystic geography" of the soul. In baptism, contended Francis and followed

---

52. Notice that the second element is essentially Nicole the Jansenist's definition of the content of desire when one prays, but it is Bremond's insistence on the first element as first that is the *mystical* hallmark.

53. Ibid., 5–16. Bremond has a delightful citation from the sermons of Aquinas: "That person does not really pray, who, rather than elevating himself to God, asks God to lower Himself to the one who prays, and who comes to prayer, not in order to stimulate the human being to will what God wills, but only to persuade God to will what human beings will. Who can tolerate such irreverence!" (ibid., 14–15).

by Bremond, supernatural gifts are given to every Christian, whereby "in Christ" a "sanctifying grace" starts to operate in the soul, a grace given to "an initial passivity" through an "internal adhesion." The upshot is that a "magnificent simplification" occurs for the believer, in which all acts of charity become outward manifestations of life at the fine point of the soul, where the human will is in process of being absorbed into the divine will, much as a painter, desiring to produce a tableau, yields with "a blind and indifferent docility" to the movements that inspire him. Then the painter (or the poet) produces his art in obedience to a single will, his own blending with that of the inspiration in a single adhesion that becomes habitual. The painter becomes one with his inspiration, just as the soul consents to God in a "despoiling of the self" in order to serve the deeper self in an act of pure love. The pain of all of this, in which a submission to sensual pleasure is finally transcended, is "the mount of Calvary" which is the "mount of lovers."[54]

Truly Bremond needed Blondel at this point, because of the danger of metaphysical confusion.

The matter might be stated this way: is prayer as Bremond understood it, a kind of second step, or quantum leap forward, along the same trajectory (the same order of being) that poetic inspiration has already established, as if poetry by its very nature displays an anticipatory openness to higher and higher levels of operation, with supernatural infusion providing the necessary "surge" (so to speak)? Or is prayer better understood by *analogy* with poetic inspiration, so that both show the same inner structure in human experience, the one being convertible into the other not along a single trajectory with a uniform direction, but rather by means of a transposition (the leap of faith) from one order of being into another (more like moving from one small house to another much larger one across a narrow walkway)? In the debates with Thomist interpreters like Maritain, and in his use of a neo-Thomist like Maréchal, this potential metaphysical confusion was much at issue. Blondel's task was to help Bremond see the snarl, and then to struggle with navigating past it (not resolve it!) successfully.

Loisy, moreover, later contended that the Académie never quite took Bremond with full seriousness, because he was not fully understood with his implied message of pure love. But perhaps Bremond himself was unclear. Let us see.

---

54. Ibid., 60–62, 72–74. Much of this from de Sales served his intention of illustrating the Tridentine emphasis on the collaboration of the free human will with the "good pleasure" of God, but Bremond uses it more to illustrate the continuity of human willing with divine willing, where artistic inspiration comes into play. What is notable, though, is that for Bremond all charitable, ethical, other-regarding action becomes a kind of artistically creative and inspired act.

16

The "Metaphysic of the Saints" I
Setting the Stage

BLOUD ET GAY BROUGHT out the long-awaited (by Bremond's fans)[1] seventh and eighth volumes of the *Histoire* with the puzzling title of "The Metaphysic of the Saints" in 1928. Taken together with the supplemental work, out in early 1929, *Introduction à la philosophie de la prière*, these tomes are the high point of Henri Bremond's work. One of the ironies of Bremond's career, pointed out by Michel de Certeau, is that volumes I–III of the *Histoire*, a product of the war years, have established Bremond's reputation (being the only ones translated into English) as a consummate raconteur of spiritual history, while the work that constitutes his message, his "philosophy" or "metaphysic," being a product of the years of slide toward the troubled 1930s, has fallen into oblivion.[2]

Aside from the most obvious reason for the irony, namely that most readership favors lively and concrete narrative over theoretical discourse, there is another more interesting contributory factor at work. What Bremond had to say in his "philosophy," often cast in his idiosyncratic terminology, can seem dated now and long superseded by more timely reflection. The theological resources on which he drew for his theorizing about mysticism, such as the work of Maréchal, are spent casings, as it were, and Blondel, illness and blindness slowly wearing him down, was entering the later, less daringly dynamic phase of his work.

The contention, however, of this chapter and the following is that Bremond's more theoretical thought deserves a fresh hearing, because it provides an important gateway into the world of spiritual challenge where we find ourselves three-quarters of a century after his death.

---

1. A number of persons, including his publisher, Francisque Gay, put pressure on Bremond to get on with the *Histoire*, taking the view that the work on prayer and poetry was only a distraction. See Goichot, EG, 210.

2. Certeau, "Henri Bremond," 24.

From the time of the prayer-and-poetry debates onward, Bremond would operate less under the influence of Blondel, and more and more out of other friendships, primarily with Loisy and the Italian Benedictine De Luca. While Blondel typically challenged Bremond to think more carefully and precisely, especially in terms of adherence to Catholic orthodoxy, the correspondence with De Luca would open another possibility, that of histories of the religious sentiment akin to his own but of other national and cultural experiences as well, while the relationship with Loisy (including new influence from Henri Bergson) would raise the matter of a universal and transcultural spirituality. It is as if Bremond were cycling through the particularity of his own French history as an access to a much wider horizon.

We recall that the problem has been there all along as the Modernist problematic. It came up with the traditionalist Jesuit training (too narrowly dogmatic), the nativist literature of Barrès and others (too nationalistic), the spirituality of Antoine Yvan and Madeleine Martin (too regional), the writing of Bossuet (Catholic and political triumphalism conjoined), etc., while characters like Thomas More and Fénelon, combined with Bérulle and Francis de Sales and Chantal, became the liberating voice of the future. Liberating because their humanism or mysticism takes them out of the constraints of this or that limiting notional or explicit construct into contact with the implicit, unlimited and infinitely "real," only to reclothe the experience, to mediate it, in newly evocative linguistic and symbolic forms.

If we take the view of Trémolières, that Bremond was engaged in a kind of laicizing process, that, having absorbed the impact of the new "religious science," he was taking the language of classical ascetical and mystical theology and shifting it in the direction of an experience-near, non-ecclesial account of the life of "pure prayer," which is the life of "pure poetry" grounded in "pure love," then it is also the case that he was gravitating by degrees in the direction of a recognition of what we have come to call "pluralism" in culture, with a recognition of inherent variation in religious expression, a variation that raises the question of a common experiential core, or at least the *possibility* of such. Nineteenth-century ethnography was, as we know, producing a very large body of research into non-European religion along with a steady growth of theorizing on the subject of "primitive" religion and religious origins. Bremond joined this conversation in the first chapter of the *Introduction à la philosophy de la prière*,[3] when, after citing a string of authorities, he opined that feelings of awe and admiration in the presence of the divine, experienced as a Personality, are the root of prayer, thus of the whole religious phenomenon.[4]

---

3. Issued in 1928 and intended to be supplemental to *Histoire*, VII and VIII as the first in a series of texts chosen to illustrate the history of thinking about prayer, the series was the brainchild of Francisque Gay and Alfred Loisy. Bremond used the volume as an expression, in essence, of his last will and testament on the subject of Ignatius and the *Spiritual Exercises* (see below), along with excerpts from a number of classical texts. The series never got past this first volume.

4. *Introduction à la philosophie de la prière* (hereafter in the notes that follow, *Introduction*), 17, and n2, referring to, among numerous others, the work of Pratt and Evelyn Underhill.

Religious vitality thus thrives on the "immediate contact" which is the defining hallmark of mysticism, thought Bremond, but that "contact" must have appropriate outward expression as a prolongation and cultivation of the initial experience. The expression is "poetry," or perhaps better stated, the "poetic state" translated into the whole range of concrete activity marked by charity and yearning for the manifestation of "pure love" in all of its efflorescence. One of the most prescient readers and utilizers of Bremond's thought, in the years immediately after his death, would be Romain Rolland (1866–1944), dramatist and novelist and international pacifist, who, in a correspondence with Freud, and then with Bremond, and despite his renunciation of dogmatic Catholicism, found the *Histoire* enormously helpful in his respectful, admiring approach to an understanding of the Hindu mystics.[5]

What makes Bremond technically engaging in "the Metaphysic of the Saints" is his focus on "religious psychology," that is, the shape and movement of the inner life in response to a religious stimulus or perception. He struggled with the "where" of mystical encounter within the inward realm ("the fine point of the soul marked by disquiet"), the "how" ("elevation" to state-like identification with the beloved representation—for Christians, Jesus), the "what" (immediate encounter with the silent and dark eternity of God understood as "pure love"), and the "then" (a personal holiness along with ascetic discipline and moral fervor grounded in "self-annihilation" and reflective of the divine nature). All of these taken together, Bremond would argue, constitute the unfolding experience of prayer in its precursors, course, and aftermath, an experience continuous with, or analogous to, arrival at the "poetic state." While he would pay heed to traditional categories by choosing the concept of "sanctifying grace," as a unifying thread, the informing spirit of thought is lyrical or poetic (Bremond is looking over his shoulder at Valéry), with holy living as a kind of inevitable outflow. Saintliness is not the product of ascetic struggle, but of exuberant response. The most challenging element, therefore, in this calculus, but the most important finally, is the characterization of the "what" as "pure love."

Political and social context provide more perspective. Eugen Weber, historian of the French interwar years and of the Action Française, has offered a vivid picture of the vigor of Catholicism during this period. Even as the life of smaller country parishes waned and they lost most of their clergy, priestly vocations were on the rise, urban religious institutions remained robust, conventual life for all of its rigidly ascetic ethos continued to thrive especially for women, youth organizations and women's and "family values" alliances flourished, social fellowships and sports clubs of all kinds had a heyday, politically aligned and partisan movements were particularly vigorous and outspoken—all in the name of the church. While, on the one hand, left-wing Catholic groups aligned with socialism and organized labor were encouraged from Rome, in fact most French Catholicism stayed right wing or weakly centrist (despite official

---

5. See Parsons, *Enigma of the Oceanic Feeling*, 111, and 210n. Bremond and Rolland had a brief correspondence (unedited).

sanction of Action Française in 1926). Indeed, the Catholic Church was often seen as the "Right at prayer" and many Catholics wondered how the church and the Republic could ever work together. The picture, then, is of a somewhat polarized church, mostly traditionalist, but in a society stagnating economically, increasingly fractured by class-divisions and culture wars, with an intelligentsia inclined to radical socialism and progressively alienated from Christianity. The politics of Vichy and a church stained by collaboration are around the corner.[6]

And in 1928 the cataclysm of the Great Depression was about to hit. This is the world into which Bremond would insert his "Metaphysic of the Saints." As we shall see, he will be accused of "quietism" in the spirituality he advocated, but it is really that he will stand for a development of the inner life that can weather the storms ahead with a view of God and grace that has the capacity for survival, then for rebirth. Anything more ebullient, more "muscular," would be false, he thought. By the time he died in 1933, "quietude" would be his theme in the unfinished *Histoire*, XI, but it is a quietude not of restful withdrawal, rather of inner gathering. First the night—perhaps a very long night—then the day.

Metaphysic?

Bremond's choice of "metaphysic" in the title for *Histoire*, VII and VIII, has led to some puzzlement, since he was writing a history, not a philosophical treatise. Certeau has argued that in VII and VIII Bremond extracts theology or philosophy *from history*, that is, he engages in an inductive process of construction rather than deducing conclusions from abstract premises or "foundations." Such an inductive method, averred Certeau, is a reflection of Bremond's use of "the genetic law of all truly spiritual language," namely, that deep experience is shrouded and hardened in conceptual expressions that simultaneously hide and reveal.[7] Jacques Le Brun varies the argument by suggesting that Bremond's procedure is a kind of Modernist "insinuation" of truth, in which he embeds his theological agenda in the "swarming mass" of his characters. Not only would explicit theorizing have been too dangerous dogmatically, it would also have been inappropriate to the nature of its object, namely, spiritual "experience" in its ineluctable concreteness.[8]

---

6. Eugen Weber, *Hollow Years*, ch. 7, "A God in Our Image." Weber notes a group of progressive Dominicans who made a strong public point of identifying with the political Left (ibid., 199). Bremond would make two seventeenth-century Dominicans, Chardon and Piny, the heroes of *Histoire*, VIII. The French Dominicans were very pleased with Bremond about this (Certeau, "Henri Bremond," 25, with a reference to Du Bos, *Journal*, V, 76). Bremond had learned in 1924 indirectly that the Dominicans, always competitive with the Jesuits, were miffed at the fact that he had thus far ignored them (see EG, 210–11).

7. Certeau, "Henri Bremond," 27–28. Bremond "wishes to draw from history its philosophical and doctrinal lesson,—a definitive 'philosophy' that the *experience* of the saints has enunciated and that the *movement of an epoch* has revealed" (ibid., 28).

8. Ibid. Le Brun argues that the form of Bremond's presentation, where philosophy has to be

But it is clear as well that Bremond wanted to outline a pattern or shape to the inner life of prayer in order to elucidate its underlying principles.[9] His exploration and assertions thus had some of the quality which would come to be known broadly as "phenomenological," that is, the effort to describe the presenting appearances of a subjective experience in such a way as to keep it recognizable to those who have the experience, while yet discerning its inner (logical) coherence.[10]

He was not yet, however, operating in the mode of the history of religions, though inclining in that direction, since the zone of his analysis was limited to literary and textual expressions. His view was that the "structure" (architectonic?) of prayer is just as valid in the present as in the past, thereby imparting a timeless quality to it, making it a "metaphysic" in a broad philosophical sense.[11] And he clearly intended it to be "philosophical," thus lay and even to a degree secular, rather than clerical and "theological," a move that Blondel very much appreciated. The idea is to take the "prayer that does not pray" and lead it forward, even if the concept of "sanctifying grace" served as a concession to the demands of traditional moral and ascetical theology. One of the attractive qualities of his whole *Histoire*, once again, is Bremond's effort to cross over (with a degree of success yet to be assessed!) the boundaries of theology, philosophy, psychology, literature, and even, in embryo, the history of religions.

There is also the question of the use of "saints" in the title. One wonders why Bremond did not use "mystics" or "mysticism," but Certeau suggested that "saints" and "mystics" were equivalents for Bremond, the two terms having been since the seventeenth century completely interchangeable as designations for the practitioners of "experimental" holiness.[12] The use of "saints" may also have had a more generalizing connotation, broadening the field of application to the whole spiritual dimension of life, especially its ethical, not just inward, aspects. His argument increasingly was that prayer/mysticism/sainthood express the entire life of all of the baptized, rightly understood, and that sanctifying grace is the core dynamic of the Christian, indeed of all

---

extracted from history, is "homologous" to its object, that is, it represents the strategy of Modernist thinking, where history "suggests" certain conclusions or insights not subject to rationalizing explication.

9. Something much like this seems to be Goichot's view in one place at least: "to disengage the fundamental and universal elements of the mystical experience, so as to make clear their simplicity and unity" (EG, 209).

10. Bremond was aware of, and approved of, the work of Max Scheler, see Bremond to Blondel, January 1, 1926 (BB, III, 233, and 235n4).

11. His own summary statement appeared in a pseudonymous review that he wrote of *Histoire*, VII and VIII, then excerpted in the *Introduction*. His intention, he said (*Introduction*, 355), was "to disengage from any 'prayed prayer' the essential elements, those that deserve to be called 'prayer,' the elements that reappear in all prayer." The story of the pseudonymous review is told by Blanchet (BB, III, 336n3) and in more detail by Goichot (EG, 235–38). It was an effort to explain what he was doing in volume VII as a preparation for volume VIII, but also a preemptive strike at critics who would deplore his attribution of mystical prayer to *habitual*, rather than *actual*, grace.

12. Certeau, "Henri Bremond," 40.

religiously grounded, existence. For the remainder of the *Histoire*, beginning with VII, the entire focus is away from reconstructing the spiritual experience of chosen, gifted, and literarily creative individuals to writers who write for the masses, who articulate the nature and processes and goals of spiritual experience for all persons. Bremond returns to Francis de Sales and Bérulle in order to chart direction, but then launches into an ocean of popular composition.

Finally, it should be noted that the title "metaphysic of the saints" is too strikingly close to Fénelon's "Maxims of the Saints" to be an accident. In a letter to Blondel, Bremond asked him for suggestions on the choice of a title for these two volumes, indicating that he was having a bit of a struggle. Seeking input also from his friend, Monbrun, he revealed that he wanted to produce a "speculative" work, and that the focus on Pure Love as the center of true prayer, a focus that rises in "un-codified form" from the "masters" of the seventeenth century leading up to Fénelon, would be preeminent. The final choice was to be his own.[13]

The Problem: Panhedonism

The two volumes of the "metaphysic of the saints" are subdivided into four sections.

Volume VII, part I, contains "the primacy of prayer," drawing on Francis de Sales, Bérulle, and Francis's early exponent Jean-Pierre Camus (1584–1652), bishop of Belley. Prayer being "commerce" and "request," issuing in the disinterested "ascent" or "elevation" of the soul to God, it is "theocentric," eschewing the "anthropocentrism" that makes devotion a means of practical results. This latter is now denominated "panhedonistic," because it is human satisfaction or pleasure, instead of God, that becomes the focus. Jansenist "victorious delectation" in election, and the Ignatian emphasis on the action that arises from prayer, are both seen as "panhedonisms," having more of the spirit of Epicurus than of Christ.[14] Protestant "emotionalism" and all forms of anti-mysticism, which smuggle in a veiled erotism as the central dynamic in religion, are included as well. Bremond argues that much of what passes as "love" with Christian teachers is a form of implicit self-gratification, "the ascetic cult of 'moi.'" This kind of asceticism is nothing but "moralism," he says, referring to an important work on the nature of love by Pierre Rousselot, to which I will return.[15]

---

13. Bremond to Blondel, early October 1927 (BB, III, 277–79, and n6). At one point he toyed with "the psychology of prayer," Bremond to Blondel, September 21, 1926 (BB, III, 254).

14. An indication that Bremond was returning to Fénelon and the theme of pure love, although there are suggestions that, in order to avoid charges of quietism Bremond was careful to omit explicit references to Fénelon (see Blanchet's note, BB, III, 335–36n2, and the citations there from Bremond's letters to Baudin in August 1927). The charge that the Jansenists are "Epicureans in disguise" goes back to Fénelon's 1714 *Pastoral Instruction in the Form of Dialogues on the System of Jansenius*, no. 23 (see Gorday, *François Fénelon*, 195–96). Bremond seems to have picked up the term "pan-hedonism" from the work of the abbé William James Baudin, with whom he maintained a correspondence about Port-Royal, and who had used the term in regard to Pascal's spirituality.

15. *Histoire*, VII, 26n1.

Blondel was waving red flags. In a letter to Bremond early in 1927 he had cautioned about the use of "theocentric" and "anthropocentric," as have many critics ever since. He agreed that, of course, God must be the unique center of religion, and that contemplation must be seen in terms of its power to maintain that perspective. But, while God has not made us for a transcendent egotism, neither must we be "the servile courtesans of a tyrannical satrap" (Blondel could turn a phrase!) whose glory is his only concern. Rather, God, needing nothing from us, acts "for our salvation," and for the beatitude that is our goal from the beginning. Thus, rightly understood, there is an anthropocentrism which is proper and valid in the light of the human vocation.[16] A little later, Blondel imagined the saying, "'Think of me, I will think of you,' says Christ to the soul united to Him."[17]

Bremond never responded directly, so far as I can see, to this perfectly coherent and proper criticism of the idea that "pure love" is an utterly disinterested adoration of God, in which all human well-being is irrelevant, if not totally forgotten. Although Blondel's criticism was well-intended, aiming to protect Bremond from the charge of quietist heterodoxy leveled against Fénelon, the problem was that Bremond was starting at the point where most people approach prayer or a conscious relationship with God. The natural tendency, so it seems, is to seek help, to be on the lookout for benefits, for the satisfaction of a need.[18] I'm just human, and I do not approach God in a search for "beatitude." My goals are more mundane, often driven by anxiety. The point of Bremond's teaching, and that of the predecessors on whom he leaned, is that this approach, as it often exists in desperate or frightened people, and as it may be justified by conditions of oppression that cry out for redress, easily ends in shipwreck on the rocks of self-interest, at least where God is concerned. And a painful learning-process is thereby entailed. I ask for baked bread, yes, and surely God wants that, but what God ultimately wants to give, *in the final analysis*, is spiritual bread. The challenge is to get egoism out of prayer, to restore, so it seems, its "proper nobility," its pure and primal nature and real purpose.[19]

Indeed, it is here that Certeau was right: Bremond is pitting the reality of experience against Blondel's lofty formulation of human destiny.[20] If God is silent, can

---

16. Blondel to Bremond, February 25, 1927 (BB, III, 267–69).

17. Blondel to Bremond, note not dated (but placed by Blanchet in October 1927) (BB, III, 284). "Divine anthropocentrism unites itself to human theocentrism," says Blondel in the same place.

18. I use the phrase "so it seems," because a "bread and circuses" view of the origins of religion, or its variant ("no atheists in foxholes"), is very widespread and makes a certain appeal to common sense, as well as to serious scholarship on the origins of religion. But Bremond worked from a different theoretical base, namely, the idea that primitives/children first develop a sense of the supernatural from feelings of wonder and awe in the face of generative power. In Bremond's language, "commerce" precedes "demand."

19. This is the argument of *Introduction*, ch. 1, "Prayer."

20. Certeau, "Henri Bremond," 38–39. What Bremond was concerned with was the experience of hitting a blank wall that most people have when they really try to pray. This is a problem of modernity, of course, the fact that God does not seem to "speak" or "manifest" anymore, especially if the sky is

people still believe, still pray?[21] And can, then, their prayer be "real," not an interested sham for propping up some chosen extraneous agenda? Bremond's answer is a firm "yes," but he had to argue a difficult counterintuitive case.

By advancing the view in his first chapter on Francis, that nurturing love is the only way out of egotism, Bremond realized that the question of whether love can ever be non-pleasurable, non-self-referential, was on the table. The second chapter then took up Francis's view of the two selves, the surface "I" and the deeper "me," a distinction equated by Bremond with Claudel's "animus" and "anima." Picking up Francis's image of the "scorched heart" or the experience of extreme and prolonged desolation or dryness in prayer, he contended that the encounter with God in the deeper self at the "fine point of the soul" cannot be a feeling, an affectively experienced surge of some kind. He cites Francis: "The lover of our souls draws us by the secret influence of his grace, which he wishes to be imperceptible, so that it may be more admirable, and that, without amusing ourselves by feeling its attractions, we may occupy ourselves more purely and more simply by uniting ourselves to his goodness."[22] The quite paradoxical implication is that the dryness at the fine point of the soul *is* the presence of God at work, since the "wall" is alive with divine energy, that spiritual desolation is the encounter with life-renewing potentialities, *if* we have the eyes of the mystic.

Bremond then moved on to a reprise of Bérulle's teaching about "elevations" which result in "adherence," about the passive contemplation of the ideal, resulting in new infusion of energy from that ideal. His primary source is a 1634 work by Claude Séguenot (1596–1676), systematizing follower of Bérulle. Adherence reflects the rhythm of a passivity that leads to reconfigured activity, a cooperating with grace that first requires a yielding to grace, so that the "state" qualities of the deep self can support the "act" qualities of the surface self. The production of poetry first requires the inner operation of the "poetic state," always remembering that "the soul should not be attached to what God is working in it, but to the God who is working in it."[23] Self-abnegation leads to a self-renewal which is no longer a self-securing, you have to lose your life in order to find it.

He then turned to Jean-Pierre Camus's interpretation of Francis in order to expound what he called the "Salesian pan-mysticism," the idea that the "passivity"

---

not pitch black, but uniformly gray!

21. "Silent" here is better than Certeau's "absent," the latter representing too much the metaphysical sub-structure of post-modern thought. Bremond's own experience, we recall, had been that God was "so hard, so reasoning, so cold" (Goichot, EG, 183, citing a letter from Bremond to Maude Petre of December 21, 1900). The interesting question: do modern people experience God as "not there" or as "indifferent," perhaps "irrelevant"?

22. *Histoire*, VII, 83n1. Cited by Bremond from Francis de Sales, *Treatise on the Love of God*, II, 2. The whole section in Francis's treatise in on the slow, percolating, quality of the divine love in the soul that opens to it, like being nurtured by maternal milk. The imagery is not particularly appealing to modern sensibilities, but Bremond's use of it is part of the effort to get away from the prejudice that mystical experience is ecstatic, overwhelming and bizarre.

23. *Histoire*, VII, 135, citing Séguenot.

experienced at the fine point of the soul is better understood as what we today prefer to call "receptivity," wherein something is given in self-forgetfulness, a gift, that is not of our own making.[24] The term "passivity" is dangerous, too redolent of contemplative monks in mountain fastnesses, too tied to the loose language of the Dionysian mystics like Benedict Canfield, whereas "receptivity," *properly understood*, denotes more a readiness for action, needing only, after waiting, an initial impulse. Camus supplied this idea by speaking of the "sanctifying" or "habitual" grace that becomes a steady "infusion" at the center. If I can let go of myself long enough, get quiet at the "wall" that is God, listen to the ideals that engage my heart and motivate me, let go of my fears, then new activation will come with the "gift" that is given, and continues to be given in a (more or less!) steady stream. Bremond calls Camus's argument the "Salesian *via media*," where "passivity" refers to the balance between a complete rejection of all ascetic activity, on the one hand, and a devotional hyper-activism, on the other.[25]

Blondel kept at it, however. He kept complaining that Bremond was setting up an image of God as the ultimate "transcendent and jealous Egotist," demanding glory and adoration as his due, ignoring the well-being of his creatures. What is "forgotten" and "annihilated" in the creature who approaches God is an illusory self of self-love, so that the self beloved by God can arise. What God wants, averred Blondel in a reference to Aristotle, is not contemplation rather than action, but *purified* action, "prattein" rather than "poiein," the former being meaningful action toward happiness, the latter mere busyness.[26]

Probably both are right, but starting from different points. Bremond was approaching the matter from the position of the individual who is in a state of religious despair, frozen and shut down, who finds God silent and cold, but who needs to persist, nonetheless, in engaging God thus experienced. Blondel is already presupposing the active God reaching out with arms of love to each of God's children, who see that love and trust it.

Another Gallery

In the second part of VII, Bremond then turned to another gallery of characters, in order to introduce colorful or exquisitely stated wrinkles into the general picture, and, again, to show how widespread was the kind of French-School spirituality that he was describing, and advocating. These are largely unknown individuals, but all writers with a certain literary flair. Bremond excerpts generously from their works

---

24. In a note to Blondel, October 10 (?), 1927 (BB, III, 284). Bremond claims that he is describing here "an anti-passive Camus who Blondelizes," the reason being that Blondel has complained about too much emphasis on "passivity," which will only lay Bremond open to charges of quietism.

25. *Histoire*, VII, 154.

26. Blondel to Bremond, November 30, 1927 (BB, III, 294–95). This letter from Blondel was a long critique of *Histoire*, VII and VIII, and I will return to it.

in order to convey the flavor, as he cycles through Pére Hercule (1603–1655), superior of a small religious order and "a facile and laughing genius who does battle with rhetoric and its models" and teaches "freedom from attachment to sensible [i.e., 'felt'] graces,"[27] then Jean-Baptiste Noulleau (1604–1672), freedom-loving Oratorian who anticipates the "social Catholicism" of Leo XIII[28] and has a "joyous and lyrical" sense of the "little people of faith" and their awareness of God's gifts, then Paul de Lagny (d. 1694), Franciscan pan-mystic with a heart for the poor and oppressed and a sense for the importance of loving God without pretending to understand God or having access to some esoteric knowledge,[29] and then Francis de Clugny (1637–1694), another Oratorian, one who had a deep conviction that the desire to be freed from guilt is a form of self-serving, that a sense of one's own imperfection is, paradoxically, necessary for perfection.[30]

Bremond concludes with, first, a section on "the 'Vine-grower' of Montmorency and the School of Heart-Prayer," a devotional touch authored by Jean Aumont (d. 1689), who popularized an image that appealed to peasant earthiness, that of the "fine point of the soul" as a "wine-cellar," where God knocks, requesting entry. Grace works like an "alambic" (distilling apparatus), where, in the "blazing furnace" of the will, transformative process slowly occurs.[31] The final section is on Louis Thomassin (1619–1695), a fellow Aixois, with an exquisite sense for the "acquiesence of the deep soul in the continual prayer of the Spirit that dwells in us."[32] "Habitual adhesion to habitual grace" is the underlying theme with Thomassin,[33] in which pure prayer is the perpetual return to a grace-induced inner state where the soul gazes upon God at the fine point in unbroken adoration. It is French School spirituality for the masses with the focus on "the one thing necessary."

The religion of the people, which is the spirituality of "pure love," when it is competently taught and faithfully practiced,[34] is thus grounded in the "sanctifying"

---

27. *Histoire*, VII, 167, 195–96.

28. Ibid., 247.

29. Ibid., 277–78.

30. Ibid., 288–302, a lengthy section dedicated to "the mysticism of sinners." "Let us resign ourselves not to sin," says de Clugny, "but to the state of being sinners." The idea is standard, as in Richard Rohr, *What the Mystics Know*, sec. 2, "God Is Found in Imperfection."

31. Ibid., 335–38. The idea is that the human heart is like the wine-press, where the flames of the "interior furnace" constantly burn up self-love in order to produce the pure wine of the love of Jesus Christ.

32. Ibid., 413.

33. Ibid., 401.

34. Goichot points to evidence that this populist agenda, so to speak, of exhibiting "religion moyenne" in the seventeenth century, had been Bremond's original intention in *Histoire*, VII, until he discovered the Dominicans Chardon and Piny, who become the central characters of volume VIII (EG, 207–8). There is then the necessity of constructing a bridge back from them to the French School, a task accomplished by including the treatment of Francis de Sales and Bérulle at the beginning of a reconstituted volume 7.

or "habitual" grace which—abstract "notion" though it be—is the reality of the thing, the lived experience, the working dynamic of popular piety back then and, implied Bremond, subject to recapture in the present as pure poetry/pure prayer.

Grace Working Within

The reasons for the choice of "sanctifying grace" as his dogmatic banner, while quite deliberate on Bremond's part, can be puzzling to us. The context was a renewal of his debate with the Jesuit Cavallera about Ignatius and the *Spiritual Exercises*. If one asks the question, "*Why* are anthropocentrism and asceticism so pernicious?," the answer is: "Pan-hedonism." The search for pleasure in one's relationship with God is the ultimate problem. But why?

Let us recall that Bremond wanted to take the life of prayer, of mysticism, of religion itself (they are all becoming coterminous by this point), away from the conscious mind or the empirical and reasoning intellect ("raison raisonnante"), but away, also, from our easily deluded sensory apparatus. When human need seeks God, there are usually efforts to "stir up" the divine presence, or to manipulate the divine will. The typical result of trying to "make" God happen ("asceticism" in Bremond's use of the term) is bondage to our own more-or-less clever agency. The mark of such agency probably at work is the sense of *pleasure* that arises in the process, the greater danger coming from highly sublimated, rather than bluntly crude, pleasures. The solution, Bremond believed, must lie in a not-doing which is a silent and inward hearkening in a state of inner quiet. *Sometimes* inspiration, poetic creativity, transformative charitable impulse and vision, will blossom forth, and I might have a sense of first *contact* with "that" which I cannot control or summon at will, but can only receive and then obey. By an act of faith I may decide to name the "that" as "God" (particularly if I have an uncanny sense that the "that" "knows me" and is thus personal).

When Bremond pictured the working of God at the "fine point" of the soul, he carefully distinguished his own approach from that of William James as he understood the American pragmatist.[35] James's delineations all pertain, claimed Bremond, to religious "experience," which is the realm of the conscious, thus superficial, aspects of religiosity, while his, Bremond's, analyses have reference to the religious "act," that is, those aspects of the divine working in a person's soul that escape conscious observation. Therefore, he opined, the concept of a "religious psychology" should be applied only to the surface, that is, to the arena in which "actual graces" come into operation. It is at this level that the individual has experiences that prepare for love, and pave the way for prayer. The encounter with love itself, however, happens only at a level out of the reach of consciousness. Psychology can study only the precursors or the effects of the union with God, but not the union itself, where "sanctifying grace," that is, the supernatural, operates. If

---

35. *Introduction*, 356–57.

the "science" of the inner life would recognize this claim, he further contended, a "true revolution" in perspective would follow for thinkers of all kinds.

The resurgent controversy over Ignatius had been very gradual in coming. As we saw, the initial exchange, pointed but polite, with Cavallera had died down in 1922, as the momentum began to build for Bremond's candidacy for the Académie and he was distracted. But there had been a publishing scheme,[36] going back to 1919, in which Bremond had agreed to edit an anthology of Catholic literature, that would include portions of the *Spiritual Exercises* with an introduction. After various frustrating permutations, Bremond ended up with a mass of notes and commentary on the *Exercises*, but the publication went nowhere.[37] By 1926–1927, as he prepared material that would become the "Metaphysic of the Saints," he was left with a head of steam about Ignatius and so decided, as he said, to heat the waters (a "good opportunity for taking back up, amplifying and orchestrating our debate")[38] and get some feedback from Cavallera at Toulouse. The result was a long provocative essay in the Strasbourg journal *Revue des sciences religieuses* for 1927.[39]

The essay operates on two levels. Both are important, but the second much more so. The first is a continuing intra-Jesuit debate about Ignatius's original intention for the *Spiritual Exercises* and how they should be understood, versus how they have been differently construed in later usage such as Bremond personally had experienced. The second, however, is a continuing reflection about the purpose of prayer, and then about the nature of a relationship with God, and what that relationship looks like in practice.

He started out by describing his efforts in the direction of a new, critical edition of the *Exercises*, noting the work of several scholars who had recently made important contributions toward the restoration of the original text.[40] His intention, he says, is thus to call for a revival of the school of Lallemant in utilizing the *Exercises*, where meditation will be rightly understood as an "ascesis," but not as prayer itself. Bre-

---

36. Laid out in detail by Goichot (EG, 186–88).

37. Bremond's collaborator in the scheme was Charles Grolleau (1867–1940), poet and translator, who would eventually produce the *Index alphabétique et analytique* to the *Histoire*. Bremond's abortive commentary on the *Spiritual Exercises* was edited and published by Jean-Claude Guy, SJ, "Henri Bremond." Some of the frustrating story was told by Grolleau in Arrou, "Henri Bremond et Charles Grolleau."

38. *Inrodution*, 24.

39. "Ascèse ou Prière? Notes sur la crise des Exercices de Saint Ignace," reproduced with additions in italics in *Introduction*, ch. 2, "Ascèse ou prière?" There had been a competitive struggle between the Toulouse Jesuit journal, the *Revue d'ascétique et de mystique*, edited by Joseph de Guibert, publishing Cavallera, and the Strasbourg journal, publishing Bremond, for dominance in their debate.

40. Included was a 1926 study by Bernard-Maître (*Introduction*, 23n: *Essai historique sur les Exercices spirituels de Saint Ignace*, published at Louvain), demonstrating the fluid nature of the text of the *Exercises* in Ignatius's time. Bernard-Maître lived on to contribute an essay at the 1966 Cerisy-La Salle conference on Bremond, "Les Exercices Spirituels de Saint Ignace de Loyola: Interprétés by Henri Bremond." He was very sympathetic with Bremond's interpretations.

mond avers that as meditation the *Exercises* do not work for many people, though the problem, he insists, is not with "method" itself, since any kind of "practice" will inevitably include a methodical dimension. In fact, within Jesuit circles themselves debates grew up about different kinds of methodical approaches, only some of them being "ascetic" in nature. He thus raises objections to the description of the *Exercises* as a "school of prayer," when in actual practice they are a school for the training of the will, where individual energies are channeled into producing the "docile instrument of God," the human will cooperating with grace in directing the individual to some particular ministry. Francis de Sales had described the *Exercises* as "the manual of the Christian soldier," and so they are in actual usage.

Now we are already used to this argument from Bremond, but there is a further wrinkle. In an Apostolic Constitution of 1922, Pius XI had, after being politically pestered by Jesuit superiors feeling besieged by criticism, clearly affirmed the status of Ignatius as the "master of the *Exercises*,"[41] thus supporting the popular retreat movement, of which the Jesuits were the leaders. There is nothing the matter with "ascesis," Bremond says, as long as we recognize that it is not prayer, and as long as we see, he says, that it is the arena for "actual grace," grace that works with our conscious efforts at self-discipline and that enables specific actions for specific purposes. Bremond does not make the connection here, but it is implied: "ascesis" is like Valéry's description of prose, i.e., a form of expression that aims at an end, and, once that purpose is served, it ceases to exist. A good thing in its proper place, we might say, but not poetry, just as "ascesis" is not prayer.

This "militarization" of the *Exercises*, argues Bremond, is precisely what Ignatius did not intend.[42] Rather than seeing his teaching as directed toward "practical results," Ignatius actually placed the emphasis on what Bremond called a "mysticism of election," that is, a spiritual state in which the exercitant is enabled to make choices under divine influence, the coming of consequent "consolations" or "desolations" being the divine sign of approval or disapproval. The imagination of the individual is thereby stimulated to read the "signs," and then to pursue an ever-deepening life of prayer under spiritual direction.[43] Bremond calls this dynamic "mysticism," because the individual is drawn into a steadily expanding, contemplative relationship with God, where *habitual grace* can work unconsciously, slowly, steadily within the confines of the "fine point" of the soul. This habitual grace is none other than sanctifying grace, the in-

---

41. Bremond interpreted this Constitution, *Summorum pontificum*, as "practical, not speculative," the intention being to support the retreat movement, but not to express a judgment on the correct interpretation of Ignatius (*Introduction*, 143).

42. Ibid., 107–8. Bremond describes the "prodigious coup d'état" by which there has been "a confounding of the rules of combat with the rules of prayer."

43. The discussion here by Goujon and Salin is especially helpful, "Henri Bremond et la spiritualité ignatienne." Cavallera disagreed with Bremond on the import of these "signs," but Goujon and Salin, focusing especially on Bremond's, and Certeau's, interest in Surin, contend that Bremond's views have been vindicated in he long run.

visible working of holiness, the pure gift, quietly and secretly generating a gradually transformative effect in the direction of charity.

The argument is pregnant at this point. Bremond had objected to the "militarizing" of Ignatius, and we know that about this time the "Camelots du roi," the rabble-rousers of the Action Française, were active in the streets of France. And we know that debates about France's military were intense at the time, since the war wounds were deep, and pacifistic tendencies were in the ascendant, with the political right always adamant for a stronger military, while the left was hesitant, if not resistant. Henri Bernard-Maître, after noting the post-WWI surge in historical scholarship on Jesuit origins, has pointed to Bremond's contention that Ignatius was not a professional soldier, but rather a gentleman engaged in chivalrous service, a well-intentioned amateur really, a kind of Don Quixote always seeking God's will, though never absolutely certain about its precise nature. The purpose, thus, of the *Exercises* is the finding of God's will without presuming to know it, a humble searching versus a presumptuous sureness.[44]

This is to say that Ignatius in effect teaches the mystical doctrine of the "discernment of spirits," looking for divine enlightenment for this or that tendency in the soul. In effect, argues Bernard-Maître (quite rightly), Bremond saw that the *Exercises* need to be understood *humanistically* in the light of Ignatius's *Autobiography*, this latter work just starting to be well-known in Bremond's time.[45] The implication was that, rightly understood, Ignatius's *Exercises* were always a work-in-progress, never a finished product—as much poetry as prose, we might say.

In his response, Cavallera once more rejected the whole notion of "ascetism," disagreeing with Bremond's Ignatian reconstructions and insisting that Ignatius's "theocentrism" was not only strong, but honored by his followers. Bremond then riposted at length by restating former points, but also by clearly separating his historical arguments from the "metaphysic" of prayer. "Ascesis," he says, is self-expending, self-assertive, dependent on grace in theory but not mentally (pray, then row like blazes!). "God" becomes an expression of our own energy, "I wish" is the watchword, aggression is the style; "prayer," on the other hand, is receptive, self-effacing, dependent on adhesion to God's will, we become expressions of God's energy, "let it be" is the watchword, enduring and suffering and experiencing and undergoing and being self-forgetful comprise the style.[46] What aggravated Bremond was the insistence that prayer, religion itself, be "practical," always directed to particular ends in the service

---

44. Bernard-Maître, "Les Exercices Spirituels." In this survey of Bremond's latest views on Ignatius, Bernard-Maître admitted to a certain "romanticism" here, but insisted that an unpitying critique of militarism as usually understood was implied (ibid., 173). In Guy's 1969 publishing of Bremond's notes, one can see his focus on Ignatius's "grandes actions . . . pour l'amour de Dieu" ("Henri Bremond," 210).

45. Henri Bernard-Maître, drawing from Bremond's (then) unpublished commentary on the *Exercises* (Bernard-Maître, "Les exercices spirituels," 171–72).

46. *Introduction*, 150–51.

of an agenda. His *particular* target was Ignatian spirituality as he believed it had been misconstrued, but his *general* goal was much larger: a protest against the relentless process of instrumentalization, and the attendant "sense of self," that marks modern technological cultures. Everything serves some utilitarian purpose that can be calculated, and I see myself as a project to be worked at (rather than to be understood and loved, we might say).[47]

I think that Bremond's protest against "asceticism" thus represents a kind of paradox, or internal contradiction perhaps, in the modernist project. Wanting, on the one hand, to embrace and affirm scientific approaches to the understanding of the past as well as the present, as well as the benefits of technology, and wanting to reform the church accordingly, modernist thinkers then have to deal with the down-side of scientific methods, which easily become impersonal and subject to technocratic manipulation. They lose "soul" in order to embrace "facts." This is why Bremond tried to have it both ways in the end—as we all must—by affirming the necessity of methods and goal-oriented disciplines as the realm of "actual graces," but the essential import as well of meanings and values, of transcendent "truth," of "habitual and sanctifying grace," as the ultimate point of reference. It is a humanist protest against science, or what we have come to call "scientism," and in spirituality the relentless drift toward materialist monisms. In Bremond's case, it was the need to push back against the growing fixation on, even worship of, industrial might and inventiveness, as in the Futurist movement. All of the challenges were there, and everything in him resisted the trends.

There is also a debate going on here about sources of strength in the human personality. A current position has it that "resilience" is a highly desirable trait, resilience being the ability to "roll with the punches" and learn from experience, sometimes bitter experience, and to become a stronger and better human being in the process. But resilience cannot be simply a matter of "trying harder," this being Bremond's gripe with the Ignatian "asceticism." "Actual graces" may enhance my ability in a specific set of circumstances, but over time there must be deeper formation of some kind, "habitual and sanctifying grace," if I am to become a more capable and compassionate person.

In any case, the debate between Cavallera and Bremond finally came to an end, as such debates are wont to do, when it became clear that they were arguing from fundamentally different assumptions, experiences and temperaments and, I would add, a different reading of modern culture and its challenges. Goichot has traced out the detailed exchange of blows in scintillating detail, entitling his final section "the truce."[48]

---

47. I touch here on the whole project of Charles Taylor, in works such as *Sources of the Self* and *A Secular Age*. In the latter, as mentioned (*Secular Age*, 510–11), Taylor points to Bremond's work as one attempt to break through the modern idea that "human flourishing" can be accomplished in a strictly immanent way by immanent means. The critique of industrial capitalism as de-humanizing is omnipresent among serious thinkers during the 1920s: Max Weber, Martin Heidegger, the Frankfurt School, etc.

48. EG, 208–9.

In other words, they agreed to disagree. Francisque Gay, always defending Bremond and always his advocate in Rome, where he had strong connections, managed to avoid any kind of censure being directed at *Histoire*, VII, and its presentations,[49] but the order came down, at the end of 1928, from Jesuit superiors to stop the quarrel, and so they did. Over time, Bremond has been the more fertile influence.[50]

Quietism and the "Passive"

Blondel, aside from reservations regarding Bremond's choice of the theocentric/anthropocentric terminology, did not have any problem with *Histoire*, VII. He seems to have found the ongoing intra-Jesuit debate with Cavallera a bit tedious, and generally encouraged Bremond to make peace. Bremond's strictures against "ascetism" made sense, he thought, although he periodically reminded Bremond that there is a good use of ascetics, and Bremond got the point as long as there was no confusion with true prayer.

The issue that was emerging, and one reason that Blondel harped on the use of "passive" and "passivity" in describing true prayer at the "fine point of the soul," was the hazard of charges of quietism. The fear that Bremond's volume VII might meet with censure from Rome was based on this distinct possibility. Any talk of "pure love" had the quietist smack as well. And we have noted that Cavallera at one point had thrown that charge against Bremond.

What is the problem here, and why is this thing called "quietism" such a threat? The issue is important because it dovetails into the highly individualized freedom for infinite variation in spiritual experience and practice that we so enjoy today. Contrariwise, the question of quietism involves our perception of religious communities as highly organized and disciplined collectives, even "militarized" collectives, in a way that Bremond was resisting, that did not "work" for him as a young novice with the Jesuits in England. It also involves our sense that religious experience and expression should have an "orderly" quality, be subject to rational control and rational implications for living. It also involves the perception (fiercely resisted by advocates) that Asian religion, especially Buddhism, with its seeming rejection of the western sense of "self" as a center of focused agency, is a spirituality of "quietistic" withdrawal and passivity.

In the classic description and definition of the term, from the papal bull of 1687, *Caelestis pastor*, condemning the teachings of the Spanish priest Michael Molinos (and with which the critics of Guyon and Fénelon associated them), "quietism" is said

---

49. See Weber, *Hollow Years*, 201, on Gay and his progressive, but futile, associations. "The spirit of Francisque Gay had a great future, but in the 1930s that was all it had."

50. Goujon and Salin ("Henri Bremond," 436–40). note that a principal vehicle of the debate, the *Revue d'ascétique et de mystique* would in time become the *Journal d'histoire de spiritualité*, and that when the first volumes of the *Dictionnaire de spiritualité* first started coming out in the 1930s, Joseph de Guibert, SJ (one of the Superiors who had shut down the debate), author of the article on Bremond, says of him in a moderately conciliatory spirit that "his true master was Fénelon."

to teach the importance of the annihilation of all activity (the soul thus returning to its origin in the essence of God), the cancellation of all content in the mind (so that anything that might be known comes directly from God), the value of the mystical death, where all consciousness of fault or imperfection ceases, where there is a "continuous inner state of immobility," so that God becomes the actor, by grace, of all that might happen. Thus, felt devotion is devalued, and the absence of various typical indicators is taken as a sign of divine presence, in order that self-love may be purged. The practical and moral consequences are that spoken prayer, various traditional devotions, the humanity of Christ, overt acts of love, resistance to temptations, the rejection of temptations, and a general downplaying of the institutional Church in favor of free-floating contemplation are all highlighted.[51] The condemnation of Fénelon's pure love teaching in the *Maxims of the Saints* was usually seen as the definitive rejection by Church authority of quietist aberrations in their most insidious form.

But there is a softer position called "semi-quietism," where some of the quietist language may be used, but shifted into an orthodox sense. And, of course, it may be the case that quietist writers employ orthodox terms in a heterodox fashion, especially if the language has a history of long and nuanced usage. A flash point is the term "passivity," beloved of quietist teachers, but with a non-quietist heritage as well. Here, then, is the point where Blondel wanted to save Bremond from trouble. For instance, in a letter of late November 1927, Blondel discusses the theme of the "crucifying trials" which we all must undergo, and argues that the phrase "activating penetration" as applied to the apparent passivity of the soul touched by grace is a good one, since in the process the soul does not lose its being, but its nonbeing.[52] Or, a little later, he confines the use of "passive" only to that moment where the soul "allows God to act" and infused grace flows.[53] Somewhat earlier, he had argued more elaborately that souls enjoying intimate communion with God only appear inert and insipid on the outside, when in fact beatifying love is at work deep within, the soul being "passive, insensible and devastated" in the divine presence—which is to say that the final passivity is not inhuman, since divine power has joined itself to human being and human possibility.[54]

Nonetheless, critics will continue to emerge with charges of quietism, despite all of the efforts at cleansing or modifying terminology, and Bremond's use of Chardon and Piny in *Histoire*, VIII, will not make things any easier. In truth, he was deeply attracted to quietist spirituality for the same reasons that he fought what he saw as "asceticism," that is, he sensed the deep modern need for an approach to prayer, and religion in general, that is constituted by "stepping back" from the empirical world into a mental zone of rest and reorientation, a place of "commerce" with God (as he put it) where "demand" becomes quiet trust and where inspiration may (not must!)

---

51. The description is taken from Le Brun, "Quiétisme: en France."
52. Blondel to Bremond, November 25, 1927 (BB, III, 291).
53. Blondel to Bremond, November 30, 1927 (BB, III, 295).
54. Blondel to Bremond, October 8, 1927, undated note attached (BB, III, 284).

happen, and action can come when the time is ready. Heterodox quietism (much modern spirituality) abuses this legitimate hunger, while seriously recognizing it. We can do better, thought Bremond (Blondel assisting).

But there is still that nagging question of "pure love" at work at the point where the soul encounters the "wall," the silence of God. Thus, Bremond moves to the second volume of the "metaphysic of the saints," the "staging" now being over, since the time for the main drama to begin had arrived.

17

The "Metaphysic of the Saints" II
The Main Act

ON THE THIRD PART of the "Metaphysic of the Saints," which is the first part of *Histoire*, VIII, Bremond bestowed the grand title "The Great Synthesis—Chardon and Piny." These chapters contain, if not the completed fabric of his design, at least its strong foreshadowing. Indeed, Chardon and Piny themselves, relatively unknown spiritual guides who would remain, and have remained, largely unknown, tend to sink into the background as the outline of Bremond's own synthesis comes center stage.

Dominican Input

Given his preoccupation with the failings of non-mystical Ignatianism, it is a bit of a surprise to discover that Bremond was very much aware of, and had a fond spot for, the Dominican heritage in France. An early indication is contained in his glowing review article done for *Études* in 1900 on the published letters of Henri Didon, just deceased Dominican priest, popular lecturer and writer, avid supporter of sports and the revival of the international Olympic Games.

Didon (1840–1900), known as a spellbinding preacher, was a controversial and colorful character, deeply devout but also a rebel against authority in the way to which Bremond always warmed. His writing and spiritual direction were, Bremond claimed, marked by a combination of "incendiary words" and deep friendships. Severely disciplined by his Order because of his radical ideas, he took the dressing-down in good spirit, then went on to pen a lively and bold interpretation of the life of Jesus. All in all, he displayed an "independence of heart" in the faithful enactment of a path-breaking ministry that was inspiring. "Let us admire," said Bremond, "how such a disposition opens to the Christ all of the great doors of this soul uniquely eager for God."[1] Perhaps the greatest credit for Didon is that he left a good mark not only on the Church,

---

1. "Lettres Spirituelles du P. Didon," 195.

but on the wider culture as well. The name of God is everywhere, Bremond insisted, in such a life. High praise.

In fact, Didon in many ways typified the whole thrust of the nineteenth-century Dominican tradition in France, reintroduced by the great Jean-Baptiste-Henri Lacordaire (1802–1861) in a practically single-handed reform movement. Against strong opposition, but with staunchness of vision and highly successful preaching at Notre Dame in Paris, Lacordaire brought the Dominican Order back to France, unencumbered by the monarchist or conservative political baggage of the longer established Orders like the Jesuits. He was politically liberal from the outset, and his Order represented the Church's determination to work with the Republic and not against it. "Liberty" was to be the Dominican watchword.[2] Elected to the Académie in 1860, he took the vacated seat of Alexis de Tocqueville. After the First Vatican Council, however, the Dominicans reverted increasingly to their more traditional role as watchdogs of orthodoxy, thus of Thomistic theology, in the process becoming more politically conservative and setting the stage for the kind of rebuke later received by Didon.

It happened, then, that in 1913 Bremond was, as he tells it,[3] on a trip to Italy, gathering materials for his projected *Histoire*, when he met with the general archivist of the Angelicum, the Dominican college in Rome. Having found that Dominican materials were simply not available in France, he had consulted a recent general history of Dominican spirituality, in which he met the view that Thomism has always reigned supreme with Dominican teachers from beginning to end. Thus all doctrine and no spirituality, in Bremond's estimation. The names of Louis Chardon (1595–1651), best known for his *Meditations on the Passion of Our Lord Jesus Christ* and especially *The Cross of Jesus* (1647), and Alexander Piny (1640–1709), whose most important works are *The State of Pure Love* (1676), *The Key of Pure Love* (1680) and *The Prayer of the Heart* (1682–83), had come up only in passing. Predictably, the Dominican archivist in Rome was dismissive of Chardon, but when Bremond took a look at Chardon's work, and later revisited that of Piny, he was stunned by the new treasures.

What he came to realize, Bremond contended, was that Dominicans were like Jesuits—especially if one set aside their characteristic theological preoccupations—in insisting on actual grace, on ascetic disciplines, and thus suppressive of some very real mystical elements in their own traditions.[4] With Chardon and Piny, however, he once again rediscovered that when hairsplitting and polemically derived doctrinal

---

2. Sheppard, *Lacordaire*, esp. ch. 8, "Return to Politics."

3. *Histoire*, VIII, 7: "In the little cell of the Father archivist I got the kind of recognizable response that had already stifled me [from reading the history of Dominican thought by Mortier]. I had come to ask for mystics; I was offered theologians."

4. Goichot contends that the above account is Bremond's "romanticized" version of how he came to appreciate Chardon and Piny, that the reality began in 1924, when he began to respond to the criticism that he had been ignoring the Dominicans in his *Histoire* (EG, 210).

predilections were put aside, the mystical mother-lode of habitual grace and the priority of "states" over "acts" came to the surface.[5]

He recognized that these two writers are totally focused on the inner life, that for them "there is a single center of perspective: the Mount of Olives, Calvary; more precisely, [these events are] meditated on ceaselessly with a singular vivacity, the mystery of the agony and of the supreme dereliction, which renews itself daily in the spiritual world; the drama of so many daily desolated little cells, the paradox of impossible prayer."[6] The core insight of Chardon and Piny, he thought, was that for the mystics "in order to love God one need not feel that one loves," that in "the psychology of the mystics . . . the distinction between surface activities and our deepest activities, thanks to which we can remain the friends of God, allows us to pray truly, and in some manner always, in the blackest of interior darknesses."[7] Therefore, the doctrine of "sanctifying grace" is "the metaphysical key to all imaginable prayer." Chardon being the theorist, and Piny the pastoral teacher, they both agree that prayer is a supernatural gift that the human subject must accept, claim, and use; habitual grace (first), and only then actual graces.[8]

In fact, what Bremond had come upon was a French adaptation (a Provençal adaptation!) of the German Dominican mystical tradition of Eckhardt and Tauler and Suso and others, at once inward in all of the ways that he so highly valued, but also strongly and intensely christological. "It is in the cross," Chardon wrote, "that the soul is amorously forced by the proper weight that sanctifying grace gives to it."[9] Everything is contained in those few words, thought Bremond, but their unpacking would require a sustained exposition containing the living heart of what he most wanted to say.

Bremond's Core Project

The working term in the statement just cited from Chardon is "amorously." What does Bremond make of it?[10]

5. Some Dominicans, like some Jesuits, Bremond insists, are "better clinicians than philosophers" (*Histoire*, VIII, 7n2).

6. *Histoire*, VIII, 14: "They have one goal: the comforting of souls. And for that they have one method: to disengage from the Cross the blessed philosophy that it conceals."

7. Ibid., 15.

8. Ibid., 3–18. Bremond observed that Reginald Garrigou-Lagrange, conservative Roman censor and traditionalist, had already published a highly glowing essay about Chardon (ibid., 18n1). Later this same authority would review with approval the notes of the first Dominican reviewer of Bremond's chapters on Chardon and Piny. Charles Du Bos was highly amused by the irony of all this, as noted by Certeau ("Henri Bremond," 25n10). Bremond was effecting here a kind of reconciliation with Thomism in revised form (see on Rousselot below).

9. *Histoire*, VIII, 21.

10. Certeau thought that everything for Bremond comes back to the "inadequation between religious knowledge and the *real assent* of faith," that is, between doctrine and experience, with a

Pure Love, Pure Poetry, Pure Prayer

If we think for a few retrospective moments over the span of his spiritual journey, we will go back, as do most commentators, to his early essay collections on *L'Inquiétude religieuse*, on *Âmes religieuses* and on *L'Enfant et la vie*. What we find there is his pedagogical-literary orientation. He was convinced early on that the religious seeking of modern people, when they acknowledge the existence of that seeking, is best satisfied through the study of literature. At first the focus is on "high" literature, as required by school-curricula, but eventually the concentration shifts to "lower" literature, as in autobiography and journals and correspondence. The reason is always the same: the "inner life" of the writer is revealed, and thus the approach to God, even when God is not named. We recall from some of the earlier essays, such as that on George Eliot, that this inner life is morally tinged, morally earnest. And we recall Bremond's interest in the moral seriousness of the English Calvinist heritage. In due course, poetry—or perhaps better stated, the poetic dimension of texts—becomes the principal literary vehicle of the passion, the horizons and the insights of this moral energy.

And then, under the weight of Jesuit formation combined with his pedagogical experience, as his attention slowly shifted toward the life of prayer as the supreme dimension of personal inwardness, he looked more closely at various religious writers who are also moral essayists. Included here were writers as diverse as Nicole and Arnold, but supremely it was to the towering genius of Newman, where "conscience" is the gateway to God, that he was most attracted. Increasingly aware of the danger of a superficial moralism, however, his interest shifted to the inwardness of mystical spirituality across the range of its literary expression. Such literature is personal, intimate, concrete. Everywhere he found expressions of religious "disquietude" like his own, the passionate seeking for genuine prayer by contrast with conventionally bourgeois piety. Biographical portraits of religiously disquieted souls, first English, then French, led him to the beginning of the *Histoire*. But the conviction is always the same: it is *literature* that matters, because the textual expression of spiritual disquietude, always deeply personal, will minister to our disquietude.[11]

The singular mark of this disquietude is, once again, that it is *moral* in nature, being not so much, as Bremond saw it, a search for truth in the abstract—an intensely rational quest as in the style of the eighteenth century—but more a function of the nineteenth-century romantic longing after beauty and goodness in the human soul artfully presented. Moral truth emanates from a purified, sanctified inwardness, captured in poetic texts, as with the mystics.

It was then the service of Newman for Bremond that the search for a morally shaped spiritual inwardness became a search for the *real* in religious experience. In

---

"philosophy of silence and spiritual passivity" as the resolution ("Henri Bremond," 26). I am suggesting, however, that for Bremond the problem is not *believing*, but *loving*.

11. Bremond's early question, taken from de Maistre,, "Who is it that really prays?," became over time the more refined query, "What does it look like, how does it express itself, when someone really prays?" It is the latter questions that enabled Bremond to identify both good and bad elements within the same person or tradition.

a modification of Pascal's "reasons of the heart," it is the spiritual truth discerned by the prayerful conscience that is the "real." So far as the Modernist project goes, that search for the real then became the progressive, historical-critical effort at recovering original states, thereby getting to the *depth* of a dogma, its moral-practical import, rather than staying at the *surface*, where outward forms are an ever-changing series of contingent manifestations, always the product of evolved conditions. Deep truth will be *moral* in nature, a revelation of the goodness in some aspect of religious thought or practice, thus its potential for nurturing and calming inquietude by means of a moral vision. This is Bremond's alliance with Blondel (always, as it were, looking over his shoulder) in the conviction that God is found in the human depth and in the church's depth, that is, *immanently*, precisely as these shape the intentional horizon, the "willed" goals, of "action."[12] The human soul experiencing deep within its spiritual core the presence of God as the morally Real, and having this experience with utter immediacy, then became the focus of Bremond's work.[13]

At this point, Bremond, of course, had options. The language of moral discourse is complex and varied. The biblical language of "covenant faithfulness," or "the call to holiness" or "the demand for righteousness," or the cry for "justice," could all have been used to describe the moral dimension of God. But the Catholic tradition in which he operated, and the literature that he treasured, made the idea of "love" the decisive category for framing the moral nature of God, and thus the moral nature of the soul in communion with God.[14] God is infinite Love requiring love on the part of finite creatures, and in Christ requiring that "natural" love become "supernatural love." The First Commandment, "You shall love the Lord your God," is everything. And this love that is commanded by the moral nature of God is at the same time the fulfillment of the nature of finite, created beings. The human heart is completed by loving God, and then in turn, loving the neighbor. That is the moral vision. God is pure Will requiring love, because God is love. For the moment, we leave to one side the critical question as to whether Bremond and his tradition have made the best, or most fruitful, choice in naming "love" as the supreme moral category for God.

12. Certeau contends that Blondel kept trying to pull Bremond in the direction of an "optimistic synthesis," where human willing, by grace, finally leads to the genuine fulfillment of human potential in beatitude, rather than to the "willing not to will" of the pure love mystics ("Henri Bremond," 52). I will suggest eventually, as a third possibility, that Bremond arrives at a "lyrical" or "poetic synthesis."

13. This is where Certeau has suggested, rightly, that Bremond, while sounding at times much like Kierkegaard, "where an internal dialectic is analyzed in order to describe an existential movement," is yet quite different (ibid., 46). For Bremond (partly because of Blondel) subjectivity is a gateway, not the thing itself.

14. Certeau demurs at this point, tending to the view that for Bremond all reference to the "objective sign" of God has disappeared, since "disinterested love" is simply the "sign of a negation," that the use of "pure" points to an absence, and that "amorous despair" is despair pure and simple (ibid., 44–45). But in Certeau's interpretation the term "amorous" is an abstraction, the Hegelian lack at the center of infinite desiring.

The deepest human hunger, always ultimately moral in nature, is expressed, then, as one contemporary writer puts it,[15] by its "eagerness to love," starting with love of Love itself, and then spreading to the love of all of God's creatures. Without the love of God, the love of the creatures would become shallow; without the love of the creatures, any professed love of God would be sterile. The challenge is to keep a socially oriented loving, such as in reform movements, from being a mere "asceticism," a mere doing, that eventually consumes its own advocates in egoism.

Precisely, moreover, because the disquieted search for the God who is Love takes a literary form, it evokes the whole range of creations by which the human imagination seeks satisfaction, especially the longing for lost childhood innocence, say, or the erotic embrace of lovers, or a mysticism of nature, or some form of utopia, where the ideal state being sought starts to become fantastic. The question, then, of the *genuineness* of love follows naturally, since, like everything else, the presenting forms of love can be superficial or just false. Thus is born the quest for "pure love," the thing itself, and this is the quest that becomes the driver for Bremond, since for him everything points in that direction for the resolution of spiritual "disquietude." This is where Fénelon comes in, with his focus on "pure love" precisely as disinterested love, and the contention that where Love is genuine or real, it always posits the glory of God or the welfare of the other not just as its chief concern, but as its *only* concern.

But there is an intellectual jump here, when the *reality* of love is equated with a hypothesized *purity*. The lineage is from Newman to Blondel, as Bremond read them, then to Fénelon and others, particularly Chardon and Piny, as Bremond read them. The reality and purity of love are a function of its agonized reach for transcendence, a transcendence that registers at the finite level in its degree of disinterestedness. Logical problems abound, of course, as in the question of whether the purity of the intention is equal to, or compromising of, the purity of the act. And there is the question of mutuality: does my desire to serve the other allow for the other's need to serve me? And so on. Bremond coined his whole technical vocabulary of "theocentric" and "anthropocentric" and "ascetic" and "panhedonistic," as well as the notion of "devout humanism," as a way at getting at these issues, which are easily evaded when an atmosphere of authoritarian certainty in religion prevails.

But the requirement seems inherently contradictory, as Blondel repeatedly reminded Bremond. Can love be "pure" in the way that Bremond desires? What can it possibly mean for a human being to will the welfare of the other, without in some way willing his/her own welfare as well? Is Bremond dealing with a moral vision or a moral fantasy? Is there a difference between those two? And if prayer is finally the seeking of God's will in order to do that will, can real prayer ever thus be possible? Can anything humanly intended ever be a fully suitable container for divine intention? This is the point at which Bremond comes to Chardon and Piny and *Histoire*, VIII. Maybe there is a *literature* of pure love that can bring us to prayer and the God who is Love.

15. Richard Rohr, *Eager to Love*.

Only when we arrive at *Histoire*, XI, and "Le procès des mystiques," will Bremond begin to show us how quietude replaces disquietude in the spiritual search, but all of the key pieces are already implied in "the metaphysic of the saints." That cold "wall" that we encounter when we try to pray *is* God present and morally powerful—precisely because it is only that coldness that can minister to our need to be purified. And it does so by overcoming our sinful sense of what our "need" is. A "hot" God, i.e., one known in raptures and bestowing bounty, virtually ensures an "interested" response from worshippers, and the satisfaction of "interest" will only prolong and deepen inquietude. It is the cold response that, as it were, "teaches" pure love, thus moral excellence. If the Beloved seems to reject me, then all the better: in my suffering I will learn what is most important by laboring to love all the harder. All good writers and poets know this to some degree or other and wrestle with it, but it is the glory of the tradition from Francis de Sales to Fénelon to have, first, stated the matter clearly, and then second, to have articulated a rounded theological response. The search for God and the life of prayer may well continue (or not), but now we know that it is the God of Love whom we are seeking, and why the journey is so difficult.

Chardon

It is clear that had he lived long enough, Bremond would have ended his study of the seventeenth century with a reprise of the Bossuet-Fénelon debates about quietism and "pure love," the *cause célèbre* of the 1690s. He refers to Fénelon constantly throughout the *Histoire*, and there are frequent references to the concept of "pure love" without any sustained exposition.[16] As it turned out, the unfinished *Histoire*, XI, contains substantial, but not definitive, attention to Fénelon's work. The problem, however, with Fénelon on the subject of "pure love" is, of course, that he was tainted with condemnation and association with Guyon's supposed heterodoxy. Bremond's discovery of Chardon and Piny, therefore, was all the more valuable: here are two impeccably orthodox spiritual teachers, completely approved by the highest doctrinal authority in the Church, teaching views of "pure love" that anticipate Fénelon without the latter's impediments.

What seems to have attracted Bremond to Chardon initially was the latter's combination of Augustinianism and its theological structure with love at the center with the tradition of German Dominican mysticism, the mysticism of Eckhardt and Tauler and Suso, which is an apophatically articulated mysticism leading to "darkness." The combination of those two led to Chardon's theology of the cross.[17]

---

16. If one consults Grolleau, *Index*, s.v. "Fénelon," it is clear that Bremond makes references to the Swan of Cambrai in every volume of the *Histoire*. It is as if he is constantly looking over his shoulder at Fénelon. See Talar, "Prayer at Twilight," 45–46.

17. References to Augustine are primarily to the *Confessions* and the theme of the "apex of the soul," where communion with God occurs. References to Tauler are to the idea of the "center of the

Bremond started out his exposition of Chardon's thought with a description of the latter's understanding of human nature. He describes the soul and God as "inclining" toward one another in an embrace, whereby all of the divine perfections are put at the service of the soul, with the soul's volitional powers potentially at the divine disposal. This "inclination" has a "cross-ward" thrust, thus making the crucifying love of God that amorous "forcing" that is the work of God's "proper weight" in the soul by means of sanctifying grace. God's presence to the soul is a function of the "divine Immensity," with the result that all natural and finite powers and operations are dependent on God; the "weight" of the divine presence is essential to the definition of humanity itself, thereby necessitating the Redemption as a fresh energizing of created potential. The soul has a "natural capacity" for God, thereby making mystical spirituality a fundamental affirmation of that same created potential.

To this Thomist-flavored description of the soul's dynamic of potency and act, God extends an invitation to pure love. But, Chardon insists, God's presence in the soul is one of absolute silence, where spiritual desolation reigns, a desolation which is the hallmark of grace at work, that same gracious love that animates the inner life of the Trinity. With a great deal of poetry Chardon develops at length this idea of a divine silence working through desolation.[18] The first stage of the mystical journey is then a fellowship with Jesus in his Cross, a fellowship in which "a marvelous system of contrary forces" is at work: "the weight of glory pulling the soul in one direction, the weight of suffering in the other."[19] The "leaning to the Cross" always produces an effort which is triumphant by virtue of the "leaning to glory." Chardon has created a real "living mechanism," says Bremond, for describing the presence of Christ in the soul as both crucifying and glorifying simultaneously. He has thus given literary expression to the theology of Aquinas.[20]

The reality of sanctifying grace, then, is this divine presence felt as a weight, drawing the predestined soul toward fearful desolations. It is the agony of being in love, where the love consumes the lover, who at the same time refuses to be seduced by pseudo-satisfactions, "the false brilliant in all its metallic splendour," as Judas knew.[21] Love is the experience of the children in the flames, consumed and yet rejoicing. One must then go through the crucifixion with Jesus, because this is the nature of love forcing itself on the faithful heart. "Love, being a movement of the heart towards what one loves, it is necessary that those who are touched by it are no longer for themselves,

---

soul" as a "vast solitude." All references are in Grolleau, *Index*, s.v. "Fénelon."

18. Bremond has this extraordinary line: "Whereas, for those souls, for whom the silence of God is synonymous with the absence of God, Chardon will wisely steer them to an identification of silence and presence" (*Histoire*, VIII, 26). There is Certeau's postmodern foot-in-the-door, so to speak, a silent presence that takes the form of an absence!

19. Ibid., 29–30.

20. "The difficult marriage of the scholastic and the rhetorical, of the Latin of St. Thomas and the French of Balzac," says Bremond (ibid., 31).

21. Ibid., 34.

but for the object that ravishes them."²² This is the "subtle and impassioned dialectic," says Bremond, in which Chardon underlines the way that grace separates the suffering soul from all other loves and attaches it more firmly to the One Love.

This love is the manifestation of Trinitarian indwelling, where love becomes the principle of the soul's activity, by which we see that the sanctifying grace in mysticism is no aberration, but rather the ultimate rationale for all religious experience and the whole Christian life. Further, it reflects a suffering inherent in all human desiring, where souls are plunged into all that is not God, all that they must endure and tolerate, in order to embrace God—since they know that only God will satisfy. Here, suggests Bremond, is the therapeutic value of poetic consciousness, the "mountain-cure" of learning to despise oneself and to breathe only in God.²³ With a touching sincerity, Bremond admits that at this point Chardon is operating at a level that he himself has not reached, but doing it with such extraordinary suppleness that one can finally see that the cruciform grace of the highest mystical consciousness belongs at the same time to the puniest of souls.

Finally, Chardon explores the "great darkness," where the "deforming catharsis" works in memory, understanding and will, so that both "pure contemplation" and "pure love" can occur.²⁴ The Thomism of this position, especially where Chardon discusses pure "knowing," is foreign to Bremond, but the idea that "pure love" is tantamount to a "pure contemplation" has great appeal. You can love only what you adore, you can love only what you "let be," you can love purely only what you do not "know" or possess mentally. Bremond concludes on Chardon by marveling at his use of Jacob wrestling with the angel as "the agony of the Cross" reaching up for pure love. We have here, asserted Bremond, "a sublime symbolic poem, worthy of being compared even to the myths of Plato."²⁵

Piny

Bremond liked Chardon, but it is also true that Chardon's scholasticism was a little intimidating. Chardon had been a theologian at Toulouse, then a writer and spiritual director in Paris. But Alexander Piny is Bremond's kind of man; he is from Aix, he is plain and straightforward without being superficial, he was mistreated (Bremond

---

22. Ibid., 37. "Nothing is more 'paradoxical' than to establish an 'affinity' between fire and cold, between a 'principle of joy' and a principle of sadness, between grace and the cross, between the beatifying presence of God and desolation, the prolonged dereliction of those who inhabit that presence."

23. Ibid., 53. It can hardly be over-emphasized at this point that it is the *poetry* of Chardon's presentation, not so much its doctrine, that enraptures Bremond.

24. Ibid., 59–60. In an interesting aside Bremond relates the superiority of imageless contemplation to the Thomist appropriation of the theological apophaticism of Dionysius (ibid., 66–67). The individual who has moved from meditation to contemplation has experiential awareness of the utter only-to-be-expressed-negatively transcendence of the Godhead.

25. Ibid., 77. Plato has been present throughout!

thinks) because of his Provençal roots, and his writing was never so well received by the Order as Chardon's. All the better, actually, as far as Bremond is concerned, as he included a long discussion of the state of Piny's *oeuvre*.[26]

The essence of Piny's thought, declared Bremond, is that "pure love" is the very heart of all mystical prayer. Rather than being a solitary act of charity (actual grace), such love is an expression of the soul united to God and manifesting itself as a unity in each one of its actions. "Whether as specific act or habitual state, pure love is an adhesion, a consenting, an acquiescence of the human will to the divine will."[27] But what is the grounding of what we might call the "adhesive dynamic" ultimately? A yielding to what is most natural, or an exterior act of moral consent, freely made but in no way necessitated by our nature? There is a slippage here between moral and physical categories, which became a bone of contention between Jesuits and Dominicans.[28] Thus, "adherence" can mean *primarily* a series of constantly repeated conscious decisions, perpetually renewed moment-by-moment, or it can refer *primarily* to a kind of physical in-dwelling (in Thomist language, a "participation") unconsciously prior to consent and then only affirmed by conscious consent. The anti-scholastic humanist in Bremond as well as the "lingering Jesuit" leaned to the former, while constantly being tugged toward the latter, i.e., from "act" thinking to "state" thinking.[29] Entailed here in modern debates is the problem of a "virtue ethic" based on character versus a "decision ethic" based on categorical principles.

Piny distinguished three stages in this acquiescence by the human will: to will what God wills, to will only what God wills, to will whatever may be simply because God wills it to be. Bremond insisted that this last, while looking fatalistic or "apathetic," is actually the "state of abandon" to the "good pleasure of God," that was Francis de Sales's ideal, and that is "pure love" in action. Furthermore, Piny argued, there can be no question here of "delight in suffering," but only an indifference to suffering and success alike, since the human will has been "disappropriated of its own," that is, has no will of its own other than God's will. The *fiat* of Christ in the Garden of Gethsemane is

---

26. Actually, as a historical note, Bremond was highly amused by the fact that despite Piny's popularity in certain distinguished circles during his own lifetime, the Dominican historian Mortier delighted in Piny's eventual obscurity, noting that Piny's works are "virtually unobtainable today." In fact, then, Bremond had literally resuscitated a kind of "subversive voice" with Piny—just the kind of recovery in which he delighted. See ibid., 82n2.

27. Ibid., 91.

28. Pointed out to me by Eugene TeSelle, private conversation.

29. This is to say that Bremond was strongly attracted to the idea that habitual grace works as a constant and uninterrupted state in the soul, although he fully recognized the heterodox, quietist danger of asserting that there is a "one continuous state" in the soul that overrides any need for discrete conscious acts of moral decision-making. The problem, or potential confusion here, however, is that a psychological/spiritual condition or "state" is being identified with an ontological status of the human soul as such.

the perfect model, the "short means" to all perfection.³⁰ One takes, consents to, what comes, whether good or bad, and *thereby* loves God.

In this vein, then, Piny moved on to the subject of temptations and trials. He argued that we must be industrious in doing what the commandments require, but then be completely accepting of the consequences, or, as we might say, the price to be paid. In the operation of our free will, we must submit to the "let-happen," since it is not the "doing" that sanctifies, but the "willing," that is, my decision to abide by what comes, good or bad. Whereas, according to Piny, "doing" is driven by results which may or may not please the doer, "willing" is a spirit that pervades all action, precisely so that "doing" might be initiated by an impulse which is the will of God. The idea is that *what* you do may be important, but the *spirit* with which you do it is even more important. What sits poorly with modern consciousness is his stress on *indifference* toward results.³¹

Piny courted quietism at this point.³² He argued that we can be over-invested in our faults as well as our successes. He urged penitents to stop worrying if they sinned, especially if the worry became obsessive and thus a mark of self-love. "I am imperfect, woe is me!" In learning to be patient with ourselves, we learn to be patient with God. "Happy are the imperfect," said Piny, reflecting Francis de Sales's spirit, if not his expression. There is the further contention that the pain of temptations and trials, especially when we succumb to them, can be, by grace, a kind of "amorous despair," in which the lover knows that he is unworthy, but continues to love nonetheless.³³

But Piny was careful here, insisted Bremond, thus separating himself from Fénelon's ultimate error, because he is clear that the lover's feeling of despair is just that, a feeling and not a true perception of the state of things.³⁴ If God casts me into hell,

---

30. Ibid., 91–96. "In loving the cross, one is assured that one loves without interest, that one loves in order to please the Well-beloved" (ibid., 95).

31. Bremond's sustained, nuanced treatment of Piny's construal of the quietistic "letting-be" is the heart of his analysis of Piny, where what is described is a posture, a sustained state of mind, rather than a situation-by-situation decision. One does not deal with temptations by either chasing them away or acting on them, but by quietly leaving them alone!

32. Bremond was very aware that many would see in Piny's approach to temptations the smoke of a quietist fire, and that his "healthy psychology" will "scandalize the unconscious [judgmentalism] of some" (ibid., 121). At another point, he notes that Piny could be accused of "metaphysical dilletantism" in the way that he approaches the agony of those who seek to love God, "splicing and dicing," we might say, their despair in highly subtle ways. Not so, says Bremond, when, in fact, Piny simply takes with utter seriousness the inexpressible despair of a lover who realizes that he may lose the Beloved (ibid., 125).

33. This is as close as Piny came to the scholastic notion of the "wound of love," in which the lover, having given himself/herself to the other in a disinterested, unconditional way, ultimately is acting contrary to the dictates of the natural desire for survival by being completely self-sacrificing to the point of death. Francis de Sales's "impossible supposition" takes the scenario a step further by imagining that the endlessly persevering lover has the perception of actually being rejected by the Beloved.

34. Bremond refers to Piny's "ponderous dexterity" in all of this, avoiding the reefs that sank Fénelon (ibid., 130–31).

I will love anyway, says the benighted lover, not realizing that such a "supposition" with regard to God is "impossible," since God does not condemn those who truly love God. But the situation can *feel* that way in the desolation of love, and then become a supreme, crucifying, purifying test for the lover of God.[35] Further, what separated Piny from Fénelon here, claimed Bremond, was his insistence that an element of hope always should remain for the lover of God in his desolation, however cold that hope may be. Bremond adds the further detail that Piny "de-sensibilizes" the experience of pure love, thus qualifying St. Bernard's sensual description of loving affections toward God, by contending that mystics do not "feel" the friendship of God, since the unity that they have with God is a unity of will, not affectivity.[36]

In further analysis of Piny's treatment of the "impossible supposition," Bremond indicated that he had consulted with a "master in theology," another Dominican, and he reproduced that expert's delineation of the logical possibilities raised by the "supposition."[37] The issue sorts out logically into three conditions: "what is the case"; "what appears to be the case"; "what one must do under the circumstances." The upshot of the assessment is that in a true evocation of the state of "pure love" there must always be some sense, even if unconscious, of the reality of God's grace, some sense of the reality of divine goodness, since, after all (here we see the effect of Blondel's input, as well), God is approached and loved not as a capricious tyrant, but as a trustworthy Father. The temptation to despair, and the fight against it, are the conditions productive of pure love. Bremond claimed that he was approaching the matter as a "historian, not a theologian," but he was tongue-in-cheek, since he was describing his own struggles.

With regard to the question of passivity, Piny emphasized that "letting-happen" is an intense activity, a loving action of submission, even if painful tedium is the result. The act of willing and the act of loving are identical, so long as one wills with the Divine Will. Psychologically, the implication is that such willing is unconscious[38] on the part of one who prays, a continuation of prayer in the face of futility that is not a conscious "ascesis"—self-conscious and pleased with itself—but a quiet, consistent, non-self-conscious rising of the soul to God. I suppose we could describe such pure love as a daily, quiet, matter-of-fact keeping-on-keeping-on, aware of the seeming lack

---

35. This equivalence of "holy despair" and "pure love" is critical for Piny, says Bremond. It is the key to everything in the life of prayer. The insight that psychological anguish, often grounded in loss, can be the pain of "wounded love," is critical, of course, in much modern psychotherapy.

36. Ibid., 134. Hence it is that Certeau, among others, has argued that Bremond here embraces, with Piny, an "affective apophaticism" ("Henri Bremond," 43).

37. *Histoire*, VIII, 137–38n. This note is apparently an inclusion based on the first review of the text by a Dominican censor, it being important for Bremond to have a Roman *imprimatur* on this volume. Goichot discusses the inclusion of this note as part of his general analysis of the fear that to the Dominican censors Piny would come off as too quietist (EG, 222).

38. Strictly speaking, however, Piny's term is not "unconscious," but "interior." The difference is subtle, to be sure, but suggests that "interior" is closer to our "preconscious," as in the usage of William James or as in a cognitivism, rather than a Freudian dynamic unconscious.

of response from God, but calmly resolved to perseverance nonetheless. It is, however, difficult to reconcile this picture with the idea of a smoldering kind of agony in the soul of the one who prays, unless the pain is very highly sublimated.[39]

In Thomist fashion, moreover, Piny evokes this idea of a passivity that is a reflection of being, an unconscious acquiescence in "what is," where suffering may be automatically entailed, in the illustration of the rock that loves God, thus "inclines towards God," by being a rock.[40] The implication is that habitual grace works in the soul by means of a deep will that is a "letting-be," a "letting-happen," that operates at the level of being itself, and not of doing. Conscious and freely willed acts are still required, and are usually the means by which one approaches God for a deeper communion, but that often these "acts" are constituted by a decision to endure, i.e., to let-be, and thus are the very opposite of a self-conscious ascetic straining.[41]

"This, it seems to me," says Bremond (in a note we have heard before!), "is the key of the mystical problem; the very sure and salutary *via media*, between the two extremes which . . . threaten to ravage the spiritual world: on the one side, an ideal quietism, perfect, which knows only the 'let-happen,' and on the other, the ideal and perfect *asceticism* (a tendency more than a doctrine) which practically, disastrously, ignores the deep activities and cultivates only the 'doing'; the first leads to inertia, the second to an agitation as infecund as dolorous."[42] Is all of this difficult? "It is easy to swim," contends Bremond, "when it is the water that bears us up; but, to abandon ourselves to that mysterious and redoubtable force, to give up our footing, takes courage."[43]

---

39. The discerning reader will have noted by now that I am pushing Bremond's understanding of "pure love" in the psychological direction of concrete loving and its ethical decisions, rather than the philosophical view of Certeau that "pure," or disinterested loving is, for Bremond, primarily an ontological category ("Henri Bremond," 51). Indeed, the latter is *implied* in Bremond's thinking, but never formalized. He is too literary.

40. *Histoire*, VIII, 144. Probably what is involved here is the Thomist idea of the part-whole relationship in understanding the relationship of self-love to love of God. A rock is a part of the universe, thus has its role to play precisely as a rock. By playing its role, by being what it is, it "participates" in the being of the totality which is ultimately grounded in the Being of God. Thus, by loving itself, i.e., being what it is, it loves God, whose Being it shares. Piny's point, however—and his radical edge—is that such love will entail a suffering which must, by grace, be quietly accepted. Goichot notes that Piny was criticized here by scholastic critics for applying the term "love" to a natural condition of being prior to the rise of subjectivity; a *metaphorical* application at best would be acceptable (EG, 224).

41. This is why the formula of "willing not to will" became salient in the discussion. Granted that the decision to endure or accept is also a decision to embrace the divine will, rather than one's own, is it fair to say that at the "fine point of the soul" all human willing ceases completely? Bremond and Piny want to answer in the affirmative, but not because the soul despairs, but rather, because the soul "hopes," placing its trust in the trustworthiness of God. This affirmation was critical in avoiding heterodox quietism.

42. *Histoire*, VIII, 145.

43. Ibid., 150.

And so, in Piny's view, the amorous union with God is the principal end of human existence.[44] And prayer is the *wanting* to pray.[45] And there is the further idea that this wanting or willing is unconscious, even when the conscious mind is in an agony of distraction. The "method" to such prayer is that of a "dis-applying" of the intellect and affections, a paralyzing of faculties, in order to produce peace and silence, so that acceptance of whatever comes is set in motion. We must always return to the fact, he says, that the union of the will with God is a subterranean current, not a raging flood. This is the prayer of abandonment to the good pleasure of God. One can be in this state of prayer at any place and at any time. In closing, Bremond notes that in the eighteenth century de Caussade, with his "practice of the presence of God," will be a kind of Jesuit Piny (also a reconciler of Bossuet and Fénelon).[46]

Ignatius Une Fois Encore

Bremond could not resist a foil, and he felt that he needed a final visit to the Ignatian tradition within the confines of the *Histoire*. The last section of volume VIII is entitled, "The Anguish of Bourdaloue and the Genesis of Asceticism," and it is a study of how the Jesuits came to resist everything for which Chardon and Piny stood. The key is in the fear of "illuminism" that grew within the Jesuit Order after the time of Ignatius, and that finally resulted in the outspoken anti-quietism of the great Jesuit preacher, Louis Bourdaloue (1632–1704), at the court of Versailles in the time of Louis XIV. Bremond's intention was to show that the "asceticism" so favored by Bourdaloue was, in fact, "pan-hedonistic" and thereby completely opposed to the idea of desolating prayer, as we saw it in the two Dominicans.

In his historical reconstruction,[47] which is a distillation of the debates with Cavallera, Bremond argued that Ignatius himself used the *Exercises* as a tool for encouraging a discipline of actual graces leading to vocational decisions, but left the subject of prayer open and flexible, trusting the Holy Spirit to provide. But, as the need for more contemplative prayer emerged in the Order, central authority intervened, making the *Exercises* into a rigid and exclusive structure that discourages individual

---

44. Thus, Piny could speak of the "natural love" "common to some degree" in every creature, which is tantamount to a "metaphysical appetite for union" (ibid., 144).

45. "Painfully experienced spiritual inaction," says Piny, is more valuable than a spiritual act actually carried out. Such inaction is actually "prayer in the most rigorous sense" (ibid., 140). There is here an echo of the Thomist idea of "natural appetites" which inherently tend toward God. On a psychological level, once I have a sense of desiring God, I have in fact begun to pray.

46. Never at a loss for the humorous touch, Bremond admitted, at the end of his exhaustive treatment of Piny's thought, that the man had a certain "idée fixe" quality about him, that could be lacking in "taste," "painfully serious" at times (ibid., 178).

47. Goichot gives special attention to Bremond's inclusion of the Bourdaloue section in *Histoire*, VIII, and to his use, already mentioned above, of Bernard-Maître's theses regarding the original nature and setting of the Ignatian *Exercises* (EG, 216–21). Bremond was moving ever closer to a benign, "mystical" interpretation of this text as the genuine, critically purified reading.

inspiration. Then, in the context of sixteenth and seventeenth century Spain, with the growing ecclesial fear of the *Alumbrados*, or spiritual "illuminati" associated with radical Franciscanism, an intellectualist-speculative approach to prayer pushed out mystical-affective tendencies. The latter came to be seen as undisciplined, individualistic, and subjective, but it also had a populist and anti-elitist dimension. The official suppression of the ideas of Balthasar Alvarez (1533–1580), spiritual director of St. Teresa of Avila and exponent of the "prayer of silence"—who is treated by Bremond at length—was the supreme manifestation of the anti-illuminist witch-hunt. But the mystical tradition of the Jesuits stayed alive, finally coming down to Louis Lallemant, already treated by Bremond in *Histoire*, V.

After an appreciation of the Jesuit theologian, Jean Crasset (1618–1692), a mediating figure between the tendency to ascetics and a true mystical spirituality, Bourdaloue is then presented as a man of contradictions, both the personification of the Jesuit asceticist tradition in his doctrine, but, in his prayer as expressed in his preaching, a "mystic in spite of himself." The classical mistake that Bourdaloue made, said Bremond, was that he confined the experience and insights of mystical contemplation to an elite few, for whom quietist inclinations are tolerable, while being too dangerous for the common people. Moreover, the internal contradiction in Bourdaloue's preaching emerges when he assigns felt consolations to mystical prayer, thus revealing his pan-hedonist tendencies, even as he eschews such experiences in favor of pure ascetics for the multitude. Pleasure in prayer is good and excellent, but only for a few. Sanctifying grace is good, as long as it produces contentment. In the final analysis, says Bremond, Bourdaloue is in agony: his real heart and his stated message are in different places. He senses that "moralism" is not the deepest truth, that the "education of the will" is not the gift given in baptism, but the practical Jesuit in his makeup has the final say.

In thirty pages of detailed "clarifications" at the end of the volume, Bremond sparred with a reviewer who had raised questions about various points in the text. The essence of the complaints seems to have been that, in his polemic against asceticism Bremond had so removed any activity of intellect or of practical method from the life of prayer as to make it vacuous, without discernible content or determination of any sort, and lacking all discipline. The critic also objected to Bremond's program of including all prayer within the scope of "mystical" prayer proper, complaining that Bremond had over-generalized, and that Piny's "letting-happen" is morally dangerous. It became clear that what the critic most feared was that Bremond had opened the door to a permissive and vague spirituality for young people, in which "anything goes," and that quietistic tendencies just feed that danger.

Bremond acknowledged the risks, while insisting that careful distinctions would be a sufficient safeguard. The point, he insisted, is that sometimes prayer begins outside the realm of grace proper, and sometimes the most inadequate prayer is already "ordered toward grace." The key idea is that there is an "essence" to prayer that arises from nature itself, where the Spirit is already beginning to pray with us; that essence is "mystical," where external forms of every kind can only be super-impositions, often counterproductive ones at that! Pan-hedonic asceticism of Bourdaloue's type only inhibits this essence by replacing it with a focus on the doing of duty or some other moral and gratifying product as the *primary* purpose. True moral enrichment will come only as a derivative gain, an aftereffect of the real thing.

Here he included a tribute again to the Jesuit Grandmaison, but also, tellingly, to the work of Pierre Rousselot—brilliant young, and controversial, Jesuit theologian, dead in the trenches in 1915—who is cited indirectly: "What is strange and properly mysterious is that, in order to will completely, there must be another who wills in me—an 'other,' that is to say, a God . . . my will is my own *only in ceasing to be my own.*" *There*, said Bremond, was Piny's point. Rousselot's implication, averred Bremond further, is that much more is involved in love than simply submitting to the higher will of the Beloved; rather, it is the actual giving up of the *moi*, of myself as a "sufficient subject," by means of a self-abandonment which is the "operation of a gift within."[48] But, the question is implied: can such self-abandonment ever be "natural," in the light of everything we think we know about human potentials and capacities? By citing Rousselot, Bremond broadened the horizon of his analysis into a reflection on the nature of love itself.

The most salient publication was Rousselot's doctoral dissertation, "*Pour l'histoire du problème de l'amour au moyen âge*,"[49] first published in 1908. Rousselot set an intellectual problem for himself: how can we understand the ability of a human being to love with a love that is not egoistic? For him as a Thomist thinker, the problem was part of a wider problematic: how can human beings really know anything, or be conscious of anything, that is not just a reflection/projection of some part of themselves?[50] His reflections on the latter question would make Rousselot controversial, but it is the former one that serves as the point of departure for the most recent analysis, that by Jacques Le Brun, on the subject of Bremond and "pure love."[51]

The Nature of Love: Rousselot

Le Brun has argued, rightly, that of all the modern literature, including that of Proust, that explores the idea of pure love as a disinterested loving, Bremond's efforts have been the most important. In fact, Bremond made the delineation of pure love to be central to the Modernist project of working from surface to depth, and then of the gap between official dogma and mystical experience. Specifically, it was by appropriating

---

48. Ibid., 390. Bremond was citing from an essay in a *Mélanges* for Grandmaison.

49. All citations will be from the English translation of Pierre Rousselot, *The Problem of Love in the Middle Ages: A Historical Contribution*.

50. Rousselot, preface to *Problem of Love*, 76.

51. Le Brun, *Le Pur Amour*, 267–88.

insights from Rousselot's work, that Bremond was able to formulate his own project more clearly.

His first mention of Rousselot came in that section of the *Apologie pour Fénelon* where he was making a positive case for Bossuet in the debates with Fénelon. We recall that in his volumes on Bossuet of 1913 Bremond demonstrated great admiration for Bossuet, not as a rigid dogmatist and street-fighter, but as an eloquent lyricist, whose spirituality, when he preached or gave spiritual direction, was far more beautiful than his authoritarian rumbling. Bremond had developed a similar theme in the 1910 volume, when he praised Bossuet's clear directness as well as his grounding in the patristic-medieval heritage—he was, after all, a beef-eating Burgundian who venerated Tradition—on the matter of pure love. Citing Rousselot's description of Bernard of Clairvaux, Bremond suggested that Bossuet was rather like Bernard, in that he had both an "explicit" and an "implicit" philosophy. The former is expressed dogmatically, in "notions," the latter lyrically in homily and confessional writing, and the two do not always agree, the "implicit" with its powerful "metaphors" being a stronger reflection of the real person.[52] In a note Bremond defended Rousselot's way of reading Bernard here, claiming that, contrary to charges of Modernism already being directed against Rousselot as an "innovator," his making of such a distinction in interpreting Bernard is *more rather than less* loyal to the past.[53]

Bremond thus touched on a key methodological element in Rousselot's way of interpreting the past, namely, distinguishing a thinker's notional arguments from the more telling underlying, suggestive metaphors. In *The Problem of Love* Rousselot had raised the question of the possibility of a non-egoistic loving, and, focusing on Christian thinkers of the thirteenth and fourteenth centuries, he had contended that two types of argument are presented, based on two types of love. The first is the "physical" (nature-based) or "Greco-Thomist" type, derived from Aristotle and most precisely formulated by Aquinas, where the love of oneself, known as "the love of desire" (*amor concupiscentiae*), is in perfect harmony with the love of God or of another party, known as the "love of the friend" (the *amor amicitiae*), since friendship is seen as the paradigm example of disinterested loving. The love of self *naturally* tends to love of God, since the deepest human longing, which is coincident with God's will, is for beatitude. God and our nature want the same ultimately. *Truly* loving oneself, and thus seeking one's salvation, with all of the interestedness implied, is tantamount to loving God as God, because it is God's will that one loves in a kind of sanctified egoism. It would be the same in loving a friend: one loves the friend without regard for one's own needs, *but* it is always the case that such loving is in fact a fulfillment of one's needs, rightly understood.

By contrast, Bernard's thinking about the "ecstatic" kind of love, an idea which he developed in his pastoral rather than dogmatic work (as in the "stages" theory of *De*

52. *Apologie pour Fénelon*, 428.
53. Ibid., 479n.

Diligendo Deo), emerges from his "habits of language," where "implicit but powerful presuppositions are dominant."[54] This love is a love that "goes out of itself" in loving the beloved, a love dualistic (between two entirely independent subjects), violent (it ignores one's natural inclination to self-preservation and thus is "wounding"), irrational (impervious to rationality, including hierarchy, thus egalitarian), and free (self-sufficient, requiring no intrinsic bond between the two parties, so that love is a pure gift, not a "necessity" of nature). Self-love and other-love are completely opposed here. One loves the beloved, no matter what, death very possibly being the result. Rousselot actually found this kind of loving in other important writers, such as Hugh of St. Victor, thus underlining a flowering of love-mysticism in the period under review.

But Rousselot took absolutely seriously Augustine's "all people desire to be happy," and he insisted with Aquinas that there *must be* a clear connection between self-love and disinterested love of the other.[55] It *must* be the case that self-love is ultimately a fulfillment, a harmonious completion, of God's will, and therefore an identity with that will. The "impossible supposition" of Francis de Sales is simply unthinkable, absurd, self-contradictory. But it is Bernard, *in his lyrical moments*, who holds out the other possibility with his "ecstatic love" and the idea of a "submitted cupidity."

What makes the ecstatic kind of love possible in Bernard, according to Rousselot (in a way that marks Rousselot as "modernist") is that it is between two "persons," and not between two "natures" as in the Greco-Thomist formulation. Consequently, it is a love that must be "given," with its purity defined negatively, that is, as free from all self-seeking. But, in the last analysis, Bernard is inconsistent, thus revealing that we must turn to Aquinas for resolution: the problem is that in the highest stage of love, the person who freely gives his love to another is so spiritualized that he/she has ceased to be a human being in any recognizable sense.[56] The ideal aim of love in the extinction of the lover's personhood is so paradoxical as to be meaningless.

What Rousselot then argued is that when scholastic thinkers turned away from poetry to organized systematic reflection, they *had* to frame their ideas in terms of the finality of natural inclinations, that is, their ultimate end as parts of God's teleologically ordered creation. If love is the most powerful of all inclinations, then its end must be a harmonious union of self-love with the love of the other, and thus of God. In scholastic language, the *appetitus* has a natural *terminus*, whose full actualization is the highest good, which is delight in the vision of God.[57]

---

54. *Problem of Love*, 143. This is the Bernard that Fénelon takes up, as Le Brun rightly notes (*Le Pur Amour*, 274).

55. Le Brun, *Le Pur Amour*, 271–74. He cites Thomas's assertion, "If one supposes that God were not the good of humankind, there would be no reason for loving God" (*Le Pur Amour*, 272). The reference is to *Summa Theologica*, IIa IIae, q.XXVI, a. 13 ad 3.

56. Rousselot, *Problem of Love*, 148–50.

57. Ibid., 210–11.

Le Brun has argued that Rousselot's presentation has to be kept in context. What he wanted was a purified Thomism, in which one recognizes that the human intellect naturally tends toward God, just as the natural will tends toward disinterested loving. The church in its many condemnations of "pure love" has misunderstood the intention of the concept, which is to state a dimension of created human potential, but not a fanatic standard fully realizable by nature alone. Rousselot's insight was to recognize that "pure love" is a kind of oxymoron supported by poetry, but not by logic, as one sees most clearly in Bernard.[58]

But it was also the case that the Middle Ages did not know the "impossible supposition," because the understanding of "nature" did not allow for it.[59] The element of sacrifice in natural loving always had to be submitted to a rational standard based on a view of the human essence. But for the modern period, with its changed views of human nature, the impossible supposition becomes a possibility. And *that* is the issue, as Bremond recognized.

It is precisely the modern age that recognizes the existence of the "moi" in a way that the earlier period did not. In other words, we are looking at the modern concept of the subjective self, in which "selfhood" is conceptualized as a free-standing psychic "space," separate and distinct from its material substrate or environment. As a "moi" I have the capacity to *give* myself or *withhold* myself as an autonomous construction, a something which is not just an instantiation of "finite nature." And that changes the game, argued Le Brun, rightly I think. The *action* of self-giving acquires a different valence, as in Blondel's thought, because the action precisely as act possesses its own thrust.

The way we might say it is that Bremond brought to the old tradition of the impossible supposition and pure love the resources of subjectively-oriented modernity, specifically of "romanticism" as he understood that category. The one who seeks to pray, who seeks God, is a romantic quester, looking for the divine within the hidden depths of his/her own inwardness, where the urge to love reveals a horizon of self-giving possibility that can bond the individual to the human other, or to the divine Other, in a communion that respects, indeed *requires*, all of the dictates of moral excellence. The "impossibility" of pure love is precisely the revelation of its transcendent horizon, its God-orientation. What makes it a true possibility even while being (seemingly) "impossible," and not just an idle and pleasurable dream, is the suffering of the subject, who must "let happen" what happens, while at the same time pushing forward. "I will love you (You) nonetheless!"[60]

58. Le Brun, *Le Pur Amour*, 283.

59. The way that Le Brun says this (ibid., 277–78) is that the medieval concept of nature manifesting as an "appetite" is now defunct, precisely because the modern perspective is not just that we have appetites, so to speak, but that we *know* we have these appetites (ibid., 277–78). In the light of such self-consciousness, everything changes.

60. A sublime selfishness, even here, with the ego in love with its own passionateness? Perhaps. That is the romantic Achilles' heel, so to speak.

Le Brun has argued that "pure love" as an illogical striving for the impossible is a "configuration," rather than a theory or system, meaning thereby that it takes the form of something "readable without necessarily being provable or making sense." In Bremond's language, not yet cast in the post-modern mode of textuality, "pure love" is a lived, rather than notional, reality, operating at the level of the human desire for God even while lacking classical theoretical grounding. His task, therefore, was to lay out, with the help of chosen mystical sources, a first effort at a "metaphysic."[61]

The one thing lacking at this point seemed to be a more thorough description of the "state" of "pure love," once one accepts that "pure love" is indeed the right formulation. That description will center on the "quietude" that displaces "disquietude," and Bremond will come to it only in *Histoire*, XI, only, that is, as his own death approached.

---

61. Le Brun has suggested the interesting possibility that Bremond's use of the term "metaphysic" for *Histoire*, VII and VIII, was inspired by Rousselot's usage, when, for instance, in reference to the texts that express the ecstatic view of love, he says, "It is admittedly a difficult and delicate task to extract a 'metaphysics' from all this lyricism, but it is a task necessary to the history of ideas" (Rousselot, *Problem of Love*, 80n5, referenced by Le Brun [*Le Pur Amour*, 275 and 410n43]).

18

Bremond's Mysticism
Friends, Foes and Critics

WITH THE COMPLETION OF *Histoire*, VII and VIII, with the outlining of the "metaphysic of prayer" as the mystical apprehension of "pure love," Bremond had mounted an argument historical, literary, and of the "sentiment," as the title of the *Histoire* suggested. The historical thesis centered on the "devout humanism" of the French School and its unfolding in derivatives. The literary thesis involved a stream of spiritual writing—mystical, confessional, practical, lyrical, personal—always descriptive of the concrete inner life of prayer, sometimes culturally elevated and sometimes plebeian, but always the instrument of the historical unfolding. The substantive thesis took the form of a structural elaboration of the religious "sentiment," that is, the psychological life of the person who prays and then writes, that person's dispositions and "states," the life of the soul at the "fine point."

In all of this Bremond's repeated claim was that he was only a historian, not a theologian. In truth, Bremond never tried to "do" theology in the form of systematic, philosophically assisted reflection. When he described God as "cold," he never speculated about why God would present Godself in such a way. But he *did* think theologically about the nature of religious experience. When he describes God as "cold," he wonders why the one who prays forms such a perception, and he then ponders the implications *both* for the subject and the object of the prayer: what is it about the devotée and the God to whom he/she prays that leads to this sense of "coldness?" In other words, how does a particular "sentiment" regarding God arise in the soul of the one who prays?

Thus, it is that Bremond's self-description as a "religious psychologist" is the most accurate, for that is truly what he was, as long as we define "psychology" in the essentially literary modes discussed earlier. His focus is always the inner life *as in literary expression, that is, in poetry or its prose substitutes.* By 1928 he was addressing two readerships. First, the church and its leading thinkers and official voices. To them, he said something like the following: our classical dogmatic theology and doctrine, along with our authoritarian power-structure, has failed to meet the spiritual needs of urbanized, industrialized populations, alienated from traditions, subservient to technical rationality, and thus chronically vulnerable to addictive, consolatory pleasure-seeking. The mystical life of prayer, Bremond might have said, has always been the church's living heart-beat, tending to "pure love," and manifested in lyrical expression of every kind. Modernism recognizes this fact, and, using the best aspects of critical method and its respect for living context in interpretation, attempts the process of historical retrieval, as long as frightened authority does not suppress that process. Friendly critics such as Blondel responded to Bremond here with discrimination, while unfriendly ones, like Georges Bernanos, howled with rage.

Second were the secular and lay critics, skeptical of religious truth-claims and cynical about motivation and spiritual integrity in Christianity, as well as in all religions. While Bremond never knew Freudian thought, we recall that Sigmund Freud's *The Future of an Illusion*, probably one of the most widely read rejections of religion as neurotic fantasy, was first published in 1927. Freud's kind of critique, in which religion is the projection of human nature onto a cosmic screen, had been around for a long time, but took on particular energy in the dark and bitter post-war and inter-war years, especially as it manifested in nationalistic cults, then Nazi ideology. To this group, Bremond said: Your rejection of religion is a rejection of the kind of transformative spiritual vitality that can build a new and better world marked by "pure love." In fact, your rejection of religion is another mode of collapse into the very technical rationality that is destroying us, instead of listening to the "depths" of our unconscious, artfully creative nature. The recovery of true aesthetic expression, especially in "pure poetry," is the first step to the recovery of mystical prayer, which is the recovery of religion.

In response to his ecclesial critics Bremond would continue to produce church-historical studies of eras, figures, movements, that caught his interest and that, in his construals, supported his agenda. On the secular front he offered new studies as well, with the discourse on "quietude" in the unfinished, posthumously organized and published *Histoire*, XI, as the most pregnant. If we wonder why Asian spiritualities, particular those of Buddhism, had already begun to capture the religious marketplace by the interwar years, and have done so even more today, consideration of what Bremond was about in this last volume of the *Histoire* is instructive. He foresaw the future.

The best way to consider what was happening with Bremond in these last years of his life, the years from 1928 to 1933, is to look more closely at these two vectors of criticism and the responses that he offered. As one might expect, he dotted i's and crossed t's to a considerable degree, but also thought through some aspects of things more deeply.

But first, some consideration of the "externals" of his life during these years. The general pattern is one of increasing honors consistent with his status as académicien combined with the discouragements of failing health and the slowly deteriorating sociopolitical context. And then the final storm-center would be Loisy.

Honors and Questions

Surely one of the most pleasant and memorable events of these years took place at Oxford University on June 27, 1928, when Bremond was honored with the conferral of the D. Litt. *honoris causa*. Writing to Monbrun shortly afterward, he rhapsodized about the trip back to England—which he had not seen for more than twenty years—and chuckled about his new cap and hood. What most pleased him, however, was the Latin discourse of presentation by Oxford's "public orator," in which he was described as "interpreter of the Muses," "sacred guide to Christian wisdom," and best of all, "most religious judge of poetry." After being formally seated with the other recipients of doctorates, he delivered an address in English (his French having been translated ahead of time by Canon Ernest Dimnet). The journal, *La Vie Catholique*, reported the event under the heading: "Oxford, la poésie pure et l'abbé Bremond."[1]

Another Oxford honorable mention came that same year. The Anglican Bishop of Oxford, Kenneth Kirk, addressing the university in the theologically oriented Bampton lectures, cited at substantial length Bremond's understanding of St. Ignatius as a chivalrous knight in the service of God, a knight "whose achievements must be the fruit of an inner communion with God."[2] Kirk was charmed by Bremond's contrast of Francis de Sales and Ignatius, and by the Bossuet-Fénelon debates over "pure love," as well as the view that prayer and morality must not be confused, that prayer always means contemplation rather than practical ascetics. The major thrust of the lectures, published as *The Vision of God: the Christian Doctrine of the* Summum Bonum, was the idea that Christian service, doing good, inevitably becomes self-centered if it is not grounded in worship, or the life of prayer. Bremond was becoming influential in Anglo-Saxon circles.[3]

He claimed also that, while at Oxford, he had a conversation with an "Oxford man" (unnamed) about the central thrust of his work. This individual posed a dilemma. If, he said, adherence to the being and work of God in us blossoms out into pure love, and if it is not in itself a first sketch of pure love, how can that identification not

---

1. Bremond to Monbrun, June 30, 1928 (BB, III, 321n). Bremond's enthusiastic use of the ideas of Middleton Murry played a role here, with the University authorities casting their vote for Murry's modern romantic-subjective, politically left-leaning, approach to poetry, rather than the more classical and traditional view represented by T. S. Eliot.

2. Kirk, *The Vision of God*. This 1934 "abridged version" of Kirk's original publication of the lectures in 1931 was claimed by Kirk to be closer to the actual spoken lectures than the longer version, according to the foreword by G. R. Dunstan. Thus, the references to Bremond would seem to be part of the original. Kirk was apparently following Bremond's publications closely.

3. In a letter to the abbé Baudin, July 21, 1931, Bremond indicated his pleasure at Kirk's use of his work, which suggested the possibility of a "synthesis" on the nature of prayer for *contemporary* use (cited by Goichot, EG, 273).

become a pure moralism, where pure love becomes another task like the others? Bremond, adroitly side-stepping, responded by citing a dictum from Sainte-Evremond, that "the spirit of Seneca is bound up with, and animated by, virtue: and, *as if it were a thing foreign to itself*, it needs to transcend itself." "Grace works in us in such a way," he averred in a kind of maxim, "that we have less need to transcend ourselves than to discover ourselves."[4] The challenge of "pure love" spirituality has to do with reconfigured inwardness, the need to know ourselves better at the "fine point," so that real action, rather than mere *ascesis*, can begin!

Indeed, the problem of the relationship between "pure love" as the heart of prayer and the demands of a Christian moral perspective, in fact of *any* moral perspective, simply would not go away. Bremond's debates with the Jesuits and mainline Ignatianism would never be resolved, but only shelved, and every critic picked at this issue in some way. The perceptions of thoughtful critics like the young Oxford man, that talk of "pure love" only redefines the nature of moral striving without doing away with its quality of striving, or that it is hopelessly vague, or that moral striving has in some way been undermined or discounted, would be perennial.

The irony of these views is that Bremond's whole intention had been from the beginning to show that true prayer is *moral* in nature, that is, an effort to commune with the moral *will* of God in pure love *before, and prior to*, efforts to live the practical implications. Perhaps, the final, summary critique from Blondel is the most intellectually incisive, as well as suggestive of the creative direction in which Bremond was moving. The problem, said Blondel in a letter to Bremond, is that you need to develop a clear view of those "dispositions" of the soul, in which a "reciprocal creation" can take place—a reciprocal creation in which each person becomes fully him/herself in the presence of God precisely by yielding to divine renewing power in a mortifying "communion of love." The problem at the level of "notions" is that such "dispositions" appear to be irreconcilable, combining heteronomy and autonomy in a single unity by making the claim that we are most fully ourselves only in that "communion of love." The "reciprocal creation" that occurs is that of the "exchange of wills," which Blondel explained as "God conferring existence on humankind through an act of self-giving, and humankind then giving itself back to God, thereby restoring God to that very place where God had seemed to withdraw, the result being the divine re-creation of humankind."[5]

Blondel wisely indicated that in the above thought "the logic of concepts succumbs in the face of such perspectives." But the idea seems to be that there is a natural affinity, or communion of substance, between the human will as God's creation and

---

4. Bremond relates this incident in a letter to Blondel, October 15, 1928 (BB, III, 332).

5. Blondel to Bremond, October 27, 1928 (BB, III, 334): ". . . une communion d'amour, en un échange des volontés, en une *création* réciproque, Dieu se donnant à l'homme pour le fair être, Dieu se rendant et se donnant à Dieu, pour restituer Dieu là où Dieu avait semblé se retirer, afin de permettre l'oeuvre divinement re-créatrice de l'homme."

God's own will, so that both wills operate in a kind of "circumincession" or circular dynamic. Sin breaks that circularity, but grace restores it in a re-creation of mutual intent for action. The mystic can then "will with God's will," but only, be it noted, because God's will has become the will of the human agent at the same time that the will of the agent has becomes God's will. It is the theme of wanting what God wants, and only what God wants, i.e., pure love in action, provided that the human agent has experienced the requisite rebirth.

Blondel had been trying to make the point since *L'Action*, namely, that human willing is *metaphysically, ontologically, not just psychologically and morally*, grounded in divine willing. The overt manifestation of that grounding is "the substantial truth of a social communion and a bond of perfection that binds men (sic) to one another."[6] The "binding" is primary, with moral expression as the concrete consequence. Blondel felt deep sympathy, thus, with Bremond's efforts in *Histoire*, VII and VIII, while being ever wary of his formulations. The worrisome element of the quietist-tending language of "passivity" nagged at him.[7]

Then came on July 2, 1928, the breathlessly awaited *nihil obstat* on VII and VIII, adjudicated by the anonymous reader to whom Bremond responded with "clarifications," printed at the end of VIII. The official censor turned out to be a Sulpician priest, Paul Vigué, with whom Bremond corresponded at length, even though the actual signing emanated from the friendly Sulpician professor of dogmatic theology, L. Labauche.[8] The *imprimatur* came, then, from the Archbishop of Paris, while the Roman Dominican censors ultimately bogged down in reservations and hesitations because of the fear of quietism and moral laxity.[9]

Indeed, it seems that as the 1920s were drawing to a close, and the economically and politically destabilizing 1930s were about to begin, questions of "moral rigor" were in the air. Avant-garde artistic and cultural movements, such as surrealism

---

6. Blanchette, *Maurice Blondel*, 89.

7. Goichot summarizes Blondel's reservations about *Histoire*, VII and VIII, noting in his final judgment that Bremond paid only lip service to Blondel's concerns, because the latter "operated with a philosophy that was not his [Bremond's] own" (EG, 226–28, citation, 228). But that is not quite true as stated. Bremond was simply not a metaphysician, and he would not let metaphysical concerns cloud the clarity of his project. His starting point—modern persons spiritually hungry but despairing and cynical—was always different from that of Blondel.

8. Ibid., 228–33. In the end Vigué agreed to the *nihil obstat*, only as long as his concerns were voiced and answered in the "Clarifications" at the end of VIII.

9. Ibid., 221–27. The Dominicans tended to balk at what they saw as a confusion of psychology and metaphysics in the work of Piny. In any case, their sense was that "the time was not right" for approval of Bremond's work. The implication was that they were too embroiled in right-wing political machinations in Rome, given their entanglement with Action Française, which, despite its official condemnation in December 1926, remained a potent presence. A good example of the warm and welcoming attitude of Dominican reviewers, combined with a clear Thomist critique, is Lavaud, "Quiétisme et pur amour; Ascèse et prière pure: A propos de deux livres récents," who levels the charge that having identified prayer as the quintessential "religious act," Bremond confuses prayer with the *operation* of grace leading to the theological virtue of love.

(including the new French embrace of psychoanalytic thought), were morally freewheeling and aggressively antinomian, while the nationalism and conservatism of right-wing movements prided themselves on maintaining strict (though self-serving) moral standards. References to "mysticism" were easily caught up in this tension, with the implication that mysticism implied irrationalism and an accompanying immoralism. Charles Du Bos, for instance, though being one of Bremond's greatest fans, went on record on more than one occasion of fearing a "mysticism" that entailed a disdain for moral discipline.[10] Bremond was fighting an uphill battle against popular, as well as academic, views, in his day and our own, of "mysticism" as a negative quantity that is chaotic, individualistic, escapist, "passive," and generally spiritually undesirable. On the political right, mysticism could be easily seen as "leftist" and degenerate.[11] If prayer does not *produce*, then what is the point? critics cried. But the return question is: produce *what*? Bremond had to look around for fresh ways of making the point, and that would bring him to the Trappist founder Armand-Jean de Rancé, as well as a host of other, lesser figures.

Dancing before the "Ark" and Rancé

Truly 1928–29 was an *annus mirabilis* for Bremond in terms of sheer productivity, and the years 1928–30 would constitute the high watermark of his influence and popularity. Invitations flowed in. Partly the product of his enhanced status after election to the Académie, the acclaim arose as well from the gradually accumulating influence of his work. With the appearance of *Histoire*, VII and VIII, and then the *Introduction à la philosophie de la prière*, the "ascesis" vs. prayer debate rumbled and rumbled. Bremond had hit a raw nerve, with pain radiating in a multitude of directions.

André Bremond, in his tribute to his brother shortly after Henri's death, felt that a major turning point had been an essay that Bremond composed as an introduction to a volume that he, André, and their brother Jean had authored on the spirituality of the Desert Fathers.[12] It was the place, thought André, where Bremond had made his distinction between "asceticism" and mysticism crystal clear, the former being "an

---

10. As described by de Lubac, citing from Du Bos's journals from 1925 and 1929 in the context of an argument that "mystical" understanding rightly construed is equivalent to the "spiritual/allegorical/symbolic" interpretation of the Bible. De Lubac saw Bremond's views as "flawed" (*Theology in History*, 195–96).

11. An easy example of the complexity of the situation is Julien Benda's notorious *The Treason of the Intellectuals*, first published in 1928. Benda lambastes the "intellectuals" of postwar France for exalting "feeling" at the expense of "thought," the mark of such "treason" being their adherence to an "artistic sensibility" which is ultimately an irrational Nietzscheanism that leads to militarist fascism. Maritain was dismissive of *Histoire*, VII and VIII, as all darkness and no light (Prévotat, "Réactions et sensibilités maurrassiennes face à l'oeuvre de Bremond," 139–40). Much of this would play into post-WWII debates about who really drained France in the interwar years of moral vigor!

12. *Les Pères du désert*. A version of this introduction was published by Bremond in the *Divertissements* collection as "Les pères du Désert."

exaggerated confidence in active ascetical discipline," to the point of excluding the Holy Spirit from the process of sanctification.[13] André, faithful Jesuit, claimed that his brother had shown that the true Ignatius teaches an "ascesis" that is a *preparation* for prayer, so that room is made for a properly mystical experience.

What Bremond actually does in that essay is to interpret the Desert Fathers, especially Pachomius, founder of Egyptian monasticism, as forerunners of Francis de Sales, teaching that ascetical discipline serves a good purpose only so long as it does not excite envy, competitiveness in the community, and spiritual triumphalism. The unspoken dogma of the Desert Fathers is that in the deepest part of the soul, a part impenetrable to demonic influences, there lies a place of certain and immediate communion with God, where the human self is forgotten, and the operation of transformative, empowering grace comes into play. The pure moral doctrine of Christ is self-forgetfulness in the practice of charity.

The remaining essays gathered in the collection *Divertissements devant L'Arche*, published in 1930, breathed the same spirit, showing that the study of devotional texts from all ages of the church's life brings to light the prevalence of mystical spirituality.[14] In one essay Bremond paid tribute to the recently deceased medievalist Charles-Victor Langlois, a pioneer in the disciplined study of sermons and pious literature, who had made available in more critical editions these "lived texts" of "the properly spiritual life," where mystical depths are increasingly coming to light. In another composition, he discussed recent work on St. Philip Neri, whom he considered "the patron saint of humorists," the model of the evangelical spirit of "childhood," of self-abandon and simplicity, filled with the idealism of mystical exaltation as well as the "street" qualities that made him popular with common folk. There is a discussion of mysticism and prophecy, where Bremond noted that a number of mystics spoke in connection with political events that affected the French monarchy, even when Church authority counseled prudence, a remarkable example being a certain Brother Fiacre, a poor and humble seventeenth-century Augustinian monk who became a model of healing and tenderness for the poor and the desperate.

Concluding essays included a piece on the admirable Monsieur Hamon, gentleman of Port-Royal and physician, who, despite his Jansenism, practiced medicine in a manner truly scientific and state-of-the-art for his time, while simultaneously pursuing a life of mystical prayer—thus exemplifying a proper separation of the natural and the supernatural. A detailed study (originally done in 1919) of Madame de Maintenon and her spiritual directors is an analysis of how these holy men tried, fruitlessly, to rein in her religiously-fueled grandiosity about her role in the destiny of the French kingdom, showing how a lack of the mystical dimension can lead to perverted religiosity.

---

13. Jean Bremond, "Henri Bremond," 46–47.

14. In this paragraph and the next, the relevant essays are "M. Ch. V. Langlois et la 'Vie Spirituelle' au Moyen Age," "Le Saint Patron des Humoristes," "Le frère Fiacre et ses trois dauphins," "Monsieur Hamon et la Médecine," "Madame de Maintenon et ses Directeurs," "La solitaire des Rochers."

Finally, he discussed a seventeenth-century female hermit known as "the solitary of Rochers," a figure venerated in Jansenist history for her penitential rigors. Deploring the use of source materials by the Jansenist-friendly historian, Gazier, he argued that ascetic rigors are sometimes exaggerated in various narratives so as to mask a dogmatic agenda, and that we need to assess these texts critically. We see that mystical spirituality produces healthy and positive moral expression, while the non-mystical easily leads to an asceticism that subverts desirable moral aspects of character.

Then came another opportunity. In the spring of 1928, the publisher of a popular series, *Figures du Passé*, proposed to Bremond that he compose a biographical study of the famous founder of the Trappist Cistercians, Armand-Jean de Rancé.[15] Bremond quickly accepted, knowing that Rancé had been a supporter of Bossuet, enemy of Fénelon, as well as opponent of the Maurist Benedictine, Jean Mabillon, and the value of sacred scholarship. Rancé had also been an ascetic extremist, hostile to the people and causes that Bremond held in high esteem. The source materials being exceedingly rich, Bremond was prepared to enjoy a feast, as he put Rancé under the microscope of religious psychology.

The result was an enormously entertaining portrait and analysis of a colorful individual. His title, *The Thundering Abbot* (with "thundering" tantamount to "raging"), suggests the tone of the book. Quickly rendered into English, its translator, F. J. Sheed, described the book as "superb" in its analysis of character, but raised the question as to whether or not it was Rancé's character that was being analyzed, whether the offered sketch was true to historical fact.[16] Many critics of the book have seen it as an out-and-out hatchet job on Rancé.[17] In truth, as the book progressed, it became a kind of allegorical construction, with Rancé standing for the doctrinaire asceticist, and Mabillon and others representing the mystical tradition of prayer. Naturally, the mystics are the true heroes. Thus, the biography is part of Bremond's defense of the moral integrity of mystical prayer.

Bremond structured the narrative as a kind of dialogue with Rancé's earlier official biographers (those appointed by the Order), questioning their idealization of Rancé, and then falling back, as he often did, on alternative sources that painted a more mixed picture. The tone throughout is catty and satirical, with Bremond frequently underlining less laudable and embarrassing details. There is thus no question that Bremond wanted to cut Rancé down to size and show that he was not the plaster saint described in Saint-Simon's famous memoirs or the biography by Chateaubriand.

In fact, Armand-Jean le Bouthillier de Rancé (1626–1700) came from an aristocratic background, by virtue of which he inherited, while being indifferently religious, various ecclesiastical benefices, thus resulting eventually in his ordination

---

15. Bremond to Baudin, May 8, 1928 (cited BB, III, 324n4).

16. *Thundering Abbot*, vi. All references are to this English translation.

17. For instance, the abbé Wehrlé in a letter to Blondel of April 29, 1929: "a methodical exercise of making everything ridiculous" (cited BB, III, 365n3).

to priesthood. About 1660 he experienced an intense conversion at the death-bed of a woman with whom he had been having an affair, leading to a step which some considered miraculous, but Bremond thought farcical: vows of total abstinence and penitential rigor. In fact, Bremond saw pretense and self-righteousness and posturing everywhere in this intense, self-dramatizing man, with his flamboyant gestures and holier-than-thou reforming impulses. After joining the Cistercian Order, Rancé spearheaded a movement for greater austerity, and finally made La Trappe the center of the Strict Observance. Violent against his critics, he acquired a reputation for storms of passion on behalf of disciplinary rigor, and on behalf of his own own sincerity in instituting such.

There are countless damning statements by Bremond along the way. For instance, "[His] soul is unfathomable not because it is too deep, but because there is no depth—only a surface." "The true ego is as far away when he storms as when he prays," and "it was generally realised that Rancé's outbursts had no more substance in them than stage bombs," etc.[18] While not being a Jansenist, Rancé is depicted as a kind of fellow-traveler of Port-Royal, fiercely opposed to the Jesuits and to Fénelon; any form of teaching that struck him as morally compromised or compromising raised his wrath. When Bremond turned to the intimate moments of Rancé's prayer-life, he found repeatedly a kind of posturing in the face of God, in which Rancé's sense of self-importance trumped any effort to listen to God and be humbled.

In the debate with Mabillon Rancé questioned the propriety of erudite study, especially the study of dogma, for those who aspire to holiness, seeing such study as irresponsible tinkering with holy things. Contrariwise, Mabillon saw study as a form of prayer. Rancé was the asceticist, while Mabillon took, in effect, the mystical position, when he said, "Christian morality has a necessary relation with the science of dogma, because true piety is founded on the knowledge of God, and usually, in proportion as that knowledge is more perfect, piety is also more solid." While ascetical effort will hold speculation cheap enough, Mabillon contended that "humble of heart we must be, but also lofty in intellect."[19] There is no question which side Bremond came down on.

He went on to trace with malicious detail the disputes that grew up around Rancé, the bitter rivalries for influence and control among his supporters and heirs, the chaos surrounding his death, finally the settling out of stability and a better balance within the Cistercians of the Strict Observance. The point of it all, said Bremond, was that in Rancé there was something not authentically Cistercian: the focus on penance rather than prayer, a preference for the details of conduct rather than the methods of the Desert Fathers and the discrete St. Benedict. Ultimately the Reform led by Rancé ended up in a good place, said Bremond, and thus "there is sufficient reason why the

---

18. *Thundering Abbot*, 141, 158. It is, of course, this tone of laughing at Rancé that infuriated critics of the book.

19. Ibid., 178–79.

Church should forever bless the memory of Rancé, yet not sufficient reason why she should ever inscribe him in the roll of her saints."[20] And the church has agreed. God does good things with flawed people, but there is no reason to imitate their flaws.

Bernanos

By the beginning of 1929 Bremond was feeling confident in his views and stating them ever more boldly. *Histoire*, VII and VIII, as well as the polemical writings against the Jesuits, seem not to have stirred any great furor at first. But then, as Goichot has described, a kind of "strange panic" set in early in the year.[21] Rumors started to circulate that the "Metaphysic of the Saints" was being considered for the Index, because some theological authorities were unhappy with it. It seems that one bone of contention lay in the fact that Bremond had minimized the "prayer of demand," as if petition and intercession were, somehow, inferior forms of prayer. Francisque Gay, Bremond's publisher and active at Rome in the machinations surrounding the condemnation of the Action Française, interceded energetically. As it turned out, while respected scholars had reservations about many of Bremond's points, nothing rose to the level of declared heterodoxy. A lot of "smoke" amounted to very little "fire."[22]

There was no question, however, about the strength of the opposition Bremond had generated. It was as much his tone, most acerbic, as we saw, in the biography of Rancé, as his substance. People were stung by his criticisms: *nobody* likes being told that his/her favorite form of prayer is "pan-hedonistic." Scholarly critics, especially Jesuits, objected to this or that aspect of his historical constructions, but the most intense resistance came from devout Catholics firmly entrenched in dogmatic orthodoxy[23]—that is, the "integrism" that hounded Blondel as well—who, rightly, recognized the kind of threat that Bremond represented.

But the most biting, pungent, profound criticism came from Georges Bernanos in the form of a novel, *The Impostor*, published in 1927, which, Bernanos later

---

20. Ibid., 289, 291.

21. EG, 238.

22. An example of the flavor of these disputes came out in the article on Bremond by de Guibert, that appeared in the first volume of the *Dictionnaire du spiritualité*, when it first appeared in the years just after Bremond's death. It is written in a spirit of cautious appreciation (Bremond was a "seductive" writer), with some affection, but also with substantive reservations (but he often lacked "exactitude"). See Trémolières's important critique of de Guibert's assessment, "The Witness to These Witnesses," 268–74.

23. Paul Claudel may be taken as the, perhaps, the best known and most respected critic, discussed by Blanchet, "Claudel lecteur de Bremond," and more briefly, with excerpts from their correspondence, by Goichot (EG, 251–52), then most fully by Marxer ("Cette curiosité," 1063–80). Claudel, a great partisan of robust joy in prayer, was dismayed by the "pan-hedonist" criticism and the whole idea of a "spiritual gourmandise" so criticized by Bremond. Marxer contends (ibid., 1078) that Claudel was a man of the "Fatherly presence of God" (Blondel as well, to a great extent), while Bremond operated in the mode of "emptiness and absence."

claimed, was not aimed expressly at Bremond, but at a certain "type" of priest. But that defense was nonsense: it *was* aimed at Bremond, and its argument is instructive.[24] What seemed to distress Bernanos, who by this time was starting to become well-known for his theologically-themed work, was religious gamesmanship, on the one hand, or arid intellectualizing on the other. Bernanos was the kind of serious—some would say *too* serious—Catholic for whom the honor of the Church and the honor of France were tightly bound together in a passionate, burning embrace. He had a complex relationship with the Action Française and with Jacques Maritain, affirming a fervent nationalism but then despising fascism, and affirming traditional orthodoxy but with little patience for theological problems and philosophical distinctions. All is blood and feeling and raw truth for him. Luke-warmness and fence-sitting of any kind are anathema.

Thus, the central priest figure of the *Impostor*, Father Cénabre, was everything Bernanos loathed in some clergy: non-believing under the disguise of religion, a specialist in the history of religions and mysticism in particular, filled with irony about everything, and an académicien. A habitué of the literary salons, Cénabre personifies "elegant skepticism." Having lost his faith, his standing in the sight of others is premised on a lie. Thus, he doles out spiritual advice which is cautious, canny and corrupt. Bernanos used this characterization and others in the novel to lash out at socialism and left-wing politics, at freethinking radicalism, at (what he saw as) moral turpitude or weakness. The problem, Bernanos thought, with these superficial, clever priests is that they do not take *evil, the reality of Satan*, seriously, and thus there is no place in them for the ferocity of real encounter with absurdity and suffering.

In one passage in *Impostor*, Bernanos described a liberal bishop, in this way: "[He] believed in Progress, and his idea of Progress was suited to his own capacities. This professor, who wore his title so proudly, was able to enrich himself with ideas without delivering his intelligence from the tyranny of his feelings. He thought with the loves and hatreds, the desires and the rancours, of his adolescence, and anything he said which was quoted for its boldness and novelty was really no more than the abstract expression of some humiliation he had suffered in his youth of which he still felt the smart."[25] It is thus no wonder that Bremond was wounded by the book. Already alienated by Bernanos's earlier work, *Sous le soleil de Satan*, with its "apocalyptic

---

24. All references are to the English translation by J. C. Whitehouse, *Impostor*. For critical commentary and analysis, Pezeril, "Bremond et Bernanos," and Salin, "De Bremond à Bernanos." Salin mounts a subtle argument that the priest in the *Impostor* is not Bremond as such but is symbolic of spiritual writing that uses mockery and irony to avoid spiritual truth.

25. Cited by Speaight, *Georges Bernanos*, 94. Speaight refers to the "Bernanosian *inferno*" of characters, such as "a former colleague of President Combes (who passed the Law of Separation of church and state in France); a ridiculous aristocrat who puts on democratic and Voltairean airs; a diplomat with a secret line to the Vatican; and his wife whose verses, like her character, are understood to be no better than they should be." It seems safe to say that with critics like Bernanos Bremond was now engaged in a "contact sport"! It is also no wonder that Pezeril, "Bremond et Bernanos," thought that Bernanos had discerned Bremond's inner, personal struggle as a refusal of "deep consent" to faith.

maledictions" reminiscent of Tertullian,[26] and despite Bernanos's claim, after advance excerpts appeared, that he had meant no personal attack, Bremond feared that this critique would add fuel to the fire about his work in Rome.[27]

Indeed, the fundamental spiritual problem for Bernanos's with Bremond's whole project—the key point, really—was his perception that Bremond was "mainlining" mysticism in a way that domesticated it, normalized it, made it a part of everyman's prayer. The result was a watering down that would weaken the church's ability to confront evil.

In the *Impostor*, the good person is Chantal de Clergerie, a young woman considering a vocation to become a Carmelite despite her well-intended, but worldly, father's efforts to dissuade her. Her father says to her, "I think your piety is strong, perhaps even enlightened, but very calm and reasonable. There's another reason why we shouldn't rush to take up thoughtlessly a way of life made specifically for mystics." Chantal is radiant, and replies, "You're absolutely right. I'm afraid I only want my own share, the beggar's share.... What you call my serenity and happiness is precisely the certainty that I'm no good for anything and the hope that as such I shall get special treatment on the Last Day. I don't look after my own interests."[28] Mysticism for Bernanos, highly supernatural from the start, is intended for a transfigured elite, who have completely broken with secular culture. The irony is that both he and Bremond are pointing to "pure love" as the ideal. The difference is that Bremond had worked out a *psychological* analysis of what it is that impedes pure love—the self-serving human ego, which is yet capable of discerning its own egotism—while for Bernanos the problem is more metaphysical, something structured into human existence at such a fundamental level that grace, when it comes, must be pure contradiction. To Bernanos Bremond's spirituality looks the pretty poems of a dilettante, while to Bremond Bernanos's piety looks like an esoteric war with reality.

Which perspective has more moral energy for God's kingdom? By the time WWII came Bernanos had fled to Brazil, where he lived quietly, and in frustrated exile, until France was liberated, and then he returned as a conservative curmudgeon. Had Bremond lived into the second War, my hunch is that he would either have toiled away at the *Histoire* in the Pyrenees, more or less insulated, or he would have gone to England in support of de Gaulle and Free France. Both men would have been acting patriotically, but the one by absconding from a conflict (as he saw it) of corrupted ideologies, while the other would have worked for the renewed inwardness that facilitates a bettered social order. Bernanos recognized the problem. In his world-famous novel, *The Diary of a Country Priest*, he has his central character say at the end, "Human agony is beyond all an act of love,"[29] a candle in the enveloping night, but, the agony,

---

26. Bremond to Blondel, end of April 1926 (BB, III, 244–45).
27. Bremond to Blondel, January 2, 1928 (BB, III, 305, and for bibliography, 306n2).
28. *Impostor*, 215.
29. *Diary of a Country Priest*, 229.

the darkness, is primary, and death is love's last word. Bremond had it the other way around. The lover seeking God will have an agonizing experience in many and varied forms, but the love is first, primary, and final, even unto death. Bremond is a humanist who can laugh (though sadly) and sing (though plaintively) because for him love is a living bond, while Bernanos in his bitterness sees the dignity and even the absurdity, but not the transformative power, of love.

Bergson

At the same time, however, Bremond's work was beginning to have strong positive resonance among some in the religious orders, who were deeply grateful to him, but even more in lay, secular circles. There was the ongoing dialogue with Valéry, but even more a growing network of connection with the highly influential philosophy of Henri Bergson and his school.

A man of the political left, whose entry into the Académie in 1914 had been strongly opposed by the Action Française, Henri Bergson (1859–1941) was, by the late 1920s, at the height of his career and influence at the Collège de France, perhaps the preeminent philosophical mind in France at that time. Best known for his anti-materialism in metaphysics, and for his anti-rationalism in epistemology, he was a champion of the élan vital as an explanation of the essential nature of animate life, and for his theory of "intuition" as the means by which we know objects as a totality or unified whole. The theory of intuition was, in turn, grounded in the concept of *durée* as experienced, subjective time. The logical mind, according to Bergson, cannot grasp motion, therefore cannot grasp fluid realities such as personality, therefore cannot grasp living or dynamic objects of any kind, but can only chop them up into discrete frozen bits. In the "sympathetic" act of intuition the mind grasps what is denied to logical reason (*An Introduction to Metaphysics*, 1903). The act of intuitive knowing is then, in fact, a function of subjective memory linking together discrete images of perception into the unity that we call "matter" in the universe (*Matter and Memory*, 5th ed., 1908).

In his most famous work, *Creative Evolution* (1908), Bergson argued that our knowledge of the world and our theory of life are codependent. Contrary to a Darwinian view of evolution, where time is broken up into self-contained moments that never cohere into a whole, the evolutionary process is actually a creative dynamic reflective of the way in which the subjective mind grasps totalities. This is to say that Bergson conceived of psychic life as something present in evolution from the beginning, because evolution is inconceivable without it. Thus, Bergson's kind of anti-rationalistic *idealism* made room for spiritual and religious perceptions of all kinds. Eventually, his *Two Sources of Morality and Religion*, 1932, would affirm religious mysticism—defined in his particular way—as a major source of moral truth.

Blondel did not like Bergson's theory of the superiority of intuitive knowledge, and they sparred a good bit. Thinking that Bergson was too quick to dismiss the value of notional knowledge and thus to court obscurantism (the charge usually brought against Bergson), Blondel preferred to let ideas of the whole emerge *out of* scientific endeavor than to pitch such notions *against* scientific endeavor.[30]

Bremond had had early indirect contact with Bergson, when they both (along with many others, including Blondel) contributed to a magazine symposium that addressed the question of the future of the "religious sentiment" in the modern age.[31] Bergson argued that the object of the religious sentiment is "something interior to the sentiment itself," based on a "felt rather than thought grasp," with ideas coming only secondarily. Bremond argued for the present and future liveliness of the religious sentiment, given the failures of rationalism in making sense of experience, thus paving the way for a true "religious psychology." Clearly, he and Bergson were on similar tracks at a general level. Thus, Bergson would always appear to Bremond as a benign thinker, despite Blondel's huffing and puffing.

Following the publication of *Histoire*, VII and VIII, Bergson wrote to Bremond, praising his work and underlining the importance of the "philosophy of religion," as he saw it, expressed therein. He contended that Bremond had exposed "that which is truly essential and *primitive*" in religion, though, as Goichot points out, Bergson was quick to assimilate Bremond's insights to his own categories as these would emerge in the *Two Sources* essay yet to come.[32]

The real influence from Bergson would actually crystallize via his aesthetically minded students, particularly Albert Thibaudet (1874–1936), essayist and literary critic for the *Nouvelle Revue Française* from 1912. In an essay that appeared at the beginning of the new year, 1929, Thibaudet lauded Bremond's work as a continuation of the grand tradition of Sainte-Beuve on Port-Royal, where a school of spirituality is held up as the essence of the French spirit, the difference being that now it is Francis de Sales and Ignatius who have that honor. Thibaudet recognized the import of Bremond's demonstration that the "problem of mysticism" is truly a *metaphysical* problem that extends beyond the borders of religion, where human effort diminishes in such a way as to allow divine grace to increase its functioning. The "impersonality" of God comes into play via the human intuition that "God" is the nameless infinite beyond all designations, enabling us to grasp the unity and wholeness of the universe. The human mind is the "screen" on which "matter" is formed, "the actor that makes a scene come alive, the verse that makes a poem, the glass reflecting light, so that the light of God can pass through, and, by means of a syllable the poem of God compose itself."[33]

---

30. See Blanchette, *Maurice Blondel*, 353–56.
31. Charpin, *La Question religieuse* (Bergson's comments, 272, Bremond's, 230–33).
32. EG, 257, for citation and comment. The letter was Bergson to Bremond, January 23, 1929.
33. Thus Goichot summarizes summarizes Thibaudet's essay of January 1, 1929, in the *Revue de*

In his memorial tribute to Bremond, Thibaudet would claim that "pure love" is "the problem of intuition in its connection with understanding, of mysticism versus dogmatism, of the opposition of the *Anima* and the *Animus*." In Bremond's case, he said, the use of intuition often took the form of the *jeu*, the "game," in which essences emerge in a Don Quixote–like way from humanistic dialogue. Truly for Bremond, he averred, the "fine point of the soul" had become "the fine point of taste!"[34] (How Bernanos must have hated that line!)

And the dialogue with Valéry always returned with renewed energy. Goichot has printed fragments from an important unedited letter from Valéry to Bremond, existing in slightly different forms in the archives of both, dated to January 1929, in which the poet, recovering from some serious illness, opened his heart to Bremond with "a tired pencil." After praising Bremond for his depictions of holy "states" and admitting that he is attracted to such, he then argued that the term "metaphysic" in VII and VIII should be replaced by "anti-physic," since the mystics seem to abhor the Creation in order to embrace an "ultra-monde" that transcends phenomena. The mystics in Bremond's portraits seem to turn the world of phenomena into a "reservoir of metaphors" and an arena of temptations, while the true poet comes at things differently: he/she *contemplates* the world in all of its given objectivity by bracketing out the ephemeral sensations of passing affectivity. The "very fine point" of the discussion, says Valéry in a twist on Bremond's phrase, is the valence of the terms "God" and "me," in which one wonders how the consciousness of God and of myself in the same instant can be "in accord" with one another.[35]

In a nuanced response that showed Bergson's influence, Bremond suggested that the "states" of the mystics cannot be objectified as something with a "before" and an "after" that allow for post-factum dissection. Any effort to discern an "accord" between an inner "state" and self-consciousness is doomed, since the latter can discern only the "prodromes" and "postludes" of the experience (recall Bremond's critique of William James). In fact, the moments of the "poetic state" are marked by a "twilight" of consciousness, followed by "gleams" where suddenly one can say only "behold, God is God." It is the Christian dogma of "Christ lives in me," where the poet has the sense of being accompanied into a darkness, followed by fire and then ascetic or intellectual energy. There is the sense of an *activité à deux* beyond all self-consciousness, an awareness of God, which easily translates into the "pagano-Valérian language"!

Paris, and cites it (ibid., 256–57). The essay, written as a long review of *Histoire*, VII and VIII, evokes Bremond's rejection of the spirituality of Port-Royal in the history of French culture in favor of the spirituality of Francis de Sales. The result, contended Thibaudet, is in effect a rejection of the specificity and "personalism" of a christocentric mysticism in favor of a mysticism of the swallowing up of the individual personality in the "impersonality" of the divine. Thus, in Bergsonian fashion, intuitive understanding tending toward union is favored over logical understanding tending to separation and distinction (Thibaudet, "Autour de la Métaphysique des Saints.")

34. "La place d'Henri Bremond dans l'histoire de la critique française."
35. Goichot, EG, 257–58.

Bremond spoke here, profoundly, of the sense of being momentarily "hermetically closed off from the spatterings of this life," a life that he, Bremond, can sing about as well as anyone.[36] Valéry's "moment," in which the poet, discerning the "real" in a way that transcends his own limited and individual subjectivity, is *nothing other than the mystic's "moments" or "states,"* since in both cases one world takes precedence over another, indeed, one is "accompanied by Another." One recognizes here Bremond's way of describing the poet/mystic's way of moving from the particular to the the universal via moments of perception; the subject, so to speak, "melts away" in the face of reality, so that, in the words of the novelist, Elizabeth Bowen, "To turn from everything to one face is to find oneself face to face with everything."[37]

Racine and Valéry

Bremond's final asseverations on Valéry's poetry and theories of inspiration came in a collection of pieces written during the 1920s and capped by a public address that he, distinguished académicien, delivered in Uzès on September 1, 1929. The occasion was the dedication of a memorial plaque commemorating a youthful sojourn in that town by Jean Racine, as he first began serious work on his poetry in 1661–62. In what was really a celebration of local heritage, and accompanied by Martin Du Gard on the outing,[38] Bremond gloried in the Provençal ambience of the event, availing himself of an opportunity for reflecting on the nature of poetic inspiration and "the pure essence of poetry."

The idea he developed, diplomatically, is that we can see in Racine's "noviciate" at Uzès the fact that good poetry is triggered by a specific environment without being a "product" of it.[39] That thesis, in which the biography of the poet and the content of his inspiration are kept in careful tension, is then expounded in a series of short interpretive essays on Racine, where Bremond constantly looked over his shoulder at Valéry and other critics. These, he felt, made the essence of poetry too much a matter of a kind of "chemical isolation," like the smell of a rose, rather than the search for something that transcends created things as such. The learning from Valéry, Bremond insisted, is that poetry as such cannot be converted to prose, that fact being the key to its mystery, a "mystery that invites us into its own silence."[40]

36. Ibid., 259, citing Bremond to Valéry (January 1929).

37. Cited by Richard Rohr, *Eager to Love*, 228.

38. Maurice Martin Du Gard described the whole event as quite an occasion with a grand dinner, a Mass in the Cathedral, and a solemn ceremony for the dedication of the plaque (MM, 385–92). A great success, according to a number of contemporary witnesses cited by Blanchet (BB, III, 362–63n1). Bremond's role at the event is a good illustration of the cultural function and standing of the académicien.

39. "Discours pour l'inauguration d'une plaque rapellant le séjour que fit Racine à Uzès, en 1661 et 1662. Le dimanche 1er septembre 1929" (*Racine et Valéry*, xvii–xxviii).

40. *Racine et Valéry*, "Avant-propos," xvi.

The dominating essay of the collection, *Racine et Valéry*, is a sustained reflection on the impossibility of correctly interpreting Racine's art by reference to his biography. This fact, argued Bremond, comes out especially clearly in the way that Racine treated his female characters, whom some have seen as demented (Mauriac) or massively passionate (Lemaître) or sadistic (Péguy), when in fact they are, as we would say, just human, but manifesting aspects of character that evoke "poetic admiration" on the part of Racine. While Racine himself was rather timid with women, and inexperienced, he created women with a spiritual dimension that rose in response to the tragic nature of their circumstances. Recalling his criticisms of Sainte-Beuve, Bremond insists that the poet's "soul" is not his history. Biographical reductionism makes the details of art all-important, while the essence is ignored. It is Valéry who teaches us to see in the artist's work not a technical virtuosity that makes experience concretely expressible, but rather a dynamic that leads away from transient particularity to a more fundamental and underlying core experience. The "inspiration" or "miracle" that empowers the poet is all-important, and is usually experienced as an "insertion" into his life independent of context. Everything human then becomes grist for the creative mill, because it has become revelatory.[41]

One particular emphasis, reflecting a perennial debate in French letters, was Bremond's preference for Racine over Corneille as the true master of French drama. Racine's *Athalie*, in which the poet's Christian sentiments were most on display, is the center-piece. Bremond argued that this is a play in which "Racine really prays" through his poetry, since it is not just the "idea of the Eternal" that is expressed but it's "sentiment." Racine's poetry here induces a "religious trance," making his poetry truly "Valéryan." The poetry manifests an incantatory power, in which a "profound zone" is opened up by the magical quality of the words. The "poetic sense" begins to yield to "devotion," and the words of Christ speak through the poet. As prayer itself begins to take over, the "vibration" created by the words subsides, and the Spirit begins to pray in us. What started out as the Muse reveals itself to be God. But finally Bremond admits that he may be confusing the "natural" and the "supernatural"![42]

In an appendix to the volume Bremond reprinted a letter that he had written to a literary critic, Ramon Fernandez, who had castigated him for his use of the word "pure," as if aesthetic activity could be separated from the "impurities" of actual life. Bremond countered that Valéry's "hyper-purism" had revivified the search for the essence of poetry that had, since Baudelaire, become a mania. The search is legitimate, Bremond argues, because it has been necessary to locate that spot within the human personality whence poetry emanates, precisely in order to avoid false understandings. How one delineates that "spot" in a rationally comprehensible way is the issue, and this is where he and Valéry differ. Bremond admits that he prefers to operate in the tradition of Aquinas, where the "reason" of "pure poetry" operates in a way that is

41. Ibid., "Biographie et poésie."
42. Ibid., "*Athalie*, poème religieux."

self-transcending, so that its "dialectic" points beyond itself, to what "reason" cannot comprehend. Poetic activity, he avers, proceeds from all that is most personal and idiosyncratic in the poet, subjected to a "crucible of purification," where the personal and the idiosyncratic are swallowed up in the transcendent. He even cited André Gide, to the effect that the writer does not merely "observe," but "invents," so that "imagination actually becomes the instrument of knowledge." In place of Gide's "invents," he substitutes "realizes," since the poet makes contact "not with notions, but with reality itself."[43]

De Luca

But the warmest reception for Bremond's work, including friendly scholarly critique, came from Italy, much of it represented most saliently in the figure of an erudite Benedictine historian of spirituality, Don Giuseppe De Luca (1898–1962). A lively correspondence between the two men, beginning in 1929, encouraged Bremond in his projects, as well as stimulating De Luca in his mature work to publish studies in the history of Italian spirituality comparable to what Bremond had done for the French heritage. De Luca made a particular contribution to Bremond's argument about the mystical elements in Jesuit tradition, and Bremond used him as part of an effort to "de-Bremondize," i.e., generalize without the party-polemics or provocative tone, his spreading influence.[44]

De Luca was an interesting man, in due course an intimate of Angelo Roncalli, who would become John XXIII. Reminiscent of Louis Duchesne, learned but fastidious about his Roman orthodoxy, yet a student of modernist historians and very much open to modernist ideas and trends. He maintained a network of contacts with ecclesiastical researchers in Italy, France and Germany, many of whom, like Bremond, were notable for discoveries in monastic libraries and repositories and for source-critical refinements in the dating and placing of ancient materials. After Bremond's death, De Luca was instrumental in gathering biographical materials, partly through exchanges with early biographers such as Martin Du Gard and Hogarth and then in collaboration with Joseph de Guibert for the early *Dictionnaire du spiritualité* essay on Bremond.[45] De Luca seems to have been responsible especially for the assessment of Bremond as a "French romantic."

43. Ibid., "Lettre à Ramon Fernandez" (reference to Gide, 241).

44. For this concept, cf. Bremond to De Luca, August 5, 1930. Bremond referred to De Luca's "mission as a historian—[to be] the Italian Bremond, wise, learned, balanced, lovable—this is willed by God" (Bernard-Maître and Guarnieri, *Don Giuseppe De Luca*, 120–21).

45. Bernard-Maître and Guarnieri, *Don Giuseppe De Luca*, ch. 1, "Le passé Henri Bremond recréé par Don De Luca." This edition of the Bremond-De Luca correspondence includes all of the known letters, not in annotated form (as with Blanchet's edition of the Bremond-Blondel material), but set out in chronological order interspersed with a connecting narrative that includes numerous excerpts from other unedited correspondence. It thus constructs a "picture" of the relationship between the

De Luca's early interest in Bremond appears to have been mediated through Bremond's own early contact with Italian Modernists whom he admired, such as Antonio Fogazzaro, and then through the non-Catholic historian Giuseppe Prezzolini, an early specialist in the study of Newman. Further, Bremond's book on Fénelon had been appreciated in Italy for its vindication of the Barnabite Lacombe, whose influence on Madame Guyon had been profound. We also recall that Bremond as a Provençal had always been attuned to Italian developments, his native region being so contiguous and historically intertwined with northern Italy. By the mid-1920s De Luca, attracted to the spiritual vitality of Modernist thought, though wary of its excesses, was functioning as a librarian in Rome at the Gregorian University, maintaining contact with Prezzolini and more and more interested in composing a history of Italian piety. Then came the publication of *Histoire*, VII and VIII, along with the increasing publicity around Bremond's debates with Cavallera. With Prezzolini's encouragement, De Luca contacted Bremond in September 1929, indicating his enthusiasm for the latter's work and revealing his own interests. Bremond responded positively.

The critical question that De Luca raised was whether Bremond had overplayed the influence of Bérulle and the French School with the consequent trend in the direction of quietism. He facilitated a three-way correspondence between himself, Bremond, and a scholar at Nijmegen, Jean Dagens, who was preparing a book on Bérulle. Out of their conversations came a request to De Luca from Bremond, that he closely examine an early work usually attributed to Bérulle in order to explore its similarities to a writing by the sixteenth-century Italian Jesuit, Achille Gagliardi (1537–1607). The result was the discovery that a work usually thought to be expressive of Bérulle's own mystical orientation turned out to be, in fact, a French rendering of an Italian Jesuit composition, thus showing that a mystical tradition for interpreting Ignatius was alive and well in Jesuit circles in Italy! Bremond had a field-day with the discovery, reserving the exploration of its significance for *Histoire*, XI, where he would discuss the mysterious "Milanese Lady" as the intermediary between Gagliardi and Bérulle.[46]

In this way, De Luca and Bremond explored many avenues of influence among Spanish, French, German and Italian mystical and spiritual writers, elucidating currents of piety and exposition broadly quietist in character. De Luca completely agreed with Bremond's contention that there was little, if any, inducement in this piety toward immorality, and he resonated profoundly with Bremond's focus on the "history of usage," as well as his essayistic, art-historical style of engagement with sources.[47] By his

---

two men, which became tender and confiding as Bremond's life-span approached its end.

46. Ibid., ch. 4. It seems that in general De Luca got Bremond to tone down the theocentric/anthropocentric antithesis, particularly with regard to the Jesuits and the *Spiritual Exercises*. De Luca, as part of "de-Bremondizing," was much more inclined to think in terms of differing emphases, shading into one another, than stark oppositions.

47. Ibid., 113–14. From the long letter of De Luca to Bremond, April 7, 1930. De Luca is dramatic: "I say to myself: why should Bremond drag himself, drag his heart, into the course of his exposition? As a historian he is too undignified; he does not take his task seriously enough," etc., "yet his soul is

moderating influence and attunement to Roman currents, De Luca helped also with the process of avoiding official censure for Bremond, though Bremond admitted at one point to Francisque Gay that he knew himself to be "vitandus" in Rome.[48]

On another occasion, Italian critics attacked Bremond's views on Pascal and Jansenism, but De Luca rose to a sustained, detailed defense. While De Luca could at times be critical of Bremond for over-simplifying or caricaturing a position, Bremond's response was that spirituality needs to be "de-ecclesiasticized" in order to make it readable and engaging,[49] with adversarial representatives who are not all good or bad but have sharply delimited positions. He promised that in a later volume he would deal with Fénelon (arch anti-Jansenist) and Duguet (arch-Jansenist) together![50] Something of a conclusion came in 1932, when Bremond wrote that he hoped that De Luca might become the Italian Bremond, but wiser, more learned, and more holy.[51] Nonetheless, he urged De Luca to be "passionate" in his presentations, running the risk of too much "moi" in what is said and how it is said, but thus conveying the sense that spirituality—its history being a prolongation of the thing itself—is a living *movement* with all of the energy involved.[52]

And so, in the period following the appearance of the "Metaphysic of the Saints," Bremond received large amounts of anxious and sometimes downright hostile criticism as his ideas disturbed some, heartfelt praise and enriching dialogue as his ideas enlivened and renewed some others in quite diverse ways, and erudite collaboration as his hypotheses and suggestions stirred further research and avenues of exploration. Without question, his work had a kind of seismic effect, creating shock waves of different kinds in the world of ecclesiastical history, but also, with his views of prayer and poetry, in the more secular space of aesthetic theory.

Indeed, there is something about symbol, about art, including religious art, that simply will not reduce to material terms, though many have tried, and do try, and will continue to try. It is clear that for Bremond, the moral aspect of pure prayer, of

---

profound," etc.

48. Ibid., 121, citing a letter of Bremond to Gay in the period of October-November 1930.

49. Bremond to De Luca, March 21, 1931 (ibid., 131).

50. Ibid., ch. 5, where the correspondence is laid out in detail by the editors. It is hard to convey how intensely, unremittingly and affectionately De Luca and Bremond went back-and-forth in these discussions. In the Bremond-Blondel correspondence, one always has the sense of a mentor talking (affectionately, but instructively) to a student, while with De Luca it more that of an older brother ("mon très cher et vénéré maître," says De Luca) to a younger ("cher Monsieur l'abbé, et très cher," says Bremond), where they are competitively pointing things out to one another.

51. Bremond to De Luca, January 16, 1932 (ibid., 137). One senses here, of course, in the repetition of the earlier expressed desire, the pathos of a scholar passing from the scene, hoping that his students will carry on. The editors of ch. 6, "Les étapes d'une 'débremondisation,'" claim that De Luca did just that by means of his many publications and the start of an ambitious, multi-volume history/encyclopedia of Italian spirituality comparable to the French *Dictionnaire de spiritualité*.

52. Ibid., 138, letter of Bremond to De Luca, January 16, 1932. The specific context was that in order to understand Port-Royal, one must discern the "movement" involved, not the "dogmatic absurdities."

mystical prayer, with its sanctifying power, is captured in the concept of "pure love." As I approach God in prayer, I am progressively no longer "for myself," but increasingly "for what God wants"—and creativity bursts forth. But why is it that that approach, so beautified by the "poetic state," should end in *silence*, rather than, say a riot of sound and color, or a torrent of inspiring eloquence? In *Histoire*, IX and X, Bremond dealt with the poetry first, and then in unfinished XI the quiet, the silence.

19

If We Die with Christ, then We Shall Sing with Him
Histoire, IX, and X—then Loisy

PUBLISHED IN 1932, THE ninth and tenth volumes of the *Histoire*, dedicated respectively to "Christian Life under the *Ancien Régime*," and "The Prayer and Prayers of the *Ancien Régime*," were doomed to be the least read and most quickly forgotten of the set. And yet, they are quite important. As surveys of sacramental and devotional practice as well as the forms and texts of both liturgical and private prayer, they are "the proof of the pudding," that is, the evidence for Bremond's claim that mystical spirituality pervaded the religious consciousness of the seventeenth century, and not just in pious books, and not just among elites, but among the most ordinary and average folk worshipping each week in their parish churches.

They are also a solid indication for his argument that religious earnestness is in its depth *about* "pure love," and not the material and practical benefits that sometimes, if not often, stimulate superficial allegiances. In fact, Bremond found his source material to be rich, exceedingly rich, with the very "lyricism" that for him was the sure sign of an inward, mystical, poetic "commerce" of the soul at its "fine point" with the sanctifying presence of God. Furthermore, the kind of moralism that so many of his opponents considered to be essential to orthodox piety—that is, the "ascetical" approach—he found to be minimal, or at least very much reduced, contrary to the conventional perceptions of the period.

All of this is to say that Bremond came to the view that the religious practice of the seventeenth century was Bérullian through and through. The function of sacramental participation, and then of the different modes of prayer, is to nurture the "habitual," often unconscious but steady, adhesion of the soul. In the current, developmental parlance of today's educational philosophy, sacraments and prayer "form" the soul so that moral affections and behavior are grounded in "character" rather than drilled regimentation or authoritarian imperatives.

When one surveys the breathtaking amount of material gathered by Bremond into these two volumes, most of it long-forgotten and wearisome for him to access, it is startling to recall that he was already in seriously failing health,[1] even as he welcomed a stream of friends and visitors to "Littlemore" at Pau, and to his mountain-retreat at Arthez-d'Asson, and even as he contemplated more works yet to come, while the political situation in France continued to deteriorate.

Mounting Catastrophe

And deteriorating it was, with anti-fascist, anticlerical, sometimes Socialist-radical partisans on the political left set in opposition to the monarchical-clerical, Action Française partisans of the political right, and efforts at centrism failing. By the early 1930s the polarization was reaching violent and hysterical levels of expression, with most of the Catholic hierarchy of France, despite Vatican denunciations of Action Française, lined up on the right. Often this alignment took the form of advocacy for stricter constraints in areas of public morality, or of support for electoral candidates articulating conservative positions. "Bolshevism" was the great fear from the right, "fascism" from the left, with efforts at compromise loudly denounced from both sides.[2]

Bremond, as we know, by virtue of his family legacy, by virtue of his personal formation in an environment that combined humanistic letters with an inward-looking spirituality, and by virtue of a temperament that allowed him to have friends in both camps, was a man of the "middle." Utterly unsympathetic with the mentality of the political right—we recall the break with Maurras and then the constant polemic against Catholic conservatism, especially that of "recent" Catholics like Péguy—he was also alienated by the traditional anticlericalism of rationalist thought, by the occasional "mob-mentality" of the political left, as well as the residues of post-Dreyfus hatred in radical circles for the Church. For him the hope of the future, the hope for harmony and charity, was always in the "correct" retrieval of a beloved tradition, where that tradition is not seen as a fossilized relic to be manipulated by authority, but as a resource enabling the life of "prayer," the life of the "poetic state," in the present.

Clearly Bremond leaned leftward politically, but *cautiously*, not so much in the form of an activist program or reformist agenda, but more in the spirit of a moral

---

1. In the correspondence with Blondel from 1928 onward there are increasingly frequent references on the part of both of these aging men to their frail health, Blondel with increasing blindness, Bremond with flu-like and pulmonary symptoms.

2. For context and lively description, including the Catholic paranoia about Freemasonry, see Weber, *Hollow Years*, esp. 196–206. This is, perhaps, the place to point out that Bremond and Blondel shared in the general anti-Wilsonian, anti-American mentality in France that followed the Versailles treaty, feeling that France had been bullied into a "bad deal" for everyone, and that Wilson's idealism was a self-serving mirage (not the "pure love" it purported to be!). As is often pointed out, however, there was a general reluctance to take into account Clemenceau's large part in the shape of the final treaty.

ideal, pure love, refurbished and reenergized by models of saintliness that are recalled by the community, then internalized by each individual, through a corporate return to the "poetry" of the sources. In such a return, the dangers of self-interested extremisms, self-interested avoidance of moral challenges and human need, and a self-interested religious dogmatism, could all be minimized.

Bremond expressed his loyalty to that ideal as a *practical program* in his turn to the devotional materials of *Histoire*, IX and X, where the focus is heavily oriented to lay, rather than clerical, forms of piety, where expression is more lyrically robust than dogmatically freighted, often in the form of liturgical or para-liturgical texts. Through his focus on such materials he shared indirectly in the widespread movement of liturgical renovation and experimentation that marked the 1930s across the Catholic-Protestant spectrum. Classicist that he was, he derided fashionable and superficial (as he saw it) popularizations, at the same time that he resisted highbrow liturgical purisms, as in the work of Dom Prosper Guéranger.[3] He very much supported any effort to return spiritual resources to the "people," by taking them out of the specialized enclaves and elite practitioner communities where they had been treasured, but also jealously guarded. The devotion of Francis de Sales and Chantal, of Bérulle and Condren and Olier, of Camus and Chardon and Piny and Fénelon, *suitably modified*, could, in the life of common prayer, and in the practical devotional habits of the faithful, be made accessible and usable across the whole life of communities.

Caussade

It was, as well, in this same period of preparation of his two volumes of community prayer texts, that Bremond had the chance to make better known a spiritual writer who has functioned as a conduit, or bridge, into the modern period for the spirituality of "pure love." We recall that Fénelon's writing is the grand embodiment of that ideal—Bremond in fact prepared an anthology of excerpts for the publisher Flammarion in 1930—but the Swan of Cambrai's extreme positions and aristocratic tone would always be a barrier. A mediating agent was thus needed, and Jean-Pierre de Caussade, SJ, (1675–1751) filled the gap. Bremond's 1931 edition, for Bloud et Gay, of Caussade's 1741 work, *Bossuet, Maître d'Oraison. Instructions spirituelles en forme de dialogues sur les divers états d'oraison suivant la doctrine de M. Bossuet. Nouvelle edition conforme a l'édition originale of 1741*, allowed him to highlight the importance of this "semi-quietist," but impeccably orthodox, writer with a popular touch. Caussade

---

3. The many histories of liturgical renewal look to the renewed, nineteenth-century European Benedictine communities as the primary source, with Guéranger's Solesmes leading the list. Much of this remained elitist (recall J.-K Huysmans's fascinations), but in the post-WWI period "went viral," as we say today. Maurice de la Taille's 1921 work, *Mysterium Fidei*, unleashed an avalanche of work and studies in liturgical renewal with patristics, medieval, and Reformation-era specialists all weighing in, as well as every conceivable kind of artist. Bremond had issues with all of this, and commented on all of the principals, as we shall see.

domesticates Fénelon's pure-love spirituality, not by watering it down, but by preserving its essence and then restructuring its presentation; in his hands, sage advice to aristocrats becomes a comprehensive spiritual perspective for the masses.

Rector of the Jesuit collège at Perpignan during the last part of his career, Caussade is best known for his authorship of *Spiritual Letters*, as well as the widely read *Abandonment to Divine Providence*, a work submerged for a time, then rediscovered in complete form only toward the end of the nineteenth century. According to Dominique Salin, the *Abandonment* became, along with Teresa of Lisieux's *Story of a Soul*, one of the principal books that sustained French Catholics during WWI,[4] and Bremond, having initially made appeal to him as far back as the *Apologie pour Fénelon*, made increasing use of him as a source of expansion and clarification in the text of the *Histoire* as it progressed, especially in the discussion of Chardon and Piny.

But the irony for Bremond in drawing increased attention to Caussade's *Instructions spirituelles* was that this work is an elaborate defense and exposition of Bossuet's views on the mystical life, with ideas from Madame Guyon and Fénelon used to elucidate Bossuet's meaning! We recall that Bossuet had originally written his work on spiritual states as a *counter* to Guyon and Fénelon, and now de Caussade was using these latter to expound the Eagle of Meaux! The result both in the *Instructions spirituelles*, and in *Abandonment*, is that we have a "Fénelonizing" of Bossuet,[5] where these two thinkers are made to agree with one another essentially (as Bremond himself contended in the *Apologie pour Fénelon*), despite technical differences. Both teachers want to honor the tradition of Francis de Sales by teaching an *orthodox* doctrine of mystical abandon, of the passive states, of pure love, and so on.[6]

Caussade provided exactly what Bremond needed in order to answer critics who fear moral laxism, or illuminism, or spiritual individualism in all of the touting of mystical spirituality. In the process, moreover, Caussade quietly circumvented, with cautious warrants from Bossuet at his pastoral best, the argument that mystical pure-love spirituality is only for an elite; on the contrary, the practice of abandonment to God's providence by living hopefully and joyfully into whatever comes is for everyone. And to sweeten the package, Caussade is another Jesuit in the tradition of Lallemant, exemplifying precisely as a Jesuit the mystical side of Ignatius.

A good example of Caussade's popularizing gift is in the analogy that he offered for understanding "how a soul in abandonment, seeking only its God, can be enveloped in darkness," where he invoked the weaver's skill: "The work is done rather like the superb tapestries that are worked stitch by stitch from the underside. The person

---

4. Salin, "Treatise on Abandonment to Divine Providence," 21.

5. Ibid., 24–27, and Michel Olphe-Galliard, "Caussade," 368–69. See also Talar, "Prayer at Twilight," 53–54n47.

6. The need for balanced views on the subject of mystical abandon is illustrated in the *DS* art. "Abandon," which is divided into two parts: "true abandon," by M. Viller, and "false abandon" (where Fénelon is firmly condemned) by the famous historian of spirituality P. Pourrat.

working at it sees their own stitch and their own needle; and when all these stitches are brought together they form magnificent shapes which appear only when everything is finished, and the good side is exhibited in the daylight. But during the time of the work, all this beauty and splendour is in darkness.... The more the soul is applying itself to its own small work, completely obscured and simple as it is, completely hidden and contemptible as it may be from the outside, the more God is making variations with it, embellishing it, enriching it with the embroidery and colours that He is mingling in with it."[7]

The glory of Caussade's work, in his deep sense that God is quietly at work in the most traumatic human misery and that faith requires submission to that hidden working, constituted a call to "pure love" in the willingness to renounce (for the time being) the normal human hunger for relief and satisfaction. It is a "big picture" adaptation of Fénelon that focuses on divine working rather than the inward-looking mysteries of human resistance and recalcitrance, and as such it embodied a spirituality well suited to the dilemmas of a battered nation struggling to rise from the ashes. A comparable struggle comes through, for instance, in Teilhard de Chardin's evolutionism in his WWI essays and the 1925 composition *The Divine Milieu*, where passive endurance is framed as a positive contribution to human progress. It was a thus a pleasure for Bremond to make Caussade's work better known, and thereby, in Charles Chauvin's words, to "keep the pot boiling."[8]

Sacraments

In late 1931, after having had portions of *Histoire*, IX, read to him, Blondel expressed great enthusiasm for what Bremond had accomplished, noting that the material had considerable appeal for intelligent and devout, but non-academic, Catholics.[9] Bremond himself was more captivated by the relationship between the hidden life of prayer and popular forms of pious practice, as he wrestled afresh with the modernist problematic of the inner-and-the-outer and their interplay.[10]

He started the volume with a survey of texts illustrative of "devotion in baptism," where dying-with-Christ and mystical incorporation into the Body of the Church serve as the key "consecratory" themes in the sacrament of initiation. Sanctifying grace begins its hidden work by means of the newly baptized person's "union with Christ," the result being that the spoken vows are an affirmation of Christ working "in us" as the energizing force in the pursuit of virtue. Ascetical practice is grounded in a prior mysticism. "I wish to be what baptism has made me," says one pious writer, harking

---

7. Cited by Salin, "Treatise on Abandonment," 33.
8. Chauvin, *Petite Vie*, 149.
9. Blondel to Bremond, December 14, 1931 (BB, III, 408).
10. *Histoire*, IX, "avant-propos." The "synthesis" to which he aspires (ibid., ii) will reveal the "spirit" embedded in the "piety."

back to the element of prior deliverance, and affirming the importance of ritualized reminders of baptism.[11] What is particularly notable, moreover, is that Bremond made extensive use of texts from Jansenist writers, especially Duguet and Quesnel, all of whom in their expounding of the meaning of baptism have a strong sense of the ethical requirements of discipleship, but are clear that these are enabled by prior grace. Nothing wrong with the best Jansenists, says Bremond, *when they pray*, since in this latter posture they are better than their doctrine. In fact, this new warmth for Jansenist writers on the part of Bremond was noted approvingly by Blondel, but also questioned by the abbé Baudin, another critic.

Blanchet has noted, a bit drily, that some sort of evolution was going on with Bremond here. A flabbergasted Baudin questioned his sincerity. How can you make such glowing use of the very spiritual movement that you so decimated in *Histoire*, IV?, said Baudin. But Bremond adopted an irenic tone, expressing some remorse at having indulged in over-statement in his criticisms of Port-Royal, that there were genuinely admirable figures, such as Saint-Cyran, among them, since in fact much of the quarreling with the Jesuits and others was based on dogmatic quibbles. Bremond was even warming a bit toward Cavallera, who had pointed out to him that no one took more of a beating from Port-Royal than the Jesuits. He even suspected that some of Port-Royal's contemporary critics, such as Vincent de Paul, were a little confused! it is easy to imagine that time and age had mellowed Bremond, but it is just as likely that he was looking to preserve the fruits of his scholarship for the Catholic mainstream of the 1930s. And that mainstream included the Jesuits as well as some Jansenist heritage.[12]

This warming toward Port-Royal continued on into Bremond's treatment of seventeenth-century Eucharistic practice, where he argued, contrary to the standard view, that the seventeenth century saw a great surge in Eucharistic participation and devotion. The test-case was the issue of frequent communion, with Arnauld's famous treatise on the subject at the center of consideration. He argued that ecclesial writers across the spectrum urged more frequent communion, basing themselves, including Arnauld (who, Bremond says, needs to be read more carefully) on a strong doctrine of the Real Presence, on the serious pursuit of holiness by the laity, and that all of the emphasis on penitential preparation, despite differences of degree and technical focus, was widespread. The idea everywhere is that all need the nourishment provided by this sacrament, that such access should not be reserved for an elite, that the critical element in preparation is purity of intention. Such is the Salesian doctrine, averred Bremond, even down to the time of Pius X (a remarkable declaration on Bremond's part).

---

11. The favored Bérullian term for mystical incorporation and adherence in baptism is, it seems, "filiation," and Bremond labors at the point that following Christ is not bare "imitation," but Christ "imitating himself" in us. This is the difference beween a legitimate and an illegitimate "ascesis" (ibid., 15–16).

12. Blanchet prints excerpts from this correspondence (BB, III, 409–10n1). He suggested that exploration of this correspondence could make a "contribution à une étude éventuelle sur l'évolution de la pensée de Bremond."

In a section on the "Holy Sacrifice" in the Mass, Bremond highlighted the way in which participation in the Eucharist became the "synthetic" act, drawing together all other aspects of worship and piety.[13] He observed a general diffusion of sacrificial theology in this period, in which the Mass became an essential component in "the common sacrifice of the priest and the faithful," with devotion increasingly understood as the internalizing of the words and actions that comprise the liturgy.[14] He noted that a trend toward certain priestly "eccentricities" at Mass, such as saying "secret" prayers quietly during the consecration, etc., or keeping the Canon of the Mass strictly in Latin, became controversial, as did the subject of translations. But the trend was set, he argued, in the direction of greater lay access and the erosion of clericalism. He offers many examples of intensified Eucharistic devotion and practice, with the implication that a Salesian fervor and style of practice were coming to predominate.

A chapter on Marian devotion attempted to refute the view of Charles Flachaire that under the influence of Bérullism and Port-Royal this devotion declined somewhat during the period. He distinguished two traditions of devotion to Mary, the first being medieval and Bernardine, taken up by the Jesuits, and the second more austere and Incarnational, emanating from Bérulle. Abuses arose on both sides, but in general the latter tradition, somewhat embraced by Port-Royal, remained more "reasonable" and restrained. Very strong popular devotion developed here by the end of the century under Grignion de Montfort, with "pure love" emphases appearing as well. A series of excursuses on particular figures underlines the vigor and theological integrity of Marian devotion by century's end.

Bremond then points to what he calls the era's "spiritual atmosphere" of the "mystical idealization" of the married state.[15] Grounded in the Incarnational theology of Francis de Sales and Bérulle, Bremond argued, this idealization manifested in a comparison with Mary's "Yes" to the Virginal Conception. Jansenist texts abound here, texts filled with great tenderness toward the marital bond, although there is then a tendency, based on the doctrine of original sin, to fall into a "Manichaean" negativity about the trials and temptations of marriage. A corresponding literature that plays up the advantages of remaining single then appeared. The right balance is hit, argued Bremond, by writers like Fénelon, who insist that every walk of life has its "crosses"

---

13. Ibid., 131–32.

14. Blondel and Bremond went back and forth about this point. In Bremond to Blondel, November 25, 1930 (BB, III, 387–88), Bremond contended that De la Taille and others overplay the theme of real "holocaust" in the sacrifice of the Mass, thus over-physicalizing everything, whereas the whole point is really the "interior sacrifice" made by each worshipper in solidarity with Christ. Blondel agreed completely (Blondel to Bremond, November 28, 1930), referring to "a false idea of the power of God, of God's sovereign majesty and sovereign egotism, that needs destruction so as to feel itself master and to judge itself as honored by its creatures," whereas in fact the sacrifice of the Mass is not just Calvary but the "whole dynamic of the Incarnation . . . the theandric union and beatific transformation" that is the process of redemption (BB, III, 389–91).

15. *Histoire*, IX, 289: "cette union mystique et sacrée."

and that sanctification resides in faithfully bearing these.[16] Unsurprisingly, the section concludes with Bremond's evoking of the humanistic approaches to child-rearing, slowly making headway at the time.

A final chapter on "the art of dying" is poignant. Bremond emphasizes that this was a time in which great emphasis was placed on the "prepared death," that is, one in which the individual through penitence and reception of the sacraments was in a state of grace at the time of death, the fear of God's judgment being very potent. He carefully analyzes a description by Boileau of the last days of the Duchesse de Luynes, as her dispositions moved from paroxysms of fear to those of the "dis-envenomed" state of companionship with the dying Savior. In a popular literary form of the "spiritual testament," Bremond saw the presence of a "constant functional inspiration," in which the dying person was enabled to express love for God as the ruler of life and death, and to entrust him/herself to that love. Oratorian devotion was especially strong here, as is seen in the "good death" of a young woman afflicted with the plague.

While the contents of *Histoire*, IX, were not those that typically engaged historians of an era, Marc Venard has pointed out that Bremond was anticipating the kind of social history that was to blossom a bit later. He was moving away from elite texts to "popular" material, and was thus opening windows into the wider spirit of the age.[17]

More elaborately and more recently, Pierre-Antoine Fabre has contended that in *Histoire*, IX and X, Bremond raised the question of the relations between individual passions and a religious sociology by showing that the spiritual atmosphere of an era is not reducible to theology as such, but rather is a "discursive elaboration," a "social inter-locution" or a "believing in the sentiment," thus a revelation of interior life into which we, too, can enter. Part of what Fabre had in mind here, following a thesis of Sophie Houdard, was that Bremond had an instinct for the way in which controversies at the popular level opened up "jeux de complémentation," in which contending parties reached mutual accommodations marked by Bergson's *durée*. Such accommodations are the product of temporal processes that reveal the "theatrical nature of history," this theatricality requiring, especially with its liturgical "moments of eternity" and ritual memory, the abolition of measured, rational time. Prayer dissolves ordered temporality in favor of a different kind of life-flow. Fabre can thus speak of a dialectical discernment of the will of God, so that debates about the practice of prayer require an antithetical give-and-take, with hearing-and-negating formulations marking an "open field."[18] The implication is that Bremond was in IX and X listening to aspects of

---

16. A "beau texte," says Bremond, ibid., 320–21n1. Indeed.

17. "Histoire littéraire et sociologie historique: deux voies pour une Histoire religieuse." The "two views" referred to in the title are Lucien Febvre's view of a quantifiable, statistical history, over against a literary and impressionistic history as with Bremond.

18. "Le temps de prier." The reference to Sophie Houdard is where Fabre discusses Bremond's use of "controversies" as a "field" of discourse and definition (ibid., 14–15).

Port-Royal and of Ignatius in fresh ways as the debates continued, and as he listened to the life of prayer within these traditions. So it is when we enter the "inner world"!

The Form of Prayer

As he entered volume X, then, Bremond took up another traditional debate about prayer, namely, the question of whether mental and unspoken prayer is superior to vocalized and expressive prayer. A central question involved the ancient prejudice—voiced by John Cassian and Teresa of Avila and Francis de Sales and many others—against parroted or mechanical prayer as insincere gibberish by comparison with the prayer "of the heart."

One would expect Bremond to be an advocate for the inwardness of purely mental prayer, but just the opposite happens.[19] At this point, his love of poetry came into play, as he noted how frequently writers who deprecate vocal prayer also manifest a fondness for liturgical forms, for the sacramentality of words and bodily expression, so that a "sur-idealism" about prayer is counterbalanced by the recognition that we are not disembodied spirits.[20] The issue is one of sincerity, so that the wisest writers acknowledge that spoken prayer, as well as mental, can be a genuine effusion of the heart, as is acknowledged, for instance, by the Port-Royalist Pierre Nicole, when he argues that loving relationships require all of the concrete behaviors of loving affections. The problem, always, is that abuse and correct usage are very close neighbors, so that too much ranting about the first can do real damage to the second. The Jansenist Duguet wisely taught the view that learning to pray with set forms, if these are taken from Scripture, is a means of stimulating the very affections that they express, so that "unreal words," in Newman's phrase, become "real" over time.

In a modern pedagogical dilemma, there is the recognition that some repetition deadens, and some enlivens, depending on the spirit in which it is embraced and utilized. Outward forms enable, or they mask. Does learning the Catechism make me a better Christian, or a dull and superficial one? Bremond was clear that it depends partly on how well the text is written, and partly on the nature of my intention as I use it.

He then raised the question of whether liturgical evolution was progressive or regressive, noting the surge in scholarship on liturgical texts and forms, along with efforts at the popularization of various liturgical reforms and practices. With one eye on Prosper Guéranger's program, he pointed to a steady tradition of "liturgical

---

19. In a shrewd, psychologically informed note Bremond observes that most study focuses either on very primitive or else very sophisticated forms of prayer, leaving out the "entre-deux" which is his real concern (*Histoire*, X, 12n2).

20. Specifically, this is a criticism of the Jesuit director, Guilloré: "the idea does not come to him that, in the living reality of a human recitation, the lips and the spirit, the words and the thoughts, the interior and the exterior, make a single reality" (ibid., 17–18).

inquietude" and "textual tinkering" manifested in the tension between a growing, enforced Roman uniformity, on the one hand, and local Gallican creativity and native expression, on the other. Here Bremond revealed himself to be a "Gallican purist" and a "localist," generally preferring the French artistry and idiosyncrasy to the centralized and imposed orthodoxy of Rome-inspired reforms.

He makes a particular example of the Jansenizing preacher and writer Nicolas Letourneux (1640–1686), who produced a popular multi-volume devotional "companion," the *L'Année chrétienne*, intended to be used by average church-folk in their regular round of parish liturgies. Though the work was quite popular, it eventually went on the Index, partly because, Bremond speculated, it presented vernacular forms of liturgical texts. But, averred Bremond, the work set a tone of high moral seriousness for the laity, while manifesting a "devout classicism" with a bit of a Cartesian temper. The main thing, though, was that Letourneux enabled intelligent participation on the part of the laity, a process that later reformers continued, so that "the liturgy lived" became a norm in ecclesial life, and "mental prayer properly called, i.e., methodic meditation," was transformed into "the public prayer of the Church," or what Bremond cleverly calls "liturgical reverie," where pious imagination could have free and creative play, while always being recalled to the sober foundation of the accepted liturgical texts.[21]

An extensive treatment of Gallican hymns followed. By "hymns" Bremond meant liturgical poetry, usually ancient texts in modified or simplified Latin forms, and set in musical format for chant. What was critical for Bremond was that the seventeenth century saw an explosion of arrangements of this material for performance and enjoyment by the laity. He cites the standard sentiment from Frédéric Ozanam that through singing children and women intuitively understand the deepest truths (one thinks also of the famous saying from Augustine that a prayer sung is prayed twice). His thesis is that the original productions of this period, done by his favorite composers, are the precious "witnesses of our national prayer under the old regime."[22] Breviaries, missals, collections of all sorts are rich with this material. He argued that the "Gallican hymn" evolved into a truly liturgical hymn in a novel way that Guéranger and other Roman reformers,[23] too besotted with their perception that most Gallican piety is also Jansenist, have failed to recognize.

Repeatedly, Bremond pointed to elements of high "lyricism" in hymnic material, though he deprecated at the same time the Cartesian-Jansenist temptation to make

---

21. Sainte-Beuve also gave quite substantial attention to Letourneux,, contending that "his great crime" was that "he wanted to introduce some role for reason and understanding into the books thus far closed up in the Sanctuary, lessening them while revering them, but also in some measure explaining the mysterious and the marvelous inherent in cultic celebration" (*Port-Royal* VI [III, 219, ed. Leroy]).

22. *Histoire*, X, 62.

23. "Romantic ultramontanism," Bremond calls this tendency (ibid., 145), offering perhaps an example of what he elsewhere called a "bad" romanticism.

hymns didactic. He contended that Gallican hymns tended to translate common prayer into verse, thus making them a true vehicle of popular piety, at the same time that they communicated basic biblical themes and symbols to ordinary worshippers.

In a description of what he called the "liturgical lyricism of the Gallican School," Bremond analyzed the function of hymns into "triumphal lyricism" (a poetic recalling of a "moment" in salvation history), then a "dramatic lyricism" (which is a reenactment for purposes of personal appropriation of that same "moment"), finally a "mystical lyricism" in prayer and poetry (an identification with the interior state of Jesus in that "moment.)" All of this is vividly illustrated by Bremond in numerous excursuses and gatherings of texts, so that one comes away with a sense of great richness, even lushness, in the liturgical-devotional life of the seventeenth century. Clearly, Bremond wanted to make a contribution to liturgical revision in his own time, as if to say "here is a native tradition that we must not forget," while acknowledging the inevitable necessity of merging this tradition with other currents. He used examples drawn from the usage at his own cathedral in Aix to show that ancient materials could be incorporated into new and approved texts, thus overcoming the anti-Gallicanism that began at the Revolution.[24]

A final section then allowed Bremond to make his over-arching point: in many of the vocal prayer-forms we can see how liturgical and quasi-liturgical texts (the "litany" forms which are explored at length) in popular practice reflected an inner life that was shaped by the literary expression of borrowed formulas. Thus, one can speak of the "art of prayer." In order to avoid mere "ascesis," moreover, in the teaching of prayer, wise writers advocated a "middle way" between vocal prayer (mechanical repetition) and discursive meditation (creative free-play with devotional themes). Hence arose a whole industry of meditative techniques, but always with the fall-back on liturgical forms that impede the tendency to egoism and self-consciousness. Bremond's thesis was that liturgical forms keep us from becoming self-focused, pull us away from ourselves into God's "bigger picture." Bypass the rational intellect, and get to the heart.

Histoire, IX and X, thus show a double movement on the part of Bremond. On the one hand, as he shifted his focus to Catholic sacramental and liturgical texts, he particularized his treatment of mystical prayer to a specifically ecclesial and Gallican arena of activity. This is to say in effect that mystical prayer, the tradition of devout humanism ending in pure love, really is the vital life of the empirical Church as a worshipping community. But, on the other hand, there is a universalizing dynamic as well, since the particularities are shown to be specific embodiments and lyrical expressions of the "inner life," of habitual and sanctifying grace manifested in the "poetic state" wherever and whenever it occurs.

24. Ibid., 141–46. In one excursus he even took J.-K. Huysmans to task for "mandarin aestheticism" in preferring the Romanized forms in the most eloquent expression of his own day to the devotion found in popular piety (ibid., 262). In another excursus he celebrated a Protestant collection, called "Le Bouquet d'Eden" of 1673, in which one sees "the influence of the Bible on the development of French language and style" (ibid., 260–61).

Valéry, therefore, *really* prays in his poetry, but so does the typical congregation at Mass when people *really* pray by entering into the dynamic of the liturgy. The outward form is not so much *essential* to the reality of what is experienced—as if that reality would dissolve without the outward form—as it is *inevitable*, given the empirical and concrete nature of culture. Furthermore, the outward expression can be critiqued for adequacy, since there is always the possibility of serious distortion. That critical factor for both Bremond and, as we shall see, for Loisy as well is "pure love."[25]

Finally, Loisy

But what about the Buddhist or Hindu or Moslem devotée, or the sincere seeker wandering in a fog? At the same time that he was creating his two volumes on prayer in the *ancien régime*, Bremond authored pseudonymously a sustained defense of Alfred Loisy, to which Loisy would eventually respond with an equally heartfelt loyalty.[26] Bremond's central point in the defense was that one maintains a true faithfulness to the integrity of one's own tradition—in this case Roman catholic Christianity—precisely by affirming its central tenets without being limited by them, without turning them into dogmatic idols.[27] A true loyalty to a particular tradition is a moral, not a doctrinal, accomplishment, an act in which one turns *outward by going inward*. In the depths of one's own heritage one discovers the level at which communion with all souls is established without losing one's specific anchorage or requiring that others lose theirs. Thus, said Bremond, Loisy for all of his rebellion was in the final analysis a true priest.[28]

---

25. This is why Goichot can refer to Bremond's view that Christian mysticism, rightly understood, is *paradigmatic* for all mystical experience, i.e., provides the critical element (EG, 295). Loisy, for all of his later focus on the "religion of humanity," cannot get away from Christian criteria of adequacy.

26. The fact of Bremond's authorship, behind the pseudonym of Sylvain Leblanc, was for a long time uncertain, but Emile Poulat's 1972 critical edition, *Une oeuvre clandestine de Henri Bremond, Sylvain Leblanc, Un clerc qui n'a pas trahi, Alfred Loisy d'après ses Mémoires*, made it certain. Interestingly, Goichot absolves Bremond of all "Nicodemism" here, that is, of using a pseudonym in order to hide from the religious authority the fact that he himself is truly a skeptic at heart (EG, 289–90). That is not the issue in his defense of Loisy.

27. Goichot refers to Leszek Kolakowski's complaint that Bremond's *Histoire* has a "naively confessional character," for all of its pretension to deal with essences (EG, 295). The complaint is reasonable, for, after all, Bremond deals with narrowly French Roman Catholic in-house disputes at exhaustive length, but it also misses the point that a meaningful portrayal of essences can only take the form of careful examination of culturally grounded masses of particular detail. The accurate grasp of "one" is at the same time the accurate grasp of "all." Further, the whole Modernist program is premised on not just the *distinction* between "deep" reality and surface manifestation, but also on their intertwined *relationship*.

28. It is also true that the meaning of the phrase "true priest" was different for Bremond and Loisy, partly because of their differing understandings of mysticism, as carefully argued by Trémolières, "Mystique et église: Le cas Bremond." Some of the turmoil created for Bremond and his friends by the publication of Loisy's *Mémoires* is captured in the passages from correspondence cited by Blanchet (BB, III, 410–12n2). The overwhelming issue seems to have been Loisy's *integrity* in word and action,

The title of *A Cleric Who Has Not Committed Treason* was, of course, a takeoff on Julian Benda's notorious 1927 essay, *The Treason of the Intellectuals*, and was occasioned by Loisy's publications of the three volumes of his *Mémoires* in 1930–31. These volumes were Loisy's *apologia* to his critics, containing large amounts of detail about persons living and dead as well as explanatory justifications for his many theological positions. Initial reviews were hostile, and Loisy's publisher, Émile Nourry, sought out Bremond for a more positive assessment. The resulting ninety-page essay is Bremond's tribute to his friend, but he used the Modernist guise of pseudonymity to avoid official censure for himself or Loisy. Unlike Benda's castigation of the French "intellectuals" for their (supposed) betrayal of the life of the mind by capitulating to politics, specifically to Germanic Nietzschean romanticism and its cult of raw power, Bremond defended Loisy for his loyalty as a true priest to the spirit of the Gospel and a Christian worldview premised on the moral goodness of humanity. However immoral the "clerks," or intellectuals, of France might be in Benda's view, there has been one "clerk," insisted Bremond, who has kept the faith, who is moral indeed. The reasoning to this conclusion is revelatory not just of how Bremond saw the meaning of Loisy's work, but also of how his own thought was developing.

From the beginning, contended Bremond, Loisy had been feeling his way along in a personal journey. He plodded his lonely way in the Church, not as a duplicitous unbeliever, but as one criticized both by skeptics who urged him to leave and by loyalists who doubted his good faith. The *Mémoires* now make all this clear. His achievement, in fact, was to salvage "from the shipwreck of his faith religion itself," so that while "his religious philosophy is debatable, like all philosophies, his probity is not."[29] His strategy has been to function as priest and critic at the same time, on the one hand assessing traditional texts as a "witness and guardian of truth," on the other hand committed to the "super-rational principles on which religious life is founded." In both modes he has been faithful, while his originality has been to follow where this process led.[30]

Indeed, Loisy had been a "mystical cleric" from the beginning, combining an intense love for the Church with an intense intellectual precocity.[31] Eventually the savant and the priest came into conflict, as the rationalizing influence of Renan on the interpretation of Scripture came into play, although Loisy always felt that reconciliation was possible. Bremond contended that Duchesne and Loisy, while similar as critics, were quite different as churchmen, Loisy being authentically mystical while

---

since the Modernists were always being accused of bad faith.

29. *Un clerc qui n'a pas trahi*, vi–vii. Citations are from the original 1931 edition.

30. Ibid., vii–viii. Leblanc (Bremond) states that Loisy is both priest and critic, and that he has betrayed neither role.

31. Ibid., 1. The whole sketch of Loisy's career is based on the tension between the priest and the savant, the mystic and the rationalist, the one for whom the substance must not be confused with its accidents, the distinction of which was essential to his whole spiritual journey. Thus, Loisy is presented very much in terms of Newman.

Duchesne was not. Loisy thought that Duchesne avoided the "big questions," while Duchesne in fact could have helped Loisy maintain a balance, a "middle way," between rationalism and traditional orthodoxy.[32] The real difference, however, was the serious, mystical intensity of Loisy's inner life—something that Duchesne avoided.

Here we have an insight into Bremond himself, since it is precisely this depth of "inner life" with its disquietudes and torments that marks one out as a "person for the future," a person for whom "faith may die, but religion be born" (Karl Barth expressed it the other way around, but that is the difference between dialectical theology and mysticism!). What Loisy had come to see is that dogma must be replaced by the religious spirit, since the church has always acknowledged that it is the substance of a dogma and not its form that ultimately matters. Where Loisy came out as he continued to struggle with these tensions was the conviction that the moral power of religion is the thing itself, a vision of moral truth, and that faithfulness lived in rectitude is the practical corollary. Leblanc-Bremond cites a passage from the first volume of the *Mémoires*, where Loisy distinguishes between the realm of "science," which is the visible world to be analyzed by reason, and the realm of "faith," inward and invisible, but also the source of vital moral discipline.[33] Until his excommunication in 1908 Loisy continued to believe that his priesthood and his critical sense could be reconciled in an affirmation of the moral truth of the church.

Close examination of Loisy's work from 1904–1908 shows, Leblanc-Bremond argued, that his faith in the Church, though no longer traditional, had become mystical, and that the very concept of "orthodoxy" had become for him a mirage. But, said Bremond, if one understands that "faith" is a profound supernatural adhesion to "all of the invisible realities of which [one] still believes that the Catholic Church is the indispensable guardian," then Loisy still had faith and had not betrayed the church.[34] Quite the contrary, "he loves the church."

But then came a whole series of frustrations for Loisy: accusations that he was a "phony," the rejection of Modernism, the Law of Separation in France, the slapping down of the Sillon, the apparent endorsement of Action Française, and Loisy was done.

But still no betrayal. The priest and the savant worked in tandem, as he churned out a productive scholarly career. He never hid his priesthood behind the professor's robes, as did so many. He desired more and more "to know the essential and living element that finds itself realized more or less imperfectly in all religions," convinced

---

32. Ibid., 10. Leblanc-Bremond laments the misunderstanding, the disconnect, between these two great historians. It is the point where one senses some fond hope that, if things had been different, Loisy could have stayed within the church.

33. Ibid., 19. One hears an echo as well of Loisy's views on the role of the church in society and in the world of education. See Harvey Hill, "Loisy's 'Mystical Faith.'"

34. Ibid., 45.

that this element grounds society, morality and humanity.³⁵ He was increasingly concerned with "obligation as a spiritual thing" and as the mystical matrix of religious development. He saw WWI as the failure of all religions, out of which was emerging something new for all of humanity. Classical atonement-theology was being replaced by a "simple devotion to the point of death," and by an ethical mysticism of "devotion to the good out of love for it." This is the "mystical flame," the "new catechism of today and tomorrow."

In a concluding section, Bremond called for a new history of Modernism, in which the real heroes will be characters like Loisy, who welcomed critical thought while remaining loyal. Loisy would have stayed in, if he had not been pushed out! Reviewing a host of "Modernist" figures, Leblanc-Bremond notes that a great deal is a matter of degree, with some staying in the church, and some not, but once we note that "Modernism" is essentially a creature of repression, we see that Loisy is the "Modernist par excellence," he for whom "the least grain of goodness matters more for humanity that the loftiest philosophy."³⁶

Certainly for Bremond Loisy's "heart" was always in the right place, but the ugliness of church politics and authority combined with a bit too much rationalism in his thought-processes made him intransigent and rigid. If he had listened a bit more to his "mystical" sense of the nature of truth, a sense that came out more and more clearly in his later writings, he would have found a way to affirm the universal in the particular, rather than to play them off against one another—as if one has to be either an orthodox Catholic or a true mystic, but not both. In any case, however, the choice was made for him, and he became a pruned branch. In their correspondence, Bremond and Loisy would wrestle endlessly with these questions, as Loisy would demonstrate in his remembrance of 1936, *George Tyrrell et Henri Bremond*.

After defending his friend, Bremond, at length, in that composition's last section, "A Religious Philosophy," Loisy compared and contrasted their two modes of thought. He was clear that Bremond was determined to live and die in the communion of the Catholic Church, while he himself had no such intention, although, he insisted (somewhat tendentiously), that that difference did not matter when it came to their shared "spiritual philosophy." He described this philosophy as "general," that is, as transcending all particular confessional allegiance, or even any particular religious tradition, so that it could not be "enclosed in the confines of a special theology, as in contemporary Catholic theology." In a shot at Blondel and others, he opined that Bremond's friends might be saddened or surprised to hear this point being made about him.³⁷

---

35. Ibid., 66. It is "religion itself" that Loisy seeks, and that is moral rather than dogmatic. As we note repeatedly, it is Blondel who keeps Bremond from going there, but it is also his sense of the concrete and specific that cannot be dissolved into abstraction that is most critical.

36. Ibid., 77, 100.

37. GT, 143–45.

Loisy set out to prove his case by citing from their shared correspondence. Without doubt, they held common commitments to the ideal of disinterested "pure love" in religion, to the struggle against fascism and the Action Française, to the need to critique political compromises and sometimes ham-fisted authoritarianism on the part of the church, to a profound respect for healthy mystical experience across religious traditions, as well as to a mutual recognition that mysticism infused with eros can lead to degenerate expression, such as in Nazism. Loisy also recognized that Bremond was reluctant to take the *metaphysical* step into an optimistic "religion of humanity," as was clear in his resistance to his, Loisy's, strictures on all religions at the time of WWI.[38] As we have seen, both Bremond and Blondel were skeptical about the flood of Wilsonian idealism that burst forth after the war, whereas Loisy was not.

In fact, Loisy was vulnerable to a rationalizing dynamic, namely, that of turning mystical experience across times and cultures into a systematic unity, that is, to see it as essentially the same thing everywhere, and thus to push for a "universal spirituality." Bremond did not take this path, sometimes described as "reductionistic" or "totalizing," because he had a view of the particularity of a tradition that blocks *that kind of* synthesis. In the "metaphysic of the saints," *Histoire*, VII and VIII, he had, to be sure, sought out a general structure, an "essence" to prayer, but he did so not in order to discard the outward forms entirely, but to purify them through a process of recall. The general structure is a heuristic, a device for thinking through a problem and engaging in critique. But for Loisy the general structure had the status of a subsistent reality, to which one could flee as an escape from the outward forms altogether.

The differing approaches, and the reasons for them, came out in how each man responded to Henri Bergson's 1932 book, *The Two Sources of Morality and Religion*.

Bergson Again

In his discussion of Bergson's treatise in "A Religious Philosophy," Loisy made it sound as if he and Bremond were in complete agreement on their understanding of Bergson's theory as well as their criticism of it. But things are not so simple, and, as noted, Loisy was highly invested in making it seem as if he and Bremond lived and thought in perfect harmony with one another.

Bergson's basic thesis was that morality and religion evolve from the same two sources in human experience and human history, the first being a primitive-instinctual and prerational intuition, the second a civilized and highly rational-intellectual transformation of the first. Both are socially shaped and generated, but on different levels, the first arising from a social grouping's need for self-preservation, and the second consisting of the mass of customs and laws that ensure stability and orderly functioning in developed society. In the case of morality a primitive sense of obligation

---

38. See ibid., 157–58, as well as my discussion *supra*.

to the group eventually gives way to the formal legal structure of society, while in the case of religion eruptions of mystical experience generate a dynamic ethos of pure love rich with mythological expression, that eventually gives way to the organization and dogmas and abstractions of static religion. The élan vital, or creative evolutionary life-force, moves society forward via an oscillating rhythm of destabilizing mystical energy, breaking through set forms for the sake of expansive love, and a stabilizing, order-producing intellectual structuring that emphasizes obedience and nationalistic loyalties. The *static* religion of order gives way to the fluid movement of *dynamic* religion and its mystically-induced pressure for change. Thus, in the total historical experience of humankind, averred Bergson, instinct and intelligence have provided the two forms of consciousness, the two sources, interacting with one another, for evolutionary advance.

Bergson developed the theory with considerable nuance and sophistication, folding it into his metaphysical system, and arguing that the mystical impulse in developed society manifests most often as saintly figures who model moral excellence and challenge the conventional status quo. He was moving very much in the direction of Catholic tradition, seeing the "high mystics" as the supreme examples of a pure love spirituality, and, as noted earlier, he very much approved of Bremond's *Histoire*.

According to Loisy, he and Bremond entirely sympathized with Bergson's exalting of primitive, instinctual, mystically-flavored experience as the intuitive kind of sensing and knowing that is the bedrock of human consciousness. They liked his description of dynamic religion, and completely agreed with his analysis of the limitations of static religion. But then they drew the line at Bergson's insistence that *both* instinct and intelligence are vital, inter-connected sources of moral and religious truth, each needing the other at different stages of development, since this argument led Bergson to over-rate, Loisy thought, the part played by monumental figures in history, and in Christian history in particular. His response to Bergson was the argument that there can be only *one* source, namely the primitive and mystical, of moral and religious experience, with pure love leading directly, through the ups and downs of contingent historical development, to the universal religion of humanity. And Bremond, as cited by Loisy, seemed to agree.[39]

One problem was that Bergson manifested a real respect for the inevitable fact of historical crystallization in powerful individuals, that mystical religion must assume discrete and particular forms of expression in such persons, that evolution inexorably moves toward these.[40] In a sense, a major presupposition of Bremond's *Histoire*, of his life's work, manifested in his loyalty to Sainte-Beuve's ideal of portraiture, is the idea that individuals in all of their idiosyncratic sharpness are the moving agents of

---

39. See Harvey Hill, "Henri Bergson and Alfred Loisy," for discussion of the Bergson-Loisy debate.

40. Ibid., 134–35. Thus Bremond could refer to Bergson's combination of two sources as "a strange mélange of élan and rusticity" (Bremond to Blondel, March 11, 1932 [BB, III, 420]).

history.[41] This is true even in *Histoire*, IX and X, where the focus is corporate, but where it is individual genius that stands out.

But there is also the fact that while Bremond made it sound as if he and Loisy were in concord, when he wrote to Blondel, things sounded different. In the autumn of 1932, he congratulated Blondel on the imminent appearance of the first volume of the latter's masterwork, *La Pensée* (actually published only in 1934), a draft of which he had just read, and described it as Blondel's *La Source unique de la religion et de la morale* in an obvious take-off on Bergson's book which had just appeared.[42] But he knew very well that insofar as Blondel can be said to be describing "one source" for religion, he meant the fully operative human *intellectus*, the rational/moral capacity, open to the *donum intelligentiae* of supernatural grace, for discerning truth, and that that *intellectus* is something quite distinct from Loisy's mysticism that moves naturally to the religion of humanity. Actually, when Bremond envisions Blondel as the advocate for one source for religion, he pictures something closer to Bergson's emphasis on civilized intellect as an essential expression of the mysterious élan vital (Bergson's substitute for the supernatural, as endless scientific critics have pointed out).

Bremond's evocation of Bergson, when he chose to do so, was more redolent of Blondel than Loisy, especially when he exalted folk piety not as a primitive and instinctual residue, but contrariwise, as an anticipation of very sophisticated thought. The reader may recall Bremond's description, back in the "turba magna" portion of *Histoire*, VI, where he describes the pious writer's evocation of the wine-cellar, where God comes knocking at the door of the "fine point of the soul." In Bremond's words, "a peasant Socrates, knowing only his catechism" expresses himself clumsily in images and symbols that, as Bergson knew, undergird in the form of poetry what a philosopher states much more abstractly, "homely wine" substituting for "metaphysical absinthe."[43] Thus it is that an ignorant man could come forth with spirituality rivaling that of the more thoughtful Francis de Sales. The peasant is a humble commoner, but he is also, in his way, a mystical genius.

It is no wonder, thus, that Loisy and Bremond were drawn to Bergson's work, but I think it was Bergson's view that mystical experience does, after all, have a content that is not only aesthetically expressed, but that constrains the mystic in an ethical direction, moving him higher on the evolutionary scale, that appealed more to Bremond than to Loisy. Both men agreed that mysticism can become erotic/demonic, as with the Nazis, and both agreed that pathological or merely egotistical elements can distort the experience. But Loisy seems to have been resistant to the idea that

---

41. A kinship with the neo-Freudian Erik Erikson's "great man" theory of historical development should be noted. Certain individuals, while developing according to endogenous epigenetic patterns common to all persons, incorporate in their personalities larger cultural-historical patterns in ways that serve as powerful change agents for whole societies.

42. Bremond to Blondel, October 3, 1932 (BB, III, 439).

43. *Histoire*, VII, 331.

some kind of conscious screening of the experience for implications and directives of an ethical character is thus necessitated, and that criteria for that screening must come from some normative source. It is the "myth" generated by the experience, then rationally interpreted, that is crucial.

Granted that mystical experience, *broadly conceived*, is universal—for, after all, poetry is universal, and thus, thought Bremond, his term "pan-mysticism" is justified—Loisy failed to see that Bremond was resistant to any construal of the *one* source for morality and religion that ultimately discards the essential import of rational reflection.[44] It is the problem again of trying to define what the mystic "knows" as a result of mystical experience, and how that experience gives rise to such "knowledge." In truth, Bergson had come very close to Bremond's French-School emphasis on "states" in relation to Jesus, but Bremond was reluctant to push this side of things onto Loisy.[45]

What Bremond did instead was to direct Loisy to his forthcoming *Histoire*, XI, on "the Procès of the Mystics" for an answer.[46] But as Loisy recognized, death intervened, and the answer remained unclear. Though perhaps not, as we shall see.

Furthermore

Along with Loisy's claim that Bremond was determined to live and die within the Catholic Church, we might also include a judgment made in 1967 by Henri Gouhier. In a discussion of a presentation by Émile Poulat on "Bremond and Modernism," in which Poulat discussed at length the nature of Loisy's *George Tyrrell et Henri Bremond*, Gouhier made the following summary statement: "It seems to me that Loisy's religion is essentially humanist and immanentist . . . on the contrary, it seems to me that all of the religious philosophy underlying Bremond's historical work is postulated on the relationship between the natural and the supernatural. I do not see how Loisy could make a rapprochement with that."[47] Gouhier had a good point, a reminder, actually, of

---

44. Loisy cites Bremond to Loisy, October 29, 1932, where Bremond expressed discomfort with Loisy's use of the phrase "one source," and even with the idea of a "source" as such (GT, 193–94). Bremond was groping after a more dynamic way of thinking about how mystical relationship is generative of moral perspective.

45. In Goichot's treatment, the Bremond-Loisy relationship, and the Sylvain Leblanc composition, are framed in terms of a dialectic between what Bremond learned from Tyrrell and what he learned from Loisy (EG, 296–305). The final result, however, is much as in my argument: in a letter to Miss Petre of September 10, 1909 (cited ibid., 297), explaining his submission after being disciplined regarding his behavior at Tyrrell's death, Bremond explained to her that "if I should abandon my Church . . . I would have no other home," and then there is Loisy's overriding claim that Bremond was determined to live and die in the Catholic Church. What I am adding is the theological influence of Blondel, and the philosophical influence of Bergson, that the concreteness of history requires specificity of commitments.

46. GT, 194, citing Bremond to Loisy, December 5, 1932.

47. Emile Poulat, "Bremond et le modernisme," comment by Gouhier in the "discussion" (EN, 92).

the enduring influence of Blondel on Bremond. Bremond himself would never have stated the matter in that fashion, since his language could be loose, but he would never have written a book entitled *La Religion*, as Loisy had done; the term would always have been plural, and he preferred to move to the more inward, more individualized, category of the *sentiment religieux*. Like Bergson, Bremond always made room for the eruptive operation of the supernatural in human history through gifted geniuses, in a way that Loisy could never do. At the same time, his difference from Bergson lay in his understanding of what it is, and how it is, that these geniuses make their gifted offering to humankind.

Furthermore, for all of the praise and approval that Bremond heaped on Loisy, it is unclear that he learned anything from him about the nature of mysticism.[48] Loisy's appropriation of the tradition of Durkheim, as well as that of Bergson, in which religion is a symbolic manifestation and reinforcement of social identity, is completely foreign to Bremond's inwardness, even in matters of community heritage, as in *Histoire*, IX and X. What Bremond was eager to affirm in Loisy was his commitment to historical methodology, as well as his personal integrity, but not a complete intellectual agreement. Loisy's 1936 tribute to Bremond was always a matter of "he agreed with me," but never "I agreed with him," thus revealing, I think, Loisy's one-way bias.

What really seemed to matter for Bremond in the relationship with Loisy was the *relationship*, the friendship and the loyalty that it required. As a result of that relationship, he saw some things that others missed or misunderstood. In similar fashion, as the discussion in *Histoire*, XI, of "quietude" in the mystical relationship would make clear, what one "knows" about God is known only in the mode of loving relationship—or in Bergson's language, only *dynamically*. Loisy complained that Bergson was over-privileging Christian language thus in describing mystical experience. Bergson was right, as Bremond knew, but he did not share Loisy's disgruntlement about that fact.

---

48. See Hill, "Henri Bergson and Alfred Loisy," 129–32. For further discussion, see also Trémolières, "Foi mystique et raison critique," and Marxer, "Entre religion et métaphysique," esp. 297–303.

20

Histoire, XI
"The Mystics on Trial," and Bremond Also

IN A FRIENDLY REVIEW of *Histoire*, IX, just after it appeared, the Jesuit Paul Doncoeur made a good point. Bremond has been accused, he said, of "offering proof of the agony of Catholicism," that "it has been reduced to being nothing more nor less than a *literary sentimentalism*." The accusation was contained in a recent essay from a biblical scholar and popular writer, Denis Saurat, who had argued that, in Bremond's view, the old idea of Catholicism as dogma was dead, poetry and the religious sentiment, the "feeling for the divine," having taken its place. But Doncoeur offered the rebuttal that one had only to read "the tableau of *Vie chrétienne sous l'Ancien Régime*" (that is, *Histoire*, IX) to find "a nobility that sufficiently witnesses to the truth of the doctrines."[1]

Bremond, calling himself in a letter to Blondel "the Catholic *du jour*," and very much in a stir, greatly appreciated Doncoeur's riposte to the "Huguenot" and "idiot" Saurat.[2] What is a bit puzzling, however, about Bremond's agitation is the fact that in all truth he himself had created the very impression that led to Saurat's kind of "idiotic" interpretation which actually was not so "idiotic." One could hardly blame a traditionalist Catholic at, say, an Académie meeting, for thinking that Bremond had done something much like what Saurat was claiming.

If one says that the truth of religion is best expressed in, and captured by, poetic form of some kind—because poetry verbalizes experience without converting it into notions and didacticism—then it is an easy step to saying that the truth of religion is *nothing but* the poetic form, a kind of aesthetic trance and a holy lyricism. And Bremond laid himself open to that charge. By arguing, as he had, that mystical experience resulting in poetry does not *know* anything more than we otherwise know, and does not necessarily end up *doing* anything more than we might otherwise do, then the

---

1. *Études*, February 20, 1932, 494–95, with reference to Denis Saurat, "Bremond et l'avenir du catholicisme," in *Les Nouvelle Revue français*, February 1932.
2. Bremond to Blondel, March 1932 (BB, III, 423–24, and notes).

claim that prayer is merely a sentimental solipsism, an empty subjectivity, for those who have a taste for that sort of thing, easily follows.

Blondel's task with Bremond, as I have often said, was to keep him from sliding down that slope, where Saurat located him, by showing that truth-claims and ethical demands are unavoidable, indeed are mandated by religious experience, because there must be a transcendent reality, an objective Something, in response to which the only outcome can be "pure love." Of course, Bremond might have said, religion *is* poetry, but then there is no such thing as *just* poetry. Poetry is not a mere leisure-time addendum to life; it registers the heart-beat of life, the *something*, the "soul," that makes life alive. He tried to make that case in *Histoire*, IX and X, but something more had to be said.

Before coming to that point, however, Bremond would receive one more incisive instruction from Blondel, who was by that time deep into the formulation of the first volume of *Pensées* and his analysis of the place of thought in sanctification. Creaturely interiority, Blondel contended, moves in the direction of unity, thus the "noetic intelligibility" of experience. This intelligibility is like a "respiratory rhythm between the particular and the universal in the cosmos," an ontological oscillation within the structure of being, including the subjective sense, or experience, or "sentiment," of being. But there is, as well, a perpetually, intrinsically, unsatisfied quality about the relationship between unity and noetic intelligibility, so that the dynamism of nature, including spiritual attunement and mystical aspiration, is always a progressive unfolding. What is more, mystical vision cannot be a narcissistic "auto-mirror," in which the mystic makes contact only with himself, since "seeing" and "knowing" will always be pushing away from the self toward the other, that is, in the direction of Being itself, where there is a Lover and a Beloved, the latter remaining beyond the full embrace of the former. I cannot "know" without "loving," and I cannot love without "knowing," but the process is always open-ended, since the Object is "veiled." This is John of the Cross as well as Aquinas, thought Blondel.[3]

For Blondel, any discourse about creaturely interiority moving in the direction of unity will be necessarily provisional, only a way-station on the road to ever new discourse, as fresh experience, itself in part the product of existing expression, calls for new verbalization. "Intelligibility" has to be a moving, fluid project always engaged in self-revision as it stimulates new thought in an endless supersession. Let us note also at this point that when Blondel talked about "creaturely interiority," he was operating in a mode foreign to both Loisy and Bergson, who, despite their differences, convert

---

3. Blondel to Bremond, March 27, 1932 (BB, III, the "Note," 423–28). Pius XI had conferred the title of "Doctor of the Church" on John in 1926. The "sanjuanist" appeal at this time was immense, as one sees in Jean Baruzi's work, especially the already mentioned 1924 study, *Saint Jean de la Croix et le problème de l'expérience mystique*, or in the skeptical philosophy of George Santayana, who considered himself an "aesthetic Catholic" and expressed admiration for John in a number of works during the 1920s and '30s. See Rosa, "Saint Jean de la Croix," for an analysis of the era's philosophical debates about how to understand John.

mystical experience into a socially-driven, socially shaped dynamic. Not so Blondel, or, I think, Bremond, for whom the interior world of mentation, of consciousness, is a furnace where experience is constantly molded into thought, operating by its own inherent dialectics. Where Bremond went *beyond* Blondel, as well as Bergson and Loisy, was in the insistence that the subjectively-shaped experience of God registers, or crystallizes, in the poetry of sacred texts.

Camus and Pure Love

As he approached, then, the end of the seventeenth century and the sunset of mysticism, Bremond looked about for a theological *littérateur* who represented every aspect of the situation. He/she would need to be a competent theologian with orthodox credentials, a spiritual mind solidly in the tradition of the French School, and a creative writer with the imagination and expressive powers of a poet. In other words, this person would be a genuine mystic who could bridge the gap from Francis de Sales and Bérulle/Condren/Olier, on the one hand, to Jean-Pierre de Caussade on the other, while incorporating some of the aesthetic excellence and perspicuity of the Fénelon-Bossuet debates along the way. The goal, briefly stated, would be to show that the mysticism embedded in Catholic prayer produces a doctrinally-notionally sound theology of grace, where the disinterestedness of pure love, the trans-rational nature of pure poetry and the non-hedonic goals of pure prayer begin to operate with a single heartbeat.

And Bremond (of course!) found, actually refound, his individual: he is Jean-Pierre Camus de Pontcarré (1584–1652), bishop of Belley, follower and popularizer of Francis de Sales, master of debate, a prelate and artist. Already important in *Histoire*, I, as well as in VII, as expounder of Francis de Sales's spirituality (though not reliable as a biographer!), he is, in *Histoire*, XI, the central character in his own right. While Caussade represented the transmission of the pure-love ethos, in the forms of spiritual direction and pastoral care, to the modern age, Camus represented its transmission as a *literary* legacy, in which fiction and poetry became, and will become even more, the tools of deep theological assertion, despite the fact that the name of Camus, champion of that legacy, is largely forgotten.[4]

With Camus becoming Bremond's last stand, his last major portrait and analysis of a pivotal figure, it is helpful to recall how Bremond had used him earlier. In the first volume he is a follower of Francis de Sales, operating with a "system of his own," "a kind of Platonism that is at once Salesian and Fénelonian," and yet he was "more convinced than the author of the *Maxims of the Saints*, more strictly faithful to the *Summa* of S. Thomas and to the *Traité de l'Amour de Dieu*."[5] He is the great defender

---

4. Except for *The Spirit of St. Francis de Sales*, originally 1641, and many times reprinted and translated (though Bremond disapproved of it as "hagiography").

5. *Histoire*, I, 119, 143. While I have only occasionally referred to the plate illustrations in the

of "pure love," but particularly in the mode of an engaging literary éclat that came out in the musical quality of his prose and his ability to evoke with humor and a childlike lyricism the joy of Christian experience.

Featured prominently again in the first of the two volumes of the "Metaphysic of the Saints," Camus is the great exponent of the Salesian "pan-mysticism," that is, the idea that all prayer, not just the high prayer of spiritual athletes, insofar as it is oriented toward God and is infused by grace, is mystical in nature. Such prayer is "easily" available to every person, in fact comes naturally, when the temptation of a "hyperactivism" is laid aside in order to rest quietly in the divine embrace. Camus represents the anti-asceticist drift of French School spirituality when it is formulated in terms of a healthy balance between the extremes of doing too little and doing too much in one's relationship with God.[6] Bremond noted, with approval, that Camus leaned toward Aquinas in his reworking of Francis de Sales, and that he had a remarkable ability to dialogue with the Jesuits and other groups. He was a practical pastor, but also a synthetic thinker—just what Bremond needed.

When Bremond turned to Camus again, in the chapter of *Histoire*, XI, entitled "The First Assaults on Pure Love," the focus was different. He wanted to portray the Bishop of Belley as a controversialist, active in the midst of the Quietist debates, engaged with the issues. The specific focus was Camus's interaction with a Jesuit author, Antoine Sirmond (1592–1643), whose book, *La défense de la vertu* (1641) was a polemical response to Camus's own treatise, *La défense du pur amour contra les attaques de l'amour-propre* (1640). Bremond saw in the Camus-Sirmond debate a "pre-quarrel" of the issues that would be at the center of Bossuet-Fénelon, where Camus, rather like Pascal, became clear that disinterested love is "only a vision," yet one that has won the battle historically. It is as if, for all of its wrongheadedness, even Port-Royal in its resistance to the Jesuits saw something, something theocentric, that the asceticist readers of Ignatius failed to discern. In a radical statement here, Bremond even contended that there is a "functional unanimity" at this point between Pascal and Fénelon![7]

Histoire, often contemporary representations of the individual being discussed in the text, these evocative pictures constitute an amusing, clever aspect of Bremond's production, carefully analyzed recently by Fabre, "L'iconographie de l'*Histoire littéraire du sentiment religieux*." The picture of Camus gives the sense of a man with a sparkling, but dry, wit, Montaigne-like in appearance (*Histoire*, XI, 221).

6. Ibid, VII, 156–57. In a letter to Baudin of May 1927 (cited BB, III, 275n6), Bremond had indicated that Camus does away with all of the "phantasmagoria of pseudo-mysticism" in Plotinus, so as to clarify the *panmysticist* position that mystical prayer is the life of all of the baptized. A little later to Blondel, October 1927, he indicated that he was presenting "an anti-passive Camus who Blondelizes with a joyful heart" (ibid., 284).

7. *Histoire*, XI, 185. The connection here is that in the tenth of the *Provinciales* Pascal is sharply critical of the Jesuit Sirmond. Thus, indirectly, Camus and Pascal end up on the same side of the argument in Bremond's construal, since Camus contends against him as well. The Camus-material first appeared as "La Querelle de pur amour au temps de Louis XIII," in *Cahier* 22 of *La Nouvelle Journée* (1932), then in *Histoire*, X, part I, broken down into a series of chapters concluding with "Les premiers assauts contre le pur amour."

The contest between Camus and Sirmond was one of discerning the meaning of the "renunciation of self" that is central to Jesus' call to his disciples—truly a classic debate on a never-ending theme. Bremond sets up the two disputants as arch-representatives of the two opposed traditions, of theocentrism and prayer on the one hand, and anthropocentrism and asceticism on the other. Even though Sirmond himself is a rather minor figure historically, the extent of his writing, the clarity of his position, and the fact that he and his views were known to Pascal and Boileau, made him a useful stand-in for the ascetical position. Bremond is emphatic at this point that what is at stake is *not* a theology of grace differing from that of Pascal, as some commentators argue, but rather the question of a *religious moralism*.[8] This is why the asceticist position, rather than being a positive doctrine or articulated stance, usually takes the form of a tendency or spirit often expressed negatively as criticism of, or satire on, the theocentrist point of view. In a metaphor that Bremond admitted is "a ridiculous comparison" (but a helpful one), he compares asceticist writers to those members of the government bureaucracy under the *ancien régime*, who were always cutting away at the monarch's power with no intention of dethroning him. They operate with the spirit of a disloyal opposition, always on the watch for opportunities to undermine the rightful structures.[9] Differently stated, asceticists *know* what the Gospel is, but for various reasons have no intention of abiding by it!

For some years before Sirmond came on the scene, Camus had been defending against an anonymous Jesuit the whole idea of "servitude" as the Salesian tradition understood it, appealing especially to Bérulle's version of Gagliardi's *Breve Compendio*, namely the *L'Abrégé de la perfection*, and using the whole mystical lexicon of adhesion to God, disappropriation, conformity to the will of God, resignation, indifference, etc. All of this language amounts, says Camus, to what is meant by disinterested love, the "pure love" of the Gospel. When Camus thus published his treatise in defense of "pure love," it is he who first makes the explicit equivalence: theocentrism = pure love.[10] It is also Camus who creates a conjunction of the teaching of Francis from the *Traité* with Bérulle's teaching in the *Abrégé*, so that Salesianism and Bérullism begin to move along the same track, the two spiritual masters expounding and clarifying one another. The theme that he works repeatedly is the contrast of the "culte de Dieu" and the "culte du moi," the latter often taking the form of an earthbound sensualism, but more subtly and in more devastating fashion, an asceticism which is a veiled form of self-love. We have here, says Bremond, the Salesian-Bérullian tradition at its best, which is simply the "evangelical philosophy of prayer."[11] The supreme irony is that it is Gagliardi the mystical Jesuit, who stands behind Bérulle, informing the very synthesis against which the Jesuit Sirmond rails.

---

8. A term that Bremond claimed to have taken from Paul Doncoeur (*Histoire*, XI, 188n1).
9. Ibid., 190.
10. Ibid, 192.
11. Ibid., 200.

And then, shortly after Camus published his 1640 treatise and before Sirmond could reply, came a discovery by the bishop of Belley: the lady Caritée, a somewhat legendary figure from *Le Livre des saintes paroles et des bonnes actions de St. Louis* by the medieval historian Jean de Joinville (c. 1224–1319). She is a lady, says Bremond, that Camus will never leave, a character from the annals of chivalry, depicted "in the fashion of an amazon from Corneille," with uncovered breasts (she is actually an "old woman" in Joinville) as she carries in one hand a torch of passionate desire for God, while with the other hand she pours water on the fires of hell.[12] Camus quickly produced in 1641 a novelistic paraphrasing and theological exposition of her legend, in which she becomes a stand-in for Francis de Sales, teaching his doctrine in every point and doing so with consummate charm.

Sirmond in his response to Caritée will laugh at Camus's credulity and playing up of this pious legend, and will appeal to the view that she is a dangerous "illuminée" kind of female. But Camus shook off the criticisms, finding in her a most useful way of making "pure love" a creature of flesh and blood. The tradition was that she was an actual woman, convicted by church authority for preaching against the ideas of heaven and hell, pleading instead for a love of God which would not be based on fear or on the hope of recompense. Saint-Cyran, champion of Port-Royal, made use of the tradition, Fénelon knew her, and Jacques Le Brun tells us that there is an equivalent character in Sufi mysticism![13]

In his Salesian-inspired defense of Caritée as a valid personification, Camus made an important distinction between "self-love" and "love of ourselves," since confusion on this matter breeds, he said, a multitude of errors. In "self-love" one willfully, and either explicitly or implicitly, renounces the final end for which love has been created, settling for a proximate end. On the other hand, the "love of self," which a pagan may well have, is a good thing, because natural and human, and it will eventually lead us to God, so long as we do not engage in renunciation of that ultimate goal, at which point it becomes "self-love."[14] When we use the term "interests," opined Camus, we ought to think not in terms of "our interests," but "our proper interests," since this latter captures the idea that often what we think of as being in our best interest is truly shortsighted when love of God is left out of the equation.[15] And, we might add, it is clearly a way to avoid the idea that "pure love" is ultimately irrational, because, says Camus, it is truly reason at its best. One cannot help noticing here how close Camus comes to Pascal, where the love of God constitutes the smarter wager, the best bet;

---

12. Ibid., 201–4, with a reproduction of a frontispiece done for the publication of Camus's *La Caritée ou le pourtraict de la vraie charité* (*Histoire*, XI, 203).

13. *Le pur amour*, 107–15, for a recounting of the whole tradition. Apparently it is Camus who actually gave her (anonymous in Joinville) the name of "Charitée."

14. *Histoire*, XI, 209.

15. Ibid., 210.

yet, at the same time Camus is *not* advocating Pascal's abandonment of "reason" as a corrupt guide for choosing "pure love." His position is more nuanced.

Furthermore, it is by means of Caritée that Camus restates Francis's "impossible supposition," in which, as an expression of "pure love," one is "indifferent" (Ignatius's term, says Camus) to one's ultimate salvation except insofar as God is pleased either to grant or withhold it. To follow God on any other terms is to do so "only coldly and imperfectly," and Camus is astounded that his Jesuit opponents would think otherwise. Even Bossuet, in his best moments, says Bremond, came close to this "Camusizing" ideal, "drowning hope itself in pure love."[16]

Does "pure love" cancel out all other loves, showing them as worthless? By no means, says Camus in a balancing statement, since "To know that the sun has the greater light is not to despise the stars or moon."[17] We should recall at this point, even though Bremond does not highlight it, that Camus was a prodigious writer of popular religious fiction, in which characters male and female display aspects of disinterested love for God.[18] In this way, Camus lets Thomas Aquinas in by the back door, making the pure love of God the apex of a hierarchical pyramid of degrees of loving, while insisting that it remains a working ideal for believers in the present, not just a perfection proper only to the state of final beatitude.

And this is where the debate with Sirmond engaged. In a complex interaction with other players, Camus had been imprisoned briefly by Richelieu, because Jesuit critics associated him with Port-Royal, and it is thus from jail that he made his defense against Sirmond's critique. The latter had argued, in accordance with Aquinas, that one is obliged to love God only within the bounds of reason, that is, "moderately." Nothing is required beyond obedience to the commandments. Pascal's criticism, then, was that this view is a permission to sin as long as certain basic boundaries are observed. Bossuet and Suarez argued in turn that the commandment to love God is a higher calling, obligatory only at the "right moment," that is, in response to a special call, which must be determined by a casuistry.

Sirmond, however, had wisely noted that the first commandment is *always* obligatory, but he made a distinction: one is commanded to love "effectively," but not always "affectively."[19] Francis de Sales had already noted that affective loving cannot

---

16. Ibid., 215. Though we are not yet at Fénelon's radical position, said Bremond (ibid., 213).

17. Ibid., 217. Camus was responding to the charge that all of his discourse had an "excessive" quality to it, as if one could love God too much. He is sensitive to the view that there is something fanatical about the idea of "pure love," something *unreasonable* about it.

18. Over 1,000 such works according to *Wikipedia*, s.v. "Jean-Pierre Camus"!

19. *Histoire*, XI, 237–38. What one sees is the Jesuit emphasis on "attrition" in penance, and not "contrition" as Port-Royal insisted. Bremond provided a long excursus on this subject, discussing the ongoing post-Tridentine debate about how much love, and what kind of love, must be present even in attrition for it to be valid as a preparation for absolution (ibid., 293–326). In Bremond's colorful exposition Sirmond had decided that the best way to "exterminate" the absurd Charitée was with the first commandment (ibid., 273).

be commanded by its very nature, but Sirmond, thought Camus, wants to free us from "right intention" altogether, i.e., from the need for an inward disposition toward love, so that we may do deeds of love for the simple reason that they are commanded. Camus claimed, then, that Sirmond maintains the name of love, but ends up with a naked obedience—which is to say in Bremond's terms, an asceticism. Contrariwise, asserted Camus, the victory of pure love is the victory of true virtue, rather than mere compliance, because it grounds virtue in pure *interior* love for God and nothing else.[20]

And so, the question arose with Camus as to whether he was after all a Jansenist, as some thought, since Sirmond and his followers attacked both him and them. In fact, insisted Bremond, they shared in a common tradition of reflection on the nature of loving God, the difference being that the Jansenists made pure love something heroic and superhuman, enabled by grace only for the elect, while for Camus and the quietist tradition pure love is subdued and often mundane, more everyday, and for everyman. Ironically Sirmond thinks of pure love as something impossible and as reserved for very few—as the Jansenists also believe—although for him this means that ordinary believers can dispense with it. All of the same arguments will later be used against Fénelon, and they will become the stock-in-trade of the suppression of quietism-mysticism by the end of the century as an "illuminé" spirituality, thus a characteristic of "enthusiasm" in the eighteenth century.[21]

Another irony with regard to Camus, noted Bremond in conclusion, was that his thought along with the figure of Charitée was picked up by Bossuet, but in a half-hearted and inconsistent way, where the duel with Fénelon would finally bring everything to a head.[22] Indeed, Camus will live on anonymously, so to speak, through absorption by larger and more prominent minds, but, so will Sirmond, argued Bremond, in the form of what he calls "Sirmondism." This is the issue of the First Commandment, and the question of whether God would command anything that is inherently beyond the possibility of flawed humankind. Would God do such a thing, and then provide us with lesser, more feasible commandments as, so to speak, a plan B?[23]

---

20. Ibid., 250.

21. The attentive reader will remember that one of the ideas beloved by George Tyrrell, in his more standard Jesuit days, was that Catholicism in England recognized the right of ordinary believers to be mediocre, so to speak, while making room for those with a higher calling—as opposed to Protestantism with its insistence that everyone has to step up to a rigorous standard. It is striking that by late in his career Bremond had moved sharply away from this position of Tyrrell, who had renounced his Thomism, while Bremond, at his later stage, is moving toward it.

22. Ibid., 281–82.

23. In an excursus, Bremond surveyed the opinions of a number of spiritual writers, including Duguet and Grou, on this question, down to the end of the *ancien régime* (ibid., 284–89). In pastoral practice, it would transmute into the attrition/contrition debates as preparation for sacramental confession. In ethics it reappears in the debate over whether agape-love can be commanded and thus formulated as a rule.

The Problem of Histoire, XI

Bremond would not live to see *Histoire*, XI, into print, and we will never know for sure what it might have looked like if he had lived a bit longer. Published in 1933, not long after his death, it was assembled at Bloud et Gay from a series of essays already composed and indicative of the direction in which the author was moving, but not yet synthesized into the finished work that he intended. André and Jean, faithful brothers, wrote later that a more complete version might eventually be published from scattered notes and fragments in an "advanced" but "utilizable with difficulty" condition, though in fact that has never happened.[24] And apparently never will happen. Goichot has examined some unpublished fragments, in which Bremond mulled over his objectives for volume XI—or even XI and XII—and has argued, given the rudimentary nature of the Guyon-Fénelon-Bossuet material, as well as Bremond's uncertainty about how much history he wanted to cover as well as the points he wanted to make about the philosophy of prayer, that a "reconstitution" of the volume-that-might-have-been is impossible.[25] It seems that Bremond mused over the possibility of writing an autobiography, so that some of these fragments are psychologically interesting as well.

As we now have it, *Histoire*, XI, "The Trial of the Mystics," is divided into two main sections, each of which is organized around a fundamental accusation brought to bear in the condemnation of mysticism. In "Anticipations and Preludes," Bremond dealt with the charge of "illuminism," that is, the idea that mystics experience private revelations from God, on the basis of which they slip by degrees into a quietism which is individualist, rebellious against all authority including that of reason, adogmatic, and inclined to the erosion of moral and disciplinary standards in the spiritual life. It is the charge that all talk of "pure love" is a coded language for sexual license. After a survey of illuminist accusations against the mystics from the time of the Spanish *Alumbrados* up to the end of the reign of Louis XIII, one can see why it was so important for Bremond to show with Camus that mystical prayer in fact results in high standards of behavior, and that charges to the contrary became early on a stereotyped calumny (mostly) devoid of truth.[26] The years of the reign of Louis XIII (1610–1643), with the developments therein, constituted the "pre-quarrel" over mysticism/quietism, anticipating, and forming a prelude to, the Quarrel itself, namely, the Bossuet-Fénelon struggle, with Madame Guyon in the background.[27]

---

24. André and Jean Bremond, preface to the collection *Autour d'humanisme*, 25.

25. Basing himself on still unpublished fragmentary material, Goichot speculated on different possible directions in which Bremond might have been going in the shaping of *Histoire*, XI, and its successors (EG, 275–85).

26. Amusingly, Bremond says that the great challenge with mystical experience is always to show that it is not "a vaguely celestial experience with hashish, nor love in the form of fleshly, rather than spiritual, desires" (*Histoire*, XI, 3).

27. *Histoire*, XI, 185.

The second major section, Bremond's last writing, consists of a series of explorations of the theme of "quietude," recalling the charge that mystical prayer, especially the so-called "prayer of quietude" or of "simple regard," is lazy, excessively passive, even a first step toward deism, skepticism and unbelief. In effect, the charge was that this quietude leads to Loisyism, or a generalized spirituality of "humanity." Convinced, however, that God truly "acts" in quietude, since there are clear "traces of God" when we enter that state, Bremond's challenge was to show that the experience of such "traces" is not an "illuminism," since the loss of self by definition cannot be the arrogant self-delusion presupposed in the accusations of the anti-mystics. The loss of self in quietude, Bremond argues, is precisely the "night of discourse," since love is not essentially discursive. However great the torrent of words about love may be, the thing itself is beyond the power of words in two ways—objectively as a reality reflective of God's ineffable presence, and subjectively as an experience that defies linguistic expression of any kind.[28]

Let us, then, look more closely at the contents of this final production in order to pick out clues as to where Bremond was headed as his work was ending and his legacy beginning.

Illuminism

We recall Joseph de Guibert's statement, which I cited in the first chapter, that Fénelon was always Bremond's "true teacher." That point is well illustrated in the first chapter of volume XI, on "Isabelle Bellinzaga, Achille Gagliardi and the Map of Love." Here Bremond tells the story, already briefly described above in the context of his relationship with Don Giuseppe De Luca, of the sixteenth-century relationship between Gagliardi, a superior of the Jesuit house in Milan, and Isabelle Bellinzaga, a wealthy laywoman known for her sanctity and respected efforts at church reform. Gagliardi having been her spiritual director, and yet having learned as much from her as she from him, Bremond made a steady comparison with Fénelon and Guyon. Gagliardi produced a manual which is both an exposition of the contemplative, mystical nature of true prayer, as well as a guide to the proper interpretation of Ignatius's *Exercises*.

Contrary to some scholarship with which he took issue, Bremond saw the manual's content as a product of Bellinzaga's mind as well as Gagliardi's, so that, as with Guyon and Fénelon, its spirituality is truly a collaboration. Gagliardi's superiors in the Company, suspicious of the influence of Bellinzaga over the Milan Jesuits, attempted restraints, but cardinal Bellarmine, despite rumors of conspiracy in church reform, defended them to Clement VIII. Eventually Bellinzaga's influence, after her death in

---

28. On what follows, see Trémolières, "Approche de l'indicible dans le courant mystique." I am intentionally fudging Trémolières's distinction of the ineffability of the divine and the unspeakability of the mystic's experience of the divine.

1624, would live on among missionary orders in the Far East,[29] while Gagliardi's *Breve Compendio*, held in suspicion by current Jesuit doctrine, would circulate under the supposed authorship of a "dame Milanaise." In this latter form, it will be discovered by several French teachers, including the young Pierre de Bérulle, who will publish his own adaptation.

Bremond contends that in the *Compendio* Gagliardi cleaned up and organized Bellinzaga's spiritual wisdom, as Fénelon did with Guyon, so that it would be doctrinally sound, carefully avoiding any advocacy of "visions" or "illuminations" as true mysticism. The very fact that the Jesuit, Étienne Binet, having no reservations about its contents, translated the *Compendio* into French shows that there is no quietism in this work, only a sound spirituality of prayer. What the work does teach is three degrees of self-abnegation in spiritual growth: "the poverty by which we are denuded of things indifferent in themselves . . . then of things very useful to the life of the spirit . . . then of things the most necessary for the establishment and the conservation of the life of the spirit." If such teaching is quietist, says Bremond, "then all of France in the time of Henri IV and Louis XIII was equally so."[30] This is Ignatius rightly understood, and proof that charges of "Guyonism" and "illuminism" were usually otiose.

Bremond then went on to trace the French roots of the supposed entanglement of illuminism and quietism with the *Alumbrados* phenomenon, beginning in early sixteenth-century Spain and coming to a head with a condemnatory Edict in Seville in 1623. "Congregated" groups of these "Enlightened ones," called "the Blessed and Perfect," fully contemplating the Godhead in this life, had migrated to Flanders, then to the Picardy region of France in the latter 1500s. Despite the charges against them, including persecution by the Inquisition, Bremond saw these people basically as reformers in the spirit of Erasmus. They were charged with teaching the sufficiency of mental prayer, with engaging in a spiritual elitism, with exalting the role of women in leadership, with discouraging the premature seclusion of women in convents, with emphasizing inward devotion over against the buying of sacraments. No "morbid asceticism" here, said Bremond![31] But the core criticism in the Edict was the charge that immorality arises from quietist theory, especially when it is taught that in certain elevated states one is freed from normal moral constraints for the reason that one *cannot* sin. This contention will shape the whole subsequent history, said Bremond, so that the concepts of "abandon" or the "prayer of simple regard" are poisoned.[32]

29. See, e.g., the interesting work of Tran Thi Tuyet Mai, *La mission*, in which the author notes the work of De Luca and Bremond on Bellinzaga and Gagliardi, highlighting Bellinzaga's primary role in producing the *Compendio*.

30. *Histoire*, XI, 54. An echo of his earlier statement (*Apologie pour Fénelon*, 436) that "if Fénelon is a quietist, half of the church was with him."

31. Ibid., 66. In fact, Bremond was impressed by the high esteem in which marriage is held by the members of these condemned conventicles as a kind of protest against forced convent life for women.

32. Ibid., 70. Bremond refers to the criticisms aimed at this caricatured quietism as an "abstract notion . . . dressed up as a stinking mannequin."

In the following short chapter, he then discussed the "first panics" of 1632 in France, in which the influence of a Capuchin friar, Archange Ripault, and his published attacks on the Illuminist heresy are central. Ripault classified these heretics into several different groups, and his descriptions are colorful and amusing. The "illuminés" are pretentious and hypocritical in ways that anticipate Molière's Tartuffe, they practice absurd forms of heavenly perfectionism that include "nudity," they have absorbed suspicious mystical thought such as that of Tauler and other esoteric mystics. Bremond shows that Ripault's descriptions are mostly borrowings from the Edict of Seville, since the language of condemnation is becoming repetitious and predictable, as well as absurd.

But then Bremond focused particularly on the "illuminés" of Picardy, and again he illustrated his conviction that women play a special role in the unfolding of the spirituality of pure love. He tells the story of a parish priest, Pierre Guérin, at Montdidier, who became the center of a reform movement and the establishment of a new religious Order, the Filles de Croix, along with special schools. Suspicions of quietist practice and teaching, coupled with charges of private revelations and sorcery and immorality, were aimed at Guérin and the sisterhood by critics. Upon examination, however, it was found that the teaching is sound and sensible, advocating moderate penitential practices and contemplative forms of prayer. Nevertheless, there were efforts at suppression, with some individuals being imprisoned, including a convent superior, Mother Madeleine de Flers of the Augustinian Hotel-Dieu in Montdidier, a good spiritual teacher who was abused and misunderstood for her wisdom and teaching about prayer and the inner life. Bremond tells her story in detail as a portrayal of the kind of evil treatment that practitioners of mystical/quietist prayer would be subjected to as the century progressed.

The tale of de Flers involved the famous Cistercian convent (suppressed at the Revolution) of Maubuisson, just outside of Paris, an institution very much in need of reform in the early years of the seventeenth century. It seems that a rocky history of efforts at disciplining the rather spoiled community of aristocratic nuns by well-intended, but ineffective, Mother-superiors, as well as by male Cistercian authority from afar, had had the result of splitting the community into pro- and anti-reform groups. Bremond recounts all of this amusing record with considerable panache, basing himself on a primary and heavily biased history by a Port-Royal nun, Madeleine de Saint-Candide Le Cerf. Attempts at austerities encouraged by Port-Royal figures failed, male spiritual directors were mocked by the laughing nuns, and finally Madeleine de Flers was brought in. She introduced mystical/quietist spiritual practices with the emphasis on self-annihilation, inner and contemplative prayer, the relaxation of overly strict regulations, and the importance of practicing "naked faith" in the face of temptations. There appears to have been some encouragement by de Flers of what her critics called "demonic" states, which, apparently, were periods of permitted regressive behavior marked by the removal of emotional constraints in order to facilitate learning and spiritual growth. Naturally, these risky, but well-meant, moves got de Flers into trouble (as they easily did not only in that day but in our own as well).

In the hostile history of all of this by Candide, de Flers was presented as a crazy "illuminé," teaching practices that lead to disobedience and moral chaos, although Bremond found the account more revelatory of Candide's irrational fears than of misbehavior by de Flers, who had sincerely tried to win Candide over. The whole thing in the end boils down to another revelation of the usual lambasting, in this case by Jansenists, of mystical prayer and quietist practice as leading to moral breakdown and degeneracy. The irony is that when an official investigation took place, de Flers was completely exonerated, and Bremond cleared her as well, since her writings reveal nothing more than a wise and mature teacher trying to reach out to a fractured and embittered community. The whole experience is a fascinating exposé of sexual politics in the religious orders of the *ancien régime*.[33]

In the next two chapters, one on the "New Panic: the Deviltries of Louviers" and one on "The Jesuits and the Diffusion of Quietism in the Time of Louis XIII," Bremond continued to trace out the same sad story of spiritual outbreaks of a mystical/quietist nature and the ensuing "panics" on the part of authorities. The Louviers disruptions, worse than Loudun in 1635, involved two priests accused of being Satanic agents, and "five hysterics" or possessed nuns, all of them charged with reading mystical writers and all charged unjustly with "abominations."

Among Jesuit writers during the time of Louis XIII, a number exemplified the tendency to look down on contemplative practice as sterile and self-centered, as leaning in the direction of quietism and illuminism, and as elitist in spirit. Yielding to "private revelations" is always the greatest danger. All in all, general hysteria, absurd exaggeration, and the ridiculous inflation associated with unjust calumny are the order of the day. On this note Bremond launched into his analysis of the work of Camus in combating the anti-mysticism and the "assault on pure love" of the Jesuit Sirmond to finish the section.

Quietude

As mentioned, we cannot know if Bremond actually intended for his treatment of "quietude" in the last part of *Histoire*, XI, to stand in a concluding position.[34] But the

33. Sluhovsky, *Believe Not Every Spirit*, ch. 5, treats the account of Madeleine de Flers, as well as the possessions at Loudun, as well as the next chapter of *Histoire*, XI, on the "deviltries" of Louviers, in great detail, with a primary focus on an understanding of demonic possession. So far as quietist/mysticism goes, he suggests that the language of "nudity" and "bareness," along with the "let-be" quality of the quietist approach to temptations, invited misunderstanding and attack. In a fragmentary note discussed by Goichot, Bremond also allowed that some of the quietist-mystics were their own worst enemies in the way that they intellectualized about their experiences, using misleading or incautious language (EG, 284).

34. Goichot raises the question of whether this last section on quietude is the doctrinal section that

assumption would be reasonable. If we recall how many times he had either said or intimated that all discourse that expresses the inner life, such as poetry, must finally yield to silence, then quiet must be the psychological, internal state corresponding to the outward fact. Motor activation (including either external or internal speech) ceases so that a rest freed from agitation can ensue. But it is not the inert rest of sleep or death, but rather of the loss of surface consciousness so that something else, from the "depth," can occupy the voided space. That depth can be described phenomenally in countless ways as dream-process, or spontaneous imagining, or detached reverie, or free-floating association, etc., but the common factor is that of release from the pressure of contingent demands or "ordinary" distractions in order to experience what "comes" or "breathes" (inspiration!) inwardly, an internal listening or attentiveness. In the classical language of the life of prayer, of "commerce with God," utilized by Bremond, this inward experiencing of what "comes" when discourse if suspended is mystical or contemplative in nature because it is marked by a "passive" acceptance or receptivity understood as a gift of God's grace.

But then an ambiguity emerges. Is the *posture* of receptivity, that is, the "quietude" itself, the gift of grace, or is it the "something" that comes when we are quiet, that constitutes the gift? The answer is unclear. We recall the Thomist criticism of Bremond here, that prayer by itself is not the same as faith, hope or love, that active charity, if all goes well, must be a grace-enabled *consequence* of prayer, because if we simply identify the quietude of prayer with grace, then we run the risk that prayer becomes a mere soother, a therapy for over-anxious modern people starved for relief. Or, in other ways, the quietude of prayer becomes an adjunct to some other end, such as removing the would-be poet's "writer's block," or improving the quality of your sleep at night, etc. And then what happens is that prayer, because of instrumentalizing, becomes a means to an end, and that is precisely what Bremond wanted to avoid with his critique of "asceticism."

What Bremond was faced with was the fact that almost all modern people, not nurtured untraumatically in a religious worldview from infancy, thus thoroughly secularized, come to religion with therapeutic goals in mind. This means that some state of anxiety is always the entry-point, and the value of religion is measured by its capacity to calm anxiety, or to address the thing/situation prompting the anxiety. Thus it is that the goal of inner quiet—whether we call it confidence or assurance or hope

---

Bremond truly intended, and then argues the thesis that the real heart of the section and its originally intended focus is the "equivocal" nature of "intellectual contemplation" in mystical experience (EG, 285). It is this equivocity that provides the basis for the panmysticist claim that all religious experience operates on a universal foundation, thus reflecting Bremond's "philosophy of prayer" as it is articulated at the notional level into the distinctly different faith traditions. That being said, however, Goichot cites an unedited text in which Bremond claimed that "the history, theology and morality of Christianity guides the interpretation of mystical experience [in such a way] that after a fashion it canalizes this experience so as to maximize its fruits, while neutralizing ('paralysant') its deviations" (ibid., 288).

or peace—is a worthy one, a necessary one, a valuable one. The problem, as all pastors know, is the question of how long individuals can stay, or return to, that inner state of calm, without the calm becoming a spiritual narcotic or end in itself, especially if it is relaxation *from* rather than relaxation *for*. The fear is always raised that "quietude" may be nothing more than escape, and thus an evoking of the seventeenth-century critique of quietist practice as morally irresponsible.

A particular practical focus for the ambiguity of quietude is the so-called "prayer of simple regard," often taught in the seventeenth century as an antidote to compulsive or anxious verbalization in prayer. One modern website describes it as prayer marked by a "momentary glance" in which I "notice God looking at me," followed by a very brief and spontaneous response, such as "Lord, bless my work!" Based on the idea of a moment-by-moment consciousness of the presence of God in the actual circumstances of daily life, it frees the one who prays from dependence on sacred setting and other artificial prompts, as well as from formality of discourse.[35] Bremond noted that the mystical Jesuits in the Lallemant tradition were very fond of the prayer of simple regard, and that Fénelon's espousal stood at the apex, with the anti-mystics in strong opposition.[36]

Bremond argued that for the classical mystics, the distinguishing mark of such simple prayer is the ceasing of discourse of any kind, including reflecting, reasoning, making resolutions, active meditation, etc.[37] He thus claimed to be in continuity with the Dionysian tradition of pseudo-Dionysius himself, Tauler, Nicolas of Cusa, and John of the Cross. He insisted, though, that the exclusion of active meditation originated in a popularization or vulgarization of the tradition, yet one that made it successful early on precisely because it reduced fatigue. He also noted that the charge that such prayer opens the floodgates to illuminism is wrong-headed, since discourse is transcended.[38] This is also why Bremond is so tirelessly insistent that the mystical prayer does not reveal anything, contains no distinctive *knowledge*, though we have noted how often Blondel balked at this claim and tried to get Bremond to state it with more nuance.

Typically, the Counter-Reformation writers made the claim that such simple prayer requires a "ligature," a "binding of powers," so that the one who prays is held in a kind of catalepsis or paralysis (Bremond suggested an "inhibition") of external

---

35. Mary Margaret Funk, http://www.spiritualityandpractice.com/practices/practices/view/21440/the-practice-of-simple-regard.

36. *Histoire*, XI, 330.

37. Ibid., 336–37, but Bremond made the helpful point as well that it is the modern context and its needs that allowed for a deepening of interior prayer. Differently stated, the modern situation of compulsive technologizing generates a reaction in the realm of subjectivity.

38. Ibid., 330–34. At one point, Bremond commented that "the present chapter is exclusively didactic," but that in a coming volume he will expound the "masters" on this subject (ibid., 333). In fact, the sections that immediately follow are fragmentary efforts to do just that, to expound the "masters," which suggests that this material consists of fragments of a larger, more comprehensive effort that would indeed have required a subsequent volume, had Bremond lived to compose it in its entirety.

motility and sensory awareness. Cognitively an even better term is "trance-state," which, as we know, can involve a complete loss of response to environmental stimuli of any kind, if the individual is highly suggestible and the trance is competently induced. Bremond argued that this movement toward what he called a "chronic impotence" or state of invited helplessness in some souls was an effort to get free of the obsession with the topsy-turvy, voluntaristic, hyper-conscientious passion for explicit methods, leading to "an introspective vigilance at every moment" in daily life.[39]

The paradox was that this kind of inhibition of powers, with perhaps a post-hypnotic restraint on certain behaviors, also released energy for free play, because imaginative capacities can begin to flow as energies shift direction within the personality. This is the openness to the "demonic" that so many critics feared. Indeed, there are dangers, as Fénelon admitted, such as utter dryness, lack of attention to practical necessities such as eating, confusion of states, etc. The counterintuitive part of it, insisted Bremond, is that there is an embrace of the void in prayer. We might call it a state of "free-fall," in which anything can, and sometimes does, happen.[40]

At this point, all of the debates that swarmed around Fénelon and the issue of "passivity" in mystical prayer came back into focus. Mystical states, he insisted, are not just negative cessations, where all activity stops, but rather cessations in which *particular* activity comes to a halt, so that higher level activity can commence.[41] There is a functional equivalent here to the well-known psychoanalytic concept of "regression in the service of the ego," or in cognitive theory to the notions of "reframing" and "stepping outside of the box."[42] What occurs may be painful or disconcerting, and so controls and discrimination are needed as well as an openness to new discoveries. The assumption, moreover, is that what "comes" in the experience will transcend discourse, that discourse as such will only block the experience, and, it can be argued, will be inadequate to the experience when it occurs.

Notice, though, in my brief citing of a popular description of the prayer of "the practice of simple regard" that *some kind* of discourse will *follow* and thus crystallize

---

39. Surely the whole tradition, in both Roman Catholic and Protestant piety, of inviting the Holy Spirit to "take control" of one's life, or to "breathe" inspiration into the soul, is a derivative of this tradition of the ligature, especially if emphasis is placed on a "gripping" or "seizing" experience. I think, though, that the difference for Bremond is in the *inwardness* of the experience, as well as its progressive and gradual character. He saw the focus on "suddenness" and "external signs" as more typical of Jansenism or Methodism! This is also why he shied away from William James's descriptions of such experiences, which tend to be of the sensational type and often redolent of pathology.

40. One is inevitably reminded of the dangers of modern "regression" therapy in which the possibility of a "psychotic decompensation" is hazarded. But this is also why Bremond was so concerned to separate out the legitimate aspects of mystical states from "merely natural" elements, which may, indeed, include mental illness, and thus trigger scathing condemnation from critics.

41. Ibid., 359–60.

42. For a classic exploration of the psychoanalytic notion of regression in the service of the ego, where the analyst becomes an analogue to the mystical teacher who accompanies the willing soul into demonic places, one cannot do better than Bakan, *Sigmund Freud and the Jewish Mystical Tradition*.

the subject-object activity that goes on within the prayer. One problem, however, with the "Lord, bless my work" kind of response is that, in Bremond's language, it reintroduces asceticism in the form of practical results to the mix. Some statement of praise or thanksgiving—or even better, simply an admiring gaze followed by an enhanced "poetic" perception of some aspect of the ordinary world—would be more in line with Bremond's prescriptions.

Bremond admits that the term "passivity" may now be unworkable because of its sinister suggestions, preferring Camus's "infusion" or "gift" (corresponding to the posture of receptivity) and he notes, by implication, the danger of what I would call an "auto-hypnosis," which is the aberration leading to a true illuminism.[43] One imagines that one hears the voice of God, when it is actually one of one's own unconscious voices directing this or that activity, usually of a self-serving nature. The spiritual results are disastrous. Bremond argued that the most one can do is to put oneself in a position where something *may* happen, something with the characteristics of pure love—this is the value of ascetic preparation—but also *may not*. Grace cannot be prompted. This is the point where Bremond hears the Thomist critique that the results of prayer are separate from the prayer itself (and that those results need to be "critiqued" before serving as an incitement to action).[44]

In fact, argued Bremond, the best way to think of the matter is to say that in prayer one is received by God, not the other way around, for whatever God wishes.[45] And the best way to receive God is first to receive oneself, because the latter act, coming first, "mimes" what is looked for, hoped for, from God, even though the two experiences operate on quite different levels.[46] Let us state the matter differently. When one tries to listen to God, all one hears at first, and perhaps for a long time, is oneself, but the process of deepening attention to what is heard can over time strip it, purify it, of those elements of the "moi" in order to lay bare the divine "traces" (to use Bremond's

---

43. In a fascinating aside, Bremond took issue with Cuthbert Butler on a "very delicate point" of the interpretation of John of the Cross. Butler had contended that John teaches "the active emptying of the mind and the silencing of the faculties" as a preparation for prayer. No, says Bremond, what John teaches is that "we prepare ourselves for receiving this emptiness and silence" (*Histoire*, XI, 356n2). It is the difference between quietude as a contrivance, and quietude as a gift. Bremond was already suspicious of spirituality as an industry.

44. Once again, Bremond demonstrates that he has slipped out of the trap of thinking that prayer *produces* anything (Aquinas would agree) by taking issue with one of his *bêtes noires*, Jean Baruzi, and his famous book on mystical knowledge in John of the Cross (*Histoire*, XI, 362). Baruzi had claimed that it is in "the depth of our emptiness that God acts." No, said Bremond, the emptiness itself is a result of God's action.

45. Ibid., 357–58. It is here that Bremond takes with all seriousness the quietist emphasis on the transpositions of wills. In true mystical prayer the divine Will replaces my own as a source of motivation. It is not a matter of my "cornering" God, but of God "cornering" me!

46. Ibid., 357–58. Was Bremond with a reference to "miming" moving in the direction of a theory of representation, of the "mimetic" presentation of reality, in this case mystical experience, in speech? It would seem so, and there is much discussion of the "indicible" aspects of mystical experience in contemporary theory, as in the work of François Trémolières.

word). This "laying bare" would not be so much a discursive process as a kind of inspired "cooking" of what one "hears" in the presence of God. The function, then, of all of the theology of self-abandon is to set up a critical criterion for assessment. Is what I discern *really* from God? Is "pure love" the result?

The proper definition of "quietude," then for Bremond is an emptying that makes room for an "infusion," in which the soul has lost interest in discursive activity, since a better way is now available.[47] In that better way one has, as it were, a sense of being "plucked," like a string on a harp, so that the resulting vibrations constitute an active response in a state that he calls "active idleness."[48] He describes grace here as "a substantial energy which penetrates by assimilating itself and [thus] creates a new life." But the further implication of the harp analogy is that we are acted upon by God only in the measure that we are disposed to our own acting. In classical terms, grace is infallible, but not irresistible!

He further discusses the idea of the "fine point of the soul" from Francis de Sales as a special zone of integration at the center of the personality, a point at which the individual, prior to and above deliberative ratiocination as such, molds knowing and willing into a unity for action. Bremond saw here a form of the Scotist "thisness" of the soul, where a radiating center of the personality operates, but it also reflects the Thomist idea that faith is an act of the whole person.[49] And we recall Blondel's view, mentioned earlier, that the human mind always presses in the direction of the noetic unity of experience in an endless process of "making meaning."

What then happens on a psychological level in and through quietude is that God "acts" in the soul so as to produce knowledge and love at a "super-discursive" level. This is the point at which Bremond, his materials in *Histoire*, XI, becoming increasingly fragmentary, moved from the "natural" to the "supernatural." It is natural in quietude to seek symptomatic relief and the expansion of self-awareness, but supernatural to seek to move in the direction of knowing and loving God, *if* the individual wishes for that and makes him/herself available for that. Bremond then realized that he had to let discursivity back into the equation because "super-discursive" knowledge must speak, for, after all, we are linguistic creatures. Activation by grace can, and must include linguistic expression, but that language will be poetry that speaks of the "unspeakable" and "impossible," that is, the vision of pure love.[50]

He reflects at some length on the distinction between a "rational" love and a "mystical" love, arguing that love which can gives reasons for itself is in the final

---

47. Trémolières, "Approches de l'indicible," 273, offers a striking image: "an inner state, a void, like the nave of a church receiving the sound of organ music, thus . . . receiving the unspeakable."

48. *Histoire*, XI, 364–65.

49. Ibid., 368–70.

50. Here again I take up the suggestions of Trémolières in "Approches de l'indicible," but suggest that what makes mystical language a language of the "unspeakable" is that it is a literary discourse of the impossible, that is, of pure love.

analysis not really love at all. A loving relationship with one's beloved happens at a level which is not subject to discourse involving analysis and distinctions. Language which would attempt to put into words the reality of love is already distanced from that reality and runs the risk of gravely distorting it.

But an acceptable discourse, insisted Bremond in one of his final points, takes the form of an interplay with quietude, in which elements of speech function as "triggers" or "discursive flashes" for times of silence, and the silence in turn functions as a point of departure for fresh elements of discourse, now changed by what has been experienced, by what one has "learned" in the meantime.[51] He compares this process to the child's experience of learning to give expression to experience through newly acquired language, and the poet's voicing of fresh intuitive understandings, where the temptations to clichés and stereotyped language either do not operate (as with the child or primitive) or are knowingly avoided (as with the poet).[52] Thus it is that quietude can often be initiated by meditation on objects, even though it will leave the objects behind, only to return by seeing the objects in a new light. There is no "wall of granite" between discursive activity and mystic quietude, but they play off one another.

He confesses to his fondness for the language of aesthetic inspiration, once again, as the best analogy for the mystic encounter with God in quietude.[53] One major reason for this fondness, he avows, is that aesthetic inspiration results in love, since the artistic creation that follows is always a labor of devotion, of the artist giving him/herself to the artistic product unconditionally and purely. Granted that ego easily interposes itself (and often does!), it does not necessarily do so, as artists who have disappeared into obscurity behind a work that endures come to know. Further, the artist who "knows" the object also "loves" it, is bonded to it both as a work-in-progress and as a finished product. So, knowledge and love go together, and quietude is the state in which they cohere and cohabitate, as it were, and where, from the center of the personality, they shape the active charity, the artistic product, of one's life.

Bremond's last thoughts, then, are on the "traces of God" in this quietude. He reflects on the language found in the mystics of being "touched" or "filled" or "seized"

---

51. And thus we are reminded of Trémolières's wise insistence (see the foreword to this work) on the "enjeux" (interplay) that always characterized Bremond's work on so many levels.

52. One is reminded of two stories about Karl Barth. One is the famous preacher's example of how Barth replied when asked to sum up the message of the Bible. His response of "Jesus loves me, this I know," etc., may be contrasted with the anecdote about his love for Mozart. His description of that artist is that "he plays and plays, and plays," that is, with a truly divine energy. Bremond would have agreed with both, while insisting that the first is "notional." He would have said that it is not the first, but the second, that came from the "child" in Barth and where he "knows" the presence of God "really." He might also have said that the content of the first statement is a "discursive spark" sending him back to a new (mystical) experience of Mozart.

53. Ibid., 395–96. In this context Bremond considered a variety of terms, including the one that has become the most popular: contemplation. Somewhat uncomfortable with "visual" language, he limited the use of this term to the highest level of discursive operation, where the mind looks at objects in a spirit of wonder, etc., whereas "intuition," his preferred term, describes discernment that becomes operative when conscious discourse ceases (ibid., 392).

by the divine presence. There is both anguish and ineffable sweetness in such moments, but these terms can be misleading. To the extent, he says, that the soul fails to feel its nothingness before God, to that extent the divine presence is unbearable. Self-love and self-consciousness become profoundly painful, as is a sense of our sinfulness. There are "sparks of God" here, he says by referencing Madame Guyon, when, in a "simple intuition," the self is lost in a "super-discursive" love for God as the only thing ultimately lovable—and in the light of whom all other things, including our flawed selves, become lovable as well. It all comes down to the "double dogma," says Bremond, of knowing, through quietude, that the presence of God is active in us all of the time, and that that presence, when we open to it, has sanctifying power.[54] Such is the whole key to mystical prayer.

The Personal Note

Perhaps as the end of his life approached, Bremond had some thoughts of his native Aix as he had known it from childhood, recognizing some of the moments of quietude that marked that era. Such is suggested by the fragments discussed by Goichot at the conclusion of his work on the *Histoire*. These moments tend to remind us that what Bremond meant by "quietude" was something inward, something at the "fine point," even while surrounded outwardly by noise, and that they contain within them the "traces" of divine presence when the individual has the sense, perhaps quite suddenly, of being struck by a "simple intuition."

In one of the childhood reminiscences cited by Goichot from autobiographical fragments, Bremond recalled an experience in which, during a religious procession at his parish church, he had the sense that something "sensationnel" was going on with an agitated older woman at the event, something in the nature of a "vision," that left him in dread of such "mysticité" ever afterward. He said that in this experience, while he not know Surin yet, the "supernaturally diabolical" became real for him. At the same time he described his early sense for holiness in some individuals, including his maternal grandfather, who was a physician for the Carmelites in Aix. He laughs at these early memories, but, as Goichot indicates, there is a kind of "unconscious awareness, a spiritual climate," surrounding his memories.[55] We might say today that he lived in an atmosphere of "liminality," filled with occasions and instants, as he had claimed with Newman, when "another world" is revealed.

It is good to remember also, that in recalling these experiences Bremond cast scorn on the opinion of Jules Lebreton, SJ, at Toulouse, that all he, Bremond, cared about in the end was the "prayer of quietude," and that he took eleven volumes to make that point.[56] But that is to miss the forest, because one tree stands out. In recall-

---

54. Ibid., 420.
55. EG, 276–77.
56. Ibid., 276.

ing his childhood experiences Bremond's concerns were always pragmatic, namely, to describe the religious psychology and practice that arise from concrete experience. He believed, thus, that the prayer of quietude served ultimately as the principal distillate of an era's struggles—which still resonate with our modern challenges.

Further, as Bremond labored to make clear, the practice of quietude *is not a substitute for a range of other practices, but is the point to which other practices come if they are conceived correctly (that is, "theocentrically")*. The distinction is absolutely critical. There are no shortcuts, despite all the exigencies of modern packaging and delivery, but only a set of practices informed by sound theology to be lived faithfully over long stretches of time. And *sometimes* grace comes.

The challenge is to get people to listen to their own experience, to cultivate an inner opening that eventually gives rise to more-or-less spontaneous effusions grounded in a sound interiority. Quietist practice was criticized as easy and quick, but one of Bremond's points was that it is neither, when rightly understood. In fact, his whole protest is against the rigid thinking and practice of conservative authoritarians, on the one hand, and the relentless vulgarizing of practice, on the other. A tough row to hoe. So Lebreton had it wrong.

In any case, the *nihil obstat* and *imprimatur* on the cobbled-together volume XI came easily in June 1933, with Bremond by that time being quite ill and disabled. The progression had been gradual, however, with his ability to write being unimpaired until close to the end. In a late summer 1932 letter to Blondel, he indicated that he was having some moderate difficulty in thinking and conversing clearly, and in a letter to Baudin a little earlier he mentioned that he was becoming fatigued easily.[57] As late as October of that year, however, he was lucid and energetic enough to compose a review article on "Saint Thomas and the Philosophy of Prayer," in which, he confided to Blondel, he was becoming fond again of Thomas only by "Blondelizing" him—another indication that he could find notionally disconcerting theologians to be attractive in the intimacy of their prayer life.[58] His final winter was hard on him, afflicted with flu in February 1933 and by March "weak and exhausted."[59] On March 20 he suffered a stroke and could no longer speak, following which he was prostrated for five months, being attended by his brothers Jean and André as well as their sister Marguerite.[60]

He died on August 17, but not before cardinal Pacelli, in a telegram of July 22, relayed a blessing from Pius XI.

Vindicated at last. And, more lately, rediscovered.

---

57. Bremond to Blondel, August 11, 1932 (BB, III, 435–36, and 436n3).

58. Bremond to Blondel, November 17, 1932 (BB, III, 443–44).

59. Bremond to Loisy and the abbé Beaudou, February 8, 1933, and March 12, 1933 (cited BB, III, 457).

60. Ibid., 457, with references. Chauvin adds the details that after the stroke Bremond lost consciousness and was paralyzed along his right side (*Petite Vie*, 158).

21

Conclusions

HENRI BREMOND'S LIFE WORK remained unfinished in at least two respects. First, he was never able to complete the *Histoire* itself, as he had gradually come to conceive it. We can only imagine how it would have unfolded, through the time of Fénelon and down through the eighteenth and nineteenth centuries to the Modernist crisis, by assembling some of the intervening pieces on Caussade and Lamennais and Gerbet and the others. We can only wonder, too, how he might have integrated his studies of his Anglican and Protestant characters into a larger fabric. Granted that his primary mode of presentation, following Sainte-Beuve, was that of *peinture*, the clustering of character sketches and personalities into a rounded picture, rather than *récit*, or temporally ordered narrative,[1] nonetheless, I have suggested that he manifested a real sense of historical development, following Newman, in the unfolding of the "idea" of pure love.

But then, second, he never finished a truly synthetic work, where he could have set out a rounded theoretical exposition of his main insights. *Prière et poésie* comes the closest, but this has to be combined with *Histoire*, VII and VIII, then with the *Introduction à la philosophie de la prière*. Still in all, key ingredients would be left out, especially from his large body of literary interpretation, as well as the work on Fénelon, as well as the material from his English years. There is also the danger, I believe, that in concentrating on his work from the 1920s, that everything will come to look like an "anti-Ignatianism," thus overplaying the disputes with the Jesuits. In fact, he had a larger vision in mind, one that I have highlighted by emphasizing his relationship with Blondel, namely, that of a history of the inner life, a "soul-history."

Early on, Bremond decided that this soul-history would, specifically, be a history of persons at prayer, because he believed that the activity of prayer is the central religious practice from which all else flows. Look at what happens when people pray, he said, and the whole meaning of their religious existence, their *sentiment* as people

---

1. The distinction comes from the *Discours de réception* of La Churne de Saint-Palaye at his Acadèmie induction in 1758 (cited by Pocock, *Barbarism and Religion*, I, 155).

of faith, comes into focus. And that *sentiment*, when closely examined, reveals that it is composed of three interactive elements: pure love expressing itself as a pure poetry which issues in pure prayer. Thus, the moral, the aesthetic and the devout all come into intimate connection. I call this linkage the love-poetry-prayer "nexus." The whole purpose of the Quietist tradition here, of which Bremond makes so much in the French seventeenth century, is, then, to refine the relationship between the "passive" and the "active" dimensions of this nexus, so that certain dangers are avoided, and the relationship between "nature" and "grace" (supernature) is clarified.

The criticism, however, that has always been directed at Bremond's kind of "history of the soul" is that it is excessively inward, creating an insulated, idealized view of psychological space, as if it were in some way an autonomous world of its own. What about context, we usually say, where material factors—political and social and economic—come into play, shaping and driving our inner lives? What about the external historical process itself? Isn't the history of the soul really the story of the ways in which religious practice acts as an outlet for motivations and desires not in fact religious in nature? Many historians would have us think so, and the question is perennial. I have tried to frame it (not put it to rest!) as the ineluctably *moral* dynamic of "pure love" spirituality. The question of the truth of the inner life, of the subjective life of spirit, as something with its own inherent laws and dynamics, is thus raised acutely, as well as the truth claim that something "real" happens there, in an encounter with an invasive Other.

Let us not forget as well that for Bremond it was always clear that the dynamics of the inner life have an enculturated quality. His earliest impulses had been to create a history of English spirituality, we recall, and then he turned to distinctively Gallican traditions of spiritual experience and writing, and eventually his influence was profound on De Luca's forays into Italian spirituality, not to mention the efforts of Romain Rolland to forge an understanding of Hindu spirituality. In *that sense* his work anticipated the current atmosphere of pluralism, in which it is recognized that each cultural experience is unique, having its own properties and wisdom. But, as noted, he was clear as well that each tradition has to be *critiqued*, since unique wisdoms also contain unique blind spots and parochialisms. And the criteria for that critique must come from somewhere—at which point Blondel reenters the picture.

The critical question that Blondel harped at, partly as a result of his debates with Maritain and the Thomists, was that of the "noetic status" of Bremond's findings: does the love-poetry-prayer nexus of his formulations result in a knowledge that is solid and objective, so that it is not just a romantic projection, a fantasy, in the final analysis? Is there a form of verbalization that (adequately) corresponds to the ineffability of that Object?

His *historical* arguments for the existence of the nexus were descriptive and normative, were contained throughout his entire corpus, especially, of course, in the *Histoire* itself, where his argument for the French School as the radiating center of "devout humanism" and its "mysticism" is the centerpiece. Exploration of the inner life of the many different characters in this tradition, and that of their opponents, will reveal the elements of the triad at work, but also the dearth of spiritual health, where these may be lacking. Thus his normative judgment. Bremond's construals of specific individuals and groups such as Bérulle or Surin or Port-Royal or the whole concept of the "French School," are endlessly debated, his books on Fénelon or Chantal or de Rancé, still highly readable, have long been replaced by more current scholarship, but his normative judgment remains provocative. His argument that the nexus is a hallmark of a distinctly *mystical* spirituality maintains its own vitality and makes him, I dare aver, a more interesting, enduring and creative representative of the best elements in Catholic Modernism than the more famous Alfred Loisy.

His *literary* arguments for the triad were based on his many essay-reviews, where he was often commenting on new critical editions of an author's work or memoirs or correspondence, or on new biographies of that author, as well as on new fiction. These judgments are more difficult to overturn, and in fact many of them hold up well. His admiration for the moral vision in George Eliot's writing, his appreciation of John Keble's poetry, his shrewd perception of the baroque religiosity of J.-K. Huysmans's religious novels, but above all his passion for Paul Valéry's sublime verse—these are still rich with insight. If we keep in mind that the love-poetry-prayer nexus is an abstract form, never, as Bremond himself insisted, perfectly realized in any one figure, then his "hermeneutic" is at many points helpful at least, sometimes brilliant at best, but not to be applied rigidly.

His judgments of *sentiment*, that is, his insights as a student of "religious psychology," are, I believe, finally the most salient for students of interiority. These are the place where his openness to a late nineteenth-century vocabulary of internal conditions and functions (sentiments, feelings, sensations, imaginations), combined with a deep awareness of the categories of mystical experience (passivity-activity, union/presence, etc.), combined with categories derived from the dogmatic tradition (acquired grace, infused grace, natural/supernatural), allowed him to engage in sophisticated discernments. While Blondel could, and did, jump on him about creating confusion at times, the fact is that he was simultaneously juggling different paradigms of inwardness in order to open up suggestive avenues of exploration—not least, it must be said, in relation to the Asian spiritualities of inwardness that now so fascinate our Western culture.

As Guibert early opined, Fénelon always remained Bremond's "master" here, he for whom the enemy of all vital religion is the ever-present "moi," the narcissistic self, trying in even the most intimate moments (*precisely* in the most intimate moments!) to corner God and make God do one's own bidding. When he took a hard look at people when they pray—better, as they *portray* themselves at prayer—and assessed what they were experiencing, including the fact that what is revealed may be as much about the person who prays as about what/whom is addressed in the prayer, he believed that he had access to an inner space where everything is exposed because everything is at stake. Recall his analysis of John Henry Newman and his solitude, and recall his damning judgment on Rancé: he is dishonest when he prays.

Nonetheless, the question of truth will not go away in a cloud of subjectivity. This is where Blondel was merciless (grindingly relentless, actually) with his student and friend, Henri Bremond. My contention throughout has been that Blondel always had the surest perception of what Bremond was up to, never failed to critique Bremond's progress, and finally was in the best position to pass judgment on how well Bremond had accomplished those goals. So it is that we need to let Blondel have the last word about this student that he loved so much and knew so clearly.

It should be evident to the reader by now that in all of the debates about the Modernists, about whether this or that figure *really* believed or actually had lost faith altogether in the course of rebelling against the authority of church and dogma, I have come down on Blanchet's side against Goichot, while suggesting that Blanchet rather over-played Bremond's endless struggle with his Jesuit experience. Goichot, in the introduction to his path-breaking work, rejected the idea that Bremond engaged constantly in a "double game" with Modernism, in which his public statements masked his private disquiets, insisting instead that he proceeded rather in a "kind of dolorous spirit" of "a night of exile,"[2] looking for a bright light to shine out and clear away the mists of disquietude. Goichot conveys the sense of a researcher, who has lost faith, desperately using his scholarship to find it again, yet *convinced* that it can be found.

Blanchet, on the other hand, insisted that Bremond never lost faith, that with Newman he persisted, whatever the cost, because an intuition constrained him. Granted, moreover, that his struggle with the Jesuits did indeed extract a heavy price, his relationship with Blondel redeemed that price in many ways—as, I believe, Blanchet recognized in his edition of their correspondence, but which he did not live to spin out into a biography. He recognized in Bremond and in Blondel the kind of churchman who loves the tradition (how else could Bremond put such vast energy into such a vast output?), but refuses to be intimidated by its (often wrong-headed or ham-fisted) guardians. And he saw where that tradition was *going*, namely, into the public arena of "spirituality"—for better or for worse.

In effect, then, I have yielded to George Tyrrell's interpretation of Bremond, and have presented here a kind of "Americanized" version by somewhat assimilating his work to that of William James. While recognizing that Bremond had strong and persistent criticisms of James's methodology and perspective in *The Varieties of Religious Experience*, I have also presented Bremond's work on souls, his preoccupation with depicted inwardness, learned from Sainte-Beuve, as a kind of variation on

---

2. EG, 11–12. See Trémolières, "Émile Goichot lecteur," 131, who honors Goichot for his emphasis on Bremond's "mobility," sometimes fatiguing for readers, but always evocative of a determination to avoid reductionist and monolithic interpretations of texts. Indeed, for Bremond, faith undergirds that "mobility."

James's work on religious varieties. This is because, in the final analysis, that is how I think Bremond's *Histoire* will long be read into the future, as are the other experts on mysticism from his era. And we must remember, once again, that it is as a "religious psychologist" that Bremond most wanted to be remembered. There is endless discussion of whether James "really" believed, just as there is with Bremond.

******

Blondel's "red flags" have been robustly in view as we have tracked Bremond's progress. The depth of their friendship and the intensity of their correspondence—so skillfully presented by André Blanchet—always having been a powerful factor in both their lives from the time of that eventful "Third Year" of Bremond's Jesuit formation in 1894. We know that Blondel was not afraid to disapprove: there had been Bremond's decision to leave the Jesuits, his actions at Tyrrell's deathbed and funeral observance, the compromising friendship with Loisy, the brouhaha with von Hügel's defense of Loisy. And it is clear that Blondel felt bound to disagree with some of what Bremond said, or overstated, or said too incautiously. Much of the disagreement involved a running, unending debate about the status of the "notional," the role of "reason," the function of "discursivity," the priority of the concrete versus the abstract in the life of faith, the exact import of historical research for dogmatic reformulations, and the degree to which, and the manner in which, the idiosyncrasies of personal "experience" should override, or qualify, the authority of communal pronouncements in the life of the individual.

And then there was the question of "ascetism" or "asceticism," Blondel agreeing that Christianity is not a moralism, yet rather more respectful than was Bremond of disciplines that "prepare" for grace. Some of this boiled down to their different postures in regard to Modernism, even though, in opposition to authoritarian neo-Thomism and its political accoutrement, the Action Française, they were in complete agreement. In Blondel's favorite language, God is no tyrant or satrap with an Ego demanding submission, grace cannot be "plastered" onto an inert human nature, and fascism posing as religion is demonic.

What was difficult for Blondel to see and accept was the fact that for the modern age philosophically encased theology would have less and less purchase for most people. Everyday pragmatism and a low tolerance for abstract thinking will predominate. Instead, it would be *art* in its many forms, with all of the risks thereof, that would have the best chance for communicating and experiencing spiritual reality. Truly, spiritual exploration was being turned over to the novelists and writers of every kind of practical, confessional and imaginative literature. Poetry was coming of age in fresh ways, not to mention music, drama, and the arena of popular entertainment. The inner world of dynamic psychology, Freudianism, was bursting onto the cultural scene, creating the deep fascination with psychoanalysis as therapy and hermeneutic that is with us still, especially in the work of Jacques Lacan and then circulating back to the interpretation of Bremond in the work of Michel de Certeau. Bremond saw this in a deep way, and rose to the challenge in the kind of work that he did as a historian and in the stance that he created as a priestly académicien. It was Bremond's service, in his friendship with Blondel, and (in Trémolières's phrase) as a "literary modernist," to keep pushing these facts in his face.[3]

But it was Blondel's service to keep reminding Bremond of a problem that in the dogmatically grounded language of the era was usually stated as the issue of the relationship between the natural and the supernatural in the life of prayer. It can be formulated as the secular-sacred relation, or as the immanent-transcendent relation, or the contrast of grace acquired and grace infused, as well. The questions are always there. Are we convinced that human flourishing requires more than human resources can provide? Where does religious experience leave off being something *induced* from below in order to be something *given or received* from above?

Nothing aggravated Blondel more than his perception that Bremond, in his desire to forge connections between mystical experience and poetry, seemed to obliterate the boundary between the human aspiration for God and an *actual transformative* relationship with God. The desire for grace and the experience of grace seemed to become coincident, thus making grace the result of human effort rather than a divine gift. We have seen Bremond, in response, twisting and turning to avoid the trap, yet always hovering on the edge. In some notes that Blondel made for him, as Bremond debated with his critics after the 1925 "pure poetry" presentation for the Académie, he likened Bremond to the "good romantic" who *divinizes* strong experience too quickly, much like a child who, warm-hearted and impulsively generous, gives himself to "inferior forms" that produce joy, but who does not yet know that true joy will require much, much more in the way of the "despoilment of imperfect satisfactions."[4]

But, to Blondel's great credit, he recognized as well that the operative word in Bremond's nexus was the term "pure," functioning as a surrogate for "supernatural," "sacred," "transcendent" and all of the other terms that denote the fact that God is God and we are not. The perennial question, a theological *crux interpretationis*, is one of being clear about where and how grace, that is, the divine gift that empowers the recipient to will what God wills, intersects created human capacity for goodness. Blondel was clear that the one who prays purely, i.e., the "mystic" as he and Bremond

---

3. One should add that to the end Bremond remained an educator, especially of children—something that one can only with difficulty imagine for the other Modernist principals. In several review-pieces included as appendices in the post-mortem AH collection, Bremond continued to plead for humanistic education that forms "taste" and the sense for beauty which is grasped by the imagination, over against a rigid technical classicism or a utilitarian scientism, the first being the fault of much French, the second of Anglo-Saxon, pedagogy.

4. BB, III, Appendix I, 477. In the final analysis, thus, Blondel registered his protest at the "supernaturalizing of the natural," which, in another vein, is the "secularizing of the Christian mystical narrative" into a mythology of the inner life, the hallmark of "romanticism" as delineated by Kirschner, *Religious and Romantic Origins*, 149–78, in a masterful analysis. Bremond saw it otherwise, and that is precisely the debate thus bequeathed to us.

defined that term, comes away from the experience "knowing" something otherwise unknown, something hidden from, but *continuous with*, our "natural" selves. The challenge, then, was to imagine how the fragile agency of human language can capture and transmit such "knowledge." As we saw in the last volume of the *Histoire*, Bremond was still at the end struggling, as do we, with the problem of this "discourse" that finally ends in silence and quietude.[5]

Love and poetry and prayer are gifts from above only to the extent that they express the purity that is their ultimate horizon. When Bremond, in preparation for that same reading to the Académie, nervously asked Blondel for critical comments on a proposed draft, the latter noted that "pure poetry seems to me pure if, instead of making us feel good and encouraging idolatries, it conducts us down into ourselves where something better and larger than ourselves awaits, like the voice of a veiled host with whom we should linger and then find—in Him alone—our true and total being."[6] Bremond was, of course, in full agreement, though probably never recognizing the extent to which most popular spirituality in the years ahead would become monistic in spirit, particularly if the influence came from (Westernized versions of) Asia, or purely instrumental, particularly if it is simply a form of applied science, or both, thus collapsing the all-important distinctions. Thus, while Bremond may have had the clearer vision of the ocean that lay ahead, Blondel may have been the better prophet of the reefs and shoals contained therein.

Of course, neither at the time of Bremond's death saw the storm coming, though both sensed it with their first opposition to Maurras and the Action Française. Both were clear that bad theology and spirituality go hand-in-hand with cruel politics and the numbing-down, finally the disintegration, of the kind of vision that produces saints of pure love and pure poetry and pure prayer. But they were equally clear that the function of this powerful nexus in dark times is the refurbishment of a true interiority, so that despair and cynicism cannot gain purchase in the listening soul, ever alert for the first signs of new grace and new life. Recalling Bremond's judgment on Surin that he made the great mistake of taking the demon's pronouncements seriously, and that Condren's virtue was that he knew how to laugh at the demons, we should remember as well that Bremond had unending enthusiasm for people of high ideals who

---

5. Michel de Certeau's solution here, as we noted in his interpretation of Bremond's "Metaphysic of the Saints" in *Histoire*, VII and VIII, was to argue that Bremond anticipated the postmodern discourse of the "absence of God." In other words, what the mystic knows is that God's presence is an absence, that the absence *is* a paradoxical presence. That is a psychological possibility: if I *know* that my friend is gone, that knowing makes him present to my consciousness. But another possibility—a better one— is that Bremond was drawing closer to the mysticism of silence that we know from the East, and that at least one theologian, Raimundo Panikkar, has framed in Christian terms, in *The Silence of God: The Answer of the Buddha*. This is the idea that by the word "God" we mean a Reality beyond being itself, so that even the word "God," tied to verbal constraints of some kind, is inadequate. In such a construal it is the privilege of the mystics to understand this limit, and thus, finally, to utilize a language that inexorably leads to silence—precisely the point that Bremond wished to make about "pure poetry."

6. BB, III, Appendix II, 483.

never gave up in the face of profound discouragements. He admired moral fortitude in the Puritans and their heirs, he was fascinated with saintly lives that made generous room for the appreciation of beauty in all its forms, he had great respect for spiritual teachers who managed to combine a passion for God with everyday common sense and practicality, but most all, I think, he was transfixed (the word is not too strong) by lives shattered by misfortune and suffering, indeed sinful as well, but radiant at the same time with loving energy, lyrical expression, and passionate prayer. It is the task of the Christian writer and historian and biographer—the painter of verbal portraits attuned to the divine purpose operative in such lives—to retrieve them as instruments for the fulfillment of our human possibility as well.

So, Bremond's question remains. Who is it that really prays? Of course, the word *really* should be in italics. The challenge is obvious. It is the challenge to see to it that *you* are that person. But better stated: to see to it that you are *becoming* that person. It was Bremond's own goal, for sure.

Bibliography

THE BIBLIOGRAPHY THAT FOLLOWS is limited to works by Bremond, and to secondary literature actually consulted for this biography. The listing of secondary literature is heavily weighted to studies that have appeared, mostly in France, since 2006. For a comprehensive, technically detailed, chronologically ordered bibliography of the entire corpus of Bremond's writings, and of secondary literature prior to 2006, the listings compiled by François Trémolières in volume 5, 337–380, of the Millon edition of the *Histoire* (HLM in Abbreviations II below) are indispensable. Professor Trémolières has also included a brief overview (ibid., 355–56) of unedited materials relative to Bremond, which are stored at several French locations: the Jesuit Archives at Vanves, the Sulpician Archives in Paris, the Bremond family archive at Aix, and especially the Bremond and Goichot fonds at the Bibliothèque nationale in Paris. This last contains the as yet unedited correspondence between Bremond and Charles Maurras.

Abbreviations I

In the bibliographical entries for "Bremond, Henri" below, the various collections in which his many essays appeared are abbreviated as follows:

AH	*Autour l'humanisme d'Érasme à Pascal.* Paris: Grasset, 1936.
AR	*Âmes religieuses.* Paris: Perrin, 1902.
DA	*Divertissements devant l'Arche.* Paris: Grasset, 1930.
EV	*L'Enfant et la vie.* Paris: Victor Retaux, 1902.
IR I	*L'Inquiétude religieuse.* First series. 2nd ed. Paris: Perrin, 1909.
IR II	*L'Inquiétude religieuse.* Second series. Paris: Perrin, 1909.
PR	*Pour le romantisme.* Paris: Bloud et Gay, 1923.

Bibliography

Abbreviations II

The various collections of scholarly essays pertaining to Bremond's life and work, appearing since 1967, are abbreviated in the bibliography as follows:

CA *Henri Bremond (1865–1933). Actes du colloque d'Aix, 19 et 20 mars 1966.* Préface de B. Guyon. Publications des Annales de la Faculté de Lettres, Aix-en-Provence. Paris: Ophrys, 1967.

EN *Entretiens sur Henri Bremond. Colloque de Cerisy, 27–31 août 1965.* Edited by Jean Dagens and Maurice Nédoncelle. Paris: Mouton, 1967.

HL *Histoire et littérature chez Henri Bremond.* Sous la direction de Étienne Fouilloux et François Trémolières. Grenoble: Jérôme Millon, 2009.

HLM Henri Bremond. *Histoire littéraire du sentiment religieux en France depuis la fin des guerres de Religion jusqu'à nos jours.* Nouvelle édition sous la direction de François Trémolières. 5 vols. Grenoble: Jérôme Millon, 2006.

LS *Littérature et spiritualité au miroir de Henri Bremond.* Textes réunis par Agnès Guiderdoni-Bruslé et François Trémolières. Grenoble: Jérôme Millon, 2012.

MM *Modernists & Mystics.* Edited by C. J. T. Talar. Washington, DC: Catholic University of America Press, 2009.

MMM *Modernisme, Mystique, Mysticisme.* Sous la direction de Giacomo Losito et Charles J. T. Talar. Paris: Honoré Champion, 2017.

****

Abercrombie, Nigel. *The Origins of Jansenism.* Oxford: Clarendon, 1936.
———. *Saint Augustine and French Classical Thought.* New York: Russell & Russell, 1938.
Ahearne, Jeremy. *Michel de Certeau: Interpretation and Its Other.* Stanford: Stanford University Press, 1995.
Amadieu, Jean-Baptiste. "Mysticisme, modernisme, et littérature: l'hétérodoxie littéraire entre deux guerres." MMM, 103–20.
Arnold, Claus. "Joseph Sauer—A German 'Modernist' in War Time." In *Roman Catholic Modernists Confront the Great War*, edited by C. J. T. Talar and Lawrence F. Barmann, 107–25. New York: Palgrave Macmillan, 2015.
Arrou, Pierre. "Henri Bremond et Charles Grolleau." *Le Divan* 246 (1943) 49–59.
Aubert, Roger. "Henri Bremond et la crise moderniste. Lumières nouvelles." *Revue d'histoire ecclésiastique* 72 (1977) 332–48.
Baldick, Robert. *The Life of J.-K. Huysmans.* Sawtry, UK: Dedalus, 2006.
Barjon, Louis. *Paul Claudel.* Preface by Paul Claudel. Paris: Éditions Universitaires, 1953.
Barmann, Lawrence F. "Baron Friedrich von Hügel and the Great War." In *Roman Catholic Modernists Confront the Great War*, edited by C. J. T. Talar and Lawrence F. Barmann. New York: Palgrave Macmillan, 2015.
———. "Le moderniste comme mystique: le baron Friedrich von Hügel." MMM, 205–44.
———. "Mysticism and Modernism in Baron Friedrich von Hügel's Life and Thought." MM, 23–38.

Bibliography

Beaumont, Keith. "The Reception of Newman in France at the Time of the Modernist Crisis." In *Receptions of Newman*, edited by Frederick D. Aquino and Benjamin J. King, 156–66. Oxford: Oxford University Press, 2015.

Bernanos, Georges. *The Diary of a Country Priest*. Translated by Pamela Morris. New York: Doubleday, 1954.

———. *The Impostor*. Translated by J. C. Whitehouse. Lincoln: University of Nebraska Press, 1999.

Bernardi, Peter J. *Maurice Blondel, Social Catholicism, and Action Francaise: The Clash over the Church's Role during the Modernist Era*. Washington, DC: Catholic University of America Press, 2009.

Bernard-Maître, Henri. "À propos de l'Histoire littéraire de sentiment religieux, une correspondence de Bremond avec Loisy (1924–1929)." *Revue d'ascétique et de mystique* 45 (1969), 161–89.

———. "Les exercices spirituels de saint Ignace de Loyola, interprétés par l'abbé Henri Bremond." EN, 167–80.

———. "Lettres d'Henri Bremond à Alfred Loisy." *Bulletin de littérature ecclésiastique* 69 (1968) 3–24, 161–84, 269–89; *Bulletin de littérature ecclésiastique* 70 (1969) 44–56.

———. "Théocentrisme et anthropocentrisme chez Henri Bremond. Une mise au point théologique de Maurice Blondel." *Revue d'ascétique et de mystique* 3 (1964) 314–18.

Bernard-Maître, Henri, and Romana Guarnieri. *Don Giuseppe De Luca et l'abbé Henri Bremond (1929-1933). De l'"Histoire littéraire du sentiment religieux en France" à l'"Archivo Italiano per la storia della Pietà" d'après des documents inédits*. Rome: Edizioni di Storia e Letteratura, 1965.

Blanchet, André. "L'abbé Bremond Quelques traits pour un portrait futur." EN, 19–30.

———. "Claudel lecteur de Bremond," suivi de Paul Claudel, "L'abbé Bremond et la prière." *Études* (1965) 155–67.

———. "Bremond et Blondel." AC, 67–74.

———, ed. *Henri Bremond et Maurice Blondel, Correspondance établie, présentée et annotée par A. Blanchet. I: Les commencements d'une amitié 1897-1904; II: Le grand dessein d'Henri Bremond 1905-1920; III: Combats pour la prière et pour la poésie 1921-1933*. Paris: Aubier, 1970, 1971, 1972.

———. *Henri Bremond 1865-1904*, suivi d'une "chronologie" par É. Goichot. Paris: Aubier, 1975.

———. "Henri Bremond: Notes autobiographiques." *Revue d'ascétique et de mystique* 41 (1965) 433–39.

———. *Histoire d'une mise à l'Index. La "Sainte Chantal" de l'abbé Bremond d'après des documents inédits*. Paris: Aubier, 1967.

———. "Péguy et Bremond." *L'Amitié Charles Péguy* 171 (1971) 1–13.

———. "Redécouverte de Bremond." AC, 11–26.

Blanchette, Oliva. *Maurice Blondel: A Philosophical Life*. Grand Rapids: Eerdmans, 2010.

Blondel, Maurice. *L'Action*. 1893. Translated by Oliva Blanchette as *Action (1893)*. Notre Dame: University of Notre Dame Press, 1984.

———. "La jansénisme et l'anti-jansénisme de Pascal." *Revue de métaphysique et de morale*, special tricentennial number (1923) 129–63.

———. *The Letter on Apologetics and History and Dogma*. Translated by Alexander Dru and Illtyd Trethowan. Grand Rapids: Eerdmans, 1994.

———. "Le problème de la mystique." *Cahiers de la nouvelle Journée* 3 (1925) 1–63.

Bibliography

Bordeaux, Henry. *Un sourcier: Henri Bremond.* Discours prononcé par M. Henry Bordeaux pour la réception de Henri Bremond à l'Académie française. Paris: Plon-Nourrit, 1924.

Bremond, André. "Henri Bremond." *Études* 217 (1933) 29–53.

Bremond, Henri. "Les acteurs d'Oberammergau." AR, 203–40.

———. *Apologie pour Fénelon.* Paris: Perrin, 1910.

———. "Apologie pour les newmanistes français." *Revue pratique d'apologétique* 3 (1906) 89–94.

———. "L'Assimilation des principes catholiques: W.-Ch. Lake (1817–1897)." IR II, 203–37.

———. "Autour de *L'Oblat*." *Le Divan* 129 (1927) 207–9.

———. "La baronne de Handel-Mazzetti." IR II, 311–70.

———. *Le Bienheureux Thomas More (1478–1535).* Paris: Victor Lecoffre, 1904. Translated as *Sir Thomas More (The Blessed Thomas More)*, by Harold Child. 2nd ed. London: Washbourne, 1920.

———. *Bossuet. Textes choisis et commentés. I: Dijon, Metz et Paris (1627–1670); II: Bossuet évêque, précepteur du Dauphin et aumônier de la Dauphine (1669–1682); III: Bossuet, évêque de Meaux (1681–1704).* Paris: Plon-Nourrit, 1913.

———. *Le charme d'Athènes.* 48-page booklet. Paris: E. Sansot, 1905.

———. *Le charme d'Athènes et autres essais.* Reissue of *Le charme d'Athènes* with additional essays by Jean Bremond and André Bremond. Paris: Bloud et Gay, 1925.

———. "*Christus vivit!*" IR I, 309–40.

———. "La conversion de Pascal." IR II, 5–42.

———. "De la foi au doute: J. R. Green (1837–1883)." IR II, 238–71.

———. "De quelques jeunes écrivains morts pour la France." *Le Correspondant* 261 (1915) 441–67.

———. "La détresse de Lammenais." IR II, 47–85.

———. *Les Deux musiques de la prose.* Paris: Le Divan, 1924.

———. "Devant des portraits d'enfants." EV, 1–32.

———. *Discours de réception à l'Académie française, Éloge de Mgr Duchesne.* Paris: Bloud et Gay, 1924.

———. "Un éducateur anglais: Édouard Thring et l'école d'Uppingham." AR, 129–202.

———. "L'éducation par les contes: La vie et l'oeuvre de Mme J. Lavergne." EV, 35–96.

———. *En prière avec Pascal.* Sermon preached for the Pascal tricentenary, July 7, 1923, Clermont-Ferrand cathedral. Published as a brochure by Bloud et Gay, 1925, revised for inclusion in the AH collection.

———. "Les étonnements d'un Anglais en France." *Études* 78 (1899) 289–309.

———. "Fénelon et la guerre." *Le Correspondant* 258 (1915) 65–90.

———. *Fléchier: Oeuvres choisies.* Paris: Bloud, 1911.

———. *Frédéric Lefèvre, Entretiens avec Paul Valéry.* Paris: Le Livre, 1926.

———. "Le frère Fiacre et ses trois dauphins." DA, 101–27.

———. *Gerbet: Dernières conférences d'Albéric d'Assise.* Paris: Bloud, 1908.

———. *Gerbet. Introduction et texts choisis.* Paris: Bloud, 1907.

———. *Henri Bremond de l'Académie française, Sainte Chantal (1572–1641).* Présentation de Didier-Marie Proton. Paris: Éditions du Cerf, 2011. Original edition, 1912.

———. *Histoire littéraire du sentiment religieux en France depuis la fin des guerres de Religion jusqu'à nos jours. IV: La Conquête mystique: l'École de Port-Royal; V: La Conquête mystique: l'École du P. Lallemant. Le P. Surin et al tradition mystique dans le Compagnie de Jésus.* Paris: Bloud et Gay, 1920.

———. *Histoire littéraire du sentiment religieux en France depuis la fin des guerres de Religion jusqu'à nos jours. VI: La Conquête mystique; Marie de l'Incarnation. Turba magna.* Paris: Bloud et Gay, 1922.

———. *Histoire littéraire du sentiment religieux en France depuis la fin des guerres de Religion jusqu'à nos jours. VII: La Métaphysique des Saints; VIII: La Métaphysique des Saints.* Paris: Bloud et Gay, 1928.

———. *Histoire littéraire du sentiment religieux en France depuis la fin des guerres de Religion jusqu'à nos jours. IX: La Vie chrétienne sous l'Ancien Régime.* Paris: Bloud et Gay, 1931.

———. *Histoire littéraire du sentiment religieux en France depuis la fin des guerres de Religion jusqu'à nos jours. X: La Prière et les prières sous la Ancien Régime.* Paris: Bloud et Gay, 1932.

———. *Histoire littéraires du sentiment religieux en France depuis la fin des guerres de Religion jusqu'à nos jours. XI: Le Procès des mystiques.* Paris: Bloud et Gay, 1933.

———. *Histoire littéraire du sentiment religieux en France depuis la fin des guerres de Religion jusqu'à nos jours.* Nouvelle édition sous la direction de François Trémolières, augmentée d'inédits et de l'*Introduction à la philosophie de prière*, avec des études d'Alain Cantillon, Pierre-Antoine Fabre, Patrick Goujon, Sophie Houdard, Jacques Le Brun, François Marxer, Dominique Salin, François Trémolières. Précédé de "Henri Bremond: un historien de la faim de Dieu" par Émile Goichot. Index, table analytique, bibliographie des études bremondiennes. 5 vols. Grenoble, France: Jérôme Millon, 2006.

———. "Huysmans." IR II, 277–310.

———. "L'idéal et la réalité dans la vie catholique." IR I, 256–308.

———. "L'inquiétude de Newman et la sérénité de Pusey." IR I, 23–90.

———. *Introduction à la philosophie de la prière. Textes choisis.* Paris: Bloud et Gay, 1929.

———. "La légende d'argent." IR II, 371–92.

———. "La légende de Boileau." PR, 1–30.

———. "Les lettres de François de Sales." AH, 83–93.

———. "Les lettres spirituelles du P. Didon." IR, II, 182–200.

———. *A Literary History of Religious Thought in France from the Wars of Religion down to Our Own Times. I: Devout Humanism; II: The Coming of Mysticism (1590-1620).* Translated by K. L. Montgomery. London: SPCK, 1928, 1930.

———. *A Literary History of Religious Thought in France. III: The Triumph of Mysticism.* Translated by K. L. Montgomery. London: SPCK, 1936.

———. *La Littérature religieuse d'avant-hier et d'aujourd'hui. À propos de la nouvelle collection "la pensée chrétienne."* Paris: Bloud, 1906.

———. "La logique de l'esprit: W. G. Ward." IR I, 169–229.

———. "La logique du coeur: M. Brunetière et l'irrationnel' de la foi." IR I, 91–130.

———. "M. Ch. V. Langlois et al 'Vie Spirituelles' au Moyen Age." DA, 47–84.

———. "M. Gladstone théologien." *Études* 70 (1897) 94–101.

———. "Manning et Newman." IR I, 230–55.

———. *Manuel illustré de la littérature catholique en France de 1870 à nos jours.* Paris: Spes, 1925.

———. "Maurice Barrès." *Le Correspondant* 257 (1923) 979–91.

———. *Maurice Barrès: Vingt-cinq ans de vie littéraire. Pages choisies.* Paris: Bloud, 1908.

———. "Mme de Maintenon et ses directeurs." DA, 146–93.

———. "Monsieur Hamon et la Médecine." DA, 128–45.

———. *The Mystery of Newman.* Translated by H. C. Corrance. London: Williams and Norgate, 1907.

———. *Newman. Le développement du dogme chrétien.* Paris: Bloud, 1904.

———. *Newman.* Vol. II, *La psychologie de la foi.* Paris: Bloud et Gay, 1905.

———. *Newman.* Vol. I, *Le développement du dogme chrétien.* Paris: Bloud, 1906. A thorough revision of the 1904 volume, with introduction by Mgr. Mignot, archbishop of Albi, along with *Newman*, vols. II and III.

———. *Newman.* Vol. III, *La Vie chrétienne.* Paris: Bloud, 1906.

———. *Nicole: Le Prisme. Des défauts des gens de bien. Des moyens de profiter des mauvais sermons. Pensées sur divers sujets de morale. Lettres choisies.* Paris: Bloud, 1909.

———. "L'Oblat." *Études* 95 (1903) 328–47.

———. *P. de Caussade, SJ. Bossuet, maître d'Oraison. Instructions spirituelles en forme de dialogues sur les divers états d'oraison suivant la doctrine de M. Bossuet. Nouvelles édition originale de 1741.* Paris: Bloud et Gay, 1931.

———. "Pascal, l'abbé de Villars et la première réfutation des *Pensées*." AH, 181–96.

———. "Pascal et les mystiques." AH, 241–59.

———. "Pascal et Valéry." AH, 260–74.

———. "La pauvresse de Pascal." AH, 172–80.

———. "Les pères du Désert." DA, 7–46.

———. "La philosophie de François de Sales." AH, 131–52.

———. *Les plus belles pages de Fénelon, choisies et commentés par Henri Bremond.* Paris: Flammarion, 1930.

———. *La poésie pure: avec un débat sur la poésie par Robert de Souza.* Paris: Grasset, 1926.

———. "Pour qu'on lise S. François de Sales." AH, 94–130.

———. *Prayer and Poetry: A Contribution to Poetical Theory.* Translated by Algar Thorold. London: Burns, Oates & Washbourne, 1927.

———. "Un prédicateur de collège: Arnold de Rugby." EV, 185–209.

———. "Le prêtre et la formation littèraire de l'enfant." EV, 113–57.

———. "La prière pour les morts." *Le Correspondant* 265 (1916) 553–57.

———. *La Provence mystique au XVIIe siècle: Antoine Yvan (1576–1653) et Madeleine Martin (1612–1678) avec deux gravures, un plan et une carte.* Paris: Plon-Nourrit, 1908.

———. "Que ferait le Christ?" AR, 241–76.

———. *Racine et Valéry: Notes sur l'initiation poétique.* Paris: Grasset, 1930.

———. "La religion de George Eliot." IR II, 86–162.

———. "Remarques sur l'éducation du sens religieux." EV, 161–84.

———. *Le Roman et l'histoire d'une conversion. Ulric Guttinguer et Sainte-Beuve d'après des correspondances inédites.* Paris: Plon-Nourrit, 1925.

———. "Un saint anglican: John Keble." AR, 3–62.

———. "Le Saint Patron des Humoristes." DA, 85–100.

———. "Sainte-Beuve ou le romantique impénitent. I. Sainte-Beuve et l'intelligence; II. Sainte-Beuve et le catholicisme." PR, 175–250.

———. *Sainte Catherine d'Alexandrie.* Paris: Henri Laurens, n.d. (1918).

———. "Saint François de Sales et sainte Chantal." *Le Correspondant* 254 (1911) 237–66.

———. "Le sécret de Port-Royal." AH, 169–72.

———. "La solitaire des Rochers." DA, 194–227.

———. "Sydney Smith et le christianisme bourgeois." IR I, 1–22.

———. *The Thundering Abbot.* Translated by F. J. Sheed. London: Sheed and Ward, 1930.

———. "Wiseman et les catholiques anglais pendant la crise d'Oxford." IR I, 131–68.
Brillant, Maurice. "L'humanisme chrétien." *Nouvelles Littéraires*, August 26, 1933.
Brown, Frederick *The Embrace of Unreason. France, 1914–1940*. New York: Knopf, 2014.
———. *For the Soul of France: Culture Wars in the Age of Dreyfus*. New York: Anchor, 2010.
Cameron, J. M. "Newman and the Empiricist Tradition." In *The Rediscovery of Newman: An Oxford Symposium*, edited by John Coulson and A. M. Allchin, 76–96. London: SPCK, 1967.
Cantillon, Alain. "Détruire et sauver Port-Royal." HLM, II, 9–21.
———. "Les marques du style." LS, 177–94.
Carroll, Andrew J. "The Philosophical Foundations of Catholic Modernism." In *George Tyrrell and Catholic Modernism*, edited by Oliver P. Rafferty, 38–55. Portland, OR: Four Courts, 2010.
Certeau, Michel de. "Henri Bremond et la 'Métaphysique des saints.'" *Recherches de science religieuse* 54 (1966) 23–60.
———. *The Mystic Fable*. Volume 1, *The Sixteenth and Seventeenth Centuries*. Translated by Michael B. Smith. Chicago: University of Chicago Press, 1992.
———. "Mystique." In *Encyclopedia Universalis*, 12:873–78. Paris: Encyclopedia Universalis, 1985.
———. *The Possession at Loudun*. Translated by Michael B. Smith. University of Chicago Press, 1990.
Chadwick, Owen. "Henri Bremond and Newman." In *The Spirit of the Oxford Movement: Tractarian Essays*, edited by Owen Chadwick, 167–97. Cambridge: Cambridge University Press, 1990.
———. *The Secularization of the European Mind in the Nineteenth Century*. Gifford Lectures, University of Edinburgh, 1973–74. Cambridge: Cambridge University Press, 1975.
Charpin, E. "Souvenirs d'un Aixois sur l'abbé Bremond." AC, 27–36.
Charpin, Frédéric. *La Question religieuse. Enquête Internationale*. Paris: Mercure de France, 1908.
Chauvin, Charles. *Petite Vie de Henri Bremond (1865–1933)*. Paris: Descléd de Brouwer, 2006.
Cholvy, Gérard. "Le restauration catholique en France au XIXe siècle." In *Migne et le renouveau des études patristiques. Actes du colloque de Sainte-flour 7-8 juillet 1975*, edited by A. Mandouze and J. Fouilheron, 61–89. Paris: Beauchesne, 1985.
Cobban, Alfred. *A History of Modern France*. Vol. 3, *France of the Republics, 1871–1962*. London: Penguin, 1965.
Cognet, Louis. "Bremond et Port-Royal." EN, 99–108.
———. *Le Jansénisme*. Paris: Presses Universitaires de France, 1964.
———. *Les Origines de la spiritualité française au XVIIe siècle*. Paris: La Columbe, 1949.
Dagens, Jean. "Introduction à Henri Bremond." EN, 1–10.
———. "De saint François de Sales à Bossuet." EN, 151–58.
Decker, Henry W. *Pure Poetry, 1925–1930: Theory and Debate in France*. Berkeley: University of California Press, 1962.
Debongnie, Pierre, and Joseph de Brandt. "Bremond (Henri)." In *Dictionnaire d'histoire et de géographie ecclésiastiques*, 10:518–29. Paris: Letouzey et Ané, 1938.
De Giorgi, Fulvio. "Saints, visionnaires, hérétiques et poètes. Mysticisme néo-catholique et modernisme orthodoxe dans le groupe de Fogazzaro." MMM, 373–400.
DeJean, Joan. *Ancients against Moderns: Culture Wars and the Making of a Fin de Siècle*. Chicago: University of Chicago Press, 1997.

De Pril, Ward. "La théologie catholique de la mystique au début du vingtième siècle." MMM, 87–102.

Descaves, Lucien. "Henri Bremond tel qu'il m'est apparu." *Nouvelles littéraires*, August 26, 1933.

Dimnet, Ernest. "Souvenirs." *Nouvelles littéraires* (August 26, 1933).

Donahue, Darcy. "The Mysticism of Saint Ignatius of Loyola." In *A Companion to Jesuit Mysticism*, edited by Robert A. Maryks, 6–35. Leiden, Netherlands: Brill, 2017.

Doyle, William. *Jansenism: Catholic Resistance to Authority from the Reformation to the French Revolution*. New York: St. Martin's, 2000.

Du Bos, Charles. *Approximations*. Deuxième Série. Paris: Corrêa, 1932; Septième Série. Paris: Corrêa, 1937. New edition, Paris: Éditions des Syrtes, 2000.

———. "Henri Bremond, historien de l'homme capable de Dieu." In *Approximations*, 1331–58. Septième Série. Paris: Fayard, 1965.

———. *Journal. I: 1921–1923*. Paris: Corrêa, 1946.

Duclos, Paul. "L'abbé Louis Beaudou, un correspondant privilegié d'Henri Bremond." *Bulletin de littérature religieuse* 90 (1989) 113–24.

Dupré, Louis. "The Christian Experience of Mystical Union." *Journal of Religion* 69 (1989) 1–13.

Dupuy, B. D. "Newman's Influence in France." In *The Rediscovery of Newman: An Oxford Symposium*, edited by John Coulson and A. M. Allchin, 147–73. London: Sheed and Ward, 1967.

Dupuy, Michel. "Jansénisme." In *Dictionnaire de spiritualité ascétique et mystique*, edited by Marcel Viller et al., 8:102–48. Paris: Beauchesne, 1974.

Egan, Harvey D. *The Spiritual Exercises and the Ignatian Mystical Horizon*. St. Louis: Institute of Jesuit Sources, 1976.

Fabre, Pierre-Antoine. "L'iconographie de l'*Histoire littéraire du sentiment religieux* et le problème de l'illustration dans la littérature spirituelle du XVIIe siècle." HL, 155–76.

———. "Le temps de prier." HLM, IV, 8–24.

Fumaroli, Marc. Preface to *Érudition et Religion aux XVIIe et XVIIIe siècles*, by Bruno Neveu, i–vi. Paris: Albin Michel, 1994.

Germain, Gabriel. "Prière et poésie." EN, 187–206.

Gibson, Ralph. *A Social History of French Catholicism 1789–1914*. London: Routledge, 1989.

Gide, André. *The Journals of André Gide*. Vol. 2, *1924–1949*. Translated and edited by Justin O'Brien. New York: Vintage, 1956.

Ginther, Clara. "Expérience pastorale et réflexion théologique: aux origines de l'interêt de George Tyrrell pour le mysticisme." MMM, 175–204.

Goichot, Émile. "Deux historiens à l'Académie. I. D'une élection à l'autre. II. À la recherche de Duchesne. III. Les avatars d'un discours de réception." *Revue d'histoire ecclésiastique* 78 (1983) 34–64, 373–96.

———. "En marge de la crise moderniste: la correspondance Bremond–von Hügel." *Revue des sciences religieuses* 48 (1974) 209–34; 49 (1975) 202–33; 53 (1979) 124–55.

———. "Henri Bremond et Alfred Loisy: à propos d'un petit livre." EN, 227–42

———. "Henri Bremond: Aux frontières de l'hagiographie." In Sanctity and Secularity during the Modernist Period, 69-101. Edited by L. Barmann and C.J.T. Talar. Bruxelles: Societe des Bollandistes, 1999.

———. "Henri Bremond: un historien de la faim de Dieu." Avant-propos, HLM, I, 13–17.

———. *Henri Bremond historien du sentiment religieux. Genèse et stratégie d'une entreprise littérature*. Paris: Ophrys, 1982.

———. "'L'Humanisme dévot' de Henri Bremond: réflexions sur un lieu commun." *Revue d'ascétique et de mystique* 45 (1969) 121–60.

———. "Une source nouvelle pour l'histoire de la spiritualité: les 'études bremondiennes.'" *Revue d'histoire de la spiritualité* 49 (1973) 91–116.

———. "Sur 'l'affaire Tyrrell': documents inédits." *Revue d'histoire ecclésiastique* 81 (1986) 95–116.

———. "Trois 'prophètes du dehors'. Henri Bremond et l'Angleterre religieuse." *Revue d'histoire et de philosophie religieuses* 65 (1985) 27–43.

Gorday, Peter. *François Fénelon, a Biography: The Apostle of Pure Love*. Brewster, MA: Paraclete, 2012.

Gouhier, Henri. "Conclusions." EN, 215–21.

———. "La Métaphysique des Saints de M. Henri Bremond." *Nouvelles littéraires*, December 29, 1928.

Goujon, Patrick, and Dominique Salin. "Henri Bremond et la spiritualité ignatienne." HLM, II, 412–43.

Goyau, Georges. "Âmes de Port-Royal." *Revue des Deux Mondes*, September 15, 1922, 329–49.

———. "Aux écoutes des âmes vivantes." *Nouvelles Littéraires*, August 26, 1933.

———. Preface to AH, 7–24.

Grandmaison, Léonce de. "L'élément mystique dans la religion." *Recherches de science religieuse* 1 (1910) 180–208.

———. "Henri Bremond à l'Académie française." *Études* 175 (1923) 557–67.

Gres-Gayer, Jacques M. "The Magisterium of the Faculty of Theology of Paris in the Seventeenth Century." *Theological Studies* 53 (1992) 424–50.

———. "The *Unigenitus* of Clement XI: A Fresh Look at the Issues." *Theological Studies* 49 (1988) 259–82.

Grolleau, Charles. *Histoire littéraire du sentiment religieux en France depuis la fin des guerres de Religion jusqu'à nos jours Index alphabetique et analytique.*. Paris: Bloud et Gay, 1936.

Guibert, Joseph de. "Bremond, Henri." In *Dictionnaire de spiritualité ascétique et mystique* 1:1928–38. Paris: Beauchesne, 1936.

Guinan, Alastair. "Portrait of a Devout Humanist. M. l'abbé Bremond." *Harvard Theological Review* 47 (1954) 15–53.

Guiral, Pierre. "Bremond et Maurras." AC, 37–50.

Gumpper, Stéphane. "La crise moderniste, entre mystique et folie. La 'psychologie des religions' en France (1899–1914)." MMM, 33–63.

Guy, Jean-Claude. "Henri Bremond et son commentaire aux Exercices de saint Ignace." *Revue d'ascétique et de mystique* 45 (1969) 191–223.

Guyon, Bernard. Preface to AC, 7–10.

Haight, Roger. "Bremond's Newman." *Journal of Theological Studies* 36 (1985) 350–79.

Harrison, Carol E. *Romantic Catholics: France's Postrevolutionary Generation in Search of a Modern Faith*. Ithaca, NY: Cornell University Press, 2014.

Hill, Harvey. "Henri Bergson and Alfred Loisy: On Mysticism and the Religious Life." MM, 104–35.

———. "Loisy's 'Mystical Faith': Loisy, Leo XIII, and Sabatier on Moral Education and the Church." *Theological Studies* 65 (2004) 73–94.

Hogarth, Henry. *Henri Bremond: The Work and Life of a Devout Humanist*. London: SPCK, 1950.

Houdard, Sophie. "Henri Bremond et le psychologie du sentiment religieux: l'impossible histoire d'un 'vide mysterieux.'" LS, 123–42.

———. "'Humanisme dévot' et histoire littéraire." HLM, I, 23–51.

Hours, Bernard. "Les historiens et l'*Histoire littéraire du sentiment religieux.*" HL, 183–212.

James, William. *The Varieties of Religious Experience: A Study in Human Nature.* Gifford Lectures on Natural Religion, Edinburgh, 1901–1902. New York: Modern Library, 1936.

Joassart, Bernard. "Henri Bremond—Hippolyte Delehaye Correspondance." *Analecta Bollandiana* 113 (1995) 365–413.

———. "Réception de l'*Histoire littéraire du sentiment religieux en France.* Parcours bollandien à travers quelques revues belges et françaises." LS, 49–80.

Jossua, Jean-Pierre. "Le jeune Bremond et la littérature." *Revue des sciences philosophiques et théologique* 84 (2000) 623–33.

Katz, Steven T., ed. *Mysticism and Philosophical Analysis.* New York: Oxford University Press, 1978.

Kerlin, Michael J. "Maurice Blondel: Philosophy, Prayer, and the Mystical." MM, 82–103.

Kerr, Ian. *John Henry Newman.* Oxford: Oxford University Press, 1988.

King, Ursula. *Spirit of Fire: The Life and Vision of Teilhard de Chardin.* Maryknoll: Orbis, 1996.

Kirk, Kenneth E. *The Vision of God: The Christian Doctrine of the* Summum Bonum. Bampton Lectures, 1928. Abridged. Oxford: Oxford University Press, 1931.

Kirschner, Suzanne. *The Religious and Romantic Origins of Psychoanalysis: Individuation and Integration in Post-Freudian Theory.* Cambridge: Cambridge University Press, 1996.

Knox, Ronald. *Enthusiasm: A Chapter in the History of Religion.* Westminster, MD: Christian Classics, 1983. Originally, Oxford University Press, 1950).

Laffay, Augustin, OP. "L'abbé Bremond suspendu *a divinis* en 1909. Le dossier romain de 'l'affaire Tyrrell.'" LS, 17–48.

Lavaud, M.-Benoît. "Quiétisme et pur amour; et prière pure: À propos de deux livres récents." *Revue Thomiste,* nouvelle série, 59 (1930) 58–74.

Le Bars, Jean. *The French Academy.* New York: Encyclopedia Press, 1913. Kindle edition.

Leblanc, Sylvain. *Un clerc qui n'a pas trahi. Alfred Loisy d'après ses Mémoires.* Paris: Nourry, 1931.

Le Brun, Jacques. "Henri Bremond et la 'métaphysique des Saints.'" HLM, III, 8–29.

———. "Humanisme dévot." *Dictionnaire de spiritualité ascétique et mystique,* 7:1028–33. Paris: Beauchesne, 1969.

———. *Le pur amour de Platon à Lacan.* Paris: Seuil, 2002.

———. "Quiétisme. II: France." *Dictionnaire de spiritualité ascétique et mystique,* 12:2805–42. Paris: Beauchesne, 2004.

Leflon, Jean. "Crise et restauration des foyers de Science Religieuse dans l'Église au XIXe siècle." In *Migne et le renouveau des études patristiques. Actes du colloque se Saint-flour 7–8 juillet 1975,* edited by A. Mandouze and J. Fouilheron, 53–60. Paris: Beauchesne, 1985.

Leonard, Ellen. *George Tyrrell and the Catholic Tradition.* New York: Paulist, 1982.

Livingston, James C., ed. *Tradition and the Critical Spirit: Catholic Modernist Writings; George Tyrrell.* Minneapolis: Augsburg Fortress, 1991.

Loisy, Alfred. *George Tyrrell et Henri Bremond.* Paris: Émile Nourry, 1936.

———. *The Gospel and the Church.* Translated by Christopher Home. Introduction by Bernard B. Scott. Reprint. Philadelphia: Fortress, 1976.

Loome, Thomas Michael. "The Enigma of Baron Friedrich von Hügel—as Modernist." *Downside Review* 91 (1973) 13–34, 123–40, 204–30.

Losito, Giacomo. Introduction to MMM, 7–16.

Lubac, Henri de. *At the Service of the Church: Henri de Lubac Reflects on the Circumstances that Occasioned His Writings*. Translated by Anne Elizabeth Englund. San Francisco: Ignatius, 1993.

———. *Theology in History*. Translated by Anne Englund Nash. San Francisco: Ignatius, 1996.

Magnard, Pierre. "La querelle des augustinismes." In *Fénelon: Philosophie et spiritualité. Actes du colloque organisé par le Centre d'Étude des Philosophes Français, Sorbonne, 27–28 mai 1994. À la mémoire de Henri Gouhier (1898-1994)*, 135–54. Genève: Librairie Droz, 1996.

Magraw, Roger. *France 1815–1914: The Bourgeois Century*. New York: Oxford University Press, 1986.

Maréchal, Joseph. *Studies in the Psychology of the Mystics*. Translated by Algar Thorold. London: Burns, Oates and Washbourne, 1927.

Marie of the Incarnation. *Marie of the Incarnation: Selected Writings*. Edited by Irene Mahoney. New York: Paulist, 1989.

Marlé, René. *Au coeur de la crise moderniste. Le dossier unédits d'une controverse, Lettres de Maurice Blondel, Henri Bremond, Fr. von Hügel, Alfred Loisy, Fernand Mourret, J. Wehrlé....* Paris: Aubier, 1960.

Martin Du Gard, Maurice. *De Sainte-Beuve à Fénelon: Henri Bremond*. Paris: Simon Kra, 1927.

———. *Les Mémorables 1918–1945*. 3 vols. Paris: Flammarion, 1999.

Marxer, François. "L'abbé Bremond ou la subjectivité entre histoire et métaphysique." HL, 13–46.

———. "'Cette curiosité des états mystiques qu'il lui était interdit de vivre': Claudel, Mounier, Maritain, Du Bos lecteurs de Bremond." HLM, II, 1046–80.

———. "L'École française: la théologie entre éblouissement théocentrique et faille christologique." HLM, I, 874–905.

———. "Entre religion et métaphysique: Maurice Blondel et 'Le problème de la Mystique.'" MMM, 259–316.

McCool, Gerald A. *Catholic Theology in the Nineteenth Century: The Quest for a Unitary Method*. New York: Seabury, 1977.

McGinn, Bernard. "Theoretical Foundations." Appendix to *The Presence of God: A History of Western Christian Mysticism*, vol. 1, *The Foundations of Mysticism*, 265–343. New York: Crossroad, 1991.

McIntosh, Mark A. *Mystical Theology: The Integrity of Spirituality and Theology*. Oxford: Blackwell, 1998.

McManners, John. *Church and Society in Eighteenth-Century France*. Vol. 2. *The Religion of the People and the Politics of Religion*. Oxford: Oxford University Press, 1998.

Meissner, W. W. *Ignatius of Loyola: The Psychology of a Saint*. New Haven: Yale University Press, 1992.

———. *To the Greater Glory—a Psychological Study of Ignatian Spirituality*. Milwaukee: Marquette University Press, 1999.

Mesnard, Jean. "Bremond et Port-Royal." AC, 95–112.

———. *Pascal*. Translated by Claude and Marcia Abraham. Tuscaloosa: University of Alabama Press, 1969.

Moisan, Clément. *Henri Bremond et la poésie pur*. Paris: minard, 1967.
Mugnier, Arthur. *Journal de l'abbé Mugnier (1879–1939)*. Paris: Mercure de France, 1985.
Nédoncelle, Maurice. "Newman selon Bremond, ou le procès d'un procès." EN, 43–60.
Neveu, Bruno. "Augustinisme janséniste et magistère romain." In *Érudition et Religion aux XVIIe et XVIIIe siècles*, 451–72. Paris: Albin Michel, 1994.
———. "Henri Bremond et l'Angleterre." *Revue des sciences philosophiques et théologiques* 84 (2000) 593–622.
———. "Sébastien Le Nain de Tillemont (1637–1698)." *Revue des sciences philosophiques et théologiques* 84 (2000) 93–104.
———. "Le statut théologique de saint Augustin au XVIIe siècle." *Revue des sciences philosophiques et théologiques* 84 (2000) 473–90.
Nicolson, Harold. *Sainte-Beuve*. Westport, CT: Greenwood, 1978.
Noël, Marie. "Souvenirs sur l'abbé Bremond." In *Notes intimes*, 333–52. Paris: Stock, 1959.
Norman, Larry F. *The Shock of the Ancient: Literature and History in Early Modern France*. Chicago: University of Chicago Press, 2011.
Olphe-Galliard, SJ,, M. "Cinq lettres d'Henri Bremond au Père Joseph de Guibert." *Bulletin de littérature ecclésiastique* 69 (1968) 185–96.
O'Malley, John W. *Trent: What Happened at the Council*. Cambridge: Harvard University Press, 2013.
Onimus, Jean. "Bremond et l'enseignement des Lettres." CA, 157–67.
Palanque, Jean-Remy. "La place des Provençaux dans l'oeuvre d'Henri Bremond." AC, 87–94.
Panikkar, Raimundo. *The Silence of God: The Answer of the Buddha*. Translated by Robert R. Barr. Maryknoll: Orbis, 1999.
Parsons, William B. *The Enigma of the Oceanic Feeling: Revisioning the Psychoanalytic Theory of Mysticism*. Oxford: Oxford University Press, 1999.
Partin, Malcolm O. *Waldeck-Rousseau, Combes, and the Church: The Politics of Anti-Clericalism, 1899–1905*. Durham, NC: Duke University Press, 1969.
Pascal, Blaise. *Pensées*. Translated by A. J. Krailsheimer. New York: Penguin, 1966.
———. *The Provincial Letters*. Translated by A. J. Krailsheimer. New York: Penguin, 1967.
Petit, Hugues. *L'Église, le Sillon, et l'Action Française*. Paris: Nouvelles Éditions Latines, 1998.
Petre, Maude D. *Autobiography and Life of George Tyrrell*. 2 vols. London: Arnold, 1912.
———, ed. *George Tyrrell's Letters*. London: Unwin, 1920.
Pezeril, Daniel. "Bremond et Bernanos." AC, 51–66.
Pierce, Andrew. "Crossbows, Bludgeons and Long-Range Rifles: Tyrrell and Newman and 'the Intimate Connection Between Methods and Their Results.'" In *George Tyrrell and Catholic Modernism*, edited by Oliver P. Rafferty, 56–75. Portland, OR: Four Courts, 2010.
Pocock, J. G. A. *Barbarism and Religion. I: The Enlightenments of Edward Gibbon (1737–1764)*. Cambridge: Cambridge University Press, 1999.
Porter, James I. "Love of Life: Lucretius to Freud." In *Erotikon: Essays on Eros, Ancient and Modern*, edited by Shadi Bartsch and Thomas Bartsherer, 113–41. Chicago: University of Chicago Press, 2006.
Portier, William L., and C. J. T. Talar. "The Mystical Element of the Modernist Crisis." MM, 1–22.
Poulat, Émile. "Bremond et le modernisme." EN, 69–87.
———. *Histoire, dogme et critique dans la crise moderniste*. Paris: Casterman, 1962.

Prévotat, Jacques. *Les catholiques et l'Action française: Histoire d'une condamnation 1899-1939*. Paris: Fayard, 2001.

———. *Une oeuvre clandestine d'Henri Bremond: "Sylvain Leblanc, Un clerc qui n'a pas trahi, Alfred Loisy d'après ses Mémoires," 1931, édition critique et dossier historique par É. Poulat*. Rome: Edizioni di Storia e Letteratura, 1972.

———. "Réactions et sensibilités maurrassiennes face à l'oeuvre de Bremond." HL, 123–48.

Proust, Marcel. *Contre Sainte-Beuve*. Paris: Gallimard, 1954.

Puhl, Louis J. *The Spiritual Exercises of St. Ignatius, Based on Studies in the Language of the Autograph*. Chicago: Loyola, 1951.

Rafferty, Oliver P. "Tyrrell's History and Theology." In *George Tyrrell and Catholic Modernism*, edited by Oliver P. Rafferty, 21–37. Portland, OR: Four Courts, 2010.

Regard, Maurice. "L'abbé Tempête ou le Silence intérieur." AC, 129–44.

Rohr, Richard. *Eager to Love: The Alternative Way of Francis of Assisi*. Cincinnati: Franciscan Media, 2014.

———. *What the Mystics Know: Seven Pathways to Your Deeper Self*. New York: Crossroads, 2015.

Rosa, Guglielmo Forni. "Saint Jean de la Croix à la Société française de philosophie." MMM, 65–86.

Rousselot, Pierre. *The Problem of Love in the Middle Ages: A Historical Contribution*. Translated by Alan Vincelette. Milwaukee: Marquette University Press, 2001.

Sainte-Beuve, Charles Augustin. *Portraits of the Seventeenth Century: Historic and Literary*. 2 vols. Translated by Katherine P. Wormeley. New York: Ungar, 1964.

———. *Port-Royal*. 3 vols. Paris: Gallimard, 1953, 1954, 1955.

Salin, Dominique. "De Bremond à Bernanos: l'énigme de l'*Imposture*." HL, 171–82.

———. "The Treatise on Abandonment to Divine Providence." *Way* 46 (2007) 21–36.

Schmidt, Leigh Eric. "The Making of Modern 'Mysticism.'" *Journal of the American Academy of Religion* 71 (2003) 273–302.

Sheppard, Lancelot C. *Lacordaire: A Biographical Essay*. London: Catholic Book Club, 1964.

Sluhovsky, Moshe. *Believe Not Every Spirit: Possession, Mysticism & Discernment in Early Modern Catholicism*. Chicago: University of Chicago Press, 2007.

———. "Mysticism as an Existential Crisis." In *A Companion to Jesuit Mysticism*, edited by Robert A. Maryks 139–65. Leiden, Netherlands: Brill, 2017.

Solignac, Aimé de. "Mystique." *Dictionnaire de spiritualité ascétique et mystique*, vol. 10. Paris: Beauchesne, 1980.

Somerville, James M. "Maurice Blondel 1861–1949." *Thought* 36 (1961) 371–410.

Sorrel, Christian. "Henri Bremond académicien français." HL, 149–70.

Speaight, Robert. *Georges Bernanos: A Study of the Man and the Writer*. New York: Liveright, 1974.

Spencer, Philip. *Politics of Belief in Nineteenth-Century France: Lacordaire: Michon: Veuillot*. New York: Fertig, 1973.

Tadié, Jean-Yves. *Marcel Proust: A Life*. Translated by Euan Cameron. New York: Penguin, 2000.

Talar, C. J. T. "Alfred Loisy and the Great War." In *Roman Catholic Modernists Confront the Great War*, edited by C. J. T. Talar and Lawrence F. Barmann, 16–52. New York: Palgrave Macmillan, 2015.

———. "Assenting to Newman: Henri Bremond's *Psychologie de la foi*." *Downside Review* 121 (2003) 251–70.

———. "The Modernist and the Mystic: Albert Houtin's *Une grande mystique*." MM, 82–103.

———. "Newman in France during the Modernist Period: Pierre Batiffol and Marcel Hébert." *Newman Studies Journal* 2 (2005) 45–57.

———. "Newman and the 'New Apologetics.'" *Newman Studies Journal* 6 (2009) 49–56.

———. "Prayer at Twilight: Henri Bremond's *Apologie pour Fénelon*." MM, 39–61.

———. "Les trois Cécile: *Une grande mystique* d'Albert Houtin." MMM, 245–58.

Talar, C. J. T., and William Portier. "The Mystical Element of the Modernist Crisis." MM, 1–22.

Taylor, Charles. *A Secular Age*. Cambridge: Harvard University Press, 2007.

Teilhard de Chardin, Pierre. "The Promised Land." In *Writings in Time of War*, edited by Pierre Teilhard de Chardin, translated by René Hague, 277–88. New York: Harper and Row, 1967.

TeSelle, Eugene. "Augustine." In *An Introduction to the Medieval Mystics of Europe*, edited by Paul E. Szarmach 19–36. Albany: State University of New York Press, 1984.

———. *Christ in Context: Divine Purpose and Human Possibility*. Philadelphia: Fortress, 1975.

———. "Engaged Intellectuals and the Politics of Culture: A Retrospective Analysis." *Annali d'Italianistica* 19 (2001) 303–25.

Thibaudet, Alfred. "Autour de la Métaphysique des Saints." *Revue de Paris*, January 1, 1929, 72–98.

———. "La place d'Henri Bremond dans l'histoire de la critique française." *Nouvelles Littéraires*, August 26, 1933.

Thirouin, Laurent. "Deux visions de Port-Royal: Sainte-Beuve et Bremond." HL, 61–102.

Thompson, William M. "An Introduction to the French School." In *Bérulle and the French School: Selected Writings*, edited by William M. Thompson. New York: Paulist, 1989.

Tran, Thi Tuyet Mai. *La mission continue de Jésus selon Mgr Lambert de la Motte (1624–1679) et le renouveau de l'évangelisation en Asie*. Paris: Cerf, n.d.

Trémolières, François. "L'abbé Bremond à l'Index." Appendix to *Approches de l'indicible*, 151–94. Rapport (*votum*) du censeur sur la *Sainte Chantal*, février–mars 1913.

———. "L'amour des lettres et le désir de Dieu: Henri Bremond, historien littérateur." In *Approches de l'indicible*, 135–50.

———. *Approches de l'indicible*. Études bremondiennes. Grenoble: Millon, 2014.

———. "Approches de l'indicible dans le courant mystique français (Bremond et Certeau lecteurs des mystiques)." In *Approches de l'indicible*, 9–46.

———. "Bremond et la poésie pure.' L'enjeu mystique d'une querelle littéraire." In *Approches de l'indicible*, 231–48.

———. "Bremond et la Visitation." In *Approches de l'indicible*, 195–212.

———. "Émile Goichot lecteur de Henri Bremond." In *Approches de l'indicible*, 121–34.

———. "Foi mystique et raison critique. Un débat de l'entre-deux guerres (Bremond, Loisy, Bergson, Baruzi)." In *Approches de l'indicible*, 47–62.

———. "L'*Histoire littéraire du sentiment religieux* d'abbé Bremond: l'unique exception d'une entreprise "moderniste" qui ait réussi?'" In *Approches de l'indicible*, 109–20.

———. "Mystique et Église: Le cas Bremond." MMM, 317–40.

———. "Note sur Henri Bremond et le 'modernisme littéraire.' Annexe: Lettre de Pie X à Caspar Decurtins, 15 septembre 1910." In *Approches de l'indicible*, 213–30.

———. "Situation de Bremond." In *Approches de l'indicible*, 63–108.

———. "'The Witness to These Witnesses': Henri Bremond." In *A Companion to Jesuit Mysticism*, edited by Robert A. Maryks, 253–78. Leiden: Brill, 2017.

Troeltsch, Ernst. *The Christian Faith*. Translated by Garrett E. Paul. Minneapolis: Fortress, 1991.

———. "Political Ethics and Christianity." In *Religion in History*, translated by James Luther Adams and Walter F. Bense, 173–209. Minneapolis: Fortress, 1991.

Tyrrell, George. "Disinterested Love." In *Essays on Faith and Immortality*, 35–39.

———. *Essays on Faith and Immortality*. Arranged by Maude Petre. London: Arnold, 1914.

———. "A Perverted Devotion." In *Essays on Faith and Immortality*, 158–71.

———. "The Prayer of Quiet." In *Essays on Faith and Immortality*, 40–42.

———. "Théologisme." *Revue pratique d'apologétique* 4 (1907) 499–526.

———. "Two Estimates of Catholic Life." Originally in the *Month* 2 (1899) 61–79. Gathered in George Tyrrell, *The Faith of the Millions: A Selection of Past Essays*, 2 vols. London: Longmans, Green, 1901.

Valéry, Paul. "L'infini esthétique." In *Art, Esthétique, Poésie (9 Conférences, Discours et Propos 1923–1939)*, edited by Paul Valéry. Kindle edition. Originally in *Art et Médecine*, 1934.

———. *Monsieur Teste*. Translated by Jackson Matthews. Princeton: Princeton University Press, 1973.

———. "Propos sur la poésie." Conférence faite à l'université des Annales, le 2 décembre 1927. In *Art, Esthétique, Poésie (9 Conférences, Discours et Propos 1923–1939)*, edited by Paul Valéry. Kindle edition.

———. "Variation sur une 'Pensée.'" *La Revue Hebdomadaire* 28 (1923) 161–70.

———. *Selected Writings of Paul Valéry*. New York: New Directions, 1950.

Varry, Dominique. "L'abbé Henri Bremond au travail." HL, 47–60.

Venard, Marc. "Histoire littéraire et sociologie historique: deux voies pour d'une Histoire religieuse." AC, 75–86.

Vidler, Alec. R. *Prophecy and Papacy: A Study of Lamennais, the Church, and the Revolution*. Birkbeck Lectures, 1952–1953. New York: Scribner, 1954.

———. *A Variety of Catholic Modernists*. Cambridge: Cambridge University Press, 1970.

Viller, M., and P. Pourrat. "Abandon." In *Dictionnaire de spiritualité ascétique et mystique*, 1:1–50. Paris: Beauchesne, 1950.

Weber, Eugen. *The Hollow Years: France in the 1930s*. New York: Norton, 1994.

Zeldin, Theodore. *A History of French Passions. I: Ambition, Love and Politics; II: Intellect, Taste and Anxiety*. Oxford: Clarendon, 1973.

Index of Proper Names

Abercrombie, Nigel, 172,199.
Ahearne, Jeremy, 224.
Alençon, Ubald d', 149.
Alvarez, Balthasar, 141, 216, 312.
Amadieu, Jean-Baptiste, 122.
Amigo, Peter Emmanuel, 102, 108.
Arnauld, Agnès, 172-173, 177-178, 180, 232.
Arnauld, Jacqueline Marie Angélique, 148, 169, 170, 177, 180.
Arnauld, Antoine ("the Great Arnauld"), 129, 172-173, 176, 180-182, 190-191, 202, 211, 260, 345.
Arnold, Claus, 147.
Arnold, Matthew, 71.
Arnold, Thomas, 31, 38, 71, 302.
Arrou, Pierre, 3, 8, 292.
Augustine of Hippo, St., 93, 129, 169, 179, 196, 199, 203, 211, 305, 316.
Aubert, Roger, 70.
Aumont, Jean, 290.

Bakan, David, 226, 275.
Baldick, Robert, 184, 187.
Barmann, Lawrence E., 67, 147.
Barjon, Louis, 275.
Barrès, Maurice, 3-5, 9, 11, 17, 22, 32, 85, 90-97, 107, 114, 128, 146, 153, 155, 158, 195, 213. 239, 243, 245-246, 282.
Baruzi, Jean, xii, 102, 242, 267, 361, 376.
Baudelaire, Charles, 260, 262, 265, 278, 335.
Baudin, William James, 286, 321, 326, 345, 380.
Baudrillart, Alfred-Henri-Marie, xii, 4-5, 6, 8, 65, 228, 240, 258.
Bautain, Louis, 99.
Beaudou, Ludovic, 257, 380.
Beaumont, Keith, 55.
Bedoyère, Michael de la, 112.
Bellesort, André, 207.
Bellinzaga, Isabelle, 369-370.
Benda, Julien, 324, 352.
Benedict XV, 146.

Bergson, Henri, 86, 240, 282, 331-332, 355-359, 362.
Bernanos, Georges, 170, 328-331.
Bernard of Clairvaux, St., 196, 211-212, 310, 315-316.
Bernard-Maître, Henri, 16, 19, 59, 73, 85, 90, 105, 148, 201, 230, 240, 292-293, 312, 336.
Bernardi, Peter J., 113,
Bernières, Jean, 237, 320.
Bérulle, Pierre de, 152-159, 164, 177, 210, 212-214, 222, 240, 282, 286, 288, 337, 342, 345, 364.
Binet, Étienne, 136.
Blanchet, André, SJ, xii, xvii, 12-13, 15, 17-18, 20-22, 24, 26-28, 31-32, 35, 39, 43, 48, 50-51, 73, 82-84, 92-95, 105, 107-109, 113, 116, 123, 134, 146, 148, 153, 182, 198, 227-229, 239, 244, 248, 257, 275, 287, 328, 384, *et passim*.
Blanchette, Oliva, 30, 76-77, 114, 116, 186, 197, 243, 323, 332.
Blondel, Maurice, ix, xiii, xvii, 7, 15, 30-33, 35, 41-44, 50-53, 57, 61, 63-64, 66-73, 75-81, 84-87, 89, 91-92, 96, 98, 100, 104-105, 107, 109, 111, 114-116, 120, 124, 126, 127-128, 135, 143-145, 147-153, 156, 168, 176, 182-183, 186, 189, 196-201, 210, 228-229, 234-245, 252, 254-255, 258, 264, 266-267, 271-272, 274, 277-278, 281-282, 285-288, 296-297, 303-304, 310, 322-323, 328, 332, 341, 346, 355, 361-362, 380, *et passim*.
Bloud, Edmond, 5, 90.
Boileau, Nicholas, 117, 243-244, 261, 263, 273.
Bonald, Louis de, 99.
Bonnefoy, François-Joseph, 84, 108.
Bordeaux, Henry, 5, 8, 9, 15, 20, 61, 82, 206-207.
Bossuet, Jacques-Bénigne, 16, 54, 105, 107, 109-111, 115, 118-119, 155, 168, 218, 223, 231, 253, 260, 282, 312, 315, 326, 342-343, 366.
Boudon, Henri-Marie, 237.
Bourbon-Parma, Sixte and Xavier, 113.
Bourdaloue, Louis, 312-313.
Bourget, Paul, 4, 5.
Bourgoing, François, 154, 158.

405

Index of Proper Names

Bowen, Elizabeth, 334.
Bradley, Arthur C., 273.
Bremond, André, 28, 31, 324-325.
Bremond, André and Jean, 11, 12, 15, 22, 368, 380.
Bremond, Émile, 12, 22.
Bremond, Jean, 144.
Bremond, Marguerite: 12, 380.
Bremond, Pierre, 12, 15-16.
Bremond, Thomasine, 12.
Brown, Frederick, 22, 32, 65, 94, 146.
Brunetière, Ferdinand, 48-50, 118, 243.
Brunschvicg, Léon, 191.
Bruyère, Cécile, 184.
Burke, Edmund, 6.
Butler, Cuthbert, 376.
Butler, Joseph, 38, 49.

Cameron, J. M., 49.
Camus, Jean-Pierre, 136, 286, 362-367.
Canfield, Benedict (Benoît de), 137, 288.
Cantillon, Alain, 173, 205-206,
Carroll, Andrew J., 64.
Catherine de Ricci, Ste., 87.
Caussade, Jean-Pierre de, SJ, 110, 117, 143, 167, 210, 216, 312, 342-345.
Cavallera, Ferdinand, 209-210, 221-222, 291-293, 312, 337, 345.
Certeau, Michel de, ix, 125, 132, 138-140, 223-225, 253, 267, 281, 283-285, 287-288, 301, 303, 306, 310, 387.
Chadwick, Owen, 28, 49, 50, 64, 90.
Chambord, Comte de, 18, 119.
Champion La Mahère, Pierre, 216.
Chantal, Jeanne de, Ste., 1, 5, 19, 88, 102, 104, 117, 119, 120-123, 125-126, 137, 163, 282, 342.
Chardon, Louis, 300-301, 304-308, 342.
Charpin. E. (Dr.), 12, 19, 22.
Charpin, Frédéric, 114, 332.
Chateaubriand, René de, 27, 184, 256, 262-263, 326.
Chaugy, Françoise-Madeleine, 117, 121.
Chauvin, Charles, 4, 8, 245, 344, 380.
Cholvy, Gérard, 19.
Claudel, Paul, 134, 240, 275, 277, 288, 328.
Clugny, François de, 290.
Cobban, Alfred, 227.
Cocteau, Jean, 240, 253.
Cognet, Louis, 172, 205.
Condren, Charles de, 154-155, 159-162, 165, 214-215, 240, 342.
Combes, Émile, 65, 80.
Crasset, Jean, SJ, 312.
Cross, John, 35.
Crouslé, Léon :107.

Dagens, Jean, 337.
Daillé, Jean, 5, 54.
David, Anne-Louis, 70.
De Giorgi, Fulvio: 145.
De Luca, Don Giuseppe, 247, 282, 336-339, 369.
De Pril, Ward: 140, 208-209.
Debongnie, Pierre: 32.
Decker, Henry W., 282, 293.
Dejean, Joan: 263.
Delacroix, Henri, 218-219, 253.
Delehaye, Hippolyte, 250.
Delplanque, Albert, 107.
Descaves, Lucien, 248.
Desert Fathers, 87, 179, 324-325.
Desmarets, Jean, 238-239.
Dessoulavy, Charles L., 102.
Dickens, Charles, 27, 232.
Didon, Henri, 299-300.
Dilthey, Wilhelm: 6.
Dimnet, Ernest, 144, 248, 320.
Doncoeur, Paul, SJ, 360, 364.
Donahue, Darcy: 209.
Doudan, Ximénès, 29.
Doyle, William: 172.
Du Bos, Charles, 249, 268, 284, 301, 324.
Ducerceau, Jean-Antoine, SJ, 273.
Duchesne, Louis, 3-6, 7, 9, 31, 64, 153, 243-245, 252, 336, 353.
Dupuy, B.D., 55-56, 62, 105.
Dupuy, Michel, 172.
Duclos, Paul: 257.

Eckhardt, Meister, 301.
Egan, Harvey D. SJ, 25.
Eliot, George, 27, 30, 32, 35-38, 86, 89, 92, 96, 302.
Erikson, Erik, 357.
Eudes, Jean, St., 159.

Fabre, Pierre-Antoine, 347, 363.
Fénelon, François, 9, 11, 16, 30, 58, 102, 104-107, 109-111, 115, 117-118, 125-126, 135, 140, 143, 148, 151, 153, 161, 167, 175, 218, 223, 231, 240, 253, 260-261, 263, 282, 285, 297, 305, 312, 326, 342-344, 365, 367, 374-375.
Fernandez, Ramon, 335.
Flachaire, Charles, 346.
Fléchier, Esprit, 117-118.
Flers, Mother Madeleine de, 371-372.
Fogazzaro, Antonio, 82, 145, 336.
Fourvière, Xavier de, 102, 108.
Francis de Sales, 5, 81, 104, 111, 117, 120-123, 126, 129, 133-134, 136-137, 141-142, 153-154, 156-157, 160, 163, 177-179, 210-211, 220, 233, 240, 251, 260, 278, 280, 282, 286, 288, 305, 309, 316, 332, 342-343, 348, 357, 377.

406

Index of Proper Names

Francis of Assisi, 46.
Freud, Sigmund, 320.
Fumaroli, Marc, 129.
Fumet, Stanislas, 253.

Gagliardi, Achille, 337, 364, 369-370.
Garrigou-Legrange, Reginald, 240, 301.
Gautier, Théophile, 135, 234.
Gay, Francisque, 5, 154, 281-282, 296, 328.
Gazier, Augustin, 172, 205, 326.
Gerbet, Philippe-Olympe, 91, 98-102, 133, 210.
Gibbon, Edward, 6, 9, 131, 256.
Gibson, Ralph :19.
Gide, André, 264, 336.
Ginter, Claire, 69.
Gladstone, William H., 38.
Goichot, Émile, ix, xii, xvii, 2, 4-5, 30, 34-35, 44, 58, 63, 68, 71, 88, 90, 101, 105, 108, 112, 133, 141, 153, 155, 167, 208-210, 220, 223, 250, 281, 285, 288, 290, 292, 294, 300, 310, 312, 321, 323, 328, 332-322, 351, 368, 372, 379, 384, *et passim*.
Gordon, Charles George, 35.
Gouhier, Henri, 127, 358.
Goujon, Patrick, and Salin, Dominique, 208, 222-223, 293, 296.
Goyau, Georges, 257.
Grandmaison, Léonce de, 105, 137, 140-142, 153, 314.
Green, John Richard, 39.
Greene, Graham, 220.
Gres-Gayer, 170.
Grolleau, Charles, 3, 8, 292, 305-306.
Grou, Nicolas, 110, 141, 167, 216, 274.
Guéranger, Dom Prosper, 144, 342, 348-349.
Guérin, Pierre, 370.
Guibert, Joseph de, SJ, 9, 112-113, 132, 209, 213, 221, 253, 292, 328, 336, 369.
Guillebert, Jean-Baptiste, 16, 19, 20, 25.
Guinan, Alastair, 102, 106.
Guiral, Pierre, 23.
Gumper, Stéphane, 254.
Guttinguer, Ulrich, 256-257.
Guy, Jean-Claude, SJ, 20, 25, 27, 292.
Guyon, Jeanne Marie Bouvier de la Mothe (Madame), 104, 106, 109-110, 122, 125, 140, 151, 162, 202, 237, 297, 305, 343, 368, 379.

Haight, Roger, 49.
Hamon, Jean, 170, 276, 325.
Handel-Mazzetti, Enrica von, 86, 115.
Harnack, Adolph von, 73.
Harrison, Carol E., 19, 66.
Hill, Harvey, 353, 356.

Hogarth, Henry, xiii, 12, 15, 34, 50, 112, 248, 251, 336.
Houdard, Sophie, 50, 210, 219, 253-254, 347.
Hours, Bernard, 251.
Hügel, Friedrich von ("the Baron"), ix, 34, 44, 52, 63, 66-69, 73, 76, 78, 83-84, 90, 102, 105, 119, 128, 147, 152-153, 163, 219.
Hugo, Victor: 19, 128, 243.
Hulst, Maurice d' (Mgr), 6, 65, 155, 258.
Huysmans, Joris-Karl, 183-187, 262, 350.

Ignatius Loyola, St., 24-27, 51, 70-71, 207-216, 250, 282, 291-294, 312, 332.

James, William, 46, 61, 129, 195, 237, 253, 291, 375, 384.
Janet, Pierre, 253.
Jansen, Cornelius, 129, 169, 173, 176.
Jean-Chrysostome, père, 237.
Jeanne des Anges, 219-220, 225.
Joan of Arc, Ste., 144, 146.
Joassart, Bernard, 250.
John of the Cross, St., 139, 150, 201, 241, 266-267, 361, 376.
John XXIII, 336.
Jossua, Jean-Pierre, 36, 52, 254.
Jovy, Ernest, 192.
Jowett, Benjamin, 35.

Katz, Steven T., 138.
Keble, John, 39-40, 46, 102.
Kerlin, Michael J., 235.
King, Ursula, 32.
Kirk, Kenneth, 320.
Kirschner, Suzanne, 386.
Knox, Ronald A., 175, 177.
Kojève, Alexandre, 269.
Kolakowski, Leszek, 351.

La Bruyère, Jean de, 47, 128.
La Fontaine, Jean de, 135.
La Rochefoucauld, François de, 107, 130, 171, 202.
Laberthonnière, Lucien, 85.
Lacordaire, Jean-Baptiste Henri, 300.
Laffay, Augustin, OP, 108-109.
Lagny, Paul de, 290.
Lake, William Charles, 38, 53.
Lallemant, Louis, SJ, 216-217, 219, 231, 292, 312.
Lammenais, Félicité de, 90-91, 96, 98-100, 129, 133, 210, 243, 256.
Langlois, Charles V., 325.
Lavaud, M.-Benoît, 323.
Le Bars, Jean, 2.
Le Brun, Jacques, 135, 267, 284, 297, 314-318, 365.

Index of Proper Names

Leblanc, Sylvain, 352-354.
Lebreton, Jules, SJ, 72, 105, 379.
Leclaire, Léon, 184.
Lefèvre, Frédéric, 271.
Leflon, Jean, 19.
Leo XIII, 28, 45, 64-66, 115, 290.
Leonard, Ellen, 70.
Letourneau, Georges, 154-155, 161, 163, 209.
Letourneux, Nicolas, 349.
Leuba, J.H., 237.
Levesque, Eugène, 107, 162.
Lilley, A.L., 106.
Livingston, James C., 71-72 .
Loisy, Alfred, xvii, 9, 43, 59, 63, 65, 67, 71-82, 84-85, 88, 102-103, 108, 112, 147-148, 156, 201, 206-207, 210, 223, 229, 244, 252, 282, 351-359, 362, 380.
Loome, Thomas, 67.
Losito, Giacomo, 140.
Louis XIV, 16, 82, 107, 117, 119, 125, 129, 181, 312.
Lubac, Henri de, 67, 139, 249, 324.

Mabillon, Dom Jean, 326-327.
Magnin, Charles, 273.
Magraw, Charles, 17, 21, 113, 116.
Mahoney, Irene, 230.
Maintenon, Madame de, 16, 109-111, 325.
Maistre, Joseph de, 90, 99, 302.
Malebranche, Nicolas, 99, 111, 129.
Mallarmé, Stéphane, 265, 268.
Manning, Henry Edward, 46.
Maréchal, Joseph, 140-143, 145, 152, 166, 274, 276, 281.
Marie of the Incarnation (Marie Guyart Martin), 227, 230-235, 254.
Maritain, Jacques, 196, 241, 255.
Marlé, René, 66-68, 73, 79.
Martène, Dom Edmond, 231, 235-236.
Martin, Dom Claude, 230, 230-236.
Martin Du Gard, Maurice, xvii, 12-13, 17, 27-28, 90-92, 95, 101-102, 108, 116, 249, 260-261, 334-336.
Marxer, François, 50, 69, 127, 131, 152, 155-156, 158, 164, 235, 242, 249, 328, 359.
Masson, Pierre-Maurice, 106, 110.
Matel, Jeanne de, 237.
Maurras, Charles, 17, 22-23, 31-32, 85, 91-94, 98, 113-116, 143, 146, 154-155, 240, 266, 341.
McGinn, Bernard, xv, 138, 145.
McIntosh, Mark, 225.
McManners, John, 172, 248.
McCool, Gerald, 65, 99.
Meissner, William W., 26, 209.
Mesnard, Jean, 191, 205.
Mignot, Eudoxe-Irénée, 54.

Mistral, Frédéric, 14.
Moisan, Clément, 282.
Monbrun, abbé Joseph, 116, 148, 153, 201, 228, 248, 321.
Montalembert, Charles Forbes René de, 90.
Montfort, Grignion de, 346.
More, Sir Thomas, 11, 81, 222.
Mugnier, abbé Arthur: 240, 248-249.
Murry, Middleton, 268, 275.
Musset, Alfred de, 19.

Naumann, Friedrich, 147.
Nédoncelle, Maurice, 49.
Neri, Philip, St., 155, 325.
Nerval, Gérard de: 265.
Neveu, Bruno, 25, 71, 82, 105, 129, 169, 179.
Newman, John Henry, 11, 25, 29-30, 32, 38, 40-62, 65, 70-71, 78, 85-87, 102, 105, 109, 120, 126, 128, 137, 160, 211-212, 251, 302, 304, 348, *et passim*.
Nicole, Pierre, 90, 107, 170, 172, 177, 180, 183, 189, 191, 202-205, 211, 214, 230, 302, 348.
Nicolson, Harold, 130, 132.
Niebuhr, H. Richard, 100.
Noël, Marie, 249, 258.
Norman, Larry F., 262.
Noulleau, Jean-Baptiste, 290.

O'Malley, John W., 169.
Olier, Jean-Jacques, 111, 151, 154-155, 159, 161-163, 168, 173, 250, 342.
Ollé-Laprune, Léon, 31, 42, 50.
Olphe-Galliard, M., SJ, 221, 343.
Onimus, Jean, 31.
Orcibal, Jean, 172, 174, 205.
Othenin D'Haussonville, Vicomte, 130.
Ozanam, Frédéric, 349.

Panikkar, Raimundo, 387.
Parsons, William B., 283.
Partin, Malcolm O., 66.
Pascal, Blaise, 48-49, 90, 93, 95-96, 117-118, 129, 167-168, 170-172, 177, 181-183, 189-197, 200-202, 206, 216-217, 220, 286, 303, 363-364, 366.
Peeters, Paul, SJ, 250.
Péguy, Charles, 116, 341.
Penon, abbé Jean-Baptiste, 19, 22, 116.
Pératé, André, 167.
Perrault, Charles, 262.
Petit, Hugues, 115.
Petre, Maude, 70, 82, 101-104, 288.
Pezeril, Daniel: 329
Pierce, Andrew, 70-71.
Piny, Alexandre, 300, 301, 304, 307-313, 323, 342.

Index of Proper Names

Pius IX, 99, 119.
Pius X, 65, 115-116, 146, 258, 345.
Pius XI, 293, 361.
Pocock, J.G.A., 381.
Poe, Edgar Allen, 265, 272.
Poulat, Émile, ix, 65, 72-73, 79, 351, 358.
Porter, James I., 163.
Portier, William L., 119, 140, 219.
Poulain, Augustin, SJ, 142-143, 145, 150, 166, 223.
Pratt, James Bissett, 231, 237, 282.
Prévotat, André, 115, 324.
Prezzolini, Giuseppe, 337.
Proust, Marcel, 131, 240, 264.
Puhl, Louis J., SJ, 212.
Pusey, Edward Bouverie, 41-42, 46.

Quesnel, Pasquier, 170-171.

Racine, Jean, 30, 49, 95, 129, 171, 262, 264.
Rancé, Armand Jean le Bouthillier, 324, 326-328, 334-335.
Ranquet, Catherine, 238.
Richeome, Louis, 135.
Rigoleuc, Jean, 216-217.
Ripault, Archange, 371.
Rodriguez, Alphonsus, 26.
Rolland, Romaine, 283.
Romanet, Marguerite, 238.
Rosette, Louis, SJ, 26
Rosmini-Sabati, Antonio, 145.
Rousseau, Jean-Jacques, 17, 253.
Rousseau, Marie, 11, 151, 162, 266.
Rousselot, Pierre, 286, 314-318.
Ruskin, John, 135.

Sabatier, Auguste, 55.
Sabatier, Paul, 46.
Saint-Beuve, Charles Augustin, 47, 49, 69, 90-91, 95, 98-100, 118, 120, 125, 127-132, 167-168, 171-175, 177-178, 189, 191, 243, 253, 256-257, 332, 335, 349, 356, 384.
Saint-Candide Le Cerf, Madeleine de, 371-372.
Saint-Cyran, abbé de (Jean Duvergier de Hauranne), 129, 168-170, 172-177, 181, 183, 190, 345, 365.
Saint- Jure, Jean Baptiste, 159.
Saint-Simon, Duc de, 2, 9, 47, 105, 109, 128.
Salin, Dominique (see under Goujon, Patrick, also): 329, 343-344.
Sangnier, Marc, 115-116.
Santayana, George, 361
Saudreau, Auguste, 145, 150, 166, 220, 223.
Saurat, Denis, 360-361.
Schmidt, Leigh Eric, 138, 140.
Scott, Sir Walter, 22, 243.
Séguenot, Claude, 288.

Sheed, Frank J., 326.
Sheppard, Lancelot C., 300.
Singlin, Antoine, 170.
Sirmond, Antoine, SJ, 363-367.
Sluhovsky, Moshe, 225-226, 372.
Smith, Sydney, 38, 46.
Solignac, Aimé, 138.
Somerville, James, 79, 81.
Sorrel, Christian, 4-5.
Souday, Paul, 5, 9, 254, 271.
Speaight, Robert, 329.
Spencer, Philip, 64, 66.
Strowski, Fortunat, 48, 117, 131, 192, 251.
Surin, Jean-Joseph, SJ, 90, 184, 201, 207, 217-221.
Suso, Henry, 301.

Tadié, Jean-Yves, 264.
Taine, Hippolyte, 97.
Talar, Charles J. T., ix, xv, 55, 58, 79, 105-107, 112-113, 119, 140, 147, 184, 219, 253, 305, 343.
Tassy, Madame, 16-17.
Tauler, Johann, 301.
Taylor, Charles, 64, 134, 294.
Teilhard de Chardin, Pierre, SJ, 32, 148, 252, 344.
Teresa of Avila, St., 139, 219, 312, 348.
Teresa of Lisieux, St., 46, 87-88, 343.
TeSelle, Eugene, xv, 2, 69, 203, 308.
Thibaudet, Albert, 332-333.
Thiers, Adolphe, 16.
Thirouin, Laurent, 131, 167.
Thomas Aquinas, St., 126, 224, 234, 242, 274, 279, 305, 315, 335-336, 361, 366, 380.
Thomassin, Louis, 290.
Thompson, William M., 164.
Thring, Edward, 31, 37.
Thureau-Dangin, Paul, 90.
Thurston, Herbert, SJ, 148.
Tillemont, Le Nain de, 172-173, 179-180.
Trémolières, François, ix, xii, xv, 25, 63, 70, 117, 122-123, 132, 141, 148, 208, 213, 221, 250, 252-254, 261, 282, 328, 351, 359, 369, 376-378, 384, 386.
Troeltsch, Ernst, 108, 147, 152.
Tyrrell, George, ix, 14, 43-44, 54, 61, 63, 67, 69-73, 76, 79, 82, 87-89, 101-105, 107-108, 111, 208-209, 228, 358, 384.
Twain, Mark, 30.

Underhill, Evelyn, 279, 282.

Valensin, Auguste, SJ, 85, 108.
Valéry, Paul, 206, 240, 249, 255, 261, 264-265, 267-271, 283, 293, 333-336, 351.
Venard, Marc, 347.
Verlaine, Paul, 260, 262, 265.
Vidler, Alec, 100, 105, 115.

Index of Proper Names

Vigué, Paul, 323.
Vincent de Paul, St., 159, 161, 175, 345.
Voltaire (François-Marie Arouet), 191.

Waldeck-Rousseau, Marie René, 65.
Ward, Josephine Hope (Mrs. Wilfrid Ward), 41, 88-89.
Ward, Wilfrid, 85, 90, 251.
Ward, William G., 40.
Watrigant, Henri, SJ, 212-213.
Weber, Eugen, 227, 283, 296, 341.
Wehrlé, abbé René, 109, 326.
Wiseman, Nicholas, 41.

Yvan, Antoine (with Martin, Madeleine), 11, 13-14, 88, 98, 134, 282.
Yves of Paris, 136-137, 154.

Zeldin, Theodore, 14, 29.
Zola, Émile, 184-185, 262.

www.ingramcontent.com/pod-product-compliance
Lightning Source LLC
Chambersburg PA
CBHW081147290426
44108CB00018B/2463